Lecture Notes in Computer Science 9432

Commenced Publication in 1973
Founding and Former Series Editors:
Gerhard Goos, Juris Hartmanis, and Jan van Leeuwen

More information about this series at http://www.springer.com/series/7409

Panos Pardalos · Mario Pavone
Giovanni Maria Farinella · Vincenzo Cutello (Eds.)

Machine Learning, Optimization, and Big Data

First International Workshop, MOD 2015
Taormina, Sicily, Italy, July 21–23, 2015
Revised Selected Papers

 Springer

Editors

Panos Pardalos
University of Florida
Gainsville, FL
USA

Mario Pavone
University of Catania
Catania
Italy

Giovanni Maria Farinella
University of Catania
Catania
Italy

Vincenzo Cutello
University of Catania
Catania
Italy

ISSN 0302-9743   ISSN 1611-3349   (electronic)
Lecture Notes in Computer Science
ISBN 978-3-319-27925-1   ISBN 978-3-319-27926-8   (eBook)
DOI 10.1007/978-3-319-27926-8

Library of Congress Control Number: 2015957789

LNCS Sublibrary: SL3 – Information Systems and Applications, incl. Internet/Web, and HCI

Printed on acid-free paper

This Springer imprint is published by SpringerNature
The registered company is Springer International Publishing AG Switzerland

Preface

MOD 2015 was the first international workshop dedicated entirely to the field of Machine Learning, Optimization and Big Data. It was held in Taormina (Messina), Sicily, Italy, during July 21–23, 2015.

By bringing together scientists, industry experts, postdoctoral, and PhD students working in data science, optimization, and machine learning, MOD aims to provide researchers with the opportunity to learn more about other research areas, where the algorithms, methods, and theories on show are likely to be relevant to their own research activity.

Machine learning, optimization, and big data researchers are now forming their own community and identity. The International Workshop on Machine Learning, Optimization and Big Data is proud to be the premier workshop in the area. As program chairs, we were honored to have such a variety of innovative and original scientific articles presented this year.

There were three plenary lectures:

Vipin Kumar, University of Minnesota, USA
Panos Pardalos, University of Florida, USA
Tomaso Poggio, MIT, USA

In addition, there were four tutorial speakers:

Peter Baumann, Jacobs University Bremen, Germany
Mario Guarracino, Italian National Research Council, Italy
Valeriy Kalyagin, National Research University - HSE, Russia
George Michailidis, University of Florida, USA
Theodore B. Trafalis, University of Oklahoma, USA

MOD 2015 received 73 submissions, and each manuscript was independently reviewed by at least five members of the Technical Program Committee in a blind review process. These proceedings contain 32 research articles written by leading scientists in the field, from 40 different countries in five continents, describing an impressive array of ideas, technologies, algorithms, methods, and applications.

We could not have organized this conference without these researchers, and we thank them all for coming. We also could not have organized MOD 2015 without the excellent work of all of the Program Committee members.

We would like to express our appreciation to the keynote and tutorial speakers who accepted our invitation, and to all authors who submitted research papers to MOD 2015.

July 2015

Panos Pardalos
Mario Pavone
Giovanni Maria Farinella
Vincenzo Cutello

Organization

General Chair

Giuseppe Nicosia   University of Catania, Italy

Conference and Technical Program Committee Co-chairs

Panos Pardalos   University of Florida, USA
Mario Pavone   University of Catania, Italy
Giovanni Maria Farinella   University of Catania, Italy
Vincenzo Cutello   University of Catania, Italy

Technical Program Committee

Ajith Abraham   Machine Intelligence Research Labs, USA
Arvind Agarwal   Xerox Research Center, USA
Agostinho Agra   University of Aveiro, Portugal
Mohammad Al Hasan   Purdue University, USA
Paula Alexandra Amaral   Universidade Nova de Lisboa, Portugal
Aris Anagnostopoulos   Sapienza University of Rome, Italy
Danilo Ardagna   Politecnico di Milano, Italy
Martin Atzmueller   University of Kassel, Germany
Chloé-Agathe Azencott   CBIO Mines ParisTech Institut Curie, France
Antonio Bahamonde   Universidad de Oviedo, Spain
Baski Balasundaram   Oklahoma State University, USA
Elena Baralis   Politecnico di Torino, Italy
Roberto Battiti   Università di Trento, Italy
Christian Bauckhage   Fraunhofer IAIS, Germany
Peter Baumann   Jacobs University Bremen, Germany
Aurelien Bellet   Télécom ParisTech, France
Daniel Berrar   Tokyo Institute of Technology, Japan
Martin Berzins   University of Utah, USA
Rajdeep Bhowmik   Cisco Systems Inc., USA
Albert Bifet   University of Waikato, New Zealand
Ernesto Birgin   University of São Paulo, Brazil
J. Blachut   University of Liverpool, UK
Konstantinos Blekas   University of Ioannina, Greece
Flavia Bonomo   Universidad de Buenos Aires, Argentina
Gianluca Bontempi   Université Libre de Bruxelles, Belgium
Christian Borgelt   European Centre for Soft Computing, Spain
Ulf Brefeld   Technische Universität Darmstadt, Germany

Arjen Hommersom	University of Nijmegen, The Netherlands
Vasant Honavar	Pennsylvania State University, USA
Frank Höppner	Ostfalia Hochschule für angewandte Wissenschaften, Germany
Xian-Sheng Hua	Microsoft Research, USA
H. Howie Huang	George Washington University, USA
Fabrice Huet	Inria Sophia Antipolis, France
Sam Idicula	Oracle, USA
Yoshiharu Ishikawa	Nagoya University, Japan
Hasan Jamil	University of Idaho, USA
Frederik Janssen	TU Darmstadt, Germany
Gareth Jones	Dublin City University, Ireland
Hachem Kadri	Aix-Marseille University, France
Valeriy Kalyagin	Higher School of Economics, Russia
Jaap Kamps	University of Amsterdam, The Netherlands
Panagiotis Karras	Skoltech, Russia
George Karypis	University of Minnesota, USA
Ioannis Katakis	National and Kapodistrian University of Athens, Greece
Saurabh Kataria	Xerox Research, USA
Kristian Kersting	TU Dortmund University, Germany
Andrzej Kochut	IBM T.J. Watson Research Center, USA
Levente Kocsis	MTA SZTAKI, Hungary
Yun Sing Koh	University of Auckland, New Zealand
Petros Koumoutsakos	ETH Zürich, Switzerland
Georg Krempl	University of Magdeburg, Germany
Sergei O. Kuznetsov	National Research University, Russia
Nicolas Lachiche	University of Strasbourg, France
Albert Y.S. Lam	Hong Kong Baptist University, Hong Kong, SAR China
Silvio Lattanzi	Google, USA
Niklas Lavesson	Blekinge Institute of Technology, Sweden
Jaan Lellep	University of Tartu, Estonia
Carson K. Leung	University of Manitoba, Canada
Jiuyong Li	University of South Australia, Australia
Kang Li	Groupon Inc., USA
Jun Li	University of Technology Sydney, Australia
Hsuan-Tien Lin	National Taiwan University, Taiwan
Weifeng Liu	China University of Petroleum, China
Xiaozhong Liu	Indiana University, USA
Paul Lu	University of Alberta, Canada
Anthony Man-Cho	The Chinese University of Hong Kong, Hong Kong, SAR China
Yannis Manolopoulos	Aristotle University of Thessaloniki, Greece
Tiziana Margaria	University of Potsdam, Germany
Enrique Frias Martinez	Telefonica, Spain

Markus Strohmaier	University of Koblenz-Landau, Germany
Johan Suykens	KU Leuven, Belgium
Domenico Talia	University of Calabria, Italy
Wei Tan	IBM, USA
Dacheng Tao	University of Technology Sydney, Australia
Maguelonne Teisseire	Cemagref - UMR Tetis, France
Panayiotis Tsaparas	University of Ioannina, Greece
Aditya Tulsyan	MIT, USA
Theodoros Tzouramanis	University of the Aegean, Greece
Satish Ukkusuri	Purdue University, USA
Giorgio Valentini	Università degli Studi di Milano, Italy
Joaquin Vanschoren	KU Leuven, Belgium
Ana Lucia Varbanescu	University of Amsterdam, The Netherlands
Carlos A. Varela	Rensselaer Polytechnic Institute, USA
Iraklis Varlamis	Harokopio University of Athens, Greece
Eleni Vasilaki	University of Sheffield, UK
Vassilios Verykios	Hellenic Open University, Greece
Herna Viktor	University of Ottawa, Canada
Maksims Volkovs	University of Toronto, Canada
D. Vucinic	Vrije Universiteit Brussel, Belgium
Jianwu Wang	University of California San Diego, USA
Liqiang Wang	University of Wyoming, USA
Marco Wiering	University of Groningen, The Netherlands
Lin Wu	UNSW, China
Yinglong Xia	IBM T.J. Watson Research Center, USA
Liguang Xie	Virginia Tech, USA
Chang Xu	Peking University, China
Qi Yu	Rochester Institute of Technology, USA
Kunpeng Zhang	University of Illinois at Chicago, USA
Nan Zhang	The George Washington University, USA
Rui Zhang	IBM Research - Almaden, USA
Ying Zhao	Tsinghua University, China
Anatoly Zhigljavsky	University of Cardiff, UK
Bin Zhou	University of Maryland, USA
Zhi-Hua Zhou	Nanjing University, China
Djamel A. Zighed	University of Lyon 2, France

Contents

Learning with Discrete Least Squares on Multivariate Polynomial Spaces Using Evaluations at Random or Low-Discrepancy Point Sets

Giovanni Migliorati$^{(\boxtimes)}$

MATHICSE-CSQI, École Polytechnique Fédérale de Lausanne,
Lausanne, Switzerland
giovanni.migliorati@gmail.com

Abstract. We review the results achieved in previous works [1,2,6,8, 10–12] concerning the analysis of stability and accuracy of discrete least-squares approximation on multivariate polynomial spaces with noiseless evaluations at random points, and the results from [9] concerning the case of noiseless evaluations at low-discrepancy point sets. Afterwards, we present some numerical examples that confirm our theoretical findings and give some insights on their potential applications. The purpose of the numerical section is twofold: on the one hand we compare the performance of discrete least squares using random points versus low-discrepancy points; on the other hand we point out further directions of research, by showing what happens when we choose fewer evaluation points than those prescribed by our theoretical analysis.

1 Introduction

Discrete least squares (hereafter shortened to DLS) are widely used for functional approximation, data fitting, prediction, and have countless applications in many scientific fields. In the present work we aim at approximating in the L^2 sense a smooth target function which depends on a multivariate random variable distributed according to a given probability density with bounded support, by computing its DLS approximation onto a properly chosen multivariate polynomial space. The DLS approximation is calculated starting from pointwise evaluations of the target function at random or deterministic point sets. In particular, our framework is an instance of the *projection learning problem* (or improper function learning problem) described in [3,13,14]. Depending on the context, two situations arise: the evaluations of the target function can be assumed noisefree (*noisefree* evaluations), or be polluted by noise (*noisy* evaluations).

Several previous contributions [1,2,6,7,10–12] have analyzed the stability and accuracy of DLS on multivariate approximation spaces, and in particular on multivariate polynomial spaces, in the case of random noiseless or noisy evaluations. One of the main results achieved, is that the DLS approximation is stable and accurate with overwhelming high probability in any dimension, provided

© Springer International Publishing Switzerland 2015
P. Pardalos et al. (Eds.): MOD 2015, LNCS 9432, pp. 1–13, 2015.
DOI: 10.1007/978-3-319-27926-8_1

a certain proportionality relation between the number of pointwise evaluations and the dimension of the underlying approximation space is satisfied. A particular feature of this analysis, in the case of approximation spaces of polynomial type, is that the number of evaluations depends on the dimension of the polynomial space but not on its "shape", which only needs to satisfy the minimal property of being downward closed. In our analysis, explicit proportionality relations between the number of evaluations and the dimension of the approximation space have been derived, for densities in the beta family including the cases of uniform and Chebyshev, and we recall these results in the following section. In [1,2,10] several estimates concerning the accuracy of DLS with noisy evaluations at random points have been proven, for several noise models and with different assumptions, under the same stability conditions obtained in the case of noiseless evaluations. For this reason, in the present paper we numerically investigate mainly the stability of DLS, since the same stability conditions apply to both cases of noiseless and noisy evaluations. We also briefly present some numerical results concerning the accuracy of DLS in the noiseless case.

Recently, in [9,15] DLS on multivariate polynomial spaces in any dimension have been analyzed, when using evaluations at low-discrepancy point sets rather than at random points. Similar conditions as those in the case of random points have been derived, for points asympotically distributed according to the Chebyshev density in [15] and for the uniform density in [9]. However, in the case of low-discrepancy points, stability and accuracy of DLS have been proven with certainty, rather than only with high probability. In the present paper we verify numerically the stability and accuracy estimates proposed in [9] in one dimension and for tensor product multivariate polynomial spaces, and compare the results with those obtained in the case of random points.

In both analyses with evaluations at random or low-dicrepancy points, the proportionality relations between number of evaluations and dimension of the approximation space are sufficient conditions ensuring the stability and accuracy of the DLS approximation, and are confirmed by our numerical tests. However, although the DLS problem can become unstable when the aforementioned proportionality relations are not fulfilled, it can be the case that a relatively accurate DLS approximation is still found up to a certain threshold. These phenomena are currently under investigation, and the present paper aims to better clarify and compare among the two cases of random and low-discrepancy points the performance of DLS in this setting.

The outline of the paper is the following: in Sect. 2 we recall some results from the theory of DLS with random evaluations, and in Sect. 3 from the theory with low-discrepancy point sets. In Sect. 4 we present some numerical results comparing the case of random points versus low-discrepancy points. Finally in Sect. 5 we draw some conclusions.

2 Stability and Accuracy of Discrete Least Squares on Polynomial Spaces with Evaluations at Random Points

In any dimension $d \in \mathbb{N}$, let $D \subseteq \mathbb{R}^d$ be a subset of the d-dimensional Euclidean space such that $D = \prod_{i=1}^{d} D_i$, with $D_i \subseteq \mathbb{R}$ being closed intervals for any $i = 1, \ldots, d$. We introduce a complete probability space (D, Σ, μ), with D being the sample space, Σ the σ-algebra of Borel sets and μ a probability measure. We denote with $y \in D$ a random variable distributed according to the measure μ. Moreover, we assume that μ is absolutely continuous with respect to the Lebesgue measure λ on D and denote with $\rho : D \to \mathbb{R}$, $\rho = d\mu/d\lambda$ the associated probability density function.

We introduce a given target function $\phi : D \to \mathbb{R}$, that we would like to approximate in the L^2 sense using pointwise evaluations $\phi(y_1), \ldots, \phi(y_m)$ in m independent and randomly chosen points $y_1, \ldots, y_m \in D$ distributed according to the measure μ. We assume that the function ϕ is well-defined at any point in D except eventually a zero μ-measure set and that $\phi \in L^2_\mu := \{f : D \to \mathbb{R} : \int_D f^2 d\mu < +\infty\}$. Hereafter, the L^2_μ norm will be simply denoted by $\| \cdot \|$, *i.e.* $\|f\| := \|f\|_{L^2_\mu(D)} = (\int_D f^2 d\mu)^{1/2}$. Moreover, $\|f\|_{L^\infty(D)} := \operatorname{ess\,sup}_{y \in D} |f(y)|$.

In general, the evaluations $\phi(y_1), \ldots, \phi(y_m)$ can be polluted by noise, coming from any source of uncertainty due to controlled or uncontrolled agents. We define the noiseless and noisy observation models as

$$\textbf{noiseless model,} \quad z_j := \phi(y_j), \quad j = 1, \ldots, m, \tag{1}$$

$$\textbf{noisy model,} \quad z_j := \phi(y_j) + \eta_j, \quad j = 1, \ldots, m, \tag{2}$$

where $y_1, \ldots, y_m \in D$ are m i.i.d. random variables distributed according to the probability measure μ, and $\eta_1, \ldots, \eta_m$ represents the noise, and denote with $z \in \mathbb{R}^m$ the vector containing the observations $z_1, \ldots, z_m$ according to the chosen model (1) or (2). In a more general framework, *e.g.* as in [10], also the noise η_j can be modeled as a random variable, which might eventually depend on y_j, *i.e.* $\eta_j = \eta_j(y_j)$. This requires the definition of a different probability space and the use of the marginal measure, see [10]. Of course the noiseless case can be seen as a particular instance of the noisy case with $\eta_j = 0$ for any $j = 1, \ldots, m$.

In the applications, experimental measurements naturally embed uncertainty, which can be modeled by means of random variables and of suitable assumptions on the type of noise polluting the measurements. However, in an abstract modeling context the main source of uncertainty is due to round-off errors when operating with finite precision calculations, and this type of uncertainty can be properly controlled making the noiseless model appropriate. As an example, we mention the recent domain of application of DLS with noiseless evaluations in the field of approximation of the solution to parametric and stochastic PDEs, see *e.g.* [1,6,11], where this methodology has been successfully analyzed. In the present paper we address only the noiseless model (1). Anyhow, both the noiseless and noisy models share the same stability conditions in our analysis, and the differences between the two cases lie in the accuracy estimates, where of course the presence of noise pollutes the overall precision of the upper bounds for the approximation error.

Unless mentioned otherwise, throughout the paper Pr and $\mathbb{E}$ refer to the probability and the expectation w.r.t. the measure μ. We define the inner product

$$\langle f_1, f_2 \rangle := \int_D f_1(y) f_2(y) d\mu(y), \quad \forall f_1, f_2 \in L^2_\mu(D), \tag{3}$$

as well as the discrete inner product

$$\langle f_1, f_2 \rangle_m := m^{-1} \sum_{j=1}^m f_1(y_j) f_2(y_j), \quad \forall f_1, f_2 \in L^2_\mu(D),$$

with $y_1, \ldots, y_m$ being any choice of m distinct points in D. These inner products are associated with the norm $\| \cdot \| = \langle \cdot, \cdot \rangle^{1/2}$ (already previously defined) and seminorm $\| \cdot \|_m := \langle \cdot, \cdot \rangle_m^{1/2}$. Notice that $\mathbb{E}(\| \cdot \|_m) = \| \cdot \|$. We denote by $V_n \subset L^\infty(D)$ any finite-dimensional subspace of $L^2_\mu(D)$ such that $n := \dim(V_n)$, and by $(\psi_i)_{1 \leq i \leq n}$ an orthonormal basis of V_n w.r.t. the inner product (3). In the present paper we confine to multivariate approximation spaces of polynomial type, and in the remaining part of this section we present the main results achieved in [1,9] concerning our analysis of the stability and accuracy properties of DLS, in the specific case of multivariate polynomial approximation spaces. For the analysis of DLS in more general multivariate approximation spaces see [1,10].

We introduce further information concerning the structure of the probability measure μ. Given a collection of (possibly different) univariate measures μ_i with corresponding densities $\rho_i : D_i \to \mathbb{R}$ for any $i = 1, \ldots, d$, we assume that μ can be expressed as a product measure $d\mu = \prod_{i=1}^d d\mu_i$. Then we introduce the family $(\varphi^i_k)_{k \geq 0}$ of $L^2_{\mu_i}$-orthonormal polynomials of degree k, *i.e.* these polynomials are orthonormal w.r.t. the weighted L^2 inner product (3) with the weight being the probability density function ρ_i associated with the measure μ_i:

$$\int_{D_i} \varphi^i_j(t) \varphi^i_k(t) d\mu_i(t) = \int_{D_i} \varphi^i_j(t) \varphi^i_k(t) \rho_i(t) d\lambda(t) = \int_{D_i} \varphi^i_j(t) \varphi^i_k(t) \rho_i(t) dt = \delta_{jk}.$$

We introduce the gamma function $\Gamma(\theta) := \int_0^{+\infty} t^{\theta-1} e^{-t} dt$ with $\mathrm{Re}(\theta) > 0$ then extended by analytic continuation, and the beta function $\mathcal{B}(\theta_1, \theta_2) := \Gamma(\theta_1)\Gamma(\theta_2)/\Gamma(\theta_1 + \theta_2)$ for any $\theta_1, \theta_2 > -1$. In the present article we focus on the univariate Jacobi weight with real shape parameters $\theta_1, \theta_2 > -1$,

$$\rho_J^{\theta_1, \theta_2}(t) := \left(2^{\theta_1 + \theta_2 + 1} \mathcal{B}(\theta_1 + 1, \theta_2 + 1)\right)^{-1} (1-t)^{\theta_1} (1+t)^{\theta_2}, \quad t \in [-1, 1], \tag{4}$$

which leads to the family of univariate Jacobi polynomials $(J_k^{\theta_1, \theta_2})_{k \geq 0}$. Remarkable instances of Jacobi polynomials are Legendre polynomials when $\theta_1 = \theta_2 = 0$, and Chebyshev polynomials of the first kind when $\theta_1 = \theta_2 = -1/2$. Notice that the weight (4) is normalized such that it integrates to one over the whole support, also known as probabilistic orthonormalization. The Jacobi weight $\rho_J^{\theta_1, \theta_2}$

corresponds, up to a translation in the parameters θ_1, θ_2 and up to an affine transformation in the support, to the standard beta probability density function. In the following we refer to the tensorized Jacobi density as the tensorization of (4) in the d coordinates, i.e. $\rho_J^{\theta_1,\theta_2}(y) = \prod_{i=1}^d \rho_J^{\theta_1,\theta_2}([y]_i), y \in D$, where the notation $[y]_i$ denotes the ith component of y. Accordingly, for the corresponding choices of the parameters θ_1 and θ_2, we refer to tensorized Chebyshev and tensorized uniform density.

Given a set $\Lambda \subseteq \mathcal{F} := \mathbb{N}_0^d$ of d-dimensional multi-indices, we define the polynomial space $\mathbb{P}_\Lambda = \mathbb{P}_\Lambda(D)$ as

$$\mathbb{P}_\Lambda := \operatorname{span}\{\psi_q : q \in \Lambda\},$$

with each multivariate polynomial basis function being defined for any $q \in \Lambda$ as

$$\psi_q(y) := \prod_{i=1}^d \varphi_{q_i}^i([y]_i), \quad y \in D, \tag{5}$$

by tensorization of the univariate families of $L_{\mu_i}^2$-orthonormal polynomials. We denote the cardinality of the multi-index set Λ by $\#(\Lambda)$. The discrete seminorm becomes a norm almost surely over $\mathbb{P}_\Lambda$, provided the points are distinct and their number satisfies $m \geq \dim(\mathbb{P}_\Lambda)$, therefore leading to an overdetermined least-squares problem. In the case of polynomial approximation we set $V_n = \mathbb{P}_\Lambda$ with $n = \dim(\mathbb{P}_\Lambda) = \#(\Lambda)$. From now on, we confine to a specific type of polynomial spaces $\mathbb{P}_\Lambda$, which are associated to multi-index sets Λ with the property of being downward closed. For any $q, p \in \mathcal{F}$, the ordering $q \leq p$ means that $[q]_i \leq [p]_i$ for all $i = 1, \dots, d$.

Definition 1 (Downward closed multi-index set). *In any dimension d, a multi-index set $\Lambda \subset \mathcal{F}$ is downward closed (or it is a lower set) if*

$$q \in \Lambda \implies p \in \Lambda, \ \forall p \leq q.$$

Let w be a nonnegative integer playing the role of spectral accuracy in the DLS approximation. In the present article, we test two types of isotropic polynomial spaces $\mathbb{P}_\Lambda$, with the set $\Lambda = \Lambda_w \subset \mathcal{F}$ being defined using the parameter w as:

$$\text{Tensor Product (TP)}: \quad \Lambda_w = \left\{ q \in \mathbb{N}_0^d : \|q\|_{\ell^\infty(\mathbb{N}_0^d)} \leq w \right\}, \tag{6}$$

$$\text{Total Degree (TD)}: \quad \Lambda_w = \left\{ q \in \mathbb{N}_0^d : \|q\|_{\ell^1(\mathbb{N}_0^d)} \leq w \right\}. \tag{7}$$

Moreover, an anisotropic polynomial space that will be mentioned in the sequel is the anisotropic tensor product space with maximum degrees $w_1, \dots, w_d$ in each one of the d coordinates, in which case

$$\text{anisotropic Tensor Product (aTP)}: \Lambda_{w_1,\dots,w_d} = \left\{ q \in \mathbb{N}_0^d : [q]_i \leq w_i, \ \forall i = 1, \dots, d \right\}. \tag{8}$$

Of course all the sets (6)–(8) are downward closed according to Definition 1.

Given the target function $\phi : D \to \mathbb{R}$, we define its continuous L^2 projection over V_n as

$$\Pi_n \phi := \arg\min_{v \in V_n} \|\phi - v\|,$$

and denote by

$$e_n(\phi) := \inf_{v \in V_n} \|\phi - v\| = \|\phi - \Pi_n \phi\|$$

its best approximation error in the L_μ^2 norm. We denote by

$$e_n^\infty(\phi) := \inf_{v \in V_n} \|\phi - v\|_{L^\infty(D)}$$

the best approximation error in the L^∞ norm. We also define the *DLS approximation* (or *discrete L^2 projection*) of the function ϕ over V_n as

$$\Pi_n^m \phi := \arg\min_{v \in V_n} \sum_{i=1}^m |z_i - v(y_i)|^2 = \arg\min_{v \in V_n} \|z - v\|_m. \tag{9}$$

The minimization in (9) corresponds to minimize the discrete seminorm containing the evaluations of the target function ϕ in the m points $y_1, \ldots, y_m \in D$. Given a threshold $\tau \in \mathbb{R}_0^+$, we introduce the truncation operator

$$T_\tau(t) := \text{sign}(t) \min\{\tau, |t|\}, \quad \text{for any } t \in \mathbb{R},$$

and use it to define the truncated DLS projection over V_n as:

$$\widetilde{\Pi}_n^m := T_\tau \circ \Pi_n^m.$$

After choosing a given ordering to enumerate the multi-indices in $\mathcal{F}$ and thus the elements of the orthonormal basis, for example the lexicographical ordering, we introduce the design matrix $\mathbf{D}$ defined element-wise as $[\mathbf{D}]_{jk} = \psi_k(y_j) \in \mathbb{R}^{m \times n}$, and the Gramian matrix $\mathbf{G} := m^{-1} \mathbf{D}^\top \mathbf{D}$. From an algebraic standpoint, the DLS projection (9) can be computed by solving the normal equations

$$\mathbf{G}\beta = m^{-1} \mathbf{D}^\top z,$$

where $\beta \in \mathbb{R}^n$ is the vector containing the coefficients of the DLS approximation of the function ϕ expanded over the orthonormal basis, *i.e.* $\Pi_n^m \phi = \sum_{k=1}^n [\beta]_k \psi_k$.

In the following we recall a result from [1], restricted to the specific case of the noiseless model. See [1, Theorem 3] for the complete theorem covering also the noisy case. More general estimates in the noisy case with several noise models have been proven in [10, Theorems 5 and 6]. We define $\zeta := (1 - \ln 2)/2 \approx 0.15$ and denote with $\|\| \cdot \|\|$ the spectral matrix norm.

Theorem 1 (from [1, Theorem 3]). *In any dimension $d \geq 1$, for any real $r > 0$ and given any finite downward closed set $\Lambda \subset \mathcal{F}$, if ρ is the tensorized Jacobi density with parameters $\theta_1, \theta_2 \in \mathbb{N}_0$ and the number of points m satisfies*

$$\frac{m}{\ln m} \geq \frac{1+r}{\zeta} (\#(\Lambda))^{2 \max\{\theta_1, \theta_2\}+2} \tag{10}$$

or, if ρ is the tensorized Chebyshev density (i.e. the tensorized Jacobi density with $\theta_1 = \theta_2 = -1/2$) and the number of points m satisfies

$$\frac{m}{\ln m} \geq \frac{1+r}{\zeta}(\#(\Lambda))^{\frac{\ln 3}{\ln 2}}, \tag{11}$$

then the following holds true:

(i) the deviation between $\mathbf{G}$ and the identity matrix $\mathbf{I}$ satisfies

$$\Pr\left\{ |||\mathbf{G} - \mathbf{I}||| > \frac{1}{2} \right\} \leq 2m^{-r}, \tag{12}$$

(ii) if ϕ satisfies a uniform bound τ over D (i.e. $|\phi| \leq \tau$ a.s. w.r.t. ρ), then one has the estimate in expectation

$$\mathbb{E}(\|\phi - \tilde{\Pi}_n^m \phi\|^2) \leq \left(1 + \frac{\zeta}{(1+r)\ln(m)} \right) e_n(\phi)^2 + 8\tau^2 m^{-r}, \tag{13}$$

(iii) one also has the estimate in probability

$$\Pr\left(\|\phi - \Pi_n^m \phi\| \geq (1 + \sqrt{2})e_n^\infty(\phi) \right) \leq 2m^{-r}. \tag{14}$$

Denoting with $K(\mathbf{G})$ the spectral condition number of the Gramian matrix $\mathbf{G}$, an immediate consequence of (12) is that

$$\Pr\left\{ K(\mathbf{G}) > \frac{1}{2} \right\} \leq 2m^{-r}, \tag{15}$$

see [10, 12], i.e. condition (10) or (11) ensures that the Gramian matrix is well-conditioned and thus the DLS approximation is stable with high probability.

3 Stability and Accuracy of Discrete Least Squares on Polynomial Spaces with Evaluations at Low-Discrepancy Point Sets

The use of deterministic point sets with good discrepancy properties rather than random points finds applications in the development of quasi-Monte Carlo methods versus the plain Monte Carlo method. Nowadays, several types of deterministic points, so-called low-discrepancy points, are available, see e.g. [4] and references therein. In the present paper, we only recall the minimal notation needed to introduce our results achieved in [9] concerning the analysis of DLS with evaluations at low-discrepancy point sets. We refer to [4,5] for a complete introduction to the topic and the precise definition of the notion of low-discrepancy point set, or to [9] for an introduction more targeted to the application in DLS approximation. Intuitively, the points in a low-discrepancy point set tend to be "evenly distributed" over the domain.

We deal with two types of low-discrepancy point sets: (t, u, d)-nets and (t, d)-sequences, defined as in the following according to [4]. For convenience, we keep the same choice of the domain $D = [0, 1)^d$ adopted in [9].

Definition 2 ((t, u, d)-**net in base** b). *Let $d \geq 1$, $b \geq 2$, $t \geq 0$ and $u \geq 1$ be integers with $t \leq u$. A (t, u, d)-net in base b is a point set consisting of b^u points in $[0, 1)^d$ such that every elementary interval of the form*

$$\prod_{i=1}^{d} \left[\frac{a_i}{b^{g_i}}, \frac{a_i + 1}{b^{g_i}} \right)$$

with integers $g_i \geq 0$, $0 \leq a_i < b^{g_i}$, and $g_1 + \ldots + g_d = u - t$, contains exactly b^t points of the net.

Definition 3 ((t, d)-**sequence in base** b). *Let $t \geq 0$ and $d \geq 1$ be integers. A (t, d)-sequence in base b is a sequence of points $(y_1, y_2, \ldots)$ in $[0, 1)^d$ such that for all integers $u > t$ and $l \geq 0$, every block of b^u points*

$$y_{lb^u + 1}, \ldots, y_{(l+1)b^u}$$

in the sequence $(y_1, y_2, \ldots)$ forms a (t, u, d)-net in base b.

A particular instance of a (t, u, d)-net, that will be tested in the numerical section in the one-dimensional case $d = 1$, is the following:

$$y_j = \frac{2j - 1}{2m} \in [0, 1), \quad j = 1, \ldots, m. \tag{16}$$

This point set is a $(0, 1, 1)$-net in base $b = m$, and it has the minimal star discrepancy among all point sets with m points in $[0, 1)$.

In the following, we recall a result from [9], in the particular case of $\delta = 1/2$, concerning the stability and accuracy of DLS in multivariate polynomial spaces of tensor product type.

Theorem 2 (from [9, Corollary 5]). *Let ρ be the tensorized uniform density (i.e. the tensorized Jacobi density with $\theta_1 = \theta_2 = 0$). In one dimension $d = 1$, if the number of sampling points m satisfies*

$$m \geq \frac{(\#(\Lambda))^2}{2}, \quad \text{with the } (0, 1, 1)\text{-net in base } b = m \text{ given by (16)}, \tag{17}$$

$$\frac{m}{\ln m} \geq C(\#(\Lambda))^2, \quad \text{with any } (t, 1)\text{-sequence in base } b, \tag{18}$$

then (21) and (22) hold true. The constant C eventually depends on the parameters t and b. In any dimension $d \geq 2$ with the set $\Lambda \subset \mathcal{F}$ being of anisotropic tensor product type (8): if the number of sampling points m satisfies

$$\frac{m}{(b+3)^{d-2} \left(1 + \dfrac{b-1}{b+3} \dfrac{\ln m}{\ln b} \right)^{d-1} \mathcal{O}(d^2)} \geq \frac{(\#(\Lambda))^2}{2} b^t, \tag{19}$$

with any (t, u, d)-net in base b with $m = b^u$ points, or

$$\frac{m}{b\,(b+3)^{d-2}\left(1 + \dfrac{2(b-1)}{b+3}\dfrac{\ln m}{\ln b}\right)^{d-1}\mathcal{O}(d^2) + \left(1 + \dfrac{\ln m}{\ln b}\right)\mathcal{O}(d)} \geq \frac{(\#(\Lambda))^2}{2}b^t,$$

(20)

with any (t, d)-sequence in base b, then (21) and (22) hold true.

$$1 \leq K\left(\mathbf{G}\right) \leq 3.$$

(21)

For any $\phi \in C^0([0,1]^d)$

$$\|\phi - \Pi_n^m \phi\| \leq \left(1 + \sqrt{2}\right) e_n^\infty(\phi).$$

(22)

4   Numerical Results

In this section we present some numerical results comparing the performances of DLS using evaluations at random versus low-discrepancy point sets. In the whole section the domain is chosen as $D = [-1,1]^d$ and we consider only the uniform density, *i.e.* the Jacobi density with $\theta_1 = \theta_2 = 0$, with the random variable y being uniformly distributed in D. In the plots displaying the results for random points, the continuous lines correspond to the mean of the condition number or to the mean of the approximation error, and the dashed lines correspond to the mean plus one standard deviation. Both the mean and the standard deviation are computed employing the cross-validation procedure described in [12, Sect. 4]. In the plots displaying the results for low-discrepancy points, the continuous lines give the value of the condition number or of the approximation error. In the following, c denotes a positive proportionality constant whose values are specified in the legend tables.

Our numerical tests confirm that, when the number of sampling points is quadratically proportional to the dimension of the polynomial space $m = cn^2$, as prescribed by condition (10) of Theorem 1 with random points or conditions (17)–(20) of Theorem 2 with low-discrepancy points, then the condition number of the Gramian matrix $\mathbf{G}$ is small (*i.e.* (15) or (21)) and the DLS approximation is accurate (*i.e.* (13), (14) or (22)). Then we test the stability and accuracy of DLS when the number of sampling points follows a linear proportionality $m = cn$ w.r.t. the dimension of the approximation space, therefore requiring fewer points than those prescribed by the quadratic proportionality $m = cn^2$.

We begin with the one-dimensional case $d = 1$, where the polynomial approximation space is the trivial one-dimensional space obtained by replacing $d = 1$ into (6). In Fig. 1 we show the condition number of the matrix $\mathbf{G}$ in the three cases of random points, equispaced deterministic points (16) and points chosen from the Sobol low-discrepancy sequence, which is a particular (t, d)-sequence in base $b = 2$. We denote with w the maximum degree of the polynomials retained

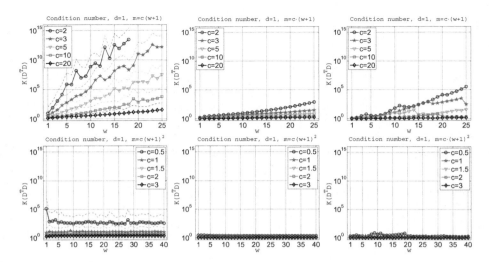

Fig. 1. Condition number $K(\mathbf{G})$ in the case $d = 1$. Top-left: $m = c(\mathrm{w} + 1)$ with random points. Top-center: $m = c(\mathrm{w} + 1)$ with deterministic equispaced points. Top-right: $m = c(\mathrm{w}+1)$ with Sobol points. Bottom-left: $m = c(\mathrm{w}+1)^2$ with random points. Bottom-center: $m = c(\mathrm{w} + 1)^2$ with deterministic equispaced points. Bottom-right: $m = c(\mathrm{w} + 1)^2$ with Sobol points.

in the space, so that $n = \mathrm{w} + 1$. Both proportionalities $m = cn$ and $m = cn^2$ between the number of sampling points m and the dimension of the polynomial space n are investigated, for different values of the proportionality constant c. The linear proportionality $m = cn$ with random points is outperformed by the choice of deterministic equispaced points and Sobol points. Moreover, in one dimension the choice of deterministic equispaced points (16) yields the lowest values of the approximation error, but its extension to higher dimensions is clearly of limited interest due to the curse of dimensionality. The quadratic proportionality $m = cn^2$ yields a bounded condition number with all the three choices of points, independently of the dimension n of the polynomial space, thus confirming the theoretical results achieved in our analysis.

In Fig. 2 we show the corresponding DLS approximation error when approximating the function $\phi(y) = \exp(y)$ over $[-1, 1]$. Clearly, with the quadratic proportionality $m = c(\mathrm{w} + 1)^2$ the DLS approximation is accurate with any choice of the sampling points, either random, equispaced or from the Sobol sequence. With the linear proportionality $m = c(\mathrm{w} + 1)$ the choice of equispaced points or Sobol points still gives an accurate DLS approximation, although without a theoretical justification. In the case of random points the results with the linear proportionality $m = c(\mathrm{w} + 1)$ are in agreement with the loss of stability seen in Fig. 1(top-left): the DLS approximation remains accurate only up to a threshold, after which the DLS problem becomes unstable and the accuracy of the approximation degenerates. Anyhow, depending on the desired accuracy, the linear

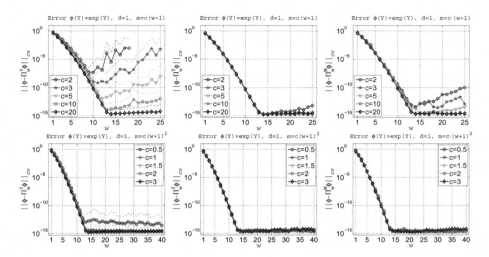

Fig. 2. Error $\mathbb{E}\left[\|\phi - \Pi_n^m \phi\|^2\right]$ in the case $d = 1$. Top-left: $m = c(\mathrm{w} + 1)$ with random points. Top-center: $m = c(\mathrm{w} + 1)$ with deterministic equispaced points. Top-right: $m = c(\mathrm{w} + 1)$ with Sobol points. Bottom-left: $m = c(\mathrm{w} + 1)^2$ with random points. Bottom-center: $m = c(\mathrm{w} + 1)^2$ with deterministic equispaced points. Bottom-right: $m = c(\mathrm{w} + 1)^2$ with Sobol points.

proportionality can still be successfully employed: for example $m = 3(\mathrm{w} + 1)$ still provides an error smaller than 10^{-8} when $\mathrm{w} = 10$, but cannot be used when smaller values for the error are sought.

Then we move to the two-dimensional case $d = 2$, where we compare the use of random points versus Sobol points. In dimension higher than one there are different ways to enrich the polynomial space, making the analysis of the approximation error more complicated than in the one-dimensional case. Usually multivariate functions are anisotropic, and some parameters are more important than others. To take into account these anisotropic features, adaptive polynomial spaces can be constructed, see *e.g.* [7], but their treatment is out of the scope of the present paper. In the following we only address the issue of stability of DLS in the multivariate case, and do not consider the issue of accuracy (that anyhow, from Theorems 1 and 2, is proven to be directly related to stability).

In Fig. 3 we show the condition number using the tensor product polynomial space (6). As in the one-dimensional case, these results confirm the theoretical findings achieved in our analysis, with the quadratic proportionality $m = cn^2$ always ensuring stability. The linear proportionality $m = cn$ exhibits the same deterioration as in the one-dimensional case, with Sobol points again performing slightly better than random points. In Fig. 4 we show the condition number using the total degree polynomial space (7), and the situation looks very similar to the case of tensor product polynomial spaces.

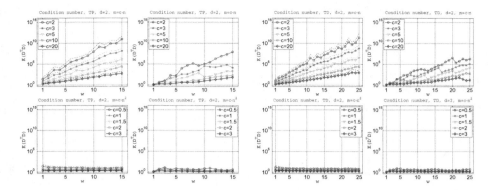

Fig. 3. Condition number in the case $d = 2$ with the tensor product polynomial space (6). Top-left: $m = cn$ with random points. Top-right: $m = cn$ with Sobol points. Bottom-left: $m = cn^2$ with random points. Bottom-right: $m = cn^2$ with Sobol points.

Fig. 4. Condition number in the case $d = 2$ with the total degree polynomial space (7). Top-left: $m = cn$ with random points. Top-right: $m = cn$ with Sobol points. Bottom-left: $m = cn^2$ with random points. Bottom-right: $m = cn^2$ with Sobol points.

5   Conclusions

In this paper we have numerically verified the theoretical results achieved in our previous analyses [1,9,12] concerning the stability and accuracy of DLS on multivariate polynomial spaces with evaluations at random or low-discrepancy point sets. In one dimension, three types of points have been compared: random points, deterministic equispaced points, and points from the Sobol sequence. In all the three cases, the numerical results confirm the theoretical estimates: stable and accurate DLS approximations are obtained when the number of points and the dimension of the approximation space satisfy the proportionality relation $m = cn^2$. The numerical results show that, in one dimension and with low-discrepancy points, the less demanding linear proportionality $m = cn$ is also enough to achieve stability and accuracy, although this claim is not supported by the theory at present time. The same does not hold in one dimension with random points, and an accurate DLS approximation is obtained only up to a threshold, after which the stability is lost and the accuracy deteriorates. In higher dimension, with tensor product and total degree polynomial spaces, the numerical results confirm the behaviour predicted by the theory, and the quadratic proportionality $m = cn^2$ again ensures stability and accuracy. As in the one-dimensional case, the linear proportionality $m = cn$ does not ensure the stability of DLS, but the gap between random and low-discrepancy points is reduced. Numerical tests with random points from [6,7,11,12] show that, using the linear proportionality $m = cn$, the stability of DLS improves when increasing the dimension, making random points more attractive. In the case of low-discrepancy points with the linear proportionality $m = cn$, the stability of DLS shows the opposite trend as the dimension increases, and low-discrepancy points seem to be more attractive than random points only in moderately high dimensions. Further investigations are needed to detect, depending on the dimension, when it is advised to choose low-discrepancy points or random points for DLS approximation.

References

1. Chkifa, A., Cohen, A., Migliorati, G., Nobile, F., Tempone, R.: Discrete least squares polynomial approximation with random evaluations - application to parametric and stochastic elliptic PDEs. ESAIM Math. Model. Numer. Anal. **49**, 815–837 (2015)
2. Cohen, A., Davenport, M.A., Leviatan, D.: On the stability and accuracy of least square approximations. Found. Comp. Math. **13**, 819–834 (2013)
3. Cucker, F., Smale, S.: On the mathematical foundations of learning. Bull. Am. Math. Soc. **39**(1), 1–49 (2001)
4. Dick, J., Pillichshammer, F.: Digital Nets and Sequences: Discrepancy Theory and Quasi-Monte Carlo Integration. Cambridge University Press, Cambridge (2010)
5. Kuipers, L., Niederreiter, H.: Uniform Distribution of Sequences. Pure and Applied Mathematics. Wiley-Interscience [Wiley], New York-London-Sydney (1974)
6. Migliorati, G.: Polynomial approximation by means of the random discrete L^2 projection and application to inverse problems for PDEs with stochastic data. Ph.D. thesis, Dipartimento di Matematica "Francesco Brioschi", Politecnico di Milano and Centre de Mathématiques Appliquées, École Polytechnique (2013)
7. Migliorati, G.: Adaptive polynomial approximation by means of random discrete least squares. In: Abdulle, A., Deparis, S., Kressner, D., Nobile, F., Picasso, M. (eds.) Proceedings of ENUMATH 2013. Lecture Notes in Computational Science and Engineering, vol. 103. Springer, Switzerland (2015)
8. Migliorati, G.: Multivariate markov-type and nikolskii-type inequalities for polynomials associated with downward closed multi-index sets. J. Approx. Theory **189**, 137–159 (2015)
9. Migliorati, G., Nobile, F.: Analysis of discrete least squares on multivariate polynomial spaces with evaluations at low-discrepancy point sets. J. Complexity **31**(4), 517–542 (2015)
10. Migliorati, G., Nobile, F., Tempone, R.: Convergence estimates in probability and in expectation for discrete least squares with noisy evaluations at random points. J. Multivar. Anal. **142**, 167–182 (2015)
11. Migliorati, G., Nobile, F., von Schwerin, E., Tempone, R.: Approximation of quantities of interest in stochastic PDEs by the random discrete L^2 projection on polynomial spaces. SIAM J. Sci. Comput. **35**, A1440–A1460 (2013)
12. Migliorati, G., Nobile, F., von Schwerin, E., Tempone, R.: Analysis of discrete L^2 projection on polynomial spaces with random evaluations. Found. Comp. Math. **14**, 419–456 (2014)
13. Poggio, T., Smale, S.: The mathematics of learning: dealing with data. Not. Am. Math. Soc. **50**, 537–544 (2003)
14. Temlyakov, V.N.: Approximation in learning theory. Constr. Approx. **27**, 33–74 (2008)
15. Zhou, T., Narayan, A., Xu, Z.: Multivariate discrete least-squares approximations with a new type of collocation grid. SIAM J. Sci. Comput. **36**(5), A2401–A2422 (2014)

Automatic Tuning of Algorithms Through Sensitivity Minimization

Piero Conca[1(✉)], Giovanni Stracquadanio[2], and Giuseppe Nicosia[1]

[1] Department of Mathematics and Computer Science,
University of Catania, Catania, Italy
{conca,nicosia}@dmi.unict.it
[2] Ludwig Institute for Cancer Research, University of Oxford, Oxford, UK
giovanni.stracquadanio@ludwig.ox.ac.uk

Abstract. Parameters tuning is a crucial step in global optimization. In this work, we present a novel method, the *Sensitive Algorithmic Tuning*, which finds near-optimal parameter configurations through sensitivity minimization. The experimental results highlight the effectiveness and robustness of this novel approach.

1 Introduction

An algorithm is a formal description of a series of steps, which provides a solution for a given problem [1]. Obviously, the output of an algorithm depends on the input data and its parameters; an algorithm can be viewed as a black-box procedure, which receives in input a set of data and returns an output representing the results. The possibility of selecting different sets of parameters potentially allows to achieve satisfactory results for different instances of a problem, thus increasing the generality of an algorithm.

Parameters tuning represents a crucial part of any experimental protocol in global optimization; indeed, parameters setting heavily affects the quality of the solutions and the speed of convergence of an optimization algorithm [2,3]. Finding good parameters values is pivotal when using stochastic algorithms [4]. Typically, parameters are set using commonly used values, or by a *trial-and-error* approach; interestingly, very few approaches have been proposed to systematically find optimal parameters settings [5–7]. Recently, Bartz-Beielstein introduced the *Sequential Parameter Optimization* (SPO) algorithm, a general framework for experimental analysis that accounts for iterative refinement of the parameters [8]. Successively, Hutter et al. proposed SPO+, an improved variant of SPO that uses log-transformations and the intensification criterion [9]. Hutter et al. also proposed PARAMILS, a method to find optimal parameters settings through local search in the parameters space [10]. An alternative approach consists of using a racing scheme where, starting from an initial set of techniques, an iterative selection is performed [11].

We address the problem of tuning an algorithm by introducing the *Sensitive Algorithmic Tuning* (SAT) method; our approach finds optimal parameters settings by minimizing the worst-case performance of the most sensitive parameters.

© Springer International Publishing Switzerland 2015
P. Pardalos et al. (Eds.): MOD 2015, LNCS 9432, pp. 14–25, 2015.
DOI: 10.1007/978-3-319-27926-8_2

We evaluate this method by tuning the *Differential Evolution* (DE) optimization algorithm [12], although, in principle, our method can be applied to any algorithm.

The paper is organized as follows: in Sect. 2 we introduce the problem of tuning algorithms and the notion of *maximum success region*. Section 3 presents the concepts of robustness and sensitivity, and describes the Morris sensitivity analysis method and the Differential Evolution algorithm. In Sect. 4, we describes the SAT algorithm. Section 5 presents the experimental results. Finally, in Sect. 6 we discuss the conclusions and future works.

2   Algorithmic Tuning

Algorithmic tuning refers to the process of finding a set of values for the parameters of an algorithm, ensuring a satisfactory solution to the problem in the average case.

A trial-and-error approach is computationally expensive and could lead to poor performances if biased by a-priori knowledge. Without loss of generality, we assume that an algorithm is defined as follows:

$$Y = A(P, X) \tag{1}$$

where A is a procedure that takes in input a problem instance P and a vector of parameters X, and returns an output Y. W.l.o.g., we assume that each parameter $x_i \in X \subset \mathbb{R}$ is constrained to an interval $[x_-, x^+]$.

Finding an optimal parameter setting is an intractable problem. Let X be a parameter setting for an algorithm A, where each parameter can take k different discrete values within the interval $[x_-, x^+]$; it follows that the number of feasible parameters settings is $k^{|X|}$. This result makes an exhaustive search intractable for large instances.

Parameters tuning generally consists in running the algorithm on a testbed problem $\bar{P}$, which shares same characteristics with the original problem P (e.g. unimodality). In this context, it becomes crucial to identify a region of the parameters space that maximizes the probability of success, which we denote as *maximum success region*.

Definition 1 (Maximum Success Region). *Let* $X = [x_-, x^+] \subset \mathbb{R}$ *be the range for the parameters of an algorithm* A. X *is called maximum efficiency region if the following condition holds:*

$$\forall x \in X : P_r(A(P, x) = S(P)) \approx 1$$

where P_r *is a function that represents the probability of obtaining the exact solution* $S(P)$ *of* P.

The concept of maximum efficiency region fits particularly well the task of tuning the parameters of optimization algorithms; in this case, the maximum efficiency region of an optimizer is the subspace of parameters, which ensures near-optimal solutions.

It should be noted that optimization methods are subject to *eager tuning*, typically by requiring a large number of objective function evaluations to ensure the convergence to an optimum. It is possible to overcome this limitation by systematically choosing the smallest parameter value ensuring a maximum success rate; this general principle is exploited by the SAT algorithm.

3   Methods

In this section, we describe a framework for robustness and sensitivity analysis that represents the basis of the *Sensitive Algorithmic Tuning* (SAT) algorithm.

3.1   Robustness and Sensitivity Estimation

Algorithmic robustness is the probability of finding a satisfactory solution to a problem, even when the parameters are not optimally tuned. In general, there is a range of values for each parameter for which near-optimality is guaranteed. W.l.o.g., we assume that an algorithm is correct if a parameters setting ensuring an optimal or suboptimal solution exists. We define the *robustness condition* ρ and the *accuracy yield* Γ as follows:

Definition 2 (Robustness Condition). *Let $X \in \mathbb{R}^n$ be a parameters setting for an algorithm A. Given a parameters set X_* obtained by perturbing X, the robustness condition ρ is defined as follows:*

$$\rho(X, X_*, A, P, \epsilon) = \begin{cases} 1 & if \mid A(P, X) - A(P, X_*) \mid \leq \epsilon \\ 0 & otherwise \end{cases} \tag{2}$$

where the robustness threshold ϵ denotes the precision in the objective function value.

Definition 3 (Yield). *Let $X \in \mathbb{R}^n$ be a parameters setting characterizing the behavior of a technique D. Given an ensemble T of parameters settings obtained by sampling the parameters space of X, the yield Γ is defined as follows:*

$$\Gamma(X, A, P, \epsilon, \rho, T) = \frac{\sum_{X_* \in T} \rho(X, X_*, A, P, \epsilon)}{|T|} \tag{3}$$

Since we consider subsets of the parameters space, we perform a Monte-Carlo sampling that generates trial settings in a specific parameters subspace. In our study, we set the robustness threshold $\epsilon = 10^{-5}$ and the number of trials $|T| = 100$.

An ad-hoc algorithmic tuning requires knowledge of the effects of the parameters on the output. In this context, the Morris sensitivity analysis technique [13] represents an interesting approach; it ranks the parameters based on their effect on the output, and does not require information about the system being analyzed [14]. In particular, a parameter is considered sensitive if variations of its value significantly affect the performance of the algorithm. In this context, the Morris technique can be used as an automated method for analyzing algorithms. We hypothesized that the identification of regions of low sensitivity could lead to an effective parameters tuning; this idea represents the basic principle of SAT.

3.2   Morris Method

Sensitivity analysis studies the influence of the input parameters on the output of a function (e.g. an algorithm), and identifies possible relations between parameters, e.g. linear and nonlinear.

The Morris method is a one-at-a-time (OAT) global sensitivity analysis technique. Given a set of parameters values, a parameter at time is modified and the variation of the output is recorded. This information is used to calculate the mean values μ and the standard deviations σ associated with each parameter. Parameters with a high μ have an important impact on the output, large values of σ indicate nonlinear relations with other parameters, whereas small mean values are associated with negligible effect.

3.3   Differential Evolution Algorithm

Differential Evolution (DE) is a stochastic *population-based* algorithm developed for global optimization in continuous spaces [12]. DE is used to solve multi-modal, multi-objective, dynamic or constrained optimization problems; it finds application in several real-world problems, such as digital filter design, fermentation processes, dispatch optimization, and several others [15–18].

DE exploits a vector of differences that is used as a perturbation operator. Given an objective function $f : \mathbb{R}^n \rightarrow \mathbb{R}$, DE starts by generating NP individuals at random, where the values of the variables are constrained in their respective lower and upper bounds. At each generation, each individual is modified according to a *crossover probability* C_r, using the following scheme:

$$x^i_{g+1} = x^i_g + F_w \times (y^i_g - z^i_g) \tag{4}$$

where x^i_{g+1} is the i−th variable of the new individual at generation $g + 1$; y_g and z_g are two individuals of the population such that $x \neq y \neq z$; and F_w is a weighting factor.

If $f(x_{g+1}) < f(x_g)$, x_{g+1} replaces x_g in the population. Typically, the algorithm stops when a predetermined number of generations (G) is reached.

The algorithm has few parameters; C_r controls the *exploring ability* of DE, F_w controls its *exploiting ability*, while NP determines the population size. In particular, for large-scale problems, DE requires large NP values and a sufficient number of generations to obtain satisfactory results.

4   Sensitive Algorithmic Tuning

The *Sensitive Algorithmic Tuning* (SAT) algorithm is a deterministic method that relies on *sensitivity analysis* and *worst-case screening* to identify maximum success regions within the parameters space.

Sensitive parameters are those that typically decrease the success or failure of an algorithm. The sensitivity of a parameter is strictly related to its uncertainty region; in general, a large parameter range makes difficult to find an optimal setting. When the value of a parameter is outside its maximum success region, we can observe an increase in sensitivity. Sensitivity minimization is a key principle in system design; it is necessary to obtain robust parameters setting, but not sufficient to guarantee near-optimal solutions. To overcome this limitation, we adopt a worst-case screening method. Given two parameters settings, SAT chooses the one providing the best solution in the worst case.

The SAT algorithm is depicted in Algorithm 1. At each step, SAT splits the parameters space of each parameter and performs Morris analysis in both regions; it then selects the subspace with the highest mean value, aiming at tuning the most sensitive parameter first. The splitting procedure can be any interval-cutting strategy [19]; in our experiments, we generate two regions by halving the range of sensitive parameters.

An example of the application of the SAT algorithm to a technique with two parameters is depicted in Fig. 1. The objective function values obtained by each parameters setting sampled during sensitivity analysis are also used for evaluating the worst case performance of the algorithm. We use two halting conditions;

Algorithm 1. Pseudo-code of the *Sensitive Algorithmic Tuning* (SAT) algorithm.

1: **procedure** $\text{SAT}(A, X_-, X^+)$
2:      $k \leftarrow 0$
3:      $M_k \leftarrow \text{Morris}(A, X_-, X^+, r, p, \Delta)$
4:      **while** $\neg \text{StopCondition}$ **do**
5:          $s_i \leftarrow \max(M_k)$
6:          $[lx_-, lx^+] \leftarrow \text{LowSplit}(X_-, X^+, s_i)$
7:          $[hx_-, hx^+] \leftarrow \text{HighSplit}(X_-, X^+, s_i)$
8:          $M_{lx} \leftarrow \text{Morris}(A, lx_-, lx^+, r, p, \Delta)$
9:          $M_{hx} \leftarrow \text{Morris}(A, hx_-, hx^+, r, p, \Delta)$
10:          **if** $\max f(M_{lx}) > \max f(M_{hx})$ **then**
11:              $[X_-, X^+] \leftarrow [lx_-, lx^+]$
12:              $M_k \leftarrow M_{lx}$
13:          **else**
14:              $[X_-, X^+] \leftarrow [hx_-, hx^+]$
15:              $M_k \leftarrow M_{hx}$
16:          **end if**
17:          $k \leftarrow k + 1$
18:      **end while**
19: **end procedure**

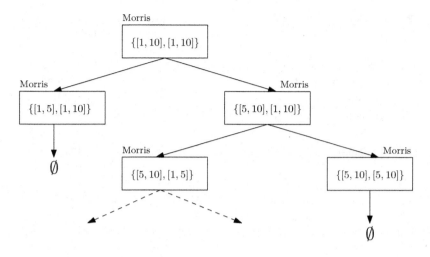

Fig. 1. Iterations of the SAT algorithm on a bi-dimensional parameter space. $\emptyset$ denotes a region that will not be furtherly splitted.

the attainment of an optimal solution in the worst case, or the impossibility of further splitting the parameters space. This strategy is useful to prevent a waste of computational effort when the parameter region is sufficiently small.

5   Experimental Results

We use the SAT algorithm for tuning DE, with the parameters reported in Table 1.

Since parameters settings are problem-dependent, we consider unimodal and multimodal numerical functions of dimensions $d = 10$ and $d = 20$ (see Table 2). Three unimodal functions are used, characterized by multiple quadratic terms. Multimodal functions take into account noise (see function f_4), quadratic and quartic terms. It should be noted that the number of local minima of f_5 increases exponentially with its dimension [20].

Table 1. Parameters of the Differential Evolution algorithm. n denotes the dimension of the problem.

Parameter	Description	X_-	X^+
NP	Population size	10	50
G	Number of generations	$n \times 25$	$n \times 250$
F_w	Weighting factor	0	1
C_r	Crossover rate	0	1

Table 2. Test problems. f^* represents the global minimum; (X_-) and (X^+) are the lower and upper bound, respectively, n denotes the dimension of the problem.

	Class	f	f^*	X_-	X^+
f_1	Unimodal	$\sum_{i=1}^{n} x_i^2$	0	-100	100
f_2	Unimodal	$\sum_{i=1}^{n}(\sum_{j=1}^{i} x_j)^2$	0	-100	100
f_3	Unimodal	$\sum_{i=1}^{n-1} 100(x_{i+1} - x_i^2)^2 + (x_i - 1)^2$	0	-30	30
f_4	Multimodal	$\sum_{i=1}^{n} i * x_i^4 + random[0,1)$	0	-1.28	1.28
f_5	Multimodal	$\sum_{i=1}^{n} x_i^2 - 10\cos(2\pi x - i) + 10$	0	-5.12	5.12

The metric adopted for evaluating the DE performance is the average value of the best solution over 10 independent runs; moreover, we apply the SAT algorithm to find a setting that ensures a worst-case result of 10^{-1}.

An extensive set of simulations is performed to achieve an optimal parameters setting for DE. Table 3 reports the results of SAT on the five testbed problems for $d = 10$. The experimental results show that SAT is able to find satisfactory settings for all the problems.

Table 3. Results for $d = 10$. f_w^* is the worst case objective function value; $v(f)$ represents the variance of the output of all the sampled settings; the lower and the upper bound of each parameter found by SAT are within brackets.

f	f_w^*	$v(f)$	NP	G	F_w	C_r
f_1	1.434×10^{-82}	1.690×10^4	$[77, 100]$	$[2000, 2500]$	$[0.55, 0.66]$	$[0.21, 0.32]$
f_2	7.737×10^{-96}	2.594×10^6	$[55, 100]$	$[2375, 2500]$	$[0.55, 0.75]$	$[0.43, 0.55]$
f_3	8.586×10^{-1}	2.095×10^9	$[77, 88]$	$[1500, 1625]$	$[0.55, 1]$	$[0.1, 0.32]$
f_4	1.482	1.597×10^{-1}	$[97, 100]$	$[4937, 5000]$	$[0.55, 0.66]$	$[0.43, 0.55]$
f_5	5.971×10^{-1}	5.9305	$[83, 88]$	$[500, 1500]$	$[0.44, 0.55]$	$[0.1, 0.325]$

On unimodal functions f_1 and f_2, we are able to obtain an upper bound on the algorithm performance that is close to the global optimum. The f_3 function represents an exception within the unimodal set: it is not surprising that the worst case result is many orders of magnitude worse than the others, due to the presence of several plateau regions that can trap the algorithm. The values of variance show that DE is highly influenced by its parameters, and the initial bounds contain many suboptimal parameters settings.

The multimodal functions are more complex, as the presence of noise and several local minima leads to a difficult tuning. Despite this complex scenario, SAT is able to find a setting that ensures near-optimal solutions in the worst case. The variance is several orders of magnitude lower with respect to unimodal functions; however, this is probably due to the smaller intervals on which the algorithm operates.

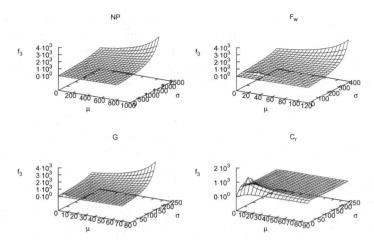

Fig. 2. Sensitivity landscape of f_3 for $d = 10$. μ, σ are reported on the x and y axis, respectively; the objective function values are reported on the z axis.

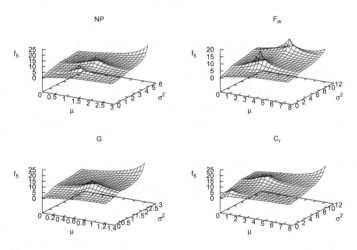

Fig. 3. Sensitivity landscape of f_5 for $d = 10$. μ, σ are reported on the x and y axis, respectively; the objective function values are reported on the z axis.

Figures 2 and 3 report the sensitivity landscapes of f_3 and f_5. The lowest function value is achieved when the sensitivity of each parameter is close to zero. This result seems to support the underlying strategy implemented in SAT. The sensitivity landscapes of the parameters are different for the two problems; for the f_3 function, the population size, the number of generations and the weighting factor show a convex shape, while the crossover probability has a spike near the maximum success region. By inspecting the sensitivity landscape of f_5, we note that the best results are obtained when the sensitivity is close to zero, but the shape of the landscape is more rugged. For all parameters, we have a high number of peaks at different points, which remarks the complexity of tuning DE in this case. Despite this rugged parameter space, SAT is able to identify the best setting.

The results for the tuning of DE when $d = 20$ are presented in Table 4.

Table 4. Results for $d = 20$. f_w^* is the worst case objective function value; $v(f)$ represents the variance of the output of all the sampled settings; the lower and the upper bound of each parameter found by SAT are within brackets.

f	f_w^*	$v(f)$	NP	G	F_w	C_r
f_1	2.322×10^{-77}	3.601×10^5	$[55, 77]$	$[4750, 5000]$	$[0.55, 1]$	$[0.21, 0.32]$
f_2	3.652×10^{-90}	5.895×10^8	$[55, 100]$	$[4750, 5000]$	$[0.55, 0.77]$	$[0.43, 0.55]$
f_3	2.830	2.193×10^{11}	$[77, 88]$	$[4000, 5000]$	$[0.1, 0.32]$	$[0.1, 0.21]$
f_4	5.402	0.795	$[32, 55]$	$[1000, 2000]$	$[0.21, 0.32]$	$[0.88, 1]$
f_5	2.985	60.316	$[77, 88]$	$[4000, 5000]$	$[0.43, 0.55]$	$[0.32, 0.55]$

On the unimodal functions f_1 and f_2, the algorithm finds a setting with a satisfactory upper bound, however this result is not as good as the one found for the smaller dimension instances. f_3 proves to be the most difficult unimodal problem of the entire set; in this case, lower accuracy than expected was obtained. The values of variance are dramatically increased, and the tuning becomes more difficult for increasing problem dimension. Although SAT was not able to find a parameters setting that matched the desired upper bound, the results required only limited computational effort.

In Figs. 4 and 5, we report the sensitivity landscape of f_3 and f_5 for $d = 20$.

The plots confirm the results obtained for lower dimensional problems. The lowest function value is always achieved when the parameters sensitivity is close to zero. The landscape for the two problems are comparable with the previous, however we observe an increase in μ and σ; for example, for f_3, the crossover probability shows a peak in the central region that is far from the maximum success region. For the f_5 function, a rugged landscape is also obtained, and we observe increased sensitivity values for all parameters. This landscape seems to remark the presence of sensitivity barriers, which makes difficult the tuning process.

Finally, we perform robustness analysis. Since parameters ranges are considered instead of single values, we have to evaluate the probability of finding satisfactory results using any setting belonging to a given parameter space. Table 5 shows the yield values of the settings for each problem. High yield values are obtained in all testbeds, except for the f_3 and f_4 functions. We conclude that the proposed settings are robust and effective, and guarantee near-optimal performances of the DE algorithm.

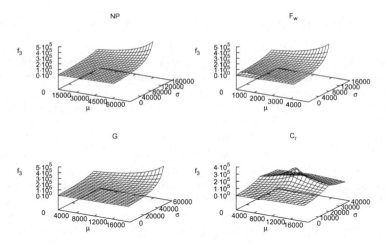

Fig. 4. Sensitivity landscape of f_3 for $d = 20$. μ, σ are reported on the x and y axis, respectively; the objective function values are reported on the z axis.

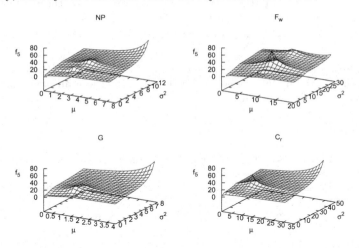

Fig. 5. Sensitivity landscape of f_5 for $d = 20$. μ, σ are reported on the x and y axis, respectively; the objective function values are reported on the z axis.

Table 5. Robustness analysis of SAT parameters. d represents the dimension, Γ is the yield.

f	d	Γ (%)	f	d	Γ (%)
f_1	10	100	f_1	20	100
f_2	10	100	f_2	20	100
f_3	10	52	f_3	20	64
f_4	10	54	f_4	20	42
f_5	10	92	f_5	20	92

6   Conclusions

Algorithm design is a complex process that should pursuit three general properties; efficiency, effectiveness and generality. These properties are strictly dependent on how algorithms parameters are configured. Parameters tuning is therefore required to ensure efficiency and effectiveness when solving a problem.

In this work, we propose the *Sensitive Algorithmic Tuning* (SAT), a new method for the automatic tuning of algorithms. SAT uses the Morris technique to determine the parameters to optimize to obtain satisfactory upper bounds on the expected performances. We evaluate the performance of SAT on the problem of tuning the *Differential Evolution* (DE) algorithm. The experimental results show the effectiveness of our approach; moreover, the discovered settings present a high degree of robustness. Interestingly, these results confirm that optimal settings are associated with a low parameters sensitivity.

We believe the parameters tuning problem should be exploited more deeply by extending the cutting strategy; for instance, an alternative *branch-and-bound* [21] approach could represent an efficient sampling strategy, where sensitivity information could be used to perform expansion and pruning of the exploring tree. We suggest the enhanced SAT algorithm could represent a valid candidate for tuning one of the most important algorithms of the Internet era: PageRank [22].

Acknowledgments. The authors would like to acknowledge Professor Angelo Marcello Anile for the useful discussions on the seminal idea of automatic algorithms tuning. Professor Anile was a continuous source of inspiration during our research work.

References

1. Cormen, T.H., Leiserson, C.E., Rivest, R.L., Stein, C.: Introduction to Algorithms. The MIT Press, Cambridge (2001)
2. Horst, R., Pardalos, P.M., Thoai, N.V.: Introduction to Global Optimization. Springer, USA (2000)
3. Floudas, C.A.: Deterministic Global Optimization. Kluwer, New York (2000)
4. Motwani, R., Raghavan, P.: Randomized algorithms. ACM Comput. Surv. (CSUR) **28**(1), 37 (1996)
5. Back, T., Schwefel, H.P.: An overview of evolutionary algorithms for parameter optimization. Evol. Comput. **1**(1), 1–23 (1993)
6. Audet, C., Orban, D.: Finding optimal algorithmic parameters using derivative-free optimization. SIAM J. Optim. **17**(3), 642–664 (2006)
7. Nannen, V., Eiben, A.E.: Relevance estimation and value calibration of evolutionary algorithm parameters. In: Proceedings of the 20th International Joint Conference on Artifical Intelligence, pp. 975–980. Morgan Kaufmann Publishers Inc. (2007)
8. Bartz-Beielstein, T.: Sequential parameter optimization - sampling-based optimization in the presence of uncertainty (2009)
9. Hutter, F., Hoos, H.H., Leyton-Brown, K., Murphy, K.P.: An experimental investigation of model-based parameter optimisation: Spo and beyond. In: Proceedings of the 11th Annual Conference on Genetic and Evolutionary Computation, GECCO 2009, pp. 271–278. ACM, New York (2009)

10. Hutter, F., Hoos, H.H., Stützle, T.: Automatic algorithm configuration based on local search. In: AAAI, vol. 7, pp. 1152–1157 (2007)
11. Birattari, M., Yuan, Z., Balaprakash, P., Sttzle, T.: F-race and iterated f-race: an overview. In: Bartz-Beielstein, T., Chiarandini, M., Paquete, L., Preuss, M. (eds.) Experimental Methods for the Analysis of Optimization Algorithms, pp. 311–336. Springer, Berlin (2010)
12. Storn, R., Price, K.V.: Differential evolution - a simple and efficient heuristic for global optimization over continuous spaces. J. Global Optim. **11**(4), 341–359 (1997)
13. Morris, M.D.: Factorial sampling plans for preliminary computational experiments. Technometrics **33**(2), 161–174 (1991)
14. Saltelli, A., Ratto, M., Andres, T., Campolongo, F., Cariboni, J., Gatelli, D., Saisana, M., Tarantola, S.: Global Sensitivity Analysis: The Primer. Wiley-Interscience, Hoboken (2008)
15. Storn, R.: Differential evolution design of an iir-filter. In: Proceedings of IEEE International Conference on Evolutionary Computation, pp. 268–273 (1996)
16. dos Santos Coelho, L., Mariani, V.C.: Improved differential evolution algorithms for handling economic dispatch optimization with generator constraints. Energy Convers. Manage. **48**(5), 1631–1639 (2007)
17. Chiou, J.-P., Wang, F.-S.: Hybrid method of evolutionary algorithms for static and dynamic optimization problems with application to a fed-batch fermentation process. Comput. Chem. Eng. **23**(9), 1277–1291 (1999)
18. Price, K.V., Storn, R.M., Lampinen, J.A.: Differential Evolution: A Practical Approach to Global Optimization. Springer, Heidelberg (2005)
19. Fusiello, A., Benedetti, A., Farenzena, M., Busti, A.: Globally convergent autocalibration using interval analysis. IEEE Trans. Pattern Anal. Mach. Intell. **26**, 1633–1638 (2004)
20. Yao, X., Liu, Y., Lin, G.: Evolutionary programming made faster. Evol. Comput. **3**(2), 82–102 (1999)
21. Fuchs, M., Neumaier, A.: A splitting technique for discrete search based on convex relaxation. J. Uncertain Syst. **4**(1), 14–21 (2010)
22. Page, L., Brin, S., Motwani, R., Winograd, T.: The pagerank citation ranking: Bringing order to the web. Technical report, Stanford InfoLab (1999)

Step Down and Step Up Statistical Procedures for Stock Selection with Sharp Ratio

A.P. Koldanov$^{(\boxtimes)}$, V.A. Kalyagin, and P.M. Pardalos

Laboratory of Algorithms and Technologies for Network Analysis,
National Research University Higher School of Economics,
Rodionova 136, Nizhny Novgorod 603155, Russia
akoldanov@hse.ru

Abstract. Stock selection by Sharp ratio is considered in the framework of multiple statistical hypotheses testing theory. The main attention is paid to comparison of Holm step down and Hochberg step up procedures for different loss functions. Comparison is made on the basis of conditional risk as a function of selection threshold. This approach allows to discover that properties of procedures depend not only on relationship between test statistics, but also depend on dispersion of Sharp ratios. Difference in error rate between two procedures is increasing when the concentration of Sharp ratios is increasing. When Sharp ratios do not have a concentration points there is no significant difference in quality of both procedures.

Keywords: Market network · Stock selection · Sharp ratio · Stepwise multiple testing statistical procedures · Holm procedure · Hochberg procedure

1 Introduction

Financial market can be considered as a complex network represented by a complete weighted graph. Market graph is a particular structure in this network [1]. It is known [10] that independent sets in market graph can be useful for portfolio optimization if one first selects stocks by Sharp ratio. In the present paper the stock selection by Shap ratio is considered in the framework of multiple hypothesis testing theory. There are two type of multiple testing statistical procedures: single-step and step-wise statistical procedures [6,13,14]. There is an intensive discussion of different properties of step-wise multiple testing statistical procedures with applications to bioinformatics last decades. In general, quality of step-wise procedures is related with degree of dependence of individual tests statistics. Important attention is paid to the case of independent statistics [3] and to the case of positive pairwise dependent statistics [2].

In this paper we investigate statistical procedures of stock selection by Sharp ratio by studying its properties as a function of the selection threshold. This point of view seems to be novel in multiple hypothesis testing but it is known to

© Springer International Publishing Switzerland 2015
P. Pardalos et al. (Eds.): MOD 2015, LNCS 9432, pp. 26–36, 2015.
DOI: 10.1007/978-3-319-27926-8_3

be an appropriate technique of data mining in market network analysis [1,11]. In our study we use a theoretical framework developed in [8,9] for stock selection with returns. Following this approach we use conditional risk as comparison criteria for different loss functions. We consider two types of loss functions: 0-1 W_1 loss function and 1-0 W_2 loss function. The first function W_1 equals 1 if there is at least one error of false rejection (error of the first kind or type I error), and equals 0 otherwise. The second function W_2 equals 1 if there is at least one error of false acceptance (error of the second kind or type II error), and equals 0 otherwise. *Conditional risk* is the expected value of the loss function.

Our main interest is a comparison of two well known multiple testing statistical procedures: Holm step down multiple test procedure [4] and Hochberg step up multiple test procedure [5]. Holm step down multiple test procedure is a statistical procedure with control of conditional risk for W_1 loss function. Theoretical estimation of conditional risk for Hochberg step up multiple test procedure is more difficult task but in practice it shows a good performance [7]. To compare above mentioned multiple testing statistical procedures we consider two extreme cases: independent individual tests statistics and linearly dependent individual tests statistics. Our main finding is: properties of procedures depend not only on relationship between individual tests statistics but also depend on dispersion of Sharp ratios. We show that the difference in error rate between two procedures is increasing when the concentration of Sharp ratios is increasing. In all cases Hochberg procedure is preferable to Holm procedure.

The paper is organized as follows. In Sect. 2 we formulate the stock selection problem and introduce conditional risk to measure a quality of statistical procedures. In Sect. 3 we introduce individual tests statistics for Sharp ratio and discuss its properties. In Sect. 4 we give a detailed description of Hochberg step up multiple test procedure for stock selection and of Holm step down multiple test. In Sect. 5 the results of comparison of stock selection statistical procedures are given and discussed. The Sect. 6 summarizes the main finding of the paper.

2 Stock Selection Problem, Decision Functions and Conditional Risk

We consider a stock market. Characteristic of stock is described by the random variable $X_i(t)$ which represent the value of attribute (price, return, volume, ...) of stock i at the moment t. Let N be the number of stocks in the financial market, n be the number of observations, $x_i(t)$ be observation of $X_i(t)$, $i = 1, 2, \ldots, N$, $t = 1, 2, \ldots, n$. We define sample space as $R^{N \times n}$ with elements $(x_i(t))$, and denote the matrix of all observations by $x = ||x_i(t)||$. We make the following assumptions:

- Random variables $X_i(t), t = 1, ..., n$ are independent for fixed i, and have all the same distribution as a random variable $X_i(i = 1, ..., N)$. This is standard assumption to model a sample of observations.
- Random vector $(X_1, X_2, ..., X_N)$ has a multivariate normal distribution with covariances matrix $\Sigma = ||\sigma_{i,j}||$ and vectors of means $\mu = (\mu_1, \mu_2, \ldots, \mu_N)$.

This assumption can be considered for example as first approximation for stocks returns multivariate distribution.

Sharp ratio for the stock i is defined by

$$Sh_i := \frac{\mu_i}{\sqrt{\sigma_{i,i}}}.$$

Selection Problem: For a given set of observations x select the stocks satisfying condition $Sh_i > Sh_0$, where Sh_0 is a given threshold. This problem is a multiple decision problem of choosing by observations one hypothesis from the set of hypotheses:

$$H_{i_1,i_2,\ldots i_N} : Sh_{i_k} \leq Sh_0, \text{ if } i_k = 0, \quad Sh_{i_k} > Sh_0, \text{ if } i_k = 1 \quad (1)$$

where $i_k \in \{0,1\}$, $k = 1,2,\ldots,N$. For a fixed threshold Sh_0 total number of hypotheses equals to $L = 2^N$.

Decision function $\delta(x)$ is a map from the sample space $R^{N \times n}$ to the decision space $D = \{d_{i_1,i_2,\ldots i_N}\}$, where $d_{i_1,i_2,\ldots i_N}$ is the decision to accept the hypothesis $H_{i_1,i_2,\ldots i_N}$, $i_k \in \{0,1\}$, $k = 1,2,\ldots,N$.

Individual Hypotheses: Formulated problem is equivalent to multiple (simultaneous) testing of individual hypothesis

$$h_i : Sh_i \leq Sh_0 \text{ vs } k_i : Sh_i > Sh_0 \; i = 1,\ldots,N. \quad (2)$$

Loss Functions: Denote by $W(H_{i_1,i_2,\ldots,i_N}, d_{j_1,j_2,\ldots,j_N})$ the loss from the decision $d_{j_1,j_2,\ldots,j_N}$ when the hypothesis $H_{i_1,i_2,\ldots,i_N}$ is true. We consider two loss functions: W_1 and W_2:

$$W_1(H_{i_1,i_2,\ldots,i_N}, d_{j_1,j_2,\ldots,j_N}) = \begin{cases} 1, \exists k \text{ such that } i_k = 0 \text{ and } j_k = 1 \\ 0, \, else \end{cases} \quad (3)$$

$$W_2(H_{i_1,i_2,\ldots,i_N}, d_{j_1,j_2,\ldots,j_N}) = \begin{cases} 1, \exists k \text{ such that } i_k = 1 \text{ and } j_k = 0 \\ 0, \, else \end{cases} \quad (4)$$

The loss functions W_1 and W_2 are traditionally used in the theory of multiple hypotheses testing [6,13]. Another type of loss functions (so called additive loss functions) was introduced in [12] and used in multiple decision theory and applications [8,9,11].

Conditional Risk: For any statistical procedure δ and true hypothesis $H_{i_1,i_2,\ldots,i_N}$ the conditional risk is defined by

$$Risk(W; H_{i_1,i_2,\ldots,i_N}, \delta) := E[W(H_{i_1,i_2,\ldots,i_N}, \delta)]$$

$$= \sum_{j_1,j_2,\ldots,j_n \in \{0,1\}} W(H_{i_1,i_2,\ldots,i_N}, d_{j_1,j_2,\ldots,j_N}) \quad (5)$$

$$P(\delta = d_{j_1,j_2,\ldots,j_N} / H_{i_1,i_2,\ldots,i_N})$$

One has for the 0-1 loss functions W_1, W_2:

$$Risk(W_1; H_{i_1, i_2, \ldots, i_N}, \delta) = 1 - P(\delta = d_{j_1, j_2, \ldots, j_N} \text{ such that } j_s = 0 \text{ if } i_s = 0)$$

$$Risk(W_2; H_{i_1, i_2, \ldots, i_N}, \delta) = 1 - P(\delta = d_{j_1, j_2, \ldots, j_N} \text{ such that } j_s = 1 \text{ if } i_s = 1)$$

Note that $Risk(W_1)$ is equal to the probability of at least one false rejection (type I error), and $Risk(W_2)$ is equal to the probability of at least one false acceptance (type II error). In multiple testing literature $Risk(W_1)$ is usually denoted as FWER (Family Wise Error Rate [6]). $Risk(W_1)$ is a generalization to multiple testing of classical significance level in individual hypothesis testing. $Risk(W_2)$ is a generalization to multiple testing of power of test in individual hypothesis testing.

3   Sample Sharp Ratio Statistics

Consider individual hypothesis (2). Sample Sharp ratio statistics is defined by

$$F_i = \sqrt{n} \frac{\overline{x}_i}{\sqrt{s_{i,i}}}, \quad \overline{x}_i = \frac{1}{n} \sum_{t=1}^{t=n} x_i(t), \quad s_{i,i} = \frac{1}{n-1} \sum_{t=1}^{t=n} (x_i(t) - \overline{x}_i)^2$$

Statistics F_i has non central Student distribution with density function [13]

$$p(x; Sh_i) = \frac{1}{2^{\frac{1}{2}(n+1)} \Gamma(\frac{1}{2}n) \sqrt{\pi n}} \int_0^\infty y^{\frac{1}{2}(n-1)} \exp(-\frac{1}{2}y) \exp[-\frac{1}{2}(x\sqrt{\frac{y}{n}} - \frac{\mu_i}{\sqrt{\sigma_{i,i}}})^2] dy$$

Uniformly most powerful test for individual hypothesis

$$h_i : Sh_i \leq Sh_0 \text{ vs } k_i : Sh_i > Sh_0$$

in the class of invariant under multiplication by a positive common constant is given by [13]:

$$\varphi(x) = \begin{cases} 1, F_i > F_0 \\ 0, F_i \leq F_0 \end{cases} \tag{6}$$

where F_0 is defined from the equation (α is significance level of the test)

$$\int_{F_0}^\infty p(x; Sh_0) dx = \alpha$$

This equation is hard to solve for a large value of n. From the other hand one can use asymtotic theory. According to general asymptotic theory [13], if $(\mu_i/\sqrt{\sigma_{i,i}}) = Sh_0$, the following individual tests statistics has asymptotically standard normal distribution

$$T_i = \sqrt{\frac{n}{1 + \frac{1}{2}Sh_0^2}} \left(\frac{\overline{x}_i}{\sqrt{s_{i,i}}} - Sh_0 \right)$$

In what follows we will replace the test (6) by the test

$$\varphi(x) = \left\{ \begin{array}{ll} 1, & T_i > c \\ 0, & T_i \leq c \end{array} \right. \tag{7}$$

where the constant c is defined from the equation $\Phi(c) = 1 - \alpha$, $\Phi(x)$ being cumulative distribution function for standard normal distribution.

4   Multiple Test Procedures

In this section we describe stepwise statistical procedures for the solution of the problem (1). First we give a general sequentially acceptance (step-up) framework for these procedures and describe in details the Hochberg procedure. Second we give a general sequentially rejective (step-down) framework and discuss in details Holm multiple tests procedure. In what follows we use the notation *H-procedure* for the Holm multiple test procedure, *Hg-procedure* for the Hochberg multiple test procedure. Associated decision functions will be denoted by δ^H and δ^{Hg} respectively.

General Sequentially Acceptance (Step-Up) Test for Stock Selection: The algorithm consists of at most N steps. At each step either one individual hypothesis h is accepted or all remaining hypotheses are rejected. For a given set of observations the decision $d_{i_1,i_2,\ldots,i_N}$ is constructed as follows: let

$$T_i(x) = \sqrt{\frac{n}{1 + \frac{1}{2}Sh_0^2}} \left(\frac{\overline{x}_i}{\sqrt{s_{i,i}}} - Sh_0 \right)$$

- Step 1: If

$$\min_{i=1,\ldots,N} T_i(x) > c_1$$

then the decision is $d_{111\ldots1}$: reject all hypotheses h_i, $i = 1, 2, \ldots, N$, else if $\min_{i=1,\ldots,N} T_i = T_{k_1}$ then accept hypothesis $h_{k_1} : Sh_{k_1} \leq Sh_0$ (put $i_s = 0, s = k_1$ for the decision $d_{i_1,i_2,\ldots,i_N}$) and go to step 2.
- ...
- Step M: Let $I = \{k_1, k_2, \ldots, k_{M-1}\}$ be the set of indexes of previously accepted hypotheses. If

$$\min_{i=1,\ldots,N; i \notin I} T_i(x) > c_M$$

then the decision is $d_{i_1,i_2,\ldots,i_N}$ with $i_s = 0, s \in I$ and $i_s = 1, s \notin I$: reject all hypotheses h_i, $i = 1, 2, \ldots, N$, $i \notin I$, else if $\min_{i=1,\ldots,N; i \notin I} T_i = T_{k_M}$ then accept hypothesis $h_{k_M} : Sh_{k_M} \leq Sh_0$ (put $i_s = 0, s \in I$ and $i_s = 0, s = k_M$ for the decision $d_{i_1,i_2,\ldots,i_N}$) and go to step (M+1).
- ...
- Step N: Let $I = \{k_1, k_2, \ldots, k_{N-1}\}$ be the set of indexes of previously accepted hypotheses. Let $l \notin I$. If

$$T_l(x) > c_N$$

then the decision is $d_{i_1,i_2,\dots,i_N}$ with $i_s = 1, s = l$ and $i_s = 0, s \neq l$: reject the hypothesis $Sh_l \leq Sh_0$
else accept hypothesis $h_l : Sh_l \leq Sh_0$ (the taken decision is $d_{00\dots00}$).

Hochberg multiple test step up procedure is obtained from general sequentially acceptive algorithm by choosing critical values c_M^{Hg}, $M = 1, 2, \dots, N$. Let $\Phi(x)$ be the standard normal distribution function. Then for a given value of significance level α, c_M^{Hg} are defined from the equations

$$\Phi(c_M^{Hg}) = 1 - \frac{\alpha}{M}, \quad M = 1, 2, \dots, N.$$

Note that $c_1^{Hg} < c_2^{Hg} < \cdots < c_N^{Hg}$. The constants C_M^{Hg} can be written as $C_M^{Hg} = u_{1-\alpha/M}$, where $u_{1-\alpha/M}$ is the $(1 - \alpha/M)$-percentile of standard normal distribution.

General Sequentially Rejective (Step-Down) Test for Stock Selection:
The algorithm consists of at most N steps. At each step either one individual hypothesis h is rejected or all remaining hypotheses are accepted. For a given set of observations the decision $d_{i_1,i_2,\dots,i_N}$ is constructed as follows:

– Step 1: If

$$\max_{i=1,\dots,N} T_i(x) \leq c_1$$

then the decision is $d_{000\dots0}$: accept all hypotheses h_i, $i = 1, 2, \dots, N$,
else if $\max_{i=1,\dots,N} T_i = T_{k_1}$ then reject hypothesis $h_{k_1} : Sh_{k_1} \leq Sh_0$ (put $i_s = 1, s = k_1$ for the decision $d_{i_1,i_2,\dots,i_N}$) and go to step 2.
– ...
– Step M: Let $I = \{k_1, k_2, \dots, k_{M-1}\}$ be the set of indexes of previously rejected hypotheses. If

$$\max_{i=1,\dots,N; i \notin I} T_i(r) \leq c_M$$

then the decision is $d_{i_1,i_2,\dots,i_N}$ with $i_s = 1, s \in I$ and $i_s = 0, s \notin I$: accept all hypotheses h_i, $i = 1, 2, \dots, N$, $i \notin I$,
else if $\max_{i=1,\dots,N; i \notin I} T_i = T_{k_M}$ then reject hypothesis $h_{k_M} : Sh_{k_M} \leq Sh_0$ (put $i_s = 1, s \in I$ and $i_s = 1, s = k_M$ for the decision $d_{i_1,i_2,\dots,i_N}$) and go to step (M+1).
– ...
– Step N: Let $I = \{k_1, k_2, \dots, k_{N-1}\}$ be the set of indexes of previously rejected hypotheses. Let $l \notin I$. If

$$T_l(x) \leq c_N$$

then the decision is $d_{i_1,i_2,\dots,i_N}$ with $i_s = 0, s = l$ and $i_s = 1, s \neq l$: accept the hypothesis

$$Sh_l \leq Sh_0$$

else reject hypothesis $h_l : Sh_l \leq Sh_0$ (the taken decision is $d_{11\dots11}$).

Different statistical procedures are obtained from general sequentially rejective test by choosing critical values c_M, $M = 1, 2, \ldots, N$. Let α be a significance level. Let $\Phi(x)$ be the standard normal distribution function. For the H-procedure one has $c_M = c_M^H$, $M = 1, 2, \ldots, N$, where c_M^H are defined from the equations $\Phi(c_M^H) = 1 - \frac{\alpha}{N-M+1}$. Note that $c_1^H > c_2^H > \cdots > c_N^H$. The constants C_M^H can be written as $C_M^H = u_{1-\alpha/(N-M+1)}$, where $u_{1-\alpha/(N-M+1)}$ is the $(1 - \alpha/(N - M + 1))$-percentile of standard normal distribution. One has $c_M^H = c_{N-M+1}^{Hg}$, $M = 1, 2, \ldots, N$.

Statistical procedure H controls the conditional risk for the loss function W_1. It means that overall error rate for these procedure is less or equal to α. Overall error rate for Hg-procedure is a subject of intensive investigations. It is known [15], for example, that Hg-procedure control the conditional risk for the loss function W_1 in the case of positive dependence of individual tests statistics T_i, T_j, $i, j = 1, 2, \ldots, N$.

5   Comparative Analysis of Step Up and Step Down Multiple Test Procedures

In this section we compare H and Hg statistical procedures. We will make a comparison using two criteria: concentration of Sharp ratios, dependence of test statistics.

Concentrated Case: Concentration of Sharp ratios can be measured by its variance. Consider the most concentrated case where all Sharp ratios are equal: $Sh_1 = Sh_2 = \cdots = Sh_N = Sh^0$. This case is of interest because in this case one can expect a maximum error rate. We consider two extreme cases for dependence of individual test statistics: random variables $T_1, T_2, \ldots, T_N$ are independent and random variables $T_1, T_2, \ldots, T_N$ are linearly dependent. In these cases it is known that H-procedure and Hg-procedure control the conditional risk for W_1 loss function. Therefore to compare the quality of procedures one has to consider the behaviour of conditional risk as a function of threshold for W_2 loss function. We start with $N = 2$. Let $Sh_0 = Sh^0$. In this case one can calculate explicitly conditional risks for W_1, W_2.

Let X_1 and X_2 are independent Gaussian random variables with the same means and variances. In this case individual tests statistics T_1 and T_2 are independent. For the W_1 loss function one has:

$$Risk(W_1; H_{0,0}, \delta^H) = \alpha - \frac{\alpha^2}{4}, \quad Risk(W_1; H_{0,0}, \delta^{Hg}) = \alpha,$$

Both procedures have FWER (Family Wise Error Rate) less or equal to α. The difference between conditional risks is $\alpha^2/4$.

For the W_2 loss function one has $Risk(W_2; H_{1,1}, \delta^H) = Risk(W_2; H_{1,1}, \delta^{Hg}) = 0$ $(Sh_0 = Sh^0)$ but the comparison can be obtained from the following relations:

$$\lim_{Sh_0 \to Sh^0 - 0} Risk(W_2; H_{1,1}, \delta^H) = 1 - \frac{3}{4}\alpha^2, \quad \lim_{Sh_0 \to Sh^0 - 0} Risk(W_2; H_{1,1}, \delta^{Hg}) = 1 - \alpha^2,$$

It means that in a neighborhood of concentration point Sh^0, Hg-procedures is more accurate than H-procedure for W_2 loss function. The difference between conditional risks is $\alpha^2/4$.

Let X_1 and X_2 are linearly dependent Gaussian random variables. In this case individual tests statistics T_1 and T_2 are lineary dependent. For the W_1 loss function one has:

$$Risk(W_1; H_{0,0}, \delta^H) = \frac{\alpha}{2}, \quad Risk(W_1; H_{0,0}, \delta^{Hg}) = \alpha,$$

Both procedures have FWER less or equal to α. The difference between conditional risks is $\alpha/2$.

For the W_2 loss function one has $Risk(W_2; H_{1,1}, \delta^H) = Risk(W_2; H_{1,1}, \delta^{Hg}) = 0$ $(Sh_0 = Sh^0)$ but the comparison can be obtained from the following relations:

$$\lim_{Sh_0 \to Sh^0 - 0} Risk(W_2; H_{1,1}, \delta^H) = 1 - \frac{\alpha}{2}, \quad \lim_{Sh_0 \to Sh^0 - 0} Risk(W_2; H_{1,1}, \delta^{Hg}) = 1 - \alpha,$$

It means that in a neighborhood of concentration point Sh^0, Hg-procedures is more accurate than H-procedure for W_2 loss function. The difference between conditional risks is $\alpha/2$.

Behavior of $Risk(W_2)$ for $N = 2$ as a function of threshold Sh_0 is illustrated on the Fig. 1. It is important to note that Hg-procedure is more accurate for $Risk(W_2)$. Moreover sensibility of conditional risk to degree of dependence between T_1 and T_2 is more important for Hg-procedure than for H-procedure. The Fig. 2 shows the behavior of conditional risk $Risk(W_2)$ for $N = 100$. The conclusion is similar: Hg-procedure is more accurate and sensibility of conditional risk to degree of dependence between $T_1, T_2, \ldots, T_N$ is more important for Hg-procedure than for H-procedure.

Non Concentrated Case: we start with illustrative example for $N = 3$. Consider the following values of Sharp rations: $Sh_1 = 1.0$, $Sh_2 = 1.5$, $Sh_3 = 2.0$.

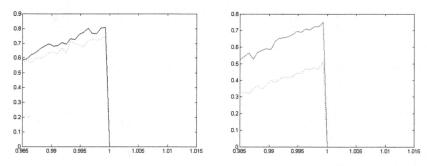

Fig. 1. Risk $Risk(W_2)$ as a function of Sh_0. Left: H-procedure. Solid line - independent random variables, dashed line - linearly dependent random variables. Right: Hg-procedure. Solid line - independent random variables, dashed line - linearly dependent random variables. Horizontal axe represents the value of Sh_0. $N = 2$, $\alpha = 0.5$, $Sh^0 = 1$.

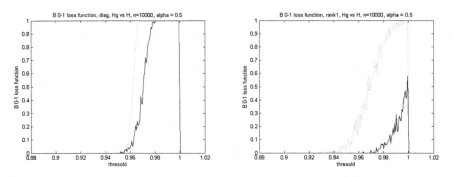

Fig. 2. Risk $Risk(W_2)$ as a function of Sh_0 for H and Hg-procedures. Solid line - Hg-procedure, dashed line - H-procedure. Left: independent random variables. Right: linearly dependent random variables. Horizontal axe represents the value of Sh_0. $N = 100$, $\alpha = 0.5$, $Sh^0 = 1$.

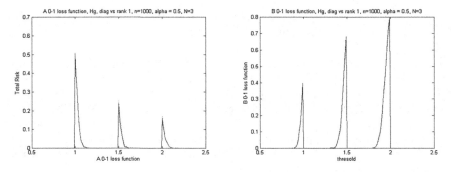

Fig. 3. Conditional risk as a function of Sh_0 for H and Hg-procedures. Left: $Risk(W_1)$. Right: $Risk(W_2)$. Horizontal axe represents the value of Sh_0. $N = 3$, $\alpha = 0.5$, $Sh_1 = 1.0, Sh_2 = 1.5, Sh_3 = 2.0$. Solid line - Hg-procedure, dashed line - H-procedure.

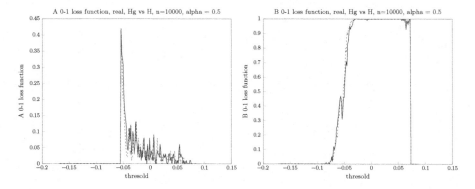

Fig. 4. Conditional risk as a function of Sh_0 for H and Hg-procedures for the real market. Left: $Risk(W_1)$. Right: $Risk(W_2)$. Horizontal axe represents the value of Sh_0. $N = 100$, $\alpha = 0.5$.

Figure 3 shows behavior of conditional risks $Risk(W_1)$, $Risk(W_2)$. In contrast with concentration case there is no difference in quality between H and Hg procedures independently from degree of dependence of random variables T_1, T_2, T_3.

Now consider the case of real stock market: NYSE stock market, $N = 100$ (we take companies greatest by capitalization), period of observations from 20.01.2010 until 06.02.2014. There is no concentration of Sharp ratios for this market and the behavior of conditional risks $Risk(W_1)$, $Risk(W_2)$ is similar to the example with $N = 3$. The Fig. 4 illustrates this behavior.

6   Concluding Remarks

Conditional risk of two well known step-wise statistical procedures (Holm and Hochberg procedures) for stock selection with Sharp ratio is investigated as a function of selection threshold. Four extreme cases are considered to emphasize a difference between two procedures:

– Concentrated Sharp ratios and independent individual tests statistics.
– Concentrated Sharp ratios and linearly dependent individual tests statistics.
– Non concentrated Sharp ratios and independent individual tests statistics.
– Non concentrated Sharp ratios and linearly dependent individual tests statistics.

In all cases both procedures control the conditional risk for W_1 loss function (Family Wise Error Rate) at a fixed level α. For W_2 loss function Hochberg procedure is preferable. Advantage of this procedure takes place with concentration of Sharp ratios. When Sharp ratios do not have a concentration points there is no significant difference in quality of both procedures. At the same time the quality of Hochberg procedure is more sensible to the degree of dependence of random variables. For the real market with concentration of Sharp ratios it is appropriate to use Hochberg statistical procedures for stock selection. From the other hand Holm procedure is more robust to the degree of dependence of individual tests statistics and can be used for all other cases.

Acknowledgement. The authors are partly supported by National Research University Higher School of Economics, Russian Federation Government grant, N. 11.G34.31. 0057 and RFFI grant 14-01-00807.

References

1. Boginski, V., Butenko, S., Pardalos, P.M.: Statistical analysis of financial networks. Comput. Stat. Data Anal. **48**(2), 431–443 (2005)
2. Cai, G., Sarkar, S.K.: Modified Simes' critical values under positive dependence. J. Stat. Plann. Infer. **136**, 4129–4146 (2006)
3. Cai, G., Sarkar, S.K.: Modified Simes' critical values under independence. Stat. Probab. Lett. **78**, 1362–1368 (2008)

4. Holm, S.: A simple sequentially rejective multiple test procedure. Scand. J. Stat. **6**, 65–70 (1979)
5. Hochberg, Y.: A sharper Bonferroni procedure for multiple tests of significance. Biometrika **75**, 800–802 (1988)
6. Hochberg, Y., Tamhane, A.: Multiple Comparison Procedures. John Wiley and Sons, New York (1987)
7. Huang, Y., Hsu, J.C.: Hochberg's step-up method: cutting corners off holm's step-down method. Biometrika **94**(4), 965–975 (2007)
8. Koldanov, P.A., Bautin, G.A.: Multiple decision problem for stock selection in market network. In: Pardalos, P.M., Resende, M., Vogiatzis, C., Walteros, J. (eds.) Learning and Intelligent Optimization. LNCS, vol. 8426, pp. 98–110. Springer, Heidelberg (2014)
9. Koldanov, P.A., Kalyagin, V.A., Bautin, G.A.: On some statistical procedures for stock selection problem. Ann. Math. Artif. Intell. doi:10.1007/s10472-014-9447-1
10. Kalyagin, V.A., Koldanov, P.A., Koldanov, A.P., Zamaraev, V.A.: Market graph and markowitz model. In: Rassias, T.M., Floudas, C.A., Butenko, S. (eds.) Optimization in Science and Engineering (In Honor of the 60th Birthday of Panos M. Pardalos), pp. 293–306. Springer Science+Business Media, New York (2014)
11. Koldanov, A.P., Koldanov, P.A., Kalyagin, V.A., Pardalos, P.M.: Statistical procedures for the market graph construction. Comput. Stat. Data Anal. **68**, 17–29 (2013)
12. Lehmann, E.L.: A theory of some multiple decision procedures 1. Ann. Math. Stat. **28**, 1–25 (1957)
13. Lehmann, E.L., Romano, J.P.: Testing Statistical Hypotheses. Springer, New York (2005)
14. Rao, C.V., Swarupchand, U.: Multiple comparison procedures - a note and a bibliography. J. Stat. **16**, 66–109 (2009)
15. Sarkar, S.K., Chang, C.K.: The simes method for multiple testing with positively dependent test statistics. J. Am. Stat. Assoc. **92**(440), 1601–1608 (1997)

Differentiating the Multipoint Expected Improvement for Optimal Batch Design

Sébastien Marmin[1,2,3]([⊠]), Clément Chevalier[4,5], and David Ginsbourger[1,6]

[1] Department of Mathematics and Statistics, IMSV,
University of Bern, Bern, Switzerland
marminsebastien@gmail.com
[2] Institut de Radioprotection et de Sûreté Nucléaire, Cadarache, France
[3] École Centrale de Marseille, Marseille, France
[4] Institute of Statistics, University of Neuchâtel, Neuchâtel, Switzerland
[5] Institute of Mathematics, University of Zurich, Zürich, Switzerland
[6] Idiap Research Institute, Martigny, Switzerland

Abstract. This work deals with parallel optimization of expensive objective functions which are modelled as sample realizations of Gaussian processes. The study is formalized as a Bayesian optimization problem, or continuous multi-armed bandit problem, where a batch of $q > 0$ arms is pulled in parallel at each iteration. Several algorithms have been developed for choosing batches by trading off exploitation and exploration. As of today, the maximum Expected Improvement (EI) and Upper Confidence Bound (UCB) selection rules appear as the most prominent approaches for batch selection. Here, we build upon recent work on the multipoint Expected Improvement criterion, for which an analytic expansion relying on Tallis' formula was recently established. The computational burden of this selection rule being still an issue in application, we derive a closed-form expression for the gradient of the multipoint Expected Improvement, which aims at facilitating its maximization using gradient-based ascent algorithms. Substantial computational savings are shown in application. In addition, our algorithms are tested numerically and compared to state-of-the-art UCB-based batch-sequential algorithms. Combining starting designs relying on UCB with gradient-based EI local optimization finally appears as a sound option for batch design in distributed Gaussian Process optimization.

Keywords: Bayesian optimization · Batch-sequential design · GP · UCB

1 Introduction

Global optimization of deterministic functions under a drastically limited evaluation budget is a topic of growing interest with important industrial applications. Dealing with such expensive black-box simulators is typically addressed

© Springer International Publishing Switzerland 2015
P. Pardalos et al. (Eds.): MOD 2015, LNCS 9432, pp. 37–48, 2015.
DOI: 10.1007/978-3-319-27926-8_4

through the introduction of surrogate models that are used both for reconstructing the objective function and guiding parsimonious evaluation strategies. This approach is used in various scientific communities and referred to as Bayesian optimization, but also as kriging-based or multi-armed bandit optimization [5, 11, 15, 16, 20, 23, 25]. Among such Gaussian process optimization methods, two concepts of algorithm relying on sequential maximization of infill sampling criteria are particularly popular in the literature. In the EGO algorithm of [16], the sequence of decisions (of where to evaluate the objective function at each iteration) is guided by the Expected Improvement (EI) criterion [19], which is known to be one-step lookahead optimal [14]. On the other hand, the Upper Confidence Bound (UCB) algorithm [1] maximizes sequentially a well-chosen kriging quantile, that is, a quantile of the pointwise posterior Gaussian process distribution. Similarly to EI [6, 24], the consistency of the algorithm has been established and rates of convergence have been obtained [23].

Recently, different methods inspired from the two latter algorithms have been proposed to deal with the typical case where $q > 1$ CPUs are available. Such synchronous distributed methods provide at each iteration a batch of q points which can be evaluated in parallel. For instance, [10] generalizes the UCB algorithm to a batch-sequential version by maximizing kriging quantiles and assuming dummy responses equal to the posterior mean of the Gaussian process. This approach can be compared with the so-called Kriging Believer strategy of [15] where each batch is obtained by sequentially maximizing the one-point EI under the assumption that the previously chosen points have a response equal to their Kriging mean. Originally, the strategies suggested in [15] were introduced to cope with the difficulty to evaluate and maximize the multipoint Expected Improvement (q-EI) [22], which is the generalization of EI known to be one-batch lookahead optimal [7, 14]. One of the bottlenecks for q-EI maximization was that it was until recently evaluated through Monte-Carlo simulations [15], a reason that motivated [11] to propose a stochastic gradient algorithm for its maximization. Now, [8] established a closed-form expression enabling to compute q-EI at any batch of q points without appealing to Monte-Carlo simulations. However, the computational complexity involved to compute the criterion is still high and quickly grows with q. Besides, little has been published about the difficult maximization of the q-EI itself, which is an optimization problem in dimension qd, where d is the number of input variables.

In this work, we contribute to the latter problem by giving an analytical gradient of q-EI, in the space of dimension qd. Such a gradient is meant to simplify the local maximization of q-EI using gradient-based ascent algorithms. Closed-form expressions of q-EI and its gradient have been implemented in the DiceOptim R package [21], together with a multistart BFGS algorithm for maximizing q-EI. In addition, we suggest to use results of the BUCB algorithm as initial batches in multistart gradient-based ascents. These starting batches are shown to yield good local optima for q-EI. This article is organized as follows. Section 2 quickly recalls the basics of Gaussian process modeling and the closed-form expression of q-EI obtained in [8]. Section 3 details the analytical

q-EI gradient. Finally, numerical experiments comparing the performances of the q-EI maximization-based strategy and the BUCB algorithms are provided and discussed in Sect. 4. For readability and conciseness, the most technical details about q-EI gradient calculation are sent in Appendix.

2   General Context

Let $f : \boldsymbol{x} \in D \subset \mathbb{R}^d \longrightarrow \mathbb{R}$ be a real-valued function defined on a compact subset D of $\mathbb{R}^d, d \geq 1$. Throughout this article, we assume that we dispose of a set of n evaluations of f, $\mathcal{A}_n = \left(\boldsymbol{x}_{1:n} := \{ \boldsymbol{x}_1, \ldots, \boldsymbol{x}_n \}, \boldsymbol{y}_{1:n} = (f(\boldsymbol{x}_1), \ldots, f(\boldsymbol{x}_n))^\top \right)$, and that our goal is to evaluate f at well-chosen batches of q points in order to globally maximize it. Following each batch of evaluations, we observe q deterministic scalar responses, or rewards, $y_{n+1} = f(\boldsymbol{x}_{n+1}), \ldots, y_{n+q} = f(\boldsymbol{x}_{n+q})$. We use past observations in order to carefully choose the next q observation locations, aiming in the end to minimize the one-step lookahead regret $f(\boldsymbol{x}^*) - t_{n+q}$, where $\boldsymbol{x}^*$ is a maximizer of f and $t_i = \max_{j=1,\ldots,i}(f(\boldsymbol{x}_j))$. In this section, we first define the Gaussian process (GP) surrogate model used to make the decisions. Then we introduce the q-EI which is the optimal one-batch lookahead criterion (see, e.g., [3,12,14] for a definition and [7,14] for a proof).

2.1   Gaussian Process Modeling

The objective function f is a priori assumed to be a sample from a Gaussian process $Y \sim \mathcal{GP}(\mu, C)$, where $\mu(\cdot)$ and $C(\cdot, \cdot)$ are respectively the mean and covariance function of Y. At fixed $\mu(\cdot)$ and $C(\cdot, \cdot)$, conditioning Y on the set of observations $\mathcal{A}_n$ yields a GP posterior $Y(\boldsymbol{x})|\mathcal{A}_n \sim \mathcal{GP}(\mu_n, C_n)$ with:

$$\mu_n(\boldsymbol{x}) = \mu(\boldsymbol{x}) + \boldsymbol{c}_n(\boldsymbol{x})^\top \boldsymbol{C}_n^{-1}(\boldsymbol{y}_{1:n} - \mu(\boldsymbol{x}_{1:n})), \text{ and} \tag{1}$$

$$C_n(\boldsymbol{x}, \boldsymbol{x}^{'}) = C(\boldsymbol{x}, \boldsymbol{x}^{'}) - \boldsymbol{c}_n(\boldsymbol{x})^\top \boldsymbol{C}_n^{-1} \boldsymbol{c}_n(\boldsymbol{x}^{'}), \tag{2}$$

where $\boldsymbol{c}_n(\boldsymbol{x}) = (C(\boldsymbol{x}, \boldsymbol{x}_i))_{1 \leq i \leq n}$, and $\boldsymbol{C}_n = (C(\boldsymbol{x}_i, \boldsymbol{x}_j))_{1 \leq i,j \leq n}$. Note that, in realistic application settings, the mean and the covariance μ and C of the prior are assumed to depend on several parameters which require to be estimated. The results presented in this article and their implementations in the R package `DiceOptim` are compatible with this more general case. More detail about Eqs. (1), (2) with or without trend and covariance parameter estimation can be found in [21] and is omitted here for conciseness.

2.2   The Multipoint Expected Improvement Criterion

The Multipoint Expected Improvement (q-EI) selection rule consists in maximizing, over all possible batches of q points, the following criterion, which depends on a batch $\boldsymbol{X} = (\boldsymbol{x}_{n+1}, \ldots, \boldsymbol{x}_{n+q}) \in D^q$:

$$\text{EI}(\boldsymbol{X}) = \mathbb{E}\left[(\max Y(\boldsymbol{X}) - T_n)_+ \mid \mathcal{A}_n \right], \tag{3}$$

where $(\cdot)_+ = \max(\cdot, 0)$, and the threshold T_n is the currently observed maximum of Y, i.e. $T_n = \max_{1 \leq j \leq n} Y(\boldsymbol{x}_j)$. Recalling that $Y(\boldsymbol{X})|\mathcal{A}_n \sim \mathcal{N}(\boldsymbol{\mu}_n(\boldsymbol{X}), C_n(\boldsymbol{X}, \boldsymbol{X}))$, and denoting $Y(\boldsymbol{X}) = (Y_1, \ldots, Y_q)^\top$, an analytic expression of q-EI at locations $\boldsymbol{X}$ over any threshold $T \in \mathbb{R}$ can be found in [8] and is reproduced here:

$$\mathrm{EI}(\boldsymbol{X}) = \sum_{k=1}^{q} \left((m_k - T) \Phi_{q, \Sigma^{(k)}} \left(-\boldsymbol{m}^{(k)} \right) + \sum_{i=1}^{q} \Sigma_{ik}^{(k)} \varphi_{\Sigma_{ii}} \left(m_i^{(k)} \right) \Phi_{q-1, \Sigma_{|i}^{(k)}} \left(-\boldsymbol{m}_{|i}^{(k)} \right) \right) \tag{4}$$

where $\varphi_{\sigma^2}(\cdot)$ and $\Phi_{p, \Gamma}(\cdot)$ are respectively the density function of the centered normal distribution with variance σ^2 and the p-variate cumulative distribution function (CDF) of the centered normal distribution with covariance Γ; $\boldsymbol{m} = \mathbb{E}(Y(\boldsymbol{X})|\mathcal{A}_n)$ and $\Sigma = \mathrm{cov}(Y(\boldsymbol{X})|\mathcal{A}_n)$ are the conditional mean vector and covariance matrix of $Y(\boldsymbol{X})$; $\boldsymbol{m}^{(k)}$ and $\Sigma^{(k)}$, $1 \leq k \leq q$, are the conditional mean vector and covariance matrix of the affine transformation of $Y(\boldsymbol{X})$, $\boldsymbol{Z}^{(k)} = L^{(k)} Y(\boldsymbol{X}) + \boldsymbol{b}^{(k)}$, defined as $Z_j^{(k)} := Y_j$ for $j \neq k$ and $Z_k^{(k)} := T - Y_k$; and finally, for $(k, i) \in \{1, \ldots, q\}^2$, $\boldsymbol{m}_{|i}^{(k)}$ and $\Sigma_{|i}^{(k)}$ are the mean vector and covariance matrix of the Gaussian vector $(\boldsymbol{Z}_{-i}^{(k)}|Z_i^{(k)} = 0)$, the index $-i$ meaning that the ith component is removed.

3   Gradient of the Multipoint Expected Improvement

In this section, we provide an analytical formula for the gradient of q-EI. Getting such formula requires to carefully analyze the dependence of q-EI written in Eq. (4) on the batch locations $\boldsymbol{X} \in \mathbb{R}^{q \times d}$. This dependence is summarized in Fig. 1 and exhibits many chaining relations. In the forthcoming multivariate calculations, we use the following notations. Given two Banach spaces E and F, and a differentiable function $g : E \rightarrow F$, the differential of g at point x, written $d_x[g] : E \rightarrow F$, is the bounded linear map that best approximate g in the neighborhood of x. In the case where $E = \mathbb{R}^p$ and $F = \mathbb{R}$, it is well known that $\forall h \in E, d_x[g](h) = \langle \nabla g(x), h \rangle$. More generally the differential can be written in terms of Jacobian matrices, matrix derivatives and/or matrix scalar products where E and/or F are $\mathbb{R}^p$ or $\mathbb{R}^{p \times p}$. To simplify notations and handle the different indices in Eq. (4), we fix the indices i and k and focus on differentiating the function $\mathrm{EI}^{(k)(i)}$, standing for the generic term of the double sums in Eq. (4). We can perform the calculation of $d_{\boldsymbol{X}} \left[\mathrm{EI}^{(k)(i)} \right]$ by noticing that $\mathrm{EI}^{(k)(i)}$ can be rewritten using the functions $g_j, 1 \leq j \leq 8$ defined on Fig. 1 as follows:

$$\mathrm{EI}^{(k)(i)} = (m_k - T) \cdot g_7 \circ G + g_4 \circ g_2 \cdot g_5 \circ G \cdot g_8 \circ g_6 \circ G, \tag{5}$$

where $G = (g_3 \circ g_1, g_4 \circ g_2)$, $\circ$ is the composition operator and $\cdot$ the multiplication operator. The differentiation then consists in applying classical differentiation formulas for products and compositions to Eq. (5). Proposition 1

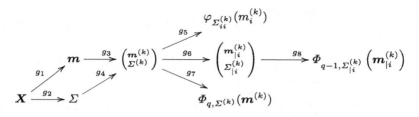

Fig. 1. Link between the different terms of Eq. (4) and the batch of points $\boldsymbol{X}$

summarizes the results. For conciseness, the formulae of the differentials involved in Eq. (6) are justified in the Appendix. The calculations notably rely on the differential of a normal cumulative distribution function with respect to its covariance matrix obtained via Plackett's formula [4].

Proposition 1. *The differential of the multipoint Expected Inmprovement criterion of Eq. (4) is given by* $d_{\boldsymbol{X}}\left[\mathrm{EI}\right] = \sum_{k=1}^{q}\sum_{i=1}^{q} d_{\boldsymbol{X}}\left[\mathrm{EI}^{(k)(i)}\right]$, *with*

$$d_{\boldsymbol{X}}\left[\mathrm{EI}^{(k)(i)}\right] = d_{\boldsymbol{X}}\left[m_k\right] \cdot g_7 \circ G + (m_k - T) \cdot d_{G(\boldsymbol{X})}\left[g_7\right] \circ d_{\boldsymbol{X}}\left[G\right] \qquad (6)$$
$$+ d_{g_2(\boldsymbol{X})}\left[g_4\right] \circ d_{\boldsymbol{X}}\left[g_2\right] \cdot g_5 \circ G \cdot g_8 \circ g_6 \circ G$$
$$+ g_4 \circ g_2 \cdot d_{G(\boldsymbol{X})}\left[g_5\right] \circ d_{\boldsymbol{X}}\left[G\right] \cdot g_8 \circ g_6 \circ G$$
$$+ g_4 \circ g_2 \cdot g_5 \circ G \cdot d_{g_6(G(\boldsymbol{X}))}\left[g_8\right] \circ d_{G(\boldsymbol{X})}\left[g_6\right] \circ d_{\boldsymbol{X}}\left[G\right],$$

where the g_j's are the functions introduced in Fig. 1. The g_j's and their respective differentials are as follow:

- $g_1 : \boldsymbol{X} \in D^q \to g_1(\boldsymbol{X}) = (\mu_n(\boldsymbol{x}_j))_{1 \le j \le q} \in \mathbb{R}^q$,
  $d_{\boldsymbol{X}}\left[g_1\right](H) = (\langle \nabla \boldsymbol{\mu}_n(\boldsymbol{x}_j), H_{j,1:d}^\top \rangle)_{1 \le j \le q}$,
  with $\nabla \boldsymbol{\mu}_n(\boldsymbol{x}_j) = \nabla \boldsymbol{\mu}(\boldsymbol{x}_j) + \left(\frac{\partial \boldsymbol{c}_n(\boldsymbol{x}_j)^\top}{\partial x_\ell}\right)_{1 \le \ell \le d} C_n^{-1}(\boldsymbol{y}_{1:n} - \mu(\boldsymbol{x}_{1:n}))$.
- $g_2 : \boldsymbol{X} \in D^q \to g_2(\boldsymbol{X}) = (C_n(\boldsymbol{x}_j, \boldsymbol{x}_\ell))_{1 \le j,\ell \le q} \in \mathcal{S}_{++}^q$. $\mathcal{S}_{++}^q$ *is the set of $q \times q$ positive definite matrices.*
  $d_{\boldsymbol{X}}\left[g_2\right](H) = \left(\langle \nabla_{\boldsymbol{x}} C_n(\boldsymbol{x}_j, \boldsymbol{x}_\ell), H_{j,1:d}^\top \rangle + \langle \nabla_{\boldsymbol{x}} C_n(\boldsymbol{x}_\ell, \boldsymbol{x}_j), H_{\ell,1:d}^\top \rangle\right)_{1 \le j,\ell \le q}$,
  with $\nabla_{\boldsymbol{x}} C_n(\boldsymbol{x}, \boldsymbol{x}') = \nabla_{\boldsymbol{x}} C(\boldsymbol{x}, \boldsymbol{x}') - \left(\frac{\partial \boldsymbol{c}_n(\boldsymbol{x})^\top}{\partial x_p}\right)_{1 \le p \le d} C_n^{-1} \boldsymbol{c}_n(\boldsymbol{x}')$.
- $G : \boldsymbol{X} \to (\boldsymbol{m}^{(k)}, \Sigma^{(k)})$, $d_{\boldsymbol{X}}\left[G\right] = \left(L^{(k)} d_{\boldsymbol{X}}\left[g_1\right], L^{(k)} d_{\boldsymbol{X}}\left[g_2\right] L^{(k)\top}\right)$.
- $g_7 : (\boldsymbol{a}, \Gamma) \in \mathbb{R}^q \times \mathcal{S}_{++}^q \to \Phi_{q,\Gamma}(\boldsymbol{a}) \in \mathbb{R}$,
  $d_{G(\boldsymbol{X})}\left[g_7\right](\boldsymbol{h}, H) = \langle \boldsymbol{h}, \nabla_{\boldsymbol{x}} \Phi_{q,\Sigma^{(k)}}(\boldsymbol{m}^{(k)}) \rangle + \mathrm{tr}(H \nabla_\Sigma \Phi_{q,\Sigma^{(k)}}(\boldsymbol{m}^{(k)}))$. $\nabla_{\boldsymbol{x}} \Phi_{q,\Sigma^{(k)}}$ and $\nabla_\Sigma \Phi_{q,\Sigma^{(k)}}$ *are the gradient of the multivariate Gaussian CDF with respect to $\boldsymbol{x}$ and to the covariance matrix, given in appendix.*
- $g_4 : \Sigma \to \Sigma^{(k)}$, $d_{g_2(\boldsymbol{X})}\left[g_4\right](H) = L^{(k)} H L^{(k)\top}$.
- $g_5 : (\boldsymbol{a}, \Gamma) \in \mathbb{R}^q \times \mathcal{S}_{++}^q \to \varphi_{\Gamma_{ii}}(a_i) \in \mathbb{R}$,
  $d_{G(\boldsymbol{X})}\left[g_5\right](\boldsymbol{h}, H) = \left(-\frac{a_i}{\Gamma_{ii}} h_i + \frac{1}{2}\left(\frac{a_i^2}{\Gamma_{ii}^2} - \frac{1}{\Gamma_{ii}}\right) H_{ii}\right) \varphi_{\Gamma_{ii}}(a_i)$

$- g_6 : (\boldsymbol{m}^{(k)}, \Sigma^{(k)}) \in \mathbb{R}^q \times \mathcal{S}^q_{++} \to (\boldsymbol{m}^{(k)}_{|i}, \Sigma^{(k)}_{|i}),$

$$d_{(\boldsymbol{m}^{(k)}, \Sigma^{(k)})}\, [g_6]\, (h, H) = \left(\boldsymbol{h}_{-i} - \frac{\boldsymbol{h}_i}{\Sigma^{(k)}_{ii}} \boldsymbol{\Sigma}^{(k)}_{-i,i} + \frac{m^{(k)}_i H_{ii}}{\Sigma^{(k)2}_{ii}} \boldsymbol{\Sigma}^{(k)}_{-i,i} - \frac{m^{(k)}_i}{\Sigma^{(k)}_{ii}} H_{-i,i}, \right.$$

$$\left. H_{-i,-i} + \frac{H_{ii}}{\Sigma^{(k)2}_{ii}} \boldsymbol{\Sigma}^{(k)}_{-i,i} \boldsymbol{\Sigma}^{(k)\top}_{-i,i} - \frac{1}{\Sigma^{(k)}_{ii}} H_{-i,i} \boldsymbol{\Sigma}^{(k)\top}_{-i,i} - \frac{1}{\Sigma^{(k)}_{ii}} \boldsymbol{\Sigma}^{(k)}_{-i,i} H^{\top}_{-i,i} \right)$$

$- g_8 : (\boldsymbol{a}, \Gamma) \in \mathbb{R}^{q-1} \times \mathcal{S}^{q-1}_{++} \to \Phi_{q-1, \Gamma}(\boldsymbol{a}) \in \mathbb{R},$
$d_{g_6(G(\boldsymbol{X}))}\, [g_8] = \langle \boldsymbol{h}, \nabla_{\boldsymbol{x}} \Phi_{q, \Sigma^{(k)}}(\boldsymbol{m}^{(k)}) \rangle + \mathrm{tr}(H \nabla_{\Sigma} \Phi_{q, \Sigma^{(k)}}(\boldsymbol{m}^{(k)})).$

The gradient of q-EI, relying on Eq. (6) is implemented in the version 1.5 of the DiceOptim R package [9], together with a gradient-based local optimization algorithm. In the next section, we show that the analytical computation of the gradient offers substantial computational savings compared to numerical computation based on a finite-difference scheme. In addition, we investigate the performances of the batch-sequential EGO algorithm consisting in sequentially maximizing q-EI, and we compare it with the BUCB algorithm of [10].

4   Numerical Tests

4.1   Computation Time

In this section, we illustrate the benefits – in terms of computation time – of using the analytical gradient formula of Sect. 3. We compare computation times of gradients computed analytically and numerically, through finite differences schemes. It is important to note that the computation of both q-EI and its gradient (see, Eqs. (4), (6)) involve several calls to the cumulative distribution functions (CDF) of the multivariate normal distribution. The latter CDF is computed numerically with the algorithms of [13] wrapped in the mnormt R package [2]. In our implementation, computing this CDF turns out to be the main bottleneck in terms of computation time. The total number of calls to this CDF (be it in dimension q, $q-1$, $q-2$ or $q-3$) is summarized in Table 1. From this table, let us remark that the number of CDF calls does not depend on d for the analytical q-EI gradient and is proportional to d for the numerical gradient. The use of the analytical gradient is thus expected to bring savings when q is not too large compared to d. Figure 2 depicts the ratio of computation times between numerical and analytical gradient, as a function of q and d. These were obtained by averaging the evaluation times of q-EI's gradient at 10 randomly-generated batches of size q for a given function in dimension d being a sample path of a GP with separable Matérn $(3/2)$ covariance function [21]. In the next section, we use the values $q = 6$ and $d = 5$ and we rely exclusively on the analytical q-EI formula which is now known to be faster.

4.2   Tests

Experimental Setup. We now compare the performances of two parallel Bayesian optimization algorithm based, respectively, on the UCB approach of [23]

Table 1. Total number of calls to the CDF of the multivariate Gaussian distribution for computing q-EI or its gradient for a function with d input variables. The last column gives the overall computational complexity.

	Φ_{q-3}	Φ_{q-2}	Φ_{q-1}	Φ_q	Total
Analytic q-EI	0	0	q^2	q	$O(q^2)$
Finite differences gradient	0	0	$q(d+1)\,q^2$	$q(d+1)\,q$	$O(dq^3)$
Analytic gradient	$q^2\frac{q(q-1)}{2}$	$q\frac{q(q-1)}{2}+q^3$	q^2+2q^2	q	$O(q^4)$

and on sequential q-EI maximizations. We consider a minimization problem in dimension $d = 5$ where $n = 50$ evaluations are performed initially and 10 batches of $q = 6$ observations are sequentially added. The objective functions are 50 different sample realizations of a zero mean GP with unit variance and separable isotropic Matérn $(3/2)$ covariance function with range parameter equal to one. Both algorithms use the same initial design of experiment of n points which are all S-optimal random Latin Hypercube designs [17]. The mean and covariance function of the underlying GP are supposed to be known (in practice, the hyperparameters of the GP model can be estimated by maximum likelihood [9]). Since it is difficult to draw sample realizations of the GP on the whole input space $D := [0,1]^d$, we instead draw 50 samples on a set of 2000 space-filling locations and interpolate each sample in order to obtain the 50 objective functions.

Two variants of the BUCB algorithms are tested. Each of them constructs a batch by sequentially minimizing the kriging quantile $\mu_n^\star(\boldsymbol{x}) - \beta_n s_n(\boldsymbol{x})$ where

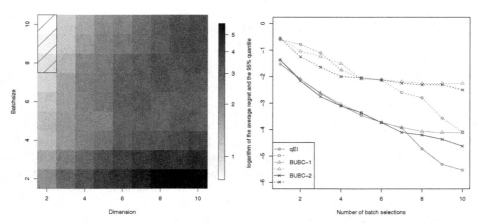

Fig. 2. Ratio between computation times of the numerical and analytical gradient of q-EI as a function of the dimension d and the batch size q. The hatched area indicates a ratio below 1.

Fig. 3. Logarithm of the average (plain lines) and 95 % quantile (dotted lines) of the regret for three different batch-sequential optimization strategies (see Sect. 4.2 for detail).

$s_n(\boldsymbol{x}) = \sqrt{C_n(\boldsymbol{x},\boldsymbol{x})}$ is the posterior standard deviation at step n and $\mu_n^\star(\boldsymbol{x})$ is the posterior mean conditioned both on the response at previous points and at points already selected in the current batch, with a dummy response fixed to their posterior means in the latter case. Following the settings of [10], in the first and second variant of BUCB, the coefficients β_n are given by:

$$\beta_n^{(1)} := 2\beta_{\text{mult}} \log\left(\frac{\pi^2 d}{6\delta}(k+1)^2\right) \text{ and } \beta_n^{(2)} := 2\beta_{\text{mult}} \log\left(\frac{\pi^2 d}{6\delta}(1+qk)^2\right) \quad (7)$$

where $\beta_{\text{mult}} = 0.1$, $\delta = 0.1$, and k is the number of already evaluated batches at time n, i.e., here, $k \in \{0, \ldots, 9\}$. The BUCB1 strategy is expected to select locations in regions with low posterior mean (exploitation) while BUCB2 is meant to favour more exploration due to a larger β_n. The minimization of the kriging quantile presented above is performed using a genetic algorithm [18]. Regarding the algorithm based on q-EI sequential maximization, we propose to use a multi-start BFGS algorithm with analytical gradient. This algorithms operates gradient descents directly in the space of dimension $qd = 30$. To limit computation time, the number of starting batches in the multi-start is set to 3. These 3 batches are obtained by running the BUCB1 algorithm presented above with 3 different values of β_{mult} equals to $0.05, 0.1, 0.2$ respectively.

At each iteration, we measure the regrets of each algorithm and average them over the 50 experiments. To facilitate the interpretation of results, we first focus on the results of the algorithms after 1 iteration, i.e. after having added only 1 batch of q points. We then discuss the results when 10 iterations are run.

Table 2. Expected and observed first batch Improvement for q-EI and BUCB batch selection methods, in average for 50 functions.

Selection rule	Average expected improvement (q-EI)	Average realized improvement
q-EI	0.672	0.697
BUCB	0.638	0.638

First Step of the Optimization. To start with, we focus on the selection of the first batch. Table 2 compares the average q-EI and real improvement obtained for the three selection rules. For the first iteration only, the BUCB1 and BUCB2 selection rules are exactly the same. Since q-EI is the one-step optimal, it is not a surprise that it performs better at iteration 1 with our settings where the objective functions are sample realizations of a GP. If only one iteration is performed, improving the q-EI is equivalent to improving the average performance. However, we point out that, in application, the maximization of q-EI was not straightforward. It turns out that the batches proposed by the BUCB algorithms were excellent initial candidates in our descent algorithms. The use of other rules for the starting batches, with points sampled uniformly or according to a density proportional to the one-point EI, did not manage to yield this level of performance.

10 Optimization Steps. The average regret of the different batch selection rules over 10 iteration is depicted in Fig. 3. This Figure illustrates that choosing the one-step optimal criterion is not necessarily optimal if more than one iteration is run [14]. Indeed, after two steps, q-EI maximization is already beaten by BUCB2, and q-EI becomes better again after iteration 7. Among the 50 optimized functions, q-EI maximization gives the smallest 10-steps final regret for only 30 % of functions, against 52 % for the BUCB1 and 18 % for the BUCB2. On the other hand, the q-EI selection rule is eventually better in average since, for some functions, BUCB is beaten by q-EI by a wide margin. This is further illustrated with the curve of the 95 % quantile of the regret which indicates that, for the worst simulations, q-EI performs better. This gain in robustness alone explains the better average performance of q-EI. Such improved performance comes at a price: the computational time of our multistart BFGS algorithm with analytical gradient is 4.1 times higher compared to the BUCB computation times.

5   Conclusion

In this article, we give a closed-form expression of the gradient of the multipoint Expected Improvement criterion, enabling an efficient q-EI maximization at reduced computational cost. Parallel optimization strategies based on maximization of q-EI have been tested and are ready to be used on real test case with the DiceOptim R package. The BUCB algorithm turns out to be a good competitor to q-EI maximization, with a lower computational cost, and also gives good starting batches for the proposed multistart BFGS algorithm. In general, however, the maximization of q-EI remains a difficult problem. An interesting perspective is to develop algorithms taking advantage of some particular properties of the q-EI function in the space of dimension qd, for example its invariance to point permutations. Other research perspectives include deriving cheap but trustworthy approximations of q-EI and its gradient. Finally, as illustrated in the application, q-EI sequential maximizations have no reason to constitute optimal decisions for a horizon beyond one batch. Although the optimal policy is known [14], its implementation in practice remains an open problem.

Acknowledgement. Part of this work has been conducted within the frame of the ReDice Consortium, gathering industrial (CEA, EDF, IFPEN, IRSN, Renault) and academic (École des Mines de Saint-Étienne, INRIA, and the University of Bern) partners around advanced methods for Computer Experiments.

6 Appendix: Differential Calculus

- g_1 and g_2 are functions giving respectively the mean of $Y(X)$ and its covariance. Each component of these functions is either a linear or a quadratic combination of the trend function μ or the covariance function C evaluated at different points of X. The results are obtained by matrix differentiation. See the Appendix B of [21] for a similar calculus.

- g_3 (resp. g_4) is the affine (resp. linear) tranformation of the mean vector $\boldsymbol{m}$ into $\boldsymbol{m}^{(k)}$ (resp. the covariance matrix Σ into $\Sigma^{(k)}$). The differentials are then expressed in terms of the same linear transformation:

$$d_{\boldsymbol{m}}\left[g_3\right](\boldsymbol{h}) = L^{(k)}\boldsymbol{h} \quad \text{and} \quad d_\Sigma\left[g_4\right](H) = L^{(k)}HL^{(k)\top}.$$

- g_5 is defined by $g_5\left(\boldsymbol{m}^{(k)}, \Sigma^{(k)}\right) = \varphi_{\Sigma_{ii}^{(k)}}\left(m_i^{(k)}\right)$. Then the result is obtained by differentiating the univariate Gaussian probability density function with respect to its mean and variance parameters. Indeed we have:

$$d_{\left(\boldsymbol{m}^{(k)}, \Sigma^{(k)}\right)}\left[g_5\right](h, H) = d_{\boldsymbol{m}^{(k)}}\left[g_5(\cdot, \Sigma^{(k)})\right](h) + d_{\Sigma^{(k)}}\left[g_5(\boldsymbol{m}^{(k)}, \cdot)\right](H)$$

- g_6 gives the mean and the covariance of $\boldsymbol{Z}_{-i}^{(k)}|Z_i = 0$. We have:

$$\left(\boldsymbol{m}_{|i}^{(k)}, \Sigma_{|i}^{(k)}\right) = g_6\left(\boldsymbol{m}^{(k)}, \Sigma^{(k)}\right) = \left(\boldsymbol{m}_{-i}^{(k)} - \frac{m_i^{(k)}}{\Sigma_{ii}^{(k)}}\Sigma_{-i,i}^{(k)}, \Sigma_{-i,-i}^{(k)} - \frac{1}{\Sigma_{ii}^{(k)}}\Sigma_{-i,i}^{(k)}\Sigma_{-i,i}^{(k)\top}\right)$$

$$d_{\left(\boldsymbol{m}^{(k)}, \Sigma^{(k)}\right)}\left[g_6\right](\boldsymbol{h}, H) = d_{\boldsymbol{m}^{(k)}}\left[g_6\left(\cdot, \Sigma^{(k)}\right)\right](\boldsymbol{h}) + d_{\Sigma^{(k)}}\left[g_6\right]\left(\boldsymbol{m}^{(k)}, \cdot\right)(H),$$

$$\text{with}: \quad d_{\boldsymbol{m}^{(k)}}\left[g_6\left(\cdot, \Sigma^{(k)}\right)\right](\boldsymbol{h}) = \left(\boldsymbol{h}_{-i} - \frac{h_i}{\Sigma_{ii}^{(k)}}\Sigma_{-i,i}^{(k)}, \ 0\right)$$

$$\text{and}: \quad d_{\Sigma^{(k)}}\left[g_6\left(\boldsymbol{m}^{(k)}, \cdot\right)\right](H) = \left(\frac{m_i^{(k)}H_{ii}}{\Sigma_{ii}^{(k)2}}\Sigma_{-i,i}^{(k)} - \frac{m_i^{(k)}}{\Sigma_{ii}^{(k)}}H_{-i,i},\right.$$

$$\left. H_{-i,-i} + \frac{H_{ii}}{\Sigma_{ii}^{(k)2}}\Sigma_{-i,i}^{(k)}\Sigma_{-i,i}^{(k)\top} - \frac{1}{\Sigma_{ii}^{(k)}}H_{-i,i}\Sigma_{-i,i}^{(k)\top} - \frac{1}{\Sigma_{ii}^{(k)}}\Sigma_{-i,i}^{(k)}H_{-i,i}^{\top}\right)$$

- g_7 and g_8 : these two functions take a mean vector and a covariance matrix in argument and give a probability in output : $\Phi_{q,\Sigma^{(k)}}\left(-\boldsymbol{m}^{(k)}\right) = g_7\left(\boldsymbol{m}^{(k)}, \Sigma^{(k)}\right)$, $\Phi_{q-1,\Sigma_{|i}^{(k)}}\left(-\boldsymbol{m}_{|i}^{(k)}\right) = g_8\left(\boldsymbol{m}_{|i}^{(k)}, \Sigma_{|i}^{(k)}\right)$ So, for $\{p, \Gamma, \boldsymbol{a}\} = \{q, \Sigma^{(k)}, -\boldsymbol{m}^{(k)}\}$ or $\{q-1, \Sigma_{|i}^{(k)}, -\boldsymbol{m}_{|i}^{(k)}\}$, we face the problem of differentiating a function $\Phi : (\boldsymbol{a}, \Gamma) \rightarrow \Phi_{p,\Gamma}(\boldsymbol{a})$, with respect to $(\boldsymbol{a}, \Gamma) \in \mathbb{R}^p \times \mathcal{S}_{++}^p$:

$$d_{(\boldsymbol{a},\Gamma)}\left[\Phi\right](\boldsymbol{h}, H) = d_{\boldsymbol{a}}\left[\Phi(\cdot, \Gamma)\right](\boldsymbol{h}) + d_{\Gamma}\left[\Phi(\boldsymbol{a}, \cdot)\right](H).$$

The first differential of this sum can be written:

$$d_{\boldsymbol{a}}\left[\Phi(\cdot, \Gamma)\right](\boldsymbol{h}) = \left\langle\left(\frac{\partial}{\partial a_i}\Phi(\boldsymbol{a}, \Gamma)\right)_{1 \leq i \leq p}, \boldsymbol{h}\right\rangle,$$

with : $\frac{\partial}{\partial a_i}\Phi(\boldsymbol{a}, \Gamma) = \int_{-\infty}^{a_1} \ldots \int_{-\infty}^{a_{i-1}}\int_{-\infty}^{a_{i+1}} \ldots \int_{-\infty}^{a_p} \varphi_{p,\Gamma}(u_{-i}, a_i)d\boldsymbol{u}_{-i} = \varphi_{1,\Gamma_{ii}}\Phi_{p-1,\Gamma_{|i}}\left(\boldsymbol{a}_{|i}\right).$

The last equality is obtained with the identity: $\forall \boldsymbol{u} \in \mathbb{R}^q, \ \varphi_{q,\Gamma}(\boldsymbol{u}) = \varphi_{1,\Gamma_{ii}}(u_i)$

$\varphi_{p-1,\Gamma_{|i}}(\boldsymbol{u}_{|i})$, with $\boldsymbol{u}_{|i} = \boldsymbol{u}_{-i} - \frac{u_i}{\Gamma_{ii}}\boldsymbol{\Gamma}_{-i,i}$ and $\Gamma_{|i} = \Gamma_{-i,-i} - \frac{1}{\Gamma_{ii}}\boldsymbol{\Gamma}_{-i,i}\boldsymbol{\Gamma}_{-i,i}^{\top}$. The second differential is:

$$d_{\Gamma}\left[\Phi(\boldsymbol{a},\cdot)\right](H) := \frac{1}{2}\text{tr}\left(H.\left(\frac{\partial\Phi}{\partial\Gamma_{ij}}(\boldsymbol{a},\Gamma)\right)_{i,j\leq p}\right) = \frac{1}{2}\text{tr}\left(H.\left(\frac{\partial^2\Phi}{\partial a_i\partial a_j}(\boldsymbol{a},\Gamma)\right)_{i,j\leq p}\right)$$

where : $\frac{\partial^2\Phi}{\partial a_i\partial a_j}(\boldsymbol{a},\Gamma) = \begin{cases} \varphi_{2,\Sigma_{\{i,j\},\{i,j\}}}(x_i,x_j)\Phi_{p-2,\Sigma_{|ij}}(\boldsymbol{x}_{|ij}) \text{ , if } i\neq j, \\ -\frac{x_i}{\Gamma_{ii}}\frac{\partial}{\partial a_i}\Phi_{\Gamma}(\boldsymbol{a},\Gamma) - \sum_{\substack{j=1 \\ j\neq i}}^{p}\frac{1}{\Gamma_{ii}}\Gamma_{ij}\frac{\partial^2}{\partial a_i\partial a_j}\Phi(\boldsymbol{a},\Gamma). \end{cases}$

References

1. Auer, P., Cesa-Bianchi, N., Fischer, P.: Finite-time analysis of the multiarmed bandit problem. Mach. Learn. **47**(2–3), 235–256 (2002)
2. Azzalini, A., Genz, A.: The R package `mnormt`: the multivariate normal and t distributions (version 1.5-1) (2014)
3. Bect, J., Ginsbourger, D., Li, L., Picheny, V., Vazquez, E.: Sequential design of computer experiments for the estimation of a probability of failure. Stat. Comput. **22**(3), 773–793 (2011)
4. Berman, S.M.: An extension of Plackett's differential equation for the multivariate normal density. SIAM J. Algebr. Discrete Methods **8**(2), 196–197 (1987)
5. Brochu, E., Cora, M., de Freitas, N.: A tutorial on bayesian optimization of expensive cost functions, with application to active user modeling and hierarchical reinforcement learning, December 2010. eprint arXiv:1012.2599
6. Bull, A.: Convergence rates of efficient global optimization algorithms. J. Mach. Learn. Res. **12**, 2879–2904 (2011)
7. Chevalier, C.: Fast uncertainty reduction strategies relying on Gaussian process models. Ph.D. thesis, University of Bern (2013)
8. Chevalier, C., Ginsbourger, D.: Fast computation of the multipoint expected improvement with applications in batch selection. In: Giuseppe, N., Panos, P. (eds.) Learning and Intelligent Optimization. Springer, Heidelberg (2014)
9. Ginsbourger, D., Picheny, V., Roustant, O., with contributions by Chevalier, C., Marmin, S., Wagner, T.: DiceOptim: Kriging-based optimization for computer experiments. R package version 1.5 (2015)
10. Desautels, T., Krause, A., Burdick, J.: Parallelizing exploration-exploitation tradeoffs with gaussian process bandit optimization. In: ICML (2012)
11. Frazier, P.I.: Parallel global optimization using an improved multi-points expected improvement criterion. In: INFORMS Optimization Society Conference, Miami FL (2012)
12. Frazier, P.I., Powell, W.B., Dayanik, S.: A knowledge-gradient policy for sequential information collection. SIAM J. Control Optim. **47**(5), 2410–2439 (2008)
13. Genz, A.: Numerical computation of multivariate normal probabilities. J. Comput. Graph. Stat. **1**, 141–149 (1992)
14. Ginsbourger, D., Le Riche, R.: Towards gaussian process-based optimization with finite time horizon. In: Giovagnoli, A., Atkinson, A.C., Torsney, B., May, C. (eds.) mODa 9 Advances in Model-Oriented Design and Analysis, Contributions to Statistics, pp. 89–96. Physica-Verlag, HD (2010)

15. Ginsbourger, D., Le Riche, R., Carraro, L.: Kriging is well-suited to parallelize optimization. In: Tenne, Y., Goh, C.-K. (eds.) Computational Intelligence in Expensive Optimization Problems. ALO, vol. 2, pp. 131–162. Springer, Heidelberg (2010)
16. Jones, D.R., Schonlau, M., William, J.: Efficient global optimization of expensive black-box functions. J. Global Optim. **13**(4), 455–492 (1998)
17. Kenny, Q.Y., Li, W., Sudjianto, A.: Algorithmic construction of optimal symmetric latin hypercube designs. J. Stat. Plann. Inf. **90**(1), 145–159 (2000)
18. Mebane, W., Sekhon, J.: Genetic optimization using derivatives: the rgenoud package for R. J. Stat. Softw. **42**(11), 1–26 (2011)
19. Mockus, J., Tiesis, V., Zilinskas, A.: The application of bayesian methods for seeking the extremum. In: Dixon, L., Szego, G. (eds.) Towards Global Optimization, vol. 2, pp. 117–129. Elsevier, Amsterdam (1978)
20. Rasmussen, C.R., Williams, C.K.I.: Gaussian Processes for Machine Learning. MIT Press, Cambridge (2006)
21. Roustant, O., Ginsbourger, D., Deville, Y.: DiceKriging, DiceOptim: two R packages for the analysis of computer experiments by Kriging-based metamodelling and optimization. J. Stat. Softw. **51**(1), 1–55 (2012)
22. Schonlau, M.: Computer experiments and global optimization. Ph.D. thesis, University of Waterloo (1997)
23. Srinivas, N., Krause, A., Kakade, S., Seeger, M.: Information-theoretic regret bounds for gaussian process optimization in the bandit setting. IEEE Trans. Inf. Theory **58**(5), 3250–3265 (2012)
24. Vazquez, E., Bect, J.: Convergence properties of the expected improvement algorithm with fixed mean and covariance functions. J. Stat. Plan. Infer. **140**(11), 3088–3095 (2010)
25. Villemonteix, J., Vazquez, E., Walter, E.: An informational approach to the global optimization of expensive-to-evaluate functions. J. Global Optim. **44**(4), 509–534 (2009)

Dynamic Detection of Transportation Modes Using Keypoint Prediction

Olga Birth[1]([⊠]), Aaron Frueh[2], and Johann Schlichter[2]

[1] Connected Drive Department, BMW Research and Technology, Munich, Germany
olga.birth@bmw.de
[2] Institute for Applied Informatics Cooperative Systems, Garching, Germany
aaron.frueh@tum.de, johann.schlichter@in.tum.de

Abstract. This paper proposes an approach that makes logical knowledge-based decisions, to determine the transportation mode a person is using in real-time. The focus is set to the detection of different public transportation modes. Hereby it is analyzed how additional contextual information can be used to improve the decision making process. The methodology implemented is capable to differentiate between different modes of transportation including walking, driving by car, taking the bus, tram and (suburbain) trains. The implemented knowledge-based system is based on the idea of Keypoints, which provide contextual information about the environment. The proposed algorithm reached an accuracy of about 95 %, which outclasses other methodologies in detecting the different public transportation modes a person is currently using.

Keywords: Knowledge representation and acquisition · Mobility and big data · Public transport modes · Context information · Real-time

1 Introduction

Detecting a users mobility mode like walking, driving or using public transport is of increasing importance in multiple applications. Appropriate and more detailed information about the used transportation mode can be provided, if the recognition was correct. Navigation systems like *TomTom* [1] or *Navigon* [2] are examples which can detect the transportation mode "driving". Those systems can track the route which a person is driving by car and show appropriate information in the event of an obstacle, like traffic jam. The provided information of such navigation systems can vary from a simple guiding to displaying obstacles and calculating a re-routing. It can also show where the next break option or fuel station can be found. *Google Maps* [3] can not only detect the transportation mode "driving" but also "walking". It can help pedestrians finding the desired destination by showing step-by-step guiding and providing help if the user took the wrong turn.

Besides the traveling modes driving and walking, which also includes running, there is another transport mode which a person can take when traveling in urban areas, which is the public transport. When it comes to public transportation,

© Springer International Publishing Switzerland 2015
P. Pardalos et al. (Eds.): MOD 2015, LNCS 9432, pp. 49–59, 2015.
DOI: 10.1007/978-3-319-27926-8_5

real-time guidance or proactive re-routing is still a deficit. Such information would be very useful to people who are visiting unknown areas and wonder, if they're using the right train. Also for users who are just interested whether they should hurry to get the chosen bus or need to know when they have to exit, real-time guidance in public transport is necessary.

There are already solutions available, which can help remind the user to exit at the next station [4,5]. In those systems the user needs to choose a route which can consist of many different transit blocks. A sequence of transit blocks can for example be "walking", "taking the subway", "walking", "taking the bus", "walking". Each of the transit blocks has a time indication which shows how long it will take the user to travel with each transportation mode. Additionally it also shows the different times for each block.

Having the chosen route of the user and the time indicator for the different transit blocks, current systems start counting back the time according to the time indicators in the transit blocks. When the first transit block ends, e.g. "walking", the next starts and the time indicators count back the time for the new block, e.g. "taking the subway". Those system have real-time data concerning delays of the public transport and they can add the delay to the time indicator in the transit block, displaying this information to the user.

The big disadvantage of those systems is that they never know if the user has really entered or left the transit block in the indicated time. They can only make assumptions based on the route a user has chosen. In that case no real-time help can be provided, if the user did not leave at the planned time or has taken the wrong train. Also delays may be shown on a route but that does not help the user if he accidentally took the wrong train.

To the best of our knowledge, there is no solution available, which can identify not only the current used public transport type and the direction of the used public transport but also the station at which the user is currently waiting and at which station the user is leaving.

We have built a system that makes logical decisions based on a knowledge-based system. We have chosen this approach, because it is not limited to our test field, which was Munich in Germany. Our designed algorithm is able to determine multiple transportation modes, including different types of public transport. Detailed information about the current used public transport is delivered. This information covers the current line, the next station while using public transportation, the entry point and the exit point.

The detection precision for any public transportation should be close or equal to the "best" (in terms of precision) state-of-the-art approach, described in Chap. 2. The total detection precision therefore should be about 93 % and specific to public transport about 83 %. We have reached an accuracy of about 95 % for the identification of the public transportation mode.

Following we will discuss the existing approaches, to identify different public transportation modes. In Chap. 3, we will describe the decision making process of our developed knowledge-based system. Furthermore, we explain the use case and the evaluation of our system. We finish this paper by providing a conclusion and outlook of future work.

2 Related Work

Existing approaches for transportation mode detection share the same pattern. They map low-level sensors to a generalized high-level behavior e.g., "on foot", "on a car", "on a bus" [8–11], without the capability of delivering detailed information, like "which bus route?", "which direction is the bus heading to?", "which entry took the person?", "which exit took the person?". The existing methodology is mostly based on a classification mode made out of mobility patterns based on historically collected data. The advantage of the approach of using low-level sensors like accelerometers, is their generalized nature. In general the acceleration sensors can be used to differentiate between motorized and non-motorized states, but the disadvantage is the mostly low probability while distinguishing between motorized states. The acceleration and declaration behavior is very similar. Partsch [8] shows, that the accelerometer data is capable to give very detailed information about the state of trams, which was tested in Dresden in Germany. They gathered very specialized information like the vibrations of the tram. Further information is mostly too inaccurate or too specific for a general approach and therefore could not be considered for the transportation mode detection.

In comparison it is notable, that algorithms that take additional contextual information into account, were able to increase their detection rate significantly. For instance Patterson [9] was able to increase the prediction accuracy from 60 % to 78 % by adding contextual information like bus stops, bus routes, and parking lots. The most interesting approach is discussed by Stenneth et al. [7]. They use a mixture of classifiers, e.g. average speed, average acceleration, average rail line closeness, average bus closeness, and candidate bus closeness. With these features and a Random Forest classification model, they reached an average accuracy of 93,42 %. The bus detection accuracy was at 85 %. The flaw with the approach described in Stenneth et al. [7] is that it always needs the live positioning data of buses and trains. Even though such information is available in bigger cities, like Chicago, New York, Washington DC or London, it is difficult to accomplish in other cities where the data is not publicly available.

This leads to the main focus of our research work. The idea to add contextual information can increase the detection rate of existing algorithms. We have built a *knowledge-based system* that makes logical decisions based on a concept hereby described as *Keypoints*. Keypoints are the data representation needed to determine the logical decisions made by the knowledge-based system. Even though it seems complex to build a knowledge-based system that logically differentiates between multiple transportation modes, the area of freedom within public transportation is limited. Public transports are bound by rails or usually do not leave their route. They generally stop at their stations and they have a certain schedule. Our proposed approach is also not limited to a restricted environment like in Stenneth et al. [7] or [8].

3 Transport Mode Detection Using Keypoints

Any location that helps identifying the current position is a Keypoint. Keypoints are also locations that give additional contextual or logical information. Details on how a Keypoint has to be identified is not further specified. As an example, a Keypoint can be identified by the location or by other sensors. This leaves a wide variety of possible points. The location of stations and stops can give logical and contextual information according to public transportation modes, like bus stations, tram stations and taxi stations. Access Points can be put in relation to other Keypoints. This could lead to a better accuracy. Certain requirements for the data representation of the Keypoints had to be fulfilled:

Flexible. The data representation is incrementally refinable and extensible. A general transport mode detection has to be extensible to further cities.

Symbolic/Numeric. The data representation should be able to incorporate knowledge that is symbolic as well as numeric.

Correlations. Knowledge can be put in correlation to one other. The system needs to do logical decisions based on the dependencies between multiple data blocks.

Transparent. Knowledge should be represented simply and explicitly.

3.1 Concept of Keypoints

For our work, we chose stations as valid Keypoints, because it was the only source of Keypoints that could be exported from map content databases, which are publicly available (e.g. *Google Maps*).

The main focus of Keypoints are the relations to each other. The relations represent the public transportation network. This was mapped to a directional graph, whereas every edge is able to represent multiple lines. Figure 1 shows on the left side the abstract representation of such a graph. The real world representative can be found aside. The orange points represent tram stations, magenta are bus stations and blue are subway stations. The small blue points are the entries of a particular subway station.

(a) Abstract Keypoint graph visualiza- (b) Real world representative of the
tion between multiple Keypoints   Keypoints in Munich

Fig. 1. Abstract Keypoint graph visualization between multiple Keypoints

It is also possible to put multiple Keypoints together, which is called a Keypoint cluster. These clusters are used as indicators, that help to identify a related "primary"-point. As an example, all entrances of a subway station would be put together to a cluster and put in relation to the subway station. If a traveler is close to a subway entrance, the Keypoint logic would return a high probability for the subway station. The reasoning behind this is, that being at the geographical location of a underground subway station, is not related to the underground station itself. Because the position is somewhere above the surface for example on a street. These special Keypoints can also be used as triggers, for example to detect a "stairs down"-motion.

An advantage of Keypoints is that it is possible to calculate probabilities according to the movement of the traveler. In principal, closer Keypoints have a higher probability than Keypoints that are further away. The following Eq. (1–7) show how the probability is calculated. The variable d_i is the distance from the current location to a particular Keypoint (for each Keypoint).

$$sumDistance = \sum_{i=0}^{n} d_i \tag{1}$$

$$\mathcal{I}(d) = (\frac{d}{sumDistance})^{-1} = \frac{sumDistance}{d} \tag{2}$$

Equation 2 calculates the inverse of the flat distance distribution between all currently weighted Keypoints. Which is the biggest percentage for the nearest Keypoint and the lowest percentage for the furthest Keypoint. On itself this returns no satisfying probability, because distributed between a high density of Keypoints, which is the case for a city like Munich, the percentage for all Keypoints is very low. However two weighting functions can be used to give a correct probability (Eqs. 3 and 4)

$$\mathcal{A}(d) \in \,]0, 2]; \mathcal{A}(d) = \{\, \Delta d d_{t-1} + 1 = \frac{d_{t-1} - d_t}{d_{t-1}} + 1, if \Delta d > -d_{t-1}1, otherwise \tag{3}$$

Equation 3 gives a differential weight. Keypoints that are approached faster are higher weighted than Keypoints that stay at the same distance. The probability of Keypoints that move away are significantly reduced. Equation 3 only uses the distance from the last measurement and the current distance between Keypoints, which makes it slightly vulnerable to oscillations. The average between the last three or five distances might give better results.

Equation 4 is an exponential weighting on the Keypoint. This weighting occurs only on distances below 200 m. Everything above this distance is kept neutral by this function.

$$\mathcal{B}(d) \in [1, 10]; \mathcal{B}(d) = 1 + 9 * e^{-d*0.026347} \tag{4}$$

Equation 5 is the final weight of one Keypoint. Divided by the total weight of all Keypoints, it is possible to calculate the probability. These calculations are simple but effective and therefore perfectly fit for mobile devices, as used for testing purposes within our work.

$$\mathcal{W}(d) = (\mathcal{I}(d) * \mathcal{A}(d) * \mathcal{B}(d)) \tag{5}$$

$$\mathcal{S} = \sum_{i=0}^{n} \mathcal{W}(d_i) \tag{6}$$

This information can be used to display points of relevance for the traveler, as Keypoints with high probabilities are a likely target. This might be further specified with the first derivation of Eq. 7, which can be calculated by the difference of the two calculations. The pool of Keypoints can further be filtered, depending on the current state of the traveler, as for example nearby locations of parking lots are of no interest if the traveler is currently using a bus.

$$\mathcal{P}(d) = 100 * \frac{\mathcal{W}(d)}{\mathcal{S}}. \tag{7}$$

3.2   Decision Making Process

The logic is separated between an upper and a lower logic. The lower logic is used within every Keypoint. Every active Keypoint has it's own state-machine. The upper logic keeps track of all Keypoints and gathers notifications of the lower logic and makes decisions about the current situation accordingly.

Upper Logic. The upper logic consists of six states, as shown in Fig. 2. The primary states are walking, car and public transport. Unknown, motorized and transition are helper states.

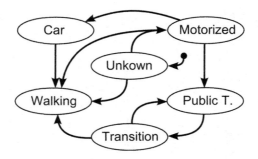

Fig. 2. Overview of the upper logic

1. The Initial State: Unkown → Walking/Motorized. The initial state is not further specified. The traveler could be in any imaginable state. The first step of the logic is therefore to differentiate between a motorized and a walking state. If the traveler is not moving at all, the logic waits until the traveler starts moving. Using the activity recognition provided by Google, this could be solved in an easy way. The activity recognition implements an accelerator based differentiation between the following states: "walking", "running", "on foot", "bicycling", "car" and "still". A high car probability is an indication for the upper logic to switch to the motorized state. Even though it is named "car", it is not able to differentiate between multiple motorized vehicles like buses or trains. If the activity recognition detects running, walking or on foot, the state can be initialized with walking. While in the unknown or walking state, the environment is searched for Keypoints and put into a plausible points list. These points are removed as soon as they leave the search area, and are currently not viable for any public transportation.

2. Walking. → Motorized → Public Transport. The transition to public transport can be best explained with Fig. 3, which represents what happens at the lower logic. Every Keypoint has its own states. If the traveler gets close enough to a Keypoint, which is illustrated by the solid circle **A**, a notification is sent to the upper logic. At this point there are two possibilities. Either the traveler is just passing by or the traveler might enter public transportation that is associated with that Keypoint. As soon as the traveler leaves circle **B**, all edges are tracked for their targeted Keypoint. The range for circle **A** is about 50 m and for circle **B** about 75 m. With the previously made assumption, that every public transportation vehicle stops at their targeted station, the algorithm can notify every targeted Keypoint. The Keypoints now track whether the traveler is approaching them or not. When the probability of one targeted Keypoint falls, then it is sorted out and the Keypoint resets itself to its initial state. If the traveler reaches the next Keypoint, it is checked if the movement speed drops below a certain margin of about five kilometers per hour. At this point a decision can be made and all lines that are assigned on that edge are possible public transportation candidates. As multiple lines can be attached to one edge, all of them have the same likelihood. With the addition of live departure times of a Keypoint, the likelihood of one line can be shifted to the most recent line departed. Without the live information these are excluded as soon as they split up their route.

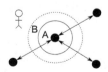

Fig. 3. Keypoint Behavior: Lower logic closeness indicator

3. The Transition State: Public Transport → Transition → Public Transport. While reaching the targeted Keypoint, the logic follows the graph and forwards the target to the next Keypoint. Hereby it prioritizes the current possible lines, but if additional lines stop at the current station or there are transitions available, they are also tracked in the background, because the traveler might change the vehicle. Figure 4 illustrates, that the current point (CP) is incremented to the targeted point (TP). The solid lines represent the possible transition points. The edges of the other possibilities are added to the secondary check and are tracked until they have been excluded.

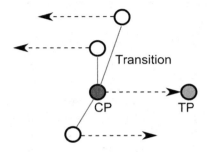

Fig. 4. Possible transitions at a transition state (CP = Current Point, TP = Targeted Point)

4. The Exit Conditions: Transition → Walking. In every transition state the fallback conditions explained below are renewed. We have implemented three fallback conditions. The first fallback condition is a timeout. The algorithm takes the distance to the next Keypoint and estimates a maximum time frame in which the next Keypoint should be reached. The time is measured as soon as the traveler leaves the current Keypoint area. The timeout is a backup mechanism, if the other fallback conditions are not triggered. The second fallback condition is a decreasing probability at the targeted Keypoint. The probability will fall significantly as soon as the traveler is moving towards a different direction. If this exceeds a certain margin, which is also calculated by the distance, then the fallback condition is triggered. This condition likely won't trigger if the traveler switches between different transportation modes at one Keypoint because the distances are too small. The third fallback condition is the activity recognition. If the activity recognition is very certain that the current activity is walking, on foot or running, then this is also a fallback condition. But the activity recognition is only tested within the transition state, because of being inaccurate within the accelerated motion of public transportation modes.

5. Motorized → Car. The differentiation between multiple motorized states is, as already mentioned, a difficult challenge. To solve this issue the algorithm uses the help of the already tracked data, the Keypoints. The motorized state is entered as soon as the probability of the "car"-State of the activity recognition is above average (about 60 %). Within this state, the surroundings are not further checked for new Keypoints and only the Keypoints that are currently within the plausible points list are taken into account. As soon as all plausible Keypoints fail their check, which means their internal logic has decided that they currently are not valid for any public transportation, then the decision is made that the traveler is currently using a car.

Lower Logic. Figure 5 illustrates the states of the lower logic. As mentioned earlier, every Keypoint has it's own state machine representing its logical status. How the Keypoint gets into the nearby state, was explained with previous Fig. 3 and its solid circle **A**. As soon as the dashed circle **B** is left, the tracking state is triggered. The dashed arrow indicates, that a transition to another Keypoints happens at this point. Whereas the Keypoint sending the notification, calculates the fallback conditions for all its edged and notifies all Keypoints targeted by those edges. Afterwards the Keypoint resets itself to it's initial state.

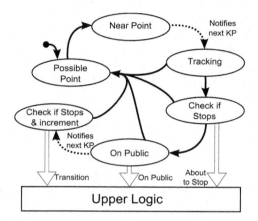

Fig. 5. The states of the lower logic

All targeted Keypoints track, if they are approached by the traveler. As soon as the traveler gets close enough to the targeted Keypoint, it switches to the "Check if Stops"-state. This closeness factor has about four times the size to the nearby factor because the traveler is moving in a faster pace and the algorithm needs to determine if the traveler will indeed slow down and stop. If the traveler stops, an "On Public" notification is sent to the upper logic, as illustrated. The logic now again notifies the next targeted Keypoint. This is done by a own state to prevent multiple "On Public" notifications to the upper logic. Instead a transition notification is sent to the upper logic, which indicates the possibility exists that the can exit the vehicle.

4 Case Study and Evaluation

In this section the evaluation procedure is discussed with the help of a proto-typical application. The prototype was developed on an Android OS Platform, using Google Nexus with Android 4.2. The goal was to deliver a simple true or false interface to verify the correctness of decisions made by the algorithm. The case study was executed in the area of Munich and the final data used for this evaluation was the first version of the data parsed by the exporter, consisting out of 3.000 Keypoints, 4.000 edges and about 260 lines. The duration of the test was 4 days. The test results met the requirements with an accuracy of 90.9 % and a recall accuracy of 96.77 %. Results that have been sent in and have been commented, that they have been underground while the wrong prediction was made have been excluded within the recall procedure, because we are until now not capable to handle underground Keypoints. Also results, that have been wrong because of graphical issues. Graphical issues existed within the center of the town where the list of possibilities exceeded the size of the notification window and were not visualized correctly.

For the sake of illustrating the results, a typical scenario has been chosen to showcase the functionality of the algorithm. The scenario chosen started in the north-east of Munich. The starting station has a total of three lines (tram 16, tram 18 and bus 50), which consists out of six possibilities. Within this test, the tram number 16 was chosen in direction of the inner city. The three possibilities going in the wrong direction sorted out quickly and were not considered as possible lines. As soon as the second station was reached, the algorithm made the correct detection of the three possibilities. The prediction narrowed down the possibilities to tram 16 after a couple of stations, because their routes split up along the way.

The target of this route was a station, where the transition was made to a different tram. The algorithm at first did not notice that the current vehicle was exited. Because the movement to the transitioning Keypoint was minimal. After about one to two minutes, the state switched from public transport to walking, due to the timeout of the original transportation mode. The transit station has about 18 public transportation possibilities in a small area. Even though this is a quite challenging scenario, the algorithm was able to detect the transition to a new public transportation. After a short period the other possibilities could be excluded and the prediction was correctly set to tram 19. The final exit of the route was the main station of Munich, which was also detected correctly.

5   Conclusion and Outlook

Our research work proves that a knowledge-based logic system has the capability to give an accurate prediction of the current used public transport type. The prediction accuracy of about 95 % showed that this approach outclasses other methodologies. The issue with this approach is, that it is highly dependent on the contextual data of the Keypoints. Errors within the database cause wrong assumptions within the decision making process. Errors made by the algorithm were mostly due to wrong or missing relations. The data was improved after the test procedure and might already deliver better results. Considering the support of even more Keypoints, like W-LAN Access points, it is likely that the accuracy could further improve. The best comparable approach, which already used additional positioning real-time information of buses, reached an accuracy of 85 %. Algorithms that use no additional contextual information are mostly below 65 % prediction accuracy.

As already mentioned the data is the most important prerequisite for the Keypoint based prediction to work. The question is how could the data collection be improved? First, crowd sourced learning of Keypoints. With anonymous position data of thousands of people, it is imaginable that a crowd-sourced algorithm can identify Keypoints. Locations with high density of people could be Keypoints. Restaurants, appartments, etc. could be excluded through map-matching. Not only the information about the current location could be analyzed, but also the missing information. For example, if people lose their GPS signal at the same point, this could indicate an underground subway entrance. The movement of a Keypoint, for example due to a construction site, also could be detected and adapted. A second thought is gamification, which is the usage of game thinking and game mechanics. A project that currently is run by Google, called Ingress [6], is a community based reality game. Where the player has the task to capture, discover and defend special points. These points consist mostly of grand buildings, monuments and statues, but also out of public transportation stops. A game that is based on the idea to deliver Keypoints would be a opportunity to gather data. The approach was built to represent any public transportation network. We further would like to understand, how well the database is expandable to other cities.

References

1. TomTom. http://www.tomtom.com/de_de/?
2. Navigon. http://www.navigon.com/portal/de/index.html
3. Google Maps. https://www.google.de/maps
4. Qixxit. https://www.qixxit.de/
5. DB Navigator. http://www.bahn.de/p/view/buchung/mobil/db-navigator.shtml
6. Ingress. https://www.ingress.com/l
7. Steneth, L., Wolfson, O., Yu, P.S., Xu, B.: Transportation mode detection using mobile phones and GIS information. In: Proceedings of the 19th ACM SIGSPATIAL International Conference on Advances in Geographic Information Systems, GIS 11, pp. 54–63. ACM, New York (2011)
8. Partsch, I., Duerrschmidt, G., Michler, O., Foerster, G.: Positioning in real-time public transport navigation: comparison of vehicle-based and smartphone-generated acceleration data to determine motion states of passengers. In: 6th International Symposium on Mobility: Economy - Ecology - Technology (2012)
9. Patterson, D.J., Liao, L., Fox, D., Kautz, H.: Inferring high-level behavior from low-level sensors. In: Dey, A.K., Schmidt, A., McCarthy, J.F. (eds.) UbiComp 2003. LNCS, vol. 2864, pp. 73–89. Springer, Heidelberg (2003)
10. Reddy, S., Burke, J., Estrin, D., Hansen, M., Srivastava, M.: Determining transportation mode on mobile phones. In: Proceedings of the 2008 12th IEEE International Symposium on Wearable Computers, ISWC2008, Washington, DC. IEEE Computer Society, pp. 25–28 (2008)
11. Reddy, S., Mun, M., Burke, J., Estrin, D., Hansen, M., Srivastava, M.: Using mobile phones to determine transportation modes. ACM Trans. Sens. Netw. **6**, 13:1–13:27 (2010)

Effect of the Dynamic Topology
on the Performance of PSO-2S Algorithm
for Continuous Optimization

Abbas El Dor[1]([⊠]) and Patrick Siarry[2]

[1] TASC INRIA (CNRS UMR 6241), Ecole des Mines de Nantes,
4 rue Alfred Kastler, 44300 Nantes, France
abbas.eldor@mines-nantes.fr
[2] LiSSi (E.A. 3956), Université de Paris-Est Créteil, 122 rue Paul Armangot,
94400 Vitry-sur-Seine, France
siarry@u-pec.fr

Abstract. PSO-2S is a multi-swarm PSO algorithm using charged particles in a partitioned search space for continuous optimization problems. In order to improve the performance of PSO-2S, this paper proposes a novel variant of this algorithm, called DPSO-2S, which uses the Dcluster neighborhood topologies to organize the communication networks between the particles. Experiments were conducted on a set of classical benchmark functions. The obtained results prove the effectiveness of the proposed algorithm.

1 Introduction

The concept of particle swarm optimization (PSO) is based on social behavior to exchange information between the particles in a swarm. Thus this property can be modelized thanks to a graph: two particles P_i and P_j of the swarm S are connected if a communication can be established between them. The set of edges between each particle P_i and its neighbours Ne_i forms the communication graph, also called the topology. Hence, the chosen topology can greatly affect the performance of the PSO algorithm. In this paper, we present a new dynamic topology, called Dcluster, which is a combination of two existing topologies (Four-clusters [7] and Wheel [6]). This topology was integrated in our proposed algorithm called PSO-2S, introduced in [2]. PSO-2S is a multi-swarm PSO algorithm using charged particles in a partitioned search space for continuous optimization problems. The performance of PSO-2S with the Dcluster topology is analysed and compared to that of PSO-2S without Dcluster, using a set of benchmark test functions. Comparisons show that the use of Dcluster improves significantly the performance of PSO-2S.

2 Particle Swarm Optimization

The particle swarm optimization (PSO) [4] is inspired originally by the social and cognitive behavior existing in the bird flocking. The algorithm is initialized with a population of particles randomly distributed in the search space,

© Springer International Publishing Switzerland 2015
P. Pardalos et al. (Eds.): MOD 2015, LNCS 9432, pp. 60–64, 2015.
DOI: 10.1007/978-3-319-27926-8_6

and each particle is assigned a randomized velocity. Each particle represents a potential solution to the problem. The particles fly over the search space, keeping in memory the best solution encountered. At each iteration, each particle adjusts its velocity vector, based on its momentum, influences of its best solution and of the best solution of its neighbors, then computes a new point to be evaluated. The displacement of a particle is influenced by three components:

1. *Physical component*: the particle tends to keep its current direction of displacement;
2. *Cognitive component*: the particle tends to move towards the best site that it has explored until now;
3. *Social component*: the particle tends to rely on the experience of its congeners, then moves towards the best site already explored by its neighbors.

In this paper, the swarm size is denoted by s, and the search space is n-dimensional. In general, a particle i has three attributes: the current position $X_i = (x_{i,1}, x_{i,2}, ..., x_{i,n})$, the current velocity vector $V_i = (v_{i,1}, v_{i,2}, ..., v_{i,n})$ and the past best position $Pbest_i = (p_{i,1}, p_{i,2}, ..., p_{i,n})$. The best position found in the neighborhood of the particle i is denoted by $Gbest_i = (g_{i,1}, g_{i,2}, ..., g_{i,n})$. These attributes are used to update iteratively the state of each particle in the swarm. The objective function to be minimized is denoted by f. The velocity vector V_i of each particle is updated using the best position it visited so far and the overall best position visited by its neighbors. Then, the position of each particle is updated using its updated velocity per iteration. At each step, the velocity of each particle and its new position are updated as follows:

$$v_{i,j}(t+1) = w v_{i,j}(t) + c_1 r_{1_{i,j}}(t) \left[p_{i,j}(t) - x_{i,j}(t) \right] + c_2 r_{2_{i,j}}(t) \left[g_{i,j}(t) - x_{i,j}(t) \right] \quad (1)$$

$$x_{i,j}(t+1) = x_{i,j}(t) + v_{i,j}(t+1) \quad (2)$$

$x_{i,j}$ is the position and $v_{i,j}$ is the velocity of the ith particle ($i \in 1, 2, ..., s$) of the jth dimension ($j \in 1, 2, ..., n$). Where w is called inertia weight, c_1, c_2 are the learning factors and r_1, r_2 are two random numbers selected uniformly in the range $[0, 1]$.

3 PSO-2S Algorithm

In this section, we present the first version of PSO-2S [2]. PSO-2S is based on three main ideas. The first is to use two kinds of swarms: a main swarm, denoted by S1, and s auxiliary ones, denoted by S2$_i$, where $1 \leq i \leq s$. The second idea is to partition the search space into several zones in which the auxiliary swarms are initialized (the number of zones is equal to the number of auxiliary swarms, thus is equal to s). The last idea is to use the concept of the electrostatic repulsion heuristic to diversify the particles for each auxiliary swarm in each zone.

To construct S1, we propose to perform the auxiliary swarms S2$_i$ several times in different areas, and then each best particle for each S2$_i$ is saved and considered as a new particle of S1. To do so, the population of each auxiliary swarm is initialized randomly in different zones (each $S2_i$ is initialized in its corresponding zone i). After each of these initializations, K displacements of particles, of each $S2_i$, are performed in the same way of standard PSO. Then the best solution found by each auxiliary swarm is added to S1. The number of initializations of $S2_i$ is equal to the number of particles in S1.

As we mentioned above the second idea is to partition the search space $[min_d,\ max_d]^N$ into several zones (max_{zone} zones). Then, we calculate the $center_d$ and the $step_d$ of each dimension separately, according to (3) and (4). The $step_d$ are similar in the case of using a square search space.

$$center_d = (max_d - min_d)/2 \tag{3}$$

$$step_d = center_d/max_{zone} \tag{4}$$

where max_{zone} is a fixed value, and d is the current dimension ($1 \leq d \leq N$).

The sizes of the zones of the partitioned search space are different ($Z_1 < Z_2 < \ldots < Z_{max_{zone}}$). Therefore, the number of particles in $S2_i$, denoted by $S2_{isize}$, depends on its corresponding zone size. Indeed, a small zone takes less particles and the number of particles increases when the zone becomes larger. The size of each auxiliary swarm is calculated as follows:

$$S2_{isize} = num_{zone} * nb_{particle} \tag{5}$$

where $num_{zone} = 1, 2, \ldots, max_{zone}$, is the current zone number and $nb_{particle}$ is a fixed value. After the initializations of the auxiliary swarms in different zones (Z_i, $S2_i$), an electrostatic repulsion heuristic is applied to diversify the particles and to widely cover the search space [3]. This technique is used in an agent-based optimization algorithm for dynamic environments [5]. Therefore, this procedure is applied in each zone separately, hence each particle is considered as an electron. Then a force of $1/r^2$ is applied, on the particles of each zone, until the maximum displacement of a particle during an iteration becomes lower than a given threshold ϵ (where r is the distance between two particles, ϵ is typically equal to 10^{-4}). At each iteration of this procedure, the particles are projected in the middle of the current zone, before reapplying the heuristic repulsion.

4   Dynamic Cluster Topology (Dcluster)

Dcluster is a dynamic topology that works as follows [1]. At each iteration, the particles are sorted in a list according to their personal best fitness in increasing order, so that the worst particle has an index equal to 1 in the list (the size of the list is equal to the size of the swarm). Then, the list is partitioned into several sub-lists which correspond to a cluster in the proposed topology. The first cluster which has the "worst" particle, called central cluster, is placed in the center of the topology. Each particle of the central cluster is connected to other clusters by one of their particles; the first worst particle of the central cluster is linked to the

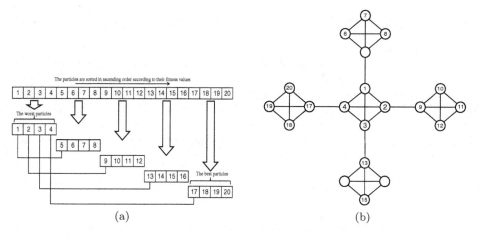

Fig. 1. (a) - The partitioning of the list into sub-lists. (b) - The structure of Dcluster topology.

Table 1. Results of DPSO-2S using Dcluster topology and PSO-2S.

Function	Search space	Acceptable error	Max. FEs	DPSO-2S		PSO-2S	
				Mean best	Suc. rate	Mean best	Suc. rate
Rosenbrock	$[-10, 10]^{30}$	0.0001	40000	2.50e+001	0.0%	**2.28e$_+$001**	0.0%
Ackley	$[-32, 32]^{30}$	0.0001	40000	**9.40e-003**	99%	3.54e-001	69%
Griewank	$[-100, 100]^{30}$	0.0001	40000	**2.19e-003**	78%	3,88e-003	72%
Rastrigin	$[-10, 10]^{30}$	0.0001	40000	**1.34e$_+$000**	30%	2.16e+000	25%
Sh. Rosenbrock	$[-100, 100]^{10}$	0.01	100000	5.25e+000	5%	**5.98e-001**	**75%**
Sh. Ackley	$[-32, 32]^{30}$	0.0001	100000	**6.26e-002**	95%	1.88e-001	86%
Sh. Griewank	$[-600, 600]^{30}$	0.0001	100000	**5.16e-003**	66%	6.11e-003	61%
Sh. Rastrigin	$[-5, 5]^{30}$	0.0001	100000	**3.14e$_+$001**	0,0%	5,36e+001	0.0%

worst particle in the second cluster, the second one is linked to the third cluster also by its worst particle, and so on, as in Fig. 1-(a). All clusters in this topology, including the central cluster, have a fully connected neighborhood. The reason why the central cluster is linked to each other cluster by only one gateway and with the worst particle of the latter is to avoid a premature convergence to a local optimum by slowing down the propagation of the information in the whole swarm. Figure 1-(b) illustrates the final structure of the proposed topology.

5   Experimental Results

Table 1 presents the settings of each problem, the number of function evaluations (Max. FEs), the success rate and the mean best value of 100 runs. The
best results among those obtained by the two algorithms are shown in bold. From
the experiments, we can notice that DPSO-2S (PSO-2S using Dcluster topology)
obtains the best results on most of the functions used. Hence, DPSO-2S algorithm outperforms PSO-2S, except for *Rosenbrock* and *Shifted Rosenbrock*.
Thus, this algorithm leads to a significant improvement over the previous
PSO-2S.

6   Conclusion

In this paper, a new dynamic topology, called Dcluster, based on two static
neighbourhood topologies was presented. Dcluster was integrated to our multi-
swarm algorithm PSO-2S. Experimental results indicate that Dcluster improves
the search performance of the previous algorithm.

In conclusion, the improvement of the PSO-2S algorithm due to the integration of Dcluster topology opens the gate to apply this dynamic topology in other
PSO algorithms.

References

1. El Dor, A., Lemoine, D., Clerc, M., Siarry, P., Deroussi, L., Gourgand, M.: Dynamic
   cluster in particle swarm optimization algorithm. Nat. Comput. **14**, 655–672 (2014).
   doi:10.1007/s11047-014-9465-2
2. El Dor, A., Clerc, M., Siarry, P.: A multi-swarm PSO using charged particles in
   a partitioned search space for continuous optimization. Comput. Optim. Appl. **53**,
   271–295 (2012)
3. Conway, J., Sloane, N.: Sphere Packings, Lattices and Groups. Springer, New York
   (1999)
4. Kennedy, J.: A new optimizer using particle swarm theory. In: Proceedings of the
   Sixth International Symposium on Micro Machine and Human Science, pp. 39–43
   (1995)
5. Lepagnot, J., Nakib, A., Oulhadj, H., Siarry, P.: A new multiagent algorithm for
   dynamic continuous optimization. Int. J. Appl. Metaheuristic Comput. **1**(1), 16–38
   (2010)
6. Kennedy, J., Mendes, R.: Population structure and particle swarm performance. In:
   Proceedings of the 2002 IEEE Congress on Evolutionary Computation, CE 2002,
   Honolulu, HI, USA, pp. 1671–1676 (2002)
7. Mendes, R., Kennedy, J., Neves, J.: The fully informed particle swarm: simpler
   maybe better. IEEE Trans. Evol. Comput. **8**(3), 204–210 (2004)

Heuristic for Site-Dependent Truck and Trailer Routing Problem with Soft and Hard Time Windows and Split Deliveries

Mikhail Batsyn[✉] and Alexander Ponomarenko

Laboratory of Algorithms and Technologies for Network Analysis,
National Research University Higher School of Economics, 136 Rodionova street,
Niznhy Novgorod, Russia
{mbatsyn,aponomarenko}@hse.ru

Abstract. In this paper we develop an iterative insertion heuristic for a site-dependent truck and trailer routing problem with soft and hard time windows and split deliveries. In the considered problem a truck can leave its trailer for unloading or parking, make a truck-subtour to serve truck-customers, and return back to take the trailer. This can be done several times in one route. In our heuristic every route is constructed by sequentially inserting customers to it in the way similar to Solomon's (1987) approach developed for simple vehicle routes. Our contributions include: heuristic insertion procedure for complex truck and trailer routes with transshipment locations; efficient randomized mechanisms for choosing the first customer for insertion, for making time window violations, and for making split-deliveries; an improvement procedure shifting deliveries in a route to earlier time; an efficient approach dealing with site-dependency feature based on the transportation problem in case of arbitrary intersecting vehicle sets and a fast vehicle assignment procedure in case of nested vehicle sets.

Keywords: Truck and trailer · Site-dependent · Soft time windows · Split-deliveries · Insertion heuristic

1 Introduction

In truck and trailer routing problems there are two types of customers: trailer-customers and truck-customers. Trailer-customers can be served both from a truck and a trailer, while truck-customers can be served only from a truck. This can be, for example, small stores in a big city to which it is impossible to drive up by a road train because of narrows streets, small parking place, and other limitations. There are two possibilities to leave a trailer. It can be left at a trailer-customer for unloading and while it is unloaded a truck can serve several truck-customers making a so-called truck-subtour and then return to take the trailer. This is efficient in terms of time because truck and trailer serve customers in parallel in this case. Another possibility is to park a trailer at a

© Springer International Publishing Switzerland 2015
P. Pardalos et al. (Eds.): MOD 2015, LNCS 9432, pp. 65–79, 2015.
DOI: 10.1007/978-3-319-27926-8_7

special transshipment location close to some truck-customer. If there are not enough goods in a truck, before it leaves for a truck-subtour, a load transfer from the trailer to the truck can be performed. If there are not enough goods in the trailer, when it is left for unloading at a trailer-customer, then the remaining goods are unloaded from the truck before it leaves.

The most simple truck and trailer routing problem is the homogeneous fleet truck and trailer routing problem which is usually referenced in literature as TTRP (Chao, 2002). In this problem all trucks and trailers are the same, have the same capacity, same travel and fixed costs and can visit every customer without any limitations except the truck-customers limitation. A number of heuristics have been suggested for this problem: Chao (2002), Scheuerer (2006), Lin et al. (2009; 2010), Villegas et al. (2011a; 2011b). Lin et al. (2011) considered the TTRP problem with hard Time Windows (TTRPTW).

Much more difficult problems are Heterogeneous Fleet TTRP problems (HFT-TRP). Different heuristics for the HFTTRP problem have been suggested by Hoff (2006), Hoff & Lokketangen (2007), Caramia & Guerriero (2010a; 2010b). Except different vehicle capacities, travel and fixed costs, for every customer there can be defined a set of vehicles which can serve it. In this case the problem is called the Site Dependent TTRP (SDTTRP). Semet (1995) developed a cluster-first route-second heuristic for the SDTTRP problem. Semet & Taillard (1993) suggested a tabu-search algorithm for the SDTTRP problem with hard time windows (SDT-TRPTW). In their formulations of these problems there are no transshipment locations and a trailer can be left only for unloading at a trailer-customer. A more general formulation with transshipment locations is presented by Drexl (2011). Along with road trains there are also single-truck vehicles. The author provides a mathematical programming model for this SDTTRPTW problem and a branch-and-price algorithm to solve it.

In this paper we consider even more general TTRP problem. We add soft time windows and split-deliveries to the SDTTRPTW problem considered by Drexl (2011). An integer linear programming model for this problem is provided in Batsyn & Ponomarenko (2014). In the current paper we further develop our heuristic suggested in Batsyn & Ponomarenko (2014). The main improvements include: new approach dealing with site-dependency feature based on the transportation problem in case of arbitrary intersecting vehicle sets; new fast vehicle assignment procedure in case of nested vehicle sets; new randomized mechanism for making soft time window violations; new insertion cases for the greedy insertion procedure. We describe our iterative insertion heuristic for the considered problem, present all possible insertion cases, and provide the pseudo-code of our algorithm. There are many cases of inserting a customer to a complex truck and trailer route because such a route can have different nodes such as: depot, trailer-customers visited by a road train, truck-customers visited by a truck without a trailer, trailer-customers at which a trailer is left for unloading, transshipment locations at which a trailer is left for parking.

In our approach many different solutions are iteratively constructed with the following randomizations. We choose the first customer in every route randomly from the most expensive (farthest) customers. Split-deliveries and soft time window violations are also made in a random way. In order to avoid making a big detour when inserting a customer, we do not insert customers for which the cost of serving it with another vehicle directly from the depot is smaller than the insertion cost. We insert customers taking into account soft time windows. If a delivery of inserted customer is started after the soft time window we apply an improvement procedure which moves all deliveries earlier in time so that instead of a late (after the soft time window) delivery at this customer we have an early (before the soft time window) delivery at some of the previous customers. This helps to compress a route and insert more customers to it.

For each customer there is a set of different vehicles which can serve it. To deal with this site-dependency feature we suggest solving a special transportation problem in which we give preference to bigger vehicles. In case where these sets for all customers are nested, instead of solving the transportation problem we propose an efficient algorithm to assign a vehicle to serve a customer.

In our formulation of the problem it is permitted to violate a given number of soft time windows and to make split-deliveries to a given number of customers. To address the soft time windows feature we suggest that during building a solution it is allowed to violate a soft time window in a random way with the probability equal to the remaining number of permitted violations divided by the expected number of possible remaining violations. We allow a split-delivery only when we insert the last customer in the current route when the remaining capacity of the vehicle is not enough to serve the total demand of this customer. This is done to load vehicles as much as possible. A split-delivery is allowed in a random way with the probability equal to the remaining number of permitted split-deliveries divided by the expected number of possible remaining split-deliveries.

2   Insertion Heuristic

The following parameters are used is the pseudo-code of the algorithm.
n - the number of customers
V - the set of all customers
K - the set of all vehicles
K_i - the set of vehicles which can serve customer i
f_k - the fixed cost of using vehicle k for delivery
Q_k - the current remaining capacity of vehicle k
q_i - the current remaining demand of customer i
s_i^k - the service time spent by vehicle k when serving customer i
op_i, cl_i - the open and close time of customer i (hard time window)
er_i, lt_i - the earliest and latest time of serving customer i (soft time window)
b_j^R - the begin time of serving customer j in route R
v_R - the number of soft time window violations in route R
c_{ij}^{kl} - the travel cost of arc (i, j) for vehicle k with/without trailer ($l = 1/l = 2$)
v - the number of permitted soft time window violations
w - the current remaining number of permitted soft time window violations

σ - the number of permitted split deliveries
s - the current remaining number of permitted split deliveries
R - the current route
S - the current solution
S^* - the best solution
$f(S)$ - the total cost of the current solution
f^* - the total cost of the best solution
U - the set of all customers sorted the most expensive (farthest) customer first
$[C_{jk}]$ - the cost matrix of the transportation problem used to assign vehicles
μ - the number of the most expensive customers from which we choose randomly
λ - the preference weight of customer direct travel cost c_{0i}^{k1}

Algorithm 1. Iterative insertion heuristic

---

function IterativeInsertionHeuristic(N)
  ▷ Builds N solutions running InsertionHeuristic()
  $S^* \leftarrow \varnothing, \quad f^* \leftarrow \infty$
  $U \leftarrow V$ ▷ the set of all customers sorted so that U_1 has maximal c_{0i}^{k1}
  $\bar{Q} \leftarrow \sum Q_k / |K|$ ▷ average vehicle capacity
  $\bar{r} \leftarrow \bar{Q}/(\sum q_i/n)$ ▷ average route size
  $m \leftarrow 0$ ▷ the total number of built routes
  $M \leftarrow 0$ ▷ the total number of customers in these routes
  $\pi \leftarrow 0$ ▷ the probability of time window violation
  $v' \leftarrow v$ ▷ backup the number of allowed time window violations
  $v \leftarrow n$ ▷ temporarily allow unlimited time window violations
  InsertionHeuristic($U, [q_j], [Q_k]$) ▷ get a solution with unlimited tw-violations
  $\pi \leftarrow (v-w)/n$ ▷ π is estimated as the ratio of time window violations to n
  $v \leftarrow v'$ ▷ restore the number of allowed time window violations
  for $i \leftarrow \overline{1, N}$ **do**
    $S \leftarrow$ InsertionHeuristic($U, [q_j], [Q_k]$)
    if $S \neq \varnothing$ **then**
      $m \leftarrow m + |S|, \quad M \leftarrow M + \sum_{R \in S} |R|, \quad \bar{r} \leftarrow M/m$
      if $f(S) < f^*$ **then**
        $S \leftarrow S^*, \quad f^* \leftarrow f(S)$
      end if
    end if
  end for
  return S^*
end function

The main function in our algorithm is IterativeInsertionHeuristic() (Algorithm 1). It makes the specified number of iterations N calling Insertion-Heuristic() function and stores the best found solution in S^*. First, all customers in set V are sorted by the direct travel cost c_{0i}^{k1} from the depot so that the first customer has maximal direct cost (is the most expensive). The sorted list of customers is stored in variable U. Note that we copy parameters $U, [q_j], [Q_k]$ each time we call InsertionHeuristic() function so that it can change them without

---

Algorithm 2. Insertion heuristic

---

function INSERTIONHEURISTIC($U, [q_j], [Q_k]$)
    ▷ Builds a solution for customers U, demands $[q_j]$, vehicle capacities $[Q_k]$
    ▷ Parameters $U, [q_j], [Q_k]$ are copied and not changed in the calling function
    $S \leftarrow \varnothing$ ▷ current solution
    $w \leftarrow v$ ▷ remaining number of soft time window violations
    $s \leftarrow \sigma$ ▷ remaining number of split-deliveries
    while $U \neq \varnothing$ **do**
        $i \leftarrow$ RANDOM($U_1, ..., U_\mu$)   ▷ choose random from the first μ most expensive
        $k \leftarrow$ CHOOSEVEHICLE($i, [q_j], [Q_k]$)
        if $k = 0$ **then**
            return $\varnothing$ ▷ not enough vehicles
        end if
        INSERTCUSTOMER($U, i, 1, R, q_i, Q_k$)   ▷ insert i to an empty route R
        $success \leftarrow$ true
        while $success$ **do**
            $success \leftarrow$ INSERTBESTCUSTOMER($U, [q_j], [Q_k], R, k$)
        end while
        $S \leftarrow S \cup \{R\}$
        $Q_k \leftarrow 0$ ▷ remove vehicle k from further consideration
    end while
    return S
end function

---

affecting their values in the main function. We also calculate here an estimation for the average route size $\bar{r}$ equal to the average vehicle capacity $\bar{Q}$ divided by the average demand. This estimation is used only for the first iteration and for next iterations we divide the total number of customers in all constructed routes by the total number of these routes. To estimate the probability π of soft time window violation we run the insertion heuristic once with an unlimited number of permitted violations v. Then we measure this probability as the fraction of soft time window violations made in the obtained solution to the total number of customers n.

We fill in the cost matrix C_{jk} for the transportation problem using the following formula:

$$C_{jk} = \begin{cases} 0, & k \in K_j \\ \infty, & \text{otherwise} \end{cases}$$

We set $C_{jk} = \infty$ for each vehicle k which cannot serve customer j. The transportation problem is solved to check that the currently available vehicles with remaining capacities $[Q_k]$ are able to serve the remaining demands $[q_j]$ of the customers with site-dependency constraints given by vehicle sets K_j containing for each customer j the vehicles which can serve it.

If these vehicle sets are nested it is possible to check it without solving the transportation problem. It is usual that for many different customers their vehicle sets are the same: $K_{i_1} = ... = K_{i_l}$. We denote these vehicle sets as $K^j = K_{i_1} = ... = K_{i_l}$. Let $K^1 \subset K^2 \subset ... \subset K^m$ be all different nested vehicle sets. When we

---

Algorithm 3. Choose the best vehicle

---

function CHOOSEVEHICLE($i, [q_j], [Q_k]$)
    ▷ Returns the best vehicle k^* for customer i, demands $[q_j]$, vehicle capacities $[Q_k]$
    ▷ Parameters $[q_j], [Q_k]$ are changed in the calling function also
    $Q_{max} \leftarrow \max(Q_k)$
    $[C'_{jk}] \leftarrow [C_{jk}]$
    for $k \in K_i$ **do**
        $C'_{ik} \leftarrow Q_{max}/Q_k$ ▷ set smaller costs for bigger vehicles
    end for
    repeat
        $[x_{jk}] \leftarrow$ TRANSPORTATIONPROBLEM($[C'_{jk}], [q_j], [Q_k]$)
        if $[x_{jk}] = \varnothing$ **then**
            return 0   ▷ not enough vehicles
        end if
        $k^* \leftarrow 0$
        for $k \in K_i$ **do**
            if $x_{ik} > 0$ and $Q_k > Q_{k^*}$ **then**
                $k^* \leftarrow k$
            end if
        end for
        if $x_{ik^*} < q_i$ and $x_{ik^*} < Q_{k^*}$ **then**
            $C'_{ik^*} \leftarrow \infty$ ▷ cannot serve total demand q_i, let's try another vehicle
        end if
    until $C'_{ik^*} = \infty$
    return k^*
end function

---

assign for customer i vehicle k from its vehicle set $K_i = K^j$, and this vehicle does not belong to smaller (nested to K^j) vehicle sets: $k \notin K^{j-1}$, then there is nothing to check. Otherwise, we need to check that this assignment is feasible and the remaining vehicles capacity is enough to serve the remaining demand.

Let us denote as $Q_{K^j} = \sum_{k \in K^j}(Q_k)$ the current total capacity of vehicles in set K^j and as $q_{K^j} = \sum_{i, K_i = K^j}(q_i)$ - the current total demand of customers for which the vehicle set is K^j. We consider that vehicles in K^1 serve all customers for which $K_i = K^1$ and then they have the remaining capacity equal to $Q_{K^1} - q_{K^1}$. Then vehicles in $K^2 \backslash K^1$ together with the remaining vehicles from K^1 serve all customers for which the vehicle set is K^2, and we have the remaining capacity of vehicles equal to $(Q_{K^2 \backslash K^1} - q_{K^2}) + (Q_{K^1} - q_{K^1})$. And so on up to the largest vehicle set K^m. We precalculate all these remaining capacities for all vehicle sets from K^1 to K^m only once, and then we only update it quickly each time we add a customer to a route. If adding a customer results in a negative value for some of the remaining capacities this means that this adding is infeasible and we cannot do it. If we assign vehicle k to serve customer i, and the smallest vehicle set K^{j_0} which contains k is smaller than $K_i = K^j$, then for each set $K^{j_0}, ..., K^{j-1}$ we check that after delivering goods to customer i the remaining vehicle capacities will be enough to serve the demands $q_{K^{j_0}}, ..., q_{K^{j-1}}$.

Function INSERTIONHEURISTIC() (Algorithm 2) sequentially constructs all routes in a solution by inserting customers one by one to the constructed route. The first customer in each route is chosen randomly from the first μ customers (μ most expensive) in the set of unserved customers U. In our experiments we take $\mu = 5$ because it provides a good balance between diversification and intensification of the search. A vehicle for each constructed route is assigned in CHOOSEVEHICLE() function. Each next customer to be inserted to the current route is chosen and inserted in INSERTBESTCUSTOMER() function.

Algorithm 4. Insert the customer to the route

---

function INSERTCUSTOMER(U, i, p, R, q_i, Q_k)
   ▷ Inserts customer i to position p in route R
   ▷ Parameters U, R, q_i, Q_k are changed in the calling function also
   $r \leftarrow |R|$ ▷ the size of route $R = (R_1, ..., R_r)$
   $R \leftarrow (R_1, ..., R_{p-1}, i, R_p, ..., R_r)$ ▷ insert customer i to position p in route R
   $q \leftarrow \min(q_i, Q_k)$ ▷ the delivered demand
   $Q_k \leftarrow Q_k - q$ ▷ update the remaining vehicle capacity
   $q_i \leftarrow q_i - q$ ▷ update the remaining customer demand
   if $q_i = 0$ **then**
      $U \leftarrow U \setminus \{i\}$ ▷ update the unserved customers list
   end if
end function

Function CHOOSEVEHICLE() (Algorithm 3) chooses the biggest vehicle feasible for customer i. It is done by setting transportation costs C_{ik} such that the bigger vehicles feasible for i have smaller costs and thus the optimal solution of the transportation problem will assign as much demand as possible to the biggest vehicle. If the biggest vehicle cannot serve the total demand q_i due to the site-dependency constraints though its capacity is enough, we forbid assignment of this vehicle by setting $C'_{ik} = \infty$ and solve the transportation problem again.

Function INSERTCUSTOMER() (Algorithm 4) inserts customer i to the specified position p in route R served by vehicle k. The remaining capacity Q_k of this vehicle and the remaining demand q_i of this customer are decreased by the value of the delivered demand q. If this customer has no remaining demand after this operation it is removed from the set of unserved customers U.

Function INSERTBESTCUSTOMER() (Algorithm 5) finds the unserved customer which has the lowest insertion cost and inserts it to the best position in the current route. Precisely we take into account the insertion cost c decreased by the direct customer cost c_{0i}^{k1} multiplied by weight λ. This is done to give preference to the most expensive (farthest) customers because it is usually more optimal to insert such customers to the solution earlier. In our experiments we take $\lambda = 1$ since it gives the best results in average.

Before choosing the best customer we decide in a random way if we allow soft time window violation and split-delivery for this customer. In average every

---

Algorithm 5. Insert the customer with the lowest insertion cost

---

function INSERTBESTCUSTOMER$(U, [q_j], Q_k, R, k)$
    ▷ Inserts the best customer from U to route R served by vehicle k
    ▷ Parameters $[q_j]$ store demands, Q_k - the remaining free capacity of vehicle k
    ▷ Parameters $U, [q_j], Q_k, R$ are changed in the calling function also
    $\bar{s} = |U|/\bar{r}$ ▷ the expected number of remaining splits (1 split per route)
    $\bar{w} = |U| \cdot \pi$ ▷ the expected number of remaining time window violations
    $split \leftarrow (\text{RANDOM}([0, 1]) < s/\bar{s})$ ▷ allow split-delivery with probability $s/\bar{s}$
    $violate \leftarrow (\text{RANDOM}([0, 1]) < w/\bar{w})$ ▷ allow tw-violation with probability $w/\bar{w}$
    $i^* \leftarrow 0$ ▷ best customer to insert to route R
    $p^* \leftarrow 0$ ▷ best position in route R to insert this customer
    $c^* \leftarrow \infty$ ▷ insertion cost for this customer
    for $i \in U$ **do**
        if $k \notin K_i$ **then**   ▷ skip customers which cannot be served by this vehicle k
            continue
        end if
        ▷ If split-deliveries are not allowed skip all them except inevitable ones
        if $(!\, split)$ & $(q_i > Q_k)$ & $(q_i < \max_{k \in K_i}(Q_k))$ **then**
            continue
        end if
        ▷ Check that after serving customer i by vehicle k the remaining
        ▷ vehicles are able to serve the remaining customers
        $q \leftarrow \min(q_i, Q_k)$ ▷ the delivered demand
        $Q_k \leftarrow Q_k - q$ ▷ try decreasing the remaining vehicle capacity
        $q_i \leftarrow q_i - q$ ▷ try decreasing the remaining customer demand
        $[x_{jk}] \leftarrow \text{TRANSPORTATIONPROBLEM}([C_{jk}], [q_j], [Q_k])$
        $Q_k \leftarrow Q_k + q$ ▷ restore the remaining vehicle capacity
        $q_i \leftarrow q_i + q$ ▷ restore the remaining customer demand
        ▷ If the remaining vehicles are not able to serve the remaining customers
        if $[x_{jk}] = \varnothing$ **then**
            continue   ▷ skip such a customer
        end if
        $p^* \leftarrow 0$ ▷ the best position in route R to insert customer i
        $c \leftarrow \text{GETINSERTIONCOST}(R, i, k, p, violate)$ ▷ find the best place for i in R
        $c_0 \leftarrow c_{0i}^{k1} + f_k/|R|$ ▷ estimation for the cost of serving i directly from depot
        if $c_0 < c$ **then**
            continue   ▷ it is cheaper to serve this customer directly from the depot
        end if
        $c \leftarrow c - \lambda \cdot c_{0i}^{k1}$ ▷ give preference $(\lambda \cdot c_{0i}^{k1})$ to farthest customers
        if $c < c^*$ **then**
            $c^* \leftarrow c, \quad i^* \leftarrow i, \quad p^* \leftarrow p$
        end if
    end for
    if $c^* = \infty$ **then**
        return false
    end if
    INSERTCUSTOMER$(U, i^*, p^*, R, q_{i^*}, Q_k)$
    if $Q_k = 0$ **then**
        return false   ▷ return false to stop building this route
    end if
    return true
end function

Algorithm 6. Calculate the best cost of inserting the customer to the route

---

function GETINSERTIONCOST($R, i, k, p^*, violate$)

    ▷ Inserts customer i to route R served by vehicle k, returns position p^* and cost

    ▷ Parameter p^* (best insertion position) is changed in the calling function also

    $c^* \leftarrow \infty$

    $r \leftarrow |R|$ ▷ the size of route $R = (R_1, ..., R_r)$

    $v_R \leftarrow$ VIOLATIONS(R)

    for $p \leftarrow \overline{1, r+1}$ **do**

        $R' \leftarrow (R_1, ..., R_{p-1}, i, R_p, ..., R_r)$ ▷ insert customer i to position p

        $\Delta^* \leftarrow 0$

        for $j \in \{i, R_p, ..., R_r\}$ **do**

            $l \leftarrow lt_j$ ▷ the latest possible begin time is the time window end lt_j

            ▷ For the second and next split-deliveries violations are not counted

            if NEXTSPLITDELIVERY(j, R') **then**

                $l \leftarrow cl_j - s_j^k$ ▷ the latest possible is close time minus service time

            end if

            $\Delta \leftarrow b_j^{R'} - l$ ▷ how greater the begin time than the latest possible time

            if $\Delta > \Delta^*$ **then**

                $\Delta^* \leftarrow \Delta, \quad j^* \leftarrow j$

            end if

        end for

        ▷ Try to shift all deliveries earlier by Δ^*

        if (! SHIFTEARLIER(j^*, R', Δ^*)) **then** ▷ if cannot satisfy hard time windows

            continue

         end if

        $v_{R'} \leftarrow$ VIOLATIONS(R')

        if $v_{R'} > v_R$ and $violate = false$ **then**   ▷ skip if R' has more tw-violations

            continue

         end if

        $c \leftarrow$ COSTDELTA(i, p, R)

        if $c < c^*$ **then**

            $c^* \leftarrow c, \quad p^* \leftarrow p$

        end if

    end for

    return c^*

end function

---

route should have one split-delivery to fully use the capacity of the vehicle. So we take the expected number of possible future split-deliveries $\bar{s}$ equal to the average number of the remaining routes in this solution. And this value is estimated as the number of unserved customers $|U|$ divided by the average route size $\bar{r}$. The expected number of possible future violations of soft time windows $\bar{w}$ is equal to the number of unserved customers $|U|$ multiplied by the probability π of soft time window violation. To provide uniform occurrence of split-deliveries and soft time window violations during construction of a solution we allow a split-delivery and a violation with probabilities $s/\bar{s}$ and $w/\bar{w}$ correspondingly.

Algorithm 7. Count the number of time window violations in the route

function VIOLATIONS(R)
    ▷ Returns the number of time window violations in route R
    $v_R \leftarrow 0$
    $r \leftarrow |R|$ ▷ the size of route $R = (R_1, ..., R_r)$
    for $p \leftarrow \overline{1,r}$ **do**
        $j \leftarrow R_p$
        ▷ For the second and next split-deliveries violations are not counted
        if NEXTSPLITDELIVERY(j, R) **then**
            continue
        end if
        if $b_j^R < er_j$ or $b_j^R > lt_j$ **then** ▷ begin time b_j^R violates time window $[er_j, lt_j]$
            $v_R \leftarrow v_R + 1$
        end if
    end for
    return v_R
end function

For every customer we check that after serving it by the current vehicle the remaining vehicle capacities will be enough to serve the remaining demands. This is done by solving the transportation problem with the cost matrix $[C_{jk}]$. The best position p^* to insert a customer is determined by function GETINSERTION-COST(). If the insertion cost of a customer is greater than the cost of serving this customer directly from the depot with another vehicle, then such customer is not inserted to the current route. This is done to avoid big detours when inserting customers.

Function GETINSERTIONCOST() (Algorithm 6) finds the best position to insert the given customer to the current route which provides the lowest insertion cost. It tries to insert the customer to every position in the route. If after insertion this or next customers in the route have late deliveries (deliveries after the soft time window), then function SHIFTEARLIER() is called to shift all the deliveries earlier so that some of the previous deliveries become early deliveries (deliveries before the soft time window). This procedure reduces the total time of the route and thus allows inserting more customers to it.

Function SHIFTEARLIER() moves the delivery for the specified customer j^* earlier by the specified time Δ^*. This requires moving earlier deliveries for some of the previous customers in the route and for some of the next customers. It moves the deliveries taking into account waiting time and split deliveries, because two vehicles cannot serve one customer at the same time. If it is not possible to move the deliveries earlier so that all hard time windows are satisfied, then SHIFTEARLIER() function returns $false$. If for example waiting time at some previous customer is greater than Δ^*, then this time is simply decreased by Δ^* and any other previous customers do not need to be moved.

Function NEXTSPLITDELIVERY() checks if the delivery to the specified customer j in route R is the second or next split delivery to this customer. This is needed because it is allowed to violate the soft time window for all split deliveries

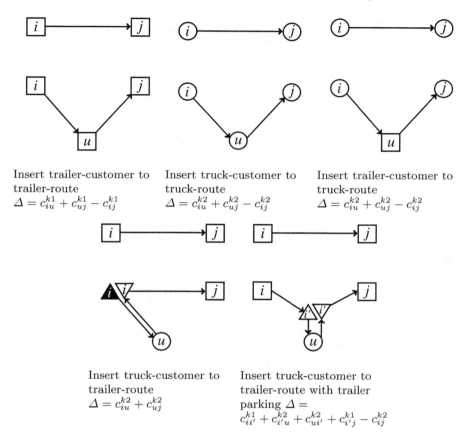

Fig. 1. Simple insertion cases

except one. So we do not count soft time window violations for the second and next split deliveries.

Function COSTDELTA() returns the insertion cost for all possible cases. These cases together with the corresponding cost deltas are shown in Figs. 1, 2, 3. The following icons are used in these figures: $\square$, a node visited by a road train; $\bigcirc$, a node visited by a truck without the trailer; $\triangle$, a node at which a trailer is left for parking; $\blacktriangle$, a node at which a trailer is left for unloading; $\triangledown$, a node at which a trailer is connected back to a truck. In each of these figures a new customer u is inserted to a route. The original route is shown above and the route after inserting this customer is shown below in each figure. An expression to calculate the cost delta is also provided.

Function VIOLATIONS() (Algorithm 7) counts the number of soft time window violations made in the given route. Note that in case of split deliveries the soft time window should not be violated only for the first split delivery to a customer. All the next split deliveries to this customer can be outside the soft time window.

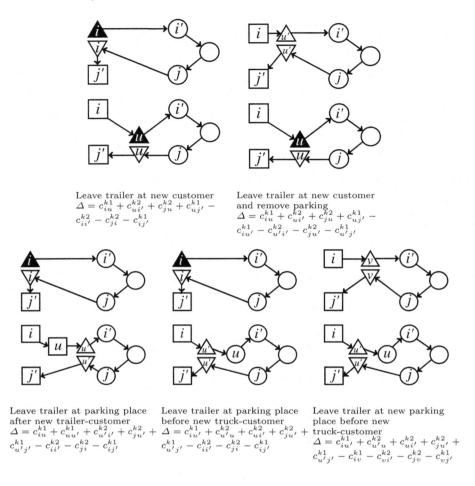

Fig. 2. Insertion cases with leaving trailer at another node

The figure contains the following cases and formulas:

Leave trailer at new customer
$$\Delta = c_{iu}^{k1} + c_{ui'}^{k2} + c_{ju}^{k2} + c_{uj'}^{k1} - c_{ii'}^{k2} - c_{ji}^{k2} - c_{ij'}^{k1}$$

Leave trailer at new customer and remove parking
$$\Delta = c_{iu}^{k1} + c_{ui'}^{k2} + c_{ju}^{k2} + c_{uj'}^{k1} - c_{iu'}^{k1} - c_{u'i'}^{k2} - c_{ju'}^{k2} - c_{u'j'}^{k1}$$

Leave trailer at parking place after new trailer-customer
$$\Delta = c_{iu}^{k1} + c_{uu'}^{k1} + c_{u'i'}^{k2} + c_{ju'}^{k2} + c_{u'j'}^{k1} - c_{ii'}^{k2} - c_{ji}^{k2} - c_{ij'}^{k1}$$

Leave trailer at parking place before new truck-customer
$$\Delta = c_{iu'}^{k1} + c_{u'u}^{k2} + c_{ui'}^{k2} + c_{ju'}^{k2} + c_{u'j'}^{k1} - c_{ii'}^{k2} - c_{ji}^{k2} - c_{ij'}^{k1}$$

Leave trailer at new parking place before new truck-customer
$$\Delta = c_{iu'}^{k1} + c_{u'u}^{k2} + c_{ui'}^{k2} + c_{ju'}^{k2} + c_{u'j'}^{k1} - c_{iv}^{k1} - c_{vi'}^{k2} - c_{jv}^{k2} - c_{vj'}^{k1}$$

3   Computational Experiments

For computational experiments we used several real-life instances with the number of customers from 55 to 300 (input data for all instances can be provided by request). All the experiments for real-life instances have been performed on Intel Core i7 machine with 2.2 GHz CPU and 8 Gb of memory. A comparison with an exact solution is possible only for very small instances of about 10 customers. Such a comparison for the first version of our heuristic can be found in Batsyn & Ponomarenko (2014).

The objective function values obtained by different algorithms are presented in Table 1. When an algorithm is not able to obtain a feasible solution it is shown as "–" in the table. We compare the suggested heuristic with an iterative greedy insertion heuristic which iteratively applies Solomon (1987) insertion procedure

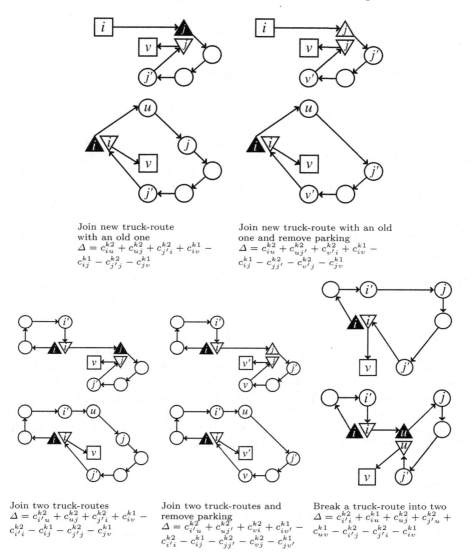

Join new truck-route
with an old one
$\Delta = c_{iu}^{k2} + c_{uj}^{k2} + c_{j'i}^{k2} + c_{iv}^{k1} - c_{ij}^{k1} - c_{j'j}^{k2} - c_{jv}^{k1}$

Join new truck-route with an old
one and remove parking
$\Delta = c_{iu}^{k2} + c_{uj'}^{k2} + c_{v'i}^{k2} + c_{iv}^{k1} - c_{ij}^{k1} - c_{jj'}^{k2} - c_{v'j}^{k2} - c_{jv}^{k1}$

Join two truck-routes
$\Delta = c_{i'u}^{k2} + c_{uj}^{k2} + c_{j'i}^{k2} + c_{iv}^{k1} - c_{i'i}^{k2} - c_{ij}^{k1} - c_{j'j}^{k2} - c_{jv}^{k1}$

Join two truck-routes and
remove parking
$\Delta = c_{i'u}^{k2} + c_{uj'}^{k2} + c_{vi}^{k2} + c_{iv'}^{k1} - c_{i'i}^{k2} - c_{ij}^{k1} - c_{jj'}^{k2} - c_{vj}^{k2} - c_{jv'}^{k1}$

Break a truck-route into two
$\Delta = c_{i'i}^{k2} + c_{iu}^{k1} + c_{uj}^{k2} + c_{j'u}^{k2} + c_{uv}^{k1} - c_{i'j}^{k2} - c_{j'i}^{k2} - c_{iv}^{k1}$

Fig. 3. Insertion cases with joined and broken truck-routes

using our insertion cases. To provide different solutions on all iterations the first customer in every route is chosen randomly from the remaining unserved customers. The solutions obtained by this approach for 100 and 100k iterations are shown in columns 2 and 3 of Table 1. The solutions of Batsyn & Ponomarenko (2014) algorithm for 100 and 100k iterations are presented in columns 4 and 5. Finally, the solutions found by the suggested new heuristic for 100 and 100k iterations are reported in columns 6 and 7.

Table 1. Computational experiments

Instance	Simple greedy, 100	Simple greedy, 100k	Batsyn & Ponomarenko (2014), 100	Batsyn & Ponomarenko (2014), 100k	New heuristic, 100	New heuristic, 100k
Novosibirsk	104026	103660	104148	103660	103757	103660
Udmurtia	–	–	1312720	1277967	1222630	1218939
Bashkortostan01	–	–	960130	941629	916792	902353
Bashkortostan07	–	–	1074651	1060665	1036272	1028024
Bashkortostan08	–	–	1027655	1021944	995317	984917
Bashkortostan09	–	–	1012611	1002596	974641	965984
Bashkortostan10	–	–	957746	945515	939019	929642
Novgorod03	–	–	–	–	1190419	1185121
Novgorod04	–	–	–	–	1082395	1073438
Novgorod05	–	–	–	–	1138652	1128973
Novgorod06	–	–	–	–	1184675	1171648
Novgorod07	–	–	–	–	1243691	1229926
Kropotkin	–	–	–	–	717075	708625

The simple greedy heuristic is able to find a feasible solution only for the first small instance of 55 customers. This is due to random assignment of vehicles and treating soft time windows as hard ones. The heuristic of Batsyn & Ponomarenko (2014) is not able to find a feasible solution for 7 instances because it always chooses the biggest available vehicle which can serve the first customer in the route and does not analyze that later a vehicle of this type will be needed for other customers which could not be served by other vehicles. The suggested heuristic obtains feasible solutions for all instances and provides the lowest costs.

4   Conclusions

In this paper we have suggested an iterative greedy randomized heuristic which efficiently addresses such features of real-life vehicle routing problems as heterogeneous fleet of vehicles, site-dependency feature, complex truck-and-trailer routes with transshipment locations, soft time windows along with hard time windows, split deliveries. To the best of our knowledge this is one of the most general formulations considered in literature for truck and trailer routing problems. We have implemented our algorithm and integrated it to the software system of a big retail company. And it shows better results on real-life instances than their experienced staff could get using their old software which partly automates construction of routes.

Currently we are working on further improvements of the suggested approach. We consider different neighbourhood structures for local search. The idea is to allow infeasible solutions during local search by penalizing them in the objective function. This makes it possible to use many different simple and efficient neighbourhoods. However due to the penalties local search will often get stuck in bad, but feasible solutions. To overcome this problem we are going to apply the tabu search approach.

Acknowledgments. The authors are supported by LATNA Laboratory, NRU HSE, RF government grant, ag. 11.G34.31.0057.

References

Batsyn, M., Ponomarenko, A.: Heuristic for a real-life truck and trailer routing problem. Procedia Comput. Sci. **31**, 778–792 (2014). The 2nd International Conference on Information Technology and Quantitative Management, ITQM 2014

Caramia, M., Guerriero, F.: A heuristic approach for the truck and trailer routing problem. J. Oper. Res. Soc. **61**, 1168–1180 (2010a)

Caramia, M., Guerriero, F.: A milk collection problem with incompatibility constraints. Interfaces **40**(2), 130–143 (2010b)

Chao, I.M.: A tabu search method for the truck and trailer routing problem. Comput. Oper. Res. **29**(1), 33–51 (2002)

Drexl, M.: Branch-and-price and heuristic column generation for the generalized truck-and-trailer routing problem. J. Quant. Methods Econ. Bus. Adm. **12**(1), 5–38 (2011)

Hoff, A.: Heuristics for rich vehicle routing problems. Ph.D. Thesis. Molde University College (2006)

Hoff, A., Lokketangen, A.: A tabu search approach for milk collection in western Norway using trucks and trailers. In: The Sixth Triennial Symposium on Transportation Analysis TRISTAN VI, Phuket, Tailand (2007)

Lin, S.-W., Yu, V.F., Chou, S.-Y.: Solving the truck and trailer routing problem based on a simulated annealing heuristic. Comput. Oper. Res. **36**(5), 1683–1692 (2009)

Lin, S.-W., Yu, V.F., Chou, S.-Y.: A note on the truck and trailer routing problem. Expert Syst. Appl. **37**(1), 899–903 (2010)

Lin, S.-W., Yu, V.F., Lu, C.-C.: A simulated annealing heuristic for the truck and trailer routing problem with time windows. Expert Syst. Appl. **38**, 15244–15252 (2011)

Scheuerer, S.: A tabu search heuristic for the truck and trailer routing problem. Comput. Oper. Res. **33**, 894–909 (2006)

Semet, F., Taillard, E.: Solving real-life vehicle routing problems efficiently using tabu search. Ann. Oper. Res. **41**, 469–488 (1993)

Semet, F.: A two-phase algorithm for the partial accessibility constrained vehicle routing problem. Ann. Oper. Res. **61**, 45–65 (1995)

Solomon, M.M.: Algorithms for the vehicle routing and scheduling problem with time window constraints. Oper. Res. **35**, 254–265 (1987)

Villegas, J.G., Prins, C., Prodhon, C., Medaglia, A.L., Velasco, N.: A GRASP with evolutionary path relinking for the truck and trailer routing problem. Comput. Oper. Res. **38**(9), 1319–1334 (2011a)

Villegas, J.G., Prins, C., Prodhon, C., Medaglia, A.L., Velasco, N.: Heuristic column generation for the truck and trailer routing problem. In: International Conference on Industrial Engineering and Systems Management IESM2011, Metz, France (2011b)

Cross-Domain Matrix Factorization for Multiple Implicit-Feedback Domains

Rohit Parimi[✉] and Doina Caragea

Kansas State University, Manhattan, USA
{rohitp,dcaragea}@ksu.edu

Abstract. Cross-domain recommender systems represent an emerging research topic as users generally have interactions with items from multiple domains. One goal of a cross-domain recommender system is to improve the quality of recommendations in a target domain by using user preference information from other source domains. We observe that, in many applications, users interact with items of different types (e.g., artists and tags). Each recommendation problem, for example, recommending artists or recommending tags, can be seen as a different task, or, in general, a different domain. Furthermore, for such applications, *explicit* feedback may not be available, while *implicit* feedback is readily available. To handle such applications, in this paper, we propose a novel cross-domain collaborative filtering approach, based on a regularized latent factor model, to transfer knowledge between source and target domains with *implicit* feedback. More specifically, we identify latent user and item factors in the source domains, and transfer the user factors to the target, while controlling the amount of knowledge transferred through regularization parameters. Experimental results on six target recommendation tasks (or domains) from two real-world applications show the effectiveness of our approach in improving target recommendation accuracy as compared to state-of-the-art single-domain collaborative filtering approaches. Furthermore, preliminary results also suggest that our approach can handle varying percentages of user overlap between source and target domains.

Keywords: Cross-domain recommender systems · Collaborative filtering · Matrix factorization · Implicit feedback

1 Introduction

The goal of a recommender system is to suggest to users items that match their interests. Collaborative Filtering (CF) is a popular implementation strategy for recommender systems because of its high-efficiency and domain independent nature [9,15]. CF approaches generally work by identifying patterns in user's *explicit* opinions (e.g., ratings) or *implicit* behavioral history (e.g., clicks) from a single data domain, and generate personalized item suggestions for that domain. However, in some real-world scenarios, user preferences for different types of

© Springer International Publishing Switzerland 2015
P. Pardalos et al. (Eds.): MOD 2015, LNCS 9432, pp. 80–92, 2015.
DOI: 10.1007/978-3-319-27926-8_8

items from multiple domains are available. For example, in the context of a music site, users can express preferences regarding *artists, tags* that they use for music, and other *users* that they are friends with. Instead of treating each type of item independently and creating a recommendation model for each task/domain separately, the user knowledge gained in one domain can be transferred to other domains. This area of research, known as cross-domain recommender systems, aims to improve the quality of recommendations in a target domain, by exploiting knowledge from one or more source domains.

One naive way to use knowledge about user preferences from multiple domains is to aggregate data about users and items from all domains into one user-item preference matrix, and use a standard CF algorithm to generate recommendations. However, such models generally recommend items from the domain in which users have preferred many items [4,7]. Furthermore, implicit user preferences across domains might mis-lead the model as implicit feedback can have different ranges [8]. To address these problems, cross-domain neighborhood-based CF approaches, which transfer similarity or neighborhood information from source domains to the target, have been originally proposed in the literature [1,2,4,16,19]. More recently, approaches based on matrix factorization have also been proposed for cross-domain recommender systems, as these techniques have better accuracy compared to neighborhood approaches [8,9]. The underlying idea of these approaches is to use the latent factors from source domains as a bridge to transfer knowledge to the target. Most of these approaches assume that items are of the same type across domains [1,2,4,12], or that the domains have explicit user feedback (binary or ratings) [1,2,4,10–12,17,19], or that the cluster level preference pattern is similar across domains [10,11]. However, in many applications, user preferences are captured through implicit feedback (e.g., clicks) and, thus, might not have the same cluster level pattern across domains, and items across domains may not be of the same type (may not even be similar).

To address these limitations, we introduce a new cross-domain recommendation problem that does not satisfy the assumptions in the literature. Our problem formulation is driven by applications such as those captured by the *Last.FM* music dataset and the *DBLP* scientometric dataset. Specifically, in *Last.FM*, we can recommend artists, friends and tags to users. Each task can be seen as a different domain. Similarly, in *DBLP*, we can recommend co-authors, conferences, and references, and we also see these tasks as different domains. In both cases, the items are of different types and highly dissimilar across domains. Furthermore, user preferences in both cases are captured through implicit feedback. The feedback corresponds to the number of artists, number of friends, and number of tags, a user interacted with, respectively, for the three domains of *Last.FM*, and number of co-authors, number of conferences, and number of references, an author interacted with, respectively, for the three domains of *DBLP*.

To tackle the above-mentioned problem, we propose a *novel* cross-domain CF approach based on matrix factorization (MF) to transfer the latent factors from source domains to the target domain. The novelty of the algorithm consists in its ability to handle *multiple* source domains with different types of *dissimilar* items and *implicit* feedback. Our assumption is that although the items are of different types and user preferences for items are different across domains, there will be some latent user information that is common for the source and target domains, and can be shared between the two. Thus, our goal is to discover, the domain independent semantic user concepts from the related source domains and transfer them to the target. We only transfer the user latent factors, given the differences in items and preferences across domains. Intuitively, our approach should be able to prevent negative transfer, to some extent, as we only require the user latent factors in source and target domains to be similar, through regularization.

In the rest of this paper, we provide an overview of the existing cross-domain approaches in Sect. 2. We define the recommendation problem addressed in this work, and present our solution in Sect. 3. In Sect. 4, we describe the datasets and evaluation methodology, and discuss the results in Sect. 5. Finally, we conclude this work with possible future directions in Sect. 6.

2   Related Work on Cross-Domain Recommender Systems

Cross-domain recommender systems are gaining popularity as many applications such as social networks and e-commerce sites have started to collect user histories for items from many domains. However, there is no unified perception of the cross-domain recommendation problem. According to the work in [4], given two domains $\mathbb{A}$ and $\mathbb{B}$, the objective of a cross-domain recommendation task can be (a) to improve the recommendation accuracy in a target domain, for example, $\mathbb{A}$, using knowledge from both domains $\mathbb{A}$ and $\mathbb{B}$, (b) to recommend items in both $\mathbb{A}$ and $\mathbb{B}$ to users in $\mathbb{A}$ and $\mathbb{B}$, or (c) to recommend items in $\mathbb{B}$ to users in $\mathbb{A}$ and vice versa. In this work, we focus on the first objective: our goal is to improve target recommendation accuracy using knowledge from two or more domains.

Some recent studies proposed several aggregation techniques for cross-domain recommender systems. For example, Berkovsky et al. [1,2] proposed approaches to transfer knowledge about user similarity, neighborhoods, and predicted item ratings, from source domains to target. Winto and Tang [19] used user preferences from multiple domains for recommender systems, while addressing the relatedness and correlation across domains. Shapira et al. [16] studied the possibility of utilizing user preferences collected from Facebook to address the sparsity and cold-start problems in recommender systems. While some of these studies concluded that cross-domain recommendations tend to be less precise than single-domain recommendations [19], other works suggested that cross-domain approaches have better recall compared to single-domain approaches [16].

Another line of research applies collective factorization or transfer learning techniques to improve target recommendation accuracy. For example, Li et al. [10,11] proposed two techniques to transfer cluster level rating information (known as the Codebook) from a dense source domain to reduce the sparsity in the target domain. Pan et al. [12] addressed the sparsity problem in the target domain by transferring user and item latent features from two auxiliary domains, an approach known as Coordinate System Transfer. Singh and Gordan [17] proposed the Collective Matrix Factorization approach to jointly factorize a user-item rating matrix and an item-context matrix by sharing the same item-specific latent features. One drawback of the previous work mentioned above is that most studies were conducted with "simulated" cross-domain data. For example, some works have simulated a cross-domain framework by partitioning a movie dataset based on genre [1], while others used different movie rating datasets as different domains [12], or transferred user rating knowledge between movies and books (as they have similarity in genre and there are many movies based on books) [10,11]. Furthermore, some works assumed explicit (Boolean or numerical) user preferences in the source and target domains [1,10–12,17,19], fixed number of source domains [10–12], dense source domains [10,11], or complete user and item overlap between source and target domains [12]. In our work, we propose an approach which can handle one or more source domains, and assumes implicit user preferences in all domains. We also assume that items are heterogeneous across domains. Finally, our approach requires only partial user overlap. Note, also, that we do not make any assumptions about data density.

3   Cross-Domain Implicit-Feedback Matrix Factorization

Problem Formulation: We define the cross-domain recommendation problem addressed in this work using a notation introduced in [4]: assume there exist a target domain T, and s auxiliary source domains, S_k, where $k \in [1,s]$, all with implicit feedback. Let U_t, U_k be the sets of target and source users, respectively, where $U_t \cap U_k \neq \emptyset$; let I_t, I_k be the sets of target and source items, respectively, where $I_t \cap I_k = \emptyset$. Our objective is to improve target recommendation accuracy (T) by exploiting user-item preferences from the s source domains.

Approach: Our approach to the problem defined earlier involves two steps: first, we follow the framework proposed in [8] to extract the user and item latent factors from the source domains with *implicit* user preferences; in the second step, we propose a *novel* way to use the latent factors from the first step as a bridge between the source and the target domains, which allows us to transfer knowledge. We describe the two steps in detail in the rest of the section.

Step 1 - Computing Source Domain Latent Factors: In this step, we find the latent user and item factors from the preference matrices for the source domains. Typically, these latent factors correspond to semantic concepts and measure the extent to which a user and an item exhibit these concepts [9]. Koren et al. [9] proposed an MF approach to identify user and item latent factors from *explicit* ratings of movies. Hu et al. [8] pointed out some drawbacks of using traditional MF approaches for implicit feedback, and proposed a new approach that can handle implicit user preferences. Given that the source domains have *implicit* feedback, we use the factorization proposed in [8], which uses two new variables to represent user feedback, namely, preference and confidence. The preference, a Boolean value denoted by p_{ui}, indicates the preference of user u for item i and takes a value 1 when u uses i. The confidence variable (c_{ui}) associates a confidence value to item i preferred by user u. The increase rate for a confidence value is controlled by a constant α which can be determined by cross-validation.

Equations (1) and (2) depict the computation of p_{ui} and c_{ui} from an implicit user feedback value r_{ui} (number of times user u preferred item i), respectively.

$$p_{ui} = \begin{cases} 1 & \text{if } r_{ui} > 0 \\ 0 & \text{if } r_{ui} = 0 \end{cases} \tag{1}$$

$$c_{ui} = 1 + \alpha r_{ui} \tag{2}$$

For a domain S_k, the user and item factors can be computed by finding x_{u_k} and y_{i_k} that minimize the objective function $\mathcal{J}$ given by Eq. (3).

$$\mathcal{J}(\mathbf{x_{u_k}}, \mathbf{y_{i_k}}) = \sum_{(u_k, i_k)} c_{u_k i_k} \left(p_{u_k i_k} - x_{u_k}^\mathsf{T} y_{i_k}\right)^2 + \lambda \left(\sum_{u_k} \|x_{u_k}^2\| + \sum_{i_k} \|y_{i_k}^2\|\right) \tag{3}$$

In Eq. (3), λ denotes the regularization parameter. The objective function can be efficiently solved using alternating least squares (ALS), and analytic expressions for user and item factors that minimizes Eq. (3) can be obtained by differentiation. Space limitations preclude us from explaining these optimizations in detail. We point the interested reader to the work in [8].

Step 2 - Integrating Source Latent Factors into Target Domain: In this step, we transfer the information captured as latent user factors from the source domains in Step 1 into the target domain through a regularization technique. To accomplish this, we use an approach similar to the approach used in Step 1, as we also have implicit user feedback in T. Specifically, we represent a user feedback (r_{ui}) using the preference (p) and confidence (c) variables given by Eqs. (1) and (2), respectively, and reconstruct the preference matrix as inner products of user and item latent factors. However, to facilitate knowledge transfer from source to target domains, we extend the objective function in Step 1 given by Eq. (3) to incorporate knowledge from source domains through regularization parameters in the factorization model, as described below.

After obtaining user and item latent factors from the source domains, we add s (number of source domains) regularization terms $\sum_{u_t} \|x_{u_t} - x_{u_k}\|^2$ to the objective function $\mathcal{J}$ for the target domain T as shown in Eq. (4).

$$\mathcal{J}(\mathbf{x_{u_t}}, \mathbf{y_{i_t}}) = \sum_{(u_t, i_t)} c_{u_t i_t} \left(p_{u_t i_t} - x_{u_t}^\mathsf{T} y_{i_t}\right)^2 + \sum_{k \,\epsilon\, [1,s]} \lambda_k \sum_{u_t} \|x_{u_t} - x_{u_k}\|^2 + \lambda \sum_{i_t} \|y_{i_t}\|^2 \tag{4}$$

In Eq. (4), x_{u_t} and x_{u_k} are the user latent factors for user u in the target T and the source S_k, respectively, and have dimensions $1 \times f$; y_{i_t} are the item latent factors in T also with dimensions $1 \times f$; f is the number of latent factors. It is possible to have a user v in T who does not have any preferences in source domain S_k, as we do not assume a complete user overlap between source and target domains. In such cases, no knowledge about v can be transferred from S_k to T and the user factors x_{v_k} will be a zero vector. The regularization parameter for user factors, λ_k, is used to control the amount of knowledge transferred from source domain S_k and to address the problem of negative transfer; λ denotes the regularization for target item factors, and s is the number of source domains.

The goal of the objective function in Eq. (4) is to factorize the user-item preference matrix in T under the constraint that the source and target user factors are similar. Intuitively, the source user factors can only be similar to the target user factors. The reason for this is that although source and target domains are related, the user factors in the source and target domains can only be similar given that bi-factorization technique used in Step 1 also integrates domain specific semantic concepts into user and item latent factors [5, 12]. By controlling the amount of knowledge transferred from source domains to the target through regularization parameters λ_k, our goal is to transfer only the domain independent part of a source S_k to the target T. Note, also, that we only use user latent factors from the s source domains when transferring knowledge to T. This is because the items are of different types across domains, according to our problem definition, and thus will not contribute to the target recommendation task.

The minimization of the proposed model defined in Eq. (4), can be performed using the alternating least squares algorithm, similar to the optimization in Step 1. Observe that, when either the user or the item factors are assumed to be known and fixed, the cost function becomes quadratic and by differentiation we can find an analytic expression for the user and the item factors, respectively. Taking the learning of the user factors as an example, we will show how to optimize x_{u_t} while fixing the item factors. We get the following updating rule for x_{u_t} when we differentiate $\mathcal{J}$ with respect to x_{u_t} and equate it to 0.

$$x_{u_t} = \frac{\sum\limits_{i_t} (c_{u_t i_t} p_{u_t i_t} y_{i_t}) + \sum\limits_{k \,\epsilon\, [1,s]} (\lambda_k x_{u_k})}{\sum\limits_{i_t} (c_{u_t i_t} y_{i_t}^{\top} y_{i_t}) + \sum\limits_{k \,\epsilon\, [1,s]} (\lambda_k I)} \tag{5}$$

Let $Y_{n \times f}$ be an item factor matrix, where n is the number of items, f is the number of factors. Let $C^u_{n \times n}$ be a diagonal matrix where $C^u_{ii} = c_{u_t i_t}$, and $p(u)$ be an $n \times 1$ vector. Using these notations, Eq. (5) can be expressed as:

$$x_{u_t} = \left(Y^{\top} C^u Y + \sum\nolimits_{k \,\epsilon\, [1,s]} \lambda_k I\right)^{-1} \left(Y^{\top} C^u p(u) + \sum\nolimits_{k \,\epsilon\, [1,s]} \lambda_k x_{u_k}\right) \tag{6}$$

Similarly, the updating rule for the item factors, y_{i_t}, is given by Eq. (7):

$$y_{i_t} = \left(X^{\top} C^i X + \lambda I\right)^{-1} X^{\top} C^i p(i) \tag{7}$$

where $X_{m \times f}$ is a user factor matrix, m is the number of users, f is the number of factors; $C^i_{m \times m}$ is a diagonal matrix, where $C^i_{uu} = c_{u_t i_t}$, and $p(i)$ is a $m \times 1$ vector. We note that the update rule for learning y_{i_t} for our model is identical to the update rule for learning y_{i_k} in Step 1 (derivation not shown), as we do not transfer any knowledge about items between source and target domains.

4 Experimental Design

Dataset Description and Preprocessing: We have used two datasets to evaluate the effectiveness of our approach in improving the recommendation accuracy in the target domain, using knowledge from multiple source domains.

Last.FM Dataset: This dataset, created by Cantador et al. [3], is a subset of the Last.FM dataset[1] and consists of the following three domains: artist domain

---

[1] http://www.lastfm.com.

in which each tuple has (*userID, artistID, #timesListened*) information, friend domain in which each tuple has (*userID, friendID,1*), tag domain in which each tuple has (*userID, tagID, #timesUsed*) information. The number of users in each domain is approximately 1.8 K. The number of items in the artist, friend, and tag domains are approximately 17 K, 1.8 K, 11 K, respectively.

Timestamps are not available for this dataset. To construct the training and test sets for the three domains, we removed users who interacted with less than three items, for example, three artists. This resulted in final datasets with approximately 1.8 K users, 1.4 K users, and 1.7 K users in the artist, friend, and tag domains, respectively. We divided the filtered data into three folds with approximately 33.3 % of a user's preferences in each fold (referred to as the *per-user CV* [14]) and used the standard 3-fold cross validation (CV) technique and use two folds as training and one fold as test.

DBLP Dataset: This dataset[2] has approximately 2×10^7 publications, and 4×10^7 citation relations [18] and we construct the following three domains: a co-author domain in which each tuple has (*authorID, coauthorID, #papersCoauthored*) information, a conference domain in which each tuple has (*authorID, conferenceID, #papersPublished*) information, and a reference domain in which each tuple has (*authorID, referenceID, #papersReferenced*) information.

Given that timestamps are available for each publication record in the dataset, we choose the data between the years 1990 and 2006 to construct the training set and data between the years 2007 to 2013 to construct the test set. As part of preprocessing, we removed any authors who co-authored with less than five authors, referenced less than five publications, and published in less than one conference, from the training set. From the test set for each domain, we removed authors who do not have any preferences in the corresponding training set. After filtering the authors as described above, we have 29,189 authors in each domain. The number of items in the co-author, conference, and reference domains are approximately, 140 K, 2.3 K, and 201 K, respectively.

When creating the training and test data for the three domains in the two datasets above, we ensure the following properties hold: a user in the test set has some history available in the training set [10,12,15], and the test set for a user does not contain items that are also in the corresponding training set for that user, as our objective is to recommend only unknown items. For the Last.FM dataset, the results we report are averaged over the three CV folds. Note that, in our experiments for the DBLP dataset, for a train user, we randomly pick 50 % of preferences from his/her training data and use only these preferences to generate recommendations. This is repeated five times, similar to CV, to account for variation in results from the algorithms and the averaged results are reported.

Evaluation Metric: For each user, the algorithm generates (*item, preference Score*) tuples as output. From this, we remove items that the user is aware of as our objective is to recommend only unknown items. Next, we sort the

---

[2] http://arnetminer.org/citation.

recommendations according to the *preferenceScore* and compute Mean Average Precision (MAP@n) and Recall@n to evaluate the algorithm [6, 16].

Experiments and Baselines: We aim to understand how our proposed Cross-domain Implicit-feedback Matrix Factorization (CIMF) approach performs on the two datasets. Towards this goal, we run three experiments for each dataset. In each experiment, we compute the accuracy of CIMF when one domain is used as target and the other two domains as sources. We compare CIMF with two Adsorption-based cross-domain approaches (WAN and WAR) that we proposed in our earlier work [13], and three single-domain approaches which use user preferences only from the target: the MF approach for *explicit* feedback data [20], the MF approach adapted for *implicit* feedback data (IMF) [8], and the item-based collaborative filtering approach (Item-CF) [15]. The implementations of MF, IMF, and Item-CF are part of the Apache Mahout software. Note that when comparing different approaches, we used a controlled evaluation protocol as indicated in [14], i.e., for all algorithms, we use the same training and test splits and compute evaluation metrics in the same way.

Parameter Settings: The parameters of the algorithms have been manually tuned and best results obtained from combinations of different parameter settings have been reported. For IMF, the following four combinations of (λ, α) were tried in the six domains: (.01, 1), (.01, 5), (.1, 1), and (.1, 5). We note that the values (.1, 5) for (λ, α) worked best for IMF in the three domains of the *Last.FM* dataset and the values (.01, 5) for (λ, α) worked best for IMF in the three domains of the *DBLP* dataset and are reported in our results. For CIMF, the values .1 and .01 are used for λ (item regularization) for the *Last.FM* and the *DBLP* datasets, respectively, as these values proved to be best for IMF in the single-domain setting for the corresponding datasets; for the source user factors, different regularization parameter values (λ_k), specifically, $\{0.1, 0.5, 1, 5\}$ are tried. For MF, we found that the values 0.1 and 0.01 for λ worked best for the three domains of the *Last.FM* and the *DBLP* datasets, respectively. For WAN and WAR approaches, five sets of (*target*, *source*) weights - (0.5, 0.25), (0.6, 0.2), (0.7, 0.15), (0.8, 0.1), (0.9, 0.05) were tried. Finally, the number of latent dimensions (f) for MF, IMF, and CIMF and the number of recommendations from the algorithm (n) were set to be 50 and 10, respectively.

5   Results

We report results for the three cross-domain approaches and the three single-domain approaches for the two datasets in Table 1.

Analysis of the *Last.FM* Dataset: As expected, our CIMF approach of transferring user latent factors from source domains outperforms the single-domain approaches in most cases considered. This can be seen from the MAP and Recall values in Table 1 for Artist, Friend, and Tag domains, respectively. Furthermore, the CIMF approach is significantly better than the WAN and WAR cross-domain approaches in two of the three domains considered. These results confirm our

Table 1. The MAP@10 and Recall@10 values of Item-CF, IMF, and MF (single-domain) and WAN, WAR, and CIMF (cross-domain) when the target domain is the Artist, Friend, Tag in *Last.FM*, and Co-Author, Conference, Reference in *DBLP*, respectively. For each target, the remaining two domains in the corresponding dataset are used as sources. The number of latent factors (f) is 50.

Target domain	Metrics	Single-domain			Cross-domain		
		Item-CF	IMF	MF	WAN	WAR	CIMF
Artist	MAP	0.0658	0.0653	0.033	**0.0950**	**0.0950**	0.0699
	Recall	**0.1537**	0.1333	0.108	0.1508	0.1483	0.1380
Friend	MAP	0.0540	0.0771	0.0135	0.0568	0.0549	**0.0915**
	Recall	0.1249	0.1601	0.0318	0.1164	0.1143	**0.1925**
Tag	MAP	0.1038	0.1087	0.0134	0.1070	0.1105	**0.1459**
	Recall	0.2310	0.2003	0.0514	0.1948	0.1962	**0.2543**
Co-author	MAP	0.0340	0.0314	0.0251	0.0240	0.0349	**0.0357**
	Recall	**0.0824**	0.0702	0.0605	0.0504	0.0696	0.0799
Conference	MAP	0.0762	0.1017	0.0124	0.0554	0.0806	**0.1020**
	Recall	0.1674	**0.2014**	0.0373	0.1172	0.1689	**0.2014**
Reference	MAP	0.0153	0.0470	0.0013	0.0309	0.0297	**0.0472**
	Recall	0.0347	0.0860	0.0041	0.0616	0.0592	**0.0866**

intuition that information about related domains can help in improving target recommendation accuracy and suggest the effectiveness of our CIMF approach to leverage information from multiple source domains. Our approach captures the correlation between related domains through latent user factors identified in each domain, while controlling the amount of knowledge to use from each source domain through regularization parameters. Among the single-domain approaches, we can also see from Table 1 that the performance of MF is significantly worse than that of IMF and Item-CF for the three domains of the *Last.FM* dataset. This is consistent with a similar observation in literature that, factorizing a user-item preference matrix by assuming an implicit preference to be an explicit rating yields poor performance [8]. Between IMF and Item-CF, the results suggest that IMF is better than Item-CF for recommending friends and tags, but slightly worse than Item-CF for recommending artists, together suggesting that IMF is a better single-domain approach for the *Last.FM* dataset.

Analysis of the *DBLP* Dataset: As can be seen from the results in Table 1 for the Co-Author, Conference, and Reference domains, our CIMF approach is generally better than the single domain approaches for all three *DBLP* domains as well, with bigger improvements observed for the Conference and Reference domains, especially when comparing CIMF to the Item-CF and MF approaches. When comparing CIMF with IMF, although there is a good improvement in the MAP and Recall values for the Co-Author domain, we observe a smaller increase in these metrics for the Conference and Reference domains. Finally, when comparing CIMF with WAN and WAR approaches, we can see from the results in

Table 1 that our CIMF approach has better MAP and Recall scores in all three domains, with bigger improvements observed for the Conference and Reference domains. This suggests that our CIMF approach is a superior cross-domain app-roach compared to WAN and WAR approaches for this dataset as well. Among the single-domain approaches, IMF is slightly worse than Item-CF when recom-mending co-authors, but is significantly better when the task is to recommend conferences and references. The weaker performance of IMF for the co-author domain most probably relates to the way in which co-author relationships are formed in real-world. Authors often collaborate with acquaintances as opposed to unknown authors. For a user, Item-CF recommends authors who frequently co-authored with the co-authors of the current user, while IMF recommends more global co-authors, which might explain why Item-CF might be a better choice among the two approaches for this domain. Finally, similar to what we observed for *Last.FM*, MF again has the lowest MAP and Recall values.

We want to emphasize that in real-world, it is possible for a user to use an item again in the future although the item has been used by that user in the past. In our experiments, for both the datasets, we only test on items that the user has not preferred in the past. However, as timestamp information is available for the *DBLP* dataset, we evaluated the performance of all algorithms without filtering preferred items from the test set. As expected, the MAP and Recall values from all algorithms increased by about 20 % to 50 % for the three domains, specifically, the MAP scores of CIMF for the Co-Author, Conference, and Reference domains are 0.0774, 0.1252, and 0.0645, respectively, and are still better than the values from other approaches. This is intuitive because authors repeat collaborations with other authors, publish in conferences in which they have published in the past, and refer papers they have cited in the past.

User Overlap Scenarios: As discussed in Sect. 3, our CIMF approach requires a partial overlap between users in source and target domains to facilitate trans-fer of knowledge. To better understand the effectiveness of our approach in improving target accuracy as compared to single-domain approaches, we con-ducted several experiments by varying the percentage of user overlap between the source and target domains, specifically, we considered 25 % overlap, 50 % overlap, and 75 % overlap. For example, 25 % overlap means that 25 % of users in target domain are in the source domains and vice versa. For each overlap scenario, we compare the performance of CIMF with the performance of IMF. From the results reported in Table 2, we can observe that our CIMF approach has better performance compared to IMF, across all percentages of overlap and for all target domains considered. This suggests that our approach can handle varying user overlap percentages between source and target domains and is effec-tive in improving target recommendation accuracy as compared to IMF. While the performance improvement of CIMF relative to IMF is considerable for the Artist, Friend, Tag, and Co-Author domains, the improvement is smaller for the Conference and Reference domains (across all overlap percentages) similar to what we have observed in Table 1. Note that when creating the training and test sets for these experiments, we only ensure that the target and source domains have the specified percentage of users in common. We do not ensure that the training set for one overlap percentage is built on top of the previous training set corresponding to the previous overlap percentage, as our main goal was to show that our approach can handle different percentages of user overlap, as opposed to showing that the performance increases with the amount of overlap.

Table 2. The MAP@10 scores of IMF and CIMF for the six target domains considered when user overlap between sources and target is varied from 25 % to 50 %, and to 75 %.

Target domain	Algorithm	Percentage	User	Overlap
		25 %	50 %	75 %
Artist	IMF	0.0651	0.0660	0.0669
	CIMF	**0.0682**	**0.0693**	**0.0690**
Friend	IMF	0.0651	0.0756	0.0773
	CIMF	**0.0705**	**0.0791**	**0.0847**
Tag	IMF	0.1008	0.1065	0.1077
	CIMF	**0.1351**	**0.1381**	**0.1460**
Co-author	IMF	0.0331	0.0324	0.0317
	CIMF	**0.0342**	**0.0351**	**0.0355**
Conference	IMF	0.0992	0.0994	0.1012
	CIMF	**0.0995**	**0.1001**	**0.1015**
Reference	IMF	0.0469	0.0470	0.0463
	CIMF	**0.0470**	**0.0472**	**0.0466**

6   Summary and Future Work

In this paper, we proposed a novel cross-domain matrix factorization approach for transferring knowledge from multiple source domains to a target domain. Our method first identifies user and item latent factors in the source domains, and later integrates the source user latent factors into the target through a regularization technique. The novelty of the algorithm includes its ability to handle multiple source domains, heterogeneous items across domains, and *implicit* feedback. Also, the algorithm requires only a partial user overlap as opposed to a complete user overlap between source and target domains. Our experimental study shows that the proposed approach was effective in improving the MAP scores in majority of the target recommendation tasks considered as compared to two previously proposed cross-domain and three single-domain approaches. Furthermore, our results show that the CIMF approach can prevent negative transfer, as we only require the user latent factors in source and target domains to be similar through the regularization terms. Finally, experiments under different user overlap scenarios produced encouraging results. As future work, we plan to create more overlapping scenarios and further test the effectiveness of our approach to improve target recommendation accuracy. Furthermore, we intend to perform similar study on other cross-domain datasets, and also to study the performance of our approach as a function of the sparsity of the target domain.

Acknowledgements. The computing for this project was performed on the Beocat Research Cluster at Kansas State University, which is funded, in part, by grants MRI-1126709, CC-NIE-1341026, MRI-1429316, CC-IIE-1440548.

References

1. Berkovsky, S., Kuflik, T., Ricci, F.: Cross-domain mediation in collaborative filtering. In: Conati, C., McCoy, K., Paliouras, G. (eds.) UM 2007. LNCS (LNAI), vol. 4511, pp. 355–359. Springer, Heidelberg (2007)
2. Berkovsky, S., Kuflik, T., Ricci, F.: Distributed collaborative filtering with domain specialization. In: Proceedings of RecSys (2007)
3. Cantador, I., Brusilovsky, P., Kuflik, T.: 2nd workshop on information heterogeneity and fusion in recommender systems (hetrec 2011). In: Proceedings of RecSys (2011)
4. Cremonesi, P., Tripodi, A., Turrin, R.: Cross-domain recommender systems. In: Proceedings of ICDMW (2011)
5. Gao, S., Luo, H., Chen, D., Li, S., Gallinari, P., Guo, J.: Cross-domain recommendation via cluster-level latent factor model. In: Blockeel, H., Kersting, K., Nijssen, S., Železný, F. (eds.) ECML PKDD 2013, Part II. LNCS, vol. 8189, pp. 161–176. Springer, Heidelberg (2013)
6. Herlocker, J.L., Konstan, J.A., Terveen, L.G., Riedl, J.T.: Evaluating collaborative filtering recommender systems. ACM Trans. Inf. Syst. **22**, 5–53 (2004)
7. Hu, L., Cao, J., Xu, G., Cao, L., Gu, Z., Zhu, C.: Personalized recommendation via cross-domain triadic factorization. In: Proceedings of WWW (2013)
8. Hu, Y., Koren, Y., Volinsky, C.: Collaborative filtering for implicit feedback datasets. In: Proceedings of ICDM (2008)
9. Koren, Y., Bell, R., Volinsky, C.: Matrix factorization techniques for recommender systems. IEEE Comput. **42**(8), 30–37 (2009)
10. Li, B., Yang, Q., Xue, X.: Can movies and books collaborate?: cross-domain collaborative filtering for sparsity reduction. In: Proceedings of IJCAI (2009)
11. Li, B., Yang, Q., Xue, X.: Transfer learning for collaborative filtering via a rating-matrix generative model. In: Proceedings of ICML (2009)
12. Pan, W., Xiang, E.W., Liu, N.N., Yang, Q.: Transfer learning in collaborative filtering for sparsity reduction. In: Proceedings of AAAI (2010)
13. Parimi, R., Caragea, D.: Leveraging multiple networks for author personalization. In: Scholarly Big Data, AAAI Workshop (2015)
14. Said, A., Bellogín, A.: Comparative recommender system evaluation: benchmarking recommendation frameworks. In: Proceedings of RecSys (2014)
15. Sarwar, B., Karypis, G., Konstan, J., Riedl, J.: Item-based collaborative filtering recommendation algorithms. In: Proceedings of WWW (2001)
16. Shapira, B., Rokach, L., Freilikhman, S.: Facebook single and cross domain data for recommendation systems. User Model. User-Adap. Interact. **23**, 211–247 (2013)
17. Singh, A.P., Gordon, G.J.: Relational learning via collective matrix factorization. In: Proceedings of ACM SIGKDD (2008)

18. Tang, J., Zhang, J., Yao, L., Li, J., Zhang, L., Su, Z.: Arnetminer: extraction and mining of academic social networks. In: Proceedings of KDD (2008)
19. Winoto, P., Tang, T.: If you like the devil wears prada the book, will you also enjoy the devil wears prada the movie? a study of cross-domain recommendations. New Gener. Comput. **26**(3), 209–225 (2008)
20. Zhou, Y., Wilkinson, D., Schreiber, R., Pan, R.: Large-scale parallel collaborative filtering for the netflix prize. In: Fleischer, R., Xu, J. (eds.) AAIM 2008. LNCS, vol. 5034, pp. 337–348. Springer, Heidelberg (2008)

Advanced Metamodeling Techniques Applied to Multidimensional Applications with Piecewise Responses

Toufik Al Khawli[1(✉)], Urs Eppelt[1], and Wolfgang Schulz[2]

[1] Department for Nonlinear Dynamics of Laser Processing (NLD),
RWTH Aachen University, Aachen, Germany
{toufik.al.khawli,urs.eppelt}@nld.rwth-aachen.de
[2] Fraunhofer Institute for Laser Technology ILT, Aachen, Germany
wolfgang.schulz@ilt.fraunhofer.de

Abstract. Due to digital changes in the solution properties of many engineering applications, the model response is described by a piecewise continuous function. Generating continuous metamodels for such responses can provide very poor fits due to the discontinuity in the response. In this paper, a new smart sampling approach is proposed to generate high quality metamodels for such piecewise responses. The proposed approach extends the Sequential Approximate Optimization (SAO) procedure, which uses the Radial Basis Function Network (RBFN). It basically generates accurate metamodels iteratively by adding new sampling points, to approximate responses with discrete changes. The new sampling points are added in the sparse region of the feasible (continuous) domain to achieve a high quality metamodel and also next to the discontinuity to refine the uncertainty area between the feasible and non-feasible domain. The performance of the approach is investigated through two numerical examples, a two- dimensional analytical function and a laser epoxy cutting simulation model.

Keywords: Metamodeling · Classification · Radial basis function network · Approximation · Multi-objective optimization · Genetic algorithm · Sequential approximate optimization · Density function

1 Introduction

In everyday engineering applications, multidisciplinary design is required where the product performance and the manufacturing plans are designed simultaneously. The main objective is then to optimize the design process in the most efficient way allowing the designer the flexibility to involve as many disciplines, objectives, and computational processes as possible. During the 1980's, virtual prototyping was successfully introduced to the engineering community. Virtual prototyping involves computer-aided design (CAD), computer-automated design (CAutoD) and computer-aided engineering (CAE) software to predict fundamental design problems as early as possible in the design process. Thus, before going into production, new products were first designed on the computer by simulation then prototyping different concepts and selecting the best were simultaneously performed [1].

© Springer International Publishing Switzerland 2015
P. Pardalos et al. (Eds.): MOD 2015, LNCS 9432, pp. 93–104, 2015.
DOI: 10.1007/978-3-319-27926-8_9

The process of learning from simulation results becomes more difficult when the simulation time as well as the number of parameters increase. This leads to the need for more efficient approximation models which are called metamodels. The main idea of these metamodels is to find a fast and cheap approximation model which is a surrogate of the expensive simulation and can be used to describe the relationship between the process parameters and criteria [2]. Once a fast metamodel is generated with a moderate number of computer experiments, it offers making predictions at additional untried inputs, and thus the conventional engineering tasks such as optimization, sensitivity analysis, or design space exploration become easily possible due to the numerous number of evaluation runs that could be performed.

Due to digital changes in the solution properties of many engineering applications (e.g. topology changes like a material cut-through), the model response is described by a piecewise function. Identifying the region of the discontinuity is not explicit, since it is defined by many other parameter relationships or other physical interactions [3]. When applying metamodels to responses with discontinuity, it can provide very poor fits because metamodels are generally applied to only continuous responses, as the reason is that they mostly apply fully-steady basis functions.

In this paper, a new smart sampling approach is proposed to generate high quality metamodels for piecewise responses. The proposed approach extends the Sequential Approximate Optimization (SAO) procedure, which uses the Radial Basis Function network (RBFN). It mainly generates accurate metamodels iteratively while adding new sampling points, which allows to approximate discrete-continuous responses. The new sampling points are added as follows: (i) in the sparse region of the feasible domain to achieve a high quality metamodel, and (ii) next to the discontinuity to refine the uncertainty area between the feasible and non-feasible domain.

The paper is organized as follows: Sect. 2 describes the formulation of the proposed methodology in detail. In this section, the radial basis function network method, classification, cross-validation, and smart sampling techniques are briefly presented. In Sect. 3, the method is applied onto two test cases, where the results of each are discussed. Finally the concluding remarks and future work are provided in Sect. 4.

2 Metamodeling Approaches for Responses with Discontinuity

After defining the design objectives, identifying the problem's input parameters and output criteria, and defining the lower and upper bounds for the domain space, a metamodel can be generated by one of the two approaches: the one-shot approach or the iterative approach.

2.1 One Shot Approach

The seven main steps typically involved in constructing a one shot metamodel are: 1- sampling the design-space; 2- evaluating the response of the reference model; 3- splitting the data; 4- interpolating the feasible data; 5- classification of the domain space;

6- merging the classification model and interpolation model; and 7- validating the metamodel as shown in Fig. 1.

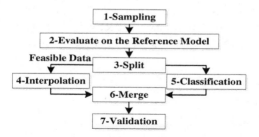

Fig. 1. Flow diagram of the one shot metamodel approach

- **Step 1.** The procedure to efficiently sample the parameter space is addressed by so-called Design of Experiments (DOE) techniques. These sampling methods are categorized either as classical sampling methods [4] such as (factorial designs, central composite design, Box-Behnken, etc...), or simulation sampling methods. Kleijnen et al. [5] proposed that experimental designs for deterministic computer simulations should be space-filling. Space-filling designs such as Latin hypercube design and orthogonal arrays design provide a high flexibility when estimating a large number of linear and nonlinear effects. The samplings determined by the methods above are generated all at once. That is why this metamodeling approach is called a "one shot approach".
- **Step 2.** A validated reference or original model (analytical functions, reduced model, full numerical simulation, or even experiments) is required for metamodeling. In this step, a discontinuity value (*DiscVal*), must be set to represent and distinguish the discontinuity in the domain space.
- **Step 3.** Split the sampling data according to the *DiscVal* to two training data sets T_F and T_C, such as

$$T_F = \{(x_F, y_F)\}_{i=1}^{n_F}, \qquad T_C = \{(x_C, y_C)\}_{i=1}^{n}, \qquad (1)$$

where indexes F, C, n_F, and n represent the feasible sampling data (no discontinuity values), the classification data (full data set), the number of feasible sampling data, and the number of the full data set respectively. The vector y_C is rescaled to values equal to either -1 that correspond to *DiscVal*, or 1 that correspond to feasible values.

- **Step 4.** Construct a metamodel of the feasible data set T_F. Out of numerous metamodeling techniques in literature [6], the Radial Basis Function Network (RBFN) is well known for its accuracy and its ability to generate multidimensional interpolations for complex nonlinear problems [7]. The radial basis function interpolant for the feasible data $F_F(x)$ is given by:

$$F_F(x) = \sum_{i=1}^{n_F} w_{F_i} h_{F_i}(\|x - x_{F_i}\|), \tag{2}$$

where n_F, h_i, $\|.\|$, correspond to the number of sampling points of the feasible set, the ith basis function, and the Euclidian distance respectively. In this work, the multiquadric function and its corresponding width r_M are chosen according to [8]. They are defined by:

$$h_F(x) = \sqrt{1 + \frac{x^2}{r_M^2}}, \quad r_M = 0.81 \cdot d, \quad d = \frac{1}{n_F} \sum_{i=1}^{n_F} d_i, \tag{3}$$

where d_i is the distance between the ith data point and its nearest neighbor. The weight vector w_F, is calculated according to:

$$w_F = \left(H_F^T H_F + \Lambda\right)^{-1} H_F^T y_F, \tag{4}$$

$$H_F = \begin{bmatrix} h_1(x_1) & h_2(x_1) & \cdots & h_{n_F}(x_1) \\ h_1(x_2) & h_2(x_2) & \cdots & h_{n_F}(x_2) \\ \vdots & \vdots & \ddots & \vdots \\ h_1(x_{n_F}) & h_2(x_{n_F}) & \cdots & h_{n_F}(x_{n_F}) \end{bmatrix}, \quad \Lambda = \begin{bmatrix} \lambda & 0 & \cdots & 0 \\ 0 & \lambda & \cdots & 0 \\ \vdots & \vdots & \ddots & \vdots \\ 0 & 0 & \cdots & \lambda \end{bmatrix}, \tag{5}$$

where λ is a regularization parameter which determines the relative importance of the smoothness of the function and

$$y_F = (y_{F_1}, y_{F_2}, \cdots, y_{F_{n_F}}). \tag{6}$$

- **Step 5.** Perform a classification task in order to decompose design space into feasible and non-feasible regions and to detect the discontinuity. By applying the Cover's theorem [9], the domain space ψ that is formed by set of n vectors x_C, can be split into two classes ψ_1 and ψ_2 by assigning a dichotomy of surfaces. This is done in Step 3 where a value of -1 is assigned to non-feasible regions and a value of 1 is assigned to feasible regions. A RBF neural network is used to perform a classification task. The domain space ψ is said to be separable if there exists a vector w_C such that:

$$C(x) = \sum_{i=1}^{n} w_{C_i} h_{C_i}(\|x - x_C\|) > 0, x \in \Psi_1,$$

$$C(x) = \sum_{i=1}^{n} w_{C_i} h_{C_i}(\|x - x_C\|) < 0, x \in \Psi_2. \tag{7}$$

The discontinuity in the domain space is defined by the equation

$$C(x) = \sum_{i=1}^{n} w_{C_i} h_{C_i}(\|x - x_C\|) = 0, \tag{8}$$

where, w_C is defined similar to Eq. (4) by considering the whole data set of size n. The first order linear spline basis and the vector y_C are defined as:

$$h(x) = |x|. \tag{9}$$

- **Step 6.** Merge the classification model and feasible interpolation metamodel in one function such as:

$$f(x) = \begin{cases} F_F(x) & if \ C(x) > 0 \\ \text{DiscVal} & if \ C(x) \leq 0 \end{cases}. \tag{10}$$

- **Step 7.** Validate the metamodel. The validation techniques are mainly used to estimate the quality of the metamodel in terms of the prediction accuracy. For quantifying the model accuracy, the Relative Mean Squared Error coefficient (*RMSE*) and the Coefficient of Determination (R^2) statistical measures are calculated on an additional data. *RMSE* percentage represents the deviation of the metamodel from the real simulation model, and is defined as:

$$RMSE = \frac{1}{nVS} \sum_{i=1}^{nVS} \left(\frac{y_i - f(x_i)}{y_i} \right)^2, \tag{11}$$

where nVS is the number of the validation data set, y_i is the output dependent variable of the validation set, and $f(x_i)$ is the metamodeling function of the parameter vector x_i. The smaller the *RMSE* value, the more accurate the metamodel is. Additionally R^2 is an error performance measure which takes into account the variance and captures how irregular the sample data is [10]. R^2 is calculated according to:

$$R^2 = 1 - \frac{MSE}{\text{variance}}, \quad \text{variance} = \frac{1}{nVS} \sum_{i=1}^{nVS} (y_i - \bar{y}_i)^2. \tag{12}$$

MSE is as defined as the relative mean squared error (similar to Eq. (11) without dividing by y_i). The closer the value of R^2 gets to 1, the more accurate the metamodel becomes.

2.2   Iterative Smart Sampling Approach

Regardless of the metamodel use, there is always a concern of achieving high accuracy with respect to the sampling size, the sampling method, and the metamodeling method. An important research issue associated with metamodeling is how to obtain a good accuracy for metamodels with reasonable sampling techniques. This was recently addressed by the Sequential Approximate Optimization (SAO) technique [11–14]. The SAO is an iterative sampling technique that reduces the number of simulation runs, and at the same time maximizes the information gain of every sampling step by adding appropriate sampling points until a predefined termination criterion is satisfied. The goal of the proposed approach, shown in Fig. 2, is to develop an adaptive sampling method that enhances the effectiveness of generating metamodels for systems that contains a discontinuity. There are two ways to enhance the accuracy of the meta-model: (1) adding infill points in the feasible sparse region (x^{SR}); (2) adding sampling point next to the discontinuity (x^{DISC}) to reduce the uncertainty in the region that lies in the range $[-1,1]$. The proposed methodology that is shown in Fig. 2 involves, in addition to the seven major steps listed before, two additional steps.

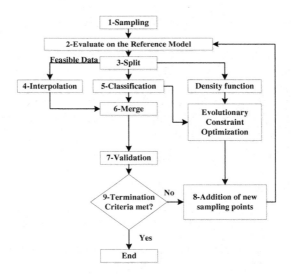

Fig. 2. Flow diagram of the proposed smart sampling method

- **Step 8.** Adding new sampling points. In order to add infill points in the feasible sparse region x^{SR}, the density function, which is proposed by Kitayama [13], is constructed according to the equation:

$$D(x) = \sum_{i=1}^{n} w_{D_i} h_{D_i}(\|x - x_C\|), \tag{13}$$

where the weights vector w_D is defined similar to Eq. (4) with considering the whole data set of size n, and y_D is a 1-by-n vector of +1. In order to achieve a response that decreases monotonically between the sampling points, the gauss basis function h_D is employed as the basis function with a width r_G chosen according to Nakayama [11]:

$$h_D(x) = \exp\left(-\frac{x^2}{r_G^2}\right), \qquad r_G = \frac{d_{\max}}{\sqrt[p]{pn}}, \qquad (14)$$

where d_{max} is the distance between the ith data point and its farthest neighbor, p is the number of parameters, and n is the number of the training points. The additional point (x^{SR}) is acquired by minimizing the multidimensional density function restricted only to the feasible region. The mathematical problem is formulated as follows:

$$
\begin{aligned}
&\min D(x) \\
&subjected \quad to \\
&C(x) > 0 \\
&l(i) < x_i < u(i) \qquad 1 \leq i \leq p,
\end{aligned}
\qquad (15)
$$

where l and u denotes the minimum and maximum ranges of every parameter, and p denotes the parameter number. Second, adding sampling point x^{DISC}, in the dichotomy metamodel to reduce the uncertainty region that ranges between -1 to 1. In this minimization problem, the threshold value in Eq. (16) was set to 0.2 in order to acquire values that lie in the range of -0.2 to 0.2. The discontinuity has a higher certainty to exist within this range. Thus the mathematical problem is formulated as follows:

$$
\begin{aligned}
&\min D(x) \\
&subjected \quad to \\
&|C(\bar{X})| \leq threshold \\
&l(i) < x_i < u(i) \qquad 1 \leq i \leq p.
\end{aligned}
\qquad (16)
$$

The constrained multidimensional optimization problem listed in Eqs. (15) and (16) are solved by interfacing the metamodel with the evolutionary genetic algorithm library NSGA-II [15].

- **Step 9.** Terminating. In this paper the iteration number is chosen to be the termination criterion. Once the maximum iteration number, set by the user, is reached, the algorithm terminates. Or else, add new sampling points are generated by going to **Step 2**.

3   Numerical Results

3.1   Two-Dimensional Analytical Function

In the first test case, the iterative smart sampling algorithm is applied on a two-dimensional piecewise function $y(x_1, x_2)$ defined by:

$$y(x_1,x_2) = \begin{cases} \dfrac{\left(x_1^2+x_2^2-62\right)^2 + \left(x_1^2+0.5x_1-0.5x_2-1.5\right)^2}{100} + 10 & \text{if } (x_1-7)^2+(x_2+7)^2 > 80 \\ NULL & \text{if } (x_1-7)^2+(x_2+7)^2 \leq 80 \end{cases},$$

in a design space limited to $-7 < x_{1,2} < 7$. The function is plotted in Fig. 3. The goal of this example is to create a metamodel that resembles the analytical function y which contains a discontinuity (*DiscVal* is set here to NULL). The algorithm starts by fitting a radial basis function and a radial basis linear classifier to a training initial data set containing 9 sampling points. The initial training experimental design set is obtained by a 3-levels full factorial design. The resulting initial metamodel, with the corresponding classification model, and density function are plotted in Fig. 4. The new proposed sampling points, which are acquired from the optimization algorithm, are illustrated by a green and white stars denoting the x^{DISC} next to the discontinuity and x^{SR} in the sparse feasible region respectively. The update procedure is repeated and this process is continued until the predefined terminating criterion (30 iterations) is met. The results in Fig. 4 show that the contour shapes in the metamodel become similar to the ones in Fig. 3 by simply adding more sampling points in the feasible region. At the same time, the gray region which represents the uncertainty in the classification model decreases while adding more sampling points next to the discontinuity.

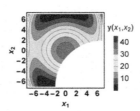

Fig. 3.   Two-dimensional analytical function example

3.2   Laser Epoxy Cutting

In this test case, the superior performance of the proposed smart sampling algorithm is demonstrated on a real design manufacturing application- laser epoxy cutting. One of the challenges in cutting glass fiber reinforced plastics by using a pulsed laser beam, is to estimate achievable cutting qualities. An important factor for the process improvement is first to detect the physical cutting limits and then to minimize the damage thickness of the epoxy-glass material. EpoxyCut, which is a tool developed by the Chair Nonlinear Dynamics of Laser Processing (NLD) of RWTH Aachen, is a reduced

Initial sampling model:

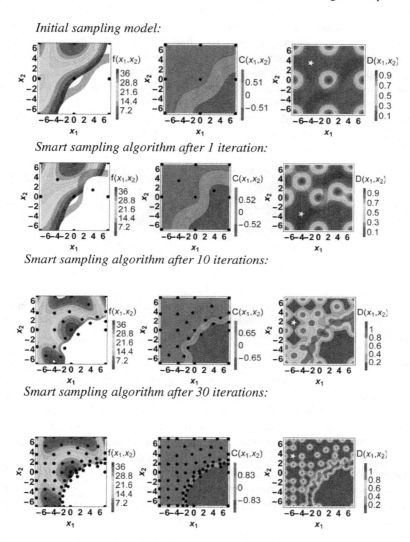

Smart sampling algorithm after 1 iteration:

Smart sampling algorithm after 10 iterations:

Smart sampling algorithm after 30 iterations:

Fig. 4. Interpolation Metamodel (Left), Classification model (Middle), Density function (Right) of the two-dimensional analytical function $y(x_1,x_2)$ for different iteration steps. The white region represents the non-feasible region. In the classification model, the gray region between the red (feasible) and blue (non-feasible) represent the uncertainty region. The density function reflects the position of the sampling points (Color figure online).

model that calculates the upper and lower cutting width, in addition to other criteria like melting threshold, time required to cut through, and damage thickness [16]. In this paper, the reduced model is considered as a black-box model. For further details on the mathematical analysis, the reader is referred to [17]. The goal of this test case is to: (i) minimize the lower cutting width while minimizing the laser power; (ii) detect the cutting limits; and (iii) efficiently generate an accurate metamodel. The laser was modeled as a Gaussian beam. The material thickness, the focal position, the beam radius, and the Rayleigh length were kept constant at 1 mm, 0 mm, 70 um, and 1.28 mm respectively. The metamodeling process parameters are selected to be the pulse duration t_P (10–1000 μs) and the laser power P_L (10–5000 W). The criterion is the cutting width at the bottom of the material W_B.

With the help of a first-order polynomial regression metamodel, a process map on a 50 × 50 Grid is generated and shown in left plot of Fig. 5.

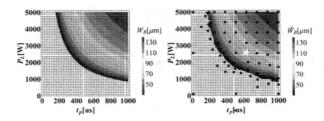

Fig. 5. Parameter space analyses of the cutting width at the bottom on laser power and pulse duration. The plots are generated by the numerical model EpoxyCut using 2500 simulations (Left) and the Metamodel using 69 simulations (Right). The big black points in the metamodel represent the sampling points generated by the smart sampling algorithm.

The white color in the contour plot represents the discontinuity (non-feasible region, no cut region) in the process domain. The physical interpretation is plausible. If the laser power or the pulse duration is not large enough to melt a specific material at the bottom of the work piece, cut through does not occur, and the relationship between the laser intensity and the cutting width bottom is determined by a discontinuity value. Otherwise if the intensity exceeds the energy material threshold, cutting occurs and the response between the laser intensity and the cutting width becomes continuous. For generating an accurate metamodel for this response, while using the minimal number of simulation runs, the proposed smart sampling algorithm is applied with a maximum of 30 iterations starting with a 3-levels full factorial model (Fig. 6).

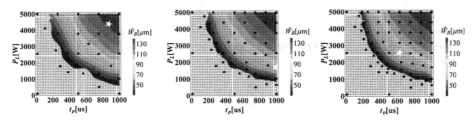

Fig. 6. Evolution of the two-dimensional Contour Plots of the metamodel after 10 iterations (Left), 20 iterations (Middle), and 30 iterations (Right)

In every iteration step, the relative mean squared error (RMSE) and the coefficient of determination (R^2) of the cutting width are calculated and plotted in Fig. 7. The results show that the quality of the metamodel improves when more training points are added till a convergence is reached. The advantage in this iterative technique is that the algorithm can be controlled by the user. If a maximum iteration number or a required quality is reached, the algorithm is terminated, and there is no need for further simulation evaluations.

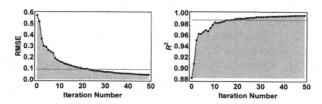

Fig. 7. The statistical measures RMSE (left) and R^2 (right) are generated to validate the quality of the metamodel. The blue line represents validation of a one shot metamodel generated from 10-levels full factorial design. The plots show that the same quality achieved by 100 sampling points from full factorial design can be achieved similarly by 60 sampling points generated by the proposed smart sampling algorithm (Color figure online).

The main advantage of using a metamodel in this process over the full scale simulation is the minimization of the time required to generate the process map. The full data set is 2500 samples in total. It takes EpoxyCut around 5 s to estimate the cutting width for one parameter set. Thus, the total computation time required for generating such a process map will be around 3.5 h. However by using the fast metamodel, it takes the metamodel, generated after 30 iterations with 69 sampling points, about 0.003 s to evaluate one run, thus for the same grid, the process map requires around 7.5 s only.

4   Conclusions

In this paper, a new smart sampling algorithm for generating metamodels with piece wise responses is proposed. The algorithm interfaces the sequential approximation optimization (SAO) and the Radial Basis Function Network (RBFN). The RBFN, with the three different basis functions- multiquadric, gauss, and linear spline, is used to construct the interpolation model, the classification model and the density function. The numerical examples indicate that the proposed algorithm provides better and more efficient results than conventionally used methods in the application cases shown, and that it can also be used in conjunction with multidimensional models. The main focus in the future work is to test the proposed algorithm on applications that have a high dimensional parameter space (5 to 8 parameters). For improving the performance of the algorithm, additional smart points will be considered such as the global optimum as well as the Expected Improvement (via Kriging-method) in the feasible domain.

Acknowledgements. The authors would like to thank the German Research Association DFG for the kind support within the Cluster of Excellence "Integrative Production Technology for High-Wage Countries" of RWTH Aachen University.

References

1. Stinstra, E.: The Meta-Model Approach FOR Simulation-Based Design Optimization. CentER, Center for Economic Research, Tilburg (2006)
2. Eppelt, U., Al Khawli, T.: Metamodeling of laser cutting, presentation and proceedings paper In: ICNAAM—12th International Conference of Numerical Analysis and Applied Mathematics, 22–28 September 2014
3. Meckesheimer, M., Barton, R., Simpson, T., Limayem, F., Yannou, B.: Metamodeling of combined discrete/continuous responses. AIAA J. **39**, 1950–1959 (2001)
4. Box, G.E.P., Draper, N.R.: Empirical Model-Building and Response Surfaces, p. 424. Wiley, New York (1987). ISBN 0-471-81033-9
5. Kleijnen, J.P., Sanchez, S.M., Lucas, T.W., Cioppa, T.M.: State of- the-art review: a user's guide to the brave new world of designing simulation experiments. INFORMS J. Comput. **17**(3), 263–289 (2005)
6. Jurecka, F.: Robust Design Optimization based on Metamodeling Techniques. Shaker Verlag, Germany (2007)
7. Orr, M.: Introduction to Radial Basis Function Networks, Centre for Cognitive Science, University of Edinburgh, Buccleuch Place, Edinburgh EH8 9LW, Scotland (1996)
8. Hardy, R.: Multiquadric equations of topography and other irregular surfaces. J. Geophys. Res. **76**(8), 1905–1915 (1971)
9. Haykin, S.: Neural Networks and Learning Machines, 3rd edn. Prentice Hall, Upper Saddle River (2009)
10. Jin, R, Chen, W., Simpson, T.W.: Comparative studies of metamodeling techniques under multiple modeling criteria. In: Proceedings of the 8th Symposium on Multidisciplinary Analysis and Optimization, Long Beach, CA (2001)
11. Nakayama, H., Arakawa, M., Sasaki, R.: Simulation-based optimization using computational intelligence. Optim. Eng. **3**, 201–214 (2002)
12. Deng, Y.M., Zhang, Y., Lam, Y.C.: A hybrid of mode-pursuing sampling method and genetic algorithm for minimization of injection molding warpage. Mater. Des. **31**(4), 2118–2123 (2010)
13. Kitayama, S., Arakawa, M., Yamazaki, K.: Sequential approximate optimization using radial basis function network for engineering optimization. Optim. and Eng. **12**(4), 535–557 (2011)
14. Kitayama, S., Srirat, J., Arakawa, M.: Sequential approximate multi-objective optimization using radial basis function network. Struct. Multi. Optim. **48**(3), 501–515 (2013)
15. Deb, K., Agrawal, S., Pratap, A., Meyarivan, T.: A fast and elitist multiobjective genetic algorithm: NSGA-II. IEEE Trans. Evol. Comput. **6**(2), 182–197 (2002)
16. Schulz, W., Al Khawli, T.: Meta-modelling techniques towards virtual production intelligence. In: Brecher, C. (ed.) Advances in Production Technology, pp. 69–84. Springer International Publishing, Switzerland (2015)
17. Schulz, W., Kostrykin, V., Zefferer, H., Petring, D., Poprawe, R.: A free boundary problem related to laser beam fusion cutting: ODE apprximation. Int. J. Heat Mass Transfer. **12**(40), 2913–2928 (1997)

Alternating Direction Method of Multipliers for Regularized Multiclass Support Vector Machines

Yangyang Xu[1], Ioannis Akrotirianakis[2]($\boxtimes$), and Amit Chakraborty[2]

[1] Rice University, Houston, TX, USA
yangyang.xu@rice.edu
[2] Siemens Corporate Technology, Princeton, NJ, USA
{ioannis.akrotirianakis,amit.chakraborty}@siemens.com

Abstract. The support vector machine (SVM) was originally designed for binary classifications. A lot of effort has been put to generalize the binary SVM to multiclass SVM (MSVM) which are more complex problems. Initially, MSVMs were solved by considering their dual formulations which are quadratic programs and can be solved by standard second-order methods. However, the duals of MSVMs with regularizers are usually more difficult to formulate and computationally very expensive to solve. This paper focuses on several regularized MSVMs and extends the alternating direction method of multiplier (ADMM) to these MSVMs. Using a splitting technique, all considered MSVMs are written as two-block convex programs, for which the ADMM has global convergence guarantees. Numerical experiments on synthetic and real data demonstrate the high efficiency and accuracy of our algorithms.

Keywords: Alternating direction method of multipliers · Support vector machine · Multiclass classification · Elastic net · Group lasso · Supnorm

1 Introduction

The linear support vector machine (SVM) [6] aims to find a hyperplane to separate a set of data points. It was orginally designed for binary classifications. Motivated by texture classification and gene expression analysis, which usually have a large number of variables but only a few relevant, certain sparsity regularizers such as the ℓ_1 penalty [4], need to be included in the SVM model to control the sparsity pattern of the solution and achieve both classification and variable selection. On the other hand, the given data points may belong to more than two classes. To handle the more complex multiclass problems, the binary SVM has been generalized to multicategory classifications [7].

The initially proposed multiclass SVM (MSVM) methods construct several binary classifiers, such as "one-against-one" [1], "one-against-rest" [2] and

© Springer International Publishing Switzerland 2015
P. Pardalos et al. (Eds.): MOD 2015, LNCS 9432, pp. 105–117, 2015.
DOI: 10.1007/978-3-319-27926-8_10

"directed acyclic graph SVM" [17]. These models are usually solved by considering their dual formulations, which are quadratic programs often with fewer variables and can be efficiently solved by quadratic programming methods. However, these MSVMs may suffer from data imbalance (i.e., some classes have much fewer data points than others) which can result in inaccurate predictions. One alternative is to put all the data points together in one model, which results in the so-called "all-together" MSVMs; see [14] and references therein for the comparison of different MSVMs. The "all-together" MSVMs train multi-classifiers by solving one large optimization problem, whose dual formulation is also a quadratic program. In the applications of microarray classification, variable selection is important since most times only a few genes are closely related to certain diseases. Therefore some structure regularizers such as ℓ_1 penalty [19] and ℓ_∞ penalty [23] need to be added to the MSVM models. With the addition of the structure regularizers, the dual problems of the aforementioned MSVMs can be difficult to formulate and hard to solve by standard second-order optimization methods.

In this paper, we focus on three "all-together" regularized MSVMs. Specifically, given a set of samples $\{\mathbf{x}_i\}_{i=1}^n$ in p-dimensional space and each $\mathbf{x}_i$ with a label $y_i \in \{1, \cdots, J\}$, we solve the constrained optimization problem

$$\min_{\mathbf{W}, \mathbf{b}} \ell_G(\mathbf{W}, \mathbf{b}) + \lambda_1 \|\mathbf{W}\|_1 + \lambda_2 \phi(\mathbf{W}) + \frac{\lambda_3}{2} \|\mathbf{b}\|_2^2, \text{ s.t. } \mathbf{W}\mathbf{e} = \mathbf{0}, \mathbf{e}^\top \mathbf{b} = 0 \qquad (1)$$

where

$$\ell_G(\mathbf{W}, \mathbf{b}) = \frac{1}{n} \sum_{i=1}^n \sum_{j=1}^J I(y_i \neq j)[b_j + \mathbf{w}_j^\top \mathbf{x}_i + 1]_+$$

is generalized hinge loss function; $I(y_i \neq j)$ equals *one* if $y_i \neq j$ and *zero* otherwise; $[t]_+ = \max(0, t)$; $\mathbf{w}_j$ denotes the jth column of $\mathbf{W}$; $\mathbf{e}$ denotes the vector of appropriate size with all *ones*; $\|\mathbf{W}\|_1 = \sum_{i,j} |w_{ij}|$; $\phi(\mathbf{W})$ is some regularizer specified below. Usually, the regularizer can promote the structure of the solution and also avoid overfitting problems when the training samples are far less than features. The constraints $\mathbf{W}\mathbf{e} = \mathbf{0}, \mathbf{e}^\top \mathbf{b} = 0$ are imposed to eliminate redundancy in $\mathbf{W}, \mathbf{b}$ and are also necessary to make the loss function ℓ_G Fisher-consistent [16]. The solution of (1) gives J linear classifiers $f_j(\mathbf{x}) = \mathbf{w}_j^\top \mathbf{x} + b_j$, $j = 1, \cdots, J$. A new coming data point $\mathbf{x}$ can be classified by the rule $\text{class}(\mathbf{x}) = \text{argmax}_{1 \leq j \leq J} f_j(\mathbf{x})$.

We consider the following three different forms of $\phi(\mathbf{W})$:

$$\text{elastic net: } \phi(\mathbf{W}) = \frac{1}{2}\|\mathbf{W}\|_F^2, \qquad (2a)$$

$$\text{group Lasso: } \phi(\mathbf{W}) = \sum_{j=1}^p \|\mathbf{w}^j\|_2, \qquad (2b)$$

$$\text{supnorm: } \phi(\mathbf{W}) = \sum_{j=1}^p \|\mathbf{w}^j\|_\infty, \qquad (2c)$$

where $\mathbf{w}^j$ denotes the jth row of $\mathbf{W}$. They fit to data with different structures and can be solved by a *unified* algorithmic framework. Note that we have added the term $\frac{\lambda_3}{2}\|\mathbf{b}\|_2^2$ in (1). A positive λ_3 will make our algorithm more efficient and easier to implement. The extra term usually does not affect the accuracy of classification and variable selection as shown in [14] for binary classifications. If λ_3 happens to affect the accuracy, one can choose a tiny λ_3. Model (1) includes as special cases the models in [16,23] by letting ϕ be the one in (2a) and (2c) respectively and setting $\lambda_1 = \lambda_3 = 0$. To the best of our knowledge, the regularizer (2b) has not been considered in MSVM before. It encourages group sparsity of the solution [22], and our experiments will show that (2b) can give similar results as those by (2c). Our main contributions are: (i) the development of a unified algorithmic framework based on the ADMM that can solve MSVMs with the three different regularizers defined in (2); (ii) the proper use of the Woodbury matrix identity [13] which can reduce the size of the linear systems arising during the solution of (1); (iii) computational experiments on a variety of datasets that practically demonstrate that our algorithms can solve large-scale multiclass classification problems much faster than state-of-the-art second order methods.

We use $\mathbf{e}$ and $\mathbf{E}$ to denote a vector and a matrix with all *ones*, respectively. $\mathbf{I}$ is used for an identity matrix. Their sizes are clear from the context.

The rest of the paper is organized as follows. Section 2 gives our algorithm for solving (1). Numerical results are given in Sect. 3 on both synthetic and real data. Finally, Sect. 4 concludes this paper.

2   Algorithms

In this section we extend ADMM into the general optimization problems described by (1). Due to lack of space we refer the reader to [3] for details of ADMM. We first consider (1) with $\phi(\mathbf{W})$ defined in (2a) and then solve it with $\phi(\mathbf{W})$ in (2b) and (2c) in a unified form. The parameter λ_3 is always assumed positive. One can also transform the MSVMs to quadratic or second-order cone programs and use standard second-order methods to solve them. Nevertheless, these methods are computationally intensive for large-scale problems. As shown in Sect. 3, ADMM is, in general, much faster than standard second-order methods.

2.1   ADMM for Solving (1) with ϕ defined by (2a)

Introduce auxiliary variables $\mathbf{A} = \mathbf{X}^\top \mathbf{W} + \mathbf{e}\mathbf{b}^\top + \mathbf{E}$ and $\mathbf{U} = \mathbf{W}$, where $\mathbf{X} = [\mathbf{x}_1, \cdots, \mathbf{x}_n] \in \mathbb{R}^{p \times n}$. Using the above auxiliary variables we can equivalently write (1) with $\phi(\mathbf{W})$ defined in (2a) as follows

$$\min \frac{1}{n}\sum_{i,j} c_{ij}[a_{ij}]_+ + \lambda_1\|\mathbf{U}\|_1 + \frac{\lambda_2}{2}\|\mathbf{W}\|_F^2 + \frac{\lambda_3}{2}\|\mathbf{b}\|_2^2 \tag{3}$$
$$\text{s.t. } \mathbf{A} = \mathbf{X}^\top \mathbf{W} + \mathbf{e}\mathbf{b}^\top + \mathbf{E}, \ \mathbf{U} = \mathbf{W}, \mathbf{W}\mathbf{e} = \mathbf{0}, \ \mathbf{e}^\top \mathbf{b} = 0.$$

The augmented Lagrangian[1] of (3) is

$$\mathcal{L}_1(\mathbf{W}, \mathbf{b}, \mathbf{A}, \mathbf{U}, \boldsymbol{\Pi}, \boldsymbol{\Lambda}) = \frac{1}{n}\sum_{i,j} c_{ij}[a_{ij}]_+ + \lambda_1\|\mathbf{U}\|_1 + \frac{\lambda_2}{2}\|\mathbf{W}\|_F^2 + \frac{\lambda_3}{2}\|\mathbf{b}\|_2^2 + \langle \boldsymbol{\Lambda}, \mathbf{W} - \mathbf{U}\rangle$$
$$+ \frac{\mu}{2}\|\mathbf{W} - \mathbf{U}\|_F^2 + \langle \boldsymbol{\Pi}, \mathbf{X}^\top\mathbf{W} + \mathbf{e}\mathbf{b}^\top - \mathbf{A} + \mathbf{E}\rangle$$
$$+ \frac{\alpha}{2}\|\mathbf{X}^\top\mathbf{W} + \mathbf{e}\mathbf{b}^\top - \mathbf{A} + \mathbf{E}\|_F^2, \tag{4}$$

---

[1] We do not include the constraints $\mathbf{W}\mathbf{e} = \mathbf{0}$, $\mathbf{e}^\top\mathbf{b} = 0$ in the augmented Lagrangian, but instead we include them in $(\mathbf{W}, \mathbf{b})$-subproblem; see the update (5a).

where $\boldsymbol{\Pi}, \boldsymbol{\Lambda}$ are Lagrange multipliers and $\alpha, \mu > 0$ are penalty parameters. The ADMM approach for (3) can be derived by minimizing $\mathcal{L}_1$ alternatively with respect to $(\mathbf{W}, \mathbf{b})$ and $(\mathbf{A}, \mathbf{U})$ and updating the multipliers $\boldsymbol{\Pi}, \boldsymbol{\Lambda}$, namely, at iteration k,

$$\left(\mathbf{W}^{(k+1)}, \mathbf{b}^{(k+1)}\right) = \underset{(\mathbf{W}, \mathbf{b}) \in \mathcal{D}}{\operatorname{argmin}} \, \mathcal{L}_1\left(\mathbf{W}, \mathbf{b}, \mathbf{A}^{(k)}, \mathbf{U}^{(k)}, \boldsymbol{\Pi}^{(k)}, \boldsymbol{\Lambda}^{(k)}\right), \tag{5a}$$

$$\left(\mathbf{A}^{(k+1)}, \mathbf{U}^{(k+1)}\right) = \underset{\mathbf{A}, \mathbf{U}}{\operatorname{argmin}} \, \mathcal{L}_1\left(\mathbf{W}^{(k+1)}, \mathbf{b}^{(k+1)}, \mathbf{A}, \mathbf{U}, \boldsymbol{\Pi}^{(k)}, \boldsymbol{\Lambda}^{(k)}\right), \tag{5b}$$

$$\boldsymbol{\Pi}^{(k+1)} = \boldsymbol{\Pi}^{(k)} + \alpha\left(\mathbf{X}^\top \mathbf{W}^{(k+1)} + \mathbf{e}(\mathbf{b}^{(k+1)})^\top - \mathbf{A}^{(k+1)} + \mathbf{E}\right), \tag{5c}$$

$$\boldsymbol{\Lambda}^{(k+1)} = \boldsymbol{\Lambda}^{(k)} + \mu\left(\mathbf{W}^{(k+1)} - \mathbf{U}^{(k+1)}\right), \tag{5d}$$

where $\mathcal{D} = \{(\mathbf{W}, \mathbf{b}) : \mathbf{W}\mathbf{e} = \mathbf{0}, \mathbf{e}^\top \mathbf{b} = 0\}$. The updates (5c) and (5d) are simple. We next discuss how to solve (5a) and (5b).

Solution of (5a): Define $\mathbf{P} = [\mathbf{I}; -\mathbf{e}^\top] \in \mathbb{R}^{J \times (J-1)}$. Let $\hat{\mathbf{W}}$ be the submatrix consisting of the first $J-1$ columns of $\mathbf{W}$ and $\hat{\mathbf{b}}$ be the subvector consisting of the first $J-1$ components of $\mathbf{b}$. Then it is easy to verify that $\mathbf{W} = \hat{\mathbf{W}}\mathbf{P}^\top, \mathbf{b} = \mathbf{P}\hat{\mathbf{b}}$ and problem (5a) is equivalent to the unconstrained optimization problem

$$
\begin{aligned}
\min_{\hat{\mathbf{W}}, \hat{\mathbf{b}}} \; &\frac{\lambda_2}{2}\|\hat{\mathbf{W}}\mathbf{P}^\top\|_F^2 + \langle \boldsymbol{\Lambda}^{(k)}, \hat{\mathbf{W}}\mathbf{P}^\top \rangle + \frac{\lambda_3}{2}\|\hat{\mathbf{b}}^\top \mathbf{P}^\top\|_2^2 + \frac{\mu}{2}\|\hat{\mathbf{W}}\mathbf{P}^\top - \mathbf{U}^{(k)}\|_F^2 \\
&+ \langle \boldsymbol{\Pi}^{(k)}, \mathbf{X}^\top \hat{\mathbf{W}}\mathbf{P}^\top + \mathbf{e}\hat{\mathbf{b}}^\top \mathbf{P}^\top \rangle + \frac{\alpha}{2}\|\mathbf{X}^\top \hat{\mathbf{W}}\mathbf{P}^\top + \mathbf{e}\hat{\mathbf{b}}^\top \mathbf{P}^\top - \mathbf{A}^{(k)} + \mathbf{E}\|_F^2.
\end{aligned}
\tag{6}
$$

The first-order optimality condition of (6) is the linear system

$$
\begin{bmatrix} \alpha \mathbf{X}\mathbf{X}^\top + (\lambda_2 + \mu)\mathbf{I} & \alpha \mathbf{X}\mathbf{e} \\ \alpha \mathbf{e}^\top \mathbf{X}^\top & n\alpha + \lambda_3 \end{bmatrix} \begin{bmatrix} \hat{\mathbf{W}} \\ \hat{\mathbf{b}}^\top \end{bmatrix} = \begin{bmatrix} \left(\mathbf{X}\boldsymbol{\Theta} - \boldsymbol{\Lambda}^{(k)} + \mu \mathbf{U}^{(k)}\right)\mathbf{P}(\mathbf{P}^\top \mathbf{P})^{-1} \\ \mathbf{e}^\top\left(\alpha \mathbf{A}^{(k)} - \boldsymbol{\Pi}^{(k)} - \alpha \mathbf{E}\right)\mathbf{P}(\mathbf{P}^\top \mathbf{P})^{-1} \end{bmatrix},
\tag{7}
$$

where $\boldsymbol{\Theta} = \alpha \mathbf{A}^{(k)} - \boldsymbol{\Pi}^{(k)} - \alpha \mathbf{E}$. The size of (7) is $(p+1) \times (p+1)$ and when p is small, we can afford to directly solve it. However, if p is large, even the iterative method for linear system (e.g., preconditioned conjugate gradient) can be very expensive. In the case of "large p, small n", we can employ the *Woodbury matrix identity* (e.g., [13]) to efficiently solve (7). In particular, let $\mathbf{D} = \text{block\_diag}((\lambda_2 + \mu)\mathbf{I}, \lambda_3)$ and $\mathbf{Z} = [\mathbf{X}; \mathbf{e}^\top]$. Then the coefficient matrix of (7) is $\mathbf{D} + \alpha \mathbf{Z}\mathbf{Z}^\top$, and by the *Woodbury matrix identity*, we have $\mathbf{P}(\mathbf{P}^\top \mathbf{P})^{-1} = [\mathbf{I}; \mathbf{0}] - \frac{1}{J}\mathbf{E}$ and

$$(\mathbf{D} + \alpha \mathbf{Z}\mathbf{Z}^\top)^{-1} = \mathbf{D}^{-1} - \alpha \mathbf{D}^{-1}\mathbf{Z}(\mathbf{I} + \alpha \mathbf{Z}^\top \mathbf{D}^{-1}\mathbf{Z})^{-1}\mathbf{Z}^\top \mathbf{D}^{-1}.$$

Note $\mathbf{D}$ is diagonal, and thus $\mathbf{D}^{-1}$ is simple to compute. $\mathbf{I} + \alpha \mathbf{Z}^\top \mathbf{D}^{-1}\mathbf{Z}$ is $n \times n$ and positive definite. Hence, as $n \ll p$, (7) can be solved by solving a much smaller linear system and doing several matrix-matrix multiplications. In case of large n and p, one can perform a proximal gradient step to update $\mathbf{W}$ and $\mathbf{b}$, which results in a proximal-ADMM [8]. To the best of our knowledge, this is the first time that the Woodbury matrix identity is used to substantially reduce[2] the computational work and allow ADMM to efficiently solve large-scale

---

[2] For the case of $n \ll p$, we found that using the Woodbury matrix identity can be about 100 times faster than preconditioned conjugate gradient (pcg) with moderate tolerance 10^{-6} for the solving the linear system (7).

multiclass SVMs. Solve (7) by multiplying $(\mathbf{D} + \alpha \mathbf{Z}\mathbf{Z}^\top)^{-1}$ to both sides. Letting $\mathbf{W}^{(k+1)} = \hat{\mathbf{W}}\mathbf{P}^\top$ and $\mathbf{b}^{(k+1)} = \mathbf{P}\hat{\mathbf{b}}$ gives the solution of (5a).

Solution of (5b): Note that $\mathbf{A}$ and $\mathbf{U}$ are independent of each other as $\mathbf{W}$ and $\mathbf{b}$ are fixed. Hence we can separately update $\mathbf{A}$ and $\mathbf{U}$ by

$$\mathbf{A}^{(k+1)} = \operatorname*{argmin}_{\mathbf{A}} \frac{1}{n}\sum_{i,j} c_{ij}[a_{ij}]_+ + \frac{\alpha}{2}\|\mathbf{X}^\top\mathbf{W}^{(k+1)} + \mathbf{e}(\mathbf{b}^{(k+1)})^\top + \frac{1}{\alpha}\boldsymbol{\Pi}^{(k)} + \mathbf{E} - \mathbf{A}\|_F^2$$

$$\mathbf{U}^{(k+1)} = \operatorname*{argmin}_{\mathbf{U}} \lambda_1\|\mathbf{U}\|_1 + \frac{\mu}{2}\|\mathbf{W}^{(k+1)} + \frac{1}{\mu}\boldsymbol{\Lambda}^{(k)} - \mathbf{U}\|_F^2.$$

Both the above problems are separable and have closed form solutions

$$a_{ij}^{(k+1)} = \mathcal{T}_{\frac{c_{ij}}{n\alpha}}\left(\left(\mathbf{X}^\top\mathbf{W}^{(k+1)} + \mathbf{e}(\mathbf{b}^{(k+1)})^\top + \frac{1}{\alpha}\boldsymbol{\Pi}^{(k)} + \mathbf{E}\right)_{ij}\right), \forall i,j, \qquad (8)$$

$$u_{ij}^{(k+1)} = \mathcal{S}_{\frac{\lambda_1}{\mu}}\left(\left(\mathbf{W}^{(k+1)} + \frac{1}{\mu}\boldsymbol{\Lambda}^{(k)}\right)_{ij}\right), \forall i,j, \qquad (9)$$

where

$$\mathcal{T}_\nu(\delta) = \begin{cases} \delta - \nu, & \delta > \nu, \\ 0, & 0 \le \delta \le \nu, \\ \delta, & \delta < 0, \end{cases}$$

and $\mathcal{S}_\nu(\delta) = \operatorname{sign}(\delta)\max(0, |\delta| - \nu)$. Putting the above discussions together, we have Algorithm 1 for solving (1) with ϕ defined in (2a).

Algorithm 1. ADMM for (1) with $\phi(\mathbf{W})$ in (2a)

Input: n sample-label pairs $\{(\mathbf{x}_i, y_i)\}_{i=1}^n$.
Choose: $\alpha, \mu > 0$ and $(\mathbf{W}_0, \mathbf{b}_0, \mathbf{A}_0, \mathbf{U}_0, \boldsymbol{\Pi}_0, \boldsymbol{\Lambda}_0), k = 0$.
while *not converge* **do**
    Solve (7); let $\mathbf{W}^{(k+1)} = \hat{\mathbf{W}}\mathbf{P}^\top$ and $\mathbf{b}^{(k+1)} = \mathbf{P}\hat{\mathbf{b}}$;
    Update $\mathbf{A}^{(k+1)}$ and $\mathbf{U}^{(k+1)}$ by (8) and (9);
    Update $\boldsymbol{\Pi}^{(k+1)}$ and $\boldsymbol{\Lambda}^{(k+1)}$ by (5c) and (5d);
    Let $k = k + 1$

2.2 ADMM for Solving (1) with ϕ defined by (2b) and (2c)

Firstly, we write (1) with $\phi(\mathbf{W})$ defined in (2b) and (2c) in the unified form of

$$\min_{\mathbf{W},\mathbf{b}} \ell_G(\mathbf{W}, \mathbf{b}) + \lambda_1\|\mathbf{W}\|_1 + \sum_{j=1}^p \lambda_2\|\mathbf{w}^j\|_q + \frac{\lambda_3}{2}\|\mathbf{b}\|_2^2, \text{ s.t.} \mathbf{W}\mathbf{e} = \mathbf{0}, \mathbf{e}^\top\mathbf{b} = 0, \qquad (10)$$

where $q = 2$ for (2b) and $q = \infty$ for (2c). Introducing auxiliary variables $\mathbf{A} = \mathbf{X}^\top\mathbf{W} + \mathbf{e}\mathbf{b}^\top + \mathbf{E}$, $\mathbf{U} = \mathbf{W}$, and $\mathbf{V} = \mathbf{W}$, we can write (10) equivalently to

$$\min \frac{1}{n}\sum_{i,j} c_{ij}[a_{ij}]_+ + \lambda_1\|\mathbf{U}\|_1 + \sum_{j=1}^p \lambda_2\|\mathbf{v}^j\|_q + \frac{\lambda_3}{2}\|\mathbf{b}\|^2$$
$$\text{s.t. } \mathbf{A} = \mathbf{X}^\top\mathbf{W} + \mathbf{e}\mathbf{b}^\top + \mathbf{E}, \ \mathbf{U} = \mathbf{W}, \ \mathbf{V} = \mathbf{W}, \ \mathbf{W}\mathbf{e} = \mathbf{0}, \ \mathbf{e}^\top\mathbf{b} = 0. \qquad (11)$$

The augmented Lagrangian of (11) is

$$
\mathcal{L}_2(\mathbf{W}, \mathbf{b}, \mathbf{A}, \mathbf{U}, \mathbf{V}, \boldsymbol{\Pi}, \boldsymbol{\Lambda}, \boldsymbol{\Gamma}) = \frac{1}{n} \sum_{i,j} c_{ij} [a_{ij}]_+ + \lambda_1 \|\mathbf{U}\|_1 + \sum_{j=1}^{p} \lambda_2 \|\mathbf{v}^j\|_q + \frac{\lambda_3}{2} \|\mathbf{b}\|_2^2
$$
$$
+ \langle \boldsymbol{\Pi}, \mathbf{X}^\top \mathbf{W} + \mathbf{e}\mathbf{b}^\top - \mathbf{A} + \mathbf{E} \rangle + \frac{\alpha}{2} \|\mathbf{X}^\top \mathbf{W} + \mathbf{e}\mathbf{b}^\top - \mathbf{A} + \mathbf{E}\|_F^2
$$
$$
+ \langle \boldsymbol{\Lambda}, \mathbf{W} - \mathbf{U} \rangle + \frac{\mu}{2} \|\mathbf{W} - \mathbf{U}\|_F^2 + \langle \boldsymbol{\Gamma}, \mathbf{W} - \mathbf{V} \rangle + \frac{\nu}{2} \|\mathbf{W} - \mathbf{V}\|_F^2, \quad (12)
$$

where $\boldsymbol{\Pi}, \boldsymbol{\Lambda}, \boldsymbol{\Gamma}$ are Lagrange multipliers and $\alpha, \mu, \nu > 0$ are penalty parameters. The ADMM updates for (11) can be derived as

$$
(\mathbf{W}^{(k+1)}, \mathbf{b}^{(k+1)}) = \operatorname*{argmin}_{(\mathbf{W}, \mathbf{b}) \in \mathcal{D}} \mathcal{L}_2(\mathbf{W}, \mathbf{b}, \mathbf{A}^{(k)}, \mathbf{U}^{(k)}, \mathbf{V}^{(k)}, \boldsymbol{\Pi}^{(k)}, \boldsymbol{\Lambda}^{(k)}, \boldsymbol{\Gamma}^{(k)}) \quad (13a)
$$
$$
(\mathbf{A}^{(k+1)}, \mathbf{U}^{(k+1)}, \mathbf{V}^{(k+1)}) = \operatorname*{argmin}_{\mathbf{A}, \mathbf{U}, \mathbf{V}} \mathcal{L}_2(\mathbf{W}^{(k+1)}, \mathbf{b}^{(k+1)}, \mathbf{A}, \mathbf{U}, \mathbf{V}, \boldsymbol{\Pi}^{(k)}, \boldsymbol{\Lambda}^{(k)}, \boldsymbol{\Gamma}^{(k)}) \quad (13b)
$$
$$
\boldsymbol{\Pi}^{(k+1)} = \boldsymbol{\Pi}^{(k)} + \alpha(\mathbf{X}^\top \mathbf{W}^{(k+1)} + \mathbf{e}(\mathbf{b}^{(k+1)})^\top - \mathbf{A}^{(k+1)} + \mathbf{E}) \quad (13c)
$$
$$
\boldsymbol{\Lambda}^{(k+1)} = \boldsymbol{\Lambda}^{(k)} + \mu(\mathbf{W}^{(k+1)} - \mathbf{U}^{(k+1)}), \quad (13d)
$$
$$
\boldsymbol{\Gamma}^{(k+1)} = \boldsymbol{\Gamma}^{(k)} + \nu(\mathbf{W}^{(k+1)} - \mathbf{V}^{(k+1)}). \quad (13e)
$$

The subproblem (13a) can be solved in a similar way as discussed in Sect. 2.1. Specifically, first obtain $(\hat{\mathbf{W}}, \hat{\mathbf{b}})$ by solving

$$
\begin{bmatrix} \alpha \mathbf{X}\mathbf{X}^\top + (\nu + \mu)\mathbf{I} & \alpha \mathbf{X}\mathbf{e} \\ \alpha \mathbf{e}^\top \mathbf{X}^\top & n\alpha + \lambda_3 \end{bmatrix} \begin{bmatrix} \hat{\mathbf{W}} \\ \hat{\mathbf{b}}^\top \end{bmatrix} = \begin{bmatrix} (\mathbf{X}\boldsymbol{\Xi} - \boldsymbol{\Lambda}^{(k)} - \boldsymbol{\Gamma}^{(k)} + \mu\mathbf{U}^{(k)} + \nu\mathbf{V}^{(k)})\mathbf{P}(\mathbf{P}^\top \mathbf{P})^{-1} \\ \mathbf{e}^\top \left(\alpha \mathbf{A}^{(k)} - \boldsymbol{\Pi}^{(k)} - \alpha\mathbf{E} \right) \mathbf{P}(\mathbf{P}^\top \mathbf{P})^{-1} \end{bmatrix},
$$
$$
(14)
$$

where $\boldsymbol{\Xi} = \alpha \mathbf{A}^{(k)} - \boldsymbol{\Pi}^{(k)} - \alpha\mathbf{E}$ and then let $\mathbf{W}^{(k+1)} = \hat{\mathbf{W}}\mathbf{P}^\top$, $\mathbf{b}^{(k+1)} = \mathbf{P}\hat{\mathbf{b}}$. To solve (13b) note that $\mathbf{A}, \mathbf{U}$ and $\mathbf{V}$ are independent of each other and can be updated separately. The update of $\mathbf{A}$ and $\mathbf{U}$ is similar to that described in Sect. 2.1. We next discuss how to update $\mathbf{V}$ by solving the problem

$$
\mathbf{V}^{(k+1)} = \operatorname*{argmin}_{\mathbf{V}} \sum_{j=1}^{p} \lambda_2 \|\mathbf{v}^j\|_q + \frac{\nu}{2} \left\| \mathbf{W}^{(k+1)} + \frac{1}{\nu}\boldsymbol{\Gamma}^{(k)} - \mathbf{V} \right\|_F^2 \quad (15)
$$

Let $\mathbf{Z} = \mathbf{W}^{(k+1)} + \frac{1}{\nu}\boldsymbol{\Gamma}^{(k)}$. According to [22], the solution of (15) for $q = 2$ is

$$
\left(\mathbf{v}^{(k+1)} \right)^j = \begin{cases} \mathbf{0}, & \|\mathbf{z}^j\|_2 \leq \frac{\lambda_2}{\nu} \\ \frac{\|\mathbf{z}^j\|_2 - \lambda_2/\nu}{\|\mathbf{z}^j\|_2} \mathbf{z}^j, & \text{otherwise} \end{cases}, \forall j. \quad (16)
$$

For $q = \infty$, the solution of (15) can be computed via Algorithm 2 (see [5] for details). Putting the above discussions together, we have Algorithm 3 for solving (1) with $\phi(\mathbf{W})$ given by (2b) and (2c).

2.3   Convergence Results

Let us denote the kth iteration of the objectives of (3) and (11) as

$$
F_1^{(k)} = F_1(\mathbf{W}^{(k)}, \mathbf{b}^{(k)}, \mathbf{A}^{(k)}, \mathbf{U}^{(k)}), \quad F_2^{(k)} = F_2(\mathbf{W}^{(k)}, \mathbf{b}^{(k)}, \mathbf{A}^{(k)}, \mathbf{U}^{(k)}, \mathbf{V}^{(k)}), \quad (17)
$$

Algorithm 2. Algorithm for solving (15) when $q = \infty$

Let $\tilde{\lambda} = \frac{\lambda_2}{\nu}$ and $\mathbf{Z} = \mathbf{W}^{(k+1)} + \frac{1}{\nu}\boldsymbol{\Gamma}^{(k)}$.

for $j = 1, \cdots, p$ **do**

   Let $\mathbf{v} = \mathbf{z}^j$;

   if $\|\mathbf{v}\|_1 \leq \tilde{\lambda}$ **then**

      Set $\left(\mathbf{v}^{(k+1)}\right)^j = \mathbf{0}$.

   else

      Let $\mathbf{u}$ be the sorted absolute value vector of $\mathbf{v}$: $u_1 \geq u_2 \geq \cdots \geq u_J$;

      Find $\hat{r} = \max\left\{r : \tilde{\lambda} - \sum_{t=1}^{r}(u_t - u_r) > 0\right\}$

      Let $v_{ji}^{(k+1)} = \text{sign}(v_i) \min\left(|v_i|, (\sum_{t=1}^{\hat{r}} u_t - \tilde{\lambda})/\hat{r}\right), \forall i$.

---

and define

$$\mathbf{Z}_1^{(k)} = \left(\mathbf{W}^{(k)}, \mathbf{b}^{(k)}, \mathbf{A}^{(k)}, \mathbf{U}^{(k)}, \boldsymbol{\Pi}^{(k)}, \boldsymbol{\Lambda}^{(k)}\right),$$
$$\mathbf{Z}_2^{(k)} = \left(\mathbf{W}^{(k)}, \mathbf{b}^{(k)}, \mathbf{A}^{(k)}, \mathbf{U}^{(k)}, \mathbf{V}^{(k)}, \boldsymbol{\Pi}^{(k)}, \boldsymbol{\Lambda}^{(k)}, \boldsymbol{\Gamma}^{(k)}\right).$$

Theorem 1. *Let $\{\mathbf{Z}_1^{(k)}\}$ and $\{\mathbf{Z}_2^{(k)}\}$ be the sequences generated by (5) and (13), respectively. Then $F_1^{(k)} \to F_1^*$, $F_2^{(k)} \to F_2^*$, and $\|\mathbf{X}^\top\mathbf{W}^{(k)} + \mathbf{e}(\mathbf{b}^{(k)})^\top + \mathbf{E} - \mathbf{A}^{(k)}\|_F, \|\mathbf{W}^{(k)} - \mathbf{U}^{(k)}\|_F, \|\mathbf{W}^{(k)} - \mathbf{V}^{(k)}\|_F$ all converge to zero, where F_1^* and F_2^* are the optimal objective values of (3) and (11), respectively. In addition, if $\lambda_2 > 0, \lambda_3 > 0$ in (3), then $\mathbf{Z}_1^{(k)}$ converges linearly.*

The proof is based on [8,10] and due to the lack of space we omit it.

3 Numerical Results

We now test the three different regularizers in (2) on two sets of synthetic data and two sets of real data. As shown in [19] the L_1 regularized MSVM works better than the standard "one-against-rest" MSVM in both classification and variable selection. Hence, we choose to only compare the three regularized MSVMs. The ADMM algorithms discussed in Sect. 2 are used to solve the three models. Until the preparation of this paper, we did not find much work on designing specific algorithms to solve the regularized MSVMs except [19] which uses a path-following algorithm to solve the L_1 MSVM. To illustrate the efficiency of ADMM, we compare it with Sedumi [18] which is a second-order method. We call Sedumi in the CVX environment [12].

3.1 Implementation Details

All our code was written in MATLAB, except the part of Algorithm 2 which was written in C with MATLAB interface. We used $\lambda_3 = 1$ for all three models.

Algorithm 3. ADMM for (1) with $\phi(\mathbf{W})$ in (2b) and (2c)

Input: n sample-label pairs $\{(\mathbf{x}_i, y_i)\}_{i=1}^n$.
Choose: $\alpha, \mu, \nu > 0$, set $k = 0$ and initialize $(\mathbf{W}_0, \mathbf{b}_0, \mathbf{A}_0, \mathbf{U}_0, \mathbf{V}_0, \boldsymbol{\Pi}_0, \boldsymbol{\Lambda}_0, \boldsymbol{\Gamma}_0)$.
while *not converge* **do**

> Solve (14); let $\mathbf{W}^{(k+1)} = \hat{\mathbf{W}}\mathbf{P}^\top$ and $\mathbf{b}^{(k+1)} = \mathbf{P}\hat{\mathbf{b}}$;
> Update $\mathbf{A}^{(k+1)}$ and $\mathbf{U}^{(k+1)}$ by (8) and (9);
> Update $\mathbf{V}^{(k+1)}$ by (16) if $q = 2$ and by Algorithm 2 if $q = \infty$;
> Update $\boldsymbol{\Pi}^{(k+1)}, \boldsymbol{\Lambda}^{(k+1)}$ and $\boldsymbol{\Gamma}^{(k+1)}$ by (13c), (13d) and (13e);

In our experiments, we found that the penalty parameters were very important for the speed of ADMM. By running a large set of random tests, we chose $\alpha = \frac{50J}{n}, \mu = \sqrt{pJ}$ in (4) and $\alpha = \frac{50J}{n}, \mu = \nu = \sqrt{pJ}$ in (12). Origins were used as the starting points. As did in [21], we terminated ADMM for (3), that is, (1) with $\phi(\mathbf{W})$ in (2a), if

$$\max\left\{ \frac{|F_1^{(k+1)} - F_1^{(k)}|}{1 + F_1^{(k)}}, \frac{\|\mathbf{W}^{(k)} - \mathbf{U}^{(k)}\|_F}{\sqrt{pJ}}, \frac{\|\mathbf{X}^\top\mathbf{W}^{(k)} + \mathbf{e}(\mathbf{b}^{(k)})^\top + \mathbf{E} - \mathbf{A}^{(k)}\|_F}{\sqrt{nJ}} \right\} \leq 10^{-5},$$

and ADMM for (11), that is, (1) with $\phi(\mathbf{W})$ in (2b) and (2c), if

$$\max\left\{ \frac{|F_2^{(k+1)} - F_2^{(k)}|}{1 + F_2^{(k)}}, \frac{\|\mathbf{X}^\top\mathbf{W}^{(k)} + \mathbf{e}(\mathbf{b}^{(k)})^\top + \mathbf{E} - \mathbf{A}^{(k)}\|_F}{\sqrt{nJ}}, \frac{\|\mathbf{W}^{(k)} - \mathbf{U}^{(k)}\|_F}{\sqrt{pJ}}, \frac{\|\mathbf{W}^{(k)} - \mathbf{V}^{(k)}\|_F}{\sqrt{pJ}} \right\} \leq 10^{-5}.$$

In addition, we set a maximum number of iterations $maxit = 5000$ for ADMM. Default settings were used for Sedumi. All the tests were performed on a PC with an i5-2500 CPU and 3-GB RAM and running 32-bit Windows XP.

Table 1. Results of different models solved by ADMM and Sedumi on a five-class example with synthetic data. The numbers in parentheses are standard errors.

Models	ADMM					Sedumi				
	Accuracy	Time	CZ	IZ	NR	Accuracy	Time	CZ	IZ	NR
Elastic net	0.597(0.012)	0.184	39.98	0.92	2.01	0.592(0.013)	0.378	39.94	1.05	2.03
Group Lasso	0.605(0.006)	0.235	34.94	0.00	3.14	0.599(0.008)	2.250	33.85	0.02	3.25
Supnorm	0.606(0.006)	0.183	39.84	0.56	2.08	0.601(0.008)	0.638	39.49	0.61	2.21

3.2 Synthetic Data

The first test is a five-class example with each sample $\mathbf{x}$ in a 10-dimensional space. The data was generated in the following way: for each class j, the first two components (x_1, x_2) were generated from the mixture Gaussian distribution $\mathcal{N}(\boldsymbol{\mu}_j, 2\mathbf{I})$ where for $j = 1, \cdots, 5$,

$$\boldsymbol{\mu}_j = 2[\cos\left((2j-1)\pi/5\right), \sin\left((2j-1)\pi/5\right)],$$

and the remaining eight components were independently generated from standard Gaussian distribution. This kind of data was also tested in [19,23]. We first chose best parameters for each model by generating $n = 200$ samples for training and another $n = 200$ samples for tuning parameters. For elastic net, we fixed $\lambda_2 = 1$ since it is not sensitive and then searched the best λ_1 over $\mathcal{C} = \{0, 0.001, 0.01 : 0.01 : 0.1, 0.15, 0.20, 0.25, 0.30\}$. The parameters λ_1 and λ_2 for group Lasso and supnorm were selected via a grid search over $\mathcal{C} \times \mathcal{C}$. With the tuned parameters, we compared ADMM and Sedumi on $n = 200$ randomly generated training samples and $n' = 50,000$ random testing samples, and the whole process was independently repeated 100 times. The performance of the compared models and algorithms were measured by accuracy (i.e., $\frac{\text{number of correctly predicted}}{\text{total number}}$), running time (sec), the number of correct zeros (CZ), the number of incorrect zeros (IZ) and the number of non-zero rows (NR). We counted CZ, IZ and NR from the truncated solution $\mathbf{W}^t$, which was obtained from the output solution $\mathbf{W}$ such that $w_{ij}^t = 0$ if $|w_{ij}| \leq 10^{-3} \max_{i,j} |w_{ij}|$ and $w_{ij}^t = w_{ij}$ otherwise. The average results are shown in Table 1, from which we can see that ADMM produces similar results as those by Sedumi within less time. Elastic net makes slightly lower prediction accuracy than that by the other two models.

Table 2. Results of different models solved by ADMM and Sedumi on a four-class example with synthetic data. The numbers in the parentheses are corresponding standard errors.

Models	ADMM							Sedumi						
	Accuracy	Time	IZ	NZ1	NZ2	NZ3	NZ4	Accuracy	Time	IZ	NZ1	NZ2	NZ3	NZ4
	Correlation $\rho = 0$													
Elastic net	0.977(0.006)	0.27	13.8	37.6	36.9	36.8	37.0	0.950(0.013)	3.75	11.0	40.2	40.0	39.5	40.4
Group Lasso	0.931(0.020)	0.46	30.4	33.7	33.4	33.2	33.2	0.857(0.022)	12.13	40.5	31.8	31.6	31.8	31.7
Supnorm	0.924(0.025)	0.52	32.6	36.6	36.1	36.4	36.2	0.848(0.020)	13.93	46.6	34.2	33.8	33.7	33.5
Models	Correlation $\rho = 0.8$													
Elastic net	0.801(0.018)	0.19	24.1	29.6	29.7	30.6	29.6	0.773(0.036)	3.74	15.7	35.4	36.3	36.0	35.7
Group Lasso	0.761(0.023)	0.38	64.0	21.4	21.2	21.3	21.2	0.654(0.023)	12.30	89.7	17.3	17.6	17.5	17.3
Supnorm	0.743(0.023)	0.45	63.1	34.1	34.0	33.9	34.2	0.667(0.016)	14.01	79.8	35.3	35.3	35.3	35.2

The second test is a four-class example with each sample in p-dimensional space. The data in class j was generated from the mixture Gaussian distribution $\mathcal{N}(\boldsymbol{\mu}_j, \boldsymbol{\Sigma}_j), j = 1, 2, 3, 4$. The mean vectors and covariance matrices are $\boldsymbol{\mu}_2 = -\boldsymbol{\mu}_1, \boldsymbol{\mu}_4 = -\boldsymbol{\mu}_3, \boldsymbol{\Sigma}_2 = \boldsymbol{\Sigma}_1, \boldsymbol{\Sigma}_4 = \boldsymbol{\Sigma}_3$, and

$$\boldsymbol{\mu}_1 = (\underbrace{1, \cdots, 1}_{s}, \underbrace{0, \cdots, 0}_{p-s})^\top, \quad \boldsymbol{\mu}_3 = (\underbrace{0, \cdots, 0}_{s/2}, \underbrace{1, \cdots, 1}_{s}, \underbrace{0, \cdots, 0}_{p-3s/2})^\top,$$

$$\boldsymbol{\Sigma}_1 = \begin{bmatrix} \rho\mathbf{E}_{s\times s} + (1-\rho)\mathbf{I}_{s\times s} \\ & \mathbf{I}_{(p-s)\times(p-s)} \end{bmatrix},$$

$$\boldsymbol{\Sigma}_3 = \begin{bmatrix} \mathbf{I}_{\frac{s}{2}\times\frac{s}{2}} \\ & \rho\mathbf{E}_{s\times s} + (1-\rho)\mathbf{I}_{s\times s} \\ & & \mathbf{I}_{(p-\frac{3s}{2})\times(p-\frac{3s}{2})} \end{bmatrix}.$$

This kind of data was also tested in [20,21] for binary classifications. We took $p = 500, s = 30$ and $\rho = 0, 0.8$ in this test. As did in last test, the best parameters for all models were tuned by first generating $n = 100$ training samples and another $n = 100$ validation samples. Then we compared the different models solved by ADMM and Sedumi with the selected parameters on $n = 100$ randomly generated training samples and $n' = 20,000$ random testing samples. The comparison was independently repeated 100 times. The performance of different models and algorithms were measured by prediction accuracy, running time (sec), the number of incorrect zeros (IZ), the number of nonzeros in each column (NZ1, NZ2, NZ3, NZ4), where IZ, NZ1, NZ2, NZ3, NZ4 were counted in a similar way as that in last test by first truncating the output solution $\mathbf{W}$. Table 2 lists the average results, from which we can see that the elastic net MSVM tends to give best predictions. ADMM is much faster than Sedumi, and interestingly, ADMM also gives higher prediction accuracies than those by Sedumi. This is probably because the solutions given by Sedumi are sparser and have more IZs than those by ADMM.

Table 3. Original distributions of SRBCT and leukemia data sets

Data set	SRBCT					Leukemia			
	NB	RMS	BL	EWS	total	B-ALL	T-ALL	AML	total
Training	12	20	8	23	63	19	8	11	38
Testing	6	5	3	6	20	19	1	14	34

3.3 Real Data

This subsection tests the three different MSVMs on microarray classifications. Two real data sets were used. One is the children cancer data set in [15], which used cDNA gene expression profiles and classified the small round blue cell tumors (SRBCTs) of childhood into four classes: neuroblastoma (NB), rhabdomyosarcoma (RMS), Burkitt lymphomas (BL) and the Ewing family of tumors (EWS). The other is the leukemia data set in [11], which used gene expression monitoring and classified the acute leukemias into three classes: B-cell acute lymphoblastic leukemia (B-ALL), T-cell acute lymphoblastic leukemia (T-ALL) and acute myeloid leukemia (AML). The original distributions of the two data sets are given in Table 3. Both the two data sets have been tested before on certain MSVMs for gene selection; see [19,23] for example.

Each observation in the SRBCT dataset has dimension of $p = 2308$, namely, there are 2308 gene profiles. We first standardized the original training data in the following way. Let $\mathbf{X}^o = [\mathbf{x}_1^o, \cdots, \mathbf{x}_n^o]$ be the original data matrix. The standardized matrix $\mathbf{X}$ was obtained by

$$x_{gj} = \frac{x_{gj}^o - \mathrm{mean}(x_{g1}^o, \cdots, x_{gn}^o)}{\mathrm{std}(x_{g1}^o, \cdots, x_{gn}^o)}, \ \forall g, j.$$

Similar normalization was done to the original testing data. Then we selected the best parameters of each model by three-fold cross validation on the standardized training data. The search range of the parameters is the same as that in the synthetic data tests. Finally, we put the standardized training and testing data sets together and randomly picked 63 observations for training and the remaining 20 ones for testing. The average prediction accuracy, running time (sec), number of non-zeros (NZ) and number of nonzero rows (NR) of 100 independent trials are reported in Table 4, from which we can see that all models give similar prediction accuracies. ADMM produced similar accuracies as those by Sedumi within less time while Sedumi tends to give sparser solutions because Sedumi is a second-order method and more accurately solves the problems.

Table 4. Results of different models solved by ADMM and Sedumi on SRBCT and Leukemia data sets

Data	Models	ADMM				Sedumi			
		Accuracy	ime	NZ	NR	Accuracy	Time	NZ	NR
SRBCT	Elastic net	0.996(0.014)	1.738	305.71	135.31	0.989(0.022)	8.886	213.67	96.71
	Group Lasso	0.995(0.016)	2.116	524.88	137.31	0.985(0.028)	42.241	373.44	96.27
	Supnorm	0.996(0.014)	3.269	381.47	114.27	0.990(0.021)	88.468	265.06	80.82
Leukemia	Elastic net	0.908(0.041)	1.029	571.56	271.85	0.879(0.048)	30.131	612.16	291.71
	Group Lasso	0.908(0.045)	2.002	393.20	150.61	0.838(0.072)	76.272	99.25	44.14
	Supnorm	0.907(0.048)	2.211	155.93	74.60	0.848(0.069)	121.893	86.03	41.78

The leukemia data set has $p = 7,129$ gene profiles. We standardized the original training and testing data in the same way as that in last test. Then we rank all genes on the standardized training data by the method used in [9]. Specifically, let $\mathbf{X} = [\mathbf{x}_1, \cdots, \mathbf{x}_n]$ be the standardized data matrix. The relevance measure for gene g is defined as follows:

$$R(g) = \frac{\sum_{i,j} I(y_i = j)(m_g^j - m_g)}{\sum_{i,j} I(y_i = j)(x_{gi} - m_g^j)}, \ g = 1, \cdots, p,$$

where m_g denotes the mean of $\{x_{g1}, \cdots, x_{gn}\}$ and m_g^j denotes the mean of $\{x_{gi} : y_i = j\}$. According to $R(g)$, we selected the 3,571 most significant genes. Finally, we put the processed training and tesing data together and randomly chose 38 samples for training and the remaining ones for testing. The process was independently repeated 100 times. Table 4 tabulates the average results, which show that all three models give similar prediction accuracies. ADMM gave better prediction accuracies than those given by Sedumi within far less time. The relatively lower accuracies given by Sedumi may be because it selected too few genes to explain the diseases.

4   Conclusion

We have developed an efficient unified algorithmic framework for using ADMM to solve regularized MSVS. By effectively using the Woodbury matrix identity we have substantially reduced the computational effort required to solve large-scale MSVMS. Numerical experiments on both synthetic and real data demonstrate the efficiency of ADMM by comparing it with the second-order method Sedumi.

References

1. Bishop, C.: Pattern Recognition and Machine Learning. Springer, New York (2006)
2. Bottou, L., Cortes, C., Denker, J.S., Drucker, H., Guyon, I., Jackel, L.D., LeCun, Y., Muller, U.A., Sackinger, E., Simard, P., et al.: Comparison of classifier methods: a case study in handwritten digit recognition. In: Proceedings of the 12th IAPR International Conference on Pattern Recognition, vol. 2, pp. 77–82 (1994)
3. Boyd, S., Parikh, N., Chu, E., Peleato, B., Eckstein, J.: Distributed optimization and statistical learning via the alternating direction method of multipliers. Found. Trends Mach. Learn. **3**(1), 1–122 (2010)
4. Bradley, P.S., Mangasarian, O.L.: Feature selection via concave minimization and support vector machines. In: Proceedings of the Fifteenth International Conference of Machine Learning (ICML 1998), pp. 82–90 (1998)
5. Chen, X., Pan, W., Kwok, J.T., Carbonell, J.G.: Accelerated gradient method for multi-task sparse learning problem. In: Proceedings of the Ninth International Conference on Data Mining (ICDM 2009), pp. 746–751. IEEE (2009)
6. Cortes, C., Vapnik, V.: Support-vector networks. Mach. Learn. **20**(3), 273–297 (1995)
7. Crammer, K., Singer, Y.: On the algorithmic implementation of multiclass kernel-based vector machines. J. Mach. Learn. Res. **2**, 265–292 (2002)
8. Deng, W., Yin, W.: On the global and linear convergence of the generalized alternating direction method of multipliers. Rice technical report TR12-14 (2012)
9. Dudoit, S., Fridlyand, J., Speed, T.P.: Comparison of discrimination methods for the classification of tumors using gene expression data. J. Am. Stat. Assoc. **97**(457), 77–87 (2002)
10. Glowinski, R.: Numerical Methods for Nonlinear Variational Problems. Springer, Heidelberg (2008)
11. Golub, T.R., Slonim, D.K., Tamayo, P., Huard, C., Gaasenbeek, M., Mesirov, J.P., Coller, H., Loh, M.L., Downing, J.R., Caligiuri, M.A., Bloomfield, C.D., Lander, E.S.: Molecular classification of cancer: class discovery and class prediction by gene expression monitoring. Science **286**(5439), 531–537 (1999)
12. Grant, M., Boyd, S.: CVX - Matlab software for disciplined convex programming, version 2.1 (2014). http://cvxr.com/cvx
13. Hager, W.W.: Updating the inverse of a matrix. SIAM Rev. **31**, 221–239 (1989)
14. Hsu, C.W., Lin, C.J.: A comparison of methods for multiclass support vector machines. IEEE Trans. Neural Netw. **13**(2), 415–425 (2002)
15. Khan, J., Wei, J.S., Ringnér, M., Saal, L.H., Ladanyi, M., Westermann, F., Berthold, F., Schwab, M., Antonescu, C.R., Peterson, C., et al.: Classification and diagnostic prediction of cancers using gene expression profiling and artificial neural networks. Nat. Med. **7**(6), 673–679 (2001)

16. Lee, Y., Lin, Y., Wahba, G.: Multicategory support vector machines. J. Am. Stat. Assoc. **99**(465), 67–81 (2004)
17. Platt, J.C., Cristianini, N., Shawe-Taylor, J.: Large margin dags for multiclass classification. Adv. Neural Inf. Process. Syst. **12**(3), 547–553 (2000)
18. Sturm, J.: Using SeDuMi 1.02, a MATLAB toolbox for optimization over symmetric cones. Optim. Methods Softw. **11**(1–4), 625–653 (1999)
19. Wang, L., Shen, X.: On L_1-norm multiclass support vector machines. J. Am. Stat. Assoc. **102**(478), 583–594 (2007)
20. Wang, L., Zhu, J., Zou, H.: Hybrid huberized support vector machines for microarray classification and gene selection. Bioinformatics **24**(3), 412–419 (2008)
21. Ye, G.B., Chen, Y., Xie, X.: Efficient variable selection in support vector machines via the alternating direction method of multipliers. In: Proceedings of the International Conference on Artificial Intelligence and Statistics (2011)
22. Yuan, M., Lin, Y.: Model selection and estimation in regression with grouped variables. J. Roy. Stat. Soc. Ser. B (Stat. Method.) **68**(1), 49–67 (2006)
23. Zhang, H., Liu, Y., Wu, Y., Zhu, J.: Variable selection for the multicategory SVM via adaptive sup-norm regularization. Electron. J. Stat. **2**, 149–167 (2008)

Tree-Based Response Surface Analysis

Siva Krishna Dasari[1]([✉]), Niklas Lavesson[1], Petter Andersson[2],
and Marie Persson[1]

[1] Department of Computer Science and Engineering,
Blekinge Institute of Technology, 371 79 Karlskrona, Sweden
siva.krishna.dasari@bth.se
[2] Engineering Method Development, GKN Aerospace Engine Systems Sweden,
Department 9635 - TL3, 461 81 Trollhättan, Sweden

Abstract. Computer-simulated experiments have become a cost effective way for engineers to replace real experiments in the area of product development. However, one single computer-simulated experiment can still take a significant amount of time. Hence, in order to minimize the amount of simulations needed to investigate a certain design space, different approaches within the design of experiments area are used. One of the used approaches is to minimize the time consumption and simulations for design space exploration through response surface modeling. The traditional methods used for this purpose are linear regression, quadratic curve fitting and support vector machines. This paper analyses and compares the performance of four machine learning methods for the regression problem of response surface modeling. The four methods are linear regression, support vector machines, M5P and random forests. Experiments are conducted to compare the performance of tree models (M5P and random forests) with the performance of non-tree models (support vector machines and linear regression) on data that is typical for concept evaluation within the aerospace industry. The main finding is that comprehensible models (the tree models) perform at least as well as or better than traditional black-box models (the non-tree models). The first observation of this study is that engineers understand the functional behavior, and the relationship between inputs and outputs, for the concept selection tasks by using comprehensible models. The second observation is that engineers can also increase their knowledge about design concepts, and they can reduce the time for planning and conducting future experiments.

Keywords: Machine learning · Regression · Surrogate model · Response surface model

1 Introduction

The design phase is an important step of product development in the manufacturing industry. In order to design a new product, the engineers need to evaluate

© Springer International Publishing Switzerland 2015
P. Pardalos et al. (Eds.): MOD 2015, LNCS 9432, pp. 118–129, 2015.
DOI: 10.1007/978-3-319-27926-8_11

suitable design concepts. A concept is usually defined by a set of design variables, or attributes. The design variables represent various design choices such as the material type or thickness of a specific part. During the design phase, several concepts are defined by providing different attribute values. Engineers may opt to use a combination of computer aided design (CAD) modeling and computer-simulated experiments instead of real experiments, in order to reduce the time, cost and risk. The simulations contribute to a better understanding of the functional behavior and predict possible failure modes in future product use [15]. They are used to identify interesting regions in the design space and to understand the relationship between design variables (inputs) and their effect on design objectives (outputs) [12]. However, one single computer-simulated experiment can take a significant amount of time to conduct. For instance, to design a part of an aero engine, an engineer has to simulate, in order to select an optimal product design, several variants where sets of parameters are studied with respect to different aspects, such as strength and fatigue, aero performance and producibility. Conducting simulations for each concept is impractical, due to time constraints. In order to minimize the time consumption and simulations, engineers use methods such as design of experiments and surrogate models, or response surface models, for design space exploration [6].

Surrogate modeling is an engineering method used when an outcome of interest cannot be directly measured [14]. The process of surrogate model generation includes sample selection, model generation and model evaluation. Sample selection is used to select a set of input samples using different types of sampling strategies (e.g., random sampling) for model generation [7]. The next step is to construct surrogate models from a small set of input samples and their corresponding outputs. The purpose of surrogate modeling is to find a function that replaces the original system and which could be computed faster [7]. This function is constructed by performing multiple simulations at key points of the design space; thereafter the results are analyzed and then the selection of an approximation model to those samples follows [7]. In machine learning, this type of learning of an approximation function from inputs and outputs is called a supervised learning problem. The approximation function is real valued so the problem is delimited to supervised regression learning. The challenge of surrogate modeling is the generation of a surrogate that is as accurate as possible by using the minimum number of simulation evaluations. This motivates the generation of surrogate models in an efficient way that can be used in concept selection.

Statistical approaches have been used to construct surrogate models using a technique called response surface methodology [4]. Engineers use statistical regression analysis to find the relationship between inputs and outputs. They usually generate regression functions by fitting a curve to a series of data points. Another engineering design strategy to generate surrogate models is the use of a black box model (e.g., support vector machines) [10]. The problem with black box models is the lack of information about the functional behavior and the mapping between inputs and outputs. Black box models can be accurate but they are not comprehensible, and there is a need to generate accurate and comprehensive surrogate models in order to understand the model behaviour. In this study, we use machine learning algorithms for response surface analysis, and we addresses the supervised regression problem with tree models. Tree models are used to create comprehensible models that are easy to interpret [22], since they reveal the mapping process between inputs and outputs. We can thus interpret and learn about the approximation function between the inputs and the outputs. The motivation for selecting tree methods in this study is, tree has a graphical structure, and tree model representation follows the divide and conquer approach and this structure provides the information about important attributes. Mathematical equations and non-linear models are difficult to understand due to the model representations [9]. We hypothesize that comprehensible models can be used to increase the understanding about design spaces with few simulation evaluations while maintaining a reasonable accuracy level. In our study, we used M5P tree and random forest tree methods for response surface modeling. These two methods have their tree nature in common, thus, we refer to them as "tree based learning" in this study.

2   Aim and Scope

The focus of this study is to use supervised machine learning algorithms for response surface models. The goal of this study is to empirically investigate how tree models perform on design samples from concept selection tasks, and to determine which regression tree induction approach yields the best performance. We hypothesize that tree models will create accurate and comprehensive models for response surfaces. The tree algorithms are applied to real-world data from the aerospace industry. Tree methods (M5P and random forests) are compared with non-tree methods (support vector machines and linear regression) to explore potential differences in various aspects of performance which is accuracy of the response surface models. This study will not focus on the choice of sampling strategy or dataset generation strategies in order to optimize the learning process. Instead, performance is measured on pre-existing and anonymized real-world data.

3   Related Work

Gorissen et al. presents a surrogate modeling and adaptive sampling toolbox for computer based design. This toolkit brings together algorithms (support vector machines, kriging, artificial neural networks) for data fitting, model selection, sample selection (active learning), hyper parameter optimization, and distributed computing in order to empower a domain expert to efficiently generate an accurate model for the problem or data at hand [10].

Ahmed and Qin used surrogate models for design optimization of a spiked blunt body in hypersonic flow conditions. This study constructed four surrogate models, namely a quadratic response surface model, exponential kriging, gaussian kriging and general exponential kriging based on the values of drag and heating responses. The authors concluded that exponential kriging surrogate produces a relatively better prediction of new points in the design space and better optimized design [1]. Haito et al. used surrogate model for optimization of an underwater glider and compared several experimental design types and surrogate modeling techniques in terms of their capability to generate accurate approximations for the shape optimization of underwater gliders. The authors concluded that combination of multi-island genetic algorithm and sequential quadratic programming is an effective method in the global exploration, and showed that the modified method of feasible direction is an efficient method in the local exploration [12].

Robert et al. introduced the use of the treed Gaussian process (TGP) as a surrogate model within the mesh adaptive direct search framework (MADS) for constrained black box optimization. Efficiency of TGP method has been demonstrated in three test cases. In all test cases, MADS-TGP is compared with MADS alone and MADS with quadratic models. Finally, the authors concluded that TGP is taking more execution time to compare with other two methods but TGP provides the quality of the solution for one of the test cases. For the other two test cases, TGP gives better solutions compared to the other methods [11].

Machine learning methods such as support vector machines, artificial neural networks have already been used extensively for surrogate models [1,10]. These methods are black box models and there are no comprehensible models that have been developed using machine learning for surrogate models. To the best knowledge of the authors, tree-based models from machine learning for response surface analysis have not been investigated for concept selection tasks in product development. Thus, this study is focused on tree methods to generate surrogate models.

4   Background

In many modern engineering problems, accurate simulations are used instead of real experiments in order to reduce the overall time, cost, or risk [7]. It is impossible to evaluate all possible concepts by conducting simulations to identify the most suitable concept. For instance, an engineer gets requirements to design a product, but he or she might not have enough time to test all concepts by conducting simulations. Thus, engineers can run few simulations using few concepts to generate a surrogate model to predict unseen concepts for design space exploration. Design optimization, design space exploration, and sensitivity analysis are possible through surrogate model generation [6].

Engineers choose a set of concepts using suitable sampling strategies. Latin hypercube sampling (LHS) is one of the most common sampling strategies currently used to select input concepts for surrogate model generation. The concepts can be changed by many different input variables such as the materials for various parts, thickness, colors, lengths, etc. The different variants of concepts are represented in 3D using CAD software. CAD/CAE (computer aided engineering) is the use of computer systems to assist in the creation, modification, analysis, or optimization of a design [2]. Through a CAD model, we can get outputs from each concept or design, which indicates how the design performs, for example strength, stiffness, weight etc. The final step is surrogate model generation based on inputs and outputs.

4.1   Methodology

In this section, we briefly introduce the studied machine learning methods for response surface modeling and the common performance metrics for regression problems. In this study, we use root mean-squared error (RMSE) [22] and the correlation coefficient [17] to evaluate the predictive performance. The RMSE is calculated as the sum of squared differences of the predicted values and the actual values of the regression variable divided by the number of predictions. This RMSE gives an idea to the engineer about the difference between actual values and predicted values. The correlation coefficient (CC) measures the strength of association between the predicted values and the actual values [17]. The following equations show the RMSE [22] and the correlation coefficient (CC) [17].

$$RMSE = \frac{1}{N} \sum_{i=1}^{n} (\hat{y} - y)^2 \tag{1}$$

Where $\hat{y}$ is the predicted value and y is the actual value.

$$CC = \sum_{i=1}^{n} \frac{\left(\hat{y}_i - \bar{\hat{y}}\right) (y_i - \bar{y})}{\sqrt{\sum_{i=1}^{n} \left(\hat{y}_i - \bar{\hat{y}}\right)^2 (y_i - \bar{y})^2}} \tag{2}$$

Where $\hat{y}_i$ is the predicted value; y_i is the actual value; $\bar{\hat{y}}$ is the mean value of the predicted values; and $\bar{y}$ is the mean value of the actual values.

The main purpose of this study is to investigate the performance of tree models for response surface analysis. Hence, we have selected the M5P algorithm and the RF algorithm. The M5P and random forests (RF) algorithms are tree models and these two models show the functional behavior between the inputs and the outputs in a comprehensible way. To compare tree model performance against a traditional benchmark, we have selected two more models linear regression (LR) and support vector machines (SVM). These algorithms are regression methods, but these two algorithms do not show the function behavior between inputs and outputs.

Linear Regression is a statistical method for studying the linear relationship between a dependent variable and a single or multiple independent variables. In this study, we use linear regression with multiple variables to predict a real-valued function. The linear regression model is considered in the following form [22].

$$x = w_0 + w_1 a_1 + w_2 a_2 + \ldots + w_k a_k \tag{3}$$

Where x is the class; a_1, a_2, ... a_k are the attribute values; w_0, w_1 ... w_k are weights. Here, the weights are calculated from the training data. The linear regression method is used to minimize the sum of squared differences between the actual value and the predicted value. The following equation shows the sum of squares of the difference [22].

$$\sum_{i=1}^{n} \left(x^{(i)} - \sum_{j=0}^{k} w_j a_j^{(i)} \right)^2 \tag{4}$$

Where the equations shows the difference between the ith instance's actual class and its predicted class.

M5P. Quinlan developed a tree algorithm called M5 tree to predict continuous variables for regression [16]. There are three major steps for the M5 tree construction development: (1) tree construction; (2) tree pruning; and (3) tree smoothing. Detailed descriptions for these three steps are available in [16]. The tree construction process attempts to maximize a measure called the standard deviation reduction (SDR).

Wang modified the M5 algorithm to handle enumerated attributes and attribute missing values [21]. The modified version of the M5 algorithm is called the M5P algorithm. The SDR value is modified to consider missing values and the equation is as follows [21].

$$SDR = \frac{m}{|T|} \times \beta(i) \times \left[sd(T) - \sum_{j \in L,R} \frac{|T_j|}{|T|} \times sd(T_j) \right] \tag{5}$$

Where T is the set of cases; T_j is the jth subset of cases that result from tree splitting based on set of attributes; $sd(T)$ is the standard deviation of T; and $sd(T_i)$ is a standard deviation of T_i as a measure error; m is the number of training cases without missing values for the attribute; $\beta(i)$ is the correction factor for enumerated attributes; T_L and T_R are the subsets that result from the split of an attribute.

SVM. This method is used for both classification and regression and it is proposed by Vapnik [20]. In the SVM method, N-dimensional hyperplane is created that divides the input domain into binary or multi-class categories. The support vectors are located near to the hyperplane, and this hyperplane separates the categories of the dependent variable on each side of the plane. The kernel functions are used to handle the non-linear relationship. The following equation shows the support vector regression function [5].

$$\bar{y}_i = \sum_{j=1}^{n} (\alpha_j - \alpha_j^*) K(x_i, x_j) + b \tag{6}$$

where K is a kernel function; α_j is a Lagrange multiplier and b is a bias. Detailed descriptions of these concepts of SVM can be found in [18,20].

Random Forest. This method is an ensemble technique developed by Breiman. It is used for both classification and regression [3], and it combines a set of decision trees. Each tree is built using a deterministic algorithm by selecting a random set of variables and random samples from a training set. To construct an ensemble, three parameters need to be optimized: (1) *ntree:* the number of regression trees grown based on a bootstrap sample of observations. (2) *mtry:* the number of variables used at each node for tree generation. (3) *nodesize:* the minimal size of the terminal nodes of the tree [3].

An average of prediction error estimation of each individual tree is given by mean squared error. The following equation shows the mean squared error (MSE) [3].

$$MSE = n^{-1} \sum_{i=1}^{n} [\hat{Y}(X_i) - Y_i]^2 \tag{7}$$

Where $\hat{Y}(X_i)$ is the predicted output corresponding to a given input sample whereas Y_i is the observed output and n represents the total number of out of bag samples.

5   Experiments and Analysis

In this section, we present the experimental design used to compare the methods for response surface modeling. We use the algorithm implementations available from the WEKA platform for performance evaluation [22]. The experimental aim is to determine whether tree models are more accurate than mathematical equation-based models. To reach this aim, the following objectives are stated:

1. To evaluate the performance of LR, M5P, SVM and RF for response surface modeling.
2. To compare tree models and non-tree models on the task of design space exploration.

5.1   Dataset Description

The algorithms are evaluated on two concept-selection data sets obtained from the aerospace industry. These datasets are from simulations and sampled by using LHS. The first dataset consists of 56 instances with 22 input features and 14 output features. The second data set includes 410 instances defined by 10 input features and three output features. In the company which is aerospace industry, engineers generate one regression model for each output feature. For this single output model, we have 14 sub data sets for the first dataset, and three sub datasets for the second dataset. We generate 14 new single-target concept-selection data sets, D1-1 to D1-14 by preserving its input features and values, and selecting a different output feature for each new data set. Using the same procedure as for the first data set, we generate three new single-target concept-selection data sets, D2-1 to D2-3.

Table 1. Performance comparison on 17 datasets

Data set	LR	M5P	RF	SVM	LR	M5P	RF	SVM
	RMSE (rank)				CC (rank)			
D1-1	0.5787(2)	0.2059(1)	2.0553(4)	0.9553(3)	0.995(2)	0.9994(1)	0.9700(4)	0.9908(3)
D1-2	10.8545(3)	5.2926(1)	10.4724(2)	11.6372(4)	0.8273(4)	0.9640(1)	0.8900(2)	0.8373(3)
D1-3	0.2838(3)	0.2726(2)	0.3155(4)	0.2545(1)	−0.1562(2)	−0.0232(1)	−0.3133(4)	−0.1696(3)
D1-4	0.0062(1)	0.0062(1)	0.0171(3)	0.0091(2)	0.9922(1)	0.9922(1)	0.9688(3)	0.9859(2)
D1-5	0.2414(3)	0.2252(2)	0.2720(4)	0.2178(1)	−0.0585(3)	0.1302(1)	−0.2878(4)	0.1817(2)
D1-6	0.0051(2)	0.0050(1)	0.0151(4)	0.0080(3)	0.9945(2)	0.9947(1)	0.9724(4)	0.9884(3)
D1-7	0.1416(3)	0.1421(1)	0.1714(4)	0.1442(2)	−0.6527(4)	−0.0952(1)	−0.3265(3)	−0.1366(2)
D1-8	0.0232(2)	0.0127(1)	0.0459(4)	0.0315(3)	0.9792(2)	0.9938(1)	0.9661(4)	0.9766(3)
D1-9	0.0907(2)	0.0888(1)	0.1067(4)	0.0928(3)	−0.6381(4)	−0.0125(1)	−0.3362(3)	−0.0495(2)
D1-10	0.0232(2)	0.0122(1)	0.0464(4)	0.0318(3)	0.9801(2)	0.9945(1)	0.9727(4)	0.9777(3)
D1-11	4.4332(3)	3.9521(2)	5.5322(4)	2.9258(1)	0.9805(3)	0.9846(2)	0.9747(4)	0.9916(1)
D1-12	0.0196(1)	0.0199(2)	0.0254(4)	0.0237(3)	0.8211(1)	0.8175(2)	0.6747(4)	0.7251(3)
D1-13	0.0419(1)	0.0419(1)	0.0482(3)	0.0466(2)	0.1186(1)	0.1137(2)	−0.0592(3)	−0.0984(4)
D1-14	0.1549(2)	0.1648(4)	0.1248(1)	0.1580(3)	0.4980(3)	0.4335(4)	0.7143(1)	0.5057(2)
D2-1	0.0676(4)	0.0647(2)	0.0602(1)	0.0661(3)	0.6655(4)	0.6995(2)	0.7482(1)	0.6853(3)
D2-2	0.1270(3)	0.0673(1)	0.0757(2)	0.1306(4)	0.5190(4)	0.9031(1)	0.8639(2)	0.5194(3)
D2-3	1.2226(2)	1.1370(1)	1.2752(4)	1.2469(3)	0.4312(3)	0.5445(1)	0.4918(2)	0.4296(4)
Avg. rank	2.29	1.47	3.29	2.58	2.64	1.41	3.05	2.70

5.2   Evaluation Procedure

We use cross-validation to maximize training set size and to avoid testing on training data. Cross-validation is an efficient method for estimating the error [13]. The procedure is as follows: the dataset is divided into k sub samples. In our experiments, we choose k = 10. A single sub-sample is chosen as testing data and the remaining k − 1 sub-samples are used as training data. The procedure is repeated k times, in which each of the k sub-samples is used exactly once as testing data and finally all the results are averaged and single estimation is provided [13]. We tuned the parameters for RF and SVM. For RF, we use a tree size of 100, and for SVM, we set the regularization parameter C to 5.0, and the kernel to the radial basis function. These parameters are tuned in WEKA [22]. We start with a C value of 0.3 and then increase with a step size of 0.3 until the performance starts to decrease. We select the number of trees starting from a low value and then increase up to 100 for improved accuracy.

5.3   Experiment 1

In this section we address the first objective. For this purpose, we trained the four methods with 10 fold cross-validation on datasets D1-1 to D1-14 and D2-1 to D2-3. For this experiment, we normalized the D2-1, D2-2 and D1-14 datasets. Table 1 shows the RMSE values, CC values and the ranks for the four methods.

Analysis: For 11 out of 17 datasets the use of the M5P tree method yields the best results with respect to the RMSE metric. The LR and SVM algorithms outperformed the other algorithms for three datasets each, and the last method: RF yields the lowest RMSE for only two datasets. When it comes to the CC performance metric, M5P tree yields the best performance for 11 datasets, and LR yields the best performance for three datasets. The other methods, RF and SVM, yield the best CC for two datasets. We observe that tree models (M5P in 11 cases and RF in 2 cases) are performing better in a majority of cases compared to the other models for LHS sampled datasets. The reason for this could be that tree models divide the design space into regions and create a separate model for each region, whereas SVM and LR create single model over the entire design space. Tree models are in general regarded as more comprehensible models than the other investigated models [9]. We observe that tree methods could be used to gain knowledge of design samples for design space exploration, by finding the decision paths from the root of the tree to the top branches. For instance, an engineer using a tree method to predict the output value y based on the input values $x_1, x_2, x_3, \ldots, x_n$, can increase his understanding of the relationship between inputs and output by analyzing their mapping. On the other hand, when the engineer wants to predict a new y value for various concepts, there is a possibility to reduce the time because the engineer has already reached an understanding about the model, and can also make informed decisions regarding future experiments.

Our experiment requires statistical tests for comparing multiple algorithms over multiple datasets. The Friedman test is a non-parametric statistical test that can be used for this purpose [8]. It ranks the algorithms for each dataset based on the performance. The best performing algorithm gets a rank of 1 and the second best algorithm gets a rank of 2 and so on, and finally it compares the average ranks of the algorithms [8]. The common statistical method for testing the significant differences between more than two sample means is the analysis of variance (ANOVA) [19]. ANOVA assumes that the samples are drawn from normal distributions [8]. In our study, the error measure samples cannot be assumed to be drawn from normal distribution hence we violate the ANOVA parametric test. The hypothesis is:

H_o: LR, M5P, SVM and RF methods perform equally well with respect to predictive performance

H_a: There is a significant difference between the performances of the methods.

The statistical test produces a p-value of 0.0003 for RMSE, and a p-value of 0.0016 for CC. The p-value is less than the 0.05 significance level. We therefore reject the null hypothesis and conclude that there is a significant difference between the performances of methods. Furthermore, we conducted post a hoc test for pairwise comparisons to see the individual differences. For this purpose, we used the Nemenyi test [8]. Table 2 shows the p-values for the pairwise comparison.

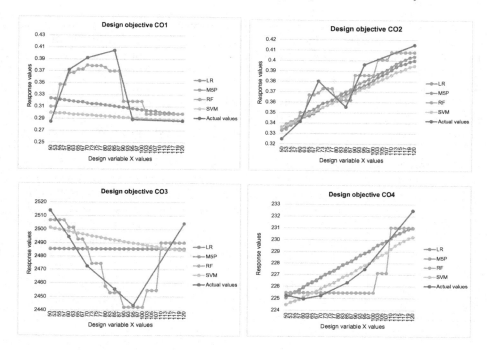

Fig. 1. Plots for four design objectives using four methods

5.4   Experiment 2

In this section, we address the second objective to compare tree models and non-tree models on the task of design space exploration. We created 14 validation datasets contain 22 features with 30 instances. The input data has the form of input 30 instances for design variable (input) X values equally distributed between 50 and 120. This input set was created based on six existing concept instances provided by an engineer, by incrementing the value of one of its inputs with a predefined step size and within a predefined interval, to explore

Table 2. Pairwise comparisons

Pairwise comparison	*RMSE p-value*	*CC p-value*
M5P-RF	0.0002	0.0015
M5P-SVM	0.0394	0.0182
M5P-LR	0.4611	0.0665
LR-SVM	0.6296	0.9667
RF-SVM	0.4611	0.8848
LR-RF	0.0394	0.6296

the response, or impact, on different design objectives (outputs) when varying a specific design variable, which design variable X values are unequally distributed in the range from 50 to 120. In general, the experiment produced as many as 14 different design objectives, but in Experiment 2 we focus on four design objectives.

The four selected design objectives are identified by the engineer as challenging outputs (design objectives CO1 to CO4), i.e., more difficult to predict and of higher priority. One of the design variables is defined by the engineer as the key input (here called design variable X value). These four design objectives and response variables have high importance in order to build a particular part in the flight engine. For example, if the product is aircraft engine, then the design variables can be length, width, curvature etc., and the design objective is to find the shape for aircraft wing. Figure 1 shows four design objectives (sub-plots), design variable X values on *x-axis* and response value on *y-axis*. For design objectives CO1, CO3 and CO4, the result of predictions is same for LR and M5P. The first observation is that RF accurately predicts the actual values, at least in the case of design objectives CO1 to CO3. The RF plot appears to have changing trends approximately following that of the labeled dataset (Actual value). The predicted output values of RF are also closest to the actual value for the majority of instances. The other models predicted output values that seems completely monotonic, and appear to almost follow a straight line. For the design objective CO4, SVM fits well to the actual values. These observations indicate an advantage for RF over the other models with regard to fitting the challenging outputs.

6   Conclusions and Future Work

The main goal was to investigate the performance of tree models for response surface modeling. We studied two tree methods (M5P and RF) and two non-tree methods (LR and SVM). Experiments were conducted on aerospace concept selection datasets to determine the performance. The results show that tree models perform at least as well as or better than traditional black-box models. We addressed the single-output regression problem for response surface models. Our future work will contrast this work with a multi-output regression approach to explore tree-based surrogate model comprehensibility further.

Acknowledgments. This work was supported by the *Knowledge Foundation* through the research profile grants *Model Driven Development and Decision Support* and *Scalable Resource-efficient Systems for Big Data Analytics*.

References

1. Ahmed, M., Qin, N.: Comparison of response surface and kriging surrogates in aerodynamic design optimization of hypersonic spiked blunt bodies. In: 13th International Conference on Aerospace Sciences and Aviation Technology, 26–28th May, Military Technical College, Kobry Elkobbah, Cairo, Egypt (2009)

2. Bell, T.E., Bixler, D.C., Dyer, M.E.: An extendable approach to computer-aided software requirements engineering. IEEE Trans. Softw. Eng. **1**, 49–60 (1977)
3. Breiman, L.: Random forests. Mach. Learn. **45**(1), 5–32 (2001)
4. Carley, K.M., Kamneva, N.Y., Reminga, J.: Response surface methodology. Technical report, DTIC Document (2004)
5. Chen, K.Y., Wang, C.H.: Support vector regression with genetic algorithms in forecasting tourism demand. Tour. Manag. **28**(1), 215–226 (2007)
6. Couckuyt, I., Gorissen, D., Rouhani, H., Laermans, E., Dhaene, T.: Evolutionary regression modeling with active learning: an application to rainfall runoff modeling. In: Kolehmainen, M., Toivanen, P., Beliczynski, B. (eds.) ICANNGA 2009. LNCS, vol. 5495, pp. 548–558. Springer, Heidelberg (2009)
7. Crombecq, K., Couckuyt, I., Gorissen, D., Dhaene, T.: Space-filling sequential design strategies for adaptive surrogate modelling. In: The First International Conference on Soft Computing Technology in Civil, Structural and Environmental Engineering (2009)
8. Demšar, J.: Statistical comparisons of classifiers over multiple data sets. J. Mach. Learn. Res. **7**, 1–30 (2006)
9. Freitas, A.A.: Comprehensible classification models: a position paper. SIGKDD Explor. Newsl. **15**(1), 1–10 (2013). http://doi.acm.org/10.1145/2594473.2594475
10. Gorissen, D., Couckuyt, I., Demeester, P., Dhaene, T., Crombecq, K.: A surrogate modeling and adaptive sampling toolbox for computer based design. J. Mach. Learn. Res. **11**, 2051–2055 (2010)
11. Gramacy, R.B., Le Digabel, S.: The mesh adaptive direct search algorithm with treed Gaussian process surrogates. Groupe d'études et de recherche en analyse des décisions (2011)
12. Gu, H., Yang, L., Hu, Z., Yu, J.: Surrogate models for shape optimization of underwater glider, pp. 3–6, February 2009
13. Kohavi, R., et al.: A study of cross-validation and bootstrap for accuracy estimation and model selection. In: IJCAI, vol. 14, pp. 1137–1145 (1995)
14. Nikolos, I.K.: On the use of multiple surrogates within a differential evolution procedure for high-lift airfoil design. Int. J. Adv. Intell. Paradigms **5**, 319–341 (2013)
15. Pos, A., Borst, P., Top, J., Akkermans, H.: Reusability of simulation models. Knowl.-Based Syst. **9**(2), 119–125 (1996)
16. Quinlan, J.R., et al.: Learning with continuous classes. In: Proceedings of the 5th Australian Joint Conference on Artificial Intelligence, Singapore, vol. 92, pp. 343–348 (1992)
17. Quinn, G.P., Keough, M.J.: Experimental Design and Data Analysis for Biologists. Cambridge University Press, Cambridge (2002)
18. Scholkopf, B., Smola, A.J.: Learning with Kernels: Support Vector Machines, Regularization, Optimization, and Beyond. MIT Press, Cambridge (2001)
19. Sheskin, D.J.: Handbook of Parametric and Nonparametric Statistical Procedures. CRC Press, Boca Raton (2003)
20. Vapnik, V.: The Nature of Statistical Learning Theory. Springer, New York (2000)
21. Wang, Y., Witten, I.H.: Inducing model trees for continuous classes. In: Proceedings of the Ninth European Conference on Machine Learning, pp. 128–137 (1997)
22. Witten, I.H., Frank, E.: Data Mining: Practical Machine Learning Tools and Techniques. Morgan Kaufmann, San Francisco (2011)

A Single-Facility Manifold Location Routing Problem with an Application to Supply Chain Management and Robotics

Emre Tokgöz[1(✉)], Iddrisu Awudu[1], and Theodore B. Trafalis[2]

[1] School of Business and Engineering, Quinnipiac University,
Hamden, CT 06518, USA
{Emre.Tokgoz,Iddrisu.Awudu}@quinnipiac.edu
[2] School of Industrial and Systems Engineering, University of Oklahoma,
Norman, OK 73071, USA
ttrafalis@ou.edu

Abstract. The location routing problem (LRP), a problem formulated for determining locations of facilities and the vehicle routes operating between these facilities, is the combination of the vehicle routing (VRP) and the facility location problems (FLP) in Euclidean space. The manifold location routing problem (MLRP) is an LRP in a Riemannian manifold setting as introduced in [14]. In seeking further advancements in the solution of LRP, MLRP improves the accuracy of the distance calculations by using geodesic distances. The shortest path distances on Earth's surface can be determined by calculating geodesic distances in local neighborhoods by using Riemannian geometry. In this work, we advance the theoretical results obtained for MLRP in [14] by incorporating support vector machines (SVM), dynamic programming, parallel programming, data mining, and Geographic Information Systems (GIS). The theory will be explained on a supply chain problem with a robotics paradigm.

Keywords: Manifold location routing problem · Riemannian manifold · Geodesics · Heuristics · Supply chain management · Geographic information systems · Data mining · Support vector machines · Robotics

1 Introduction

Allocating a facility and transportation from this facility location to the customers are two important problems in supply chain management. Location routing problem (LRP), a combination of the vehicle routing (VRP) and facility location (FLP) problems in Euclidean space, is solved to determine the best location of a facility and the corresponding cost effective operations from this facility to its suppliers and demand points [6]. LRP is a cost minimization mixed integer nonlinear programming problem that can be solved in a discrete or a continuous (planar) surface platform. It employs the Weber problem (WP) as a sub-problem for minimizing the Euclidean distance between a facility and a given set of customers on the plane. FLP and VRP are both well-known NP-hard problems. We refer to [5, 9] for overviews of FLP and VRP respectively. The most recent

© Springer International Publishing Switzerland 2015
P. Pardalos et al. (Eds.): MOD 2015, LNCS 9432, pp. 130–144, 2015.
DOI: 10.1007/978-3-319-27926-8_12

improvement on the location routing problem is introduced in [14] by assuming manifold surfaces.

The surface assumption in the statements of LRP had been either planar or spherical (see for example [1, 6, 10, 12]) before the manifold surface assumption introduced in [14]. Manifold location routing problem (MLRP) an LRP with manifold surface assumption, is introduced in [14]. The manifold surface assumption is a more realistic surface assumption than the planar or spherical surface assumptions used for solving the LRPs in the literature noting that the surface of earth is a manifold surface. MLRP employs geodesics on the Riemannian manifold surface to determine the shortest path distance between the facilities, suppliers, and demand points. For an overview of MLRP we refer to [14].

In Sect. 2, information about the use of support vector machines (SVM), dynamic programming, parallel programming, data mining, and Geographic Information Systems (GIS) are explained. In addition, incorporation of these concepts to the MLRP introduced in [14] are explained in this section. The assumptions, notation and formulation of the MLRP are explained in Sect. 3. The solution methodology for MLRP is explained in Sect. 4. MLRP algorithm details are explained in Sect. 5. Section 6 is dedicated to a supply chain management problem as an example to the MLRP formulated in this work. Section 7 is devoted to the summary of the ideas presented in this work.

2   A New Manifold Location Routing Problem

In this section, incorporation of the support vector machines (SVM), dynamic programming, parallel programming, data mining, and Geographic Information Systems (GIS) concepts to improve (i.e. advance) the statement of the MLRP are explained.

2.1   Riemannian Geometry and Geodesics

A Riemannian manifold (RM) is a differentiable manifold M in which each tangent space is equipped with an inner product. The inner product defines a Riemannian metric that has smooth variation from point to point. Bernhard Riemann introduced the corresponding geometry [11] in which the metric properties vary from point to point (See for example [2]). The change of a Riemannian manifold surface (RMS) is measured by determining how much it deviates from being planar (corresponding to curvature 0) in a local neighborhood. S^n, n-dimensional sphere, with curvature 1, and $\mathbb{R}^n$, n-dimensional Euclidean space with curvature 0 are commonly used Riemann manifolds in applications. If the curvature of a surface changes from a flat to a spherical surface then the curvature changes from 0 to 1.

In [14], the distances between customers and a facility to be allocated are measured on compact connected Riemannian Manifold Surfaces (CCRMS); a generalization of planar surfaces. The shortest path geodesic distances are the shortest distances between the customers and a possible location of the facility to be allocated. Therefore the planar WP is changed to the Manifold WP (MWP) Restatement of the WP is considering CCRMS to determine the shortest path geodesics is used for distance calculations. The main contribution in [14] is to provide a heuristic algorithm solution to the MLRP by using Riemannian surfaces and geodesic distances. A special case of the MLRP is the planar LRP when the curvature of the Riemannian surface is zero in 2-dimensional space. In the case when the road surface changes from flat to mountain, the curvature varies from zero (corresponding to the flat surface) to a positive curvature at each local neighborhood throughout the surface towards the mountain. In this case, the geodesics are the roads that connect certain intersections in the local regions. The shortest path geodesic between two locations on this surface is the geodesic with the shortest distance between them. This consideration is possible by using a one-to-one and onto map $\varphi : U \subset M \rightarrow \mathbb{R}^n$ called homeomorphism. By using a homeomorphism, each open neighborhood U in the topology of the manifold M can be mapped to an open neighborhood φ (U) in the Euclidean space. A connected Riemannian manifold carries the structure of a metric space whose distance function is the arc-length of a minimizing geodesic. Let M be a connected Riemannian manifold and γ: $[a,b] \rightarrow M$ be a parameterized differentiable curve in M with the velocity vector γ'. The length of γ between a and b is defined by the equality

$$l(\gamma) = \int_M h(\gamma'(t), \gamma'(t))dt = \int_a^b \nabla \gamma(t)dt \qquad (1)$$

where ∇ is the Levi-Civita connection; See for example [2, 4, 8] for details.

2.2   Weighted Support Vector Machines (WSVM)

Given two class sets, the basic idea of weighted support vector machines (WSVM) is to find a maximal margin separating hyper-plane giving the greatest separation between the classes in a high dimensional feature space. WSVM is particularly useful for reducing the effect of noise/outlier while determining the separating hyper-plane between two data classes [15]. In this work, SVM is employed for domain reduction from RMS to MMR by using the different signatures of the demand and supply points. We assign signature −1 to demanding customers and +1 to suppliers. The amount demanded by each demander is assigned as its signature and the amounts of goods supplied by each supplier is assigned to be its weights. This domain reduction will be a valuable contribution to the solution of the multi-facility Weber problem noting that LRP is an NP-hard problem [13]. On the contrary to the general WSVM, outliers plan an important role in the facility allocation solution since the maximum marginal region is a part of the facility allocation solution to be explained later. The kernel trick [15] can be employed for determining an SVM solution with the corresponding MMR. The facility is planned to receive from suppliers and distribute to demanding customers via robots. A robot in this context is a machine capable of carrying out a complex series of actions automatically, especially one programmable by a computer.

The weights w_i assigned to the demanding customers and suppliers play an important role in the allocation of the facilities. The existing customer data is considered to be the training data set represented by

$$\{(c_i, \ s_i, \ w_i)\}, \ c_i \in \mathbb{R}^N, \ s_i \in \{-1, 1\}, \ w_i \in \mathbb{R} \ \& \ i = 1, 2 \ldots n$$

In particular, the quadratic WSVM programming problem is [15]

$$\min\Phi(\rho) = \frac{1}{2}\rho^T\rho + C\sum_{i=1}^{n} w_i\xi_i, 1 \leq i \leq n$$

subject to

$$s_i(<\rho, \varphi(c_i)> + b) \geq 1 - \xi_i, \quad 1 \leq i \leq n$$
$$\xi_i \geq 0, \qquad 1 \leq i \leq n \tag{3}$$

A common technique to solve this minimization problem is by solving its corresponding dual problem [15]. We assume each existing customer has a demand list consisting of a fixed number of products.

2.3   Weighted Network Design, Dynamic Programming and Parallel Programming

The discrete locations of the facility will be determined by designing a weighted customer network. This weighted network is formed by the weights assigned to the customers in the WSVM quadratic programming problem formulation. In this network, the demand and supply points are the vertices, and the edges are the geodesics between these nodes. The distances between the nodes are the weights assigned to the edges. After determining the MMR and the corresponding separating hyper-plane as a result of the WSVM, a set (k number) of discrete feasible discrete locations are determined for facility allocation in MMR. Dynamic programming is employed to determine the best location of the facility by calculating the distances to the suppliers and demanding customers. Parallel programming is employed for

- Implementation of pathway calculations between the facility, customers, and suppliers;
- Projections of customer locations from the manifold surface to Euclidean surface;
- Solving the 2-objective functions (4) and (5) is formulated below.

3   Manifold Location Routing Problem (MLRP)

We assume the following for the MLRP introduced in this work:

- Supply and demand points, and the facility are assumed to be located on a CCRMS;
- Demand points are assigned signature −1 and suppliers are assigned +1 signature for the SVM solution;
- Only robots are assumed to operate between suppliers, demanding customers, and the facility to be allocated;
- A set of robots are assumed to operate only between the facility and the suppliers, and the rest of the robots are assumed to operate between the demanding customers and the facility;

- Operating robots ensure that the transportation problem is balanced at all times;
- The surface of the domain is well defined and accessible through GIS by the robots to determine and update the pathways;
- Parallel programming is employed by the robots to determine the supply levels of the facility with supply and demand tables structured for the demanding customers and suppliers.
- Distances between the customers and possible locations of the facility are calculated by using geodesic distances;
- Customers and suppliers have known demands and locations;
- Robots are the operating vehicles that are capacitated and homogeneous;
- Facility to be allocated is incapacitated;
- All the robots have the same capacity;
- The number of robots to be operated do not exceed the upper bound of the number of robots;
- The number of robots to be used will be derived as a result of the problem stated;
- There is no fixed cost for operating robots;
- Each robot route starts and finishes at the facility to be allocated;

The following notions will be used for the model formulation and the rest of the paper:

M CCRMS corresponding to the local region on Earth's surface.

C Set of demanding customers' c_i, $i \in I_1 = \{1, 2...m_1\}$.

S Set of suppliers' s_i, $i \in I_2 = \{1, 2...m_2\}$.

φ Homeomorphism defined for projection from M to $\mathbb{R}^2$.

a_k Demander locations on M with the coordinates $c_k = \left(\varphi \left(x_k^1 \right), \varphi \left(y_k^1 \right) \right)$ on $\mathbb{R}^2$.

a_0 Facility location on M with the Euclidean coordinate $c_0 = (\varphi (x_0), \varphi (y_0))$ on $\mathbb{R}^2$.

b_k Supplier locations on M with the coordinates $d_k = \left(\varphi \left(x_k^2 \right), \varphi \left(y_k^2 \right) \right)$ on $\mathbb{R}^2$.

E_1 Set of demanding customers and the facility with the facility indexed to be 0.

E_2 Set of suppliers and the facility with the facility indexed to be 0.

γ_{ij} Parametric geodesic on M connecting demanding customers' a_i and a_j.

β_{ij} Parametric geodesic on M connecting suppliers' b_i and b_j.

V_1 Set of robots operating between demanding customers and the facility $v_1 = 1, 2... n_1$ with $|V_1| \leq n_1$.

V_2 Set of robots operating between suppliers and the facility $v_2 = 1, 2... n_2$ with $|V_2| \leq n_2$.

v_{max}^i The maximum capacity of robot v^i.

D The demand set with $d_i \in D$ corresponding to the demander $c_i \in C$, $i \in I_1$.

K The supplier set $t_i \in D$ corresponding to the supplier $s_i \in S$, $i \in I_2$.

$$\delta_{ijk} = \begin{cases} 1 & \text{if nodes } i \text{ and } j \text{ are connected via route } k \\ 0 & \text{otherwise} \end{cases}$$

Similar to the 1-objective mixed integer nonlinear programming (MINLP) model introduced in [14], the following 2-objective MINLP supply chain management problem is formulated as a balanced transportation problem with transportation assumed to be via robots:

$$min \sum_{i,j \in E_1, \, v \in V_1} \int_M \left\| \gamma'_{ij}(t) \right\| dz \delta_{ijv} \tag{4}$$

$$min \sum_{i,j \in E_2, \, v \in V_2} \int_M \left\| \beta'_{ij}(t) \right\| dz \delta_{ijv} \tag{5}$$

subject to

$$\sum_{j \in E_p} \delta_{ijv} - \sum_{j \in E_p} \delta_{jiv} = 0 \qquad \forall i \in E_p; v \in V_p \text{ for all } p = 1, 2 \tag{6}$$

$$\sum_{i \in E_1, j \in C_1} \delta_{ijv} d_i \leq v^i_{max} \qquad \forall v \in V_1 \tag{7}$$

$$\sum_{i \in E_2, j \in C_2} \delta_{ijv} t_i \leq v^i_{max} \qquad \forall v \in V_2 \tag{8}$$

$$\sum_{v \in V_1, i \in U_1, j \in E_1 - U_1} \delta_{ijv} \geq 1 \qquad \forall U_1 \subset C \tag{9}$$

$$\sum_{v \in V_2, i \in U_2, j \in E_2 - U_2} \delta_{ijv} \geq 1 \qquad \forall U_2 \subset S \tag{10}$$

$$\sum_{v \in V_1, i \in E_1} \delta_{ijv} = 1 \qquad \forall j \in C \tag{11}$$

$$\sum_{v \in V_2, i \in E_2} \delta_{ijv} = 1 \qquad \forall j \in S \tag{12}$$

$$\sum_{j \in E_1} \delta_{0jv} \leq 1 \qquad \forall v \in V_1 \tag{13}$$

$$\sum_{j \in E_2} \delta_{0jv} \leq 1 \qquad \forall v \in V_2 \tag{14}$$

$$\sum_{j \in I_1} d_j - \sum_{i \in I_2} t_i \leq 0 \qquad \forall i, j \in E_1, E_2 \tag{15}$$

$$\delta_{ijv} \in \{0, 1\} \qquad \forall i, j \in E_1, E_2; v \in V_1, V_2 \tag{16}$$

The minimization of the total transportation cost on the manifold setting M is indicated by the objective functions (4) and (5). Traffic flow for visiting each demander and supplier by the same robot is managed by constraints (6) when p = 1 and p = 2 respectively. During the transportation, the maximum capacity of the vehicles for suppliers and demanding customers cannot be violated by constraints (7) and (8). Existences of sub-tours are declined by constraints (9) and (10) ensuring that there exist at least one robot leaving any subset of demanding customers and suppliers. Each demander and supplier belongs to one and only one tour as a result of the constraints (11) and (12) in their respective groups. Each robot leaves the facility either once or never used for transportation as a result of constraints (13) and (14) noting that not all the robots are necessarily used for transportation. The transportation of supply and demand is balanced by the constraint stated in (15). The conditions for decision variables are stated in (16). Two of the continuous variables are the locations of the customers and suppliers in the Euclidean space and the third continuous variable is the parameter z for the geodesic on the manifold M. The numerical results known in the literature for the MLRP are incomparable with the numerical results obtained in this work since the known data sets used for the LRP are not for general manifold settings. This difference in numerical results arises naturally from the change in the surface assumption from planar surfaces to the Riemannian manifold surfaces.

4   Solution Methodology

Solutions to the LRP in the Euclidean space are obtained by using sequential, iterative, and hierarchical methods (see for example [3, 7, 11, 12]). In this section, a similar solution methodology to the one used in [14] is implemented with various additional concepts included to solve the MLRP stated in this work.

4.1   Main Steps of the Algorithm

The first step of the algorithm for solving MLRP is mapping the demanding customers' and suppliers' locations from M to $\mathbb{R}^2$ by using homeomorphisms. A homeomorphism (for example orthogonal projection) can be used for projecting demander locations and another homeomorphism can be used for supplier location projections. In addition the geodesic distances on the manifold surface between the suppliers and demanding customers are calculated by using the inner product defined on M and mapped from M to $\mathbb{R}^2$. These geodesic distances include all possible roads between the suppliers' network and the demanding customers' network within the compact connected domain on the surface of M. These lengths correspond to the lengths of the roads in the network formed by the customers in the Euclidean space. Therefore the metric choice on M determines the metric to be used in the Euclidean space.

In [14] the location of the facility for the MLRP solution is determined by using a heuristic approach with a method named linked chain method (LCM). LCM is defined to be a method of chaining z open balls with the center of the ith open ball being the best location of the center of the step $(i-1)^{st}$ open ball, i = 0,1,...,z. The center of each B_i is determined by solving the routing problem within the disk obtained by the interior of B_i for all i. The radius of the circle B_i is determined by calculating the distance between the ith and $(i-1)^{st}$ open balls. The radius of each consecutive circle is modified dynamically. The stopping criteria for adding circles to the LCM is when a sufficiently small distance between the $(z-1)^{st}$ and z^{th} circles is obtained. In this work, the second step of the algorithm is designed to first reduce the domain from M to MMR and then solving the LRP in the Euclidean space by employing dynamic programming. The initial location of the facility is determined randomly "close" or on the separating hyper-plane from k feasible locations within MMR that are also feasible locations on M for the facility allocation. In this step WSVM is initially employed for domain reduction from M to MMR with the separating hyper-plane determined.

The third step of the algorithm is projecting the results obtained in the second step from $\mathbb{R}^2$ to M and determining a feasible location of the facility on M. The cost effective facility location determined on $\mathbb{R}^2$ may or may not be a feasible location on M, therefore a local neighborhood search is necessary on M for the best allocation of the facility in the case when the solution is not feasible on M.

The fourth and last step of the algorithm is robots' service to the existing demanding customers and suppliers. Every robot that serves to the demanding customers keep track of the existing orders of the customers online as an order table. A robot is assigned to fulfill the orders of the customers in order to fulfill the existing demands received in order. Therefore robots are required to data mine for updating the routes to serve customers based on the updated demand tables of the customers. These robots report the goods demanded by the demanding customers to the facility and add this data to the supply table. Parallel computing and updating the corresponding demand tables are necessary for supply chain's organizational management. Similarly robots that are required to pick-up from suppliers have to data mine to keep track of the demand tables and pick-up goods from suppliers to keep the transportation balanced. Updating the routes is a necessity for pick-ups from the suppliers based on their supply tables and changing routes of pick-ups. Parallel computing and updating the corresponding supply tables are necessities for organizational skills. The main steps of the algorithm are summarized in the following table and its details will be explained in Sect. 5.

1ʳᵗ Step **Projection from M to $\mathbb{R}^2$**

Sub-Step (1) *Supplier & Demander location projections*

    (1.a) Use a homeomorphism to project the demanding customers' and suppliers' locations from the surface of M to R^2

    (1.b) Use the same homeomorphism to project the obstacles

Sub-Step (2) *Geodesic projections*

    (2.a) Determine the geodesics and the corresponding distances between suppliers and demanding customers that do not pass through though the obstacles on M. These are the shortest paths between the suppliers and demanding customers

    (2.b) Assume the homeomorphism used in (1.a) and (1.b) are the same to project the geodesic distances to $\mathbb{R}^2$

    (2.c) Assign the distances determined in (2.a) as the distances between the demanding customers and suppliers on $\mathbb{R}^2$

2ⁿᵈ Step **Facility allocation on $\mathbb{R}^2$**

Sub-Step (3) *Initial facility location*

    (3.a) Determine the MMR region and the separating hyper-plane by employing the WSVM solution. Reduce the domain to MMR

    (3-b) Determine k number of feasible locations for the facility within the MMR close to the separating hyper-plane by choosing a random feasible location.

Sub-Step (4) *Facility location determination*

    (4.a) Use the geodesic distances determined in (2a) and apply dynamic programming by using the k feasible locations within the MMR after determining all geodesic distances from these locations to the suppliers and demanding customers

    (4.b) Determine the best possible location of the facility with the corresponding pathways to the suppliers and demanding customers in $\mathbb{R}^2$

3ᵗʰ Step **Projection from $\mathbb{R}^2$ to M**

Sub-Step (5) *Projections of the new facility location and determined paths to M*

    (5.a) Use the inverse map of the homeomorphism determined in (1.a) to project the allocated facility and the corresponding minimum cost routes from $\mathbb{R}^2$ to M

    (5-b) Determine a feasible location for the facility on M by employing a local search within the local region if the projected location from $\mathbb{R}^2$ to M is not feasible

4ᵗʰ Step **Data Mining & Transportation System via Robots**

Sub-Step (6) *Transportation via Robots*

    (6.a) The robots are required to data mine for updating the routes to serve customers based on the demand tables received from the customers. Parallel computing and updating the corresponding demand tables are necessary for organizational skills.

    (6.b) The robots are required to data mine for updating the routes for pick-ups from the suppliers based on the supply tables of the

suppliers. Parallel computing and updating the corresponding supply tables are necessary for organizational skills.

Fig. 1. Proposed algorithm to solve the MLRP

4.2   Computational Complexity of the Algorithm

It is well known that LRP is an NP-hard problem noting that both routing and location problems are NP-hard on the Euclidean surface [13]. Similarly, the MLRP introduced in [14] is an NP-hard problem. Therefore the MLRP that we introduced for the supply chain management problem that we introduced in this work is also an NP-hard problem. The main computational challenges for solving the MLRP are pathway length calculations (the integrals givens in (4) and (5)) between the suppliers and demanding customers on the RMS and solving the routing problem in the Euclidean space at every circle of the LCM. The time complexity of projection from $\mathbb{R}^2$ to M and determining the best location of the facility on the manifold can be a constant, therefore can be negligible in computational complexity calculations in the case when the feasible solution is within a closed region on the RMS. It can also be the complexity of the proposed algorithm in the case when the feasible location of the facility is too far from the solution on the CCRMS after using the proposed algorithm.

5   MLRP Algorithm Details

In this section, we explain the details of the heuristic algorithm given in Fig. 1 for solving the Manifold Location Routing Problem (MLRP). These details include projection of the demander locations; supplier locations; the robot routes from the manifold to the planar surface; determining the location of the facility after solving the WSVM by applying dynamic and parallel programming; and mapping back the locations of the location of the facility to the manifold setting.

5.1   Projection from M to $\mathbb{R}^2$

The first step of allocating a facility on a local Earth surface (on M) is by projecting the customer locations and all possible route lengths between these customers from the surface of M to $\mathbb{R}^2$. This initial step is necessary because calculations on a Riemannian manifold are not easy and require projection from M to $\mathbb{R}^2$. We use the same projection map used in [14] to map from M to $\mathbb{R}^2$. Therefore we use the following homeomorphism to map the locations of the demanding customers and suppliers from the Riemannian manifold surface M to the Euclidean surface $\mathbb{R}^2$

$$\varphi : M \to R^2$$
$$a_j \mapsto \left(x_j^1 \cos\theta, y_j^1 \sin\theta \right) \tag{17}$$
$$b_i \mapsto \left(x_i^2 \cos\theta, y_i^2 \sin\theta \right)$$

where a_j represents the locations of the demanding customers, b_i represents the locations of the suppliers, and θ are randomly generated angles for suppliers and demand locations in local regions [2]. The choice of the homeomorphism changes the customer locations in the Euclidean space that would affect the LRP solution in the Euclidean space. Our choice of homeomorphism defined in (17) yields to projection of customer locations to a circular setting. The radius of the circles formed by the customers can be easily obtained from (17) by using the formula

$$R_k^\theta = \sqrt{x_k^2 + y_k^2} \tag{18}$$

that depends on projection angle θ. Another homeomorphism that can be employed for projection can be the orthogonal projection. Figure 2 displays the projection of the customers from surface of the compact connected Riemannian manifold M to the Euclidean space by using the homeomorphism introduced in (17). Figure 3 displays the projected customer locations on $\mathbb{R}^2$.

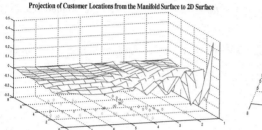

Fig. 2. Projected customer locations from M to $\mathbb{R}^2$

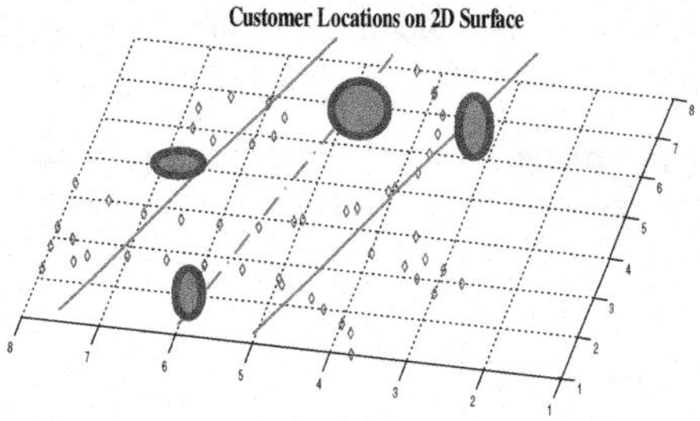

Fig. 3. Projected customer locations on $\mathbb{R}^2$

All possible pathway lengths among customers are calculated by using (4) and (5), and the corresponding geodesic functions can be pre-determined by using GIS (Geographic Information Systems). The geodesics determined between customers on the RMS are projected from M to $\mathbb{R}^2$ and the lengths of these geodesics are assigned to be the edge lengths between the nodes of demander-supplier-facility network formed in $\mathbb{R}^2$. It is important to note that the metric used on the manifold defines the metric used on the RMS. This is due to the fact that the norm we use for the distance calculations is the norm used on the projected Euclidean surface.

5.2 Facility Location on $\mathbb{R}^2$ with WSVM, Dynamic Programming, and Parallel Programming

In this section the allocation of the facility is explained with the corresponding WSVM solution. The MMR region is determined first with the corresponding hyper-plane solution. The next step is to determine the set of discrete locations where the continuous FLP becomes discrete FLP. The location of the facility is set after applying dynamic and parallel programming. Figure 4 displays the paths that can be determined as a result of a possible discrete location chosen that is close to the separating

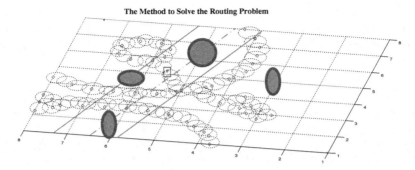

Fig. 4. A solution to the routing problem is sketched starting from one of the randomly chosen feasible facility locations after applying WSVM solution. Dynamic and parallel programming is used for facility allocation. In this figure an initial location of the facility f_0 is pointed (Color figure online).

hyper-plane. Parallel programming is applied for k discrete locations. The blue spots represent the obstacles within the domain.

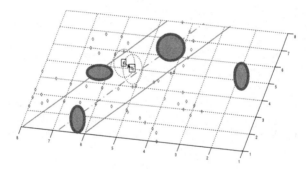

Fig. 5. Second phase of determining the best robot routes from the facility to a customer by dynamic programming.

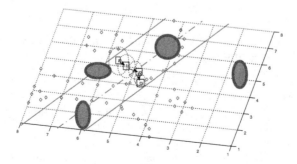

Fig. 6. Fourth phase of determining the best robot routes from the facility to a customer by dynamic programming.

Figures 4, 5 and 6 display the neighborhood geodesic search that robots can follow. Dynamic and parallel programming are implemented to determine the location of the facility.

5.3   Projection from $\mathbb{R}^2$ to M

The third step of the algorithm is to map the shortest path distribution routes and the facility location back to the RM surface by using the inverse map φ^{-1} of the homeomorphism φ defined in (17):

$$\varphi^{-1}: \quad \begin{aligned} \mathbb{R}^2 &\rightarrow M \\ (x_k, y_k) &\mapsto (\varphi^{-1}(x_k\cos\theta), \varphi^{-1}(y_k\cos\theta)) \end{aligned} \tag{19}$$

Customer location data is pre-existing on M, therefore it is not necessary to map the customer data from the Euclidean surface back to the RM surface.

5.4   Data Mining and Transportation System

We consider a balanced transportation problem as the last step of the algorithm. The robots follow the geodesic paths to pick-up goods from suppliers and travel to distribute goods to demand points for supply chain management. The transportation problem is assumed to be balanced for efficient demand-supply flow within the network. The robots update and keep track of the supply and demand tables of demanding customers and suppliers. Robots can update their routes by using GIS information that is assumed to be achievable online and calculate the geodesic distances accordingly.

6   An Example

Allocation of a facility for serving its customers and receiving goods from suppliers based on the MLRP solution with the WSVM approach will be explained in this section. In this example, we assume there are 3 suppliers, 6 demand points, and a

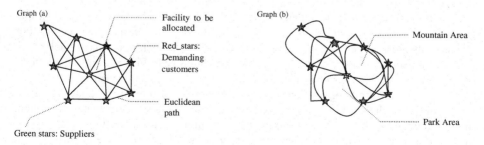

Fig. 7. Graph (a) Network formed by the Euclidean distances in the Euclidean space. **Graph (b)** Network formed in the Euclidean space by mapping the routes from RM surface.

facility satisfies the assumptions stated for the MLRP. The geodesic distances between the customers, suppliers, and facility are calculated by using functions generated randomly. This information can be obtained by using GIS data in real life applications.

In Fig. 7 we consider the initial phase of the routing problem with the corresponding possible routes for the formed networks on the Euclidean and RM surfaces. In this setting, the initial location of the facility is determined by using the MMR region and the corresponding separating hyper-plane solution. In Fig. (7-a) the Euclidean robot routes are calculated on the planar setting with the MMR represented by two solid lines and the separating hyper-plane in the middle by a dashed line. In Fig. (7-b) the routes are the geodesics projected from the RM surface to the Euclidean surface. These geodesics are length minimizing with respect to the routes considered on the RM

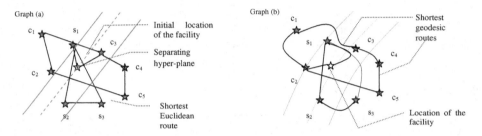

Fig. 8. Graph (a) Shortest path route determined from the location of the facility that is determined by the MMR solution by using Fig (7-a) **Graph (b)** Shortest path route determined in the Euclidean space by mapping the routes from RM surface from the new location of the facility.

surface. These differences between the routes would have a big impact on the supply chain cost optimization since the routes can be effected by areas such as parks, mountains etc. Figure 7-b contains more realistic information than Fig. 7-a based on the path lengths calculated on Earth's surface. The MMR region and the separating hyper-plane have curved structure on M.

Both Figures 8-a and 8-b follow the corresponding counterparts given in Fig. 7. Robot routes for both pick-up and delivery are displayed from the finalized location of the facility after applying dynamic and parallel programming in Fig. (8-a) and the corresponding geodesic routes and distances on RM surface in Fig. (8-b). The distribution and pick-up routes can change from Figs. 8-a to 8-b. This is due to the fact that geodesic distances can make a big impact on the allocation direction of the facility. For example, there is a difference in the final location of a robot before it returns back to the facility after serving customers between Figs. 8-a and 8-b. In Fig. 8-a, the robots visits c_3 as the last customer however in Fig. 8-b the same robot has to visit c_2 last.

The choice of the Riemann metric plays an important role in the distance calculations in the Euclidean space since it is assigned to be the distance between customers in the Euclidean space as pointed out in [14]. It is important to note that the change in the homeomorphism does not make a difference in the allocation of the facility since it is a 1–1 and onto map used to determine a location on the RMS. However the metric choice can make a difference in the computational complexity of the algorithm chosen.

Initial routing – 1st phase for customers

Figure (8-a): Path followed	c_3	c_1	c_2	c_5	c_4
: Path lengths	1.2	1.9	1.45	2.3	1.1
Figure (8-b): Path followed	c_2	c_1	c_3	c_4	c_5
: Path lengths	1.2	1.92	1	1.55	2.6

Initial routing – 2nd phase for customers

Figure (8-a): Path followed	c_2	c_1	c_3	c_4	c_5
: Path lengths	0.7	1.45	1.9	0.9	1.1
Figure (8-b): Path followed	c_3	c_2	c_1	c_4	c_5
: Path lengths	0.99	2.89	2.378	1.62	1.92

Initial routing – 1st phase for suppliers

Figure (8-a): Path followed	s_1	s_3	s_2
: Path lengths	1.02	1.6	1.65
Figure (8-b): Path followed	s_1	s_2	s_3
: Path lengths	1.5	1.5	1.8

Initial routing – 2nd phase for suppliers

Figure (8-a): Path followed	s_1	s_2	s_3
: Path lengths	1.02	1.5	1.65
Figure (8-b): Path followed	s_3	s_2	s_1
: Path lengths	0.8	1.8	1.5

Fig. 9. Customer-supplier-facility distance calculations for the first two phases where dynamic and parallel programming are used for calculations on the Euclidean and RM surfaces for solving the LRP problem.

This is due to the fact that a homeomorphism if chosen to be a complicated function will yield to more calculations. Figure 9 below describes the first two phase implementations of MLRP by using the information provided in Figs. 8-a and 8-b. Parallel programming is employed for distance calculations between suppliers, customers, and the facility. Dynamic programming and GIS are implemented for determining the road to follow on the existence surface.

7 Summary

In this work we introduced weighted support vector machines (SVM), dynamic programming, parallel programming, data mining, and Geographic Information Systems (GIS) as a part of the Manifold Location Problem introduced in [14]. In [14], the facility allocation was determined by employing a heuristic approach. In this work we employed WSVM to determine the location of a facility by employing dynamic and parallel programming techniques. Demanding customers are assigned -1 and suppliers are assigned $+1$ as a part of the WSCM approach. The MMR and separating hyper-planes are also determined as a part of this solution. The location of the facility is determined by designing a weighted network of the demanding customers and suppliers. These weights are used for the WSVM solution. A basic application of this theory is explained on a supply chain management problem in which the robots follow the geodesic paths to pick-up goods from suppliers and travel to distribute goods to demanding customers. The transportation problem is assumed to be balanced for efficient demand-supply flow within the network. The robots update and keep track of the supply and demand tables of demanding customers and suppliers. Robots can update their routes by using GIS information that is assumed to be achievable online and calculate the geodesic distances accordingly. The LRP is solved by following a similar method used in [14].

Acknowledgement. Dr. Theodore Trafalis was supported by RSF grant 14-41-00039 and he conducted research at National Research University Higher School of Economics.

References

1. Aly, A., Kay, D., Litwhiler, J.: Location dominance on spherical surfaces. Oper. Res. **27**, 972–981 (1979)
2. Do Carmo, M.P.: Differential geometry of curves and surfaces. Prentice Hall Inc., Englewood Cliffs (1976)
3. Aras, N., Yumusak, S.: Altınel, IK: solving the capacitated multi-facility Weber problem by simulated annealing, threshold accepting and genetic algorithms. In: Doerner, K.F., Gendreau, M., Greistorfer, P., Gutjahr, W.J., Hartl, R.F., Reimann, M. (eds.) Metaheuristics: Progress in Complex Systems Optimization, pp. 91–112. Springer, USA (2007)
4. Cheeger, J., Ebin, D.G.: Comparison Theorems in Riemannian Geometry. North Holland Publishing Company, American Elsevier Publishing Company Inc., Amsterdam, New York (1975)
5. Daskin, M.S.: What you should know about location modeling. Naval Res. Logis. **55**, 283–294 (2008)
6. Drezner, Z., Wesolowsky, G.O.: Facility location on a sphere. J. Oper. Res. Soc. **29**, 997–1004 (1978)
7. Gamal, M.D.H., Salhi, S.: Constructive heuristics for the uncapacitated continuous location-allocation problem. J. Oper. Res. Soc. **52**, 821–829 (2001)
8. Jost, J.: Riemannian Geometry and Geometric Analysis, 6th edn. Springer, New York (2011)
9. Laporte, G.: What you should know about the vehicle routing problem. Naval Res. Logis. **54**, 811–819 (2007)
10. Prodhon, C., Prins, C.: A survey of recent research on location-routing problems. Euro. J. Oper. Res. **238**(1), 1–17 (2014)
11. Riemann, B: Grundlagen für eine allgemeine Theorie der Functionen einer veränderlichen complexen Grösse. Inauguraldissertation, Göttingen (1851)
12. Salhi, S., Nagy, G.: Local improvement in planar facility location using vehicle routing. Ann. Oper. Res. **167**, 287–296 (2009)
13. Sherali, H.D., Noradi, F.L.: NP-hard, capacitated, balanced p-median problems on a chain graph with a continuum of link demands. Math. Oper. Res. **13**, 32–49 (1988)
14. Tokgöz, E., Alwazzi, S., Theodore, T.B.: A heuristic algorithm to solve the single-facility location routing problem on Riemannian surfaces. Comput. Manage. Sci. **12**, 397–415 (2014). doi:10.1007/s10287-014-0226-6. Springer
15. Yang, X., Song, Q., Wang, Y.: A weighted support vector machine for data classification. Int. J. Pattern. Recog. Artif. Intell. WSPC **21**(5), 961–976 (2007)

An Efficient Many-Core Implementation for Semi-Supervised Support Vector Machines

Fabian Gieseke[(✉)]

Institute for Computing and Information Sciences, Radboud University Nijmegen,
Toernooiveld 212, 6525 EC Nijmegen, The Netherlands
fgieseke@cs.ru.nl

Abstract. The concept of semi-supervised support vector machines extends classical support vector machines to learning scenarios, where both labeled and unlabeled patterns are given. In recent years, such semi-supervised extensions have gained considerable attention due to their huge potential for real-world applications with only small amounts of labeled data. While being appealing from a practical point of view, semi-supervised support vector machines lead to a combinatorial optimization problem that is difficult to address. Many optimization approaches have been proposed that aim at tackling this task. However, the computational requirements can still be very high, especially in case large data sets are considered and many model parameters need to be tuned. A recent trend in the field of big data analytics is to make use of graphics processing units to speed up computationally intensive tasks. In this work, such a massively-parallel implementation is developed for semi-supervised support vector machines. The experimental evaluation, conducted on commodity hardware, shows that valuable speed-ups of up to two orders of magnitude can be achieved over a standard single-core CPU execution.

Keywords: Semi-supervised support vector machines · Non-convex optimization · Graphics processing units · Big data analytics

1 Introduction

The classification of objects is a fundamental task in machine learning and *support vector machines* (SVMs) [4,20,22] belong to the state-of-the-art models to address such scenarios. In their original form, support vector machines can only take labeled patterns into account. However, such labeled data can be scarce in real-world applications, whereas unlabeled patterns are often available in huge quantities and at low cost. *Semi-supervised learning* schemes aim at taking both labeled and unlabeled patterns into account to improve the models' performances [6,28]. The corresponding extension of support vector machines takes the additional unlabeled part of the data into account by searching for the partition of the unlabeled patterns into two classes such that a subsequent application of a support vector machine yields the best overall result [2,14,23].

© Springer International Publishing Switzerland 2015
P. Pardalos et al. (Eds.): MOD 2015, LNCS 9432, pp. 145–157, 2015.
DOI: 10.1007/978-3-319-27926-8_13

Various authors have demonstrated the usefulness of this concept. One main drawback, however, is the computational runtime needed to solve or to approximate the underlying combinatorial task. A quite recent trend in big data analytics is to resort to *graphics processing units* (GPUs) to speed up the involved computations. These devices, which have formerly only been used in the context of computer graphics, can nowadays also be applied to accelerate general-purpose computations (e.g., multiplication of matrices). While modern GPUs offer massive parallelism (e.g., thousands of compute units on a single device), the specific hardware properties have to be taken into account in order to achieve a satisfying performance. In some cases, this requires a careful redesign of a given algorithm to make it amenable to such devices.

Contribution: We propose a massively-parallel variant of the single-core implementation for semi-supervised support vector machines recently proposed by Gieseke et al. [12]. The experimental evaluation shows that a single GPU device can yield speed-ups of up to two orders of magnitude over the corresponding CPU single-core implementation. Since modern desktop computers can accommodate multiple many-core devices, one can dramatically reduce the practical runtime needed to train these models given standard commodity hardware.

2   Background

We start by providing the mathematical background of semi-supervised support vector machines and the key ideas of general-purpose computations on GPUs.

2.1   Semi-Supervised Support Vector Machines

Let $T_l = \{(\mathbf{x}_1, y_1'), \ldots, (\mathbf{x}_l, y_l')\} \subset X \times \mathbb{R}$ be a set of labeled patterns and $T_u = \{\mathbf{x}_{l+1}, \ldots, \mathbf{x}_{l+u}\} \subset X$ a set of unlabeled ones, where X is an arbitrary set. Support vector machines are of the form [18, 20, 22]

$$\inf_{f \in \mathcal{H}, b \in \mathbb{R}} \frac{1}{l} \sum_{i=1}^{l} \mathcal{L}\big(y_i', f(\mathbf{x}_i) + b\big) + \lambda ||f||_{\mathcal{H}}^2, \tag{1}$$

where $\lambda > 0$ is a *regularization parameter*, $\mathcal{L} : \mathbb{R} \times \mathbb{R} \to [0, \infty)$ a *loss function* and $||f||_{\mathcal{H}}^2$ the squared norm in a *reproducing kernel Hilbert space* $\mathcal{H} \subseteq \mathbb{R}^X = \{f : X \to \mathbb{R}\}$ induced by a *kernel function* $k : X \times X \to \mathbb{R}$. The first term of the objective measures how well the model fits the data, whereas the second term penalizes "complex" models. Popular choices for the loss functions are, e.g., the *square loss* $\mathcal{L}(y, t) = (y - t)^2$ or the *hinge loss* $\mathcal{L}(y, t) = \max(0, 1 - yt)$, where the latter one yields the concept of a classical support vector machine [19, 22].

Semi-Supervised Extension. Given few labeled patterns only, support vector machines might yield an unsatisfying classification accuracy. For many real-world

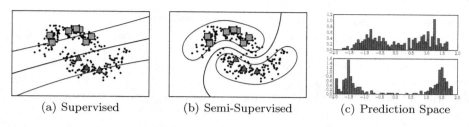

(a) Supervised	(b) Semi-Supervised	(c) Prediction Space

Fig. 1. Support vector machines only take labeled patterns (red squares and blue triangles) into account. In contrast, semi-supervised support vector machines make use of additional unlabeled patterns (black points) by enforcing the model not to go "through" the induced high-density areas, see Figure (b). This corresponds to penalizing predictions for the unlabeled patterns that are close to zero, see Figure (c), where the top figure corresponds to the supervised and the bottom one to the semi-supervised model (Color figure online).

scenarios, however, additional unlabeled patterns $T_u = \{\mathbf{x}_{l+1}, \ldots, \mathbf{x}_{l+u}\} \subset X$ are available and can often be obtained without much additional effort. The concept of semi-supervised support vector machines addresses these scenarios. In a nutshell, one searches for the partition of the unlabeled patterns into two classes such that a subsequent (slightly modified) support vector machine yields the overall best result [2,14,23]. From a mathematical point of view, one searches for a partition vector $\mathbf{y}^* = (y_1^*, \ldots, y_u^*)^\mathrm{T} \in \{-1, +1\}^u$, an offset term $b^* \in \mathbb{R}$, and a model $f^* \in \mathcal{H}$ that are optimal w.r.t.:

$$\underset{f \in \mathcal{H}, b \in \mathbb{R}, \mathbf{y} \in \{-1,+1\}^u}{\text{minimize}} \frac{1}{l} \sum_{i=1}^{l} \mathcal{L}\big(y_i', f(\mathbf{x}_i) + b\big) + \frac{\lambda'}{u} \sum_{i=1}^{u} \mathcal{L}\big(y_i, f(\mathbf{x}_{l+i}) + b\big) + \lambda ||f||_{\mathcal{H}}^2$$

Here, $\lambda' > 0$ is an additional parameter that determines the influence of the unlabeled patterns. Using the hinge loss and given a fixed $(f, b) \in \mathcal{H} \times \mathbb{R}$, the optimal partition vector $\mathbf{y}$ is given as $y_i = \text{sgn}(f(\mathbf{x}_{l+i}) + b)$ [9]. This leads to the *effective loss* defined on the unlabeled patterns, which is given by $\mathcal{L}^e(f(\mathbf{x}) + b) = \max(0, 1 - |f(\mathbf{x}) + b|)$ and which penalizes predictions "around" zero, see Figs. 1(c) and 2(a). The *representer theorem* [19] shows that any optimal solution $(f, b) \in \mathcal{H} \times \mathbb{R}$ for the induced continuous problem has the form

$$f(\cdot) = \sum_{j=1}^{n} c_j k(\mathbf{x}_j, \cdot) + b \tag{2}$$

with $\mathbf{c} = (c_1, \ldots, c_n)^\mathrm{T} \in \mathbb{R}^n$, $b \in \mathbb{R}$, and $n = l + u$. Thus, using $||f||_{\mathcal{H}}^2 = \sum_{i=1}^{n} \sum_{j=1}^{n} c_i c_j k(\mathbf{x}_i, \mathbf{x}_j)$, the overall problem can be formulated as continuous (non-convex) optimization task of the form:

$$\underset{\mathbf{c} \in \mathbb{R}^n, b \in \mathbb{R}}{\text{minimize}} \frac{1}{l} \sum_{i=1}^{l} \mathcal{L}\big(y_i', f(\mathbf{x}_i) + b\big) + \frac{\lambda'}{u} \sum_{i=1}^{u} \mathcal{L}^e\big(f(\mathbf{x}_{l+i}) + b\big) + \lambda ||f||_{\mathcal{H}}^2 \tag{3}$$

To avoid unbalanced solutions, an additional balancing constraint is usually considered. In the remainder of this work, we follow Chapelle and Zien [9] and include a constraint of the form $\frac{1}{u}\sum_{i=1}^{u} f(\mathbf{x}_{l+i}) + b \approx b_c$, where b_c is an estimate of the expected ratio between both classes (obtained via the labeled patterns or fixed by the user). By centering all patterns w.r.t. to the mean of the unlabeled patterns in feature space, this constraint can simply be enforced by fixing $b = b_c$.[1]

Related Work. The concept of semi-supervised support vector machines stems from Vapnik and Sterin [23], who named it *transductive support vector machines*. The first practical approaches that tackled the combinatorial nature of the task have been proposed by Joachims [14] and Bennet and Demiriz [2]. The former approach is based on a label-switching strategy, which is also related to more recent techniques [1,21]; the latter approach makes use of mixed-integer programming solvers to obtain a globally optimal solution. Various other optimization approaches have been proposed, including semi-definite programming [3,26], branch-and-bound strategies [7], or gradient-based techniques [9,12]. We refer to Chapelle *et al.* [6,8] and Zhu and Goldberg [28] for an overview.

Few GPU-based implementations have been proposed for support vector machines and their variants. For instance, Catanzaro *et al.* [5] resort to GPUs for speeding up the training phase of standard support vector machines. Wen *et al.* [24] make use of this implementation to accelerate a local search scheme that addresses a variant of the problem outlined above. In particular, the approach is based on small subsets of the data and resorts to Catanzaro *et al.*'s implementation to speed up the intermediate SVM tasks. To the best of our knowledge, no GPU-based implementation that is specifically devoted to the task induced by semi-supervised support vector machines has been proposed so far.

2.2   Massively-Parallel Computations on GPUs

Modern graphics processing units are based on thousands of compute units. Originally, such devices were only used to accelerate computer graphics. Nowadays, however, they can also be used for so-called *general-purpose computations on graphics processing units* (GPGPU) such as matrix multiplications. Various adaptations of standard machine learning tools have been proposed in recent years and the potential of such massively-parallel implementations has been demonstrated for different application domains [5,11,13,25].

In contrast to CPUs, which exhibit complex control units and function mechanisms that are optimized for sequential code execution, GPUs rely on simplified control units and are generally designed for "simple tasks" that are executed in a massively-parallel manner [10]. Two key ingredients for an efficient GPGPU implementation are (1) exposing sufficient parallelism to the many-core device and (2) reducing the memory transfer between the host system and the device(s).

---

[1] More precisely, we assume $\sum_{i=1}^{u} \Phi(\mathbf{x}_{l+i}) = \mathbf{0}$, where $\Phi(\mathbf{x}) = k(\mathbf{x}, \cdot)$ is the feature mapping induced by the kernel k. Centering the data can be achieved by adapting the kernel matrices in the preprocessing phase, see, e.g., Schölkopf and Smola [20].

The tasks assigned to a GPU are executed in parallel based on the *single instruc-tion multiple data*-paradigm (SIMD), meaning that all threads can only execute the same instruction in a single clock cycle, but have access to different memory locations. Most of the GPGPU implementations aim at "separating" the com-putationally intensive parts from the remaining computations such that these parts can be conducted efficiently on the many-core device.

3   Optimization on Many-Core Systems

In its original form, the continuous objective associated with semi-supervised support vector machines is not differentiable, which rules out the use of, e.g., gradient-based optimization techniques. One way to tackle this problem is to resort to differentiable surrogates for the objective [9]. In this section, we build upon our previous work [12] and describe the modifications needed to make the implementation amenable to an efficient execution on modern GPUs.

3.1   Differentiable Objective

Following Gieseke *et al.* [12], we consider the *modified logistic loss* $\mathcal{L}(y, f(\mathbf{x})) = \frac{1}{\gamma} \log \left(1 + \exp(\gamma(1 - y_i' f(\mathbf{x}_i)))\right)$ as replacement for the hinge loss and $\mathcal{L}^e(f(\mathbf{x})) = \exp(-3(f(\mathbf{x}_{l+i}))^2)$ as replacement of the effective loss defined on the unlabeled patterns [9, 27], see Fig. 2. This yields

$$F_{\lambda'}(\mathbf{c}) = \frac{1}{l} \sum_{i=1}^{l} \frac{1}{\gamma} \log \left(1 + \exp\left(\gamma(1 - y_i' \sum_{i=1}^{n} c_i k\left(\mathbf{x}_i, \cdot\right))\right)\right) \tag{4}$$
$$+ \frac{\lambda'}{u} \sum_{i=l+1}^{n} \exp\left(-3\left(\sum_{i=1}^{n} c_i k\left(\mathbf{x}_i, \cdot\right)\right)^2\right) + \lambda \sum_{i=1}^{n} \sum_{j=1}^{n} c_i c_j k(\mathbf{x}_i, \mathbf{x}_j)$$

as new differentiable objective. As pointed out by Gieseke *et al.* [12], one can compute the objective value $F_{\lambda'}(\mathbf{c})$ in $\mathcal{O}(n^2)$ time for a given vector $\mathbf{c} \in \mathbb{R}^n$. This also holds true for the gradient $\nabla F_{\lambda'}(\mathbf{c})$, which can be written as

$$\nabla F_{\lambda'}(\mathbf{c}) = \mathbf{K}\mathbf{a} + 2\lambda\mathbf{K}\mathbf{c} \tag{5}$$

with $\mathbf{a} \in \mathbb{R}^n$ and coefficients defined as

$$a_i = \begin{cases} -\dfrac{1}{l} \cdot \dfrac{\exp(\gamma(1 - f(\mathbf{x}_i)y_i'))}{1 + \exp(\gamma(1 - f(\mathbf{x}_i)y_i'))} \cdot y_i' & \text{for } i \leq l \\[3mm] -\dfrac{6\lambda'}{u} \cdot \exp\left(-3(f(\mathbf{x}_i))^2\right) \cdot f(\mathbf{x}_i) & \text{for } i > l \end{cases},$$

To reduce the computational complexity and memory requirements, one can integrate kernel matrix approximation schemes such as the *subset of regressors* framework [18], which replaces (2) by $\hat{f}(\cdot) = \sum_{k=1}^{r} \hat{c}_{j_k} k(\mathbf{x}_{j_k}, \cdot) + b$, where $R =$

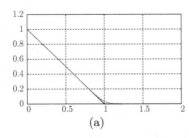 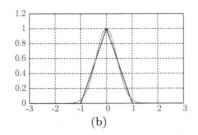

(a)   (b)

Fig. 2. Figure (a) shows the hinge loss $\mathcal{L}(y,t) = \max(0, 1 - yt)$ (black) and a differentiable surrogate $\mathcal{L}(y,t) = \frac{1}{\gamma}\log(1 + \exp(\gamma(1 - yt)))$ with $y = +1$ and $\gamma = 20$ (blue). Figure (b) shows the associated effective loss function $\mathcal{L}(t) = \max(0, 1 - |t|)$ (black) along with its differentiable surrogate $\mathcal{L}(t) = \exp(-st^2)$ with $s = 3$ (blue) (Color figure online).

$\{j_1, \ldots, j_r\} \subseteq \{1, \ldots, n\}$ is a subset of indices. This leads to a runtime of $\mathcal{O}(nr \cdot k_T)$ for computing all involved matrices and to $\mathcal{O}(nr)$ per function and gradient evaluation, where k_T depicts the runtime to conduct a single kernel computation $k(\mathbf{x}_i, \mathbf{x}_j)$ [12]. In the following, we consider this kernel matrix approximation scheme, where the non-approximation case can be obtained by setting $r = n$.

3.2   Algorithmic Framework

Following Gieseke *et al.* [12], we consider a particular instance of the quasi-Newton family of optimization tools, called the *L-BFGS* method [17]. As justified below, this variant is particularly well-suited for the aspired many-core implementation since the optimization-related matrices (approximations of the Hessian's inverse) are updated on the fly based on a small amount of past iterations. This will lead to a *linear* instead of a quadratic memory and time consumption for all steps that will be executed on the host system.

General Optimization Workflow. We consider a simple, yet effective way to take advantage of both the resources of the host system as well as the ones of the many-core device: First, all computationally intensive tasks are conducted on the GPU device (e.g., the computation of kernels matrices, matrix-vector multiplications, centering patterns in feature space). Note that all kernel matrices as well as auxiliary matrices for centering the data in feature space are only materialized on the GPU (only the labeled and unlabeled training patterns have to be copied to the device). Second, most of the linear-time operations are conducted via the CPU. The reason for this is that the overhead for invoking a GPU call is usually larger than the actual computation time on the host system.[2]

---

[2] A linear-time operation on, e.g., $n = 10000$ elements does not yield sufficient parallelism for a modern GPU with thousands of compute units.

Algorithm 1. GPU-QN-S^{3}VM

Require: A set $T_l = \{(\mathbf{x}_1, y_1'), \ldots, (\mathbf{x}_l, y_l')\}$ of labeled and a set $T_u = \{\mathbf{x}_{l+1}, \ldots, \mathbf{x}_n\}$ of unlabeled training patterns, model parameters λ', λ, and a sequence $0 = \alpha_1 < \alpha_2 < \ldots < \alpha_\tau$.

1: Copy training data from host to device   [host $\xrightarrow{\mathcal{O}(dn)}$ gpu]
2: Initialize all kernel matrices   [gpu: $\mathcal{O}(nr \cdot k_T)$ time]
3: Center data in feature space   [gpu: $\mathcal{O}(nr)$ time]
4:
5: Initialize $\mathbf{c} = \mathbf{0} \in \mathbb{R}^n$ [host: $\mathcal{O}(n)$ time]
6: **for** $i = 1$ **to** τ **do**
7:     $\mathbf{c}_0 = \mathbf{c}$ [host: $\mathcal{O}(n)$ time]
8:     Initialize $\mathbf{H}_0 = \delta\mathbf{I}$ [host: $\mathcal{O}(n)$ time]
9:     $j = 0$
10:     **while** termination criteria not fulfilled **do**
11:        Copy candidate solution $\mathbf{c}_j$ to device   [host $\xrightarrow{\mathcal{O}(n)}$ gpu]
12:        Compute $F_{\lambda' \cdot \alpha_i}(\mathbf{c}_j)$ and $\nabla F_{\lambda' \cdot \alpha_i}(\mathbf{c}_j)$ [gpu: $\mathcal{O}(nr)$ time; host: $\mathcal{O}(n)$ time]
13:        Copy $F_{\lambda' \cdot \alpha_i}(\mathbf{c}_j)$ and $\nabla F_{\lambda' \cdot \alpha_i}(\mathbf{c}_j)$ back to host   [host $\xleftarrow{\mathcal{O}(n)}$ gpu]
14:        Compute $\mathbf{H}_j$ on the fly (m rank-1 updates)   [host: $\mathcal{O}(n)$ time]
15:        Compute search direction $\mathbf{p}_j = -\mathbf{H}_j \nabla F_{\lambda' \cdot \alpha_i}(\mathbf{c}_j)$ [host: $\mathcal{O}(n)$ time]
16:        Update $\mathbf{c}_{j+1} = \mathbf{c}_j + \beta_j \mathbf{p}_j$ [host: $\mathcal{O}(n)$ time]
17:        $j = j + 1$
18:     **end while**
19:     $\mathbf{c} = \mathbf{c}_j$
20: **end for**

In general, the overall process consists of (1) invoking the outer optimization engine (which resorts to function and gradient calls) and (2) the function and gradient calls themselves. For the sake of exposition, we briefly sketch the involved steps as well as the runtimes and involved memory transfers between host and device, see Algorithm 1: In Steps 1–3, the training data (assuming $X = \mathbb{R}^d$) are copied from host to device and all involved matrices are materialized on the GPU (data centering is done by adapting the kernel matrices). The initial candidate solution $\mathbf{c}$ is initialized on the host system in Step 5. Afterwards, the local search takes place (Steps 6–20). Since $\alpha_0 = 0$, the first iteration corresponds to the initialization of $\mathbf{c}$ via a purely supervised model. Note that, for each iteration, only linear-time operations are conducted on the CPU and only a linear amount of data is transferred between host and device (Steps 8–18). The computationally intensive parts are conducted on the GPU (Step 12). Assuming m to be constant, all operations on the host system take linear time per iteration.[3]

GPGPU Implementation. The above framework resorts to function and gradient calls in each iteration, which are mostly conducted on the GPU. However, a series of linear-time operations is needed for both the objective and gradient calls (e.g., operations to avoid numerical instabilities [12]). Since these operations do not yield sufficient parallelism for today's many-core devices, we conduct these operations on the host system as well (the experimental evaluation confirms that the runtime for these steps is very small). For all matrix-vector

---

[3] Nocedal and Wright [17] point out that small values for the parameter m are usually sufficient to achieve a satisfying convergence rate in practice (e.g., $m = 3$ to $m = 50$).

multiplications, we resort to highly-tuned linear algebra packages available for GPUs (see Sect. 4). For the remaining computations, we make use to several manually designed GPU kernels. Due to lack of space, we only mention the key techniques applied:

(1) *Fusion of Operations*: The objective and gradient calls involve a series of matrix and array operations. To achieve a satisfying performance, it is crucial to fuse all these operations as much as possible such that unnecessary data movements from global memory of the GPU device to the compute units are avoided.

(2) *Memory Access:* For the remaining GPU kernels, all memory operations are conducted in a coalesced manner if possible. This is, in particular, important for various operations that yield one- or two-dimensional sums of arrays (e.g., for the data centering preprocessing step).

Again, despite the space needed for the training data, only $\mathcal{O}(n)$ additional space is allocated on the host system; all remaining arrays are initialized on the GPU.

4   Experiments

The potential and possible pitfalls of semi-supervised support vector machines have already been analyzed extensively in the literature [6,8,28]. We therefore focus on the computational speed-ups that can be achieved using modern GPUs.

4.1   Experimental Setup

We make use of commodity hardware for all experiments. In particular, the test system is a standard desktop computer with an `Intel(R) Core(TM) i7--3770` CPU running at 3.40 GHz (4 cores; 8 hardware threads), 16 GB RAM, and a `Nvidia GeForce GTX770` GPU having 1536 shader units and 4 GB RAM. The operating system is `Ubuntu 12.04` (64 Bit) with kernel `3.8.0--44` and CUDA 5.5 (graphics driver version 319.23).

Both the CPU-based implementation as well as its many-core analog are implemented in `Python` (version 2.7.6) using efficient linear algebra packages for computations involving matrices. For the CPU implementation, these computations are efficiently supported via the `NumPy` package (version 1.9.1), which, in turn, resorts to linear algebra routines (linked against `blas` and `lapack` libraries). For the many-core approach, we resort to manually designed `CUDA` [10] kernels that are invoked via `PyCUDA` [16] (version 2014.1) as well as to `scikit-cuda` (version 0.5.0), which provides `Python` interfaces to, e.g., `CUBLAS` [16]. The L-BFGS scheme is implemented via the `fmin_l_bfgs_b` procedure provided by the `SciPy` [15] package (version 0.15.1) with parameters $m = 25$, $pgtol = 0.0001$, and $factr = 10^{12}$ being fixed for all experiments.

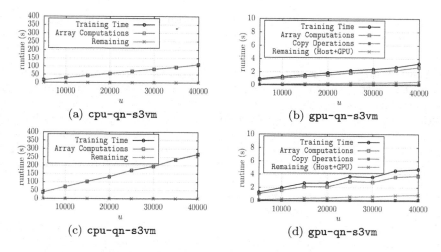

Fig. 3. Runtime analysis of `cpu-qn-s3vm` and `gpu-qn-s3vm` given the `mnist8m` (top row, classes 1 and 7) and the `epsilon` data set instance (bottom row); model parameters are fixed to $\lambda = 0.001$ and $\lambda' = 0.1$. Further, the number $l = 100$ labeled patterns are used, whereas the number u of unlabeled patterns is varied from 5000 to 40000.

We focus on a direct runtime comparison between the implementation described in Gieseke *et al.* [12] and its GPU variant, called `cpu-qn-s3vm` and `gpu-qn-s3vm`, respectively.[4] Note that we do not take other implementations into account since (a) the runtime performance of the CPU version has been evaluated extensively in the literature [12] and since (b) the practical runtime heavily depends on the involved parameters (such as stopping criteria). A meaningful comparison therefore has to take both the runtimes *and* the associated classification accuracies into account, which we leave over for future work.[5] For all comparisons, single floating point precision is used for both implementations.

We make use of both a linear and an RBF kernel function [20] and resort to dense data set instances for all runtime experiments. In particular, we consider subsets of the `mnist8m` and the `epsilon` data sets.[6] Further, we set $r = \min(5000, n)$ such that thousands of unlabeled patterns can be considered.

4.2   Results

For the sake of exposition, we focus on two data set instances; it is worth pointing out, however, that similar runtime results were observed for other data sets as

---

[4] Our CPU version is a manually tuned variant of the publicly available code [12] (version 0.1), which is by a factor of two faster than the original version.

[5] The most significant part of the runtime of `cpu-qn-s3vm` is spent on matrix operations (see below), which are efficiently supported by the `NumPy` package; we therefore do not expect significant performance gains using a pure, e.g., `C` implementation.

[6] Available at http://www.csie.ntu.edu.tw/~cjlin/libsvmtools/datasets/.

well in the course of the experimental evaluation (especially in case of larger data sets with more than 10,000 patterns).

Runtime Analysis. The optimization process of the GPU variant takes place both on the host system and on the many-core device. As described in Sect. 3, only linear-time operations are conducted on the host system, whereas the computational intensive parts are executed on the GPU. In Fig. 3, the runtimes of the different phases for both cpu-qn-s3vm and gpu-qn-s3vm are shown for a varying number u of unlabeled patterns on two data sets. The total runtime corresponds to the training time, which is, in turn, split up into (1) array computations, (2) remaining computations, and (3) copy operations between host and GPU (only for gpu-qn-s3vm). The most significant part of the runtime of cpu-qn-s3vm is spent on array computations.

It can be clearly seen that the GPU implementation can greatly speed up these computationally intensive parts. The analysis of gpu-qn-s3vm also shows that both the runtime for the copy operations as well as the one for the remaining computations on the host system are very small compared to the overall runtime of cpu-qn-s3vm (which is an important ingredient for achieving good speedups). Thus, one can basically separate the computational intensive parts (kernel matrix computation, fitness and gradient evaluations, ...) from the remaining parts of the optimization process. This is in line with the algorithmic framework depicted in Algorithm 1, since only linear-time operations have to be performed on the host system and since only $\mathcal{O}(n)$ data are moved from host to device and back per iteration.

Speed-Ups and Model Parameters. Semi-supervised support vector machines are sensitive w.r.t. to appropriate assignments for the involved model parameters. For this reason, an exhaustive tuning phase (based on, e.g., cross-validation and grid-search) is usually conducted, which requires significant computational resources. The GPU implementation can greatly reduce the practical runtime needed for this phase. To investigate the practical benefits of the GPU framework in this context, we consider the epsilon data

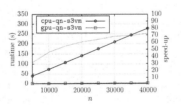

Fig. 4. Runtime comparison between the CPU implementation and its many-core variant for $\lambda = 1$, $\lambda' = 1$, $\sigma = 1 \cdot s$.

set and vary the model parameter assignments. In particular, we make use of an RBF kernel with kernel width σ, where we consider multiples of an approximate of the average distance s between all training patterns [12]. In Fig. 4, the runtimes and the induced speed-ups of gpu-qn-s3vm over cpu-qn-s3vm are provided for $\lambda = 1$, $\lambda' = 1$, and $\sigma = 1 \cdot s$. It can be seen that a valuable speed-up (green, dotted) of about 80 can be achieved (GPU vs. single CPU core). Similar results are obtained for other parameter assignments as well, see Fig. 5 (a single parameter assignment was changed for each plot).

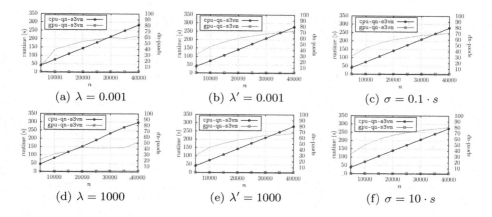

Fig. 5. Runtime comparisons between `cpu-qn-s3vm` and `gpu-qn-s3vm` for varying u and different model parameters (single CPU core vs. single GPU device).

5   Conclusions

Modern graphics processing units offer massive parallelism and can effectively reduce the practical running time in case the specific hardware properties are taken into account. We propose a massively-parallel implementation for semi-supervised support vector machines and show that practical speed-ups of about up to 80 can be achieved (GPU vs. single CPU core). Since standard desktop computers can nowadays easily accommodate up to four such GPU devices, one can significantly reduce the training time (grid search), even compared to powerful multi-core CPUs. To the best of our knowledge, the implementation provided is the first one that directly addresses the optimization task induced by semi-supervised support vector machines. We expect this implementation to be useful for real-world applications as well as for future extensions of this learning concept (e.g., stability analysis based on many models).

Acknowledgements. The author would like to thank the anonymous reviewers for their careful reading and detailed comments. This work has been supported by the *Radboud Excellence Initiative* of the Radboud University Nijmegen. The author also would like to thank *NVIDIA* for generous hardware donations.

References

1. Adankon, M., Cheriet, M., Biem, A.: Semisupervised least squares support vector machine. IEEE Trans. Neural Netw. **20**(12), 1858–1870 (2009)
2. Bennett, K.P., Demiriz, A.: Semi-supervised support vector machines. In: Advances in Neural Information Processing Systems, vol. 11, pp. 368–374. MIT Press (1999)
3. Bie, T.D., Cristianini, N.: Convex methods for transduction. In: Advances in Neural Information Proceedings Systems, vol. 16, pp. 73–80. MIT Press (2004)

4. Boser, B.E., Guyon, I.M., Vapnik, V.N.: A training algorithm for optimal margin classifiers. In: Haussler, D. (ed.) Proceedings 5th Annual Workshop on Computational Learning Theory, pp. 144–152. ACM, New York (1992)
5. Catanzaro, B., Sundaram, N., Keutzer, K.: Fast support vector machine training and classification on graphics processors. In: Proceedings of the 25th International Conference on Machine Learning, pp. 104–111. ACM, New York (2008)
6. Chapelle, O., Schölkopf, B., Zien, A. (eds.): Semi-Supervised Learning. MIT Press, Cambridge (2006)
7. Chapelle, O., Sindhwani, V., Keerthi, S.S.: Branch and bound for semi-supervised support vector machines. In: Advances in Neural Information Processing Systems 19, pp. 217–224. MIT Press (2007)
8. Chapelle, O., Sindhwani, V., Keerthi, S.S.: Optimization techniques for semi-supervised support vector machines. J. Mach. Learn. Res. **9**, 203–233 (2008)
9. Chapelle, O., Zien, A.: Semi-supervised classification by low density separation. In: Proceedings of the 10th International Workshop on Artificial Intelligence and Statistics, pp. 57–64 (2005)
10. Cheng, J., Grossman, M., McKercher, T.: Professional CUDA C Programming. Wiley, New Jersey (2014)
11. Coates, A., Huval, B., Wang, T., Wu, D.J., Catanzaro, B.C., Ng, A.Y.: Deep learning with COTS HPC systems. In: Proceedings of the 30th International Conference on Machine Learning, pp. 1337–1345. JMLR.org (2013)
12. Gieseke, F., Airola, A., Pahikkala, T., Kramer, O.: Fast and simple gradient-based optimization for semi-supervised support vector machines. Neurocomputing **123**, 23–32 (2014)
13. Gieseke, F., Heinermann, J., Oancea, C., Igel, C.: Buffer k-d trees: processing massive nearest neighbor queries on GPUs. In: Proceedings of the 31st International Conference on Machine Learning, JMLR W&CP, vol. 32, pp. 172–180. JMLR.org (2014)
14. Joachims, T.: Transductive inference for text classification using support vector machines. In: Proceedings of the International Conference on Machine Learning, pp. 200–209 (1999)
15. Jones, E., Oliphant, T., Peterson, P., et al.: SciPy: open source scientific tools for Python (2001–2015). http://www.scipy.org/
16. Klöckner, A., Pinto, N., Lee, Y., Catanzaro, B., Ivanov, P., Fasih, A.: PyCUDA and PyOpenCL: a scripting-based approach to GPU run-time code generation. Parallel Comput. **38**(3), 157–174 (2012)
17. Nocedal, J., Wright, S.J.: Numerical Optimization, 1st edn. Springer, New York (2000)
18. Rifkin, R., Yeo, G., Poggio, T.: Regularized least-squares classification. In: Advances in Learning Theory: Methods, Models and Applications. IOS Press (2003)
19. Schölkopf, B., Herbrich, R., Smola, A.J.: A Generalized Representer Theorem. In: Helmbold, D.P., Williamson, B. (eds.) COLT 2001 and EuroCOLT 2001. LNCS (LNAI), vol. 2111, pp. 416–426. Springer, Heidelberg (2001)
20. Schölkopf, B., Smola, A.J.: Learning with Kernels: Support Vector Machines, Regularization, Optimization, and Beyond. MIT Press, Cambridge (2001)
21. Sindhwani, V., Keerthi, S.S.: Large scale semi-supervised linear SVMs. In: Proceedings of the 29th Annual International ACM SIGIR Conference on Research and Development in Information Retrieval, pp. 477–484. ACM, New York (2006)
22. Steinwart, I., Christmann, A.: Support Vector Machines. Springer, New York (2008)

23. Vapnik, V., Sterin, A.: On structural risk minimization or overall risk in a problem of pattern recognition. Autom. Remote Control **10**(3), 1495–1503 (1977)
24. Wen, Z., Zhang, R., Ramamohanarao, K.: Enabling precision/recall preferences for semi-supervised SVM training. In: Proceedings of the 23rd ACM International Conference on Information and Knowledge Management, pp. 421–430. ACM, New York (2014)
25. Wen, Z., Zhang, R., Ramamohanarao, K., Qi, J., Taylor, K.: Mascot: fast and highly scalable SVM cross-validation using GPUs and SSDs. In: Proceedings of the 2014 IEEE International Conference on Data Mining (2014)
26. Xu, L., Schuurmans, D.: Unsupervised and semi-supervised multi-class support vector machines. In: Proceedings of the National Conference on Artificial intelligence, pp. 904–910 (2005)
27. Zhang, T., Oles, F.J.: Text categorization based on regularized linear classification methods. Inf. Retr. Boston **4**, 5–31 (2001)
28. Zhu, X., Goldberg, A.B.: Introduction to Semi-Supervised Learning. Morgan and Claypool, San Rafael (2009)

Intent Recognition in a Simulated Maritime Multi-agent Domain

Mohammad Taghi Saffar[(✉)], Mircea Nicolescu, Monica Nicolescu,
Daniel Bigelow, Christopher Ballinger, and Sushil Louis

Computer Science and Engineering Department, University of Nevada Reno, Reno, NV, USA
msaffar@unr.edu, bigelowdc@gmail.com
{mircea,monica,caballinger,sushil}@cse.unr.edu

Abstract. Intent recognition is the process of determining the action an agent is about to take, given a sequence of past actions. In this paper, we propose a method for recognizing intentions in highly populated multi-agent environments. Low-level intentions, representing basic activities, are detected through a novel formulation of Hidden Markov Models with perspective-taking capabilities. Higher level intentions, involving multiple agents, are detected with a distributed architecture that uses activation spreading between nodes to detect the most likely intention of the agents. The solution we propose brings the following main contributions: (i) it enables early recognition of intentions before they are being realized, (ii) it has real-time performance capabilities, and (iii) it can detect both single agent as well as joint intentions of a group of agents. We validate our framework in an open source naval ship simulator, the context of recognizing threatening intentions against naval ships. Our results show that our system is able to detect intentions early and with high accuracy.

Keywords: Intent recognition · Scene understanding · Action recognition · Multi-agent system · Activation spreading · HMM

1 Introduction

Plan recognition is the process of selecting the most suitable plan that an agent is undertaking based on a sequence of observed atomic actions [1]. Usually a plan is formally defined as a set of low-level actions with a partial order relation defined to represent ordering between these low-level actions, and the observable evidence for a plan is a sub-sequence of one of the many different ways of linearization of the low-level actions which satisfy the ordering. The body of work in this area like [2, 3] has little prediction power in the sense that it is required to observe the whole plan or many low-level actions to robustly detect the underlying plan. Another important shortcoming is that previous approaches like [4, 5] do not consider (soft) real-time constraints that are inherent to the

This work has been supported by the Office of Naval Research, under grant number N00014-09-1-1121.

P. Pardalos et al. (Eds.): MOD 2015, LNCS 9432, pp. 158–170, 2015.
DOI: 10.1007/978-3-319-27926-8_14

nature of applications such as human robot interaction. Another limitation of current systems is that they cannot detect collective plans effectively.

In this paper we propose a new distributed hierarchical architecture to detect individual or collective intentions in a crowded simulated multi-agent system. Our approach brings several key contributions: (i) the system has predictive power, which means it can detect intentions well before they are being realized, (ii) the system works in real-time, processing data while it is being gathered and (iii) the system can detect intentions of individual agents towards other agents, as well as joint intentions. The basic idea of our method is that the hierarchical structure of activities is represented as an interconnected network of nodes representing various actions. The observation of certain basic actions increases the strength of corresponding nodes, which begin to send activation to nodes that represent related activities. Activities that accumulate the highest level of activation are considered most likely to be performed by the agent. Nodes may correspond to either *low-level* (one-on-one agent) intentions or *high-level* (joint) intentions. Low-level intentions are detected using a new formulation of Hidden Markov Models (HMM), which are implemented to run in parallel on GPU with CUDA technology [6] for higher speed. To detect joint intentions we use a distributed network of connected nodes, where the lowest level nodes get their activation values from HMMs and higher level nodes receive activation from lower level nodes.

The rest of this paper is organized as follows. In the next section a brief overview of previous research is presented. Section 3 introduces the infrastructure of the proposed approach, which we later use to implement and evaluate our intent recognition system. The following section introduces our formulation for low-level intent recognition based on HMMs. Section 5 describes our distributed activation spreading network (ASN) to detect multi-agent intentions followed by experimental results in Sect. 6. Finally the last section provides conclusions and future directions to extend this work.

2   Previous Work

As stated in [7], it is not enough to simply recognize the intentions of each individual agent towards others. To obtain a good prediction of joint intents, it is also necessary to infer the shared plan of the agents as a group. [8, 9] utilize HMMs for intent recognition, however the problem domain has only a few number of agents. In [10], Banerjee *et al.* present a formalization of multi-agent plan recognition by representing a plan library as a set of matrices and observation of actions as another matrix. The matching in this formalism is NP-Complete and cannot handle goal abandonment or plan interleaving. In [4], Zhuo *et al.* focus on the problem of partial observability. Using the formulation in [10], they assume that some actions are unknown and try to marginalize on these unknown actions while finding the best match in the plan base. This work still cannot handle plan interleaving and does not scale well to large plan libraries. In [11], the authors proposed a theoretical framework with a combined top-down and bottom-up approach. In the top-down approach the system reasons about global goals and their decomposition into plans. In bottom-up the system observes atomic actions and merges them into plan segments. No experimental evaluations were provided in this work. Some new approaches in plan recognition use dynamic networks of connected nodes such as Dynamic Neural Fields [12] or semi-Markov decision process graphs [13] to represent tasks for applications like active learning, intent inference and joint intention understanding. Dynamic Neural Fields (DNF) [14, 15] have first been introduced as a simplified mathematical model for neural processing based on recurrent interactions, which neglects the temporal dynamics of individual neurons and uses average firing rate. The main idea behind DNF-models for intent representation is that a distributed network of reciprocally connected neurons forms a complex dynamical system, which can represent and process intent-related information in its activation patterns.

3   Infrastructure

We evaluate our approach for multi-agent intent recognition in the context of detecting threatening intentions against Navy ships, using an open-source naval ship simulator [16] as the base for our simulation framework. We built a fully functioning test-bed for intent recognition systems on top of this simulator. The open source naval simulator [16] is very appropriate for our problem, as it supports the simulation of multiple ships, operates in real-time, and is deterministic (which allows for precise reproduction of experiments). A snapshot of the simulation environment is shown in Fig. 1(a).

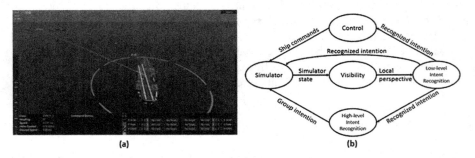

Fig. 1. (a) Screen-shot of the simulator environment. (b) Intent recognition system architecture

For better modularity and for decoupling the intent recognition system from the simulator, we created separate processes for controlling the simulation and for intent recognition. These two components would communicate via the Robot Operating System (ROS) [17], using its publish/subscribe approach. To make the experiments realistic we implemented a visibility module to filter out any information that is hidden from the viewpoint of an entity in the simulator (ships, oil platforms, airplanes, helicopters, etc.). This module considers any landscape in the line of sight between two entities and publishes local state vectors for each pair of entities. The state vector contains the following local information: the distance between the entities (*dist*), the angle of line connecting them (*cross angle*), the direction (*orientation*) and speed of movement for each entity, and finally a visibility flag showing if the second entity is visible from the first entity's viewpoint. Finally, another component was added to the simulator for visualizing detected intentions. The components and their connections are shown in Fig. 1(b).

4 Low-Level Intent Recognition

Following previous work in using HMMs for intent recognition [8, 9], our HMM formalism is based on the idea of *perspective taking*. As shown in Fig. 1(b), the input to this layer is simply the local perspective state generated by the visibility module and the output is the recognized intention for each pair of entities. We use HMMs to capture pairwise interactions between entities. An intention that an agent can have towards any other agent is represented as a set of Hidden Markov Models. An HMM is a probabilistic method to model a Markov process with unobserved states, and consists of a set of hidden states, a probability distribution on transitions between hidden states (transition probability), a set of visible or observable states, and a probability distribution on observing visible states given that the system is in a particular hidden state (emission probability). In our particular low-level intent recognition problem, each possible low-level intention is modeled as a separate set of HMMs. In each HMM, we are trying to recognize the intention of only a single entity (actor) towards another entity (target). We denote the intention of actor A towards target T as $I_A^T \in \bigcup_{k=1}^{m} i_k$ in which i_k represents the kth low-level intention in our system and m is the total number of low-level intention types. Any low-level intention i_k has a set of corresponding HMMs $M_k = \bigcup_{j=1}^{s} m_k^j$ that have different number of hidden states ranging from 1 to s hidden states.

Previous work [11] suggests that to accurately model an intention as a HMM, we need to have a meaningful interpretation of hidden states such as sub-activities of the particular intention being modeled. This break-down typically requires expert knowledge about the domain at hand, which is not always available. In addition, in many domains it is possible to have multiple ways of accomplishing an intention, which is precluded if we allow only a single model for each intention. Following these observations we therefore employ a set of HMMs M_k for each low-level intention i_k in our system. These models have different numbers of hidden states. To detect the intention of an actor towards a target, we use cross-validation to select the best model for each intention.

For our particular naval ship domain we are interested in detecting the following 5 different low-level intentions: *approach* (one boat heads directly to another), *pass* (one boat passes another in opposite directions), *overtake* (one boat passes another in the same direction), *follow* (one boat maintains the same distance and heading with respect to another) and *intercept* (one boat heads toward a point of another boat's trajectory). A schematic representation of these intentions is shown in Fig. 2(a). Formally the set of observable states is a set of tuples of the form $T = \langle d, \alpha, o_A, o_T, \delta \rangle$ in which $d \in \{+, -, =\}$ is the change in distance between actor and target, $\alpha \in \{+, -, =\}$ is the change in the angle between the actor's current direction of movement and the straight line from actor towards target,

$o_A, o_T \in \{facing, not\ facing\}$ are the orientations of actor towards target and orientation of target towards actor respectively, and finally $\delta \in \{the\ same, not\ the\ same\}$ is the difference in headings for the actor and the target. Figure 2(b) shows the observable states defined above. The set of all possible tuples T forms the alphabet of observable states and contains a total of 72 different tuples.

For each one of the 5 intentions, we created 4 different models with different number of hidden states ranging from 1 to 4. We chose 4 because we believe that the low-level intentions we are trying to detect at this stage are not complex enough to need more than 4 hidden states. To train the HMM models, we generated 20 different two-boats examples for each intention in our simulator, each with randomized starting boat configurations. We then computed observable variables for each frame of each generated example, and trained our models with the Baum-Welch algorithm [18].

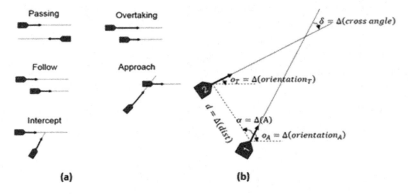

Fig. 2. (a) Low-level intentions in naval ship domain. (b) Local state vector for a sample configuration of entities (Observable states are changes in these measurements not their absolute value)

Once the HMMs for each intention have been trained, recognizing intent becomes a problem of pattern classification. At runtime, we calculate the observable variables for each agent in a scene with respect to every other agent, and we determine the model that is most likely to have generated a given sequence of observables with the forward algorithm [19], which, given an HMM and a sequence of observable variables, returns the log-likelihood of the given HMM generating that particular sequence. We compute this likelihood for each trained model and choose the one with the highest probability.

The approach to intent recognition presented so far is shown to work quite well in the work presented in [8, 9]. However, it is subject to some constraining assumptions. First, while the algorithm will work in its current form for scenarios involving multiple agents, the forward algorithm is computationally complex and the intent recognition process cannot scale to scenarios involving many agents while still performing in real-time. Since this approach is based on the idea of perspective taking, for n number of entities in the environment we need to detect $n^2 - n$ number of intentions. If we have m number of low-level intentions and for each low-level intention we have s different

HMMs, then for detecting each intention we need to apply the forward algorithm for $m \times s$ HMMs, which means that for each frame we have to run the forward algorithm $m \times s \times (n^2 - n)$ times, which becomes infeasible for real-time intent recognition. Second, the HMM-based approach to intent recognition assumes that each agent's intention towards each other agent is completely independent of all other intentions. While this simplifying assumption is not a problem for low-level intentions such as *passing*, *overtaking*, or *approaching*, it presents difficulties when attempting to model intentions that involve coordinated efforts among multiple agents.

In our early experiments with the ship simulator, we discovered that without parallelization, the HMM method tends to stop performing in real-time when more than 5 agents are present in the scenario. However we can take advantage of the independence assumption and parallelize each step of our algorithm. We calculate the observable variables independently and in parallel for each pair of agents in the scene, using a CUDA kernel. Once each sequence of observable variables has been calculated, we use the parallel implementation of the forward algorithm presented in [20] to calculate the log-likelihood for each intention, for each pair of agents simultaneously. Once this has been done, another CUDA kernel is used to choose the most likely intention for each pair of agents (or no intention, if all likelihoods are below a certain threshold). This parallelization significantly increases the speed of the intent recognition process.

5   High-Level Intent Recognition

As discussed in Sect. 2, the general approach to multi-agent plan recognition defined by [10] is to maintain a library of joint plans and search for plans that contain the list of observed actions as a subsequence. In the naval ship domain, a joint plan for creating a *Blockade* might involve at least three agents performing an *intercept*. The problem with using a plan library is twofold. First, plan libraries might become quite large, slowing the search process, which becomes an issue if real-time computation is desired. Second, goal abandonment or plan interleaving is not easily supported. In this paper we propose to address these problems by using activation spreading in a hierarchical intent network for the task of high-level intent recognition. An ASN can be represented as a set of neurons that are connected to each other via synaptic connections. Mathematically, an ASN is a directed graph $G = \langle V, E \rangle$ in which $V = \{v_1, \dots, v_n\}$ is a finite set of vertices (neurons) and $E = \{e_1, \dots, e_k\}$ is a set of directed edges (synapses) connecting two vertices. For simplicity, we use the e_{ij} notation to represent an edge from v_i to v_j. Each vertex v_i has an activation value A_i and each edge e_{ij} has a weight w_{ij}. There is also a firing threshold F and a decay factor D associated with the network. Our basic approach for activation spreading inference is shown in Fig. 3.

```
for i = 1..n
  A_i = 0
set A_i = x; x > F for some origin nodes
for each i so that A_i > F and v_i is unfired
  for each j so that e_ij ∈ E
    A_j = max(A_j + (A_i * w_ij * D), 0)
  repeat
repeat
```

Fig. 3. Our basic activation spreading inference algorithm

The activation spreading network allows us to encode complex, possibly hierarchically structured intentions, through the topology of the network. In the network, low-level nodes correspond to the low-level intentions recognized by the HMM approach discussed in Sect. 4. We create one low-level node for each pair of agents and each low-level intention that can occur between them. In our work, this means that for each pair of nodes (i, j), we will have 5 low-level nodes associated with the five different intentions. Nodes that represent higher-level intentions receive activations from the low-level nodes or other high-level intentions. For simplicity we use 1 as the weights for the connecting edges, the decay factor D is set to 0.95 and the firing threshold F is set to 0. For example, for the *Blockade* example, we would connect all the low-level nodes corresponding to the *intercept* intention (from all entities to a given target) to a higher-level node, representing *Blockade*. It is also relatively simple to encode multiple intentions in a single network as shown in Fig. 4. To recognize high-level intentions we run the algorithm from Fig. 3 by running it in a continuous loop, where at each step activation is set on the low-level nodes (based on the maximum likelihood selection of forward probabilities of HMMs with different number of hidden states for each low-level intention at this time-step) and propagated through the graph as described above. At each time step activation values decay based on the following formula. $A_i = A_i \times D$. Activation will accumulate in the various nodes and detecting an intention can be done by checking that the activation level of a node is above a certain threshold.

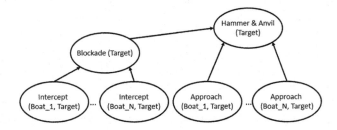

Fig. 4. Activation network to detect blockade and hammer and anvil intentions

Encoding intentions in activation networks addresses the problem of maintaining a library of plans to recognize, as well as the problem of performing an exhaustive search of that plan library. Using a topology-based approach to encoding intentions, it is possible to add new intentions without a significant increase in the size of the network.

In our method, we simply need to monitor the activation levels of the nodes corresponding to high-level intentions to determine if such an intention is likely. This also solves the problem of simultaneous execution of plans, as the structure of the network will encode all possible recognizable intentions, and activation will spread appropriately from any firing low-level nodes. However, it is still necessary to encode each high-level intention by hand, and specify the topology of the network accordingly. In the naval ship domain, it is very desirable to also assign a *general threat level* to the state of the scene, in addition to particular high-level intentions. To do that we add a *threat level* node to our activation network for each target agent and we connect it to all hostile intentions (low-level intentions like *intercept, approach*, etc. and high-level intentions like *Blockade* and *Hammer and Anvil*) towards that target. The degree of threat for each agent will then be proportional to the activation level of its corresponding *Threat Level* node.

6 Experimental Results

To test the baseline accuracy of the HMM-based approach to low-level intent recognition, we trained models for 5 different intentions: *approach, pass, overtake, follow*, and *intercept*. We then generated 200 two-agent scenarios using the simulation system, resulting in 40 test scenarios for each of the individual intentions. All of our statistics represent the average performance of the intent recognition system over the 40 relevant scenarios. For a quantitative analysis of the intent recognition system, we used three standard measures for evaluating HMMs [21]: *Accuracy rate* is the proportion of test scenarios for which the final recognized intention was correct. *Average early detection* is $\frac{1}{N} \sum_{i=1}^{N} \frac{t_i^*}{T_i}$ where N is the number of test scenarios, T_i is the total runtime of test scenario i, and t_i^* is the earliest time at which the correct intention was recognized consistently until the end of scenario i. *Average correct duration* is $\frac{1}{N} \sum_{i=1}^{N} \frac{C_i}{T_i}$ where C_i is the total time during which the correct intention was recognized for scenario i.

For reliable intent recognition, we want the accuracy rate and the average correct duration to be close to 100 %, and the average early detection to be close to 0 %. The results of our experiments are shown in Table 1. As can be seen, the system is able to detect all intentions correctly and for most of the simulation time. It also performs well in terms of early detection for the *approach, intercept*, and *follow* behaviors, recognizing them consistently within the first 12 % of the completion of the action.

The poor performance of *pass* and *overtake* intentions on early detection rate is mainly because of the lack of distinguishing observable variables in our HMM-based module. This is especially true when the agents have come close to each other. The only difference between *pass* and *overtake* at this point would be *change in angle from target to actor* which is likely not enough for a distinct classification.

Table 1. Performance of low-level intent recognition system

Intention	Accuracy (%)	Average early detection (%)	Average correct duration (%)
Approach	100	8.95	90.9
Pass	100	68.0	96.5
Overtake	100	56.8	64.6
Follow	100	1.92	99.3
Intercept	100	11.3	88.8

To evaluate the effectiveness of parallelizing the intent recognition process, we implemented both serial and parallel versions of the HMM-based intent recognition algorithm and ran them on 17 scenarios containing varying numbers of agents. We then recorded the average frame rate over each scene. The performance of the serial implementation quickly drops below an acceptable frame rate for real-time systems, but the parallel implementation maintains a speed of about 40 frames per second.

To evaluate the performance of our proposed approach for multi-agent intent recognition, we first need to create more complex scenarios involving multiple agents. To this end, we created 7 different scenarios in our simulator in which naval vessels needed to recognize potentially hostile intentions (*approach* and *intercept*) as enemy ships maneuvered to attack. In all of the scenarios there are high-value target ships (vessels, aircraft carriers and oil platforms) which could be the target of coordinated attacks.

In scenario 1 (16 ships in total), a convoy of naval vessels is attempting to traverse the straits. As they do so, a pair of other ships passes close by to the convoy, creating a distraction. Shortly after this, more ships break free of a group of trawlers, and begin a suicide run towards the convoy in an attempt to damage it.

Scenario 2 (17 ships) is constructed similarly: a group of naval vessels is attempting to exit the harbor. As they travel towards the harbor mouth, a ship that had been behaving like a fishing boat comes about and begins a run towards the naval vessels.

In scenario 3 (7 ships), the naval vessels are traveling through a channel, while passing some container ships. As this happens, a small boat accelerates to a position behind one of the container ships and hides there until it is abreast of the navy vessels. At this point, it breaks from hiding and attacks the navy vessels.

In scenario 4 (14 ships, 1 oil platform and a helicopter), two naval vessels are patrolling around an oil platform. There is a helicopter on the platform. A small boat starts a suicide run towards one of these vessels to create a diversion and at the same time another boat breaks free from a fishing boat swarm to attack the oil platform.

In scenario 5 (an aircraft carrier, a jet fighter and 16 ships), an aircraft carrier and another naval vessel are moving in a congested area with big tankers and fishing boats. A boat hides behind a tanker waiting for the carrier to get close to attack it. Another boat starts a suicide run towards the carrier from the other side at the same time.

Scenario 6 and 7 are examples of scenarios in which more complex intentions (in which agents must cooperate to perform a task) may occur. In scenario 6 (4 ships), a naval vessel is attempting to pass through a channel when some other ships emerge from hiding behind nearby islands and intercept it, forming a blockade. Scenario 7 (7 ships) begins similarly, but once the channel is blocked by the blockading ships, an additional pair of ships approaches from behind in order to attack and cut off its escape.

In performing a quantitative analysis of the more complex scenarios, we first define key intentions as those intentions that make up actions that are threatening to the naval vessels in the scene. The accuracy rate for our system is 100 % for key intentions in complex scenarios, which means all key intentions were correctly recognized in all complex scenarios. In addition, it can be seen in Table 2 that the early detection rate for the key intentions is below 9 %. In every case, the key intentions were recognized almost as soon as they began. It is worth mentioning that we have the ground truth for intentions in each of the scenarios. The total time T_i that a particular intention is active is the total time for that particular intention to be active in the ground truth. The system is able to detect the intention with the highest likelihood without any pre-segmentation of the observation trace: as new behaviors are performed in the scenario, the system is capable of transitioning from one detected intention to another. We only use the ground truth information for the qualitative evaluation.

Table 2. HMM-based intent recognition in complex scenarios

Scenario	Key intentions	Average early detection ratio for key intentions (%)
1	approach, intercept	1.50
2	approach, intercept	2.31
3	approach, overtake	3.03
4	Intercept	0.00
5	approach, intercept	5.04
6	approach, intercept	4.23
7	approach, overtake, intercept	8.40

In order to quantitatively evaluate our activation network based approach to high-level intent recognition, we designed two scenarios, scenario 6 and 7, in which cooperative intentions were taking place. Table 3 shows the results for each of the three intentions we wanted to recognize. Blockade 1 refers to the blockade executed in the blockade scenario, and blockade 2 refers to the blockade executed as the first step of the hammer and anvil scenario. As shown in the table, the activation network based approach performed very well for each intention. All of them were classified correctly, therefore the accuracy rate of our ASN-based approach to multi-agent intent recognition is 100 % and each was recognized within the first 6 % of the scene.

Table 3. ASN-based intent recognition

Scenario	Early detection rate (%)
Blockade 1	3.12
Blockade 2	3.10
Hammer and anvil	5.23

Figure 5 shows activation levels for nodes in our ASN corresponding to high-level intentions, the threat level and the detection threshold values we are using to detect high-level intentions. It is important to note that the absolute value as thresholds for detecting hammer and anvil is actually equal to the initial threshold value for that intention plus any positive difference between the activation level of blockade and the blockade threshold. This is because hammer and anvil is placed higher in the topology of the network compared to blockade and the weight of their connection is 1, therefore the minimum activation level for hammer and anvil is always greater than or equal to the blockade activation level. If we used a fixed threshold we might wrongly detect a hammer and anvil if the activation level of the blockade node becomes greater than hammer and anvil fixed threshold. It is difficult to perform a quantitative analysis of the threat level indicator, due to the ambiguity inherent in defining a "level of threat" for any given scenario. However, it can be seen in Fig. 5 that the activation level of the *threat level* node does behave as expected. That is, as the number of hostile low-level intentions increases, so does the threat level.

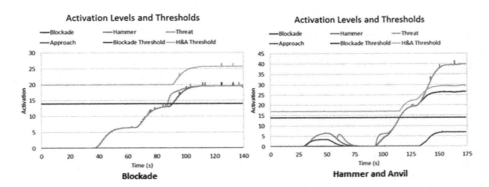

Fig. 5. Activation levels for the blockade and hammer and anvil in scenarios 6 and 7

7   Conclusion and Future Work

In this paper we presented a novel approach to multi-agent intent recognition for the real-time domain of naval ships. The proposed approach consists of two components - for detecting low-level single actor intentions and for recognizing high-level multi-agent (joint) intentions. The low-level intent recognition system is based on the idea of perspective taking for intent recognition, by utilizing Hidden Markov Models (HMMs) with local perspective observable states. In order to be suitable for real-time processing, this part of the system is implemented by parallelizing different parts of the recognition algorithm as CUDA kernels. We also showed that the HMM-based approach is not enough to represent and recognize joint plans and intentions, and for this purpose we proposed using Activation Spreading Networks (ASNs). We showed how ASNs can be used to encode high-level intentions and how the activation spreading algorithm can be modified for intent recognition. We conducted several experiments to evaluate the performance of our approach in the naval ship simulator environment. Our experimental results show that the proposed approach is able to detect intentions reliably under different circumstances, while also being able to detect these intentions very early.

As future work, we plan to extend this approach by adding learning capabilities in order to automatically generate the activation spreading network from a training set, rather than manually encoding its topology. Another shortcoming of the ASN approach is that in its current form, it is not able to represent any sequential constraints between actions in different plans. We will try to solve this issue by introducing different types of nodes and edges for the activation network. We will also investigate ways to handle missing information, which is inevitable in real world problems because of partial observability of the environment or failing sensors.

References

1. Kautz, H.A., Allen, J.F.: Generalized plan recognition. AAAI **86**, 32–37 (1986)
2. Geib, C.W., Goldman, R.P.: A probabilistic plan recognition algorithm based on plan tree grammars. Artif. Intell. **173**(11), 1101–1132 (2009)
3. Levine, S.J., Williams, B.C.: Concurrent plan recognition and execution for human-robot teams. In: Twenty-Fourth International Conference on Automated Planning and Scheduling (2014)
4. Zhuo, H.H., Li, L.: Multi-agent plan recognition with partial team traces and plan libraries. IJCAI **22**(1), 484 (2011)
5. Zhuo, H.H., Yang, Q., Kambhampati, S.: Action-model based multi-agent plan recognition. In: Advances in Neural Information Processing Systems, pp. 368–376 (2012)
6. Luebke, D.: CUDA: Scalable parallel programming for high-performance scientific computing. In: 5th IEEE International Symposium on Biomedical Imaging: From Nano to Macro, ISBI 2008, pp. 836–838 (2008)
7. Demiris, Y.: Prediction of intent in robotics and multi-agent systems. Cogn. Process. **8**(3), 151–158 (2007)
8. Kelley, R., King, C., Tavakkoli, A., Nicolescu, M., Nicolescu, M., Bebis, G.: An architecture for understanding intent using a novel hidden markov formulation. Int. J. Humanoid Robot. **5**(2), 203–224 (2008)
9. Kelley, R., Tavakkoli, A., King, C., Nicolescu, M., Nicolescu, M., Bebis, G.: Understanding human intentions via hidden markov models in autonomous mobile robots. In: The 3rd ACM/IEEE international conference on Human robot interaction, pp. 367–374 (2008)
10. Banerjee, B., Kraemer, L., Lyle, J.: Multi-agent plan recognition: formalization and algorithms. In: AAAI (2010)

11. Azarewicz, J., Fala, G., Heithecker, C.: Template-based multi-agent plan recognition for tactical situation assessment. In: Artificial Intelligence Applications, pp. 247–254 (1989)
12. Erlhagen, W., Mukovskiy, A., Bicho, E.: A dynamic model for action understanding and goal-directed imitation. Brain Res. **1083**(1), 174–188 (2006)
13. Hayes, B., Scassellati, B.: Discovering task constraints through observation and active learning. In: IROS (2014)
14. Wilson, H.R., Cowan, J.D.: A mathematical theory of the functional dynamics of cortical and thalamic nervous tissue. Kybernetik **13**(2), 55–80 (1973)
15. Amari, S.: Dynamics of pattern formation in lateral-inhibition type neural fields. Biol. Cybern. **27**(2), 77–87 (1977)
16. Nicolescu, M., Leigh, R., Olenderski, A., Louis, S., Dascalu, S., Miles, C., Quiroz, J., Aleson, R.: A training simulation system with realistic autonomous ship control. Comput. Intell. **23**(4), 497–516 (2007)
17. Quigley, M., Conley, K., Gerkey, B., Faust, J., Foote, T., Leibs, J., Wheeler, R., Ng, A.Y.: ROS: an open-source robot operating system. In: ICRA Workshop on Open Source Software (2009)
18. Baum, L.E., Petrie, T., Soules, G., Weiss, N.: A maximization technique occurring in the statistical analysis of probabilistic functions of Markov chains. Ann. Math. Stat. **41**, 164–171 (1970)
19. Rabiner, L.: A tutorial on hidden Markov models and selected applications in speech recognition. Proc. IEEE **77**(2), 257–286 (1989)
20. Liu, C.: cuHMM: a CUDA Implementation of Hidden Markov Model Training and Classification. Johns Hopkins University, Baltimore (2009)
21. Nguyen, N.T., Phung, D.Q., Venkatesh, S., Bui, H.: Learning and detecting activities from movement trajectories using the hierarchical hidden Markov model. In: CVPR, pp. 955–960 (2005)

An Adaptive Classification Framework for Unsupervised Model Updating in Nonstationary Environments

Piero Conca[1]([✉]), Jon Timmis[1], Rogério de Lemos[2,3], Simon Forrest[4], and Heather McCracken[4]

[1] The University of York, York, UK
pieroconca@gmail.com, jon.timmis@york.ac.uk
[2] University of Kent, Canterbury, UK
[3] CISUC, University of Coimbra, Coimbra, Portugal
[4] NCR Labs, Dundee, UK

Abstract. This paper introduces an adaptive framework that makes use of ensemble classification and self-training to maintain high classification performance in datasets affected by concept drift without the aid of external supervision to update the model of a classifier. The updating of the model of the framework is triggered by a mechanism that infers the presence of concept drift based on the analysis of the differences between the outputs of the different classifiers. In order to evaluate the performance of the proposed algorithm, comparisons were made with a set of unsupervised classification techniques and drift detection techniques. The results show that the framework is able to react more promptly to performance degradation than the existing methods and this leads to increased classification accuracy. In addition, the framework stores a smaller amount of instances with respect to a single-classifier approach.

1 Introduction

Due to the dynamic nature of the world, there are several real-world applications in which the distribution of the data collected from a system is expected to change. This phenomenon, known as *concept drift*, may degrade the performance of a classifier whose model is not updated according to the distribution of the changing data [15].

Several approaches have been developed to cope with datasets containing concept drift [8]. They make use of supervision, namely, intermittent information about the true classes of the data instances that is used to measure the performance of a classifier and potentially update its model [15].

Some of the existing techniques resort to ensemble classification, a technique which combines multiple classifiers with a technique of decision fusion and provides increased generalisation with respect to single classifiers [13]. For the problem of concept drift, a common approach consists of training the classifiers

The first author would like to thank the NCR corporation for sponsoring this project.

P. Pardalos et al. (Eds.): MOD 2015, LNCS 9432, pp. 171–184, 2015.
DOI: 10.1007/978-3-319-27926-8_15

at different time steps, while supervision is used to assess their performances and therefore to re-compute their weights accordingly, or to create and delete classifiers [4]. Another class of techniques, semi-supervised techniques, combines classification with clustering to limit the amount of supervision required and therefore reduce the costs and, more generally, the problems associated with labelling [11].

Although supervision can be employed in several applications, there are certain scenarios in these applications in which the classes of the instances ceased to be known, after the initial supervision that generates a model. We claim that this problem should be investigated in more detail to identify the cases in which the information provided by the unlabelled data can be used to update a classification model in the presence of concept drift. For this purpose, we propose an adaptive framework that consists of an *ensemble classifier*, a mechanism of *self-training* and a mechanism of *drift inference*. The adaptive framework is able to handle concept drift because it incorporates self-training, namely, the combination of input vectors and their respective classes generated by the ensemble to train new classifiers, which are added to the ensemble to update its model. The framework also features a technique of drift inference that analyses the differences between the decisions of the classifiers to determine when to trigger the replacement of old classifiers with new ones. A set of experiments involving different classification techniques and data distributions is performed. The experiments show that the contributions of the framework are: reduced storage requirements with respect to a single classifier and quick adaptation to concept drift which leads to higher classification performance than the comparative techniques.

The rest of the paper is organised as follows. Section 2 describes classification approaches that use different amounts of supervision. Section 3 describes a set of unsupervised techniques for classification and drift detection. Section 4 defines the major aspects of the adaptive framework, from the ensemble of classifiers to the replacement strategy. The results of the experiments are illustrated in Sect. 5. Section 6 presents the conclusions of this work.

2   Classification and Detection of Concept Drift

Concept drift is a growing area of research in machine learning, and several approaches have been presented to deal with this problem. The main differences between these approaches are: the use of mechanisms for change detection, the memory management strategy, the learning strategy, the use of single rather than ensemble classifiers and the types of classification techniques, among others [8]. However, the aspect that is more relevant to our work is the amount of supervision that is used to update a model. The classification techniques that deal with concept drift can be classified into *supervised*, *semi-supervised* and *unsupervised* techniques.

Supervised techniques receive information about the true class of each instance after classification. This information, which may be delayed, is used to measure the classification performance and update the model accordingly. Ensemble classifiers, which consist of a collection of classifiers and a technique to fuse their decisions (e.g., weighted or majority voting), represent a large class of supervised techniques [12]. An approach consists of training classifiers using chunks of data containing instances along with their respective classes that are provided intermittently. Supervision is used to assess the performance and, therefore, recompute the weights of the existing classifiers and to create or delete classifiers.

There are cases in which providing supervision for every instance is not feasible. That could be due, for example, to the rate at which instances are presented or to the costs associated with labelling [11]. Semi-supervised techniques update a classification model by means of small amounts of labelled data and generally larger amounts of unlabelled data.

In some scenarios, a classification model can be updated without using supervision. For example, the concept of *self-training*, initially developed for the problem of semi-supervised learning of static distributions, has also been used to deal with this problem [14]. In this context, unlabelled instances and their predicted classes that are determined by a model are used to generate an up-to-date model of the data. A potential avenue for classifying changing data with no supervision could be the combination of on-line clustering and semi-supervised clustering. In particular, semi-supervision could form an initial set of clusters from data with labels and then those clusters could be updated to concept drift using on-line clustering.

The majority of methods for drift detection measure the error rate of a classifier and, therefore, require supervision in order to operate [10]. There are other methods that do not make use of supervision to detect drift. These methods, which generally operate on the features of the data, are related to the areas of signal processing, comparison of density estimations, statistical analysis, among others [6]. These methods generally compare the similarity between two datasets recorded at different times in order to reveal the presence of concept drift.

3   Related Work

A set of unsupervised techniques for model updating and drift detection are described, respectively, in Sects. 3.1 and 3.2. They are used for the comparisons of the experimental part (Sect. 5).

3.1   Classification Techniques: Unsupervised Model Updating

A single-classifier technique that uses self-training and a fixed-size window to classify data streams with no supervision is described in [14]. The window initially contains instances with their true classes and are used to train a model. Then, only unlabelled instances are generated. Each of these is classified and is added to the window along with its predicted class. Then, the oldest instance within the window is discarded and a new model is generated. These steps are repeated for every instance that is presented.

As mentioned in Sect. 2, classification of data with concept drift and no supervision could be tackled by combining on-line clustering with semi-supervision. The on-line clustering techniques CluStream and DenStream [1,3] use a two-level clustering approach: rather than to store a large numbers of instances in memory, a set of *micro-clusters* maintains statistics about the instances that have been observed, which are discarded; high-level clustering is then applied to the set of micro-clusters. Semi-supervised clustering is used to aid the formation of clusters by means of a set of labelled instances. A method consists of forming clusters that contains only instances from a specific class [2]. That class can also be used as a label to the cluster. This information could be used to classify new instances based on the cluster they are associated with.

3.2   Unsupervised Drift Detection Techniques

For unsupervised data, concept drift can be detected by measuring the similarity between the distributions of two different datasets generated at different points in time [6]. The technique by Hido et al. measures the error of a classifier trained on that data to detect drift [9], while the method Friedman-Rafsky builds a tree from the data and then measures the interconnection between nodes associated with different datasets [7].

4   The Adaptive Framework

This section provides an outline of the adaptive framework by describing the characteristics of the ensemble classifier, the technique of self-training and the mechanism of drift inference.

The backbone of the framework being proposed consists of an ensemble containing a fixed set of classifiers of the same type, while majority voting is adopted to fuse the decisions of the classifiers. This approach was adopted for its simplicity, as it should simplify the analysis of the functioning of the framework. The ensemble is divided in two pools of classifiers: *mature* and *naïve*. Only mature classifiers take part to the voting, while naïve classifiers are iteratively trained with new data. Naïve classifiers can become mature if concept drift is detected.

The operation of the framework is divided into a *training* phase and an *online* phase. Supervision about the true classes of data instances is limited to the training phase, which has the purpose of training the mature classifiers. In this phase the data distribution does not change. During the on-line phase, affected by concept drift, only feature vectors are provided without any information about their classes. New classifiers are generated at runtime combining these feature vectors and the classes that the voting system assigns to them. A description of the pseudo-code of both phases and the mechanism of drift inference follows.

4.1   Pseudo-code of Training, Testing and Inference of Drift

The inputs to the training procedure are the training set D_{training} and the threshold th_{training}, as shown in the pseudo-code of the Algorithm 1 (line 1). The result is a set of mature classifiers that fill the pool E_{M}, which is initially empty (line 2). The instances D_i of the set D_{training} are couples in the form $(\mathbf{x}_i, y_i)$ where $\mathbf{x}_i$ is a vector of features $(x_{i_1}, \ldots, x_{i_m})$ and y_i is its class. A while loop then iterates through the instances of D_{training} (line 6). Data instances D_i from D_{training} are copied, one at a time, into the temporary storage D_{temp} (line 7), until D_{temp} contains at least th_{training} instances of class "+1" and th_{training} instance of class "−1" (line 9). When this happens, a new classifier is trained and added to E_{M} and D_{temp} is emptied (lines 11–13). The purpose of the parameter th_{training} is to avoid the collection of datasets containing only instances of a single class, which would not allow the training of new classifiers. If there are no instances left in D_{training}, E_{M} is returned (line 16).

When E_{M} has been created, supervision ceases. In order to deal with drift, ineffective classifiers need to be replaced with new classifiers to avoid degradation of classification performance. For some aspects, the online testing procedure (Algorithm 1, line 18) is similar to the training phase. The major difference is that the instances used to train new classifiers, in this case, are generated at runtime by coupling feature vectors $\mathbf{x}_i$ with their respective decisions generated by the ensemble $voting(\mathbf{x}_i)$ (lines 23–24). When at least th_{online} instances with associated class "+1" and th_{online} instances with class "−1" are gathered (line 27), a new classifier is created and added to the ensemble, and an existing classifier is deleted. The combination of new data and decisions by the existing model allows the framework to incrementally update its model in order to deal with the changing distribution. The classifiers that are created in the first iterations of the on-line phase serve to populate the pool of naïve classifiers E_{N} and to make the inference of drift operative. When E_{N} contains $\lfloor ratio_{\text{NaiveMature}} * |E_{\text{M}}| \rfloor$ classifiers (lines 31–32), every new classifier generated is initially added to the naïve set (line 34). However, if concept drift is not inferred by INFERDRIFT() then the oldest naïve classifier in the pool is deleted (line 40). If drift is inferred, a mature classifier is deleted and a naïve one is promoted to mature (lines 35–38).

The framework introduces a technique of drift inference that monitors the similarity between naïve and mature classifiers. For simplicity let us assume that the speed of drift and the time to collect the data that trains a classifier are such that the change of $p(\mathbf{x})$ is neglectable during that time. If concept drift modifies $p(\mathbf{x})$, the models of the naïve classifiers, trained on new data, are expected to differ from those of the mature classifiers, trained with older distributions. The similarity between two classifiers is estimated by measuring the Hamming distance between their decisions over a time window. In fact, if the vectors collected allow to generate a good estimate of the underlying data distribution, then the Hamming distance represents a computationally undemanding measure of the similarity between two classification models. In particular, the framework uses a symmetric matrix H in which the element H_{ij} contains the Hamming distance between the classifiers i and j.

Algorithm 1. Pseudo-codes of the procedures of training, testing and inference of drift.

```
 1: procedure TRAIN(D_training, th_training)
 2:     E_M ← ∅
 3:     i ← 1
 4:     j ← 1
 5:     D_temp ← ∅
 6:     while i ≤ |D_training| do
 7:         D_temp ← D_temp ∪ {D_i}
 8:         i ← i + 1
 9:         if              (|{D_k ∈ D_temp|class(D_k) = +1}| ≥ th_training)     ∧
       (|{D_k ∈ D_temp|class(D_k) = −1}| ≥ th_training) then
10:             train(E_{M_j}, D_temp)
11:             E_M ← E_M ∪ {E_{M_j}}
12:             j ← j + 1
13:             D_temp ← ∅
14:         end if
15:     end while
16:     return E_M
17: end procedure
```

```
18: procedure TEST(E_M, E_N, D_test, th_online)
19:     i ← 1
20:     j ← 1
21:     D_temp ← ∅
22:     while i ≤ |D_test| do
23:         D_i ← (x_i, VOTING(E_M, x_i))
24:         D_temp ← D_temp ∪ {D_i}
25:         UPDATEHAMMINGMATRIX(H, D_i, E_M, E_N)
26:         i ← i + 1
27:         if              (|{D_k ∈ D_temp|class(D_k) = +1}| ≥ th_online)     ∧
       ({D_k ∈ D_temp|class(D_k) = −1}| ≥ th_online) then
28:             TRAIN(E_j, D_temp)
29:             j ← j + 1
30:             drift ←INFERDRIFT(H, FIFO_ID, th_ID)
31:             if |E_M| ≤ |E_N| then
32:                 E_N ← E_N ∪ {E_j}
33:             else
34:                 E_N ← E_N ∪ {E_j}
35:                 if drift = true then
36:                     DELETECLASSIFIER(E_M)
37:                     E_l ← SELECT (E_N)
38:                     E_M ← E_M ∪ {E_l}
39:                 else
40:                     DELETECLASSIFIER(E_N)
41:                 end if
42:             end if
43:             D_temp ← ∅
44:         end if
45:     end while
46:     return
47: end procedure
```

48: **procedure** INFERDRIFT($H, FIFO_{\text{ID}}, th_{\text{ID}}$)
49:     $temp \leftarrow 0$
50:     **for** j in $[1, \ldots, |E_{\text{M}}|]$ **do**
51:         **for** i in $[1, \ldots, i]$ **do**
52:             $temp \leftarrow temp + H_{ij}$
53:         **end for**
54:     **end for**
55:     $d_{\text{M}} \leftarrow 2 * temp/(|E_{\text{M}}| * (|E_{\text{M}}| + 1))$
56:     **for** j in $[|E_{\text{M}}| + 1, \ldots, |E_{\text{M}}| + |E_{\text{N}}|]$ **do**
57:         **for** i in $[|E_{\text{M}}| + 1, \ldots, i]$ **do**
58:             $temp \leftarrow temp + H_{ij}$
59:         **end for**
60:     **end for**
61:     $d_{\text{N}} \leftarrow 2 * temp/(|E_{\text{N}}| * (|E_{\text{N}}| + 1))$
62:     **for** i in $[|E_{\text{M}}| + 1, \ldots, |E_{\text{M}}| + |E_{\text{N}}|]$ **do**
63:         **for** j in $[|E_{\text{M}}| + 1, \ldots, |E_{\text{M}}| + |E_{\text{N}}|]$ **do**
64:             $temp \leftarrow temp + H_{ij}$
65:         **end for**
66:     **end for**
67:     $d_{\text{MN}} \leftarrow temp/(|E_{\text{N}}| * (|E_{\text{M}}|))$
68:     POP($FIFO_{\text{ID}}$)
69:     **if** $d_{\text{MN}} > d_{\text{N}} \wedge d_{\text{MN}} > d_{\text{M}}$ **then**
70:         ATTACH($FIFO_{\text{ID}}, 1$)
71:     **else**
72:         ATTACH($FIFO_{\text{ID}}, 0$)
73:     **end if**
74:     **return** $sum(FIFO_{\text{ID}}) > \lfloor FIFO_{\text{ID}_{\text{size}}} * th_{\text{ID}} \rfloor$
75: **end procedure**

After a new classifier has been created the procedure INFERDRIFT() is invoked (lines 28, 30 and 48). It calculates the mean distances between mature classifiers (d_{M}, lines 50–55), between naïve classifiers (d_{N}, lines 56–61) and between mature and naïve classifiers (d_{MN}, lines 62–67). If d_{MN} is higher than both d_{M} and d_{N}, a 1 is added to a First-In-First-Out (FIFO) queue of size $FIFO_{\text{ID}_{\text{size}}}$, otherwise a 0 is added to the queue (lines 69–72). Drift is inferred if the sum of the values within the FIFO queue is higher than $\lfloor FIFO_{\text{ID}_{\text{size}}} * th_{\text{ID}} \rfloor$ (line 74), where the parameter th_{ID} controls the sensitivity of the technique.

The replacement strategy determines how the pools of classifiers are updated. When drift is inferred, the naïve classifier with minimum Hamming distance from the other naïve classifiers is promoted and the mature classifier having maximum Hamming distance from the naïve classifiers is deleted.

5 Experiments

Two experiments are presented here to evaluate the classification performance and the use of memory resources of the adaptive framework, as well as its capability to detect concept drift. Two datasets are employed, they feature different distributions and concept drift characteristics. Moreover comparisons are presented in order to place the framework in the context of existing methods.

5.1 Evaluation of the Classification Capabilities of the Framework

This experiment evaluates the classification performance and the memory consumption of the framework on a dataset with different characteristics. Its distribution is similar to that of the dataset presented in [5] and consists of four "clusters" of points C_1, C_2, C_3 and C_4, each with a bivariate Gaussian distribution. Cluster C_1 is labelled with class "+1", while the remaining clusters have class "−1". A concept drift containing high-overlapping between the classes and different drift schemata is generated by changing the mean values (μ_x and μ_y) and the standard deviations (σ_x and σ_y) of the clusters according to the patterns of Table 1. Initially, a model is trained using 500 instances generated from a stationary distribution corresponding to instance $i = 1$ of Table 1. The data D_{test} used to evaluate the framework consists of 10^6 instances.

Table 1. Concept drift of the dataset used to evaluate the classification performance of the framework and the comparative techniques (from [5]).

		$0 < i/|D_{\text{test}}| \leq 1/3$		
cluster	μ_x	μ_y	σ_x	σ_y
C_1	8	5	1	1
C_2	2	5	1	$1+6i/|D_{\text{test}}|$
C_3	5	8	$3-6i/|D_{\text{test}}|$	1
C_4	5	2	$3-6i/|D_{\text{test}}|$	1
		$1/3 < i/|D_{\text{test}}| \leq 2/3$		
cluster	μ_x	μ_y	σ_x	σ_y
C_1	$8-9(i/|D_{\text{test}}|-1/3)$	5	1	1
C_2	2	5	1	3
C_3	$5+9(i/|D_{\text{test}}|-1/3)$	8	1	1
C_4	$5+9(i/|D_{\text{test}}|-1/3)$	2	1	1
		$2/3 < i/|D_{\text{test}}| \leq 1$		
cluster	μ_x	μ_y	σ_x	σ_y
C_1	$5-9(i/|D_{\text{test}}|-2/3)$	$5+9(i/|D_{\text{test}}|-2/3)$	1	1
C_2	$5-9(i/|D_{\text{test}}|-2/3)$	2	1	$3-6(i/|D_{\text{test}}|-2/3)$
C_3	8	8	1	1
C_4	8	2	1	1

In order to identify potential advantages and disadvantages of the framework (FW), its performance is compared against the performances of a set of alternative methods that do not require supervision to update their models, these techniques are: the single classifier that uses self-training (SC-NO) and the clustering algorithms CluStream (CS) and DenStream (DS) with semi-supervision, described in Sect. 3. In order to avoid the training of a new model for every instance that is observed, the single classifier uses nonoverlapping windows for this experiment. The measure of accuracy, calculated as the number of instances that are correctly classified divided by total number of instances, is used to evaluate the performance of the techniques. In particular, if a technique is able discriminate between the classes then its accuracy at the end of a run is expected to be close to 1. By contrast, due to the imbalance of this dataset, values of accuracy around 0.75 or smaller are associated with a poor ability to classify points of different classes correctly. The parameters of the techniques are determined empirically in order to provide a combination of good model representation in the training phase and good ability to update the model during concept drift. The parameters of the framework are configured as follows: $th_{training} = 23$, $th_{online} = 25$, $ratio_{NaiveMature} = 0.4$, $FIFO_{ID_{size}} = 10$ and $th_{ID} = 0.1$. The single classifier has a window of size 500. Clustream has an horizon of 1000 instances, 1000 micro-clusters with a radius of 2 units and $k = 4$. DenStream has the following parameters: $\mu = 4$, $\beta = 0.03$, the initial number of micro-clusters is 500, ϵ and θ of the low-level DBSCAN have, respectively, values 0.5 and 3, while ϵ and θ of the high-level DBSCAN have values 1.2 and 1. For the descriptions of the parameters of Clustream and DenStream the reader is referred to their respective articles [1,3].

The framework and the single classifier are tested on the technique of SVM. The values of accuracy are calculated over two hundred runs, this value was determined using the A-test, a statistical technique that evaluates the similarity between two sets of values. In this context, by comparing different sets, each containing the values of accuracy of multiple runs, the A-test is used to determine how many times the experiment must be repeated in order to obtain results with low variability [16]. The values of accuracy of the framework and the comparative methods show that the framework and the single classifier are the only techniques that are able to classify this dataset (Fig. 1). In particular, both techniques classify the data correctly in 93 out of 200 runs. Morevoer, their performances in terms of accuracy have been compared using the Mann-Whitney test, which measures the likelihood of two sets of values being generated from the same distribution without making any assumption about the type of distribution of the data. According to the Mann-Whitney test, the distributions of the values of accuracy of the two techniques are not statistically significantly different with a confidence level of 0.995, and therefore their performances on this dataset are not distinguishable. An analysis of the results of Clustream showed that this technique is able to provide high accuracy only for two runs, however the values across these runs are affected by large variations.

An analysis of the memory consumption of the framework and the single classifier revealed that the framework maintained in memory, on average, 103 instances in order to train a new classifier, and it never used more than 310 instances. By contrast, the single classifier is not able to maintain high per-

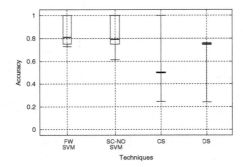

Fig. 1. Distributions of the values of accuracy of the framework and the comparative techniques.

formance with window sizes smaller than 400 instances and, however, the best results are obtained when 500 instances are stored. This means that the framework uses, on average, a number of instances that is four to five times smaller than that of a single classifier. However, the framework makes use of multiple classifiers, which could increase the computational cost with respect to using only a classifier. However, this depends on the classification technique that is adopted. A tecnique whose training time increases considerably for large inputs could benefit from the use of multiple classifiers trained on fewer instances.

5.2 Evaluation of the Concept Drift Detection Capabilities of the Framework

This experiment evaluates the capability of the framework to detect drift. For this reason, a dataset is presented with the goal of highlighting the characteristics of the inference of drift with respect to the comparative methods. Different from the previous experiment which employed a distribution with a gradient, for this experiment the distribution of each class is uniform and has a squared shape with edges of unitary length. The position of the center of class "+1" is fixed and has coordinates (1,1). The position of the center of class "−1", with initial coordinates (3,1), does not change for the first 250,000 instances, after that it drifts linearly to the position (4,1) which is reached when 500,000 instances have been generated. The initial absence of concept drift has the purpose of evaluating the specificity of the inference of drift. The concept drift that follows is such that it would not affect the performance of a previously established linear model that separates the classes, in fact class "−1" moves away from class "+1". This phase is aimed at verifying the capability of framework to recognise this particular type of concept drift. After that, the center of class "−1" moves in the opposite direction and reaches the final position (2,1) when 1,000,000 instances have been observed. In this part of the dataset, since the distance between the centers of the classes decreases, a model operating on the data needs to be updated in order to avoid performance degradation.

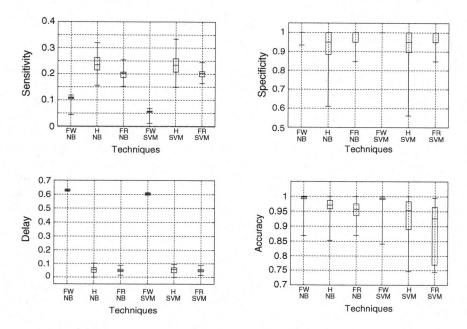

Fig. 2. Distributions of the values of sensitivity, specificity, delay of detection and classification accuracy of the framework with the different unsupervised drift detection techniques.

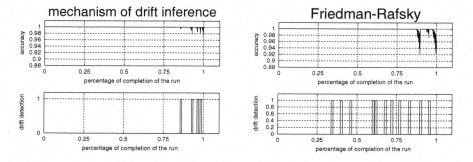

Fig. 3. Comparison of the values of accuracy and the detection of drift over a run of the technique of drift inference and the Friedman-Rafsky method.

The inference of drift of the framework is compared against the technique by Hido et al. (H) and the technique by Friedman and Rafsky described (FR) in Sect. 3. In order to provide a fair comparison, each comparative technique is integrated within an instance of the framework and when it detects concept drift the model is actually updated. The batch of instances collected in the first iteration is stored in memory and its similarity with subsequent batches is estimated, one at a time. When the distributions of two batches are different according to technique being used, drift is detected and the data batch stored in memory is replaced with the last batch observed.

The parameters of the instances of the framework are configured as follows: $th_{training}=45$, $ratio_{NaiveMature}=1.0$, $th_{ID}=1.0$, $th_{online}=100$ (when SVM are use in place of naïve Bayes, $th_{online}=400$), while $FIFO_{ID_{size}}$ has the value 40 for the inference of drift and 60 for the comparative methods. Sensitivity, specificity and delay of detection of the detection techniques are measured. Moreover, classification accuracy at the end of a run is also recorded. Sensitivity measures the ability to detect drift when this is ongoing and is calculated by the formula $\frac{TP}{TP+FN}$ (TP=drift present and detected; FN= drift present and not detected). Specificity measures the rate of false alarms and is expressed by the formula $\frac{TN}{TN+FP}$ (TN=drift absent and not detected; FP= drift absent but detected). Delay of detection is calculated as the ratio between the number of instances before drift is detected and the total number of intances. For this experiment, the framework uses naïve Bayes (NB) and SVM classifiers.

The results, shown in Fig. 2, highlight that the framework has higher specificity than the comparative methods. This means that drift is detected only when it is ongoing. However, the framework has lower sensitivity and higher delay of detection than the other two methods. This is caused by the fact that during the first part of the dataset the classes are separable, hence the Hamming distances between the decisions of the classifiers in the ensemble are null and drift is not detected, but that does not affect the classification accuracy. However, in the second part of the concept drift, the center of class "-1" moves towards the center of class "$+1$", the Hamming distances are no longer null and drift can be inferred. When this happens, the framework reacts promptly to performance degradation as shown in Fig. 3 and this leads to a higher accuracy than the comparative methods (Fig. 2).

6 Conclusions

This paper has introduced an adaptive framework which deals with the problem of classification of data affected by concept drift without the aid of external supervision. The framework uses feedback of its decisions, namely self-training, for training new classifiers. In this way, the model of new classifiers combines information regarding concept drift, but also memory about previous states. The iterative replacement of old classifiers with new classifiers allows the model of the framework to adapt to concept drift. In order to perform replacement only when drift occurs, a mechanism for inferring drift analyses the differences between the decisions of the classifiers of the ensemble.

A set of experiments featuring different classification techniques and different datasets has been performed with the purpose of evaluating the ability of the framework to deal with concept drift. The outcome of that experiments has shown that our framework affords good classification performance, but it stores fewer instances with respect to a single-classifier approach. This result may be related to the property of incremental learning that characterises ensemble methods. In fact, the same amount of data that is required to train a single classifier with high accuracy is split into smaller batches, each of which trains a member of the ensemble. Although these classifiers may be less accurate than a single-classifier, the generalisation that follows from their combination provides the same level of classification performance. Moreover, the technique of drift inference of the framework affords quicker model updating and, therefore, smaller performance degradation with respect to the comparative methods, thus providing higher classification accuracy.

There are several directions in which the framework could be developed. One possibility would consist of changing the values of its parameters (parametric optimization) or the set of features (adaptive feature selection) at runtime. In fact, the initial parametric setting of the framework and its classifiers might need retuning to classify effectively data affected by concept drift. The framework could also learn new combinations of input features to obtain better discrimination between the classes and therefore higher classification performance. Another interesting possibility would be the use of different classification techniques. Adding new techniques could be useful, for instance, to process new types of data or different types of concept drift.

References

1. Aggarwal, C.C., Watson, T.J., Ctr, R., Han, J., Wang, J., Yu, P.S.: A framework for clustering evolving data streams. In: Proceedings of the Twenty-nineth International Conference on Very Large Data Bases, VLDB 2003, vol. 29, pp. 81–92. VLDB Endowment, Berlin (2003)
2. Basu, S., Banerjee, A., Mooney, R.J.: Semi-supervised clustering by seeding. In: Proceedings of the Nineteenth International Conference on Machine Learning, ICML 2002, pp. 27–34. Morgan Kaufmann Publishers Inc., San Francisco (2002)
3. Cao, F., Ester, M., Qian, W., Zhou, A.: Density-based clustering over an evolving data stream with noise. In: Proceedings of the Sixth SIAM International Conference on Data Mining, SDM 2006, pp. 328–339. SIAM (2006)
4. Dietterich, T.G.: Ensemble methods in machine learning. In: Kittler, J., Roli, F. (eds.) MCS 2000. LNCS, vol. 1857, pp. 1–15. Springer, Heidelberg (2000)
5. Ditzler, G., Polikar, R.: An ensemble based incremental learning framework for concept drift and class imbalance. In: The 2010 International Joint Conference on Neural Networks (IJCNN), pp. 1–8, July 2010
6. Dries, A., Rückert, U.: Adaptive concept drift detection. Stat. Anal. Data Min. 2(5–6), 311–327 (2009)
7. Friedman, J.H., Rafsky, L.C.: Multivariate generalizations of the Wald-Wolfowitz and Smirnov two-sample tests. Ann. Stat. 7, 697–717 (1979)
8. Gama, J., Žliobaitė, I., Bifet, A., Pechenizkiy, M., Bouchachia, A.: A survey on concept drift adaptation. ACM Comput. Surv. (CSUR) 46(4), 44 (2014)
9. Hido, S., Idé, T., Kashima, H., Kubo, H., Matsuzawa, H.: Unsupervised change analysis using supervised learning. In: Washio, T., Suzuki, E., Ting, K.M., Inokuchi, A. (eds.) PAKDD 2008. LNCS (LNAI), vol. 5012, pp. 148–159. Springer, Heidelberg (2008)
10. Gonçalves Jr., P.M., de Carvalho Santos, S.G., Barros, R.S., Vieira, D.C.: A comparative study on concept drift detectors. Expert Syst. Appl. 41(18), 8144–8156 (2014)

11. Li, P., Wu, X., Hu, X.: Mining recurring concept drifts with limited labeled streaming data. ACM Trans. Intell. Syst. Technol. **3**(2), 29:1–29:32 (2012)
12. Nishida, K., Yamauchi, K., Omori, T.: ACE: Adaptive classifiers-ensemble system for concept-drifting environments. In: Oza, N.C., Polikar, R., Kittler, J., Roli, F. (eds.) MCS 2005. LNCS, vol. 3541, pp. 176–185. Springer, Heidelberg (2005)
13. Polikar, R.: Ensemble based systems in decision making. IEEE Circ. Syst. Mag. **6**(3), 21–45 (2006)
14. Sahel, Z., Bouchachia, A., Gabrys, B., Rogers, P.: Adaptive mechanisms for classification problems with drifting data. In: Apolloni, B., Howlett, R.J., Jain, L. (eds.) KES 2007, Part II. LNCS (LNAI), vol. 4693, pp. 419–426. Springer, Heidelberg (2007)
15. Tsymbal, A.: The problem of concept drift: Definitions and related work. Technical report, Trinity College Dublin, Ireland (2004)
16. Vargha, A., Delaney, H.D.: A critique and improvement of the "CL" common language effect size statistics of McGraw and Wong. J. Educ. Behav. Stat. **25**(2), 101–132 (2000)

Global Optimization with Sparse and Local Gaussian Process Models

Tipaluck Krityakierne[1]([✉]) and David Ginsbourger[1,2]

[1] Department of Mathematics and Statistics, IMSV,
University of Bern, Bern, Switzerland
{tipaluck.krityakierne,ginsbourger}@stat.unibe.ch
[2] Idiap Research Institute, Martigny, Switzerland
ginsbourger@idiap.ch

Abstract. We present a novel surrogate model-based global optimization framework allowing a large number of function evaluations. The method, called SpLEGO, is based on a multi-scale expected improvement (EI) framework relying on both sparse and local Gaussian process (GP) models. First, a bi-objective approach relying on a global sparse GP model is used to determine potential next sampling regions. Local GP models are then constructed within each selected region. The method subsequently employs the standard expected improvement criterion to deal with the exploration-exploitation trade-off within selected local models, leading to a decision on where to perform the next function evaluation(s). The potential of our approach is demonstrated using the so-called Sparse Pseudo-input GP as a global model. The algorithm is tested on four benchmark problems, whose number of starting points ranges from 10^2 to 10^4. Our results show that SpLEGO is effective and capable of solving problems with large number of starting points, and it even provides significant advantages when compared with state-of-the-art EI algorithms.

Keywords: Black-box optimization · Expected improvement · Kriging

1 Introduction

In real world engineering optimization problems, the objective function is often a black box whose derivatives are unavailable, and function values are obtained from time-consuming simulations. To reduce the computational cost, in surrogate model-based optimization, the objective function is approximated with an inexpensive surrogate (also known as response surface model or metamodel). An auxiliary optimization problem on this surrogate is then solved in each iteration to determine at which point to evaluate the objective function next. The new data point is used to update the surrogate, and thus it is iteratively refined. Several popular response surface models such as radial basis functions, Gaussian process models (kriging), polynomials, and support vector regression have been successfully applied in this context (see, e.g. [5,8,10,13,14,19,23]).

© Springer International Publishing Switzerland 2015
P. Pardalos et al. (Eds.): MOD 2015, LNCS 9432, pp. 185–196, 2015.
DOI: 10.1007/978-3-319-27926-8_16

Thanks to its flexibility and efficiency, the EGO (Efficient Global Optimization) algorithm proposed by Jones [8] has become a very popular GP-based global optimization algorithm. It is based on the expected improvement criterion and more generally on ideas from Bayesian Optimization, following the seminal work carried out by Mockus and co-authors (see [9] and references therein). While EGO provides an elegant way to model the objective function and deal with the exploration versus exploitation trade-off, the computational cost and the storage requirements, nevertheless, have become major bottlenecks obstructing its practical application. Although quantifying complexity of EGO with hyperparameter re-estimation is a difficult task, EGO is known to be very slow and crash when the total number of observation points exceeds a few thousands. This is due to the training and prediction costs of GP that scale as $\mathcal{O}(N^3)$ and also the storage that scales as $\mathcal{O}(N^2)$, where N is the number of data points in the training set.

To circumvent this limitation, a number of sparse GP models have been proposed in the literature of GP regression (e.g. [3,15,16,21]). The idea behind these sparse models is generally to use a small number ($M << N$) of inducing points (also known as support points) to represent the full data points; as a result, the number of computations and storage requirements are reduced to $\mathcal{O}(NM^2)$ and $\mathcal{O}(NM)$, respectively. It is known that these approaches are related and can also be viewed within a single unifying framework. See [11] for details.

While some recent publications put a focus on Bayesian Optimization with a large number of points [18,22], to the best of our knowledge, no attempt has yet been made to integrate sparse GP within a global optimization framework. This work is intended as a contribution to the new area of applying GP-based global optimization to a larger number (typically, tens of thousands) of data points, which can be viewed somewhat as an extension to Bayesian Optimization.

In Sect. 2, we give necessary background regarding GP regression, Sparse Pseudo-input Gaussian Process models, as well as EI and EGO. In Sect. 3, we introduce the Sparse and Local EGO (SpLEGO) framework. A simple example of application on a one-dimensional problem and several numerical experiments that illustrate algorithm effectiveness in higher dimensions are presented in Sect. 4. Some comments on the proposed method as well as perspectives of future work are also given in this section. Finally, we conclude our work in Sect. 5.

2 Background

2.1 Problem Formulation and Notation

We consider a global optimization problem of the form:

$$\min_{\mathbf{x} \in D} f(\mathbf{x}) \tag{1}$$

where $f : D \subset \mathbb{R}^d \to \mathbb{R}$ is assumed continuous and $D = [\mathbf{a}, \mathbf{b}] = \prod_{i=1}^d [a_i, b_i]$ $(a_i, b_i \in \mathbb{R} : a_i < b_i)$. The objective function f is assumed to be expensive and without any derivative information available (referred to as "black box" henceforth).

The goal of this paper is to develop a GP-based global optimization algorithm that can find near globally optimal solutions when the number of starting points (or allowable function evaluations) is relatively large.

2.2 Gaussian Process Modeling

Suppose that we have observed the vector of outputs $f(\mathbf{X}) = [f(\mathbf{x}_1), ..., f(\mathbf{x}_N)]^T$ at the training input points $\mathbf{X} = \{\mathbf{x}_1, ..., \mathbf{x}_N\}$. Assume a Gaussian Process prior $f \sim \mathrm{GP}(\mu_0(\cdot), K(\cdot, \cdot))$ where μ_0 and K are a given mean function and covariance kernel, respectively. For a fixed $\mathbf{x} \in D$, the posterior of $f(\mathbf{x})$ knowing $f(\mathbf{X})$ is $f(\mathbf{x})|f(\mathbf{X}) \sim \mathcal{N}(\mu_N(\mathbf{x}), \sigma_N^2(\mathbf{x}))$. Taking $\mu_0(\cdot) = 0$, we have [12]

$$\mu_N(\mathbf{x}) = K(\mathbf{x}, \mathbf{X}) K(\mathbf{X})^{-1} f(\mathbf{X}) \tag{2a}$$

$$\sigma_N^2(\mathbf{x}) = K(\mathbf{x}, \mathbf{x}) - K(\mathbf{x}, \mathbf{X}) K(\mathbf{X})^{-1} K(\mathbf{X}, \mathbf{x}), \tag{2b}$$

where $K(\mathbf{X}, \mathbf{x})$ is defined as $[K(\mathbf{x}_1, \mathbf{x}), ..., K(\mathbf{x}_N, \mathbf{x})]^T$. $K(\mathbf{X}) := K(\mathbf{X}, \mathbf{X})$ (assumed invertible here) is defined analogously. One example (among many others, see [20]) of a commonly used covariance kernel is the squared exponential:

$$K(\mathbf{x}, \mathbf{x}') = \sigma^2 \exp\left(-\frac{1}{2} \sum_{k=1}^{d} \theta_k (\mathbf{x}_k - \mathbf{x}'_k)^2\right), \tag{3}$$

where $\Psi = \{\sigma^2, \theta_1, ..., \theta_d\}$ are the hyperparameters, whose values are often obtained by maximizing the log marginal likelihood:

$$\mathcal{L}(\Psi) = -\frac{1}{2} \log |K_\Psi(\mathbf{X})| - \frac{1}{2}\mathbf{f}(\mathbf{X})^T K_\Psi^{-1}(\mathbf{X}) \mathbf{f}(\mathbf{X}) - \frac{N}{2} \log(2\pi). \tag{4}$$

Evaluating any of Eqs. 2a, 2b or 4 relies on the inversion of the $N \times N$ covariance matrix $K_\Psi(\mathbf{X})$, and so GP modelling is prohibitively expensive when the size of the training data set becomes large.

2.3 Expected Improvement and EGO

As in most surrogate-based optimization methods, EGO [8] starts by constructing a space-filling design in the decision space $\{\mathbf{x}_1, ..., \mathbf{x}_{N_0}\} \subset D$, for some $N_0 \geq 1$. The objective function is then evaluated at these design points and an initial GP model is fitted. The algorithm selects the next function evaluation point(s) by maximizing the expected improvement (EI) criterion, which depends both on the prediction $\mu_{N_0}(\mathbf{x})$ and on the associated uncertainty $\sigma_{N_0}^2(\mathbf{x})$ from Eqs. 2a and 2b.

More generally, for $N \geq N_0$, let $f_{\min} = \min\{f(\mathbf{x}_1), ..., f(\mathbf{x}_N)\}$ be the current best objective function value. EI, defined as the expectation of the improvement brought by evaluating f at a candidate point, can be calculated analytically:

$$\text{EI}_N(\mathbf{x}) = \mathbb{E}_N\left[\max\left(0, f_{\min} - f(\mathbf{x})\right)\right] \tag{5a}$$

$$= (f_{\min} - \mu_N(\mathbf{x}))\Phi\left(\tfrac{f_{\min} - \mu_N(\mathbf{x})}{\sigma_N(\mathbf{x})}\right) + \sigma_N(\mathbf{x})\phi\left(\tfrac{f_{\min} - \mu_N(\mathbf{x})}{\sigma_N(\mathbf{x})}\right), \tag{5b}$$

where $\mathbb{E}_N$ is the expectation taken with respect to posterior distribution given the first N observations, and Φ and ϕ are the standard Gaussian cdf and pdf, respectively. In EI algorithms such as EGO, at each iteration a function evaluation is performed at a point maximizing EI, i.e. $\mathbf{x}_{N+1} \in \text{argmax}_{\mathbf{x}\in D}\,\text{EI}_N(\mathbf{x})$, and the GP model is then updated with the new evaluation result. Figure 1 shows an example of GP model based on five observations (Left) and the corresponding EI criterion (Right). By assigning large values to inputs $\mathbf{x}$ whose $f(\mathbf{x})$ is likely to be less than $f_{\min}$ and/or whose prediction variance is high, the EI criterion provides a good balance between exploration of unexplored regions and exploitation of promising regions with low predictive mean.

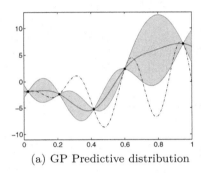 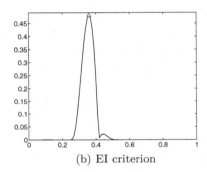

(a) GP Predictive distribution   (b) EI criterion

Fig. 1. A GP model and the corresponding expected improvement function. In Panel (a) the dots represent the training data. The black dashed line is the (unobserved) objective function. The shaded area represents the point-wise mean (middle red line) plus and minus twice the prediction standard deviation at each input value. In Panel (b), the point that attains the max EI is depicted by a blue triangle (Color figure online).

One remark regarding EI-optimal points shall be given before we turn to the next section. Let us consider the bi-objective optimization problem:

$$\min_{\mathbf{x}\in D} F(\mathbf{x}) = \left(\mu_N(\mathbf{x}),\, -\sigma_N^2(\mathbf{x})\right). \tag{6}$$

Since EI is decreasing in $\mu_N(\cdot)$ and increasing in $\sigma_N(\cdot)$, if $\mathbf{x}$ maximizes the EI criterion then $\mathbf{x}$ is automatically in the Pareto set of the bi-objective problem above. In situations when the EI formula (Eq. 5b) is not applicable, using this Pareto optimality property instead can come in handy, as we will see in Sect. 3.

2.4   Sparse Pseudo-input Gaussian Process

To circumvent the time-complexity, storage bottlenecks, and potential singularity problems for a large covariance matrix, a number of computationally efficient

sparse GP approximations have been proposed in the machine learning literature. In this section, we give a brief review of a particular method called Sparse
Pseudo-input Gaussian Process (SPGP) [16]. The SPGP method is based on a
low-rank approximation to the full GP covariance using a small set of induc-
ing points $\bar{\mathbf{X}} = \{\bar{\mathbf{x}}_1, ..., \bar{\mathbf{x}}_M\}$. In SPGP, the inducing points are referred to as
"pseudo-inputs" since they do not need to be a subset of the input training data
but are rather inferred along with the kernel hyperparameters.

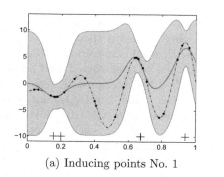

(a) Inducing points No. 1

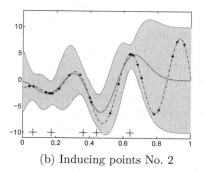

(b) Inducing points No. 2

Fig. 2. SPGP predictive distribution obtained using different sets of inducing points

We first give two examples of SPGP predictive distribution using different
sets of inducing points in Fig. 2. The black dots correspond to 25 training points.
The locations of the inducing points are shown as crosses. The shaded areas
represent the point-wise SPGP predictive means plus and minus twice the standard deviations at each input value. Again, the dashed black line represents the
(unobserved) objective function. We can see that the predictive distribution is
significantly influenced by the locations of the inducing points.

Coming to the SPGP equations, let us assume a zero mean GP prior on
the objective function, $f \sim \mathrm{GP}\left(0, K\left(\cdot, \cdot\right)\right)$. Without going into the details of its
derivation, it turns out that SPGP can be considered as a standard GP with a
particular covariance function [16]:

$$K^S(\mathbf{x}, \mathbf{x}') = Q(\mathbf{x}, \mathbf{x}') + \delta_{\mathbf{x},\mathbf{x}'}\left[K(\mathbf{x}, \mathbf{x}) - Q(\mathbf{x}, \mathbf{x})\right], \qquad (7)$$

where $Q(\mathbf{x}, \mathbf{x}') = K\left(\mathbf{x}, \bar{\mathbf{X}}\right) K\left(\bar{\mathbf{X}}\right)^{-1} K\left(\bar{\mathbf{X}}, \mathbf{x}'\right)$ and $\delta_{\mathbf{x},\mathbf{x}'}$ is Kronecker's delta. After
matrix simplifications, the predictive mean and variance of SPGP boil down to
formula involving only calculations with matrices of manageable dimensionality:

$$\mu^S\left(\mathbf{x}\right) = K\left(\mathbf{x}, \bar{\mathbf{X}}\right) H^{-1} K\left(\bar{\mathbf{X}}, \mathbf{X}\right) \Lambda^{-1} f\left(\mathbf{X}\right) \qquad (8a)$$

$$\sigma^{S2}\left(\mathbf{x}\right) = K\left(\mathbf{x}, \mathbf{x}\right) - K\left(\mathbf{x}, \bar{\mathbf{X}}\right)\left(K\left(\bar{\mathbf{X}}\right)^{-1} - H^{-1}\right) K\left(\bar{\mathbf{X}}, \mathbf{x}\right), \qquad (8b)$$

where $\Lambda = \mathrm{diag}\left(K\left(\mathbf{X}\right) - Q\left(\mathbf{X}\right)\right)$ and $H = K\left(\bar{\mathbf{X}}\right) + K\left(\bar{\mathbf{X}}, \mathbf{X}\right) \Lambda^{-1} K\left(\mathbf{X}, \bar{\mathbf{X}}\right)$.
Consequently, the pseudo-inputs $\bar{\mathbf{X}}$ can be considered as extra hyperparameters

of the model and can be estimated jointly with the kernel hyperparameters (of size $Md + |\Psi|$) by maximizing the log marginal likelihood as in Eq. 4. Note that since here $K_{\Psi,\bar{\mathbf{X}}}^S(\mathbf{X})$ can be written as a sum of a low rank part and a diagonal part, it can be inverted in $\mathcal{O}(NM^2)$. See [16] for more details.

3   Sparse and Local GP for Global Optimization

We wish to have an EGO-like algorithm that offers expected improvement but can also handle a large number of starting points. One natural extension of EGO in such a situation is to partition the whole decision space into smaller subregions, $D = \cup_{i=1}^r R_i$, e.g. where each region R_i would contain no more than k training input points. Local GP models could then be constructed, and a point $w_i \in R_i$ maximizing the local $\mathrm{EI}^{(i)}$ could be identified within each region R_i. Finally, one could take the best point among all w_i (with the largest local EI) as an approximation to the solution point corresponding to the true global EI.

While this may seem simple and appealing at first glance, such an approach would actually raise a few issues, and could be very computationally expensive in practice especially because of the potentially large number of local GP models to build and maintain. Our proposed algorithm, called SpLEGO (**Sp**arse and **L**ocal **EGO**), on the other hand, takes advantage of space partitioning while remaining at a more reasonable computational cost through some kind of pruning.

Given $\mathbf{X}_N = \{\mathbf{x}_1, ..., \mathbf{x}_N\}$ and $\mathbf{Y}_N = \{f(\mathbf{x}_1), ..., f(\mathbf{x}_N)\}$, the specific steps of SpLEGO are given in Algorithm 1.

Algorithm 1. SpLEGO Framework

---

1. Build a sparse GP model using $M << N$ inducing points $\mathcal{I}_{\mathrm{IP}} = \{\bar{\mathbf{x}}_1, ..., \bar{\mathbf{x}}_M\}$.
2. Identify center points for local models, $V = \{v_1, ..., v_r\}$:
   (a) Generate a Quasi-random sequence, e.g. Sobol sequence, $Q = \{u_1, ..., u_q\} \subset D$.
   (b) Compute the sparse predictive mean and variance for all $u \in Q$.
   (c) Identify the Pareto front with the two objectives, $F_1(\mathbf{x}) = \mu^S(\mathbf{x})$ and $F_2(\mathbf{x}) = -\sigma^{S2}(\mathbf{x})$. Let $v_1, ..., v_r \in Q$ be the points in the Pareto set.
3. For $i = 1 : r$,
   (a) Identify a subregion R_i around v_i.
   (b) Build a local GP model.
   (c) Calculate local $\mathrm{EI}^{(i)}$. Let $w_i \in \mathrm{argmax}_{\mathbf{x} \in R_i} \mathrm{EI}^{(i)}(\mathbf{x})$, i.e. $w_i \in R_i$ maximizes the local $\mathrm{EI}^{(i)}$ using the local GP in Step 3b. Note that the global $f_{\min} = \min \mathbf{Y}_N$ is used as a threshold when calculating all local $\mathrm{EI}^{(i)}$'s.
4. Let $i_0 \in \mathrm{argmax}_{1 \leq i \leq r} \mathrm{EI}^{(i)}(w_i)$, $\mathbf{x}_{N+1} \leftarrow w_{i_0}$ and $y_{N+1} \leftarrow f(\mathbf{x}_{N+1})$.
5. Update $\mathbf{X}_{N+1} \leftarrow \mathbf{X}_N \cup \{\mathbf{x}_{N+1}\}$, $\mathbf{Y}_{N+1} \leftarrow \mathbf{Y}_N \cup \{y_{N+1}\}$, and $N \leftarrow N + 1$.
6. Go back to Step 1.

To grasp a big picture of the entire domain, SpLEGO first constructs a sparse global GP model (Step 1 of Algorithm 1). Following the same philosophy of EI criterion that favors regions with high uncertainty and low mean predictions, non-dominated points are then identified from a space filling sequence, where evaluations are done on the the two competing objectives (mean and variance) obtained from the sparse GP model (Step 2).

From the trade-off point-of-view, input points in a vicinity of Pareto-optimal points define interesting regions. Thereby, local GP models are built within each of these regions (Step 3b). Finally, the next evaluation point is taken as the point that attains the overall maximum local EI across all subregions (Step 4).

Steps 3a and b of Algorithm 1 need further clarification. While different approaches can be used to define a subregion R_i in Step 3a, in this work we define R_i to be a hyperrectangle $\left[\min\left(\mathbf{X}_N^{(i)} \cup \{v_i\}\right), \max\left(\mathbf{X}_N^{(i)} \cup \{v_i\}\right)\right]$, where $\mathbf{X}_N^{(i)} \subset \mathbf{X}_N$ is a set of k-nearest input neighbors of v_i, and the minimum and maximum are taken component-wise. Next, two possibilities of a local GP model in Step 3b are presented:

V1. Exact Local GP: Use the k points in $\mathbf{X}_N^{(i)}$ (with their corresponding exact observations) to build a local GP in the region R_i.

V2. Globalized Local GP: Use a combination of the k points in $\mathbf{X}_N^{(i)}$ and M noisy inducing points in $\mathcal{I}_{\text{IP}}$ from Step 1.

The details of the GP posterior used in version V2, which combines exact responses from the ith local model ($1 \leq i \leq r$) and noisy responses from the inducing points of the SPGP model, are as follows: Let $\mathbf{X}_N^{(i)} = \left\{\mathbf{x}_{N,1}^{(i)}, \dots, \mathbf{x}_{N,k}^{(i)}\right\}$ and $f\left(\mathbf{X}_N^{(i)}\right) = \left[f\left(\mathbf{x}_{N,1}^{(i)}\right), \dots, f\left(\mathbf{x}_{N,k}^{(i)}\right)\right]^T$ be the exact k input-output observations from region i. Let $\bar{\mathbf{X}}_M = \{\bar{\mathbf{x}}_1, \dots, \bar{\mathbf{x}}_M\}$ be the (noisy) inducing points, with SPGP predictive means $\mu^S(\bar{\mathbf{X}}_M)$ and variances $\tau^2 = \sigma^{S2}(\bar{\mathbf{X}}_M)$. Writing $\tilde{\mathbf{X}}_N^{(i)} = \left[\mathbf{X}_N^{(i)}, \bar{\mathbf{X}}_M\right]$ and $\Delta = \text{diag}(\tau^2)$, the predictive mean and variance of the combined local GP in region i are given by

$$\mu_N^{(i)}(\mathbf{x}) = K\left(\mathbf{x}, \tilde{\mathbf{X}}_N^{(i)}\right)\left[K\left(\tilde{\mathbf{X}}_N^{(i)}\right) + \begin{pmatrix} \mathbf{0} & \mathbf{0} \\ \mathbf{0} & \Delta \end{pmatrix}\right]^{-1}\left[\begin{matrix} f\left(\mathbf{X}_N^{(i)}\right) \\ \mu^S(\bar{\mathbf{X}}_M) \end{matrix}\right] \tag{9a}$$

$$\sigma_N^{(i)2}(\mathbf{x}) = K(\mathbf{x},\mathbf{x}) - K\left(\mathbf{x},\tilde{\mathbf{X}}_N^{(i)}\right)\left[K\left(\tilde{\mathbf{X}}_N^{(i)}\right) + \begin{pmatrix} \mathbf{0} & \mathbf{0} \\ \mathbf{0} & \Delta \end{pmatrix}\right]^{-1} K\left(\tilde{\mathbf{X}}_N^{(i)}, \mathbf{x}\right). \tag{9b}$$

One can view Step 3b as a refinement phase. The difference between the two versions is the use of inducing points in SpLEGO-V2. While SpLEGO-V1 focuses on refining the selected regions of interest using only the exact evaluation points in the region R_i, SpLEGO-V2 uses information from both the nearby exact observations and the sparse global model.

Let us remark that although it seems out of reach here to specify the complexity of EGO or SpLEGO, the overall complexity of a typical step of the two algorithms are dominated by $\mathcal{O}(N^3)$ and $\max\left\{\mathcal{O}\left(NM^2\right), \mathcal{O}\left(k^3\right), \mathcal{O}\left(dN^2\right)\right\}$, respectively. Therefore, when $N \gg M, k, d$ (which is our case), it appears that SpLEGO will be more efficient than EGO.

4   Applications

4.1   A Didactic Example

Figure 3 illustrates the application of SpLEGO with a simple didactic example. SPGP is used in Step 1 of the algorithm. Panels (a) and (b) correspond to Steps 1 and 2. Panel (c) corresponds to Step 3a. Here, four Pareto optimal points are used to define the same number of subregions R_i with $k = 3$ points each. Finally, Panel (d) corresponds to Step 3c where the local $\mathrm{EI}^{(i)}$'s are calculated within each R_i.

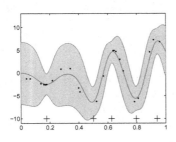
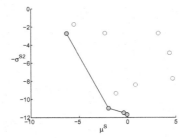

(a) SPGP with five inducing points.   (b) A Pareto front for two objectives: SPGP mean and negative variance.

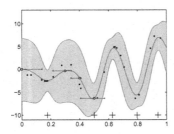
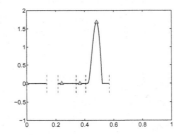

(c) Pareto optimal points (green dots) and their subregions R_i (blue lines).   (d) Local EIs and points attaining their maxima (blue triangles).

Fig. 3. A step-by-step application with a simple didactic example (Color figure online)

4.2   Numerical Experiments

Test Problems. SpLEGO is assessed on four benchmark problems. The test functions have between 4 and 10 dimensions and are summarized in Table 1.

Table 1. Summary of test problems

Problem	Domain	N_1	N_2
Rastrigin [6]	$[-20, 20]^{10}$	100	0
Hartmann [4]	$[0, 1]^6$	400	5×200
Ackley [1]	$[-1, 3]^{10}$	280	4×280
Shekel [4]	$[0, 10]^4$	5000	1×5000

Initial Data. To examine method applicability, we create the initial data in a way that the points are packed in some regions but not completely filling the space. The initial designs are composed of two types of samples:

I1: Latin Hypercube Designs of size N_1
I2: clusters of uniformly distributed points of size N_2.

The total number of initial points is therefore $N_0 = N_1 + N_2$, where N_1, N_2 for each test problem are given in Table 1. For example, the initial design of Hartmann-6D consists of $N_0 = 1400$ points: a Latin Hypercube Design ($N_1 = 400$) and five clusters of 200 uniformly distributed points ($N_2 = 1000$).

Experimental Results. Ten trials are performed for both EGO and SpLEGO. Parameter values used in numerical experiments for SpLEGO are $M = 20$, $q = 500$, $k = 50$ (Steps 1, 2, and 3a of Algorithm 1). Here, we implement SpLEGO-V2. The plots of the average best objective function value ($\min_{1 \leq n \leq N} f(\mathbf{x}_n)$) versus number of sample size N (starting from N_0) are shown in Fig. 4. The top left panel of Fig. 4 corresponds to Rastrigin-10D. With a relatively small initial design of size $N_0 = N_1 = 100$ we did not expect SpLEGO to work that well; nevertheless, we see that our method outperforms EGO on this test problem. With a larger number of initial data, SpLEGO again outperforms EGO on Hartmann-6D and Ackley-10D (top right and bottom left panels). Finally, the bottom right panel illustrates the feasibility of using our method for very large N_0 (size 10^4) on Shekel-4D test function. Note that EGO is no longer feasible. For this test function, the results based on two versions of SpLEGO are shown.

Recall that while SpLEGO-V1 only relies on exact points from the neighbourhood R_i, SpLEGO-V2 incorporates furthermore the inducing points of SPGP when fitting local GPs. The algorithm achieves better results with SpLEGO-V2 for this example, note however that, in general the results may vary from problem to problem.

4.3   Comments and Perspectives of Future Work

Since SPGP relies on a set of inducing points (which is changed in every iteration), whether or not SPGP leads to regions containing the global minimum is still an open problem. Nevertheless, the presented results are promising for

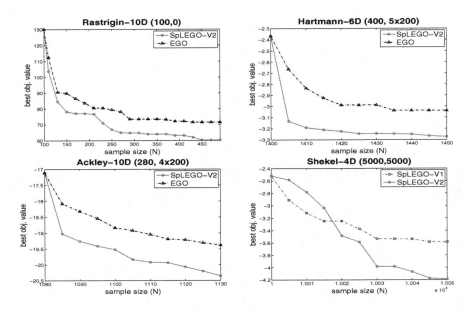

Fig. 4. Average best function value (10 trials) versus the number of sample size N. Initial sample size is $N_0 = N_1 + N_2$ where (N_1, N_2) is specified in each figure.

future research. One way to possibly improve the method is to incorporate also secondary non-dominated fronts in Step 3 when building local GP models and calculating local EIs. For example, in Fig. 5a, the first point on the secondary non-dominated front ($\mu^S \approx -5$, $-\sigma^{S2} \approx -2$) looks more promising than the last point on the Pareto front ($\mu^S \approx 0$, $-\sigma^{S2} \approx -12$). As expected, this point on the secondary front turns out to be the point at $x = 0.8$ in the decision space (Fig. 5b). In this example, we see that considering also the second front allows the algorithm to find a much wider spread of solutions.

In addition, Step 3c can be modified to allow SpLEGO to perform expensive function evaluations in a (synchronous or asynchronous) parallel way [7]. Instead of selecting only one point per iteration, several points from the pool of $\{w_i : i = 1, ..., r\}$ could be selected (in order of maximum local EI, from largest to smallest) and sent to the compute nodes. Once all the nodes have been taken, the next points wait in queue until the next node becomes available. Also, several candidate points may be considered for those regions with high potential, and possibly an arbitrage may be done between points from different subregions depending both on local EI and multipoint EI values [2].

One final remark about SPGP is that since $Md + |\Psi|$ hyperparameters need to be estimated, the standard SPGP method becomes no longer affordable for high dimensional data sets. Fortunately, [17] addresses this limitation by performing supervised dimensionality reduction in which the input space is projected to a low dimensional space. Problems of up to 10^2 dimensions and 10^4 number of training input points were considered in [17]. Consequently, this extension may

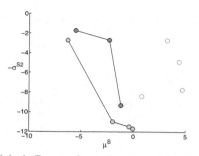 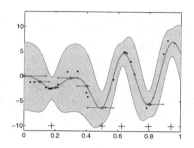

(a) A Pareto front for two objectives: SPGP mean and negative variance

(b) Pareto optimal point (green dots), second optimal (magenta dots), and its subregion R_i (blue line)

Fig. 5. Secondary non-dominated front and the corresponding subregions (Color figure online)

allow SpLEGO to be applied to solve global optimization problems where both the number of data points N and the input dimension d are large.

5 Conclusions

In this paper, SpLEGO, an extension of the EGO algorithm for handling a large number of starting points, was introduced and demonstrated on several test problems. SpLEGO is based on a multi-scale EI framework for global optimization that uses both sparse and local GP models. First, in the global scale, the space is partitioned using a Pareto-front approach with respect to the predictive mean and variance obtained from the sparse model. In the local scale, the algorithm zooms in specific regions around Pareto-optimal points, builds local GP models, and the next sample point is defined as the overall EI-optimal point among the maximizers of the several local EI criteria. The already obtained results demonstrate the effectiveness and robustness of our proposed method, yet there is still much room for improvement, particularly in developing adapted models and subregions for higher-dimensional problems, and also in handling the case of clustered points using some dedicated preliminary approach.

References

1. Ackley, D.H.: A Connectionist Machine for Genetic Hillclimbing. Kluwer, Dordrecht (1987)
2. Chevalier, C., Ginsbourger, D.: Fast computation of the multipoint expected improvement with applications in batch selection. In: Giuseppe, N., Panos, P. (eds.) Learning and Intelligent Optimization, pp. 59–69. Springer, Heidelberg (2014)
3. Csató, L., Opper, M.: Sparse on-line gaussian processes. Neural Comput. **14**(3), 641–668 (2002)

4. Dixon, L.C.W., Szegö, G.P.: The global optimization problem: an introduction. Towards Glob. Optim. **2**, 1–15 (1978)
5. Forrester, A.I.J., Keane, A.J.: Recent advances in surrogate-based optimization. Progr. Aerosp. Sci. **45**(1), 50–79 (2009)
6. Hansen, N., Finck, S., Ros, R., Auger, A., et al.: Real-parameter black-box optimization benchmarking 2009: noiseless functions definitions (2009)
7. Janusevskis, J., Le Riche, R., Ginsbourger, D., Girdziusas, R.: Expected improvements for the asynchronous parallel global optimization of expensive functions: potentials and challenges. In: Hamadi, Y., Schoenauer, M. (eds.) LION 2012. LNCS, vol. 7219, pp. 413–418. Springer, Heidelberg (2012)
8. Jones, D.R., Schonlau, M., Welch, W.J.: Efficient global optimization of expensive black-box functions. J. Glob. Optim. **13**(4), 455–492 (1998)
9. Mockus, J.: Bayesian approach to global optimization. Springer, The Netherlands (1989)
10. Myers, R.H., Anderson-Cook, C.M.: Response Surface Methodology: Process and Product Optimization using Designed Experiments, vol. 705. Wiley, New York (2009)
11. Quiñonero-Candela, J., Rasmussen, C.E.: A unifying view of sparse approximate gaussian process regression. J. Mach. Learn. Res. **6**, 1939–1959 (2005)
12. Rasmussen, C.E., Williams, C.K.I.: Gaussian Processes for Machine Learning. The MIT Press, Cambridge (2006)
13. Regis, R.G., Shoemaker, C.A.: A stochastic radial basis function method for the global optimization of expensive functions. INFORMS J. Comput. **19**(4), 497–509 (2007)
14. Roustant, O., Ginsbourger, D., Deville, Y.: DiceKriging, DiceOptim: two R packages for the analysis of computer experiments by kriging-based metamodeling and optimization. J. Stat. Softw. **51**, 1–55 (2012)
15. Smola, A.J., Bartlett, P.: Sparse greedy gaussian process regression. In: Advances in Neural Information Processing Systems, vol. 13. Citeseer (2001)
16. Snelson, E., Ghahramani, Z.: Sparse gaussian processes using pseudo-inputs. In: Schölkopf, B., Weiss, Y., Platt, J. (eds.) Advances in Neural Information Processing Systems, vol. 18. MIT Press, Cambridge (2006)
17. Snelson, E., Ghahramani, Z.: Variable noise and dimensionality reduction for sparse gaussian processes. In: Proceedings of the 22nd International Conference on Uncertainty in Artificial Intelligence (2006)
18. Snoek, J., et al.: Scalable bayesian optimization using deep neural networks (2015). arXiv preprint arXiv:1502.05700
19. Sóbester, A., Leary, S.J., Keane, A.J.: On the design of optimization strategies based on global response surface approximation models. J. Glob. Optim. **33**(1), 31–59 (2005)
20. Stein, M.L.: Interpolation of Spatial Data: Some Theory for Kriging. Springer, New York (1999)
21. Titsias, M.K.: Variational learning of inducing variables in sparse gaussian processes. In: International Conference on Artificial Intelligence and Statistics, pp. 567–574 (2009)
22. Veenendaal, G.V.: Tree-GP: a scalable bayesian global numerical optimization algorithm. Master's thesis, Utrecht University, The Netherlands (2015)
23. Wang, G.G., Shan, S.: Review of metamodeling techniques in support of engineering design optimization. J. Mech. Des. **129**(4), 370–380 (2007)

Condense Mixed Convexity and Optimization with an Application in Data Service Optimization

Emre Tokgöz[1][(✉)] and Hillel Kumin[2]

[1] School of Engineering, Quinnipiac University, Hamden, CT 06518, USA
Emre.Tokgoz@quinnipiac.edu
[2] School of Industrial and Systems Engineering, University of Oklahoma,
Norman, OK 73071, USA
hkumin@ou.edu

Abstract. Elements of matrix theory are useful in exploring solutions for optimization, data mining, and big data problems. In particular, mixed integer programming is widely used in data based optimization research that uses matrix theory (see for example [13]). Important elements of matrix theory, such as Hessian matrices, are well studied for continuous (see for example [11]) and discrete [9] functions, however matrix theory for functions with mixed (i.e. continuous and discrete) variables has not been extensively developed from a theoretical perspective. There are many mixed variable functions to be optimized that can make use of a Hessian matrix in various fields of research such as queueing theory, inventory systems, and telecommunication systems. In this work we introduce a mixed Hessian matrix, named condense mixed Hessian matrix, for mixed variable closed form functions $g : \mathbb{Z}^n \times \mathbb{R}^m \to \mathbb{R}$, and the use of this matrix for determining convexity and optimization results for mixed variable functions. These tasks are accomplished by building on the definition of a multivariable condense discrete convex function and the corresponding Hessian matrix that are introduced in [14]. In addition, theoretical condense mixed convexity and optimization results are obtained. The theoretical results are implemented on an M/M/s queueing function that is widely used in optimization, data mining, and big data problems.

Keywords: Continuous convexity · Discrete convexity · Hessian matrix · Optimization · Data mining

1 Convexity and Optimization of Real and Discrete Variable Functions

Matrix theory is widely used by researchers to solve problems in big data, data mining, and optimization. In particular, a continuous variable functions' Hessian matrix can be used for determining local and global convexity results that help

© Springer International Publishing Switzerland 2015
P. Pardalos et al. (Eds.): MOD 2015, LNCS 9432, pp. 197–208, 2015.
DOI: 10.1007/978-3-319-27926-8_17

determine local and global optimization results. An important and well-known implementation of the Hessian matrix is to determine a closed form optimization solution for multivariable C^2 functions in $\mathbb{R}^m$. The convexity of a multivariable C^2 function $f : \mathbb{R}^m \to \mathbb{R}$ can be determined by observing the positive definiteness of the corresponding Hessian matrix

$$H_f = \left[\frac{\partial^2 f}{\partial x_i \partial x_j} \right]_{m \times m} \tag{1}$$

It is well known [11] that f is convex if and only if H_f is positive semi-definite. A function f with positive definite Hessian matrix H_f has a unique minimum point.

Discrete convexity and the discrete analogue of the Hessian matrix in $\mathbb{Z}^n$ are introduced for multi-variate discrete functions by several researchers (see for example [9]). The classical definition states that a discrete function of a single variable is convex if its first forward difference is increasing or at least non-decreasing, as defined in [1,3] and others in the literature. Some of the discrete convex function definitions and their introducers are; discretely convex functions in [7], integrally-convex functions in [2], $M^\natural$-convex functions in [10], $L^\natural$-convex functions, L-convex functions and M-convex functions in [4], strongly discrete convex functions in [16], and D-convex and semi-strictly quasi D-convex functions in [15]. Discrete Hessian matrices corresponding to multivariable discrete L, $L^\#$, M, and $M^\#$ functions are introduced in [5,8]. Condense discrete convexity of multivariable discrete functions introduced in [14] is a generalization of the integer convexity definition introduced in [3] from one dimensional discrete space to multi-dimensional discrete space. In [14], a condense discrete convex set U is defined to be the set of points that coincides with a real convex set on the integer lattice which is large enough to support the second difference of a given condense discrete function. The union of condense discrete convex sets is assumed to be a condense discrete convex set, and a condense discrete convex function is defined as follows:

Definition 1. A discrete function $g : U \to \mathbb{R}$ on a condense discrete convex set $U \subset \mathbb{Z}^n$ is defined to be condense discrete convex if its quadratic expression $\frac{1}{2} x^T A x$ in the neighborhood U is strictly positive where A is the symmetric coefficient matrix of the quadratic expression of g. g is called condense discrete concave if $-g$ is condense discrete convex. A is called the discrete coefficient matrix of g.

The condense discrete convexity of a function $g : \mathbb{Z}^n \to \mathbb{R}$ for $n \geq 1$ and its corresponding positive definite discrete Hessian matrix

$$H_g = [\nabla_{ij} g]_{n \times n} \tag{2}$$

are shown to be equivalent where the first difference of g is defined by

$$\nabla_i g(x) = g(x + \delta_i) - g(x)$$

and the second difference of g is defined by

$$\nabla_{ij}\left(g\left(x\right)\right) = g\left(x + \delta_i + \delta_j\right) - g\left(x + \delta_i\right) - g\left(x + \delta_j\right) + g\left(x\right) \qquad (3)$$

with δ_i representing the integer vectors of unit length at the ith position of the function g [14].

The convexity of a discrete variable function can differ based on the way the discrete convexity is defined. For instance, in [16], an adaptation of Rosenbrock's function $g : \mathbb{Z}^2 \rightarrow \mathbb{R}$

$$g(x, y) = 25(2y - x)^2 + \frac{1}{4}(2 - x)^2 \qquad (4)$$

is shown to fail the discrete convexity definition of Miller [7], whereas in [14], the function defined in Eq. (4) is shown to be a condense discrete convex function in $\mathbb{Z}^2$. For further details of condense discrete convexity and optimization results see [14].

In this paper, our main goals include introducing condense mixed convexity the concept of and a Hessian matrix for condense mixed convex functions defined in $\mathbb{Z}^n \times \mathbb{R}^m$. The results introduced in this work can be used for data mining, big data, and optimization applications. Mixed integer programming is widely used in data based optimization research that uses matrix theory (see for example [13]). The Hessian matrix we introduce in this work will be particularly useful for determining closed form convexity and optimization of functions with multiple mixed variables. The condense mixed convexity will be constructed by using the definitions and results obtained for condense discrete convexity in [14]. An M/M/s queueing system optimization problem with an algorithmic mixed convexity solution is introduced in the last section for data service optimization where the number of servers is assumed to be the discrete variable and the service rate is assumed to be the continuous variable.

2   Condense Mixed Convexity and Minimization

In this section, function and set definitions of condense mixed convexity, and local and global minimum of a C^1 condense mixed convex function are introduced. In addition, mixed convexity and corresponding minimization results are stated and proven.

Definition 2. Let $V_1 \subseteq \mathbb{Z}^n$ be a condense discrete convex set and $V_2 \subseteq \mathbb{R}^m$ be a real convex set. A condense mixed convex set is the set of the form $V = V_1 \times V_2 \subseteq \mathbb{Z}^n \times \mathbb{R}^m$. Throughout this paper, g will be assumed to be a C^2 function with respect to its real variables unless stated otherwise, and the indices i, j, and k, l will be used for the integer and real variables, respectively.

A mixed function $g : V \rightarrow \mathbb{R}$ on a condense mixed convex set $V \subseteq \mathbb{Z}^n \times \mathbb{R}^m$ is defined to be condense mixed convex if its quadratic expression

$$g\left(x, y\right) = \frac{1}{2}x^T A x + x^T B y + \frac{1}{2}y^T C y + d^T x + e^T y + f \qquad (5)$$

in the neighborhood V is strictly positive where d and e are constant coefficient vectors of x and y, respectively, and f is a constant. A and C are assumed to be symmetric coefficient matrices of the quadratic expression of g with respect to x and y, respectively. h is called condense mixed concave if $-h$ is condense mixed convex. The quadratic expression of the function mentioned above is the quadratic form of the function within a local neighborhood.

Proposition 1. *Let $g : V \to \mathbb{R}$ be a condense mixed convex function defined on a condense mixed convex set $V \subseteq \mathbb{Z}^n \times \mathbb{R}^m$ with its quadratic expression given in (5). The coefficient matrix H_g corresponding to g is the symmetric matrix*

$$H_g = \begin{bmatrix} [\nabla_{ij}(g)]_{n \times n} & \left[\frac{\partial}{\partial y_k}\nabla_j(g)\right]_{n \times m} \\ \left[\nabla_i \frac{\partial}{\partial y_l}(g)\right]_{m \times n} & \left[\frac{\partial^2 g}{\partial y_k \partial y_l}\right]_{m \times m} \end{bmatrix} \tag{6}$$

Proof. The symmetry of the matrix $[\nabla_{ij}(g)]_{n \times n}$ in the mixed Hessian matrix H_g follows from [14]. Clearly

$$\frac{\partial^2 g}{\partial y_k \partial y_l} = \frac{\partial^2 g}{\partial y_l \partial y_k}$$

yields to a symmetric matrix. The off diagonal block matrices of H_g satisfy the symmetry condition

$$\frac{\partial}{\partial y_k}(\nabla_j g(x,y)) = \frac{\partial}{\partial y_k}(g(x + \delta_j, y) - g(x,y))$$

$$= \frac{\partial}{\partial y_k}g(x + \delta_j, y) - \frac{\partial}{\partial y_k}g(x,y)$$

$$= \nabla_j \frac{\partial}{\partial y_k}g(x,y)$$

for all j and k. Therefore H_g is a symmetric matrix.

By the definition of condense mixed convex function,

$$\nabla_{ij}(g(x)) = a_{ij}$$

holds for all i and j [14]. Therefore

$$A = [a_{ij}]_{n \times n} = [\nabla_{ij}g]_{n \times n}$$

Straightforward calculations indicate

$$\left[\frac{\partial^2 g}{\partial y_k \partial y_l}\right]_{m \times m} = C$$

The off diagonal elements satisfy

$$
\begin{aligned}
\frac{\partial}{\partial y_k} \nabla_j \left(g\left(x,y\right) \right) &= \frac{\partial}{\partial y_k} \left(\left(x + \delta_j\right)^T By - x^T By + d^T \left(x + \delta_j\right) - d^T x \right) \\
&= \frac{\partial}{\partial y_k} \left(x^T By + \delta_j^T By - x^T By + d^T \delta_j \right) \\
&= \frac{\partial}{\partial y_k} \left(\delta_j^T By + d^T \delta_j \right) \\
&= b_{jk}
\end{aligned}
$$

Proposition 2. *The coefficient matrix H_g of a condense mixed convex function $g : V \to \mathbb{R}$ given in Proposition 1 satisfies the properties of the mixed Hessian matrix corresponding to real convex functions. That is, H_g is linear with respect to the condense mixed functions, symmetric, and vanishes when g is mixed affine.*

Proof. Let $g_t : W_t \to \mathbb{R}$, $t = 1, 2$, be condense mixed functions where W_t are mixed convex sets (for $t = 1, 2$) with the corresponding coefficient matrices

$$
H_{g_t} = \begin{bmatrix} A_{g_t} & B_{g_t} \\ B_{g_t} & C_{g_t} \end{bmatrix}, \ t = 1, 2
$$

Note that

$$
\begin{aligned}
\frac{\partial}{\partial y_k} \nabla_j \left(g_1 + g_2\right) &= \frac{\partial}{\partial y_k} \left\{ g_1 \left(x + \delta_j, y\right) + g_2 \left(x + \delta_j, y\right) - \left[g_1 \left(x, y\right) + g_2 \left(x, y\right) \right] \right\} \\
&= \frac{\partial}{\partial y_k} \left(g_1 \left(x + \delta_j, y\right) - g_1 \left(x, y\right) \right) + \frac{\partial}{\partial y_k} \left(g_2 \left(x + \delta_j, y\right) - g_2 \left(x, y\right) \right)
\end{aligned}
$$

indicating

$$
\begin{aligned}
\left[\frac{\partial}{\partial y_k} \nabla_j \left(g_1 + g_2\right) \right]_{n \times m} &= \left[\frac{\partial}{\partial y_k} \nabla_j \left(g_1\right) \right]_{n \times m} + \left[\frac{\partial}{\partial y_k} \nabla_j \left(g_2\right) \right]_{n \times m} \\
&= B_{g_1} + B_{g_2}
\end{aligned}
$$

Therefore, by using the symmetry property obtained in Proposition 1,

$$
\begin{aligned}
H_{g_1 + g_2} &= \begin{bmatrix} \left[\nabla_{ij} \left(g_1 + g_2\right) \right]_{n \times n} & \left[\frac{\partial}{\partial y_k} \nabla_j \left(g_1 + g_2\right) \right]_{n \times m} \\ \left[\frac{\partial}{\partial y_k} \nabla_j \left(g_1 + g_2\right) \right]_{m \times n} & \left[\frac{\partial^2}{\partial y_k \partial y_l} \left(g_1 + g_2\right) \right]_{m \times m} \end{bmatrix} \\
&= \begin{bmatrix} A_{g_1 + g_2} & B_{g_1} + B_{g_2} \\ B_{g_1} + B_{g_2} & \frac{\partial^2 g_1}{\partial y_k \partial y_l} + \frac{\partial^2 g_2}{\partial y_k \partial y_l} \end{bmatrix} \\
&= \begin{bmatrix} A_{g_1} + A_{g_2} & B_{g_1} + B_{g_2} \\ B_{g_1} + B_{g_2} & C_{g_1} + C_{g_2} \end{bmatrix} \\
&= \begin{bmatrix} A_{g_1} & B_{g_1} \\ B_{g_1} & C_{g_1} \end{bmatrix} + \begin{bmatrix} A_{g_2} & B_{g_2} \\ B_{g_2} & C_{g_2} \end{bmatrix} \\
&= H_{g_1} + H_{g_2}
\end{aligned}
$$

which also proves the linearity of the second difference operator with respect to the condense discrete functions. The symmetry condition is proven in Proposition 1.

Considering the condense mixed affine function g, i.e.

$$g(x,y) = \sum_{i=1}^{n} d_i x_i + \sum_{k=1}^{m} w_k x_k$$

the second difference operator vanishes since $\nabla_i(g) = b_i$ and $\nabla_{ij}(g) = 0$ for all i and j. Similarly $\nabla_i \frac{\partial}{\partial y_k} = 0$ and $\frac{\partial^2}{\partial y_k \partial y_l} = 0$ for all i, k, and l.

Now assume we have a mixed quadratic function of the form

$$g(x,y) = \frac{1}{2} x^T A x + x^T B y + \frac{1}{2} y^T C y$$

Next the strict condense mixed convexity of mixed variable functions will be defined.

Theorem 1. *A function $g : V \to \mathbb{R}$ is strict condense mixed convex if and only if the corresponding mixed Hessian matrix H_g is positive definite in V.*

Proof. In the case when $m = 0$ the proof follows from Theorem 1 in [14]. In the case when $n = 0$ the result is well known from real convexity theory. Consider the mixed function

$$g(x,y) = \frac{1}{2} x^T A x + x^T B y + \frac{1}{2} y^T C y$$
$$= ax^2 + 2bxy + cy^2$$

where $a, b, c \in \mathbb{R}$ and $(x,y) \in \mathbb{Z} \times \mathbb{R}$. We prove the case for a 2×2 matrix and the $(n+m) \times (n+m)$ matrix case follows similarly. Let $z = (x,y)$. Suppose H_g is positive definite.

Case 1. If we let $z = (1,0)$, then

$$g(z) = ax^2 + 2bxy + cy^2 = a > 0$$

Case 2. If we let $z = (0,1)$, then

$$g(z) = ax^2 + 2bxy + cy^2 = c > 0$$

To show $H_g > 0$ for any $z \neq 0$ consider the following cases.

Case 1. If we let $x = (x,0)$ with $x \neq 0$. Then,

$$g(x) = ax^2 + 2bxy + cy^2 = ax^2 > 0 \Leftrightarrow a > 0$$

Case 2. If we let $x = (x,y)$ with $y \neq 0$. Let $x = ty$ for some $t \in \mathbb{R}$. Therefore we have

$$g(x) = \left(at^2 + 2bt + c\right) y^2$$

where $g(z) > 0 \Leftrightarrow \varphi(t) = at^2 + 2bt + c > 0$ since $y \neq 0$. Note that

$$\varphi'(t) = 2at + 2b = 0$$
$$\Rightarrow t^* = -\frac{b}{a}$$
$$\varphi''(t) = 2a.$$

If $a > 0$ then

$$\varphi(t) \geq \varphi(t^*) = \varphi\left(-\frac{b}{a}\right) = \frac{-b^2}{a} + c$$
$$= \frac{1}{a}\det\begin{bmatrix} a & b \\ b & c \end{bmatrix}$$

Therefore if $a > 0$ and the determinant given above is positive then $\varphi(t) > 0$ for all $t \in \mathbb{R}$. Conversely, if $g(z) > 0$ for every $z \neq 0$ then $\varphi(t) > 0$ for some t, therefore

$$\varphi(t) > 0 \Rightarrow a > 0, \;\; and \;\; 4b^2 - 4ac = -4\det(H_g) < 0$$
$$\varphi(t) > 0 \Leftrightarrow a > 0 \;\; and \;\; \det(H_g) > 0$$

which completes the proof.

To obtain minimization results for a given condense mixed convex function, the given condense mixed convex function will be required to be C^1 with respect to all of its variables.

Following [14], let

$$\mathbb{Z}^n \times \mathbb{R}^m = \overset{\infty}{\underset{i=1}{\cup}} S_i \times \overset{\infty}{\underset{j=1}{\cup}} R_j$$

where $S_i \times R_j$ are non-empty sufficiently small condense mixed convex neighborhoods to support a quadratic expression of g, $\underset{i \in I}{\cap} S_i \neq \emptyset$ for all S_i where S_i have at least one common element for all $i \in I$, I is a finite index set, and $\{(s_i, r_j)\}$ is a singleton in $\mathbb{Z}^n \times \mathbb{R}^m$.

The partial derivative operator of a C^1 mixed function $g : \mathbb{Z}^n \times \mathbb{R}^m \to \mathbb{R}$ will be denoted by

$$Dg(x) := \left(\frac{\partial g}{\partial x_1}, \frac{\partial g}{\partial x_2}, ..., \frac{\partial g}{\partial x_n}, \frac{\partial g}{\partial y_1}, \frac{\partial g}{\partial y_2}, ..., \frac{\partial g}{\partial y_m}\right) x$$

Definition 3. The local minimum of a condense mixed C^1 function $g : \mathbb{Z}^n \times \mathbb{R}^m \to \mathbb{R}$ is the minimal value of g in a local neighborhood $\underset{i \in I}{\cup} S_i \times \underset{j \in I}{\cup} R_j$ which is also the smallest value in a neighborhood $M = N \times R$ where I is a finite index set and $R = \underset{j \in I}{\cup} R_j$. The global minimum value of a condense mixed convex function $g : \mathbb{Z}^n \times \mathbb{R}^m \to \mathbb{R}$ is the minimum value of g in the entire mixed space $\mathbb{Z}^n \times \mathbb{R}^m$.

Define the set of local minimums of a C^1 condense mixed convex function g by

$$\Theta = \{\rho = (\rho_1, ..., \rho_n, \alpha_1, ..., \alpha_m) : \rho_i \in \{\lceil \gamma_i \rceil, \lfloor \gamma_i \rfloor\} \subset \mathbb{Z} \; \forall i, \alpha_j \in \mathbb{R} \; \forall j\} \subset \mathbb{Z}^n \times \mathbb{R}^m$$

where $Dg(\gamma, \alpha) = 0$ holds for $(\gamma, \alpha) \in \mathbb{R}^{n+m}$. In this paper, the solutions in Θ where $\rho_i = \lceil \gamma_i \rceil$ or $\rho_i = \lfloor \gamma_i \rfloor$ are considered for the multivariable mixed function g.

Lemma 1. *Let* $g : M \to \mathbb{R}$ *be a* C^1 *condense mixed convex function in* $M \subset \mathbb{Z}^n \times \mathbb{R}^m$. *Then there exists a local minimum value in* M *such that*

$$g_0 = \min_{\beta \in \Theta} \{g(\beta)\}$$

Proof. Let $g : M \to \mathbb{R}$ be a C^1 strict condense mixed convex function. Suppose $Dg(x, y) = 0$ holds in some neighborhood

$$S = \bigcup_{i \in I} S_i \times \bigcup_{j \in I} R_j \subseteq M$$

for all $(x, y) \in M$. Therefore, the local minimum of the C^1 function g is obtained when the system of equations

$$\frac{\partial g(x)}{\partial x_i} = \lim_{t \to 0} \frac{g(x + t\delta_i) - g(x)}{t} = 0$$

$$\frac{\partial g(x)}{\partial y_j} = 0$$

are solved simultaneously for all i, $1 \leq i \leq n$, and for all j, $1 \leq j \leq m$. This indicates the existence of a $(\gamma, \alpha) \in \mathbb{R}^{n+m}$. For the integer variables in the domain $\mathbb{Z}^n$, we take the ceiling and floor of the components of γ_i to obtain the minimal point which consist of integer numbers $\lfloor \gamma_i \rfloor$ or $\lceil \gamma_i \rceil$ for all i, $1 \leq i \leq n$. This gives a local minimum point $(\beta, \alpha) \in \Theta$ since there exists a unique minimum value of a real convex function and the corresponding value $g_0 = \min_{\beta \in \Theta} \{g(\beta)\}$.

Suppose $Dg(x, y) \neq 0$ for some x and y. Then either $Dg(x, y) > 0$ or $Dg(x, y) < 0$ holds which in either case the minimum value is obtained for the boundary values of M for x and y satisfying $Dg(x, y) \neq 0$.

The following theorem for condense mixed convex functions has a similar statement to the results obtained for real and condense discrete convex functions. It is evident that a condense mixed convex function can have more than one global minimum point.

Theorem 2. *Let* $g : \mathbb{Z}^n \times \mathbb{R}^m \to \mathbb{R}$ *be a* C^1 *strict condense mixed convex function which has local and global minimum points. Then the set of local minimum points of* g *form a set of global minimum points and vice versa.*

Proof. Suppose $g : \mathbb{Z}^n \times \mathbb{R}^m \to \mathbb{R}$ is a C^1 condense mixed convex function. Let

$$\bigcup_{i=1}^{\infty} S_i \times \bigcup_{j=1}^{\infty} R_j = \mathbb{Z}^n \times \mathbb{R}^m$$

where $S_i \times R_j$ are sufficiently small condense mixed neighborhoods supporting quadratic expression of g for all i and j, and $\bigcap_{i=1}^{\infty} S_i = \emptyset$. Let Φ_1 be the set of local minimum points of g in $\mathbb{Z}^n \times \mathbb{R}^m$, and Φ_2 be the set of global minimum points of g in $\mathbb{Z}^n \times \mathbb{R}^m$.

Let $g : \mathbb{Z}^n \times \mathbb{R}^m \to \mathbb{R}$ be a C^1 condense mixed convex function and suppose g has global minimum points in $\mathbb{Z}^n \times \mathbb{R}^m$. Noting that g is strict mixed convex, there exists a collection of

$$S_i \times R_j \subset \bigcup_{i \in I_0} S_i \times \bigcup_{j \in I_0} R_j$$

where the global minimum points are located. Considering the quadratic expression of g in the neighborhood $S_i \times R_j$, the solution set of $Dg(z) = 0$ gives the set of local minimums in $S_i \times R_j$. Therefore for all $z_2 \in \Phi_2$ there exists a set of vectors $z_1 \in \Phi_1$ such that $\min_{z_1 \in \Phi_1} g(z_1) = g(z_2)$ which indicates $\Phi_2 \subset \Phi_1$ since

$$\bigcup_{i \in I_0} S_i \times \bigcup_{j \in I_0} R_j \subset \mathbb{Z}^n \times \mathbb{R}^m$$

Now suppose there exists a vector $z_0 = (x_0, y_0)$ in a local neighborhood

$$M_1 = \bigcup_{i \in I_1} S_i \times \bigcup_{j \in I_1} R_j$$

such that $z_0 \notin \Phi_2$ (Note that z_0 is not necessarily an element of Φ_1 since it is a local minimum in a local setting). z_0 is a local minimum which is not a global minimum in M_1, therefore there exist z_1 and z_2 such that $g(z_0) > g(z_1) > g(z_2)$ in

$$M_2 = \bigcup_{j \in J} \left(\bigcup_{i \in I_j} S_i \right) \times \bigcup_{j \in J} \left(\bigcup_{i \in I_j} R_i \right) \supset M_1$$

where z_2 becomes the new local minimum of the local neighborhood M_2. Therefore z_2 is the new local minimum of M_2 where z_0 is not a local minimum of M_2. Suppose z_2 is a local minimum that is not a global minimum otherwise it would be an element of Φ_2. Continuing to enlarge the local obtained neighborhoods in this way to the entire space $\mathbb{Z}^n \times \mathbb{R}^m$, a set of points in a local neighborhood V of $\mathbb{Z}^n \times \mathbb{R}^m$ is obtained where local minimum points $z \in \Phi_1$ satisfy $g(z) < g(\overline{z})$ for all $\overline{z} \in \mathbb{Z}^n - V$. Therefore $z \in \Phi_2$ and hence $\Phi_1 \subset \Phi_2$ which completes the proof.

3   Applications in Data Service Optimization

Consider a parallel channel queueing system in which data arrive according to a Poisson process with the arrival rate λ. In each channel, service follows the same negative exponential distribution with the service rate μ. Data does not wait for service by the server if there is a free channel. Otherwise it joins the queue and waits for service. The queue discipline is FIFO. It is well known that steady-state exists for this system if $\rho = \frac{\lambda}{s\mu} < 1$ [6]. Assuming this to be the case, the expected number in the system is found to be

$$E(s, \mu) = s\rho + \frac{\rho P_s}{(1 - \rho)^2} \cdot$$

where

$$P_s = \frac{\left(\frac{\lambda}{\mu}\right)^s P_0}{s!}$$

and

$$P_0 = \left[\left(\sum_{j=0}^{s-1} \frac{\left(\frac{\lambda}{\mu}\right)^j}{j!}\right) + \frac{\left(\frac{\lambda}{\mu}\right)^s}{s!}\left(\frac{1}{1-\rho}\right)\right]^{-1}$$

Let the discrete decision variables be the number of servers s and the continuous decision variable be the service rate μ. Assume that there are fixed costs c_1, c_2, and c_3 associated with the number of servers, the service rate, and the expected number of data in the system [6]. Thus, we can define the following closed form optimization problem:

$$\min_{(s,\mu)\in\mathbb{Z}\times\mathbb{R}} \Psi(s,\mu) = c_1 s + c_2 \mu + c_3 E(s,\mu) = c_1 s + c_2 \mu$$

$$+ c_3 \left\{ \frac{\lambda}{\mu} + \frac{\lambda\mu\left(\frac{\lambda}{\mu}\right)^s}{(s-1)!\,(s\mu-\lambda)^2\left[\left(\sum_{j=0}^{s-1}\frac{\left(\frac{\lambda}{\mu}\right)^j}{j!}\right) + \frac{\left(\frac{\lambda}{\mu}\right)^s}{s!}\left(\frac{s\mu}{s\mu-\lambda}\right)\right]} \right\}$$

$$\tag{7}$$

$$subject\ to : \mu > 0, \lambda > 0, s = 1, 2, 3, \ldots$$

where c_1, c_2, and c_3 are arbitrary positive constants and $\lambda < s\mu$. The mixed convexity of this problem can be determined by applying the condense mixed convexity definition, and therefore by determining the conditions under which the corresponding mixed Hessian matrix is positive definite. Noting that the second difference, the second differential, and difference of the differential of the linear term $c_1 s + c_2 \mu$ are zero, the Hessian matrix would have the form

$$H_\Psi = \begin{bmatrix} \nabla_{11}(\Psi) & \frac{d}{d\mu}(\nabla_1(\Psi)) \\ \nabla_1\left(\frac{d}{d\mu}(\Psi)\right) & \frac{d^2\Psi}{d\mu^2} \end{bmatrix}$$

$$= \begin{bmatrix} \nabla_{11}(E) & \frac{d}{d\mu}(\nabla_1(E)) \\ \nabla_1\left(\frac{d}{d\mu}(E)\right) & \frac{d^2 E}{d\mu^2} \end{bmatrix}$$

that solely depends on the expected value. The following algorithm, requiring symbolic programming, can be implemented for determining both theoretical and numerical computational mixed convexity results. This algorithm can be particularly useful for functions with complex structures such as the one given in Eq. (7). We do not implement the computations for Eq. (7) in this work due to space limitation.

```
Algorithm.
syms c1 c2 c3 alpha mu rho s
rho = lambda/mu
PSI(s,mu) = c1*s + c2*mu + c3*(lambda/mu + lambda*mu*(rho^s)/(fact(s-1)
*(s*mu-lambda)^2*(sum(rho^j/fact(j),0,s-1)+((rho^s)/fact(s))
*(s*mu/(s*mu-lambda))))
d1M = diff(PSI,mu)
d2M = diff(PSI,mu,2)
Difference1 = PSI(s+1,mu)-PSI(s,mu)
diff_Difference1 = diff(Difference1,mu,1)
Difference2 = PSI(s+2,mu)-2PSI(s+1,mu)+PSI(s,mu)
DetH = d2M*Difference2 - (diff_Difference1)^2
If (DetH>0) then PSI is condense mixed convex
else PSI is not condense mixed convex
```

The optimization problem can be reorganized to have a more complicated structure: It is possible to assume that the arrival rate λ is a continuous decision variable in addition to the existing variables s and μ; therefore, the minimization problem will have domain $(s, \mu, \lambda) \in \mathbb{Z} \times \mathbb{R}^2$. The linear costs can be assumed nonlinear functions with variables c_1, c_2 and c_3 which would yield to an optimization problem with the decision variables $(s, \mu, \lambda, c_1, c_2, c_3) \in \mathbb{Z} \times \mathbb{R}^5$.

References

1. Denardo, E.V.: Dynamic Programming. Prentice-Hall, Englewood (1982)
2. Favati, P., Tardela, F.: Convexity in nonlinear programming. Ric. Operativa **53**, 3–44 (1990)
3. Fox, B.: Discrete optimization via marginal analysis. Manag. Sci. **13**, 210–216 (1966)
4. Fujishige, S., Murota, K.: Notes on L-/M-convex functions and the separation theorems. Math. Prog. **88**, 129–146 (2000)
5. Hirai, H., Murota, K.: M-convex functions and tree metrics. Jpn. J. Indus. Appl. Math. **21**, 391–403 (2004)
6. Kumin, H.: On characterizing the extrema of a function of two variables, one of which is discrete. Manag. Sci. **20**, 126–129 (1973)
7. Miller, B.L.: On minimizing nonseparable functions defined on the integers with an inventory application. SIAM J. Appl. Math. **21**, 166–185 (1971)
8. Moriguchi, S., Murota, K.: Discrete Hessian matrix for L-convex functions. IECE Trans. Fundam. **E88-A**, 1104–1108 (2005)
9. Murota, K.: Discrete Convex Analysis. SIAM, Philadelphia (2003)
10. Murota, K., Shioura, A.: M-convex function on generalized polymatroid. Math. Oper. Res. **24**, 95–105 (1999)
11. Rockafellar, R.T.: Convex Analysis. Princeton University Press, Princeton (1970)
12. Stoer, J., Witzgall, C.: Convexity and Optimization in Finite Dimensions I. Springer, Berlin (1970)
13. Tawarmalani, M.: Convexification and Gobal Optimization in Continuous and Mixed-Integer Nonlinear Programming: Theory, Algorithms, Software, and Applications. Springer, USA (2002)

14. Tokgöz, E., Nourazari, S., Kumin, H.: Convexity and optimization of condense discrete functions. In: Pardalos, P.M., Rebennack, S. (eds.) SEA 2011. LNCS, vol. 6630, pp. 33–42. Springer, Heidelberg (2011)
15. Ui, T.: A note on discrete convexity and local optimality. Jpn. J. Indust. Appl. Math. **23**, 21–29 (2006)
16. Yüceer, U.: Discrete convexity: convexity for functions defined on discrete spaces. Disc. Appl. Math. **119**, 297–304 (2002)

SoC-Based Pattern Recognition Systems for Non Destructive Testing

Omar Schiaratura[2]([✉]), Pietro Ansaloni[1], Giovanni Lughi[1], Mattia Neri[1],
Matteo Roffilli[1], Fabrizio Serpi[1], and Andrea Simonetto[1]

[1] Bioretics S.r.l., Pula, Italy
info@bioretics.com
http://www.bioretics.com
[2] CRS4 S.c.a.r.l., Pula, Italy
omar.schiaratura@crs4.it
http://www.crs4.it

Abstract. Non Destructive Testing (NDT) is one of the most important aspect in modern manufacturing companies. Automation of this task improves productivity and reliability of distribution chains. We present an optimized implementation of common pattern recognition algorithms that performs NDT on factory products. To the aim of enhancing the industrial integration, our implementation is highly optimized to work on SoC-based (System on Chip: an integrated circuit that integrates all components of a computer into a single chip.) hardware and we worked with the initial idea of an overall design for these devices. While perfectly working on general purpose SoCs, the best performances are achieved on GPU accelerated ones. We reached the notable performance of a PC-based workstation by exploiting technologies like CUDA and BLAS for embedded SoCs. The test case is a collection of toy scenarios commonly found in manufacturing companies.

Keywords: Non-destructive testing · SoC · ARM · CUDA · OpenCL

1 Introduction

In order to create a product of high quality and to meet customer's expectations, the manufacturer needs to fulfill specific requirements planned for achieving a successful product. In this context, quality is intended as how much a product is suitable for the purpose it has been developed. That is, how much the product has the properties and the capabilities the producer warrants and how much it meets market needs [1].

In this scenario, most of the potential defects are visual patterns that prevent the perceived quality. Nowadays, these defects can be detected by automatic systems via destructive quantitative measures taken over samples, and matched to standard ranges. Unfortunately, these measures are not easy to obtain, and even if they are taken, they result in having a negative impact on the process

© Springer International Publishing Switzerland 2015
P. Pardalos et al. (Eds.): MOD 2015, LNCS 9432, pp. 209–221, 2015.
DOI: 10.1007/978-3-319-27926-8_18

layout as well as on costs [2]. In many production chains, the aforementioned measures could be taken by a human-like analysis on images of the products.

Pattern Recognition algorithms have shown to be reliable in such analysis and to have great performances even in difficult operative conditions found in industrial environments [3]. These techniques, mainly when based on Machine Learning, are greed for computational power (GFlops) that should be yielded by devices often in a non server farm environment. Thus, it is absolutely necessary to use the last generation of HPC technologies that can enable those methodologies in a as little as possible space, typically the dimension of a credit card.

SoCs allow optimal exploitation of the packaging space and permit the creation of modular systems (serial, parallel and distributed ones) depending on the required computational power. The advantage is that you do not need to invest in proprietary (es. DSP, FPGA), very expensive (es. blade server), or big form factor infrastructures.

In fact, when the issues related to the computational power are solved with traditional HPC systems, these introduce new problems such as electrical power consumption, the physical space they need, and a suitable cooling apparatus. In a research environment, physical space is not relevant, since there are laboratories with HPC clusters aimed at computational purposes.

In an industrial context you could need an integrated system in a short physical space, able to perform material recognition in real time on a moving machine, as well as to take care of power consumption.

An embedded COTS based system[1], developed on top of a SoC, yields a low impact solution concerning cost, physical space, power consumption and low overheating.

2   State of the Art

Embedded systems introduce new challenges as well as new issues to face. They have particular characteristics that affect the whole development and testing process. This complex domain includes:

1. a development process that considers both the hardware and the software parts of the whole system;
2. complex specifications;
3. platform-dependent constraints (CPU, memory, power consumption, peripherals);
4. quality constraints;
5. very short time-to-market constraint.

Each application sector needs to take into account the difficult identification of general tools and techniques, so ad-hoc methods are needed.

---

[1] Commercial Off The Shelf: products that are commercially available and can be bought "as is".

Table 1. Technical features of SoCs.

Model	CPU	# of Cores	Clock (Mhz)	RAM (MB)	Extensions	GPU	Cost (€)	Advantages
Raspberry Pi	ARM11 Broadcom BCM2835	1	700	512	vfp	Broadcom Video- Core IV	45, 00	diffusion, sdk aimed at graphics
Wandboard	Cortex A9 Freescale i.MX6 Quad	4	792	2048	vfp, NEON	Vivante gc2000, gc355, gc320	100,00	top-notch performance
Intel Galileo	x86 Intel Quark x1000	1	400	256	/	/	60,00	x86 compatibility
lime A20	Cortex A7 Allwiner A20	2	1000	/	vfp, NEON	dual core Mali 400	33,00	good price- performance ratio
Nvidia Jetson TK1	Cortex A15	4	1900	2048	vfp, NEON, Cuda	Kepler	192,00	high performance

NDT-VT[2] literature is filled with methodologies, techniques and instruments that support traditional product testing, but few examples can be found concerning testing with advanced pattern recognition and machine learning systems. The most advanced systems in industry, are based on proprietary PLCs solutions that are difficult to maintain or modify. Hence, the necessity to design a new system (Table 1).

ARM based SoCs have a BUS internal structure that interconnects the following devices:

1. more than one CPU Core;
2. GPU core;
3. interfaces for sensor, debug and/or development systems (i.e. PC, monitor, HD, etc.).

Technical features of different kind of platforms available have been evaluated, choosing the most promising ones. The choice has been made based on the following criteria:

1. diffusion of the platform, documentation and support;
2. advanced CPU extensions availability;
3. ease of interfacing with external devices;
4. computational power of the CPU and number of cores.

The Raspberry Pi platform has a good support for the developers, the most complete and the best documented HW/SW video features, while its computational unit performance suffers from the quite old ARM11 vfp[3] architecture.

The Lime is a good low cost alternative, considering its dual core CPU, its Mali card, and the support for the NEON[4] technology.

---

[2] Non Destructive Testing - Visual Testing.
[3] Vector Floating Point: an ARMv11 floating point architecture.
[4] Arm general purpose SIMD engine.

The Wandboard and Jetson TK1 are the top-notch solutions amongst the ARM based systems. They include both a quad core CPU and multiple GPUs, as well as a sufficient amount of RAM. The last one has also Cuda support.

The Intel Galileo suffers from a performance gap when compared to its competitors. Its price is high and lacks of video support, but the system is Arduino platform compatible; it can execute x86 standard code without x86 advanced optimizations.

3   System Implementation

A complete NDT system can be represented as in Fig. 1. In details, the I/O part receives an analog or digital signal as input (receiver transducer) from an external hardware like a video camera, an X-ray machine, an infrared sensor, and so on.

The signal, typically analog, is amplified by the interface and then converted to a digital form. After conversion, the obtained digital signal, is processed by a micro-controller that will pass it to the classification sub-system.

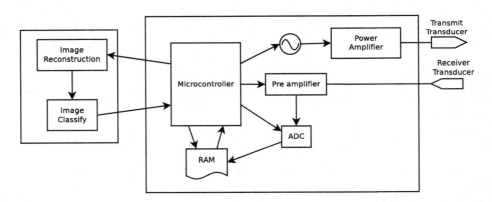

Fig. 1. Block diagram of a NDT system. The smaller block on the left side is the classification subsystem; transducers on right side represent the I/O subsystem.

We have been focused on HW optimizations in the classification sub-system expanded in Fig. 2 with highlight of the modules composing the classification parts.

Part of the system shown in Fig. 1 has been simulated implementing an ad-hoc framework in the Python programming language with the support of the openCV library. The framework task is to extract the objects of interest from the images and then input them to the classification system.

The process of classification can be summarized as follows:

1. the image is processed and isolated from the background (i.e. objects of interest are selected);

  (a) each segment is resized and then transformed via mathematical operators (i.e. Fourier, Wavelet or Ranklet). These transforms yield underlying texture characteristics of the segment (features) useful for classification purpose [4];
  (b) the classification algorithm (SVM [5], Neural Networks, etc.), that also takes in input a model of the defects, classifies the processed segment;
  (c) finally, the signal is normalized and an output is sent, that indicates the state of the analyzed segment (good or bad).

The system in Fig. 2 is very modular, and each block has an independent interface, so it can be easily replaced without or with minor change to other blocks. Transformation and classification blocks are the ones that need an optimized implementation. Our choice (see [6] for a detailed description of the workflow) for the transformation is a Haar DWT of computational complexity O(n). The second one is a SVM classifier which has O(n²) complexity for each sample, using a polynomial kernel function.

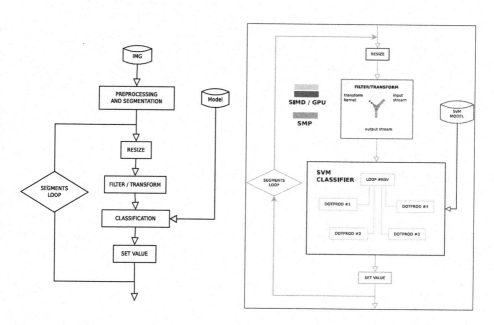

Fig. 2. Serial workflow (sx) and with optimized loops (dx).

The classification stage was improved in several ways:

1. grouping the segments and making different logic units process them. Code distribution is done over different SoCs connected to each other in a serial or parallel configuration;

2. executing parallel code for each segment, so that the code is distributed over the cores (SMP);
3. speeding up the computationally more expensive parts via vectorized instructions (SIMD - NEON), and GPU processing.

4   Evaluating GPU for Classification Problems

Systems like Wandboard and Jetson TK1 allow using complex GPGPU languages like CUDA [7], OpenCL [8] and GLSL [9], which would enable to combine CPU and GPU in compute-intensive tasks. The first one supports OpenCL and GLSL, while the second supports CUDA, GLSL and OpenCL with limitations. The OpenCL Jetson TK1 API is only available for Android operating systems. GLSL support on Wandboard isn't complete, and doesn't handle 32 bit float textures.

Using OpenCL makes it possible to write code that runs transparently on both GPUs and CPUs at the cost of a performance degradation in case of CPUs-only systems.

CUDA is a more mature architecture, but it is only available in Nvidia HW.

GLSL is more complex to program and optimize, while it best fits on graphics-visualization code. We are using BLAS [10] implementations in our applications: we adopt cuBLAS, clBLAS, ATLAS, handmade GLSL and OpenCL code.

For the classification system's peculiarity, it is also interesting to exploit the GPU in the data acquisition from the camera, in conjunction with the CPU for the execution of the classifier, so that objects acquisition and elaboration can be done in real time.

4.1   OpenCL

To support clBLAS on ARM, we made a porting of AMD source code on ARM freescale i.MX6 quad which supports the complete openCL EP[5] 1.1 specifications.

At this time, our porting is able to execute scalar product (dot), matrix product (gemm) and matrix product between vectors (ger). The dot product has some stability issues yet, while the matrix-vector product (gemv) is under working.

4.2   GLSL

GLSL is the shading language of the openGL [11] library that enables GPUs to be used like CPUs for computing purpose, but the following is also important to understand other GPGPU technologies.

GPUs work following the SPMD paradigm[6]. SPMD approach is called *stream processing* and is similar to that used in FPGAs. The program is seen as an

---

[5] Embedded Profile.
[6] Single Program Multiple Data is a kind of parallel architecture.

atomic operation that is executed over a continuous stream of input data. GPUs have more logical units that operate simultaneously executing parallel threads, as many as the computational units they contain.

Within shaders, it is possible to use SIMD instructions, exploiting thread innate internal parallelism.

4.3   How to Solve Main Limitations of GP Computing

There are several limitations for shaders to be run on a GPU architecture:

1. maximal dimension for computed data,
2. data transfer from main to GPU memory,
3. more complex programs to be written.

As the graphic card memory is limited and usually smaller than the main one, when computing is there executed, data dimension is bounded from memory space. To avoid an out of memory during computations, we had implemented a block version of linear algebra algorithms like gemv, and we allocate memory only when needed, interleaving memory allocation with computational parts (Fig. 3).

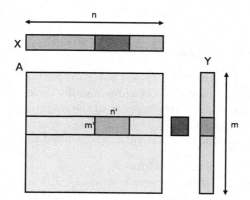

Fig. 3. gemv memory schema (y = Ax). Each GPU cycle threats the dark color parts of data and blue internal buffer is used as global memory to merge results each time (Color figure online).

Data saved in the main memory (CPU memory) need to be uploaded first to the GPU memory in order to be used. While the GPU is optimized for data transfer from CPU to GPU memory, exploiting DMA and buffering techniques, it is too slow when it transfers back from the GPU to the CPU memory. We have optimized the flows of the program and reordered the operations needed to allow the few memory data transfer as possible; in the classification parts, the matrices are uploaded to the GPU memory, only the first time and the results are transferred back to CPU memory only at the end of computation.

To obtain the best optimization of the architecture, data has been mapped to textures of dimension equal to a power of 4, with a 0 padding of unnecessary data (Table 2).

Table 2. Test performance on Jetson TK1 GLSL matrices - Near computation time the whole time with data transfer in secs *100.

Op	256	Whole	1024	Whole	4096	Whole
SDOT	0,29	10,83	0,28	10,78	0,25	10,76
SGEMV	0,25	11,61	0,85	15,33	7,51	31,66
SGER	0,23	12,03	0,31	13,83	2,03	26,68
SGEMM	0,36	13,18	3,04	01,92	37,89	2166

There are usually some additional limitations in the use of some SoCs, that have been found:

1. openGLES [12] is needed in place of openGL;
2. limited number of cycles within a shader;
3. limits in the type of data and subroutines.

4.4 GPGPU Code Implementations

In Table 3 are shown the architecture and SW used for testing. The OS versions for ARM systems are the ones supported by manufacturer, and for the reference architecture the one that has better support in the major number of technologies than other OSs.

We consider four fundamental operations, executed in single precision:

1. dot - scalar product between vectors,
2. gemv - product between matrix and vector,
3. gemm - product between matrices,
4. ger - matrix product between two vectors.

The tests have been run with vectors of dimension 256, 1024, 4096 and in some cases of 8192. In addition, square matrices of dimension 256, 1024 and 4096 have been used too. Next to the computation time for GPUs implementations, it's shown the whole time including the data transfer time from GPU to CPU.

In Tables 4, 5 and 6 are shown the results of the matrix product operations (capable of exploiting better the GPUs HW), for the two best ARM architectures and two control architectures.

Scalar product suffers from the fact that the algorithm cannot exactly run parallel. It consists of an initial parallel phase and then a reduction phase.

The results are identical to the CPU vector optimized BLAS, with the same error with respect to non optimized plain CPU code. The errors affect the seventh

Table 3. Platforms used for GPU algorithms evaluations.

Architecture	Operating system	Compiler	Supports
Jetson TK1	ARM HF Ubuntu 14.04 based	Gcc-4.8 armhf	Cuda, GLSL
Wandboard quad	ARM SF Ubuntu 12.04 based	Gcc4.6 arm	OpenCL, limited GLSL
Intel core 2 1,6 ghz	Ubuntu 14.10 x86_64	Gcc 4.8 x86_64	OpenCL, GLSL, Cuda
Nvidia GeForce 320M		Mac OSX 10.9	
Intel I7 2,7 GHZ	Ubuntu 11.04 x86_64	Gcc 4.6 x86_64	SW OpenCL, GLSL
Intel GMA 3000	Mac OSX 10.7		

Table 4. Test performance on SGEMM with 256×256 matrices in secs.

Board	C code	blas	openCL		Cuda		GLSL	
Wandboard	0,13	0,24	0,16	0,19	X	X	X	X
Jetson TK1	0.12	0.012	X	X	0,00010	0,0026	0,0036	0,13
Core2 1,6 Mhz	0,013	0,0059	0,0051	0,042	0,0022	0,011	0,041	0,61
Core I7 2,7 Ghz	0,0072	0,0029	0,0042	0,0062	X	X	0,019	0,24

significant digit in the 10 numerical base. The C vector version has a greater propagation error, which is solved using the Kaham sum vectors algorithm [13].

These errors rarely affect the classification phase, and they are difficult to detect in the experimental phase as well. Overall, these errors usually have a negligible impact on the final result.

Platforms that support GLSL show performance boosts compared to CPU implementations.

Increasing matrix dimension, the memory transfer bottleneck impact decreases. With 4096×4096 matrices the speed up is 200x considering the whole time, while the CPU blas implementation lacks in performance.

For shorter matrices dimensions, the GPU execution time is near CPU time, but transfer degrades the whole performance of the systems.

The Jetson TK1 board confirms its more powerful GPU and great performance of CUDA GPUs.

5   Evaluation of the Classifier Performances

Algorithm performances have been evaluated through the execution of several benchmarks:

Table 5. Test performance on SGEMM with 1024×1024 matrices in secs.

Board	C code	blas	openCL		Cuda		GLSL	
Wandboard	17,18	28,67	0,16	0,28	X	X	X	X
Jetson TK1	1,22	0,54	X	X	0,00019	0,026	0,030	1,02
Core2 1,6 Mhz	1,15	0,34	0,0067	0,12	0,071	0,062	0,032	0,66
Core I7 2,7 Ghz	0,41	0,19	0,0033	0,025	X	X	0,019	0,26

Table 6. Test performance on SGEMM with 4096×4096 matrices in secs.

Board	C code	blas	openCL		Cuda		GLSL	
Wandboard	1110,39	1827,5	0,2	3,38	X	X	X	X
Jetson TK1	90,33	34,89	X	X	0,016	0,21	0,39	21,67
Core2 1,6 Mhz	71,09	21,52	0,0065	1,49	0,0029	0,11	0,0062	2,30
Core I7 2,7 Ghz	27,88	11,85	0,0032	0,39	X	X	0,022	0,56

Table 7. Execution of a test prediction expressed in seconds.

Board	# of Cores	Block C	Block Blas	GPU CUDA
Galileo	1	878,98	X	X
Raspberry Pi	1	363,50	96,94	X
Lime A20	1	194,17	83,39	X
Lime A20	2	95,40	45,65	X
Wandboard	1	109,12	20,62	X
Wandboard	2	61,22	14,83	X
Wandboard	4	36,74	12,10	X
Jetson TK1	1	19,16	7,28	5,16
Jetson TK1	2	14,00	7,28	X
Jetson TK1	4	9,45	7,28	X
Xeon E54440 2.83 Ghz	1	9,70	1,70	X
Xeon E54440 2.83 Ghz	2	5,53	1,37	X
Xeon E54440 2.83 Ghz	4	3,00	1,19	X
Core i7 4790k 4,00 Ghz	1	6,03	0,89	0,66
Core i7 4790k 4,00 Ghz	2	3,94	0,65	X
Core i7 4790k 4,00 Ghz	4	1,97	0,53	X

1. on a GPU cluster x86 with a generic model for image recognition. The same tests have been done, in a second moment, on SoC systems;
2. toy test on SoC systems, GPGPU and CPU x86.

Table 8. Different execution times for the single SVM and Wavelet transform in prediction.

Board	# of Cores	Wavelet	Block C SVM	Block Blas SVM	Cuda SVM
Galileo	1	39,94	839,03	X	X
Raspberry Pi	1	15,24	348,26	81,70	X
Lime A20	1	34,94	159,22	48,45	X
Lime A20	2	"	60,46	10,70	X
Wandboard	1	8,69	100,43	11,93	X
Wandboard	2	"	52,52	6,14	X
Wandboard	4	"	28,05	3,41	X
Jetson TK1	1	3,78	15,44	3,56	1,44
Jetson TK1	2	"	10,28	3,56	X
Jetson TK1	4	"	5,73	3,56	X
Xeon E54440 2.83 Ghz	1	0,80	8,91	0,90	X
Xeon E54440 2.83 Ghz	2	"	4,73	0,57	X
Xeon E54440 2.83 Ghz	4	"	2,20	0,39	X
Core i7 4790k 4,00 Ghz	1	0,38	5,65	0,55	0,28
Core i7 4790k 4,00 Ghz	2	"	3,56	0,27	X
Core i7 4790k 4,00 Ghz	4	"	1,59	0,15	X

The tests have been executed both with standard optimizations for the compiler and with Blas libraries, the latter giving the best performance.

A camera has been installed on the systems for the tests over SoCs, while the ad-hoc framework realized with Python simulates the rest of the system. In addition, the moving objects to be recognized have been simulated by a video stream.

Image pre-processing can be efficiently implemented on SoCs hardware using high optimized library as OpenCV [14].

Tables 7 and 8 show results for a classification problem. The first table shows elapsed time against the number of threads, while the second one shows elapsed time separately for classification (SVM) and feature extraction (Wavelet).

The classifier was implemented in standard C, in multi-threading and with a Blas implementation, while the Wavelet transform was executed in single core mode with the compiler optimizations.

The training phase was executed off-line on a standard PC to obtain the model used for the classification.

In prediction phase, the model is read from the disk and is written in XML format, and this results in a longer time for the system to start up.

In order to obtain more accurate results, classification and pre-processing cycles were repeated for 1000 times, introducing each time numerical noise in the original image, so that classification of different objects could have been simulated by introducing vanishing cache coherency.

As expected, Wandboard and Jetson TK1 are the fastest boards, since they have a shorter reading time of the model than the SoC competitors. The Raspberry Pi on a single core was competitive with the Lime A20, thanks to a more efficient I/O system (shorter reading time from the disk), even though it is one generation behind the Lime if considering ARM architecture.

Results for x86 high-end systems are showed too.

The differences in performance of this architecture from the others are many, but mainly they are due to a faster clock and a CPU/Memory system optimized for high performance, while the ARM architecture is optimized for power consumption.

We argue that overall performances are quite satisfactory, if considered to be the result of preliminary tests, and a margin of improvement is expected.

Actual results are comparable with the theorized ones.

As a basis for comparison, a quad-core i7 2,7 GHz should have a computational power peak of 86 GFlops (8 operations for each clock cycle and core), while an ARM Cortex A8 quad-core 1 GHz has a 18 GFlops peak.

6   Conclusion

We had highly optimized the design of our pattern recognition software to embed it in an ARM SoC based HW.

For a real time environment, the best choice is the use of a device based on ARM Cortex A8 and further, while for a general purpose detection is sufficiently powerful an ARMv6 architecture. The Cortex A15 based boards like Jetson provide the best performance both in only CPU and CPU-GPU computations. The internal classifier, which is based on linear transformations, is the most computational power consumptive, so we focused on it the most optimization effort.

This statement is valid when using a Wavelet transform as a feature selection part, where using other transformations like Ranklets needs more powerful computational units to obtain the same performance. The wavelets are very efficient and its CPU SIMD optimized implementations are sufficient for all fields of utilization.

Due to GPU utilization, it would be interesting evaluating CNNs (Convolutional Neural Networks) [15] approach to our problems and the utilization of Wavelet scattering networks [16].

A focus on the acquisition process, especially for real time camera acquisition images, must be necessary to avoid its influence on classification time, to perform this last in real time during acquisitions without performance losses.

The use of graphics boards APIs make it possible. The choice of the operating system is Linux due to the manufacturers' support; almost all producers have its customized and optimized version for device drivers and they provide for source code and specifications on how to use Linux on boards. Even if the performance tuning is code dependent, we have focused on optimizing vector and matrix linear algebra operations when possible, without penalizing the whole system performance, so the results can be generalized over other systems and SoC based HW, thanks to our modular frameworks.

Acknowledgments. The authors acknowledge partial financial support from Sardegna Ricerche and from the Sardinian Regional Authority under grant number G28F14000010002 for project "COACH - Choice on a Chip" (call "Incentivo Ricerche Polaris").

References

1. Montgomery, D.C.: Introduction to Statistical Quality Control, 5th edn. McGraw-Hill, New York (2009)
2. Hocken, R.J., Pereira, P.H. (eds.): Coordinate Measuring Machines and Systems, 2nd edn. CRC Press, Boca Raton (2012)
3. Chen, C.H. (ed.): Handbook of Pattern Recognition and Computer Vision, 4th edn. World Scientific Publishing, River Edge (2010)
4. Tian, D.P.: A review on image feature extraction and representation techniques. Int. J. Multimedia Ubiquit. Eng. 8(4), 385–396 (2013)
5. Vapnik, V.: The Nature of Statistical Learning Theory. Springer, New York (1995)
6. Roffilli, M.: Advanced Machine Learning Techniques for Digital Mammography. Technical report UBLCS-2006-12, University of Bologna (2006)
7. Wilt, N.: "The CUDA Handbook". All day (2013)
8. Khronos OpenCL Working Group: "The OpenCL specifications". Howes, L., Munshi, A. (eds.) (2014)
9. Rost, R.J., Licea-Kane, B.M., Ginsburg, D., Kessenich, J.M., Lichtenbelt, B., Malan, H., Weiblen, M.: OpenGL Shading Language, 3rd edn. Addison Wesley, Reading (2009). Paperback
10. NetLib Home of BLAS. http://www.netlib.org/blas/. Accessed 26 February 2015
11. Shereiner, D.: OpenGL Programming Guide, 7th edn. Addison-Wesley, Reading (2013). Paperback
12. Ginsburg, D., Purnomo, B., Shreiner, D., Munshi, A.: OpenGL ES 3.0 Programming Guide, 2nd edn. Addison-Wesley, Reading (2014). Paperback
13. Kahan, W.: Further remarks on reducing truncation errors. Commun. ACM **8** (1965)
14. Pulli, K., Baksheev, A., Kornyakov, K., Eruhimov, V.: Real-time computer vision with OpenCV. Commun. ACM **51**, 61–69 (2012)
15. Convolutional Neural Networks. http://deeplearning.net/tutorial/lenet.html. Accessed 26 February 2015
16. Bruna, J., Mallat, S.: Invariant Scattering Convolution Networks (2012)

Node-Immunization Strategies in a Stochastic Epidemic Model

Juan Piccini$^{(\boxtimes)}$, Franco Robledo, and Pablo Romero

Facultad de Ingeniería, Universidad de la República, Julio Herrera y Reissig 565,
11300 Montevideo, Uruguay
{piccini,robledo,romero}@fing.edu.uy

Abstract. The object under study is an epidemic spread of a disease through individuals. A stochastic process is first introduced, inspired in classical Susceptible, Infected and Removed (SIR) model. In order to jeopardize the epidemic spread, two different immunization strategies are proposed. A combinatorial optimization problem is further formalized. The goal is to minimize the effect of the disease spread, choosing a correct immunization strategy, subject to a budget constraint. We are witness of a counter-intuitive result: in non-virulent scenarios, it is better to immunize common individuals rather than communicative ones. A discussion is provided, together with open problems and trends for future work.

Keywords: Epidemic model · Susceptible · Infected and removed model · Stochastic process · Combinatorial optimization problem

1 Introduction

Ironically, a cornerstone in the mathematical analysis of epidemiology has not been published in the scientific literature. The work by Lowell Reed and Wade Frost on Susceptible, Infected and Removed (SIR) model was considered by its authors as too slight a contribution [4]. The most valuable aspects of SIR model is its simplicity: closed formulas are met, an epidemic spread can easily be carried out on a computer, and it connects deterministic and stochastic models in an elegant fashion. For those reasons, SIR model is the starting point in teaching and understanding epidemic propagation. However, it assumes a full-mixed population with random contacts. Several subsequent authors in the field believe a more realistic model is inspired by networks, where nodes represent individuals, and the epidemic spread takes places in the links [14]. The interest of the topic is increased with the current threaten of bioterrorism as a letal weapon over an induced pandemia [13]. The reader can find other authoritative works about SIR epidemics on graphs in the related literature [10–12]. Simulations carried-out on small-world networks confirm that there exists an extinction threshold [10–12,15]. There, the epidemic propagation is carried out through graphs with either potential or exponential degree distribution as distinguished characteristics. However, for social network applications an asymmetric

© Springer International Publishing Switzerland 2015
P. Pardalos et al. (Eds.): MOD 2015, LNCS 9432, pp. 222–232, 2015.
DOI: 10.1007/978-3-319-27926-8_19

right-tailed distribution shows to be more suitable. Specifically, if nodes represent people and links are contacts, most individuals have a reduced number of neighbors, that keep in contact daily. Aspects such as network awareness and node-ageing has been suggested by Barabasi in order to define realistic evolutionary network models [1]. Explicit characterizations of extinction and probability distribution of the epidemic outbreak are currently available by means of percolation theory. Kena and Robins use percolation techniques and random mixing using classical SIR model [7]). An empirical study using SIR model is performed by Macdonald and Shakarian. They find centrality measures and detect main spreaders of a disease [9]. The goal of this work is to develop immunization methods to cope with an epidemic propagation. As a mathematical framework, a realistic stochastic process for epidemic propagation is here introduced, together with a score for different immunization strategies. This process is more realistic than classical SIR model.

This article is organized in the following manner. In Sect. 2, classical SIR model is described as a reference to study epidemic propagation. In order to introduce a more realistic model for disease propagation, a stochastic process is introduced in Sect. 3. A combinatorial problem is formally presented in Sect. 4. There, the goal is to choose among a set of feasible immunization strategies, in order to minimize the peak of the epidemic spread. There, the precise meaning of "peak" will be formalized in terms of the underlying stochastic process. Two extremal immunization strategies are proposed. On one hand, we consider a *greedy* immunization notion, were nodes with the highest degree are immunized first, called *HighDegree*. On the other, we pick nodes with low degree uniformly at random, called *LowFirst*. Section 5 introduces classical random graphs as opposite to lattices, as well as efficiency measures for simple graphs. Two random graphs are generated in this work as a case study for disease propagation. Section 6 introduces two massive random graphs used in the simulation of the stochastic process. Then, the performance of strategies *HighDegree* and *LowDegree* is analyzed on the lights of these graphs. Finally, Sect. 7 contains concluding remarks and trends for future work.

The main contributions of this article are summarized in the following items:

- We propose a realistic stochastic process to simulate and understand the evolution of an disease spread.
- A combinatorial optimization problem is formally presented, where the decision variable involves a set of immunization strategies, and the goal is to minimize the infection in the population subject to a budget constraint.
- A greedy notion for the previous combinatorial problem is introduced, where nodes with high degree are immunized first.
- We explicitly show that greedy is not the best option; indeed, a better result is achieved when nodes with low degree are immunized in some scenarios (precisely, in two graphs with 2000 nodes). We will discuss how this counterintuitive result is possible, in terms of the underlying topology and different virus-types.
- Open problems are presented, arising from the stochastic process and the global optimum for the combinatorial problem.

2   SIR Model

Probably the most-studied class of epidemic models is classical SIR model. There, individuals are Susceptible (S), Infected (I), or Removed (R). The last category represents those individuals that are immune after being recovered of the disease. Iinfected individuals have random contacts with others (from any of the three states) at a mean rate β. They are removed (recovered) at a mean rate γ. If a susceptible receives a contact, it turns infected.

If we consider a big population of n individuals, SIR epidemic model can be described by the following system of non-linear differential equations:

$$\frac{ds}{dt} = -\beta is, \frac{di}{dt} = \beta is - \gamma i, \frac{dr}{dt} = \gamma i,$$

being $s(t) = S(t)/n, i(t) = I(t)/n, r(t) = R(t)/n$ the respective proportions of classes at time t. The last equation can be omitted, since $s + i + r = 1$ [5]. The model assumes standard incidence and recover (I-output) at a rate $\gamma I/n$. This represents a waiting time (or residence time in class I) of $e^{-\gamma t}$ time units, with mean $1/\gamma$. Since such period is small, the model lacks of a vital dynamics (i.e., natural death and birth). Therefore, it is suitable just to describe diseases with fast propagation and conclusion. Furthermore, they provide immunity to infected individuals, for instance, influenza. In computer viruses, we can interpret this as an antivirus program that, once updated, infection is no longer allowed.

SIR model is suitable for a completely-mixed population, where the assumption of uniformly random contact selection is plausible. All individuals have the same number of contacts in a given time unit, and those contacts are equally likely to propagate the disease. However, in real-life applications, we rarely meet all the requirements that must be fulfilled to apply SIR model. Individuals do not contact randomly, and full-mixtures should be replaced by networks [10–12]. Links represent those pair of individuals with a potential epidemic spread between them. Neighboring nodes represent individuals that potentially contact during the disease (i.e. in real life, partners, mates, friends, people that travel together occasionally, among others). The approach from Percolation Theory gives us information about asymptotic size of infected population, usually under some assumptions such that random mixing or same types of mixing [7]. An overview of mixing and its relation with percolation theory can be found at [6].

It is neither consistent nor realistic to assume the infection probability between pairs of nodes to be identical. It is possible to find some pairs that have higher probability of infection than others. Furthermore, it is not realistic to assume that an infectious-susceptible contact is equivalent to an infection. The capacity of the infectious to spread susceptible with which it has contact may vary over time. The existence of a link between infected and susceptible nodes is not a guaranteed contagion of the susceptible one. The time-window during which an infected node can spread has a non-deterministic (nor fixed) length. In fact, an infected node does not have to contact all its susceptible neighbors at a time. This is our motivation to propose a more realistic stochastic process for disease propagation, in the sense that includes the previous concerns.

3   Stochastic Process

We are given a simple graph $G = (V, E)$, where nodes represent individuals and links are relation between nodes (i.e., possible infection channels). Time is slotted, and the starting point $(t = 0)$ is defined as follows:

- Certain selected nodes $V^* \subset V$, called *immunized nodes*, are removed, and the process takes place in the subgraph induced by $V' = V - V^*$, denoted by G'. Observe that $V^* = \emptyset$ implies no immunization at all.
- A single *infected node* $x_0 \in V'$ is chosen uniformly at random (the zero case). All nodes from V' but x_0 are *susceptible nodes*.

Infected nodes might affect neighboring nodes from G' over time, and then susceptible nodes may become infected ones. If a node is infected at time t_i, it can affect neighboring susceptible nodes during a random time-window $[t_i, t'_i]$. It is reasonable to assume that although this time-window is random and this length varies from an infected node to another, it fluctuates around a mean value. Therefore, we represent the time-window picking a normal distribution with parameters (μ, σ), where $\mu > 0$ represents the mean length of the time-window and σ denotes its standard deviation. Time t'_i is then picked using the rule $t'_i = t_i + |X_i|$, being X_i a normally distributed random variable, $X_i \sim N(\mu, \sigma)$. The parameters (μ, σ) are called the *virus-type of the disease*. Once t'_i is reached, that infected node is in removed state. When an infected node contacts a susceptible one, the probability of spread varies over time, depending on the state of the infected node. An infected node will affect a susceptible neighboring node at $t \in [t_i, t'_i]$ if and only if its *infectivity profile* $f(t) > u$, being $f(t) = \exp\left\{-\frac{1}{(t'_i - t)(t - t_i)}\right\}$ a *bump function* and u a random number in the compact set $[0, 1]$. Function f represents the capacity of the node to spread the disease. This is in agreement with real life, where the infectivity is first monotonically increasing, then it presents a maximum, and later it is monotonically dicreasing.

Definition 1. *The number of infected nodes* $\{X_t\}_{t \in \mathbb{N}}$ *is the stochastic process under study.*

We want to minimize the overall effect of the disease spread. Formally:

Definition 2. *The peak of the disease spread in graph G with immunization set V^* and virus-type (μ, σ) is the first moment of the maximum achieved by the process:* $p(G, V^*, \mu, \sigma) = E(\max_{t \in \mathbb{N}}\{X_t\})$

4   Node Immunization Problem and Heuristics

In this paper, we formulate the performance of different immunization strategies by means of a combinatorial optimization problem. Given a simple graph $G = (V, E)$ and virus-type (μ, σ), we want to minimize the peak of the epidemic spread

$p(G, V^*, \mu, \sigma)$ among all feasible immunization sets V^*. The Node Immunization Problem is formulated as follows:

$$\min_{V^*} p(G, V^*, \mu, \sigma) \tag{1}$$

$$s.t.$$

$$|V^*| \leq N \tag{2}$$

The reasons leading to include Constraint (2) in the combinatorial problem are twofold. The first reason is related with a real budget constraint. Even though the desease is propagated through links, the protection takes place in the nodes. The second is related with a requirements associated with immunization heuristics: In order to fix the constraint N, let C be the number of nodes that can be immunized with the available resources.

The critical degree is the first degree g^* such that an epidemic spread occurs (the peak exceeds the 5 % of total population), once we remove all nodes from the set $V^* = \{v \in V : deg(v) \geq g^*\}$. Now, let us focus on the development of naive immunization strategies suitable for the combinatorial problem. A small number of individuals with a big link action will have a higher impact than a highly populated group with a sparse number of links. If we immunized these nodes, we would remove its edges of the graph. At first glance, the best nodes to protect should be those with the highest degree.

Nevertheless, the link density is not the only matter, but the quality of those links. This means that if a node-group has several links but they are mostly locally defined (like a clique or quasi-clique), then the immunization of those nodes will not mine the link structure, in the sense that it should be better to immunize a set of nodes V^* with large amount of external links. This suggests another approach: instead of immunizing nodes of higher degree, immunize randomly chosen nodes (those likely to have low degree, since these nodes are the majority of the population). In order to have a strong contrast with the greedy notion, we will choose nodes with low degree. Specifically, the following immunization strategies will be considered in this article:

- *HighDegree*: the greedy notion, where nodes are sort in terms of degree (nodes with the same degree are sort randomly). The immunization takes place in nodes with the highest degree, meeting at the same time Constraint (2).
- *LowDegree*: analogously, but nodes with the lowest degree are selected first, meeting Constraint (2).
- *Raw*: when no immunization takes place ($V^* = \Phi$), we have Raw immunization strategy, which is the cheapest one in practice (but naturally, its performance is low as we will see in Sect. 6).

5   Random Graphs and Efficiency

Let $G = (V, E)$ a graph with $|V| = n, |E| = m$. There are $C^m_{n(n-1)/2}$ possible spanning subgraphs with m edges in the complete graph K_n. In Erdös-Rënyi rule for random graph generation, a number $t < \frac{n(n-1)}{2}$ is fixed, and a subgraph with t edges is selected uniformly at random. This type of random graphs have typically low diameter, since the random connection between nodes connects every pair of nodes with the same probability [3]. Also, the number of clusters is small, because if a is connected to b and b is connected to c, the probability of the $a-c$ connection is the same that for every pair of nodes. This kind of graph is the example of networks with purely random connections, leading to homogeneous Random Mixing. On the other hand we have Lattices: highly regular graphs with high diameter where the connection $a - c$ has higher probability provided a is connected to b and b is connected to c. From Lattices we can obtain other kind of random graphs (by "rewiring "pairs of nodes at random) that inherits these properties. In order to measure the presence of clusters the concepts of *Global and Local Efficiency* are introduced in [8]. Let us consider a simple graph $G = (V, E)$ with adjacency matrix $A = (a_{i,j})$ and distance matrix $D = (d_{i,j})$.

Definition 3. *The efficiency between nodes v_i and v_j is $e_{i,j} = \frac{1}{d_{i,j}}$.*

Definition 4. *The mean efficiency $Eff(G)$ is the normalized expected value over all node pairs: $Eff(G) = \frac{1}{n(n-1)} \sum_{i \neq j} \frac{1}{d_{i,j}}$.*

The mean efficiency $Eff(G)$ is maximized when $G = K_n$ is the complete graph.

Definition 5. *The global $GEff(G)$ is the ratio between the mean efficiency of G and K_n: $GEff(G) = \dfrac{Eff(G)}{Eff(K_n)}$.*

Note that $0 \leq GEff(G) \leq 1$ and $GEff(G)$ makes sense even if G is not connected. An analogous notion is considered locally for single nodes.

Definition 6. *Let v_i be a node, N_i its neighbor set and G_i the subgraph induced by N_i. The Local Efficiency is the mean of $GEff(G_i), i = 1, \dots, n$:*

$$LEff(G) = \frac{1}{n} \sum_{i=1}^{n} GEff(G_i)$$

This concept measures the fault tolerance of the graph G. In other terms, it represents the efficiency of the communication between neighbors of a node i when it is removed. On one hand, random graphs present low diameters and then low values of $d_{i,j}$. This implies high values of Global Efficiency. The low probability of clusters implies low Local Efficiency. On the other, Lattices present low values of Global Efficiency (high diameters) but high values of Local Efficiency.

6   Performance Analysis

In order to test the effectiveness of different immunization strategies, two graphs with 2000 nodes have been generated. These graphs were built choosing a predetermined node-degree distribution, and using Havel-Hakimi theorem. To avoid the pure exponential or potential node-degree distributions, we use Gamma distribution (rounded to closest integer values). Let us consider the candidate degrees $(d_1 \geq d_2 \geq \cdots \geq d_{2000})$ of a graph. Havel-Hakimi theorem helps to determine whether such graph exists:

Theorem 1. *The sequence $d_1 \geq d_2 \geq \cdots \geq d_{2000}$ is graphic if and only if the sequence is graphic $d_2 - 1 \geq d_3 - 1 \cdots \geq d_{d_1+1} - 1 \geq d_{d_1+2} \cdots \geq d_p$ is graphic.*

Once we have a graphic sequence, a recursive method to produce the graph is offered by the work from Bayati [2]. This method generates a graph chosen uniformly at random from the set of all graphic graphs with 2000 nodes and prescribed degrees. In this way, we generated two graphs with 2000 nodes, called $2000A$ and $2000B$. These graphs present low values of Global Efficiency as Lattices, and low values of Local Efficiency, as Random Graphs:

$$GEff(2000A) = 0.2564,$$
$$LEff(2000A) = 0.0079,$$
$$GEff(2000B) = 0.2158$$
$$LEff(2000B) = 0.0043.$$

Both graphs are sketched in Fig. 1.

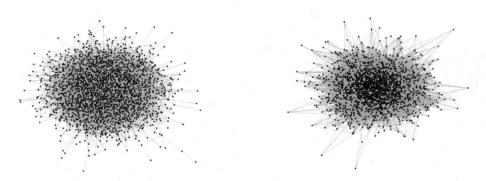

Fig. 1. Left: Graph $2000A$. Right: Graph $2000B$

Simulations were carried-out for different virus-types (μ, σ) in both graphs. In order to perform a faithful comparison of both strategies, one-hundred independent simulations were considered with $t_f = 100$ time slots for each graph, using Crude Monte Carlo. The time-window is generated using a normal distribution with parameters (μ, σ), with mean $\mu \in \{3, 5, 10, 20\}$ and standard deviation $\sigma = 1$. Higher values for μ imply that an infected individual will have more time to infect contacted susceptible individuals. When μ is extremely large, the existence of a link will practically guarantee a positive infection if the neighbor node is susceptible. Figure 2 presents the temporal evolution of X_t in a 100-run average (or mean-epidemic), for $HighDegree$ (red) and $LowDegree$ (blue), with Raw as a reference (green) for the set of virus types $(\mu, \sigma) \in \{(3,1),(5,1),(10,1),(20,1)\}$ in Graph $2000A$.

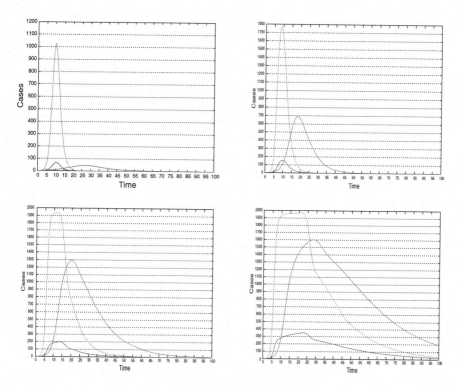

Fig. 2. Performance in Graph 2000 A for virus types $(3,1)$, $(5,1)$, $(10,1)$ and $(20,1)$. $HighDegree$ (red), $LowDegree$ (blue), Raw (green) (Color figure online).

All simulations for $HighDegree$ were carried out using the critical node set V^* for the set of removed nodes. Analogously, $LowDegree$ is performed choosing nodes whose degree is below the critical one g^* (see Section refcop).

Curiously enough, $LowDegree$ outperforms both $HighDegree$ and Raw heuristics for virus type $(20,1)$. Therefore, the graph connectivity has low sensibility to a high-degree node-deletion via immunization. This fact suggests that nodes with higher degree tend to connect each other. Therefore, the deletion of their links do not undermine the link-structure of the graph as much if we eliminate the links of the N low degree nodes. For virus-type $(10,1)$, an epidemic spread takes place in $HighDegree$ if we remove all nodes with degree $d \geq 7$. With virus type $(5,1)$ the situation is similar to the previous case, as it could be expected if the topology is in fact relevant. For less virulent diseases it is

expected to get a lower influence in the underlying network topology. As the
disease is less virulent and the topological influence is decreased, *HighDegree*
tends to be more effective.

An analogous performance analysis is carried out in Graph 2000*B*.

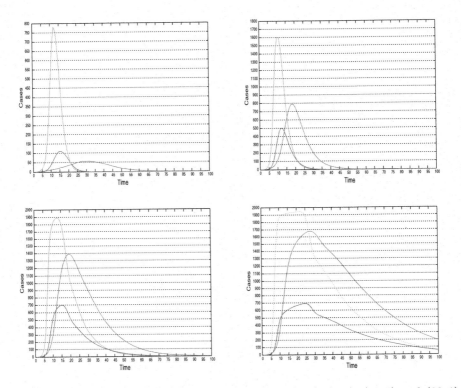

Fig. 3. Performance in Graph 2000B for virus types $(3,1)$, $(5,1)$, $(10,1)$ and $(20,1)$.
HighDegree (red), *LowDegree* (blue), *Raw* (green) (Color figure online).

Figure 3 presents the temporal evolution X_t of infected individuals in a 100-
run average (or mean-epidemic). As in previous instances, the difference between
both strategies tends to vanish when the disease is less virulent (less influence
of the underlying topology). This points out a huge amount of internal links
between nodes with the highest degree.

7   Concluding Remarks

The effects of an epidemic propagation under two different immunization heuristics has been discussed. For that purpose, we built two massive random graphs
(with Gamma degree distribution and using the strength of Havel-Hakimi theorem), and develop a SIR-based model simulations with different virulence levels.

Two "opposite" heuristics have been proposed. On one hand a *greedy* notion, called *HighDegree* heuristic, immunizes N nodes with the highest degree first. The intuition here is that they could infect more neighbors in the same time-window. On the other hand, *LowDegree* heuristic picks N nodes with lower degree uniformly at random, and immunizes them. They are computationally efficient, since the number of elementary operations is linear with the order of the input graph. If we do not immunize nodes we have *Raw* heuristic. As expected, both heuristics outperform *Raw*.

A counter-intuitive result is that *LowDegree* heuristic outperforms *HighDegree* in some scenarios. A possible explanation would be the following: when we have low values of μ, the number of infected individuals from the neighbor-set N_i is small, and only infected nodes of high degree have a chance to spread disease, since they have a number of contacts many times greater than low-degree nodes and this compensate the low number of trials (time). So, deletion of high-degree nodes is more effective and *HighDegree* is better.

On the other hand, when we have high values of μ low degree nodes ended by infecting all its neighbors further nodes of high degree, because they have comparatively few neighbors and more time to each one. Graph with a low local efficienct are highly sensible to node deletions, regardless of the degree (see Sect. 5). The deletion of low-degree nodes disconnects the graph more effectively, and *LowDegree* is better. As real social networks are adequately modeled by random graphs, simulations will assist in order to study virtual versions of real epidemics. This tool provides a systematic way to produce essays of control and disease prevention, which is an essential element to design adequate strategies to cope with epidemics.

As a future work, we will develop a greedy randomized heuristics in order to find outstanding immunization strategies. More sophisticated ideas should be considered in order to detect high-performance immunization strategies, understanding the underlying graph topology as an input of the heuristic. It is worth to remark that the problem is purely combinatorial when the virus-type is increased without bound, and can be expressed in terms of graph theory and network connectivity. The complexity of this combinatorial problem is still open.

References

1. Barabasi, A.: Linked: The New Science of Networks. Perseus Publishing, Cambridge (2002)
2. Bayati, M., Kim, J.H., Saberi, A.: A sequential algorithm for generating random graphs. In: Charikar, M., Jansen, K., Reingold, O., Rolim, J.D.P. (eds.) RANDOM 2007 and APPROX 2007. LNCS, vol. 4627, pp. 326–340. Springer, Heidelberg (2007)
3. Bollobás, B.: Random Graphs. Academic Press, London (1985)
4. Fine, P.E.: A commentary on the mechanical analogue to the reed-frost epidemic model. Am. J. Epidemiol. **106**(2), 87–100 (1977)
5. Hethcote, H.W.: The mathematics of infectious diseases. SIAM Rev. **42**(4), 599–653 (2000)

6. Keeling, M.J., Eames, K.T.: Networks and epidemic models. J. Royal Soc. Interface **2**(4), 295–307 (2005)
7. Kenah, E., Robins, J.M.: Network-based analysis of stochastic SIR epidemic models with random and proportionate mixing. J. Theor. Biol. **249**(4), 706–722 (2007)
8. Latora, V., Marchiori, M.: Efficient behavior of small-world networks. Phys. Rev. Lett. **87**, 198701 (2001)
9. Macdonald, B., Shakarian, P., Howard, N., Moores, G.: Spreaders in the network SIR model: an empirical study (2012). CoRR abs/1208.4269
10. Newman, M.E.J.: Spread of epidemic disease on networks. Phys. Rev. E **66**(1), 016128 (2002)
11. Newman, M.E.J.: The structure and function of complex networks. SIAM Rev. **45**(2), 167–256 (2003)
12. Newman, M.E.J., Strogatz, S.H., Watts, D.J.: Random graphs with arbitrary degree distributions and their applications. Phys. Rev. E **64**(2), 026118 (2001)
13. Roberts, F.S.: Bioterrorism: Mathematical Modeling Applications in Homeland Security. Frontiers in Applied Mathematics. Society for Industrial and Applied Mathematics, Philadelphia (PA) (2003)
14. Santhanam, G.R., Suvorov, Y., Basu, S., Honavar, V.: Verifying intervention policies to counter infection propagation over networks: a model checking approach. In: AAAI (2011)
15. Shirley, M.D., Rushton, S.P.: The impacts of network topology on disease spread. Ecol. Complex. **2**(3), 287–299 (2005)

An Efficient Numerical Approximation for the Monge-Kantorovich Mass Transfer Problem

M.L. Avendaño-Garrido[✉], J.R. Gabriel-Argüelles, L. Quintana-Torres, and E. Mezura-Montes

Universidad Veracruzana, Xalapa, Veracruz, Mexico
{maravendano,jgabriel,lquintana,emezura}@uv.mx

Abstract. The approximation scheme for the Monge-Kantorovich mass transfer problem on compact spaces proposed in [7] is improved. The upgrade presented is inspired on a meta-heuristic algorithm called Scatter Search in order to reduce the dimensionality of the problem. The new approximation scheme solves finite linear programs similar to the transport problem but with lower dimension. A numerical example is presented and compared with the scheme studied in [7].

Keywords: Mass transfer problem · Finite linear program · Transport problem · Meta-heuristic algorithm

1 Introduction

In the late XVIII century, Gaspard Monge proposed the mass transfer problem (see [18]). Monge wanted to find an optimal transportation plan to move a mound to a hole. The cost of that transportation plan was in function of the distance. The solution assigns each particle of the mound its corresponded place in the hole.

In the mid XX century, Leonid Kantorovich proposed the problem of translocation of masses (see [14]). That problem consisted in minimizing the work to move an initial mass distribution to a final mass distribution. The problem was considered in compact metric spaces, Borel sets and a non-negative continuous cost functions. Kantorovich found that if the cost function is a distance, the translocation mass problem is a generalization of the Monge problem (see [13]). Hence, this problem is called the Monge-Kantorovich (MK) mass transfer problem. The MK problem is widely studied in [21] by Villani.

In several works, approximations schemes for the MK problem are posed as: Anderson et al. studied an algorithm on the unit interval [0,1] (see [1,2]), Hernández-Lerma and Lasserre gave a general approximation scheme based on infinite-dimensional linear programs, that scheme can be applied to the MK problem (see [12]), González-Hernández et al. proposed a general approximation scheme for the MK problem on Polish spaces (see [9]). Recently, Gabriel et al.

© Springer International Publishing Switzerland 2015
P. Pardalos et al. (Eds.): MOD 2015, LNCS 9432, pp. 233–239, 2015.
DOI: 10.1007/978-3-319-27926-8_20

studied a numerical approximation scheme on compact spaces (see [7]) and Bosc and Mèrigot have proposed others numerical approximations for the MK problem (see [4,17], respectively).

The MK problem appears in several areas of mathematics as Differential Geometry, Stochastic Control, Information Theory, Matrix Theory, Probability Theory among others (see [20]). Moreover, the Kantorovich metric is defined trough a MK problem and it is used in different applications as: probability metrics [19], control of cancer radiotherapy [11], image registration and warping [10], limit theorems and recursive stochastic equations [20], computers science [5], phylogenetic trees [6], among others.

This work presents an improvement to the approximation scheme for the MK problem on compact spaces given in [7]. The proposed improvement uses a meta-heuristic algorithm called Scatter Search (see [16]) in order to make the algorithm more efficient. The new scheme solves Linear Programs (LP) seem to Transport (T) problems but with lower dimension, in Sect. 3 more details are given.

2   The MK Problem and Its Numerical Approximation

In this section, the MK problem is described and the scheme to obtain an approximation for it given in [7] is detailed as well.

Let X_1 and X_2 be two metric spaces, endowed with the corresponding Borel σ-algebras $\mathbb{B}(X_1)$ and $\mathbb{B}(X_2)$, respectively, a measurable function $c : X_1 \times X_2 \to \mathbb{R}$ and two probability measures ν_1 and ν_2 on X_1 and X_2, respectively.

Consider the linear space of finite signed measures $M(X_1 \times X_2)$ on $\mathbb{B}(X_1 \times X_2)$ endowed with the topology of weak convergence and the convex cone of non-negative measures $M^+(X_1 \times X_2)$ in $M(X_1 \times X_2)$.

If μ is in $M(X_1 \times X_2)$, the marginals of μ on X_1 and X_2 are denoted by $\Pi_1\mu$ and $\Pi_2\mu$, and are given by

$$\Pi_1\mu(A) := \mu(A \times X_2) \text{ and } \Pi_2\mu(B) := \mu(X_1 \times B),$$

for all $A \in \mathbb{B}(X_1)$ and $B \in \mathbb{B}(X_2)$.

The MK problem is stated as follows:

$$\text{MK} \qquad \text{minimize:} \quad \langle \mu, c \rangle := \int_{X_1 \times X_2} c \, d\mu \qquad (1)$$

$$\text{subject to:} \quad \Pi_1\mu = \nu_1, \quad \Pi_2\mu = \nu_2, \quad \mu \in M^+(X_1 \times X_2). \qquad (2)$$

A feasible solution for the MK problem is a measure μ in $M(X_1 \times X_2)$ that satisfies (2) and $\langle \mu, c \rangle$ is finite. If the set of feasible solutions for the MK problem $\mathcal{S}$ is non empty, the problem is consistent, in that case its optimum value is

$$\inf(\text{MK}) := \inf\{\langle \mu, c \rangle | \mu \in \mathcal{S}\}.$$

The MK problem is solvable, if there exists a feasible solution $\widehat{\mu}$ that attains the optimum value. Moreover, $\widehat{\mu}$ is the optimal solution for the MK problem and its minimum is $\langle \widehat{\mu}, c \rangle$.

Let X_1 and X_2 be compact metric spaces and $c(x, y)$ a continuous function as in [7].

Remark 1. By the Proof of Proposition 3.1 in [7], for a given sequence of positive numbers $\{\varepsilon_n\}$ such that $\varepsilon_n \downarrow 0$, there exists two probability measure sequences $\{\nu_1^n\}$ on $\mathbb{B}(X_1)$ and $\{\nu_2^n\}$ on $\mathbb{B}(X_2)$, with supports on finite sets contained in X_1^n and X_2^n respectively, where $\bigcup_n X_1^n$ and $\bigcup_n X_2^n$ are denumerable dense sets in X_1 and X_2, respectively. Moreover, the sequences $\{\nu_1^n\}$ and $\{\nu_2^n\}$ weakly converges to ν_1 and ν_2, respectively.

Hence, for each positive integer n, it is defined the following MK problem:

$$\text{MK}^n \quad \text{minimize:} \quad \langle \mu, c \rangle$$
$$\text{subject to:} \quad \Pi_1 \mu = \nu_1^n, \quad \Pi_2 \mu = \nu_2^n, \quad \mu \in M^+(X_1 \times X_2).$$

Taking the set $X^n = X_1^n \times X_2^n$, each MK^n problem can be discretized by a transportation problem T^n as:

$$\text{T}^n \quad \text{minimize:} \quad \sum_{(x,y) \in X^n} c_{xy} \lambda_{xy}^n$$
$$\text{subject to:} \quad \sum_{y \in X_2^n} \lambda_{xy}^n = a_x^n, \qquad \text{for all } x \in X_1^n,$$
$$\sum_{x \in X_1^n} \lambda_{xy}^n = b_y^n, \qquad \text{for all } y \in X_2^n,$$
$$\lambda_{xy}^n \geq 0, \qquad \text{for all } (x, y) \in X^n.$$

where $c_{xy} = c(x, y)$, $a_x^n = \nu_1^n(\{x\})$ and $b_y^n = \nu_2^n(\{y\})$ with $x \in X_1^n$ and $y \in X_2^n$.

Remark 2. For each n, as ν_1^n and ν_2^n are probability measures, we have that

$$\sum_{x \in X_1^n} a_x^n = \sum_{y \in X_2^n} b_y^n = 1,$$

hence, the respective T^n problem has an optimal solution (see [3]).

If $\{\widehat{\lambda}_{xy}^n\}$ is the optimal solution of T^n problem, it is defined the measure:

$$\widehat{\mu}^n(\cdot) = \sum_{(x,y) \in X^n} \widehat{\lambda}_{xy}^n \delta_{(x,y)}(\cdot)$$

where $\delta_{(x,y)}$ denotes the Dirac measure concentrated at (x, y) in $X_1 \times X_2$.

In practice, for each n, the previous approximation scheme can be implemented by solving the T^n problem. Nevertheless, as n increases the machine execution time becomes high and it is difficult to compute it.

3   Improvement Scheme

To decrease the time of execution, an approximation scheme inspired on a meta-heuristic algorithm called Scatter Search (see [8]) is implemented. Such proposal reduces the number of variables of the T^n problem and it allows to obtain much better approximations in less time.

Meta-Heuristic Algorithm. A sequence of linear programs (LP^n) is constructed under the following steps:

1. For n given, resolve the T^n problem and take as reference set

$$R^n = \{(x, y) \text{ such that } \widehat{\mu}^n(x, y) \neq 0\}.$$

2. Add additional points to R^n using a deterministic method to construct the set $\widetilde{R}^{n+1}$ such that $\widetilde{R}^{n+1} \subset X^{n+1}$.
3. Using the set $\widetilde{R}^{n+1}$ construct the following LP^{n+1} problem

$$LP^{n+1} \text{ minimize:} \sum_{(x,y) \in \widetilde{R}^{n+1}} c_{xy} \lambda_{xy}^{n+1}$$

$$\text{subject to:} \sum_{y:(x,y) \in \widetilde{R}^{n+1}} \lambda_{xy}^{n+1} = a_x^{n+1}$$

$$\text{for all } x \text{ such that } (x, y) \in \widetilde{R}^{n+1},$$

$$\sum_{x:(x,y) \in \widetilde{R}^{n+1}} \lambda_{xy}^{n+1} = b_y^{n+1}$$

$$\text{for all } y \text{ such that } (x, y) \in \widetilde{R}^{n+1},$$

$$\lambda_{xy}^{n+1} \geq 0 \quad \text{for all } (x, y) \in \widetilde{R}^{n+1},$$

and resolve it. Take as new reference set

$$R^{n+1} = \{(x, y) \text{ such that } \widehat{\mu}^{n+1}(x, y) \neq 0\},$$

where

$$\widehat{\mu}^{n+1}(\cdot) = \sum_{(x,y) \in \widetilde{R}^{n+1}} \widehat{\lambda}_{xy}^{n+1} \delta_{(x,y)}(\cdot)$$

with $\{\widehat{\mu}^{n+1}\}$ the optimal solution of the LP^{n+1} problem.
4. Repeat Steps 2 and 3 until stop condition.

Remark 3. The extreme points set of the T^{n+1} problem is the extreme points set of the LP^{n+1} problem, if the variables λ_{xy}^{n+1} with (x, y) in $(\widetilde{R}^{n+1})^c$ are the non-basic variables of the T^{n+1} problem, where the set $(\widetilde{R}^{n+1})^c$ is given by $X^{n+1} - \widetilde{R}^{n+1}$ (see [3]).

Note that the decisive condition is "the variables λ_{xy}^{n+1} with (x, y) in $(\widetilde{R}^{n+1})^c$ are the non-basic variables of the T^{n+1} problem". That is, the most significant step is constructing the set $\widetilde{R}^{n+1}$ such that it let be satisfied with $card(\widetilde{R}^{n+1}) <<$ $card(X^{n+1})$ as possible. The Scatter Search is used because it does not involve randomness and without randomness it is easier to satisfy the above condition.

Considering the meta-heuristic algorithm the convergence and the convergence order of the new scheme can be established and proved. Moreover, they are equivalent to the convergence and the convergence order of the proposed scheme in [7].

4   Numerical Example

Finally, the proposed scheme is illustrated with an example and it is compared with the scheme given in [7]. In the example, X_1 and X_2 are $[0, 1]$ with the usual topology, $\nu_1 = \nu_2$ are the Lebesgue measure and the sets $X_1^n = X_2^n$ are given by

$$\left\{ \frac{k}{2^n} \text{ with } 0 \leq k \leq 2^n \right\}.$$

The cost function is $c(x, y) = xy$, this function is an example in [15] because it satisfies conditions of existence and uniqueness.

By Remark 3 the minimum value of the T^n and LP^n problems are the same. However, the comparison is based on their number of variables. As $card(X_1^n) = card(X_2^n) = 2^n$, the T^n problems have $(2^n)(2^n)$ variables, that is, the cost of solving the T^n problems increases quickly when n increases. In Table 1 the number of elements in $\widetilde{R}^n$ that are taken to construct the LP^n problem is showed. It can be noted that the number of variables of the LP^n problem is remarkably much lower than the number of variables of the T^n problem. The results of the

Table 1. Number of variables of the problems

Problem	No. variables	Optimum value
T^8	65536	0.1666679
LP^8	——	——
T^9	262144	0.166667
LP^9	1024	0.166667
T^{10}	1048576	0.1666667
LP^{10}	2048	0.1666667
T^{11}	4194304	——
LP^{11}	4096	0.1666667
T^{12}	16777216	——
LP^{12}	8192	0.1666667

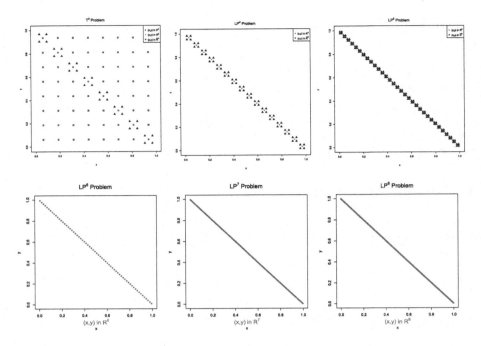

Fig. 1. Solution of the cost function $c(x, y) = xy$.

LP^8 problem are not presented because it requires the solution of the T^7 problem. The results for the T^{11} and T^{12} problems are not reported because of the hight cost of their implementation.

On the other hand, the sets introduced in the proposed scheme are illustrated graphically to show their performance at each iteration. The algorithm is started with $n = 3$ because it is suitable to show the sets X^n, $\tilde{R}^n$ and R^{n+1}. If n larger than 3 is taken, it is difficult to visualize the sets. In the first image of Fig. 1, the points in the set X^3 are in blue square, the points in the set R^3 are in red circle and the points in the set $\tilde{R}^4$ are in green triangle. In the second and third images of Fig. 1, next two iterations are showed. In the remaining images of Fig. 1, only the points in sets R^6, R^7 and R^8 are showed because the points are too close and it is difficult to visualize them.

5   Conclusion and Future Work

The MK problem solution can be approximated by the finite LP solution. The finite LP is obtained using a meta-heuristic algorithm inspired on Scatter Search and it has remarkably lower dimension that the respective T problem used in the approximation scheme studied in [7]. The convergence and the convergence order of the new scheme can be established as a consequence of the main results in [7]. Finally, a numerical example is presented to illustrate the new scheme and to compare it with the previous scheme.

As future work, the meta-heuristic algorithm inspired on Scatter Search could be applied to solve the Kantorovich-Rubinstein mass transshipment problem and the Kantorovich metric.

References

1. Anderson, E., Nash, P.: Linear Programming in Infinite-dimensional Spaces. Wiley, New York (1987)
2. Anderson, E., Philpott, A.: Duality and an algorithm for a class of continuous transportation problems. Math. Oper. Res. **9**, 222–231 (1984)
3. Bazaraa, M.S., Jarvis, J.J., Sherali, H.D.: Linear Programming and Network Flows. Wiley-Interscience, New Jersey (2010)
4. Bosc, D.: Numerical approximation of optimal transport maps. SSRN (2010)
5. Deng, Y., Du, W.: Kantorovich metric in computer science: a brief survey. Electron. Notes Theoret. Comput. Sci. **353**(3), 73–82 (2009)
6. Evans, S., Matsen, F.: The phylogenetic kantorovich-rubinstein metric for environmental sequence samples. J. Roy. Stat. Soc.: Ser. B (Stat. Methodol.) **74**(3), 569–592 (2012)
7. Gabriel, J., González-Hernández, J., López-Martínez, R.: Numerical approximations to the mass transfer problem on compact spaces. IMA J. Numer. Anal. **30**, 1121–1136 (2010)
8. Glover, F.: A template for scatter search and path relinking. In: Hao, J.-K., Lutton, E., Ronald, E., Schoenauer, M., Snyers, D. (eds.) AE 1997. LNCS, vol. 1363, pp. 1–51. Springer, Heidelberg (1998)
9. González-Hernández, J., Gabriel, J., Hernández-Lerma, O.: On solutions to the mass transfer problem. SIAM J. Optim. **17**, 485–499 (2006)
10. Haker, S., Zhu, L., Tannenbaum, A., Angenent, S.: Optimal mass transport for registration and warping. Int. J. Comput. Vision **63**, 225–240 (2004)
11. Hanin, L., Rachev, S., Yakovlev, A.: On the optimal control of cancer radiotherapy for non-homogeneous cell population. Adv. Appl. Probab. **25**, 1–23 (1993)
12. Hernández-Lerma, O., Lasserre, J.: Approximation schemes for infinite linear programs. SIAM J. Optim. **8**, 973–988 (1998)
13. Kantorovich, L.: On a problem of monge. J. Math. Sci. **133**(4), 225–226 (2006)
14. Kantorovich, L.: On the translocation of masses. J. Math. Sci. **133**(4), 1381–1382 (2006)
15. Levin, V.: Optimality conditions and exact solutions to the two-dimensional monge-kantorovich problem. J. Math. Sci. **133**(4), 1456–1463 (2006)
16. Martí, R., Laguna, M., Glover, F.: Principles of scatter search. Eur. J. Oper. Res. **169**, 359–372 (2006)
17. Mèrigot, Q.: A multiscale approach to optimal transport. Computer Graphics Forum **30**(5), 1583–1592 (2011)
18. Monge, G.: Mémoire sur la théorie des déblais et des remblais. De l'Imprimerie Royale, Paris (1781)
19. Rachev, S.: Probability Metrics and the Stability of Stochastic Models. Wiley, New York (1991)
20. Rachev, S., Rüschendorf, L.: Mass Transportation Problems, vol.I and II. Springer, New York (1998)
21. Villani, C.: Optimal Transport: Old and New, vol. 338. Springer, Heidelberg (2008)

Adaptive Targeting for Online Advertisement

Andrey Pepelyshev[1]([✉]), Yuri Staroselskiy[2], and Anatoly Zhigljavsky[1,3]

[1] Cardiff University, Cardiff, UK
{pepelyshevan,ZhigljavskyAA}@cardiff.ac.uk
[2] Crimtan, London, UK
yuri@crimtan.com
[3] University of Nizhnii Novgorod, Nizhnii Novgorod, Russia

Abstract. We consider the problem of adaptive targeting for real-time bidding for internet advertisement. This problem involves making fast decisions on whether to show a given ad to a particular user. For intelligent platforms, these decisions are based on information extracted from big data sets containing records of previous impressions, clicks and subsequent purchases. We discuss several strategies for maximizing the click through rate, which is often the main criteria of measuring the success of an advertisement campaign. In the second part of the paper, we provide some results of statistical analysis of real data.

Keywords: Online advertisement · Real-time bidding · Adaptive targeting · Big data · Click through rate

1 Introduction

Online advertising is an important form of marketing where advertisements shown to a user may depend on the user browsing behaviour. Advertising platforms collect big data which may include records of previous conversions, clicks, impressions, visited webpages, account information and search requests. A large part of online advertisements goes through prominent technology companies like Google, Yahoo, Bing and Facebook, which are able to collect enormous amounts of data on the user behaviour, see e.g. [4,6,8,12,19]. Some part of online advertisement spend goes through independent ad exchanges where advertising platforms have less information about users [14]. The present paper deals with the latter case.

Ad exchanges as well as search providers use Real-Time Bidding (RTB), which is a popular way of delivering online advertising, see [3,9,13,20]. As reported in [5], spending on RTB in the US during 2014 increased by 137 % and reached \$10 billion and RTB has 45 % of the total spend in online advertising. In contrast to traditional advertising on TV and fixed contracts on showing fixed advertisements on specific websites, RTB enables a demand side to find a favorable ad campaign and submit a bid for a request depending on parameters of the request and behaviour data (i.e. a track record of a user). In our case the demand side is represented by an advertising platform whose core business is

© Springer International Publishing Switzerland 2015
P. Pardalos et al. (Eds.): MOD 2015, LNCS 9432, pp. 240–251, 2015.
DOI: 10.1007/978-3-319-27926-8_21

in delivering efficient advertisements on websites, see [14]. Marketing managers expect that online advertising brings customers at cheaper costs and granular targeting capabilities although the traditional offline advertisement is continued.

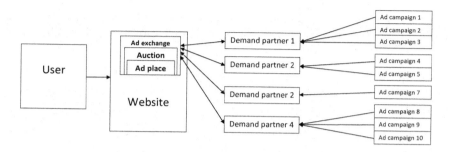

Fig. 1. The scheme of real-time bidding for online advertising.

In Fig. 1 we show the scheme of the RTB system, which consists of 4 components: a user, a webpage with embedded ad place, demand partners (advertising platforms) and ad campaigns; see [17,20] for more detail.

The process of delivering online advertisements occurs billions times each day and consists of the following steps:

- A user comes to a webpage of a web site, where advertisement can be delivered using auction via an ad exchange.
- The web site via the ad exchange notifies several demand partners that there is a possibility to show an ad via bid request (real time auction). Each bid request contains information about user (user id, time of request, IP, geo, user agent) and information about the site (site, url, minimal bid). To make efficient decision demand side can store and analyze information about bid requests. Due to the enormous amount of bid requests storage and analysis of this data is a true big data challenge.
- If a demand partner decides to deliver an ad for the given request, it responds with a bid and a particular advertisement. The demand partners are usually required to return a bid in a short time (e.g. 100 ms) while the webpage is loaded by a user. The bid is given in a certain currency (often USD) multiplied by 1000, corresponding to the commonly adopted cost-per-mille pricing model.
- The website via the ad exchange decides which demand partner won the auction (based on their bids) and delivers the ad of the winner. Note that ad exchanges are working as the second price auction model; that is, the winner pays the second highest bid.
- If a demand partner wins, it delivers the ad and can store information about ad delivery in order to analyze historical efficiency. Note that the user is given the right to opt out from targeted advertisement delivery via demand platform site opt out or via ad itself. In such case the demand partner doesn't store user related information.

- If the user clicks on the delivered ad, the advertiser can store the information about clicks.
- If the user visits the advertised site which contains code of the advertiser, the demand partner can store the information about the visit and can use it to optimize campaign efficiency further.
- If the user buys a product on the advertised site, the demand partner can store the purchase information to evaluate optimization strategies on historical data.

The advertiser has to solve the problem of maximizing either the click through rate (CTR) or the conversion rate by targeting a set of requests under several constraints:

 (i) Budget (total amount of money available for advertising),
 (ii) Number of impressions (total amount of ad exposures),
 (iii) Time (ad campaign is restricted to certain time period).

Campaign size in programmatic segment varies between \$5000 and \$500000 per month and the advertisement company running a campaign needs to choose from 5 mln to 500 mln requests out of 50 bln available ones.

One of the main characteristics of an ad campaign is average cost-per-action (CPA) or average cost per conversion. To identify those parameters of bid request/ impressions, which caused the click/conversion, we have to use all logs.

The problem of adaptive targeting for ad campaigns was addressed in proceedings of the annual WWW conference and in a dozen of papers, however, many of them deal with the sponsored search, see e.g. [8,12,19]. Some papers, for example [2,16], use the look-alike idea implying that a new request will lead to the click/conversion if the new request is similar to (look like one of) the previous successful requests. In 2014 two Kaggle contests were organized [see https://www.kaggle.com/c/avazu-ctr-prediction and https://www.kaggle.com/c/criteo-display-ad-challenge] on algorithms for predicting the CTR using datasets with subsampled non-click records (the CTR for one dataset is about 17%). The algorithms proposed by many teams are based on different approaches, mainly, ensembles of field-aware factorisation machines (FFM) [15], follow-the-regularized-leader (FTRL) methodology [11], gradient boosting machines (GBM) [7], and are now publicly available, give approximately the same performance with respect to the logarithmic loss criterion

$$logloss = -1/N \sum_{i=1}^{N} (y_i \log(p_i) + (1 - y_i) \log(1 - p_i)),$$

where N is the size of the test set, p_i is the predicted probability of click for the i-th request, and $y_i = 1$ if the i-th request leads to click and $y_i = 0$ otherwise.

All the main strategies mentioned above make learning either about the parameters of the model (like in FFM and FTRL) or the response function directly depending on X. This learning constitutes the main objective at the initial phase of any advertisement campaign. At a later stage in the campaign, when either models or estimates of the response function can be considered satisfactory, they are used for improving the selection of users with the purpose to increase (or even maximize) the CTR. The cost of impressions on the learning stage should be kept on the lowest level but it should be increasing as the choice of users becomes more intelligent since we should be prepared to pay higher price for the users that are more likely to click on our ad.

The present paper is organized as follows. In Sect. 2 we present the formal description of the problem of maximizing the CTR and propose an adaptive strategy which consists of estimating the preference characteristic for a new request and suggesting a relevant bid price; this strategy is based on the 'look-alike' principle and does not use any parametric models similar to those used by FFM and FTRL. In Sect. 3 we perform an analysis of data provided to us by an advertising platform. Specifically, we give the descriptive statistics in Sect. 3.1 and perform the multidimensional scaling in Sect. 3.2. Finally, we evaluate the performance of the proposed strategy in Sect. 3.3 and investigate the sensitivity of the strategy to the choice of factors in Sect. 3.4. Conclusions are given in Sect. 4.

2   Adaptive Strategy for Maximizing the CTR of an Ad Campaign

Suppose that the ad we want to show is fixed. Consider the problem of maximization of the click through rate by an adaptive targeting procedure which should yield the decision whether to show or not the ad to a request from a webpage visited by a user. If the procedure decides to show the ad, it has to propose a bid.

The adaptive decision should depend on the current sample of impressions and clicks which contain the users to whom we have shown the ad before and who have clicked on the ad. We will treat the sample size N as time. We can increase the size of the sample by including all our previous impressions of the same advertisement, so that N could be very large.

Features of an i-th request: $X_i = (x_{i,1}, \ldots, x_{i,m})$, $i = 1, \ldots, N$, where m is the number of features (factors). We equate the i-th request to X_i. Suppose that the requests leading to the click on the ad are $X_{j_1}, \ldots, X_{j_K}$, where $1 \leq j_1 < j_2 < \ldots < j_K \leq N$ and $K = K(N) < N$. Our running performance criterion of the advertising campaign is the click through rate (CTR) defined by $p_N = K/N$. It is clear that the CTR p_N changes as N grows.

We make the following important assumption of independence: if we choose a request with features $X = (x_1, \ldots, x_m)$ then the probability of a click is p_X; different events ('click' or 'no click') are independent. We assume that all possible vectors $X = (x_1, \ldots, x_m)$ belong to some set $\mathbb{X}$ (which is partly discrete and possibly has difficult structure). We also assume that for any two points X and $X' \in \mathbb{X}$ we can define some kind of measure $d(X, X')$ which can be considered as distance (it does not have to satisfy mathematical axioms of the distance function). The properties we require for $d(X, X')$ are: (a) $d(X, X') \geq 0$ for all

$X, X' \in \mathbb{X}$; (b) $d(X, X) = 0$ for all $X \in \mathbb{X}$; (c) small values of $d(X, X')$ indicate on a large degree of similarity between X and X'; (c') large values of $d(X, X')$ indicate on a large degree of dissimilarity between X and X'; (d) $d(X, X') = \infty$ if X and X' can be considered as unrelated (or totally dissimilar).

If $\mathbb{X}$ is a discrete set with all features $X = (x_1, \ldots, x_m) \in \mathbb{X}$ given on the nominal scale then we can use the Hamming distance

$$d(X, X') = \sum_{j=1}^{m} \delta(x_j, x'_j), \quad \delta(x_j, x'_j) = \begin{cases} 1 & x_j = x'_j, \\ 0 & x_j \neq x'_j, \end{cases}$$

or the weighted Hamming distance $d(X, X') = \sum_{j=1}^{m} w_j \delta(x_j, x'_j)$, where the coefficients w_j are positive and proportional to the importance of the j-th feature (factor), $j = 1, \ldots, m$.

The purpose of the strategy for maximizing the CTR is to adapt the feature sets for the new requests we will be showing the ad to increase p_N as N increases. Formally, if we assume that $N \to \infty$ then our aim is devising a strategy such that $\lim_{N \to \infty} p_N$ is maximum. In practice, we are given N_{total}, the total number of requests to be exposed to an ad. Correspondingly, we want to maximize $p_{N_{total}}$.

The natural adaptive strategy is an evolutionary one which prefers new requests in the vicinity of the requests that were successful previously, i.e. which follow the look-alike idea. To define the preference criterion, for all N we need an estimator $\hat{p}_N(X)$ of the function $p(X)$, which is defined for all $X \in \mathbb{X}$. We do not need to construct the function $\hat{p}_N(X)$ explicitly; we just need to compute values of $\hat{p}_N(X)$ for a given X, where X is a request which is currently on offer for us. We hence suggest the following estimator $\hat{p}_N(X)$:

$$\hat{p}_N(X) = \frac{\sum_{k=1}^{K} \exp\{-\lambda_N d(X, X_{j_k})\}}{\sum_{i=1}^{N} \exp\{-\lambda_N d(X, X_i)\}} + \varepsilon_N, \tag{1}$$

where λ_N and ε_N are some positive constants (possibly depending on N). The sum in the numerator in (1) is taken over all users which have clicked on the ad. If all these (good) requests are far away from X then the value $\hat{p}_N(X)$ will be very close to zero. The constant ε_N is a regularization constant. As $\varepsilon_N > 0$ there is always a small probability assigned to each X, even if in the past there were no successful requests that were similar to X. Theoretically, as $N \to \infty$, we may assume that $\varepsilon_N \to 0$.

Alternative way of determining the estimator of $p(X)$ is the logistic model constructed by the FFM and FTRL approaches [11,15] or the tree-based model constructed by the GBM methodology [7].

Using an estimator $\hat{p}_N(X)$ for $p(X)$, we can suggest how much the advertising platform can offer for the request X in the bidding procedure. For example, the demand side can offer larger bids if $\hat{p}_N(X) \geq p_*$, where p_* is the desired probability we want to reach. Another strategy: the amount of money the advertising platform offer for X is proportional to the difference $\hat{p}_N(X) - K/N$, if this difference is positive.

In the strategy above, we can remove old data from the sample by always keeping the sample size equal to N_0 (assuming $N_0 < N$); in this case the estimator (1) changes to

$$\hat{p}_{N,N_0}(X) = \frac{\sum_{k=1}^{K} 1_{[j_K \geq N-N_0]} \exp\{-\lambda d(X, X_{j_k})\}}{\sum_{i=N-N_0}^{N} \exp\{-\lambda d(X, X_i)\}} + \varepsilon; \qquad (2)$$

in this estimator there is no need to change λ and ε as the sample size is constant (it is always equals N_0). In (2), $1_{[j_K \geq N-N_0]}$ is the indicator of the event $j_K \geq N - N_0$.

3 Analysis of Real Data

Since descriptive statistics for big data are important tools for understanding the data structure, see [1], we show some figures for two ad campaigns named as ad campaign 1 and ad campaign 2. For different subsets of data, we depict the estimator of the CTR computed as $\hat{p} = K/N$ with the 95 %-confidence interval $(\hat{p} - 1.96\sqrt{\hat{p}(1-\hat{p})/N}, \hat{p} + 1.96\sqrt{\hat{p}(1-\hat{p})/N})$, where K is the number of clicks and N is the number of impressions in the selected subset. We use the descriptive statistics to study the influence of each factor on the CTR that helps us to reduce the number of factors for the adaptive strategy.

The estimated CTR for all data is $\hat{p} = 1.7 \cdot 10^{-4}$ for ad campaign 1 and $\hat{p} = 2.4 \cdot 10^{-4}$ for ad campaign 2. These values will serve as a baseline for comparing the CTRs for different subsets of data.

3.1 Descriptive Statistics of the CTR for Two Ad Campaigns

In Fig. 2 we show the CTR on different days. We can see that CTR slightly depends on days. We can observe that the largest CTR of ad campaign 1 was on Dec 20 and the few preceding days, which can be explained by Christmas shopping. The CTR of ad campaign 2 is larger at weekends since the structure of bid requests is different at weekends.

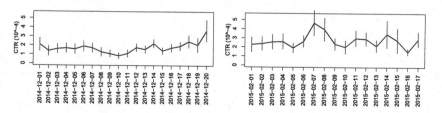

Fig. 2. The click through rate multiplied by 10^4 at different days for ad campaign 1 (left) and ad campaign 2 (right).

In Fig. 3 we show the CTR at different hours. We can see that the CTR for ad campaign 1 is larger from 22:00 to 22:59, which can be explained by activity of certain group of users. The CTR for ad campaign 2 is higher from 9:00 to 9:59 and from 19:00 to 19:59, when a group of users usually use internet in the morning and the evening.

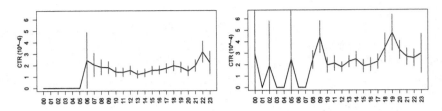

Fig. 3. The click through rate multiplied by 10^4 at different hours for ad campaign 1 (left) and ad campaign 2 (right).

In Fig. 4 we can see that the CTR is nearly the same for many websites except very few websites where the CTR is larger. It is quite natural that the largest CTR is for the website http://www.preloved.co.uk, which is a large classified advertising site. Another large CTR occurs for the website http://www.express.co.uk, which is a portal of the newspaper "Sunday Express"; however, the confidence interval is wide because the number of impressions is small. It is worth noting that the CTR for the websites of other newspapers, "Independent" and "Telegraph", is very close to the average value.

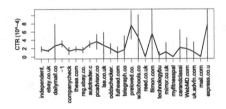

Fig. 4. The click through rate multiplied by 10^4 for 25 websites with largest numbers of requests for the ad campaign 2.

In Fig. 5 we can observe that the CTR does not depend on ad exchange but depends on the user agent. Specifically, the CTR is larger than average for MSIE and smaller than average for Safari.

In Fig. 6 we can see that the CTR for some cities and postcodes significantly differs from the average value. In particular, we can observe that the CTR for London is large but the CTR for Uxbridge and Trowbridge is small. However, the largest CTR occurs for the postcode PO standing for Portsmouth but the number of requests with postcode PO is quite small. The second largest CTR is for the postcode EC standing for Eastern Central, an area in central London. Also the CTR is well above average for postcodes CV (Coventry) and BN (Brighton).

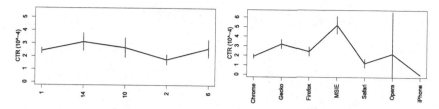

Fig. 5. The click through rate multiplied by 10^4 for different ad exchanges and user agents for the ad campaign 2. The x-tick labels of the left plot are the identification numbers of ad exchanges.

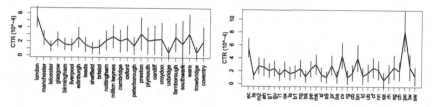

Fig. 6. The click through rate multiplied by 10^4 for 25 cites and 33 postcodes with largest numbers of requests for the ad campaign 2.

3.2 Multidimensional Scaling

In Fig. 7 we show the multidimensional scaling (MDS) performed by the SMA-COF algorithm (see [10]) where we have used the Hamming distance for measuring the closeness between points $X, X' \in \mathbb{X}$. The MDS finds the association between the original high-dimensional points and points in a smaller dimension preserving the similarity of distances between points. Formally, the MDS for the dimension 2 is a solution of

$$\min_{z_1,\dots,z_n \in \mathbb{R}^2} \sum_{i=1}^{n} \sum_{j=1}^{n} (D_{ij} - ||z_j - z_i||_2)^2$$

where $D_{i,j}$ is the distance between the i-th request and the j-th request. We considered the set $\mathbb{X}$ with 7 factors: website, ad exchange, city, postcode, device type, user agent, user behaviour category. Since the multidimensional scaling is a hard computational problem we extract a subsample of the points from the data. We repeated the MDS for different subsamples and found that the pattern of 2D points very much repeats.

In Fig. 8 we show the supervised multidimensional scaling proposed in [18] with $\alpha = 0.2$, which is a solution of

$$\min_{z_1,\dots,z_n \in \mathbb{R}^2} \frac{1-\alpha}{2} \sum_{i=1}^{n} \sum_{j=1}^{n} (D_{ij} - ||z_j - z_i||_2)^2 + \alpha \sum_{i,j:y_j > y_i} (y_j - y_i) \sum_{s=1}^{2} (D_{ij} - (z_{js} - z_{is}))^2,$$

where $y_i = 1$ if the i-th request led to the click and $y_i = 0$ otherwise. Certainly, the supervised multidimensional scaling gives better separation between the

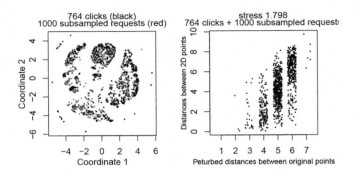

Fig. 7. The multidimensional scaling by SMACOF algorithm.

two groups: the users that have clicked on the ad and the users that haven't. However, the results of supervised scaling are hard to use in the adaptive strategy considered above. On the other hand, the classification obtained from unsupervised scaling are easy to use in such procedures.

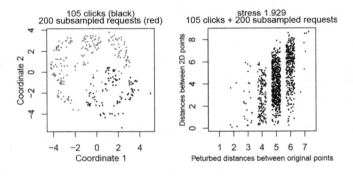

Fig. 8. The supervised multidimensional scaling.

3.3   Evaluation of the Adaptive Strategy

To investigate the performance of the adaptive strategy for the database of requests for ad campaign 2, we split the database of impressions into 2 sets: the training set $\mathbb{X}_p(T)$ of past records with dates until the certain time T (where T is interpreted as the present time) and the test set $\mathbb{X}_f(T)$ of future records with dates from the time T. We also define the set

$$L(r) = \{X_j \text{ from } \mathbb{X}_p(T): \min_{clicked \ \tilde{X}_i \in \mathbb{X}_f(T)} d(X_j, \tilde{X}_i) \leq r\};$$

that is, $L(r)$ is a set of requests where we have shown the ad and the minimal distance to the set of clicked requests from the set of past records is not greater than r. In other words, the set $L(r)$ is an intersection of the set of our requests with the union of balls of radius r centered around the clicked past requests. Here we also consider X_j with 7 factors: website, ad exchange, city, postcode, device type, user agent, user behaviour category.

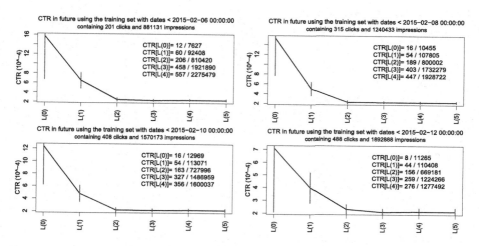

Fig. 9. The click through rate multiplied by 10^4 for the sets $L(r)$, $r = 0, 1, \ldots, 5$, for several values of T.

In Fig. 9 we show the click through rate for the sets $L(r)$, $r = 0, 1, \ldots, 5$, for several values of T. Recall that the ad campaign 2 starts on 2015-02-01 and finishes on 2015-02-17.

It is natural that the CTR for the set $L(r)$ decreases as r increases. We can observe that the CTR for $L(0)$ and $L(1)$ is very large but the number of impressions from $L(0)$ and $L(1)$ is small.

To be specific, for the time moment T=2015-02-08 the size of the set $L(r)$ is 10455 for $r = 0$, 107805 for $r = 1$, 800002 for $r = 2$, 1732279 for $r = 3$, and 1928722 for $r = 4$; and the number of clicked impressions in the set $L(r)$ is 16 for $r = 0$, 54 for $r = 1$, 189 for $r = 2$, 403 for $r = 3$ and 447 for $r = 4$.

Overall we can see that the CTR for $L(1)$ is significantly larger than the CTR for $L(2)$ at all times T.

3.4   The CTR for Different Choices of Factors

Let us perform the sensitivity analysis of the CTR for sets $L(r)$ for the ad campaign 2. In Table 1 we show the CTR for several sets $L(r)$ with T=2015-02-08 and different choices of factors. We can observe that the device type has no influence and the ad exchange has a small influence on the CTR for sets $L(0)$ and $L(1)$, consequently such factors can be removed from the model (and computations). The postcode has no influence on the CTR for the set $L(0)$ but has some influence on the CTR for the set $L(1)$.

Table 1. The CTR multiplied by 10^4 for several sets $L(r)$ with T=2015-02-08 and different choices of factors. Abbreviation of factors are Be:behaviour category, We:website, Ex:ad exchange, Ci:city, Po:postcode, De:device type, Ag:user agent.

Factors	CTR[$L(0)$]	CTR[$L(1)$]	CTR[$L(2)$]	CTR[$L(3)$]	CTR[$L(4)$]
Be,We,Ex,Ci,Po,De,Ag	15.3	5.01	2.36	2.33	2.32
We,Ex,Ci,Po,De,Ag	5.13	2.43	2.35	2.33	2.33
Be, Ex,Ci,Po,De,Ag	11.69	2.81	2.35	2.31	2.33
Be,We, Ci,Po,De,Ag	12.29	3.89	2.31	2.29	2.33
Be,We,Ex, Po,De,Ag	7.62	2.46	2.32	2.32	2.33
Be,We,Ex,Ci, De,Ag	14.96	2.45	2.32	2.32	2.33
Be,We,Ex,Ci,Po, Ag	15.27	5.09	2.38	2.33	2.32
Be,We,Ex,Ci,Po,De	4.87	3.37	2.20	2.33	2.33
Be,We,Ex,Ci, Ag	14.93	2.48	2.32	2.32	2.33
Be,We, Ci, Ag	11.99	2.38	2.29	2.33	2.33
Be,We, Ci,Po, Ag	12.27	3.88	2.34	2.29	2.33

In contrast, the user agent, the user behaviour category, and the city are very influential factors. It is very surprising that the postcode has no influence but the city has a big influence on the CTR for the set $L(0)$. However, the postcode is highly important to have the large value of the CTR for the set $L(1)$.

4   Conclusions

We have considered the problem of maximizing the CTR from the view-point of an advertising platform working with independent ad exchanges. We have discussed and studied an adaptive strategy which is based on the look-alike idea. We have tested the performance of the strategy. In particular, we have found out that the strategy of showing ads to requests from the set $L(1)$ yields the CTR which is 2.5 times larger than the CTR for the original ad campaign.

Acknowledgement. The paper is a result of collaboration of Crimtan, a provider of proprietary ad technology platform and University of Cardiff. Research of the third author was supported by the Russian Science Foundation, project No. 15-11-30022 "Global optimization, supercomputing computations, and application".

References

1. Abello, J., Pardalos, P.M., Resende, M.G. (eds.): Handbook of Massive Data Sets, vol. 4. Springer Science and Business Media, New York (2002)
2. Aly, M., Hatch, A., Josifovski, V., Narayanan, V.K.: Web-scale user modeling for targeting. In: Proceedings of the 21st International Conference Companion on World Wide Web, pp. 3–12. ACM (2012)

3. Chakraborty, T., Even-Dar, E., Guha, S., Mansour, Y., Muthukrishnan, S.: Selective call out and real time bidding. In: Saberi, A. (ed.) WINE 2010. LNCS, vol. 6484, pp. 145–157. Springer, Heidelberg (2010)

4. Edelman, B., Ostrovsky, M., Schwarz, M.: Internet advertising and the generalized second price auction: selling billions of dollars worth of keywords. Am. Econ. Rev. **97**(1), 242–259 (2007)

5. eMarketer: US programmatic ad spend tops $10 Billion this year, to double by 2016 (2014). http://www.emarketer.com/Article/US-Programmatic-Ad-Spend-Tops-10-Billion-This-Year-Double-by-2016/1011312

6. Evans, D.S.: The online advertising industry: economics, evolution, and privacy. J. Econ. Perspect. **23**(3), 37–60 (2009)

7. Friedman, J.H.: Greedy function approximation: a gradient boosting machine. Ann. Stat. **29**(5), 1189–1232 (2001)

8. Jansen, B.J., Mullen, T.: Sponsored search: an overview of the concept, history, and technology. Int. J. Electr. Bus. **6**(2), 114–131 (2008)

9. Google: the arrival of real-time bidding. Technical report (2011)

10. de Leeuw, J., Mair, P.: Multidimensional scaling using majorization: SMACOF in R. SMACOF. J. Stat. Softw. **31**(3), 1–30 (2009)

11. McMahan, H.B.: Follow-the-regularized-leader and mirror descent: equivalence theorems and L1 regularization. In: International Conference on Artificial Intelligence and Statistics, pp. 525–533 (2011)

12. McMahan, H.B., Holt, G., Sculley, D., et al.: Ad click prediction: a view from the trenches. In: Proceedings of the 19th ACM SIGKDD International Conference on Knowledge Discovery and Data Mining, pp. 1222–1230 (2013)

13. Muthukrishnan, S.: Ad exchanges: research issues. In: Leonardi, S. (ed.) WINE 2009. LNCS, vol. 5929, pp. 1–12. Springer, Heidelberg (2009)

14. Nicholls, S., Malins, A., Horner, M.: Real-time bidding in online advertising (2014). http://www.gpbullhound.com/wp-content/uploads/2014/09/Real-Time-Bidding-in-Online-Advertising.pdf

15. Rendle, S.: Factorization machines. In: 2010 IEEE 10th International Conference on Data Mining (ICDM), pp. 995–1000. IEEE (2010)

16. Tu, S., Lu, C.: Topic-based user segmentation for online advertising with latent dirichlet allocation. In: Cao, L., Zhong, J., Feng, Y. (eds.) ADMA 2010, Part II. LNCS, vol. 6441, pp. 259–269. Springer, Heidelberg (2010)

17. Wang, J., Yuan, S., Shen, X., Seljan, S.: Real-time bidding: a new frontier of computational advertising research. In: CIKM Tutorial (2013)

18. Witten, D.M., Tibshirani, R.: Supervised multidimensional scaling for visualization, classification, and bipartite ranking. Comput. Stat. Data Anal. **55**(1), 789–801 (2011)

19. Yang, S., Ghose, A.: Analyzing the relationship between organic and sponsored search advertising: positive, negative or zero interdependence? Mark. Sci. **29**(4), 602–623 (2010)

20. Yuan, S., Wang, J., Zhao, X.: Real-time bidding for online advertising: measurement and analysis. In: ADKDD (2013)

Outlier Detection in Cox Proportional Hazards Models Based on the Concordance c-Index

João Diogo Pinto[1], Alexandra M. Carvalho[1], and Susana Vinga[2]($\boxtimes$)

[1] Instituto de Telecomunicações, Instituto Superior Técnico,
Universidade de Lisboa, Lisboa, Portugal
[2] IDMEC, Instituto Superior Técnico, Universidade de Lisboa, Lisboa, Portugal
susanavinga@tecnico.ulisboa.pt

Abstract. Outliers can have extreme influence on data analysis and so their presence must be taken into account. We propose a method to perform outlier detection on multivariate survival datasets, named *Dual Bootstrap Hypothesis Testing* (DBHT). Experimental results show that DBHT is a competitive alternative to state-of-the-art methods and can be applied to clinical data.

1 Introduction

Survival analysis, the field that studies time-to-event data, has become a relevant topic in clinical and medical research. In many medical studies time to death is the event of interest, hence, it is usually named *survival time*. However, other important measures may also be considered, such as the time between response to treatment or the time to the onset of a disease.

Survival analysis is specifically tailored to deal with unknown survival times for a subset of the study group, a phenomenon called *censoring*. The most common type is *right-censoring*, addressed in this work; it occurs when the event is beyond the end of the follow-up period. Survival data is typically denoted by $D = \{(X_1, Y_1), \ldots, (X_N, Y_N)\}$, where each X_i is a p-dimensional vector of covariates and $Y_i = (t_i, \delta_i)$, where t_i is the event or censoring time and δ_i the censoring indicator.

There are several definitions of an outlier. Hawkins [4] defines it "as an observation that deviates so much from other observations as to arouse suspicion that it was generated by a different mechanism than the remaining data". In the survival field, Nardi and Schemper [6] define outlying observations as individuals whose survival time is too short, or too long, with respect to the values of its covariates.

In this work, we propose to perform outlier detection in survival analysis taking profit from Harrel's *concordance c-index* [3] and extending the work in [5]. The concordance c-index measures the model's ability of predicting a higher relative risks to individuals whose event occurs first. The relative risk is estimated from the output of the model for each individual; in a Cox Proportional hazards model, for instance, the relative risk corresponds to the hazard ratio.

P. Pardalos et al. (Eds.): MOD 2015, LNCS 9432, pp. 252–256, 2015.
DOI: 10.1007/978-3-319-27926-8_22

2   DBHT

Bootstrapping [2] is a resampling technique to unveil the underlying distribution of the data. It is used when this distribution is unknown or simplifying assumptions are not reasonable. Given a dataset D with N observations, one *bootstrap sample* is obtained by sampling, with replacement, N observations from D.

We propose to improve the *bootstrap hypothesis test* (BHT) described in [5]. In the BHT method, the procedure removes one observation from the dataset and then assesses the impact of each removal on concordance. This has the undesired effect that, with less observations to fit, concordance tends to increase, which potentially increases the number of "false positives", signalling inliers as outliers.

The proposed method, called dual bootstrap hypothesis test (DBHT), overcomes this problem. In starts by generating two histograms from two antagonistic versions of the bootstrap procedure – the *poison* and the *antidote* bootstraps – and then compare them using a statistical test. The *antidote* bootstrap excludes the observation under test from every bootstrap sample. On the other hand, the *poison* bootstrap works by forcing the observation under test to be part of every bootstrap sample. Both the poison and antidote bootstraps have the same number of observations in each bootstrap sample.

The general strategy is as follows. For each observation i we make the hypothesis that the observation is "poison" (meaning that the observation is an outlier). To test it, we compare the histograms of concordance variation ΔC between the *antidote* and *poison* bootstraps. If the observation is indeed an outlier, we expect the *antidote* bootstrap to push the histogram for higher values of ΔC. Conversely, we expect the *poison* bootstrap to generate lower values of ΔC. The more the *poison* histogram is to the left of the *antidote* histogram, the more outlying the observation is. We consider $\Delta C_{antidote}$ and ΔC_{poison} two real random variables with the following hypothesis:

$$H_0 : E\left[\Delta C_{antidote}\right] > E\left[\Delta C_{poison}\right];$$
$$H_1 : E\left[\Delta C_{antidote}\right] \leq E\left[\Delta C_{poison}\right].$$

To calculate the p-value of the test we use a independent two sample Welch's t-test.

DBHT is a *soft-classifier* and a *single-step* method with the output being an outlying measure for each observation. From this, it is possible to extract the k

---

Algorithm 1. Dual Bootstrap Hypothesis Test

Input: input dataset D, the survival model and number of bootstrap samples B.
Output: a p-value for each observation
for all $d_i \in D$ **do**
    $D_{-i} = D \setminus d_i$ {remove observation i from the original dataset}
    Generate B *poison* bootstrap samples
    Generate B *antidote* bootstrap samples from D_{-i}
    Compute the B values of ΔC_{poison} and store them in vector psn
    Compute the B values of $\Delta C_{antidote}$ and store them in vector ant
    From psn and ant compute the p-value using a t test for equality of means
end for
return the vector of p-values

most outlying observations. Pseudo-code of the DBHT procedure can be found in Algorithm 1.

In Fig. 1, *poison* and *antidote* histograms for an outlier (on the left) and inlier (on the right) can be found.

3   Results

Herein, we assess the performance of DBHT in 12 synthetic datasets. Its performance is compared with two concordance-based methods [5] – *one step deletion* (OSD) and *Bootstrap hypothesis test* (BHT) – and with outlier detection methods commonly employed on survival data, namely, *martingale residuals* (MART), *deviance residuals* (DEV) , *likelihood displacement statistic* (LD) and *DFBETAS* (DFB).

The model chosen to recreate survival times was the Cox proportional hazards. The simulated observations were generated from two different Cox models, a general trend model $\beta = \beta^G$ and an outlier model $\beta = \beta'$. From the Cox hazard function, the distribution of T is given by $F(t|X) = 1 - \exp\left[-H_0(t) \cdot \exp(\beta X)\right]$. The vector of covariates X characterizing each individual was generated from a three-dimensional normal distribution with zero mean with identity covariance matrix. The survival times were generated using the methodology explained in [1], each observation time as function of the covariate vector X given by $T = H_0^{-1}\left[-\log(U) \cdot \exp(-\beta X)\right]$, where U is a uniform random variable distributed in the interval $[0, 1]$.

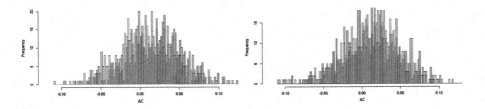

Fig. 1. On the left, contrast between antidote (blue) and poison (red) bootstrap histograms of concordance variation, for a typical outlier. On the right, antidote (blue) and poison (red) bootstrap histograms of concordance variation, for a typical inlier (Colour figure online).

Several scenarios were simulated. For each one, the vector of covariates was given by $X_i \sim N(0, \mathbf{I})$, where $\mathbf{I}$ is the identity matrix. Each simulated dataset contains 100 observations with hazard functions

$$h_i(t) = \begin{cases} h_0(t) \exp\{\beta^G \mathbf{X}\} & 1 \leq i \leq n - k \\ h_0(t) \exp\{\beta' \mathbf{X}\} & n - k < i \leq n, \end{cases}$$

Table 1. Outlier configurations used in the simulated data (left). Average of TPR (middle) and average of AUC (right) grouped by outlier scenarios.

Scen.	Θ'	$\|\beta'\|/\|\beta^G\|$	β'	MART	DEV	LD	DFB	OSD	BHT	DBHT	MART	DEV	LD	DFB	BHT	DBHT
1	180°	1	(-1,-1,-1)	0.29	0.36	0.43	0.36	0.47	0.43	**0.47**	0.70	0.70	0.74	0.68	0.78	**0.82**
2	180°	0.2	(-0.2,-0.2,-0.2)	0.22	0.25	0.31	0.29	0.32	0.31	**0.34**	0.65	0.65	0.70	0.64	0.71	**0.75**
3	180°	5	(-5,-5,-5)	0.50	0.58	0.59	0.52	0.63	0.59	**0.65**	0.80	0.80	0.78	0.77	0.86	**0.90**
4	135°	0.2	(-0.143,0,-0.283)	0.22	0.23	0.30	0.28	0.30	0.29	**0.32**	0.64	0.64	0.69	0.63	0.71	**0.73**
5	135°	5	(-3,0,-7.07)	0.44	0.54	0.52	0.48	**0.58**	0.53	0.58	0.78	0.77	0.74	0.75	0.82	**0.84**
6	90°	0.2	(-0.245,0,-0.245)	0.21	0.22	**0.28**	0.26	0.27	0.26	**0.28**	0.63	0.63	0.67	0.63	0.68	**0.71**
7	90°	5	(6.12,0,-6.12)	0.40	**0.50**	0.40	0.41	0.44	0.37	0.42	**0.76**	**0.76**	0.66	0.73	0.70	0.72
8	0°	0.2	(0.2,0.2,0.2)	0.18	0.18	**0.23**	0.22	0.22	0.20	**0.23**	0.62	0.62	0.66	0.62	0.65	**0.68**
9	0°	5	(5,5,5)	0.32	**0.36**	0.18	0.25	0.09	0.06	0.07	**0.74**	0.72	0.61	0.69	0.60	0.60
10	180°	10	(-10,-10,-10)	0.53	0.63	0.64	0.57	0.68	0.60	**0.70**	0.83	0.83	0.80	0.81	0.87	**0.92**
11	0°	10	(10,10,10)	0.38	**0.46**	0.24	0.32	0.14	0.11	0.12	**0.78**	0.76	0.61	0.73	0.59	0.61
12	135°	10	(-7.15,0,-14.15)	0.49	**0.60**	0.54	0.51	**0.60**	0.52	**0.60**	0.80	0.80	0.74	0.78	0.81	**0.86**

where the pure model $\beta^G = (1,1,1)$ and β' taking 12 different vectors; see Table 1.

When assessing the performance of outlier detection methods on the simulated data it has to be taken into account that the observations are randomly generated from distributions: the inliers from the general distribution β^G, and the outliers from an outlying distribution β'. It may happen that observations initially intended to be inliers may be drawn from the lower or upper tail of the distribution and may configure an outlier, and vice-versa. Our performance assessment assumes that for each scenario the observations generated from general distribution are inliers and the observations generated from the outlying distribution are outliers.

We used two metrics to analyse the results, the *true positive rate* (TPR), also known as *sensitivity*, and the *area under the ROC curve* (AUC). For datasets with k outliers the TPR will measure for each scenario the fraction of true outliers found in the top-k most outlying observations indicated by each method. The AUC provides us a threshold-independent outlier detection ability. The AUC is not applicable to the output of the OSD method, because it does not provide an outlying score for every observation. The TPR and AUC are the mean of 50 runs per simulation configuration. Results are depicted in Table 1.

4 Conclusion and Future Work

DBHT has shown promising results, being the best method in nine of the 12 simulated outlier scenarios. On the three scenarios where β' is collinear with β^G, the performance of DBHT, BHT and OSD is poor; in these scenarios outliers have the same hazard direction as inliers, and so concordance fails to capture them as it does note take into account the difference in predicted hazards. This kind of outliers are typically very well detected by residual-based methods, so DBHT may be useful when used jointly with these methods. Future applications include outlier detection for oncological patients.

Acknowledgments. Work supported by Fundação para a Ciência e a Tecnologia (FCT) under contracts LAETA (UID/EMS/50022/2013) and IT (UID/EEA/50008/2013), and by projects CancerSys (EXPL/EMS-SIS/1954/2013) and InteleGen (PTDC/DTP-FTO/1747/2012). SV acknowledges support by Program Investigador (IF/00653/2012) from FCT, co-funded by the European Social Fund through the Operational Program Human Potential.

References

1. Bender, R., Augustin, T., Blettner, M.: Generating survival times to simulate Cox proportional hazards models. Stat. Med. **24**(11), 1713–1723 (2005)
2. Efron, B.: Bootstrap methods: another look at the jackknife. Ann. Stat. **7**, 1–26 (1979)
3. Harrell, F.E., Califf, R.M., Pryor, D.B., Lee, K.L., Rosati, R.A.: Evaluating the yield of medical tests. Jama **247**(18), 2543–2546 (1982)
4. Hawkins, D.M.: Identification of Outliers, vol. 11. Springer, The Netherlands (1980)
5. Pinto, J., Carvalho, A.M., Vinga, S.: Outlier detection in survival analysis based on the concordance c-index. In: Proceedings of BIOINFORMATICS, pp. 72–82 (2015)
6. Nardi, A., Schemper, M.: New residuals for COX regression and their application to outlier screening. Biometrics **55**(2), 523–529 (1999)

Characterization of the #k–SAT Problem in Terms of Connected Components

Giuseppe Nicosia and Piero Conca$^{(\boxtimes)}$

Department of Mathematics and Computer Science,
University of Catania, Catania, Italy
{nicosia,conca}@dmi.unict.it

Abstract. We study the #k–satisfiability problem, that is the problem of counting the number of different truth assignments which satisfy random Boolean expressions having k variables per clause. We design and implement an exact algorithm, which we will call *Star*, that solves #k–SAT problem instances. We characterize the solution space using the connected components of a graph G, that is a subgraph of the n dimensional hypercube representing the search space.

1 Introduction

Standard experimental methods for studying $\mathcal{NP}$–complete problems use a random generator of the problem instances and an exact algorithm, possibly optimized by means of heuristics, to solve the instances [1,2]. By analyzing the results with *ad hoc* measures (e.g. number of recursive calls), one can obtain important information about the problem (e.g. hard and easy distributions, phase transitions, topological characterization of the search space, etc.) [3].

Statistical physics models can serve as a source of inspiration for understanding $\mathcal{NP}$–complete problems. As a matter of fact, during the last decade, theoretical computer science has witnessed the development of several new methodologies based on statistical physics for investigating the nature and properties of $\mathcal{NP}$–complete problems [4–6]. This, for example, has lead to the determination of the computational complexity of k–satisfiability from characteristic *phase transitions* [7].

Thanks to this connection between such different fields, new algorithms capable of producing notable results have been developed. For instance, it has been shown the existence of an intermediate phase below the phase transition threshold in k–SAT problems and a powerful class of optimization algorithms have been presented and tested successfully on the largest existing benchmark of k–satisfiability [8].

In our work, we apply the experimental method to the analysis of #k–SAT problem, i.e. the problem of counting how many truth assignments satisfy a given instance of k–SAT [9]. In particular, we designed and implemented an exact algorithm and, for our experiments, we used the A. van Gelder's k–SAT

© Springer International Publishing Switzerland 2015
P. Pardalos et al. (Eds.): MOD 2015, LNCS 9432, pp. 257–268, 2015.
DOI: 10.1007/978-3-319-27926-8_23

problem instance generator, MKCNF.C[1]. Algorithms for counting the number of solutions to instances of SAT have been proposed in [10–12], and the computational complexity has been studied in [13].

Our research shows that the number of solutions grows exponentially in proximity of the threshold of the transition phase. This result is confirmed by the rigorous work presented in [14].

2   #k–SAT Problem

When we face a problem we want to known if a solutions exists and, in this case, we may also want to know how many solutions exist and if it is possible to produce all the solutions [15].

Let the relation $R(x, y) =$ "y satisfies x" be a polynomially-balanced, polynomial-time-decidable binary relation. The counting problem associated with R consists of determining the number of pairs $(x, y) \in R$ [16]. In this context, $\#\mathcal{P}$ is the class of all counting problems associated with polynomially–balanced polynomial–time–decidable relations.

As a particular example, #SAT is defined as the problem of computing the number of different truth assignments that satisfy a Boolean expression [16]. An interesting problem associated with it is the #k–SAT problem. An instance of the #k–SAT problem consists of a set V of variables with $\mid V \mid = n$, a collection C of clauses over V, where $\mid C \mid = m$, such that each clause $c \in C$ has $\mid c \mid = k$ literals. The problem consists of finding all the different satisfying truth assignments for C.

It can be shown that #SAT is $\#\mathcal{P}$–complete [16], i.e. it belongs to the class $\#\mathcal{P}$, and any other problem in $\#\mathcal{P}$ can be reduced to #SAT in polynomial time.

3   Counting the Solutions of k–SAT

We present now our novel algorithm to count the solutions of an instance of k–SAT by describing the pseudo-code of the algorithm and the procedure it uses.

3.1   Sorting the Clauses

First, we present a preprocessing procedure which determines the *frequency of variables*, i.e. how many times a variable occurs in clauses, and the *frequency-weight of clauses*, i.e. the sum of the frequencies of the variables occurring in it. We then sort the clauses in nonincreasing order.

3.2   The Algorithm Star

The algorithm being proposed, that we call "Star", uses a list L to compute the number of solutions of an instance of #k–SAT. In particular, the list L has size n, which is the number of boolean variables representing partial solutions.

---

[1] Available at ftp://dimacs.rutgers.edu/pub/challenge/satisfiability/contributed/ UCSC/instances.

> **Procedure Preprocessing** (V, C, k)
>
> compute the frequency $f(i)$ of every variable $i \in V$, $1 \leq i \leq n$.
> compute the frequency–weight $\Phi(j)$ of every clause $j \in C$, $1 \leq j \leq m$, where $\Phi(j) = \sum_{h=1}^{k} f(var(c_{j,h}))$.
> sort C respect to Φ such that $\Phi(1) \geq \Phi(2) \geq \ldots \geq \Phi(m)$.
>
> **end Preprocessing**
> *Comment:* $c_{j,h}$ represents the hth literals of the jth clause, while the function $var(c_{j,h})$ returns the corresponding variable of the literal.

For any $v \in L$, the ith boolean variable $v[i]$ can assume one of the following values: 0 (false), 1 (true) or "$*$"; where the symbol "$*$" denotes the possibility of a variable to be true or false independent of the values of the others variables.

Let us inspect, now, the code of the recursive algorithm Star. The algorithm has three parameters: the list L of current partial solutions, the index i of a clause, and a pointer P which is the index of an element–vector v of L that the procedure will process in the next recursive call. Three different cases are possible.

- In the first case, v (pointed by P) satisfies the i-th clause c_i, so we move to the next element–vector in L. In this way, a new region of the search space can be explored. The number of solutions and the length of L remain unchanged.
- In the second case, v has at least a "$*$" value for one of the variables occurring in a literal of c_i, (e.g., the literal $c_{i,j}$) and the other variables occurring in the clause have values which do not satisfy the clause. In this case we create a copy v' of v and insert it in L after v. In vector v, "$*$" is replaced with the value that makes the literal $c_{i,j}$ true, while the "$*$" in v' is replaced with the value that makes $c_{i,j}$ false.

  The function $value\_of(c_{i,j})$ returns the value that if assigned to the variable j makes $c_{i,j}$ true. In this way, v satisfies the clause c_i and we can move to the next element–vector in L.

  This is the *expansion* case. The number of solutions remains the same, however the length of L is increased by one. In particular, the set of solutions represented by the old v is substituted by two modified copies, in such a way that the variable $var(c_{i,j})$ of the literal $c_{i,j}$ is given both boolean values *true* and *false*. Thus, a compact representation of a group of solutions is partitioned into two subgroups, without loss of solutions. In particular, notice that only one element of v has been changed, from "$*$" to a boolean value, and all the boolean values already set remain unchanged. So, it now satisfies clause i and all clauses that were previously satisfied.
- In the last case, vector v does not satisfy the clause c_i, therefore it is deleted from L and the next vector is analyzed. If L if empty, the procedure is terminated because the given k–SAT instance is unsatisfiable.

Algorithm. $Star(L, i, P)$

    if $is\_empty(L)$ **then**
        return $null$;
    if $P.v$ satisfies c_i **then** /* case 1 */
        $P \leftarrow P.next$;
    else
        for $j = 1$ **to** k **do**
            if $P.v[c_{i,j}] ==$ "$*$" **then** /* case 2 */
                Let Q be a copy of P;
                $Q.v[c_{i,j}] \leftarrow \neg value\_of(c_{i,j})$;
                $P.v[c_{i,j}] \leftarrow value\_of(c_{i,j})$;
                $Q.next \leftarrow P.next$;
                $P.next \leftarrow Q$;
                $P \leftarrow P.next$;
                goto $label$ 1;
            endif
        endfor
        $Q \leftarrow P$; /* case 3 */
        $P \leftarrow P.next$;
        $free(Q)$;
    endif
    if $is\_not\_empty(P)$; $\rightarrow label$ 1
        return $Star(L, i, P)$
    elif $(i < m)$
        $P \leftarrow L$;
        return $Star(L, i + 1, P)$;
    else
        return L;
    endif

end Algorithm

This is the *contraction* case. The length of L is reduced and, in turn, the search space is reduced and the number of candidate solutions decreases.

If $i = m$ and the pointer P is **null**, the algorithm terminates and returns the list L of solutions.

3.3　The Main Program

By inspecting the code of the main program Counting–$\#k$–SAT, we see that, first, there is a call to the preprocessing phase using the parameters V, C and k to initialize the list of solutions.

Initially, the list L contains only a vector $\{*\}^n$ that represent the space of all the possible solutions. The first call to the algorithm Star uses the parameters $(L, 1, P)$. The last step of the main program Counting–#k–SAT is to process the list ℓ returned by the Algorithm Star, to obtain the number of solutions, ns, of the input instance. We observe the number of solutions of the k–SAT instance is given by

$$\sum_{v \in L} 2^{num(v)}$$

where $num(v)$ returns the number of stars in v.

Counting-#k-SAT (V, C, k)
Input: A set of n variables, V, and a set of m k–clauses, C.
Output: ns, the number of solutions.

Preprocessing(V, C, k)
$L.vector \leftarrow \{*\}^n$;
$L.next \leftarrow null$;
$P \leftarrow L$;
$\ell \leftarrow Star(L, 1, P)$;
$ns \leftarrow PostProcessing(\ell)$;
$G \leftarrow MakeGraph(\ell)$;
$DFS(G)$;
end Counting-#k-SAT

Later in the paper, we will discuss the last two statements of the main program.

3.4   An Example

Let us consider the following formula of 3–SAT:

$$F = (A \vee B \vee C) \wedge (A \vee \neg B \vee C) \wedge (A \vee B \vee \neg C). \tag{1}$$

Initially, we have:

$$L \rightarrow ***. \tag{2}$$

We examine the first clause. The second case of the star algorithm applies, and let us choose A as a variable with assigned "$*$" value. We have:

$$L \rightarrow 1** \rightarrow 0**. \tag{3}$$

Now we consider the second element of L. The value that is assigned to A, that is "0", does not satisfy the formula. The remaining values are "$*$", therefore, the second case applies. At this point, we choose the variable B and obtain:

$$L \rightarrow 1** \rightarrow 01* \rightarrow 00*. \tag{4}$$

Let us consider the third element of L. Again, the second case applies and, by choosing C (the only variable left), we obtain:

$$L \to 1** \to 01* \to 001 \to 000. \tag{5}$$

Then we consider the fourth element of L. The third case applies, since the assignment "$0,0,0$" does not satisfy the first clause, and this element is eliminated. At this point, the first clause has been analyzed. The space of solutions is represented by:

$$L \to 1** \to 01* \to 001. \tag{6}$$

We now analyze the second clause case and the first element of L. Since A has value 1, the second clause is satisfied. The third case applies and we move to the next element. In this case A is given the value 0 and B the value 1. C has the value "$*$"; the second clause is not satisfied by the assigned values and one of its literals has value "$*$". Therefore, the second case applies:

$$L \to 1** \to 011 \to 010 \to 001. \tag{7}$$

We move on to the third element of L. The third case applies and the element is deleted from L. We obtain:

$$L \to 1** \to 011 \to 001. \tag{8}$$

Moving on to the third element of L we see that the third case of the algorithm Star applies. Therefore, the list remains unchanged.

We now consider the third clause. Using the first and second element of L we are in the first case of the algorithm. With the last element of L we are in the third case, so it is deleted from L. Thus, we have:

$$L \to 1** \to 011. \tag{9}$$

that represents the set of satisfying truth assignments. It turns out that we have 5 assignments which satisfy 1, these are:

$$L \to 100 \to 101 \to 110 \to 111 \to 011 \tag{10}$$

4 Correctness of the Program

We now prove that the algorithm being presented is correct, i.e. it finds all and only the truth assignments that satisfy the formula. We begin by observing that algorithm Star analyzes the clauses of a formula sequentially. Each clause is processed only once and when it has been processed, the program moves to the next one.

Lemma 1. *When working with the ith clause, all the elements in L represent truth assignments which satisfy the first $i-1$ clauses. Moreover, all the elements in L that precede the one pointed by P represent truth assignments which satisfy the ith clause. If P is null, all the elements in L satisfy the ith clause.*

Proof. We prove the lemma by induction on the number of clauses, h, analyzed by algorithm Star.

If $h = 0$, L is null and the lemma is vacuously true. Let us assume that algorithm Star is analyzing clause i, and the recursive call is being called with the following arguments: $Star(L, i, L)$. By induction, all the elements in L represent truth assignments which satisfy the first $i - 1$ clauses. While working with the ith clause, if the second case and the third case of the algorithm do not apply, all the elements remain unchanged. Moreover, when P moves forward it leaves behind elements which also satisfy the ith clause. If P points to an element which does not satisfy c_i, the element is deleted. Then, P moves forward leaving behind only elements which satisfy c_i. If P points to an element v for which the second case applies, the element *splits* in L is replaced by two other elements. The first one, which is going to be left behind by P, is obtained by replacing a star symbol "$*$" with a boolean value in order to satisfy clause c_i. All other variables remain unchanged. Therefore, any clause previously satisfied by v are also satisfied by this new element, which, by construction, satisfies c_i as well. The lemma is proven.

Theorem 1. *The algorithm Star is correct.*

Proof. Let us prove that when the algorithm returns, the elements in L represent all and only the truth assignments which satisfy the m clauses.

We observe that Star terminates when $i = m$ and P is null. Therefore, from the lemma above, all the elements in L represent truth assignments which satisfy the m clauses. It remains to be proved that these are the only truth assignments which satisfy the given clauses. This is guaranteed by the fact that the algorithms considers the whole search space and elements are deleted when they do not satisfy a clause.

We also remark that if the given formula is unsatisfiable, the algorithm is still correct. Indeed, if it halts because L is empty, without having examined all the clauses, that is because it could not find truth assignments which satisfy a first group of clauses.

5   Computational Complexity

The computational complexity of our algorithm is exponential. It is possible to build an example of a formula that would force the program to require exponential time to count all the satisfying assignments. Consider an instance of #2–SAT with $2n$ variables e n clauses defined as follows: $(A \vee B) \wedge (C \vee D) \wedge (E \vee F) \wedge \dots$. Applying the algorithm Star to such an instance, one can see that after having examined the first clause L will contain two clauses. After having examined the second clause, it will contain 4 clauses, and so on. When Star returns L it will have 2^n elements, and the algorithm would have made $3 * 2^n$ recursive calls.

In general, for an instance of #k–SAT with $k * n$ variables and n clauses, the number of recursive calls might be $(k + 1) * k^n$ which is asymptotically better than a brute force search with complexity 2^{kn}.

6   Experimental Results

Given a combinatorial problem **P**, a *solution space* of **P** is defined by a couple (S, f) where S is a finite set of configurations (or nodes) and f a cost function which associates a real number to each configurations of S. Two common measures are the minimum and the maximum costs which give rise to combinatorial optimization problems. The search space for the k–SAT problem is (S, f) where S is the set of all possible truth assignments (configurations) and the cost function for k–SAT computes only the number of satisfied clauses from truth assignment s for formula F :

$$f_{sat}(s) = \#\text{SatisfiedClauses(F,s)},$$

for $s \in S$. Given a search space (S, f), a *search landscape* is defined by a triplet (S, n, f) where n is a neighborhood function

$$n : S \to 2^S - \{0\}$$

It can be conveniently viewed as weighted graph $H = (S, n, f)$ where the weights are defined on the nodes, not on the edges. The search Landscape H for the k–SAT problem is a n *dimensional hypercube* (with n being the number of boolean variables). Combinatorial optimization problems are often hard to solve since such problems may have large and complex search landscapes. The notion of landscape is an important concept which might help understand the behavior of search algorithms and heuristics and to characterize the difficulty of a combinatorial problem. In the program Counting–#k–SAT, the statement

$$G \leftarrow MakeGraph(\ell);$$

builds a graph G from the list of solutions returned by Star. G is a subgraph of the n dimensional hypercube H. Finally, the statement $DFS(G)$ calls the procedure *Depth First Search* to compute the connected components (CCs) of G, and the number of vertices of each connected component. The CCs of G, give us some interesting topological information on the structure of the solution space. As a case study, let us consider the problem #3–SAT with $| V |= 10$ variables. We use A. van Gelder's k–SAT problem instance generator to create satisfiability formulas.

In Fig. 1 we can see how the total number of solutions and the connected components' cardinality decrease rapidly as the ratio between number of clauses and number of variables increases. The curve of number of CCs has the shape of a bell in which the maximum is located at $\alpha = 3.0$ and has a long tail on the right hand side. Each point in the plot has been averaged over 10000 different instances. Moreover, for the 3–SAT problem the phase transition is located at $\alpha = 4.256$ where the number of CCs is about 2 and the CC's cardinality is lower than number of CC. One can observe that for $\alpha = 0.5$ and 1.0 there is only one CC, which contains all the solutions to the problem instance. In this case, the total number of solutions is equal to the cardinality of the CC.

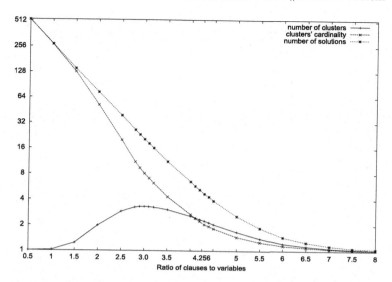

Fig. 1. Number of solutions, number of connected components and CCs' cardinality versus α for #3–SAT problem with $n = 10$ variables.

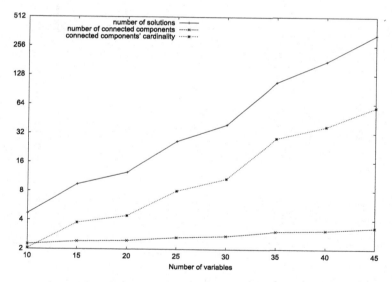

Fig. 2. Number of Solutions, number of connected components and CC's cardinality at phase transition $\alpha_c(3) = 4.256$ versus number of variables n for #3–SAT problem.

For $\alpha > 1.0$ we do not have just one CC, but we have several with high cardinalities. When α reaches the critical value 3.0 the number of CCs starts decreasing, and they have smaller and smaller cardinalities. These results are consistent with known theoretical results [6].

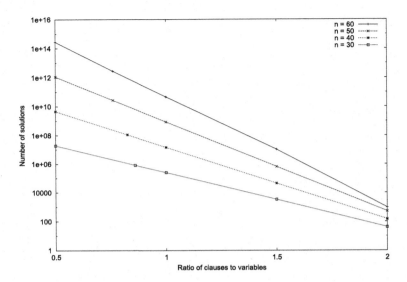

Fig. 3. Number of solutions for #2sat problem.

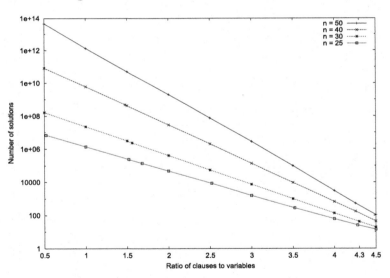

Fig. 4. Number of solutions for #3–sat problem.

If instead we set $\alpha = 4.256$ and let n vary from 10 to 45, we obtain the results shown in Fig. 2. It can be observed that in this case the number of CCs is basically constant (it varies on average from 2.25 to 3.33). The number of solutions and the cardinality of the CCs grow, instead, exponentially.

Figures 3 and 4 show the number of solutions for #2–SAT and #3–SAT respectively, for n ranging between 25 to 60. In the semi–log plot we can observe

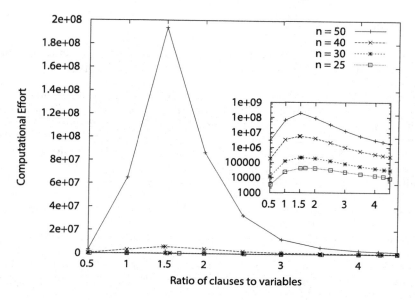

Fig. 5. Star Algorithm's computational effort for the #3–sat problem.

straight lines with increasing slope as the number of variables increases. For these results we generated from 50000 to 100000 random instances for each value of n.

The algorithm Star has been used to determine experimentally the phase transition between hard and easy distributions of instances for the #3–SAT problem. We found, for our algorithm, a threshold value $\alpha_{\#c}(3) = 1.5$, representing the ratio between the number of clauses and the number of variables. Such experimentally found value (see Fig. 5) tells us that the closer we are to the threshold, the harder it becomes to solve the counting problem computationally. The further we are from such value, the easier it becomes to count all the satisfying assignments.

7   Final Comments

In this paper we have introduced a new exact algorithm for the counting problem #k–SAT. The found experimental results are consistent with the theoretical results found during the last years [5–8]. The given algorithm not only determines the number of solutions but it also presents (for some values of n and α) the graphs of the solutions. To our knowledge, this is the first time that the solution space of k–SAT is characterized in terms of connected components. For 3–SAT we have seen how for the phase transition, $\alpha_c = 4.256$, the number of connected components is independent from the number of variables. Experimental results seem to point out that our algorithm makes its biggest computational effort for #3–SAT, in the proximity of $\alpha_{\#c} = 1.5$.

References

1. Ermon, S., Gomes, C.P., Selman, B.: Computing the density of states of boolean formulas. In: Cohen, D. (ed.) CP 2010. LNCS, vol. 6308, pp. 38–52. Springer, Heidelberg (2010)
2. Ermon, S., Gomes, C., Selman, B.: A flat histogram method for computing the density of states of combinatorial problems. In: Proceedings of the Twenty-Second International Joint Conference on Artificial Intelligence, pp. 2608–2613 (2011)
3. Montanari, A., Shah, D.: Counting good truth assignments of random k-SAT formulae. In: Proceedings of the Eighteenth Annual ACM-SIAM Symposium on Discrete Algorithms, SODA '07, pp. 1255–1264 (2007)
4. Mitchell, D., Selman, B., Levesque, H.: Hard and easy distributions of SAT problems. In: AAAI, vol. 92, pp. 459–465 (1992)
5. Hogg, T., Huberman, B.A., Williams, C.P.: Phase transitions and the search problem. Artif. Intell. 81(1), 1–15 (1996)
6. Monasson, R., Martin, O., Zecchina, R.: Statistical mechanics methods and phase transitions in optimizations problems. Theor. Comput. Sci. 265(1), 3–67 (2001)
7. Monasson, R., Zecchina, R., Kirkpatrick, S., Selman, B., Troyansky, L.: Determining computational complexity from characteristic phase transitions. Nature 400(6740), 133–137 (1999)
8. Mézard, M., Parisi, G., Zecchina, R.: Analytic and algorithmic solution of random satisfiability problems. Science 297(5582), 812–815 (2002)
9. Vaisman, R., Strichman, O., Gertsbakh, I.: Model counting of monotone conjunctive normal form formulas with spectr. NFORMS J. Comput. 27(2), 406–415 (2015)
10. Birnbaum, E., Lozinskii, E.L.: The good old Davis-Putnam procedure helps counting models. J. Artif. Intell. Res. 10, 457–477 (1999)
11. Dubois, O.: Counting the number of solutions for instances of satisfiability. Theor. Comput. Sci. 81(1), 49–64 (1991)
12. Zhang, W.: Number of models and satisfiability of sets of clauses. Theor. Comput. Sci. 155(1), 277–288 (1996)
13. Littman, M.L., Pitassi, T., Impagliazzo, R.: On the complexity of counting satisfying assignments. Unpublished manuscript, vol. 328, p. 329 (2001)
14. Boufkhad, Y., Dubois, O.: Length of prime implicants and number of solutions of random CNF formulae. Theor. Comput. Sci. 215(1), 1–30 (1999)
15. Garey, M.R., Johnson, D.S.: Computers and Intractability, vol. 29. W.H. Freeman, New York (2002)
16. Papadimitriou, C.H.: Computational Complexity. John Wiley and Sons Ltd., Chichester (2003)

A Bayesian Network Model for Fire Assessment and Prediction

Mehdi Ben Lazreg$^{(\boxtimes)}$, Jaziar Radianti, and Ole-Christoffer Granmo

Centre for Integrated Emergency Management,
University of Agder, Grimstad, Norway
{mehdi.b.lazreg,jaziar.radianti,ole.granmo}@uia.no
http://www.ciem.uia.no

Abstract. Smartphones and other wearable computers with modern sensor technologies are becoming more advanced and widespread. This paper proposes exploiting those devices to help the firefighting operation. It introduces a Bayesian network model that infers the state of the fire and predicts its future development based on smartphone sensor data gathered within the fire area. The model provides a prediction accuracy of 84.79 % and an area under the curve of 0.83. This solution had also been tested in the context of a fire drill and proved to help firefighters assess the fire situation and speed up their work.

Keywords: Bayesian network · Indoor fire · Smartphone sensors

1 Introduction

The international association of fire and rescue services reported approximately a million fires in buildings or domestic houses around the world in 2012 alone. These fires unfortunately left 23.7 thousand victims [9]. Thousands of people around the world are affected directly or indirectly by fire. Such facts have previously motivated numerous works in the field of automated fire detection that tried to find some solution to prevent fires and limit the casualties.

During a fire, people tend to leave the building, however, there are potential rescuers going in and trapped victims inside carrying smartphones. In this paper, we propose a model for fire assessment and prediction based on a Bayesian network and smartphone sensors. The number of smartphone user has been growing considerably and is expected to grow even further. Moreover, these smartphones are more and more equipped with advanced sensor technology. The sensor data is gathered from the smartphone located in the fire zone and fed to the Bayesian network. Bayesian networks are capable of handling uncertainty in data which is a common issue when dealing with fire incidents [14]. In addition, they can be adapted to deal with different fire scenarios. To assess the fire status in a specific room, the Bayesian network uses the sensor data along with the estimated state of the fire in neighbouring rooms. The model follows the fire

© Springer International Publishing Switzerland 2015
P. Pardalos et al. (Eds.): MOD 2015, LNCS 9432, pp. 269–279, 2015.
DOI: 10.1007/978-3-319-27926-8_24

development from its ignition until it reaches a fully developed status in addition to forecasting its development.

The topic of automated fire detection and prediction has been extensively studied in the review by Mahdipour et al. [1]. In their review of the subject they showed that most studies focus on detecting fire and reducing the rate of false fire alarm. Various methods have been investigated, including image and video processing, computer vision and statistical analysis to enhance fire detection. These methods focus only on detecting the fire, whereas our method not only detects but follows the development of the fire. Other researches have focused on detecting and predicting fire development by means of wireless sensor networks in context of outdoor and residential area fires. Bahrepour et al. [3] use wireless sensor network (combination of temperature, ionisation, CO and photoelectric sensors) along with machine learning techniques that includes decision tree neural network and naïve Bayes to detect outdoor and indoor fire. Ma [4] used sensor network (temperature, smoke thickness and CO) and neural network fusion algorithm to compute the probability of a fire generated by coal occurs. Nonetheless, those methods are limited only on detecting the fire and they did not take into consideration the sate of the fire in neighbouring rooms as a factor in the fire's propagation. Matellini et al. [5] used Bayesian networks to model the fire development within dwellings from the point of ignition through to extinguishment. Cheng et al. [6] modelled the building as a direct acyclic graph and used Bayesian networks to model fire dynamics in the building and determine the probability of the fire spread from a room to another. However, these methods do not use sensors as a basis for detecting and predicting the fire, but only use the state of the fire in different rooms of the building to deduce its development. Combining Bayesian network with sensor technology with taking into consideration the state of the fire in neighbouring rooms to assess and predict the fire state can be considered as the main contribution of this paper.

The paper is organised as follows: Sect. 2 provides a brief introduction to Bayesian networks. Section 3 presents the fire assessment and prediction model. In Sect. 4, we evaluate the model based on two criteria: its performance for assessing the fire and its usefulness in case of fire. We finally conclude this work in Sect. 5, and reveal the possible future direction.

2   Bayesian Network

A Bayesian Network (BN) represents a set of random variables and their conditional dependencies using a directed acyclic graph (DAG) [7]. In brief, a BN is composed of [14]:

- Directed acyclic graph: contain a set of nodes and directed edges connecting one node to another in a way that starting from a node A there is no sequence of edges that loops back to node A. In a BN, the nodes may represent an observable quantity, latent variable, unknown parameter or hypotheses. The edges represent the causal relationship between two events represented by two nodes: an edge directed from node A to node B implies that the occurrence of an event represented by node A has a direct impact on the occurrence of another event represented by node B. In a DAG, family terminology is used to describe the relationship between nodes. Hence the parents of A ($pa(A)$) are a set of nodes that have an edge directed to A. The children of A are a set of nodes that are reached by an edge generated from A.

– A set of probabilities: each node in the DAG is assigned a probability distribution if it is a root node or a conditional probability distribution if it is not. Those probabilities express the likelihood that the event symbolised by a certain node accrues.

Bayesian network is based on the fundamental assumption of causal Markov condition [8]. This assumption specifies that each node in the DAG of the BN is conditionally independent of its non-descendent nodes given its parents. To further explain this assumption, let us consider a $DAG = (V, E)$ where V represents the set of nodes in the DAG and E is the set of edges between those nodes. Let $X \in V$ be a node in this DAG. Let $child(X)$ be the set of all the children of X and $pa(X)$ the set of all parents (direct causes of X). The causal Markov condition can be expressed formally as follows

$$\forall X, Y \in V; Y \notin child(X) \Rightarrow P(X|Y, pa(X)) = P(X|pa(X)). \tag{1}$$

From Eq. (1), it can be concluded that for any BN composed of a set of nodes $\{X_1, X_2, ..., X_n\}$ the joint probability is given by

$$P(X_1, X_2, ..., X_n) = P(X_n|X_1, X_2, ..., X_{n-1})P(X_1, X_2, ..., X_{n-1})$$
$$= P(X_1)P(X_2|X_1)...P(X_n|X_1, X_2, ..., X_{n-1})$$
$$= \prod_{k=1}^{n} P(X_k|pa(X_k)).$$

3   Fire Assessment and Prediction Model Based on Bayesian Network

3.1   Fire Assessment

A fire is a dynamic process that evolves through time. Its status at a present time t depends on that at previous time steps [6]. One might then think of using a dynamic Bayesian network (DBN) to capture fire dynamics. However, for each node a DNB keeps other nodes for each time step. Thus, DBN is more complicated and consequently more process consuming [14]. Since we intend to run the application on mobile devices with limited power and battery life, the application of a simple BN is preferable. The Bayesian network presents each room in the building by a node (see Fig. 1(b)). This choice was motivated by the work done by Cheng et al. [6] and Granmo et al. [15] who also used Bayesian network to model indoor hazards.

A fire normally goes through five stages (dormant, growing, developed, decaying and burnt out) [6]. In this research, we only focus on the first three stages for two main reasons. First, this choice simplifies the classification process. Second, it allows us to model the fire at it most dangerous stages (growing and developed). Therefore, the fire in a room R can be dormant, growing or developed. Let S be a set representing the fire state in a room

$$S = \{dormant, growing, developed\}.$$

Smartphones come with a variety of sensors. The most appropriate in case of fire are: temperature, humidity, pressure and light from which the visibility can be deduced. Let O be the set of observed sensor data in R

$$O = \{temperature, humidity, visibility, pressure\}.$$

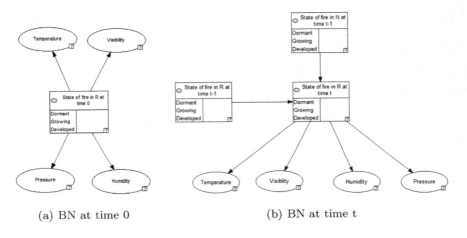

(a) BN at time 0   (b) BN at time t

Fig. 1. BN for real time fire assessment

At time 0, the fire state in R influences the observed sensor's values recorded in that room. This is modelled by edges going from the node representing the fire status in the BN to the nodes representing each sensor (Fig. 1(a)). Furthermore, to model the dynamic aspect of the fire at a time $t > 0$, we added to the model in Fig. 1(a) a node that represents the status of the fire in a room at previous time step. Moreover, the fire in R depends also on the situation of the fire in neighbouring rooms. Therefore, a node representing the fire state in the neighbouring room at previous time step is added to the BN. Note that the graph in Fig. 1(b) only represented one neighbouring room for simplicity. In reality, R can have multiple neighbours. In that case edges are added between each neighbour and R. If we had used a DNB to model the fire we would end up with 12600 nodes for a 30 min fire simulation for each room in the building instead of the 7 nodes that we have in our model.

Let R_t be the random variable representing the state of the fire in R and N_t that of the neighbouring room at a time t. The BN infers the fire state in R

at time 0 based on the value of temperature, humidity, visibility and pressure collected by the phone sensors placed in R. At a time t, we add the fire state in R at $(t-1)$ and the fire state in the neighbouring room N as a factor in the inference process (Fig. 1). This inference is performed using the joint probability distribution of the random variable in the network expressed as follows

$$P(R_0, O) = P(R_0|O)P(O) \text{ if } t = 0 \tag{2}$$

$$P(R_t, R_{t-1}, N_{t-1}, O) = \frac{P(R_{t-1})P(N_{t-1})P(R_t|R_{t-1}, N_{t-1})P(R_t|O)P(O)}{P(R_t)} \text{ if } t > 0. \tag{3}$$

Finally, at each time step the probability distribution of a node representing the fire state in a room at a time t will be passed to the node that represents its former state as virtual evidence for the next iteration. Unlike normal evidence or soft evidence where the evidence of an observed event is deterministic like in the case of temperature provided by a sensor-, the virtual evidence uses a likelihood ratio to present the confidence toward the observed event. In our case, since the observed state of the fire at a time t is derived from the BN with a certain probability and thus uncertain, it is more appropriate to pass it to the node presenting the previous state as a virtual evidence. The whole process of fire assessment for a single room R is summarised in Algorithm 1.

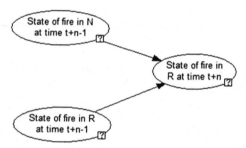

Fig. 2. BN for fire forecasting

3.2 Fire Prediction

In addition, the BN should be able to forecast the state of the fire at a future time $(t+n)$. For this we designed a BN illustrated in Fig. 2. The network in Fig. 2 is similar to the network designed for fire assessment. The only difference is the lack of node representing the sensor data since the sensor data provided by the smartphone sensors is only known at the present time. Thus, at each future time step $(t+n)$ the state of the fire in room R is inferred from the state of the fire in R and its neighbouring rooms in the previous time step $(t+n-1)$. The joint probability distribution would be as follows

$$P(R_{t+n}, R_{t+n-1}, N_{t+n-1}) = P(R_{t+n-1})P(N_{t+n-1})P(R_{t+n}|R_{t+n-1}, N_{t+n-1}). \tag{4}$$

The probability distribution of the fire in R at time $(t+n)$ is then passed to the node representing the probability distribution of the fire in R at time $(t+n-1)$ as virtual

---

Algorithm 1. Algorithm for fire assessment using BN

---

1 **Loop**
2 | **forall the** $o_i \in O$ **do**
3 | | o_i = registered sensor data
4 | **end**
5 | **forall the** $s_i \in S$ **do**
6 | | If (t=0) infer $P(R_0 = s_i|O))$
7 | | Else infer $P(R_t = s_i|O, R_{t-1}, N_{t-1}))$
8 | **end**
9 | virtual evidence$(R_{t-1})= R_t$
10 | $t++$
11 **EndLoop**

Algorithm 2. Algorithm for fire prediction using BN

---

1 **while** $t \leq T$ **do**
2 | **forall the** $s_i \in S$ **do**
3 | | infer $P(R_t = s_i|R_{t-1}, N_{t-1})$
4 | **end**
5 | virtual evidence $(R_{t-1})= R_t$
6 | $t++$
7 **end**

---

evidence. This process is done recursively until a final time T in the future is reached $(t + n = T)$. The whole process of fire prediction is summarised in Algorithm 2.

As Algorithms 1 and 2 suggest we need to infer $P(R_t|O, R_{t-1}, N_{t-1}))$ from Eqs. 3 and 4. To do that we need to compute $P(R_t, R_{t-1}, N_{t-1}, O))$ and $P(O)$ with are respectively known as the most probable explanation and the probability of evidence problem. These problem are difficult problems known to be NP-complete and PP-complete problem respectively [14]. Therefore, Eqs. 3 and 4 cannot be solved directly to obtain the probability of each state of the fire due in general to high computational complexity. However, different algorithms have been developed to approximate a solution for those equations. We used one of the fastest and most precise of them: the Estimated Posterior Importance Sampling algorithm for Bayesian Networks (EPIS-BN) [12]. It is based on using loopy belief propagation [13] to compute an approximation of the posterior probability over all nodes of the network. The loopy belief propagation is based on approximating the problem of computing $P(R_t|O, R_{t-1}, N_{t-1}))$ by computing $P(R_t|R_{t-1}, N_{t-1}))$ and $P(O|R_t = s_i)$ where $P(R_t|O, R_{t-1}, N_{t-1})) = \alpha P(R_t|R_{t-1}, N_{t-1}))P(O|R_t)$. Then, it uses importance sampling to refine this approximation. Importance sampling allows to approximate a function by another function called importance function. It is used to approximate $P(O|R_t)$.

4   Test Results and Discussion

4.1   Test Settings

We used the third floor of the University of Agder building as the scenario for our model. The floor contains 5 classrooms, 30 offices, 7 group rooms, 4 computer labs, 2 meeting rooms, 12 corridors and 3 stairways used as escape routes from the fire. The building is an interesting case study since it is large enough to be a challenge for firefighters in the event of a fire: based on our meeting with firefighter they stated that they rarely phase a fire spreading in a building of this amplitude. Each room in the building will be represented by a BN as described in Figs. 1 and 2.

The network described in the previous section is trained and tested using data obtained from several fire simulations runs produced using the fire dynamics simulator (FDS) [11]. The FDS permits the imitation of the geometry of a building and its material properties, the definition of fuel that triggers fire, and the placement of devices such as visibility and temperature sensors in the simulated environment in such a way that fire parameter data can be measured and collected. A user needs first to build a 3D space object called mesh to make a fire simulation, which will be used to construct the 3D building geometry being the target of fire simulations. The user can define the fire cause and starting point and thermal properties of the building material. For our BN experiments, we created a model of the third floor of our university building that follows all the real dimensional size and the detailed rooms and furniture.

For completing the model, the user can place devices and sensors such as sprinklers, smoke detectors, heat flux gauges and produce the quantity outputs, for example, temperature, visibility and so on. The type of sensors placed in each room in this 3D university building is in line with our research goals, i.e. to get information about the temperature, humidity, visibility, and pressure. We run this simulation twice with different starting points of the fire. During those simulations, all defined sensors would register all the data produced in this simulation. The output of the fire parameters produced by FDS comes as a table containing the value of temperature, humidity, visibility and pressure in each room at each second for 30 min as well as the corresponding fire state to those values.

As we have seen in Sect. 2 the BN is composed of a DAG (described in Figs. 1 and 2) and for each node a probability distribution representing the likelihood that an event represented by that node accuses. We trained one BN based on the table produced by the FDS simulations for all the rooms (we ended up with 128 fire examples). This allows to learn those probability distributions. This includes $P(R_t|R_{t-1}, N_{t-1})$, $P(temperature|R_t)$, $P(pressure|R_t)$.... Once learned those probabilities are used in the inference process to solve Eqs. 3 and 4. The building structure is then loaded into the app. It consist of a table with the room its location and neighbours. Copies of the trained BN nodes are then created for each room based on this table.

Further, We simulate two another set of fire scenarios to test the BN. The lines containing the sensor data are retrieved consecutively from the table produce by FDS and fed as evidence to the Bayesian network. The results of this test are the probabilities of each fire state in each room as a function of time. Thus, the BN prediction varies from room to room and from time step to time step.

We have implemented the BN using JSMILE, a Java interface of SMILE (Structural Modelling, Inference, and Learning Engine) [10]. It allows the creation, editing and use of Bayesian network for probabilistic reasoning and decision making under uncertainty.

4.2   Performance Testing

First, we present the results of a test on a specific scenario from the scenarios we used to test our BN. The results for two representative rooms ($R1$ and $R2$) are presented in Figs. 3 and 4. These Figures show the probability of a dormant, growing and developed fire in the two rooms as a function of time as well as the actual state of the fire (black line). Room $R1$ is the neighbouring room toe the fire starting point whereas room $R2$ is located on the opposite side of the building and thus it is the furthest room to the fire starting point. For $R1$ (Fig. 3), the predicted probabilities match the actual state of the fire. The delay of detecting the growing phase of the fire is 3 s. For Room $R2$ (Fig. 4), the BN is not sure about its fire state predictions, especially during the growing phase of the fire. This can be due to a conflict between the sensors' data obtained from the simulation and the fire state in neighbouring rooms: the neighbouring rooms experience a developed fire that should propagate to $R2$ however the sensors' data suggest that the fire is dormant in the mentioned room. In spite of not distinguishing between the growing and developed state of the fire in room R2, the BN was able to at least detect that there is fire in the room (regardless of its state) with a delay of 30 s. In the remaining rooms, the results vary from room to room but they similar to the results presented for room $R1$ and $R2$ with delays to detect the growing and developed state of the fire varying from 3 to 67 s.

Overall the test set, to calculate the overall accuracy of our model, we first take the most probable state as the predicted state. Then, for each room we compute the percentage of the correct classifications. Finally, we average the result over all the room in the building, The overall accuracy of the Bayesian network is then 84.79 %. The model also has an overall area under the curve (AUC) of 0.83. The AUC allows to test the ability of the BN to predict each state of the fire. The AUC can be viewed as the probability that the model gives a higher probability to the fire state that is actually correct. An AUC of 0.83 means that, given an instance from the test set, the model has an 83 % chance of giving a higher probability to the correct state of the fire for that instance. The AUC is a useful metric even if the state of the fire are imbalanced (in our case the growing state is less frequent the two other states). It was extended to evaluate multi class classification problem by Hand et al. [2] who proposed to use the formula in Eq. 5 where c in the number of classes and $A(i, j)$ is the AUC of the binary classification of two classes i and j out of the c classes:

$$AUC = \frac{2}{c(c-1)} \sum_{i<j} A(i,j). \tag{5}$$

4.3   Game Scenario Testing

As mentioned in the previous section, we implemented the BN model in an Android app, and tested this fire development and prediction app in a serious game. We used a fire scenario simulated by FDS to get the sensor data and feed them to the BN. In this game, a group of players (9 persons), acting as firefighters, conducted a search and rescue operation, while another group (13 persons) played victims trapped in the rooms during the indoor fire hazard, with one person acted as the MCU (Medical Care Unit). The game took place at the University of Agder (UiA) and two game sessions of 30 min each had been planned, i.e. one without and one with app support. We focused

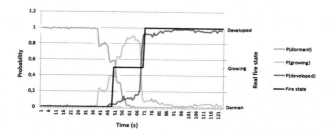

Fig. 3. Fire state probabilities in room R1

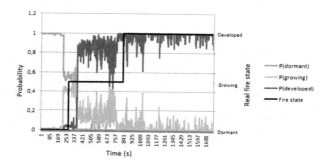

Fig. 4. Fire state probabilities in room R2

on a hypothetical situation where the fire had grown, and several victims were trapped inside.

We hypothesised that the rescue operation with app support (2nd session) would be faster than without app support (1st session). The game goal was to search for victims trapped in the 3rd floor, and rescuing them by moving them all the way to the MCU located by the main entrance of the UiA building. All victims that were saved had to be reported to the CM, who monitored the overall progress of the rescue operation performed by all three rescuer groups. No exact script was given to them as how to act, communicate and interact, except that they were informed on the outline of the roles, tasks, scenarios, prior to the game.

In the session without app, the players should check the room one by one and reported to MCU if the room was clearnobody inside. The communication mode was walkie-talkie software on the smartphone. In that session, each burning room would be marked over time by a fire marker, based on a predefined fire spread. In the scenario with the app, the fire information was available on the smartphone and users could observe the fire spread from room to room by the mean of a heat map. The BN-based fire assessment and prediction app served as a decision support and a basis for rescuers to act while saving the victims. The deployment of the app was conducted in two ways: by sending the app directly to the players to download in advance, and by preparing ten devices with the app installed. The app usage was explained in the briefing, and repeated before the 2nd session was started. In fact, familiarising the players with the app was crucial to the success/failure of the game goal.

The quantitative data collected from this game is about the number of victims saved in the first and second sessions. The game testing shows that the rescue process

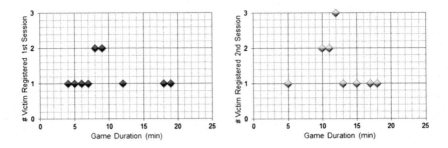

Fig. 5. Number of saved victims as function of time

was faster with the app. Figure 5 shows the time and the number of victims being saved without the fire assessment/prediction app (left) and with the app (right). The horizontal axis indicates the duration of the game in minutes while the vertical axis shows the number of victims saved, as registered by the MCU. The rescue process took 15 min in the first experiment, and 13 min in the second experiment. This time was counted from the moment the first victim was found. In the second session, 11 victims were saved in the last 8 min. On the contrary, the saved victims were spread over a longer time during the first round. There was a longer delay before the rescuers could find the first victim in the second experiment (Fig. 5, right). The reason for this was that the players needed some adjustment to use the app, and some of them experienced technical issues at the beginning of the app use. Further, most of the players relied more on the real-time fire assessment than on the prediction feature while performing their rescue task. This is due to the fact that the rescuers (as they reported in the briefing) had to deal with the real-time assessment of fire situation while trying to save the victim at the same time, and thus could not spend time on "additional" task such as checking where fire would develop in the future.

Hence, we learnt from the game that being able to see how the fire develops over time was useful in a fire situation to decide where the safest place to escape is, but there was a barrier in practice regarding the usage of the prediction feature. The interview with real firefighters who were present during the game indicated that placing the app with the firefighters' leader, who normally does not go inside the building, can relieve the firefighter from that extra task. The leader can then inform the team members about the future fire situation while the firefighters can concentrate on finding the victims. This could be a better design for future testing the usefulness of fire prediction feature.

5 Conclusion

This paper proposes a model that uses smartphone sensors along with Bayesian network to assess fire situation and predict its development. The Bayesian network infers the probability of each state of the fire based on the sensor data collected from smartphones in the fire area and the state of the fire in the previous time step. It provides an overview of the fire situation along with forecasting its development. The test of the model performance shows that the computed probabilities match the actual state of the fire in 84.79 % of the cases and an area under the curve of 0.83. This solution also helps facilitate and speed up the work of firefighters in order the save more lives as revealed from field experience. The future directions of this work would be to use smoke and temperature sensors in the building alongside the smartphones as well as figuring out the optimal number of sensors needed inside the building to still achieve an acceptable prediction accuracy of the fire. We also plan to develop our model to include fire development from one floor to another.

References

1. Elham, M., Chitra, D.: Automatic fire detection based on soft computing techniques: review from 2000 to 2010. Artif. Intell. Rev. **42**(4), 895–934 (2014)
2. David, H., Till, R.: A simple generalisation of the area under the ROC curve for multiple class classification problems. Mach Learn. **45**(2), 171–186 (2001)
3. Bahrepour, M., van der Zwaag, B.J., Meratnia, N., Havinga, P.: Fire data analysis and feature reduction using computational intelligence methods. In: Phillips-Wren, G., Jain, L.C., Nakamatsu, K., Howlett, R.J. (eds.) IDT 2010. SIST, vol. 4, pp. 289–298. Springer, Heidelberg (2010)
4. Ma, X.-M.: Application of data fusion theory in coal gas fire prediction system. In: International Conference on Intelligent Computation Technology and Automation (ICICTA) (2008)
5. Matellini, D.B., Wall, A.D., Jenkinson, I.D., Wang, J., Pritchard, R.: A bayesian network model for fire development and occupant response within dwellings. In: IEEE Conference on Prognostics and System Health Management (PHM) (2012)
6. Cheng, H., Hadjisophocleous, G.V.: The modelling of fire spread in buildings by bayesian network. Fire Saf. J. **44**(6), 901–908 (2009)
7. Stephenson, T.A.: An Introduction to Bayesian Network Theory and Usage. IDIAP researsh institue Martigny, Switzerland (2000)
8. Hausman, D.H., Woodward, J.: Independence Invariance and the Causal Markov Condition. Oxfor University Press, Oxford (1999)
9. Brushlinsky, N.N., Ahrens, M., Skolov, S.V., Wagner, P.: World fire statistics. In: International Association of Fire and Rescue Service (2014)
10. Druzdzel, M.J.: SMILE: structural modeling, inference, and learning engine and GeNIe: a development environment for graphical decision-theoretic models. In: Proceedings of the Sixteenth National Conference on Artificial Intelligence and the Eleventh Innovative Applications of Artificial Intelligence Conference Innovative Applications of Artificial Intelligence (1999)
11. Kevin, M., Howard, B., Ronald, R.: Fire dynamics simulator technical reference guide. National Institute of Standards and Technology (2007)
12. Yuan, C., Druzdzel, M.J.: An importance sampling algorithm based on evidence pre-propagation. In: The Conference on Uncertainty in Artificial Intelligence (2003)
13. Murphy, K., Weiss, Y., Jordan, M.: Loopy belief propagation for approximate inference: an empirical study. In: Proceedings of the Fifteenth Annual Conference on Uncertainty in Artificial Intelligence (1999)
14. Van Harmelen, F., Lifschitz, V., Porter, B.: Handbook of Knowledge Representation, 1st edn. Elsevier, San Diego (2008)
15. Granmo, O.-C., Radianti, J., Goodwin, M., Dugdale, J., Sarshar, P., Glimsdal, S., Gonzalez, J.J.: A spatio-temporal probabilistic model of hazard and crowd dynamics in disasters for evacuation planning. In: Ali, M., Bosse, T., Hindriks, K.V., Hoogendoorn, M., Jonker, C.M., Treur, J. (eds.) IEA/AIE 2013. LNCS, vol. 7906, pp. 63–72. Springer, Heidelberg (2013)

Data Clustering by Particle Swarm Optimization with the Focal Particles

Tarık Küçükdeniz[✉] and Şakir Esnaf

Department of Industrial Engineering, Engineering Faculty,
Istanbul University, Istanbul, Turkey
{tkdeniz,sesnaf}@istanbul.edu.tr

Abstract. Clustering is an important technique in data mining. In unsupervised clustering, data is divided into several subsets (clusters) without any prior knowledge. Heuristic optimization based clustering algorithms tries to minimize an objective function, generally a clustering validity index, in the search space defined by the dimensions of the data vectors. If the number of the attributes of the data is large, then this will decrease the clustering performance. This study presents a new clustering algorithm, particle swarm optimization with the focal particles (PSOFP). Contrary to the standard particle swarm optimization (PSO) approach, this new clustering technique ensures high quality clustering results without increasing the dimensions of the search space. This new clustering technique handles communication among the particles in a swarm by using multiple focal particles. The number of focal particles equals to the number of clusters. This approach simplifies the candidate solution representation by a particle and therefore reduces the effect of 'curse of dimensionality'. Performance of the proposed method on the clustering analysis is benchmarked against K-means, K-means++, hybrid PSO and the CLARANS algorithms on five datasets. Experimental results show that the proposed algorithm has an acceptable efficiency and robustness and superior to the benchmark algorithms.

Keywords: Data clustering · Clustering analysis · High dimensional data · Particle swarm optimization · Focal particles

1 Introduction

Advances in technology has made information easy to capture and inexpensive to store, thus the amount of data stored in various databases increased dramatically. These data contain useful but hidden information that may be critical for the decision-making processes of the enterprises. Data mining is the general name of the techniques that are used to extract information from a very large amount of data [11]. Clustering is a major technique in data mining, which refers to a process of dividing data into several subsets while maintaining maximum similarity among the data within the same cluster and keeping minimum similarity among different clusters. Its applications can be seen in customer segmentation,

© Springer International Publishing Switzerland 2015
P. Pardalos et al. (Eds.): MOD 2015, LNCS 9432, pp. 280–292, 2015.
DOI: 10.1007/978-3-319-27926-8_25

document clustering and information retrieval, web data analysis, image segmentation, anomaly detection, biology, medicine and many other areas. Clustering is an unsupervised process, thus true knowledge about the class that each data object belongs to is not known by the clustering algorithm. If the true class label of data is known to the algorithm and used in the analysis then the method is named classification.

When we look at the history of clustering techniques, we see that many unsupervised clustering algorithms have been developed. K-means is one of the well-known of them. K-means clustering algorithm is easy to implement and very efficient, however suffers from several drawbacks. The objective function of the K-means is not convex hence it may contain many local minima. The outcome of the K-means algorithm is heavily dependent on the initial choice of the centroids [2]. In order to achieve better clustering performance, fuzzy c-means (FCM) clustering algorithm is introduced by Bezdek [4].

Clustering is also an application field in mathematical optimization when it is done by searching for the global minima of a clustering performance function. This approach makes it possible to apply heuristic algorithms to clustering analysis. Particle swarm optimization (PSO) is a population based heuristic algorithm, which maintains a population of particles where each particle represents a potential (candidate) solution to an optimization problem. Merwe and Engelbrecht used PSO in data clustering [22]. They also developed an hybrid approach, which combines PSO and K-means algorithm to achieve better clustering performance.

Merwe and Engelbrecht's original PSO data clustering approach inspired many works. Ji et al. clustered mobile networks by applying PSO to weighted clustering algorithm [12]. Correea et al. categorized sample types of biological databases with PSO [7]. Chen et al. tested PSO clustering algorithm on four different datasets. They analyzed the performance of standard PSO clustering algorithm in their paper [6]. Cui et al. applied PSO to the document clustering problem [8]. Attributes of documents defined as the dimensions of the particles. Omran et al. applied PSO to the image classification problem [18,19]. Their algorithm is a binary PSO model which dynamically adjusts the number of clusters. Kumar and Arasu proposed a particle swarm optimization based clustering method to medical databases [14]. Their modified particle swarm optimization based adaptive fuzzy K-modes algorithm produces good results in terms of precision and accuracy. Rana et al. gives a detailed literature review of PSO applications to data clustering [20]. Readers can also refer to [16] for further literature survey on nature inspired metaheuristic algorithms for data clustering.

Although each of these studies provide a number of improvements and innovations for clustering applications of PSO, all of them remains faithful to the Merwe and Engelbrecht's standard particle representation. But this representation creates a disadvantage by increasing the dimensions of the particles by the number of features of a data vector times the number of desired clusters (Fig. 1). Most stochastic optimization algorithms, including particle swarm optimization, suffer from this 'curse of dimensionality', which simply put, implies that their performance deteriorates as the dimensionality of the search space increases [23]. Bouveyron *et al.* advises dimension reduction or subspace clustering as the primary ways of avoiding the curse of dimensionality [5].

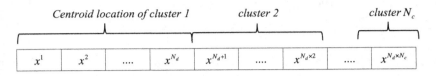

Fig. 1. Particle structure of the standard PSO. Each particle contains the centroids for all clusters.

The proposed method in this study,unlike the standard PSO approach, achieves high quality clustering results without increasing the number of dimensions. To do so, instead of a whole representation of a candidate solution by a particle (including all centroids of all clusters as in Fig. 1), in the proposed method, each particle represents only one centroid in the search space. Therefore, the number of dimensions of a particle equals the number of data vector features. Despite this major change in the particle representation, the proposed version of PSO's adherence to the standard PSO principles is provided by the changes made in the structure of the communication between particles.

One of the main configurational properties of PSO is topology or structure of connections between particles. Several approaches are developed to obtain good performance. In the *gbest* model, each particle is connected to all other particles (Fig. 2a). In the *lbest* model, each particle is connected to a predefined number of other particles (Fig. 2b). In star topology, which is a *lbest* model, one of the particles in the swarm become the focal particle and all other particles are connected to this focal particle (Fig. 2c). Therefore, all communication in the swarm is transmitted through this focal particle.

The proposed PSO variant in this study, addresses a star topology based new PSO clustering method. In this method there are several focal particles in the swarm. Other particles are connected to their nearest focal particle and all communication passes through these focal particles. There are several studies about focal particles in PSO [13,21]. However, we couldn't find any study on multiple focal particles in a swarm with dynamically changing neighborhoods among particles.

In this study, we aim to prove that, by decreasing the number of dimensions with the help of this multiple focal particle topology, our proposed PSO variant achieves high quality clustering results with less computation cost than other heuristics in high dimensional datasets. In the following sections, first data clustering is defined as an optimization problem. Then, in the third section, particle swarm optimization technique is introduced and the method of data clustering with particle swarm optimization is explained. In the fourth section particle swarm optimization with the focal particles method is introduced. This method

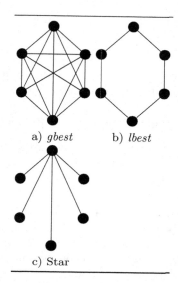

a) *gbest*   b) *lbest*

c) Star

Fig. 2. Swarm topologies: *gbest* topology - Each particle is connected to each other. *lbest* topology - Each particle is connected to a number of other particles. Star topology - Each particle is connected to a focal particle.

is applied on five datasets and, results and the conclusion is given at the end of this study.

2 Data Clustering

When the data clustering problem is treated as an optimization problem, the aim is to find optimal centroids of clusters rather than finding optimal partition of the data vectors [1]. The dataset to be clustered is represented as a set of vectors $D = \{x_1, x_2, ..., x_m\}$ where m is the number of data objects x_i. A data object can have any number of dimensions. These dimensions of data is called attributes or features. A cost function is to be defined for clustering optimization problem. In clustering analysis these cost functions are validity indexes. A comprehensive review of the clustering methods can be found in [15, 16, 24].

2.1 Validity Indexes

Several validity indexes are defined to assess the performance of the clustering algorithms. In optimization based data clustering, these validity indexes (or similarity indexes) are used to calculate the fitness of the current solution. The most basic validity index is the sum of distances between the data vectors and their assigned cluster centroids in the vector space. This index is called clustering error index [1] and given in the Eq. (1).

$$J_e = \sum_{j=1}^{N_c} [\sum_{\forall x_i \in C_j} d(x_i, o_j)] \tag{1}$$

where d is the distance of the data vector x_i to its assigned centroid. N_c denotes the number of clusters (provided by the user). o_j denotes the centroid vector of cluster C_j.

Another validity index is quantization error (2) from [22].

$$J_q = \frac{\sum_{j=1}^{N_c} [\frac{\sum_{\forall x_i \in C_j} d(x_i, o_j)}{|C_j|}]}{N_c} \tag{2}$$

Here $| C_j |$ is the number of data vectors belonging to cluster C_j. This quantization error is the average distances of the data vectors to their assigned centroids. The quantization error used in the Eq. (2) allows for division by zero. In our study, if a division by zero was encountered, the fitness of the particle was approximated to infinity.

One another well-known validity index is Silhouette value. The silhouette value for each point is a measure of how similar that point is to points in its own cluster, when compared to points in other clusters. Higher silhouette means a better assignment of data vectors to clusters. Formula for silhouette value is given in (3).

$$S(x_i) = \frac{b(x_i) - a(x_i)}{max\{a(x_i), b(x_,)\}} \tag{3}$$

where $a(x_i)$ is the average distance from the ith point to the other points in the same cluster as i, and $b(x_i)$ is the minimum average distance from the ith point to points in a different cluster, minimized over clusters. Silhouette value is in between -1 and $+1$. There are several other validity indexes for data clustering, a brief list of them can be seen in [16].

The distance parameter in the Eqs. (1) and (2) can be Euclidian, cosine or any other distance metric. In data clustering euclidian distance, given in the Eq. (4), is one of the most frequently used metric. But at some special occasions like document clustering, cosine distance is more suitable [25].

$$d(x_i, o_j) = \sqrt{\sum_{k=1}^{N_d} (x_{ik} - o_{jk})^2} \tag{4}$$

Here N_d is the data dimension, i.e. the number of attributes of each data vector.

3   Particle Swarm Optimization

Swarm optimization algorithms are inspired by the efforts to model the social systems of birds and bees. Particle swarm optimization is developed by Kennedy and Eberhart in 1995 [9]. In PSO, each particle represents a position in N_d dimensional space. PSO algorithm moves particles through this multi-dimensional search space to search for an optimal solution. A particle's movement is affected by three factors; (1) Particle's own velocity vector, $\vec{v}_i$ - (2) Particle's best position found thus far, $\vec{p}_i$ - (3) Best position found by the particles in the neighborhood of that particle, $\vec{y}_i$.

In the first step of the algorithm, velocity of a particle is calculated as in (5) and then this value is added to the current position of the particle as given in (6). If $\vec{x}_i$ is the current position of the particle, $\vec{v}_i$ is the current velocity of the particle and $\vec{p}_i$ is the personal best position of the particle then the velocity of the particle for the next iteration is;

$$\begin{aligned} \vec{v}_{i,k}(t+1) = {} & w\vec{v}_{i,k}(t) + c_1 r_{1,k}(t)(\vec{p}_{i,k}(t) - \vec{x}_{i,k}(t)) \\ & + c_2 r_{2,k}(t)(\vec{y}_{i,k}(t) - \vec{x}_{i,k}(t)) \end{aligned} \tag{5}$$

$$\vec{x}_i(t+1) = \vec{x}_i(t) + \vec{v}_i(t+1) \tag{6}$$

where w is the inertia weight, c_1, c_2 are positive constants, called the cognitive and social acceleration factors respectively. $r_{1,k}(t)$, $r_{2,k}(t) \backsim U(0,1)$, and $k = 1, ..., N_d$ [22].

3.1 Data Clustering with Particle Swarm Optimization

In PSO, every particle represents a candidate or potential solution. The model employed by the particle should point a solution of the problem by its own. In Merwe and Engelbrecht's [22] method, a particle is constructed as in 7.

$$\vec{x}_i = (o_{i1}, o_{i2}, ..., o_{ij}, ...o_{iN_c}) \tag{7}$$

where o_{ij} corresponds to the j_{th} centroids represented by the i_{th} particle. Thus, if a data vector consists of N_d dimensions, then a particle will have $N_d \times N_c$ dimensions.

PSO algorithm tries to minimize an objective function iteration by iteration. In data clustering mode, this objective function should be chosen carefully to achieve a good clustering result at the end of the iterations or when a termination criteria for the PSO is reached. Merwe and Engelbrecht [22] have chosen quantization error (2) as the fitness function.

4 Particle Swarm Optimization with the Focal Particles

As it is explained before, in PSO, a particle is a representation of a whole solution, thus a particle should have $N_d \times N_c$ dimensions. This usually yields the so-called 'curse of dimensionality' problem. To overcome this ineffectiveness, we have developed a new clustering approach, namely particle swarm optimization with the focal particles (PSOFP). In this new approach each particle represents only one centroid in the search space. If N_c is the number of clusters, then N_c

number of particles are chosen as the final representatives of clustering solution. These particles are the focal particles to which all other particles in the swarm are connected to their nearest. This neighborhood structure is similar to Fig. 3. This approach results in less dimensionality in particles. Therefore, it is expected to have less computational cost than the standard approaches. In the next section we have benchmarked PSOFP's performance with other clustering algorithms.

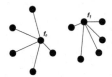

Fig. 3. f_0 and f_1 are the focal particles. There are 13 particles in total. This is an example for a two cluster problem.

In PSOFP, a particle is constructed as in (8).

$$\vec{x}_i = (o_i) \tag{8}$$

where $\vec{x}_i$ is a centroid in the search space. Algorithm 1 displays the pseudo code of PSOFP algorithm. To start PSOFP, a swarm with l particles are initialized with the particle formation given in (8). Swarm initialization of PSOFP is similar to the standard PSO. Then, randomly selected N_c number of these particles are labeled as focal particles. The swarm size should be bigger than N_c. At each iteration, the fitness value of each particle is calculated. To do this calculation, first centroid locations represented by the focal particles are combined together to make a candidate solution. Then, for each non-focal particle, the particle's position vector (the centroid it represents) is overwritten to the corresponding place in the candidate solution. This process is illustrated in the Table 1.

In this illustrative example, a swarm with 8 particles is initialized. We are trying to cluster our data vectors into three clusters. Thus, the first three particles are assigned as the focal particles. The data vectors are in two dimensions, therefore each particle has two dimensions. To calculate the fitness value of the fourth particle,

– First a candidate solution is built by the focal particles as: {10; 18; 45; 26; 21; 34}. The first two columns of the candidate solution is the centroid of the first cluster and the third and the fourth terms are the centroid of the second cluster, the last part is the centroid of the third cluster.
– Then, we calculate the nearest focal particle to the fourth particle using the selected distance metric. It is the second focal particle in this example.
– In the candidate solution, places belonging to the second focal particle is replaced with the current particle's position: {10; 18 ; 38; 30; 21; 34}. Fitness of the fourth particle is calculated by using this final candidate solution.

Table 1. An illustrative example for the PSOFP fitness calculation process.

Particle Nr.	Focal?	Position vector $(x_1; x_2)$
1	True	10; 18
2	True	45; 26
3	True	21; 34
4	False	38; 30
5	False	12; 22
6	False	5; 52
7	False	15; 42
8	False	45; 22

Another difference from the standard PSO is, focal particles in PSOFP will not have their own inertia weight component. Focal particles are only affected by their own personal best and the best performances of the other particles that are connected to these focal particles. At the end of each iteration, particles, including the focal, move in the search space. When these movements finishes, the neighborhood structure of the swarm is to be updated. Each particle, except focal ones, will be connected to its nearest focal particle. To do this, the distances among focal and non-focal particles are calculated again.

5   Application and Results

Table 2 shows the datasets used for benchmarking. IRIS, WINE, CMC and Gesture Data are from UCI benchmark datasets. RAND1 is a randomly generated dataset which includes $500 \times U(0, 100)$, $1000 \times U(500, 1500)$ and $1000 \times U(2500, 3000)$ values.

Table 2. Benchmark datasets

Name	Data vectors	Data attributes	Clusters
IRIS	150	4	3
WINE	178	13	3
CMC	1473	9	3
Gesture Data	4833	18	5
RAND1	2500	25	3

The following methods are used for benchmarking:

- Standard K-Means Clustering Algorithm

Require:
   · Dataset: $D = \{x_1, x_2, ..., x_m\}$
   · The number of clusters: N_c
Initialisation:
   · Initialize the position $\vec{x}_i$ and velocity $\vec{v}_i$ of $l > N_c$ number of particles randomly. Each particle contains one randomly generated centroid vector (o_i) in the search space.
   · Define the set of focal particles S_F, where the number of focal particles equal to N_c

foreach *iteration* **do**
   forall the *particle i* **do**
      · x_i: Position of the particle i
      · f_i: The index of the focal particle that particle i is connected to
      · x_{f_i}: Position of the focal particle that particle i is connected to
      · x_{S_F}: All focal particles' positions
      · generate a candidate solution by replacing the x_{f_i} in the x_{S_F} with the x_i
      · calculate the fitness of particle: $J(x_i)$ by a clustering validity index

      `// Compare the particles current fitness with its` *pbest*:
      if $J(x_i) < J(p_i)$ **then**
       | $p_i = x_i$
      end
   end
   forall the *particle i* **do**
      · *Define neighborhood*: If i is non-focal then assign i to its nearest focal particle
      · $y_i = \text{MIN}(p_i \in S^i_{neigh})$ where S^i_{neigh} is the neighborhood of i
      · Change the velocity of the particle i according to the equation (5)
      if $v_i > v_{max}$ **then**
       | $v_i = v_{max}$ `// Check if the velocity is out of limits`
      end
      Calculate the position of i according to the equation (6)
      if $x_i > x_{max}$ **then**
       | $x_i = x_{max}$ `// Check if the position is out of limits`
      end
      if $x_i < x_{min}$ **then**
       | $x_i = x_{min}$ `// Check if the position is out of limits`
      end
   end
end

Algorithm 1. Pseudo code for PSOFP algorithm

– K-means++ Algorithm: Arthur and Vassilvitskii's K-means++ algorithm [3], is an improvement to the standard K-means for choosing better initial values and therefore avoiding poor results.

- Merwe's [22] hybrid PSO data clustering method: In hybrid PSO, the result of K-means clustering feed into PSO as a particle, i.e. the solution of K-means algorithm is where the PSO starts.
- CLARANS: Ng and Han [17] introduced the algorithm CLARANS (Clustering Large Applications based upon RANdomized Search) in the context of clustering in spatial databases. Authors considered a graph whose nodes are the sets of k medoids and an edge connects two nodes if they differ by exactly one medoid.

We have paralleled the benchmarking tests on a 16 processor computer. Due to the random nature of k-means and particle swarm algorithms, all methods have been run 160 times. The test computer had 16 Intel Xeon E5 2.90 Ghz processors with 30 GB of RAM. 8 parallel runs are done at the same time. We also tried paralleling the fitness evaluation process in a single run. But due to the high information preprocessing overhead, parallel evaluation of fitness functions in a single run was slower than the serial evaluation. Our test computer was on the Amazon EC2 cloud computing servers. We refer to [10] for a discussion on parallelization in data mining applications.

PSO and PSOFP algorithms are initialized with 100 particles. Permitted maximum iteration count is 4000, but iterations stop when there is less than 0.0001 improvement in the global best value during the last 250 iterations. Equation 5 is used for velocity calculations, $w = 0.90$, $c_1 = c_2 = 2.05$. In standard PSO, the $gbest$ model is chosen. Selection of the fitness function is an important process in heuristic optimization. We choose quantization error (2) as the fitness function. Quantization error and Silhouette values of each method is reported in the Table 3. CPU time column is the mean CPU time for 160 runs. $Mean$ and $Min.$ columns of quantization error represent the average and the best value obtained from 160 runs. $Max.$ column of Silhouette value represents the best value achieved among 160 runs for the Silhouette index. $S.D.$ column gives the standard deviation of runs.

When we refer to the quantization error, proposed PSOFP algorithm outperforms all other algorithms on the benchmark datasets. The mean value of the quantization error of PSOFP on five datasets is 3.71 %, 4.16 %, 4.06 % and 1.65 % lower than the K-means, K-means++, PSO Hybrid and CLARANS algorithms respectively. When we compare the best valued achieved by each algorithm (minimum values), PSOFP is 7.64 %, 7.59 %, 6.42 % and 7.78 % better than these algorithms. Standard deviation is an indicator of the representation strength of reported average errors. In all datasets, except RAND1, standard deviation of PSOFP is lower than the benchmarking algorithms. This shows that proposed PSOFP is a robust clustering technique. Silhouette value is another useful index to analyze the clustering performance. Values nearer to $+1$ is better for the Silhouette index. Silhouette values of PSOFP is equal or slightly better than the benchmarking algorithms. Only, in RAND1 dataset CLARANS algorithm is 2.23 % better than the PSOFP on the average.

As the CPU time column of the Table 3 indicates, due to the less number of dimensions of the search space in the PSOFP method, PSOFP is much faster, at the same time more successful in the term of clustering validity, than the standard PSO. Its computational time is 45.03 %, 5.00 %, 39.66 %, 64.54 % and 9.25 % less than the standard PSO algorithm in WINE, IRIS, CMC, Gesture and RAND1 datasets respectively. Although CLARANS algorithm gives better results than the PSOFP on RAND1 dataset, its computational time in this dataset is 4.3 times higher than the PSOFP.

Table 3. Benchmark results over 160 runs for each method.

Dataset	Algorithm	CPU time	Quantization error			Silhouette		
			Mean	Min	S.D.	Mean	Max	S.D.
WINE	K-Means	0.53	101.58	97.87	3.91	0.726	0.73	0.01
	K-Means++	0.45	99.84	97.87	3.43	0.729	0.73	0.02
	PSO Hybrid	668.75	100.67	97.87	3.73	0.728	0.73	0.01
	CLARANS	14,937.00	99.61	97.15	2.11	0.726	0.74	0.02
	PSOFP	367.61	96.72	95.51	1.59	0.726	0.75	0.14
IRIS	K-Means	0.44	0.65	0.64	0.02	0.724	0.74	0.06
	K-Means++	0.35	0.65	0.64	0.01	0.725	0.74	0.05
	PSO Hybrid	257.98	0.65	0.64	0.01	0.730	0.74	0.04
	CLARANS	356.86	0.65	0.64	0.00	0.730	0.74	0.02
	PSOFP	245.08	0.61	0.53	0.02	0.735	0.74	0.13
CMC	K-Means	11.38	3.83	3.83	0.00	0.645	0.65	0.01
	K-Means++	9.66	3.83	3.83	0.00	0.645	0.65	0.01
	PSO Hybrid	832.80	3.83	3.83	0.00	0.645	0.65	0.01
	CLARANS	654.77	3.83	3.83	0.00	0.645	0.65	0.01
	PSOFP	502.53	3.83	3.82	0.002	0.643	0.65	0.00
Gesture	K-Means	15.54	1.51	1.47	0.021	0.534	0.60	0.001
	K-Means++	12.56	1.50	1.47	0.023	0.523	0.60	0.001
	PSO Hybrid	1,470.71	1.59	1.37	0.046	0.532	0.70	0.003
	CLARANS	867.90	1.54	1.48	0.025	0.535	0.67	0.002
	PSOFP	521.51	1.46	1.19	0.02	0.536	0.71	0.00
RAND1	K-Means	25.11	369.23	334.71	134.11	0.952	0.98	0.11
	K-Means++	24.74	388.58	334.71	160.07	0.905	0.98	0.33
	PSO Hybrid	682.72	360.31	334.71	114.50	0.947	0.98	0.21
	CLARANS	2,664.28	334.80	334.71	0.00	0.978	0.98	0.00
	PSOFP	619.60	354.26	334.71	85.67	0.957	0.98	0.10

6   Conclusions

In this study a new approach is presented for clustering analysis using particle swarm optimization with the focal particles. In standard PSO, each particle is a representation of the final solution, however, this increases the number of dimensions a particle has. In PSOFP, each particle is a representation of only one point in the search space, therefore the number of dimensions are lower than the standard PSO. We analyzed the performance effect of this dimensionality reduction to the clustering performance. We selected three small and two large datasets and benchmarked proposed PSOFP algorithm with the standard K-means, K-means++, hybrid PSO and CLARANS algorithms. Each algorithm has run 160 times. The Amazon EC2 cloud computing platform is used and 8 parallel runs has been made each time. Also, we tried paralleling the objective function evaluation of particle swarm optimization. This approach didn't accelerate the clustering analysis due to the high information overhead among parallel processes.

Quantization error and Silhouette values are chosen as the performance criteria for benchmark tests. The results indicated that while maintaining better or equal clustering performance with the benchmarking algorithms, PSOFP was faster than the standard PSO algorithm. This shows that the dimensionality reduction approach of the PSOFP is an efficient and robust strategy in heuristic-based data clustering analysis.

As the future work, an improved fully parallel approach for focal particles can be studied. We employed Euclidian distance as the distance metric in our calculations. But cosine metric is also known to be a good representative for the similarity among data objects in high dimensional space. The performances of the algorithms can be compared by using cosine distance metric.

References

1. Abdel-Kader, R.: Genetically improved PSO algorithm for efficient data clustering. In: Second International Conference on Machine Learning and Computing (2010)
2. Ahmadyfard, A., Modares, H.: Combining PSO and k-means to enhance data clustering. In: International Symposium on Telecommunications, IST 2008, pp. 688–691. IEEE (2008)
3. Arthur, D., Vassilvitskii, S.: k-means++: the advantages of careful seeding. In: Proceedings of the Eighteenth Annual ACM-SIAM Symposium on Discrete Algorithms, pp. 1027–1035. Society for Industrial and Applied Mathematics (2007)
4. Bezdek, J.C.: Fuzzy Mathematics in Pattern Classification. Cornell University, Ithaca (1973)
5. Bouveyron, C., Girard, S., Schmid, C.: High-dimensional data clustering. Comput. Stat. Data Anal. **52**(1), 502–519 (2007)
6. Chen, C.-Y., Ye, F.: Particle swarm optimization algorithm and its application to clustering analysis. In: 2004 IEEE International Conference on Networking, Sensing and Control, vol. 2, pp. 789–794. IEEE (2004)
7. Correa, E.S., Freitas, A.A., Johnson, C.G.: A new discrete particle swarm algorithm applied to attribute selection in a bioinformatics data set. In: Proceedings of the 8th Annual Conference on Genetic and Evolutionary Computation, pp. 35–42. ACM (2006)
8. Cui, X., Potok, T.E., Palathingal, P.: Document clustering using particle swarm optimization. In: Proceedings of the 2005 IEEE Swarm Intelligence Symposium, SIS 2005, pp. 185–191. IEEE (2005)

9. Eberhart, R.C., Kennedy, J.: A new optimizer using particle swarm theory. In: Proceedings of the Sixth International Symposium on Micro Machine and Human Science, New York, NY, vol. 1, pp. 39–43 (1995)

10. García-Pedrajas, N., de Haro-García, A.: Scaling up data mining algorithms: review and taxonomy. Prog. Artif. Intell. **1**(1), 71–87 (2012)

11. Hatamlou, A., Abdullah, S., Nezamabadi-pour, H.: A combined approach for clustering based on k-means and gravitational search algorithms. Swarm Evol. Comput. **6**, 47–52 (2012)

12. Ji, C., Zhang, Y., Gao, S., Yuan, P., Li, Z.: Particle swarm optimization for mobile ad hoc networks clustering. In: IEEE International Conference on Networking, Sensing and Control, vol. 1, pp. 372–375. IEEE (2004)

13. Kennedy, J., Mendes, R.: Population structure and particle swarm performance (2002)

14. Kumar, R.S., Arasu, G.T.: Modified particle swarm optimization based adaptive fuzzy k-modes clustering for heterogeneous medical databases. J. Sci. Ind. Res. **74**, 19–28 (2015)

15. Maimon, O.Z., Rokach, L.: Data Mining and Knowledge Discovery Handbook, 1st edn. Springer, US (2005)

16. Nanda, S.J., Panda, G.: A survey on nature inspired metaheuristic algorithms for partitional clustering. Swarm Evol. Comput. **16**, 1–18 (2014)

17. Ng, R.T., Han, J.: Efficient and effective clustering methods for spatial data mining. In: Proceedings of VLDB, pp. 144–155 (1994)

18. Omran, M., Salman, A., Engelbrecht, A.P.: Image classification using particle swarm optimization. In: Proceedings of the 4th Asia-Pacific Conference on Simulated Evolution and Learning, Singapore, vol. 1, pp. 18–22 (2002)

19. Omran, M.G., Salman, A., Engelbrecht, A.P.: Dynamic clustering using particle swarm optimization with application in image segmentation. Pattern Anal. Appl. **8**(4), 332–344 (2006)

20. Rana, S., Jasola, S., Kumar, R.: A review on particle swarm optimization algorithms and their applications to data clustering. Artif. Intell. Rev. **35**(3), 211–222 (2010)

21. Reyes-Sierra, M., Coello, C.A.C.: Multi-objective particle swarm optimizers: a survey of the state-of-the-art. Int. J. Comput. Intell. Res. **2**(3), 287–308 (2006)

22. Van der Merwe, D.W., Engelbrecht, A.P.: Data clustering using particle swarm optimization. In: The 2003 Congress on Evolutionary Computation, CEC'03, vol. 1, pp. 215–220. IEEE (2003)

23. van den Bergh, F., Engelbrecht, A.P.: A cooperative approach to particle swarm optimization. IEEE Trans. Evol. Comput. **8**(3), 225–239 (2004)

24. Xu, R., Wunsch, D.: Survey of clustering algorithms. IEEE Trans. Neural Netw. **16**(3), 645–678 (2005)

25. Zhao, Y., Karypis, G.: Comparison of agglomerative and partitional document clustering algorithms. Technical report, DTIC Document (2002)

Fast and Accurate Steepest-Descent Consistency-Constrained Algorithms for Feature Selection

Adrian Pino Angulo$^{(\boxtimes)}$ and Kilho Shin

Graduate School of Applied Informatics, University of Hyogo, Kobe, Japan
apinoa85@gmail.com, yshin@ai.u-hyogo.ac.jp

Abstract. Realizing a good balance to the fundamental trade-off between accuracy and efficiency has been an important problem of feature selection. The algorithm of INTERACT was an important breakthrough, and the algorithms of SDCC and LCC were stemmed from INTERACT. LCC has fixed a certain theoretical drawback of INTERACT in accuracy, while SDCC has improved accuracy of INTERACT by expanding the search space. However, when comparing SDCC and LCC, we find that SDCC can output smaller feature sets with smaller Bayesian risks than LCC (advantages of SDCC) but can show only worse classification accuracy when used with classifiers (disadvantages). Furthermore, because SDCC searches answers in much wider spaces than LCC, it is a few ten times slower in practice. In this paper, we show two methods to improve SDCC in both accuracy and efficiency and actually propose two algorithms, namely, FAST SDCC and ACCURATE SDCC. We show through experiments that these algorithms can output further smaller feature sets with better classification accuracy than SDCC. Their classification accuracy appears better than LCC. In terms of time complexity, FAST SDCC and ACCURATE SDCC improve SDCC significantly and are only a few times slower than LCC.

1 Introduction

Feature selection is important not only to find good models that describe specific phenomena with a small number of explanatory variables but also to improve efficiency and accuracy of machine learning algorithms.

In this paper, we study feature selection from the efficiency and accuracy points of view. By *efficiency*, we simply mean the time complexity of algorithms. By contrast, the meaning of *accuracy* is not explicit. In this paper, when we say that a feature selection algorithm is more accurate than another, we mean that classifiers on average exhibit a better classification accuracy when used with the former than when used with the latter.

In large, feature selection includes two main approaches, namely, the *filter approach* and the *wrapper approach*. The filter approach only takes advantage of intrinsic properties of datasets for feature selection. By contrast, the wrapper approach specifies a particular classifier algorithm and aims to select feature sets

© Springer International Publishing Switzerland 2015
P. Pardalos et al. (Eds.): MOD 2015, LNCS 9432, pp. 293–305, 2015.
DOI: 10.1007/978-3-319-27926-8_26

that optimize the performance of the classifier. Despite of this difference, both of the approaches share the same framework that is composed of two basic gears: a *search strategy* and an *evaluation function*. In the well known survey by Molina et al. [1], the search strategy is further decomposed into search organization and generation of successors, and an evaluation function is referred to as an evaluation measure.

The search strategy represents sequences of theoretical and/or heuristic decisions on feature sets leveraging responses of the evaluation function. The evaluation function, on input of feature sets, evaluates their appropriateness. In the filter approach, an evaluation function is a mathematical function, while it returns the results of running a specified classifier in the wrapper approach.

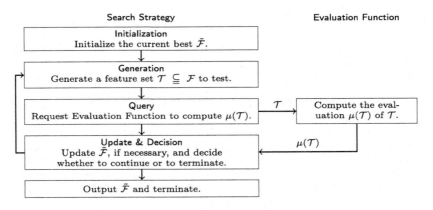

Fig. 1. The basic framework of feature selection of the filter and wrapper approaches. $\mathcal{F}$ is the entire feature set of a dataset $\mathcal{D}$, and $\tilde{\mathcal{F}}$ denotes the current best feature subset.

Figure 1 depicts this framework. In Initialization, the current best feature set $\tilde{\mathcal{F}}$ is set to an appropriate initial value. For example, we let $\tilde{\mathcal{F}} = \emptyset$ for forward selection and $\tilde{\mathcal{F}} = \mathcal{F}$ for backward elimination, where $\mathcal{F}$ denotes the entire feature set of the dataset $\mathcal{D}$ input. In Generation, the search strategy generates a feature set $\mathcal{T}$ that is to be investigated and then requests the evaluation function to evaluate $\mathcal{T}$. In Update & Decision, based on $\mu(\mathcal{T})$ returned from the evaluation function, the search strategy updates $\tilde{\mathcal{F}}$, if necessary, and decides whether it should continue the search or should terminate it by outputting $\tilde{\mathcal{F}}$.

In the remainder of this paper, we are interested in the filter approach and assume that an evaluation function is a statistical or information theoretic function. An important requirement for such evaluation functions is that it can evaluate *interaction* among features: more than one features are said to *interact* with one another, when they are not relevant to classes individually but show strong relevance to classes as a set. For example, a simple sum of individual relevance scores such as $\mu(\mathcal{T}) = \sum_{F \in \mathcal{T}} \mathrm{SU}(F, \mathrm{C})$ cannot evaluate interaction among features, where $SU(F, C)$ denotes the symmetric uncertainty between a feature F and the class C: We let F_1 and F_2 be binary features such that $\Pr(F_1 = a, F_2 = b) = \frac{1}{4}$ for $a = 0, 1$ and $b = 0, 1$ and determine the class label by $C = F_1 \oplus F_2$; Although F_1 and F_2 determine C, we have $\mu(\{F_1, F_2\}) = SU(F_1, C) + SU(F_2, C) = 0$.

A *consistency measure*, by contrast, can evaluate interaction among features. We introduce the *Bayesian risk* as an example. To illustrate, for a dataset $\mathcal{D}$, we view a feature of $\mathcal{D}$ as a random variable and a feature set $\mathcal{T}$ as a joint variable. Then, we let $\Omega_{\mathcal{T}}$ denote the sample space of $\mathcal{T}$, C denote a variable that describes classes and $\Pr_{\mathcal{D}}$ denote the empirical probability distribution of $\mathcal{D}$. With these notations, the Bayesian risk is defined by

$$\mathfrak{Br}(\mathcal{T}) = 1 - \sum_{x \in \Omega_{\mathcal{T}}} \max\{\Pr_{\mathcal{D}}[\mathcal{T} = x, C = y] \mid y \in \Omega_C\}.$$

This function is also referred to as the *inconsistency rate* in [2]. The Bayesian risk has two important properties, that is, *determinacy* and *monotonicity*, and we introduce the notion of *consistent feature sets* to explain the properties.

Definition 1. *For a dataset $\mathcal{D}$ described by $\mathcal{F}$, a feature subset $\mathcal{T} \subseteq \mathcal{F}$ is consistent, iff, $\Pr_{\mathcal{D}}[C = y \mid \mathcal{T} = x] = 0$ or 1 for all $x \in \Omega_{\mathcal{T}}$ and $y \in \Omega_C$.*

Then, the determinacy and monotonicity properties are described as follows.

Determinacy. $\mathfrak{Br}(\mathcal{T}) = 0$, if, and only if, $\mathcal{T}$ is consistent in $\mathcal{D}$.
Monotonicity. $\mathfrak{Br}(\mathcal{T}) \geq \mathfrak{Br}(\mathcal{U})$, if $\mathcal{T} \subseteq \mathcal{U} \subseteq \mathcal{F}$.

Formally, a consistency measure is defined as a function that returns real numbers on input of feature sets that has the determinacy and monotonicity properties. The *consistency-based feature selection*, on the other hand, is characterized by use of consistency measures as the evaluation function.

INTERACT [2] is the first instance of consistency-based feature selection algorithms that have practical performance in both time efficiency and prediction accuracy. LCC [3] is a modification of INTERACT to fix the problem that INTERACT may return irrelevant feature sets because of accumulation of errors. SDCC [4] is a further modification of LCC, which aims to select *better* feature sets than LCC by enlarging the search range of LCC based on the steepest descent method. In fact, it can be verified through experiments that SDCC can select feature sets smaller in size with smaller Bayesian risks. However, it has been also shown that, in combination with classifiers, the feature sets selected by SDCC could only exhibit lower prediction accuracy than those selected by LCC. At the same time, SDCC is much slower than LCC because of its larger search range. The objective of this paper is to solve these problems of SDCC. In fact, we will propose two new algorithms, namely FAST SDCC and ACCURATE SDCC, which drastically improve SDCC in both prediction accuracy and time-efficiency.

2   SDCC and LCC: A Comparison

In this section, we identify the problems of SDCC that we address in this paper.

2.1   The Algorithms of INTERACT, LCC and SDCC

INTERACT [2] was an important breakthrough in the research of consistency-based feature selection. It selects an answer from a small number of candidates, to be specific, $|\mathcal{F}|$ feature subsets. Nevertheless, it can exhibit high accuracy when used with classifiers. Figure 2(a) depicts the algorithm: INTERACT receives a dataset $\mathcal{D}$ that is described by a feature set $\mathcal{F}$ and a threshold δ; In Initialization, INTERACT sorts the features in $\mathcal{F}$ into $(F_1, \ldots, F_{|\mathcal{F}|})$ in the increasing order of the symmetric uncertainty $\mathrm{SU}(F, \mathrm{C})$ and then sets $\tilde{\mathcal{F}}$ to $\mathcal{F}$; Starting from $i = 1$, INTERACT lets $\mathcal{T} = \tilde{\mathcal{F}} \backslash \{F_i\}$ and computes $\mathfrak{Br}(\mathcal{T}) - \mathfrak{Br}(\tilde{\mathcal{F}})$, which is non-negative by the monotonicity property; If $\mathfrak{Br}(\mathcal{T}) - \mathfrak{Br}(\tilde{\mathcal{F}}) \leq \delta$, INTERACT judges that the feature F_i is not important and eliminates it from $\tilde{\mathcal{F}}$; INTERACT repeats the steps of Generation, Query and Update & Decision until it tests all the features.

Although INTERACT presented good balance between accuracy and efficiency, Shin and Xu [3] have found that $\mathfrak{Br}(\mathcal{T}) - \mathfrak{Br}(\tilde{\mathcal{F}})$ can accumulate, and consequently, INTERACT may output feature sets whose Bayesian risks are high for a certain class of datasets. They also proposed a new algorithm, namely, *Linear Consistency Constrained* (LCC), that solves this problem. Figure 2(b) depicts the algorithm.

The difference of LCC from INTERACT is slight: The criteria to eliminate F_i is on $\mathfrak{Br}(\mathcal{T})$ instead of on $\mathfrak{Br}(\mathcal{T}) - \mathfrak{Br}(\tilde{\mathcal{F}})$. Therefore, an output $\tilde{\mathcal{F}}$ of LCC is *minimal* in the sense that both of $\mathfrak{Br}(\tilde{\mathcal{F}}) \leq \delta$ and $\mathcal{G} \subsetneq \tilde{\mathcal{F}} \Rightarrow \mathfrak{Br}(\mathcal{G}) > \delta$ hold.

Steepest Descent Consistency Constrained (SDCC) [4] is further stemmed from LCC and aims to improve the prediction performance of LCC by expanding the search range of LCC. Figure 2(c) depicts the algorithm of SDCC. LCC is based on INTERACT. The size of $\tilde{\mathcal{F}}$ decreases by one for each iteration: When $\tilde{\mathcal{F}}$ is the current best feature subset, SDCC asks the evaluation function to calculate the Bayesian risk scores of all of the subsets that are obtained by eliminating a single feature from $\tilde{\mathcal{F}}$. If the minimum of the Bayesian risks computed is no greater than δ, SDCC updates $\tilde{\mathcal{F}}$ with one of the subsets that yield the minimum. The outputs of SDCC are minimal in the same sense as stated above. Hence, if $\tilde{\mathcal{F}}$ is the final output, SDCC evaluates $(|\mathcal{F}| + |\tilde{\mathcal{F}}|)(|\mathcal{F}| - |\tilde{\mathcal{F}}| + 1)/2$ feature subsets.

Both in LCC and SDCC, the parameter δ is used to pursue a good balance of the fundamental tradeoff between the size and the Bayesian risk value of outputs. The greater δ is, the more likely the algorithms output feature sets smaller in size with greater Bayesian risks.

2.2   Comparison of SDCC with LCC Based on Experiments

Figure 3 shows experimental results to compare SDCC with LCC. As we expected, the feature sets that SDCC select are smaller in size and better in the collective Bayesian risk than those selected by LCC (Fig. 3(a) and (b)): LCC eliminates the first feature F that satisfies $\mathfrak{Br}(\tilde{\mathcal{F}} \setminus \{F\}) \leq \delta$ from $\tilde{\mathcal{F}}$, while SDCC tests all $F \in \tilde{\mathcal{F}}$ and eliminates the feature F that minimizes $\mathfrak{Br}(\tilde{\mathcal{F}} \setminus \{F\})$. Therefore, an increase of the Bayesian risk by eliminating a single feature for SDCC is smaller

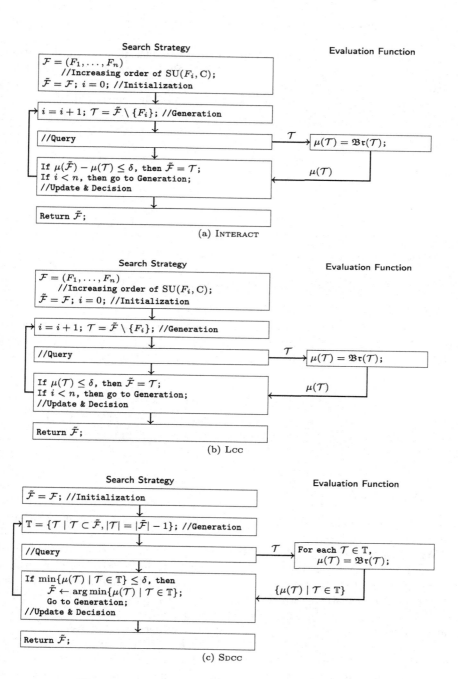

Fig. 2. The algorithms of INTERACT, LCC and SDCC

than for Lcc, and hence, Sdcc can eliminate more features and can approach δ closer.

By contrast, when we applied the Naïve Bayes classifier to those feature sets, the prediction accuracy (measured by AUC-ROC) obtained from Lcc were better than that from Sdcc (Fig. 3(c)). This finding may confuse us, because Sdcc searches answers in wider ranges than Lcc and hence should be better.

(a) Number of features   (b) Collective Bayesian risk   (c) Accuracy of Naïve Bayes

Fig. 3. Comparison between Sdcc and Lcc.

Also, the table below shows a comparison in run-time in seconds between Lcc and Sdcc with eight datasets from Table 1 using a PC with Intel Core i3 2.6 GHz. Sdcc turns out to be 10 to 400 times slower than Lcc.

	Arr	Opt	Wav	Mfa	Mfo	Mka	Mpi	Sem
Lcc	0.398	1.268	0.632	1.388	0.729	0.665	0.976	0.787
Sdcc	43.83	14.04	6.557	107.2	6.638	5.054	140.3	127.6

2.3   Problems of Sdcc

We decompose the aforementioned problems of Sdcc in accuracy and efficiency into more concrete problems.

With respect to the problem in accuracy, the difference between Sdcc and Lcc that may justify it is that, while Sdcc only considers the collective relevance of feature sets, Lcc evaluates the relevance of the individual member features in addition. To illustrate, we use an example depicted by Fig. 4. Figure 4 is the Hasse diagram of $\mathcal{F} = \{F_1, F_2, F_3, F_4\}$, and the gray nodes represent the feature subsets whose Bayesian risk is zero. Furthermore, we assume $\delta = 0$. Lcc investigates $\mathfrak{Br}(\{F_2, F_3, F_4\}), \mathfrak{Br}(\{F_1, F_3, F_4\}), \mathfrak{Br}(\{F_1, F_4\})$ and $\mathfrak{Br}(\{F_1\})$ and finally outputs $\{F_1, F_4\}$. On the other hand, the solid lines represent an example of the paths that Sdcc can track. In the first iteration, Sdcc finds $\mathfrak{Br}(\{F_1, F_2, F_3\}) = \mathfrak{Br}(\{F_1, F_2, F_4\}) = \mathfrak{Br}(\{F_1, F_3, F_4\}) = 0$ and updates $\tilde{\mathcal{F}}$ by one of them arbitrarily. If it uses $\{F_2, F_3, F_4\}$, it finally outputs $\{F_2, F_4\}$.

Compared between these two outputs, $\{F_1, F_4\}$ could be better because of $SU(F_1, C) + SU(F_4, C) = 0.5 > SU(F_2, C) + SU(F_4, C) = 0.4$. Therefore, the first problem of SDCC can be described as follows.

Problem 1. SDCC selects a minimal feature set with $\mathfrak{Br}(\mathcal{F}) \leq \delta$ arbitrarily.

A possible cause of low efficiency of SDCC is because:

Problem 2. SDCC performs unnecessary investigation of $\mathfrak{Br}(\mathcal{T}) \leq \delta$.

For example, SDCC verifies $\mathfrak{Br}(\{F_2, F_3\}) > 0$ in the second iteration, and this is totally unnecessary, because it has verified $\mathfrak{Br}(\{F_1, F_2, F_3\}) > 0$ in the first iteration: $\mathfrak{Br}(\{F_2, F_3\}) > 0$ is inferred by monotonicity.

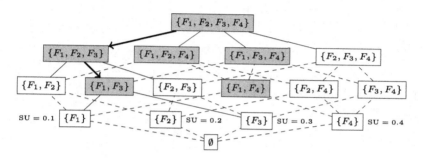

Fig. 4. An example of search paths by SDCC.

3   FAST SDCC and ACCURATE SDCC

FAST SDCC and ACCURATE SDCC are developed to solve Problems 1 and 2.

Figure 5 depicts the algorithm of FAST SDCC. In each iteration of `Repeat`, FAST SDCC finds F that minimizes $\mathfrak{Br}(\{\tilde{\mathcal{F}} \setminus \{F\})$ first and then minimizes $SU(F, C)$, and eliminate it from $\tilde{\mathcal{F}}$. The following are the differences from SDCC.

1. The features in $\mathcal{F}$ are sorted in the incremental order of $SU(F, C)$ (Line 1).
2. The variable ξ' holds the smallest $\mathfrak{Br}(\tilde{\mathcal{F}} \setminus \{F\})$ evaluated so far in the current iteration, and F' is the first feature with $\mathfrak{Br}(\tilde{\mathcal{F}} \setminus \{F'\}) = \xi'$ (Line 15).
3. $SU(F', C)$ is the smallest value of $SU(F, C)$ assuming $\mathfrak{Br}(\tilde{\mathcal{F}} \setminus \{F\}) = \xi'$.
4. The variable ξ holds $\mathfrak{Br}(\tilde{\mathcal{F}})$. If $\mathfrak{Br}(\tilde{\mathcal{F}} \setminus \{F\}) = \xi$ is observed, F' is set to F, and the current iteration of `Repeat` is terminated (Line 11 to 13).
5. For a feature $F \in \mathcal{F}$, $\delta(F)$ is $\mathfrak{Br}(\tilde{\mathcal{F}} \setminus \{F\})$ that has been computed the most recently for some $\tilde{\mathcal{F}}$ (Line 10).
6. Therefore, if $\delta(F) \geq \xi'$, $\mathfrak{Br}(\tilde{\mathcal{F}} \setminus \{F\}) \geq \xi'$ always holds by the monotonicity property, and FAST SDCC does not compute $\mathfrak{Br}(\tilde{\mathcal{F}} \setminus \{F\})$ (Line 9).

1 Sort $\mathcal{F}$ in the increasing	1 Sort $\mathcal{F}$ in the increasing
2 order of $SU(F, C)$	2 order of $SU(F, C)$
3 $\tilde{\mathcal{F}} = \mathcal{F}$; $\xi = \mathfrak{Br}(\mathcal{F})$;	3 $\tilde{\mathcal{F}} = \mathcal{F}$; $\xi = \mathfrak{Br}(\mathcal{F})$;
4 //Assume $\xi \leq \delta$	4 //Assume $\xi \leq \delta$
5 For each $F \in \mathcal{F}$, $\delta(F) = 0$;	5 For each $F \in \mathcal{F}$, $\delta(F) = 0$;
6 Repeat	6 Repeat
7 $\xi' = \delta$; $F' = \text{Nil}$;	7 $\xi' = \delta$; $\vartheta' = \infty$; $F' = \text{Nil}$;
8 For each $F \in \tilde{\mathcal{F}}$ from 1st	8 For each $F \in \tilde{\mathcal{F}}$ from 1st
9 If $\delta(F) \leq \xi'$	9 If $\delta(F) \leq \xi'$
10 $\delta(F) = \mathfrak{Br}(\tilde{\mathcal{F}} \setminus \{F\})$;	10 $\delta(F) = \mathfrak{Br}(\tilde{\mathcal{F}} \setminus \{F\})$;
11 //	11 $\vartheta = \vartheta_\alpha(\tilde{\mathcal{F}}, F)$;
12 If $\delta(F) = \xi$	12 If $\delta(F) = \xi$ and $\vartheta < \vartheta'$
13 $F' = F$;	13 $F' = F$;
14 Break from For;	14 Break from For;
15 Else If $\delta(F) < \xi'$	15 If $\delta(F) < \xi'$
16 $\xi' = \delta(F)$; $F' = F$;	16 $\xi' = \delta(F)$;
17 End For;	17 If $\vartheta \leq \vartheta'$
18 If $F' = \text{Nil}$	18 $\vartheta' = \vartheta$; $F' = F$;
19 Break from Repeat;	19 End For;
20 $\tilde{\mathcal{F}} = \tilde{\mathcal{F}} \setminus \{F'\}$; $\xi = \xi'$;	20 If $F' = \text{Nil}$
21 End Repeat;	21 Break from Repeat;
22 Return $\tilde{\mathcal{F}}$;	22 $\tilde{\mathcal{F}} = \tilde{\mathcal{F}} \setminus \{F'\}$; $\xi = \xi'$;
	23 End Repeat;
	24 Return $\tilde{\mathcal{F}}$;

Fig. 5. The algorithms of FAST SDCC (left) and ACCURATE SDCC (right)

Item 4 solves **Problem** 1 of SDCC, and Item 6 solves **Problem** 2. In particular, FAST SDCC behaves identically to LCC, if $\delta = 0$.

FAST SDCC jointly uses $\mathfrak{Br}(\tilde{\mathcal{F}} \setminus \{F\})$ and $SU(F, C)$. In this regard, ACCURATE SDCC (Fig. 5) aims to use these measure in more flexible way by leveraging

$$\vartheta_\alpha(\tilde{\mathcal{F}}, F) = \alpha \cdot SU(F, C) + (1 - \alpha) \cdot \frac{\mathfrak{Br}(\tilde{\mathcal{F}} \setminus \{F\}) - \mathfrak{Br}(\mathcal{F})}{\delta - \mathfrak{Br}(\mathcal{F})},$$

where α satisfies $0 \leq \alpha \leq 1$. If $\mathfrak{Br}(\tilde{\mathcal{F}} \setminus \{F\}) \leq \delta$, $0 \leq \vartheta_\alpha(\tilde{\mathcal{F}}, F) \leq 1$ holds.

This function may remind the reader of the well known feature selection algorithm of mRMR [5]. mRMR tries to find an optimal balance between the accumulative relevance to classes and the internal correlation of features through a similar evaluation function. In contrast, the function above finds a balance between the collective relevance (measured by the Bayesian risk) and the accumulative relevance (measured by the symmetric uncertainty)

In each iteration of **Repeat**, ACCURATE SDCC finds F that minimizes $\vartheta_\alpha(\tilde{\mathcal{F}}, F)$ under the condition of $\mathfrak{Br}(\tilde{\mathcal{F}} \setminus \{F\}) \leq \delta$. This can be proven as follows. For convenience, we let $\tilde{\mathcal{F}} = (F_1, F_2, \ldots, F_k)$.

1. As the features in $\mathcal{F}$ are sorted (Line 1), $SU(F_i) \geq SU(F_j)$ holds for $i > j$.

2. When ACCURATE SDCC starts to evaluate F_i, $\vartheta' = \min_{j=1,\ldots,i-1} \vartheta_\alpha(\tilde{\mathcal{F}}, F_j)$, $\xi' = \min_{j=1,\ldots,i-1} \mathfrak{Br}(\tilde{\mathcal{F}} \setminus \{F_j\})$ and $\mathfrak{Br}(\tilde{\mathcal{F}} \setminus \{F_k\}) = \xi'$ hold (Line 16 & 18).
3. $\delta(F_i) < \xi'$ is necessary for $\vartheta_\alpha(\tilde{\mathcal{F}}, F_i) < \vartheta'$ (Line 9): Otherwise, $\vartheta_\alpha(\tilde{\mathcal{F}}, F_i) \geq \vartheta_\alpha(\tilde{\mathcal{F}}, F_k) \geq \vartheta'$ follows from $\mathfrak{Br}(\tilde{\mathcal{F}} \setminus \{F_i\}) \geq \delta(F_i) \geq \mathfrak{Br}(\tilde{\mathcal{F}} \setminus \{F_k\})$ and $SU(F_i, C) \geq SU(F_k, C)$.
4. If $\mathfrak{Br}(\tilde{\mathcal{F}} \setminus \{F_i\}) = \xi$, $\vartheta_\alpha(\tilde{\mathcal{F}}, F_j) \geq \vartheta_\alpha(\tilde{\mathcal{F}}, F_i)$ holds for any $j > i$. Hence, F_i yields the minimum $\vartheta_\alpha(\tilde{\mathcal{F}}, F)$ (Line 15 and 16).

4   Experimental Evaluation

We investigate the performance of the FAST SDCC and ACCURATE SDCC through experiments using the datasets described in Table 1. We run FAST SDCC, ACCURATE SDCC, SDCC and LCC on these datasets with the same δ that varies in $\{0, 0.01, \ldots, 0.1\}$. For α of ACCURATE SDCC, we use 0.75, which has turned out to optimize the algorithm through experiments. Figure 6 shows the accuracy value of each classifier when α is modified. Note that when α is 1, ACCURATE SDCC is equivalent to a simple filter based on SU ranking and when α is 0, the output is the same that FAST SDCC. The values plotted in the charts of this section are the averages across the 16 datasets.

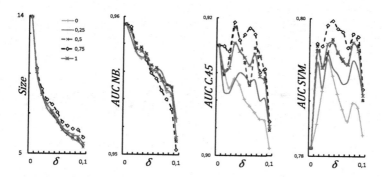

Fig. 6. Classification accuracy by AUC-ROC and size for different values of α.

4.1   Comparison in Classification Accuracy

To compare the feature selection algorithms in terms of classification accuracy, we use three classifiers, namely, *Naïve Bayes (NB)*, *C4.5* and *Support Vector Machine (SVM)*. The procedures of the experiments are as follows.

1. We run the 4 feature selection algorithms on the 16 datasets with the 11 values of δ and obtain $4 \cdot 16 \cdot 11 = 704$ datasets with the selected feature sets.

Table 1. Datasets used in the experiments. The columns headed by #Ex., #Ft. and #Cl. show the number of examples, features and class labels, respectively

Dataset	#Ex.	#Ft.	#Cl.	Dataset	#Ex.	#Ft.	#Cl.
DERMATOLOGY:DER	366	34	6	SPECTROMETER:SEP	531	100	48
ARRHYTHMIA:ARR	452	279	16	MFEAT-FACTOR:MFA	2000	216	10
KR-VS-KP:KvK	3196	36	2	MFEAT-FOURIER:MFO	2000	76	10
PENDIGITS:PEN	10992	16	10	MFEAT-KARHUNEN:MKA	2000	64	10
MUSHROOM:MUS	8124	22	2	MFEAT-PIXEL:MPI	2000	240	10
OPTIDIGITS:OPT	5620	64	10	MFEAT-ZERNIKE:MZE	2000	47	10
NURSERY:NUR	12960	8	5	SEGMENT:SEG	2310	19	7
WAVEFORM:WAV	5000	40	3	SEMEOIN:SEM	1593	256	10

2. For each dataset obtained, we perform the ten-fold cross validation with the 3 classifiers and compute the averages of the obtained AUC-ROC measurements.

Figure 7 shows the plots of these values. For every classifier, inferiority of SDCC to the other three seems evident. When using *NB*, as δ increases *Fast* and *Accurate Sdcc* algorithms do not drastically output different results in terms of accuracy as *Sdcc* and *Lcc* do it. This means that even when low quality sets are feasible outputs, *Fast* and *Accurate Sdcc* seems to better avoid be trapped by local optima. Recently, in [6] was proposed to use $\delta = 0.01$.

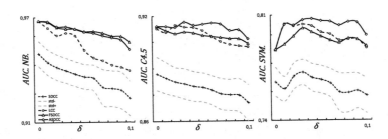

Fig. 7. Classification accuracy by AUC-ROC.

The accuracy reached by the three learning algorithms fixing $\delta = 0.01$ is maximum when *Accurate Sdcc* is used. Figure 8 shows the plots of the averaged ranks to apply the Bonferroni Dunn multiple comparison test. When a plot of a feature selection algorithm falls in the gray area of each chart, the algorithm is statistically significantly inferior to the top ranked algorithm with the significance level 10 %. Therefore, the observed inferiority of SDCC is verified. We compare the other three. With NB, FAST SDCC and ACCURATE SDCC perform the best. In particular, the difference from Lcc is statistically significant for many values of δ. With C4.5 and SVM, we observe that ACCURATE SDCC outperforms the

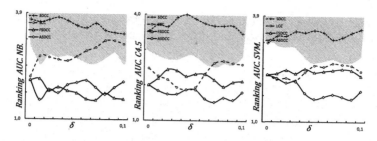

Fig. 8. Ranking of classification accuracy.

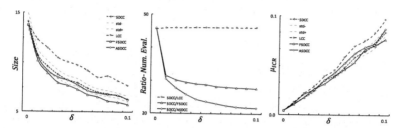

Fig. 9. Size, ratio of number of evaluation and Bayesian risk.

other two, but its superiority cannot be statistically verified by the Bonferroni Dunn test, which is known to be relatively conservative.

Overall, we can conclude that FAST SDCC and ACCURATE SDCC improve the accuracy performance of SDCC significantly, and their performance are at least comparable with and probably better than that of LCC. FAST SDCC and ACCURATE SDCC consistently select feature sets smaller in size than LCC (Fig. 9).

4.2 Comparison in Time-Efficiency

We measure the time-efficiency of the algorithms by the number of times in which the algorithms compute Bayesian risks since the time to compute Bayesian risks is dominating in the entire execution time of the algorithms. Chart in the center of Fig. 9 shows plots of the averaged ratios of SDCC to the other algorithms.

We see that FAST SDCC and ACCURATE SDCC compute as many Bayesian risks as LCC for $\delta = 0$, that is, they are as fast as LCC. This is because FAST SDCC and ACCURATE SDCC give up further search in each iteration of Repeat when they detect the first occurrence of $\mathfrak{Br}(\tilde{\mathcal{F}} \setminus \{F\}) = \mathfrak{Br}(\mathcal{F})$ (Lines 12 to 14 in Fig. 5), and hence, they behave exactly the same as LCC. For $\delta > 0$, the chart indicates that SDCC computes Bayesian risks 30 times more than FAST SDCC, while it does about 20 to 30 times more than ACCURATE SDCC.

Also, Table 2 shows the actual run-time of the algorithms for each dataset measured in seconds for $\delta = 0.01$. The averaged run-time ratios of SDCC and LCC, FAST SDCC and ACCURATE SDCC are 45.7, 34.6 and 33.4, respectively, and are very closed to the ratios in the numbers of computation of Bayesian risks.

Consequently, we can conclude that FAST SDCC and ACCURATE SDCC are 20 to 30 times faster than SDCC and a few times slower than LCC.

Table 2. Run-time (sec.) with $\delta = 0.01$ (Intel Core i3 2.6 GHz and 8 GB memory)

	ARR	OPT	WAV	MFA	MFO	MKA	MPI	SEM
FSDCC	0.504	1.239	0.971	1.586	0.927	0.694	1.399	1.420
ASDCC	0.532	1.268	0.930	1.448	0.929	0.691	1.468	1.452
LCC	0.398	1.268	0.632	1.388	0.729	0.665	0.976	0.787
SDCC	43.839	14.041	6.557	107.201	6.638	5.054	140.312	127.602

5   Conclusion

We have identified two important problems of SDCC and have proposed two new feature selection algorithms, namely, FAST SDCC and ACCURATE SDCC, that fix the problems and improve the performance of SDCC in both accuracy and efficiency. The degree of improvement is remarkable. Our experiments have shown that the improvement in accuracy is statistically significant, and FAST SDCC and ACCURATE SDCC are about 20 and 30 times faster than SDCC. Compared with LCC, FAST SDCC and ACCURATE SDCC are only a few times slower but exhibit comparable or better accuracy. Besides, the size of outputs by FAST SDCC and ACCURATE SDCC is fairly smaller than LCC and the difference between FAST SDCC and LCC is statistically significant.

Acknowledgment. This work was partially supported by the Grant-in-Aid for Scientific Research (JSPS KAKENHI Grant Number 26280090) from the Japan Society for the Promotion of Science.

References

1. Molina, L., Belanche, L., Nebot, A.: Feature selection algorithms: a survey and experimental evaluation. In: Proceedings of IEEE International Conference on Data Mining, pp. 306–313 (2002)
2. Zhao, Z., Liu, H.: Searching for interacting features. In: Proceedings of International Joint Conference on Artificial Intelligence, pp. 1156–1161 (2007)
3. Shin, K., Xu, X.M.: Consistency-based feature selection. In: Velásquez, J.D., Ríos, S.A., Howlett, R.J., Jain, L.C. (eds.) KES 2009. LNCS, vol. 5711, pp. 342–350. Springer, Heidelberg (2009)
4. Shin, K., Xu, X.M.: A consistency-constrained feature selection algorithm with the steepest descent method. In: Torra, V., Narukawa, Y., Inuiguchi, M. (eds.) MDAI 2009. LNCS, vol. 5861, pp. 338–350. Springer, Heidelberg (2009)

5. Peng, H., Long, F., Ding, C.: Feature selection based on mutual information: criteria of max-dependency, max-relevance and min-redundancy. IEEE Trans. Pattern Anal. Mach. Intell. **27**(8), 1226–1238 (2005)
6. Shin, K., Fernandes, D., Miyazaki, S.: Consistency measures for feature selection: a formal definition, relative sensitivity comparison, and a fast algorithm. In: 22nd International Joint Conference on Artificial Intelligence, pp. 1491–1497 (2011)

Conceptual Analysis of Big Data Using Ontologies and EER

Kulsawasd Jitkajornwanich[1(✉)] and Ramez Elmasri[2]

[1] Geo-Informatics and Space Technology Development Agency (Public Organization),
Ministry of Science and Technology of Thailand, 120 The Government Complex,
Chaeng Wattana Road, Lak Si, Bangkok 10210, Thailand
kulsawasdj@gistda.or.th
[2] Department of Computer Science and Engineering,
The University of Texas at Arlington, 701 S Nedderman Dr, Arlington, TX 76019, USA
elmasri@cse.uta.edu

Abstract. Large amounts of "big data" are generated every day, many in a "raw" format that is difficult to analyze and mine. This data contains potential hidden meaningful concepts, but much of the data is superfluous and not of interest to the domain experts. Thus, dealing with big raw data solely by applying a set of distributed computing technologies (e.g., MapReduce, BSP [Bulk Synchronous Parallel], and Spark) and/or distributed storage systems, namely NoSQL, is generally not sufficient. Extracting the full knowledge that is hidden in the raw data is necessary to efficiently enable analysis and mining. The data needs to be processed to remove the superfluous parts and generate the meaningful domain-specific concepts. In this paper, we propose a framework that incorporates conceptual modeling and EER principle to effectively extract conceptual knowledge from the raw data so that mining and analysis can be applied to the extracted conceptual data.

Keywords: Conceptual modeling · Big data · NoSQL · Distributed computing

1 Introduction

Enormous amounts of data are rapidly generated every day in almost every application domain. These raw data could be thought of as a huge data warehouse, which contains hidden and meaningful information. However, to analyze the available raw data directly from its original formats is not easy as the data is often in a format that is difficult to analyze and is usually 'big'.

Although there is no formal definition of big data, 3 V definition: volume, variety, and velocity, is often used to describe big data by its characteristics [1, 28]. In any given domain, big data contains potential hidden meaningful concepts as well as superfluous data that are not of interest to the domain experts. As a result, dealing with big data solely by applying a set of distributed computing technologies such as MapReduce [2], BSP (Bulk Synchronous Parallel) [3], and Spark [4]; and/or distributed storage systems namely NoSQL databases [7] may not be an efficient way to discover the knowledge

© Springer International Publishing Switzerland 2015
P. Pardalos et al. (Eds.): MOD 2015, LNCS 9432, pp. 306–317, 2015.
DOI: 10.1007/978-3-319-27926-8_27

hidden in the data. To enable analysis, the big data need to be pre-processed so that the superfluous parts are removed (also known as a "cleaning" of the raw data) and the meaningful domain-specific knowledge is extracted.

Ontology, a specification of conceptualization [14], has practically been used in knowledge modeling as it allows domain-specific knowledge to be formalized and reasoned about in a logical way. ER (Entity-Relationship) and EER (Enhanced-ER) models/diagrams are excellent tools to communicate concepts, and can also be easily converted to relational tables. Our goal is to enable big data in any given domain to be analyzed by utilizing conceptual modeling (through ontologies) and EER to represent the domain-specific knowledge in the data. The formalized concepts are developed based on consulting with domain experts in the area of knowledge covered by the raw data.

An overview of our framework is shown in Fig. 1. The advantages of our framework include the capture of domain-specific conceptual knowledge (which is typically much smaller in size, compared to the raw data), accommodating existing traditional analysis as well as facilitating new knowledge discovery, and better system performance by applying distributed technologies (e.g., map-reduce, HDFS [Hadoop Distributed File System], etc.) to clean and convert the raw data. Our framework also offers more robust and user-friendly analysis by storing the final conceptual knowledge in a relational database.

The organization of this paper is as follows. We describe our framework in Sect. 2. A case study that adopted the framework is discussed in Sect. 3. We use big raw rainfall data in our case study. Finally, conclusion and future work are discussed in Sect. 4. In the case study, we briefly describe formalization of rainstorm ontology concepts [10–12] and translate them into EER. The mapping algorithms are implemented and the comparison experiments are performed. We also give some examples of how analysis and mining can be done on the resulting conceptual storm data.

2   Framework Description

There are four main components in our framework as shown in Fig. 1, each of which is described in the following subsections.

2.1   Developing and Formalizing Domain-Specific Concepts into an Ontology with the Assistance of Domain Experts

The first process is to study a particular domain (where the big raw data comes from), come up with the domain-specific concepts, and formalize them into an ontology. This requires a literature review in the application domain as well as working with the domain experts to determine the important concepts that are needed. Investigation as to how their research is currently conducted using the traditional data processing methods is also required; some traditional methods (or more complex analysis) could be improved (or realized) by utilizing available big data analysis tools such as map-reduce/Hadoop [6].

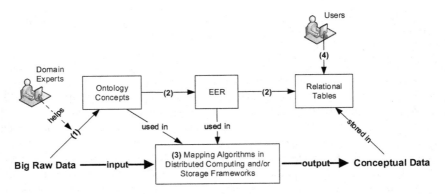

Fig. 1. Framework architecture

The developed ontology must satisfy the domain experts' requirements and capture not only the essential concepts that they are looking for but also other potential concepts–which may not have been previously identified, but could be of benefit to them. This can also help the domain users to better understand their own datasets. The hidden insight and conceptual relationships can consequently lead them to the knowledge that was not previously discovered. Thus, further complex analysis and mining can be applied.

2.2 Translating the Domain-Specific Ontology to EER and Mapping the EER to Relational Tables

In the context of big data, an RDBMS (Relational Database Management System) is usually not a preferred option and often labeled as incompatible with the needs of big data analysis and mining. Their key features, however, are well recognized, in term of user-friendly analysis capabilities. The concepts of NoSQL databases, on the other hand, spread rapidly and caught a lot of attention as tools for big data storage and analysis/mining in the past few years [8, 9, 23] (as of now, there are more than 200 different NoSQL databases available in the market [7]). The main advantages of NoSQL databases include high availability, fast key-value access, horizontal scalability, fault-tolerance, and dynamic/semi-structured datatype support.

However, the emerging of NoSQL does not primarily intend to replace the conventional relational database but instead complement it as one application may work for one system but not for the other depending upon the application scenario. Some features of RDBMS are not readily available on NoSQL such as strong consistency, full support on relational features (e.g., join, group by) across partitions/nodes, normalization, and fully-developed declarative query language [29, 30].

Our framework combines the benefits from both systems (RDBMS and NoSQL) together. We use a distributed storage system (HDFS) during the processing steps and load the final conceptual outputs into a relational database.

To store the final conceptual outputs in a relational database, we translate the formalized domain concepts from the previous process to an EER model, which will later be mapped to relational tables. The general ideas of ontology-to-EER translation are as follows:

- An object in ontology becomes an entity in EER, and a class becomes an entity type.
- A datatype property (a relation between an object and a data value [31]) in ontology becomes an attribute or derived attribute of an entity in EER.
- An object property (a relation between objects [31]) in ontology becomes an attribute (of an entity) that is generally a foreign key. However, in some cases depending on the application ontology, an object (or datatype) property can be mapped to an entire new entity to better suit the required types of analysis (e.g., storm centers as we will see in Sect. 3.2: Fig. 4).
- Other ontology concept specifications are translated through the use of EER features such as primary and foreign keys, cardinality and participation constraints, specialization and generalization, stored procedures, UDFs, triggers, etc.

The EER-to-relational tables mapping process is done by using the techniques described in [14].

2.3 Designing and Implementing Mapping Algorithms to Convert the Raw Data to the Conceptual Data

To design mapping algorithms, four main factors are taken into account: (1) structure and format of the big raw data, (2) choices of distributed computing/storage framework, (3) domain-specific ontology, and (4) EER model corresponding to the ontology.

Understanding the structure and format of the big raw data helps in optimizing the computation, I/O, and buffer usage in the raw data-to-conceptual data mapping algorithms. Three aspects of big raw data are considered: data representation (i.e., examining how the raw data is formatted and interpreted), data transmission (i.e., determining delivery method, transmission frequency, and downtime period of the raw data), and data integrity (i.e., ensuring the consistency of the raw data). Next, we make a decision as to which distributed technology should be used. The selected technology should take full advantage of the characteristics of the raw data as well as other available resources (e.g., hardware). The ontology is used to ensure the formalized domain concepts are correctly identified. Finally, the corresponding EER model is used to convert the final conceptual outputs into relational database-compatible format. In addition, since the final conceptual data is now stored in a relational database, the verification process can also be done through SQL.

2.4 Performing Analysis and Mining on the Conceptual Relational Data

After the algorithms are executed on the big raw datasets, we now have the extracted conceptual data stored in a relational database. The size of the conceptual relational outputs are usually significantly reduced when compared to the size of the big raw data as the superfluous parts are removed and the raw data is summarized/converted into meaningful domain-specific concepts. The analysis and mining tasks can then be easily conducted by a domain user on the conceptual knowledge base both directly via SQL [5] and indirectly by extracting the conceptual data from the relational database.

3   Case Study: Rainfall Precipitation Data

In this section, we show a case study by which the proposed framework has been adopted. Our big raw data is rainfall precipitation datasets, *MPE (Multisensors Precipitation Estimate)* [24], retrieved from NOAA: National Weather Service (NWS) [21, 22] in the hydrology domain. We describe how each process of the framework is applied to our big raw rainfall data in the following subsections.

3.1   Rainstorm Formalization

In the hydrology domain, rainfall precipitation data is one of the hydrological observation types that most hydrologists work with (they also work with other types of datasets, such as soil moisture, river/stream levels, and watersheds). Rainfall-related analysis usually involves three characteristics of the data: rainfall statistical properties, correlation among storm characteristics (such as DDF: Depth-Duration-Frequency [13]), and focusing on the extreme precipitation values. However, the majority of these tasks are based on a location-specific analysis [13, 15, 16]. This prevents the analysis tasks from extracting storm-specific (or called 'overall' [10–12]) spatio-temporal aspects of the storms, which include storm movement (trajectory) and speed. After consulting with the hydrology experts, we introduced a partial rainstorm ontology that can eliminate this limitation and also support traditional location-based analysis. In the resulting ontology, three formalizations of rainstorms are introduced [10]: *local storm*, *hourly storm*, and *overall storm*.

Our ontology formalization considers the raw data framework, which we briefly describe now. The rainfall precipitation data is recorded hourly in a text file format. The data is reported for a regular grid structure called HRAP: Hydrologic Rainfall Analysis Project [17, 18], where each grid location is approximately 4 km by 4 km (see Fig. 2). Each grid (site) location has a unique identifier, from which a lat/long coordinate can be derived. The format of the raw data contains four attributes: row number in the text file, site location, precipitation value, and observation time. Each line in the data file represents a precipitation value at a particular site during a particular hour.

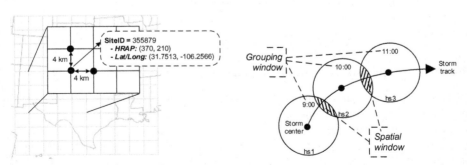

Fig. 2.   Example of site location in HRAP   **Fig. 3.**   An overall storm and its hourly storms

Informally, a *local storm* is a site-specific storm, which considers each site location independently when analyzing a storm. An example of local storms is the sequence of storms (separated by a certain number of hours with zero precipitation—inter-event time [15, 19, 20]) that occurred at site location 586987 last month. An *hourly storm* has an orthogonal concept to local storm. It considers a specific time point (hour) instead of a particular site location, and includes all contiguous locations that have precipitation during the same hour. The last storm formalization, *overall storm*, considers both location and time together when analyzing a storm. The result is the capture of storm as a whole, allowing storm movement, speed, and other overall storm characteristics that could not be found in most hydrology papers to be materialized [13, 15, 16, 19, 20]. An overall storm can be viewed as a sequence of hourly storms as they progress through time, as long as they have a spatial overlap from one hour to the next. The combination of hourly storms that form an overall storm satisfies two requirements: *grouping window* and *spatial window* [10]. Figure 3 shows an example of how an overall storm moves over time.

Each of the three types of rainfall concepts will have specific features. We will discuss these in the next section, when we develop the EER diagram for these concepts.

3.2 Ontology Translation and Mapping

To translate the domain ontology to an EER model for storing the final conceptual outputs in a relational database, we take into account the formalized domain-specific concepts and the characteristics of the raw rainfall data, and use the methodology described in [14]. Our rainstorm ontology is translated to an EER, which later be mapped to the database schema (as shown in Figs. 4 and 5) containing 8 relational tables.

`LocalStormHours` stores local storms information for each hour of every site; its characteristics are summarized into `LocalStorms`. Each local storm is uniquely identified by (`YearID`, `LSID`); `YearID` indicates a particular year where the local storms are identified. `HourlyStormSites` and `HourlyStorms` contain precipitation value for each site of an hourly storm, and its statistics, respectively. Each hourly storm can be uniquely identified by (`DatetimeUTC`, `HSID`) as the rainfall data files are recorded hourly and each file is independent from others.

`OverallStormHourlyStorms` stores information of all hourly storms combined into an overall storm. The primary key (denoted by underline) for this table is (`DateTimeUTC`, `HSID`) because an hourly storm can belong to only one overall storm. Technically, this table could be further mapped to `HourlyStorms` by having (`YearID`, `OSID`) as a foreign key (denoted by arrow) to `OverallStorms`. However, we mapped it into a separate table because the hourly storm statistics (`Hourly-Storms`) is calculated at the end. Having a separated `OverallStormHourly-Storms`, we do not need to wait until hourly storm identification is concluded in order to identify overall storms. Hourly storm and overall storm identifications can run concurrently. `OverallStormTracks` contains track information of the overall storms for each hour. Note that the `OverallStormTracks` table is derived from the relationships among the entity types: `Overall Storm`, `Hourly Storm`, `Centers`, and `Time Point` in Fig. 4.

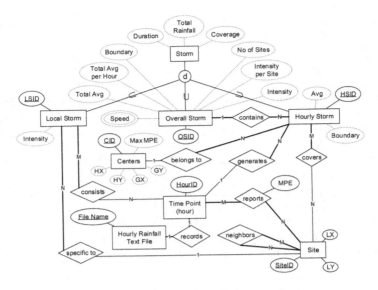

Fig. 4. EER diagram for rainstorm ontology

3.3   Implementation of Storm Identification System

In this process, we developed mapping algorithms designed specifically to take full advantage of the structure and format of the big raw rainfall data in extracting its domain-specific ontology. The map-reduce (MR) paradigm is selected as our distributed computing framework as it is one of the well-known and efficient tools in analyzing big data across multiple machines. Our implemented mapping algorithms are called *MR-based Storm Identification System* [11, 12]. Three main components of the system consist of MR-based- local storm identification (MR-LSI), hourly storm identification (MR-HSI), and overall storm identification (MR-OSI). With map-reduce, we can efficiently utilize our cluster of 19 servers as we can see in our comparison experiment between previous (non-MR) approach and MR-based approach (see Table 1).

To compare the system performance of the MR-based approach [11, 12] with the previous (non-MR) approach, we use a rainfall dataset (MPE) from October 2010 to December 2011 covering 37,413 site locations in Texas, retrieved from NOAA-NWS [10]. In the non-MR approach, the dataset is resided in a relational database and the identification process is done on a single server. The server runs on Microsoft Windows Server 2008 Enterprise OS with 2.83 GHz Intel Xeon quad-core processors, 20 GB of RAM, 500 GB of local disk, and 10 TB of external disk. In the MR-based approach, we use the same dataset but is in a textual format (which covers much more site locations [i.e., Texas and some surrounding areas]). The experiment is done on a Hadoop cluster of 1 master node and 18 worker nodes. All nodes have the same hardware specification (except local disks: 1.5 TB in worker node and 3 TB in master node): 3.2 GHz Intel Xeon quad-core processors and 4 GB of RAM. The cluster is operated by Rocks Cluster 6.3 OS and has Hadoop 1.0.3 installed in every node.

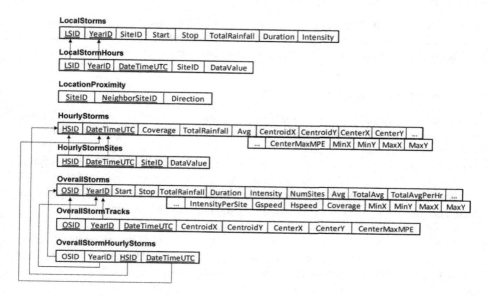

Fig. 5. Database schema corresponding to the rainstorm EER

The computational time comparison between the non-MR implementations and the MR-based implementations is shown in Table 1. The experiments of the two approaches

Table 1. Comparison of processing time between non-MR and MR-based approaches

| Regions / Number of Raw Data Records | Number of Sites | Processing Time (in hrs.) | | | | | |
| | | Previous Non-MR Approach | | | MR-based Approach | | |
		LSI	HSI	OSI	LSI	HSI	OSI
1. East Texas (48,953,130)	4,643	8.67	1.44	1.24			
2. Edwards Plateau (73,415,532)	6,962	8.72	1.23	2.25			
3. High Plains (31,711,927)	3,008	4.5	0.32	0.57			
4. Low Rolling Plains (24,965,521)	2,368	3.35	0.28	0.27			
5. North Central (59,082,957)	5,604	8.66	1.17	1.64			
6. South Central (31,102,334)	2,949	4.28	0.67	0.42			
7. South Texas (31,949,386)	2,933	3.97	0.48	0.60			
8. Lower Valley (5,324,898)	601	0.55	0.07	0.08			
9. Trans-Pecos (65,136,216)	6,177	6.86	0.55	1.16			
10. Upper Coast (22,863,789)	2,168	3.88	0.57	0.39			
TOTAL	37,413	53.44	6.78	8.62	less than 3 hrs. for all sites (incl. 37,413 sites in Texas)	less than an hour for all sites	less than 3 hrs. for all sites

give the same results but the MR-based approach is executed significantly faster. The MR-based approach allows programs to be executed distributedly on multiple machines and hence the efficiency of the storm analysis is increased.

3.4 Conceptual Analysis of Rainfall Data

In this section, we show some examples of how rainfall data can be analyzed by using our extracted storm data. From the experiment mentioned in Sect. 3.3, we extend it to the entire rainfall dataset for 16 years from 1997 to 2012. The conceptual storm data is extracted, summarized, and stored in a relational database. The size of the conceptual storm data is less than 1 % of the size of the raw rainfall data as shown in Table 2.

We divide the analysis and mining tasks into two groups: (1) traditional hydrology analysis and (2) more flexible/robust analysis and mining [26]. We only discuss the first of these in this paper due to space limitations.

Most traditional rainfall analysis is based on location, meaning each site or region (set of sites) is considered separately when analyzing a storm. The goal is to investigate characteristics of storms at a particular location. These analyzed characteristics will then be used in creating an efficient/cost-effective hydraulic control structure (e.g., storm drain [to route localized runoff] and parking lot design for effective draining) and designing river flow or flooding prediction models [25]. As mentioned, the traditional rainfall analysis can be divided into three categories [13, 15, 16, 25]: (1) storm statistical properties, (2) relationships between/among characteristics of storms, and (3) focusing on extreme precipitation values of storms. Some examples of the first item are as follows (for more examples in other analyses, please refer to [26]).

Table 2. Number of (conceptual) storm records in each component and year

Year	Num Raw MPE Records	MR-LSI Num Storms	MR-HSI Num Storms	MR-OSI Num Storms	Num Storm Records	Reduction in Raw Data Size (%)
1997	731,786,250	3,944,877	298,561	150,886	4,394,324	0.60
1998	1,451,804,250	6,372,104	455,575	235,409	7,063,088	0.49
1999	1,450,644,000	5,842,579	434,440	218,516	6,495,535	0.45
2000	1,453,627,500	6,138,978	439,557	225,029	6,803,564	0.47
2001	1,451,804,250	6,663,672	496,213	248,550	7,408,435	0.51
2002	1,451,804,250	6,827,462	448,670	196,531	7,472,663	0.51
2003	1,451,804,250	7,606,046	441,303	196,330	8,243,679	0.57
2004	1,455,782,250	12,526,769	545,125	237,457	13,309,351	0.91
2005	1,451,804,250	10,169,983	479,560	210,777	10,860,320	0.75
2006	1,450,478,250	10,354,175	519,978	227,517	11,101,670	0.77
2007	1,448,489,250	12,819,729	643,383	282,021	13,745,133	0.95
2008	1,455,782,250	10,371,608	544,036	248,001	11,163,645	0.77
2009	1,451,638,500	10,958,887	547,164	248,294	11,754,345	0.81
2010	1,451,141,250	10,108,909	546,926	247,449	10,903,284	0.75
2011	1,451,804,250	7,143,676	382,009	183,112	7,708,797	0.53
2012	1,455,782,250	9,024,720	481,920	225,075	9,731,715	0.67
TOTAL	22,515,977,250	136,874,174	7,704,420	3,580,954	148,159,548	0.66
AVERAGE	1,407,248,578	8,554,636	481,526	223,810	9,259,972	0.66

In storm statistical properties analysis, each characteristic of storms is analyzed separately for its statistical properties. The storm characteristics include inter-event time, total rainfall, and duration. There are six main statistics studied: mean (average) inter-event time between storms, mean total rainfall at a particular location, number of storms during the study period, total duration of all local storms, distribution of total rainfall values over the various storms, and distribution of storm durations [15]. Each statistical property is analyzed for a particular inter-event time. Most statistics can directly be calculated using pre-computed attributes (such as query SQL1). For statistics that were not pre-computed, they can also be easily calculated by using SQL (see SQL2). In our analysis, we use $h = 6$ h as the inter-event time. To determine the statistical properties for other inter-event times ($h = 8$, 12, 16, …), we just need to change the *inter-event-count* parameter [26] in the local storm identification program and re-run it.

SQL1. Determine mean total rainfall, number of storms, total duration for a given location

1:	SELECT	(AVG(TotalRainfall)|COUNT(*)|SUM(Duration))
2:	FROM	LocalStorms
3:	[WHERE	(SiteID = < site > |SiteID IN < region >)]

SQL2. Determine mean storm inter-event time for a given location (a site or region)

1:	SELECT	AVG(L2.Start–L1.Stop)
2:	FROM	LocalStorms L1 JOIN LocalStorms L2
3:		ON L1.YearID = L2.YearID AND L1.LSID = L2.LSID-1
4:	[WHERE	(SiteID = < site > |SiteID IN < region >)]

---

4 Conclusion and Future Work

In this paper, we propose a generalized analysis framework for big data in a given domain by utilizing conceptual modeling and EER. We show how the framework can be applied through a case study by using big raw rainfall datasets in the hydrology domain. In the rainfall case study, we overviewed the formalization of the partial rainstorm ontology and translated it into an EER. The MR-based storm identification system is implemented based on the developed rainstorm ontology. Finally, we show some examples of how traditional hydrology analysis can be done by utilizing SQL capabilities over the conceptual storm data. In addition to traditional hydrology analysis, we are working on more complex mining tasks [27], such as pattern matching of storms based on storm shape and trajectory, directional analysis of storm progression using Markov models, and other approaches to identify and classify storms based on their characteristics. These results will be communicated in future work.

Although our ontology-guided framework can accommodate a domain-specific and user-friendly analysis of big data by converting raw data to conceptual data, the extracted conceptual data may be too large to fit in a relational database, even if it is distributed or parallel. Thus, there are options to either perform an analysis in a finer sub-domain or convert the EER/relational tables concepts to a NoSQL system; in the latter option, some RDBMS features might be sacrificed.

References

1. Embley, D.W., Liddle, S.W.: Big data—conceptual modeling to the rescue. In: 32nd International Conference on Conceptual Modeling (2013)
2. Dean, J., Ghemawat, S.: MapReduce: simplified data processing on large clusters. In: 6th Symposium on Operating Systems Design and Implementation (2004)
3. Valiant, L.G.: A bridging model for multi-core computing. In: 16th Annual European Symposium (2008)
4. Apache. Apache Spark™. http://spark.apache.org
5. Zou, B., Ma, X., Kemme, B., Newton, G., Precup, D.: Data mining using relational database management systems. In: 10th Pacific-Asia Conference (2006)
6. Lam, C.: Hadoop in Action. Dreamtech Press, New Delhi (2011)
7. Edlich, S.: List of NOSQL Databases. http://nosql-database.org
8. Amazon. Amazon DynamoDB. http://aws.amazon.com/dynamodb
9. MongoDB. http://www.mongodb.org
10. Jitkajornwanich, K., Elmasri, R., Li, C., McEnery, J.: Extracting storm-centric characteristics from raw rainfall data for storm analysis and mining. In: 1st ACM SIGSPATIAL International Workshop on Analytics for Big Geospatial Data (2012)
11. Jitkajornwanich, K., Gupta, U., Elmasri, R., Fegaras, L., McEnery, J.: Using mapreduce to speed up storm identification from big raw rainfall data. In: 4th International Conference on Cloud Computing, GRIDs, and Virtualization (2013)
12. Jitkajornwanich, K., Gupta, U., Shanmuganathan, S.K., Elmasri, R., Fegaras, L., McEnery, J.: Complete storm identification algorithms from big raw rainfall data. In: 2013 IEEE International Conference on Big Data (2013)
13. Overeem, A., Buishand, A., Holleman, I.: Rainfall depth-duration-frequency curves and their uncertainties. J. Hydrol. **348**, 124–134 (2008)
14. Elmasri, R., Navathe, S.: Fundamentals of Database Systems, 6th edn. Pearson Education, New Delhi (2010)
15. Asquith, W.H., Roussel, M.C., Cleveland, T.G., Fang, X., Thompson, D.B.: Statistical characteristics of storm interevent time, depth, and duration for eastern New Mexico, Oklahoma, and Texas. Professional Paper 1725, US Geological Survey (2006)
16. Lanning-Rush, J., Asquith, W.H., Slade, Jr., R.M.: Extreme precipitation depth for Texas, excluding the trans-pecos region. Water-Resources Investigations Report 98–4099, US Geological Survey (1998)
17. NOAA's national weather service. The XMRG File Format and Sample Codes to Read XMRG Files. http://www.nws.noaa.gov/oh/hrl/dmip/2/xmrgformat.html
18. Consortium of universities for the advancement of hydrologic science, Inc. (CUAHSI). ODM Databases. http://his.cuahsi.org/odmdatabases.html
19. Asquith, W.H.: Depth-duration frequency of precipitation for Texas. Water-Resources Investigations Report 98–4044, US Geological Survey (1998)
20. Asquith, W.H.: Summary of dimensionless Texas hyetographs and distribution of storm depth developed for texas department of transportation research project 0–4194. Report 0–4194-4, US Geological Survey (2005)

21. National Oceanic and Atmospheric Administration (NOAA). National Weather Service River Forecast Center: West Gulf RFC (NWS-WGRFC). http://www.srh.noaa.gov/wgrfc

22. Unidata. What is the LDM? https://www.unidata.ucar.edu/software/ldm/ldm-6.6.5/tutor-ial/whatis.html

23. Chang, F., Dean, J., Ghemawat, S., Hsieh, W.C., Wallach, D.A., Burrows, M., Chandra, T., Fikes, A., Gruber, R.E.: Bigtable: a distributed storage system for structured data. In: 7th USENIX Symposium on Operating Systems Design and Implementation (2006)

24. NOAA. MPE: Multisensor Precipitation Estimate. http://www.erh.noaa.gov/marfc/Maps/xmrg/index_java.html

25. Mishra, S.K., Singh, V.P.: Soil Conservation Service Curve Number (SCS-CN) Methodology. Kluwer Academic Publishers, Boston (2003)

26. Jitkajornwanich, K.: Analysis and modeling techniques for geo-spatial and spatio-temporal datasets. Doctoral Dissertation, The University of Texas at Arlington (2014)

27. Cheng, T., Haworth, J., Anbaroglu, B., Tanaksaranond, G., Wang, J.: Spatio-Temporal Data Mining. Handbook of Regional Science. Springer, Heidelberg (2013)

28. IBM Big Data and Analytics Hub. Understanding Big Data: e-book. http://www.ibmbigdatahub.com/whitepaper/understanding-big-data-e-book

29. Jin, R. NoSQL and Big Data Processing: Hbase, Hive and Pig, etc. http://www.cs.kent.edu/~jin/Cloud12Spring/HbaseHivePig.pptx

30. Widom, J. NoSQL Systems: Overview. http://openclassroom.stanford.edu/Main-Folder/courses/cs145/old-site/docs/slides/NoSQLOverview/annotated.pptx

31. World Wide Web Consortium (W3C). OWL Web Ontology Language Guide. http://www.w3.org/TR/owl-guide/

A Parallel Consensus Clustering Algorithm

Olgierd Unold$^{(\boxtimes)}$ and Tadeusz Tagowski

Department of Computer Engineering, Faculty of Electronics,
Wroclaw University of Technology, Wyb. Wyspianskiego 25,
50-370 Wroclaw, Poland
olgierd.unold@pwr.edu.pl

Abstract. Consensus clustering is a stability-based algorithm with a prediction power far better than other internal measures. Unfortunately, this method is reported to be slow in terms of time and hard to scalability. We presented here consensus clustering algorithm optimized for multi-core processors. We showed that it is possible to obtain scalable performance of the compute-intensive algorithm for high-dimensional data such as gene expression microarrays.

Keywords: Clustering · Consensus clustering · Multi-core · Microarray data analysis

1 Introduction

Following the survey by Handl et al. [11], clustering can be viewed as a process of making a choice of: (a) a distance function, (b) a clustering algorithm, and (c) a validation method. However, according to the same article of Handl et al., the subject literature pays more attention to clustering algorithms, rather than to validation methods. Meanwhile, however, the identification of an adequate validation measure seems to be a central part of clustering, especially clustering biological data.

Microarray data analysis involves, among others, clustering of high-dimensional gene expression microarray data [2]. A wide range of clustering methods for microarray data analysis have evolved, ranging from partitional and hierarchical clustering, biclustering, flat and partition-based clustering, fuzzy clustering, model-based clustering, optimization-based clustering, network-based clustering, ensemble clustering, to hybrid approaches [19]. As noted in [11], clustering post-genomic data has to struggle with high-dimensional data, often with noise and/or missing values. Moreover, clustering prediction is expected to discover the inherent biological structure in a data [12]. In the light of above-mentioned facts, the use of internal, data-centric validation measures appears to be the most fundamental issue in clustering biological data, including microarray data.

. The research is financed by Wroclaw University of Technology statutory grant.

P. Pardalos et al. (Eds.): MOD 2015, LNCS 9432, pp. 318–324, 2015.
DOI: 10.1007/978-3-319-27926-8_28

In the literature, a number of internal clustering validation measures (ICVMs for short) have been proposed (e.g. [11, 15]). The stability-based methods [3–7, 9, 10, 13, 14, 17] are those approaches, among the different ICVMs, which are less biased than standard internal validation methods when comparing clustering with different similarity measures. Moreover, Giancarlo et al. [8] showed, that stability-based methods outperform other internal measures on microarray data in terms of prediction. The main drawback is that the stability-based ICVMs are the slowest in terms of time. Giancarlo et al. reported also a lack of scalability for the most precise internal validation measures. Consensus clustering (CC for short), by Monti et al. [17], turned out to be a stability-based method with the best precision, although the method is placed among the slowest.

Based on the above considerations, this paper focuses on a multi-core consensus clustering algorithm (MCCC for short), which parallelizes all calculations. The MCCC algorithm has been written as a R statistical programming language package [21], including the code for parallel execution on several CPUs.

2 Consensus Clustering

Original Consensus clustering method proposed by Monti et al. in [17] performs multiple runs of a single clustering algorithm in order to produce a set of consensus matrices. The multiple runs are performed on re-sampled parts of the given data set. Consensus matrices are then used to assess stability of resulting clusters for each proposed number of clusters. By analysing contents of consensus matrices, and changes in empirical cumulative distributions of those matrices it is possible to find the best suited number of clusters for given data.

Algorithm 1. Consensus-Clustering $(D, Resample, H, P, a, k_{min}, k_{max})$
1: **input:** D is the input dataset
2: **input:** $Resample$ is the re-sampling scheme used for extracting a subset of the dataset
3: **input:** H is the number of $Resample$ and an algorithm a runs performed on D
4: **input:** P is the percentage of rows extracted each time in the sub-sampling procedure
5: **input:** a is the clustering algorithm used
6: **input:** k_{min} and k_{max} set a range of expected number of clusters in the dataset
7: **output:** M_s^k is the consensus matrices for each $k_{min} \leq k \leq k_{max}$
8: **for** $k_{min} \leq k \leq k_{max}$ **do**
9:    initialize to empty connectivity matrices
10:   **for** $1 \leq h \leq H$ **do**
11:      perform $Resample$ on D and assign to $D^{(h)}$
12:      group elements in $D^{(h)}$ in k clusters using algorithm a
13:      build a connectivity matrix based on clustering algorithm's a results for k
14:   **end for**
15:   using connectivity matrices build a consensus matrix M_s^k for k
16: **end for**
17: **return** M_s^k

To produce consensus matrices the procedure needs a dataset, a re-sampling method for perturbation of the data set, a clustering algorithm, number of runs of the algorithm, percentage of vectors taken from the dataset in each resampling procedure, and a range of expected number of clusters. Having those parameters, the procedure performs for each expected number of clusters multiple runs of re-sampling and clustering algorithms on the data, so as all clustering algorithms are performed on a perturbed part of the dataset. For each expected number of clusters two matrices keep the results of clustering algorithms. First matrix, called an identity matrix, identifies how many times two vectors where placed in the same clusters in all the runs of clustering algorithm for given expected number of clusters. Second matrix, called a connectivity matrix, says how many times two points were in the re-sampled dataset in all the runs. The quotient of those matrices is the aforementioned consensus matrix. The procedure can be described by the pseudo-code Algorithm 1.

2.1 Multi-core Implementation of Consensus Clustering

Procedure of *consensus clustering* described in [17] is the natural candidate for parallelization. It requires many repeated and independent runs of one clustering algorithm for each proposed number of clusters. Results of those multiple runs are then processed in order to build consensus matrices for each proposed number of clusters.

Algorithm 2. MultiCore-Consensus-Consensus $(D, H, P, a, k_{min}, k_{max}, c)$

1: **input:** D is the input dataset
2: **input:** H is the number of sub-sampling steps performed on D
3: **input:** P is the percentage of rows of the dataset randomly extracted each time in
      the sub-sampling procedure
4: **input:** a is the clustering algorithm to perform on each sub-sampled dataset
5: **input:** k_{min} and k_{max} set a range of probable number of clusters in the dataset
6: **input:** c is the number of cores to use for parallelization
7: **output:** M_s^k is the consensus matrices for each $k_{min} \leq k \leq k_{max}$
8: **for** $k_{min} \leq k \leq k_{max}$ dividing iterations among c cores **do**
9:      initialize to empty connectivity matrices
10:     **for** $1 \leq h \leq H$ **do**
11:         using P perform *subsampling* on D and assign to $D^{(h)}$
12:         group elements in $D^{(h)}$ in k clusters using algorithm a
13:         build a connectivity matrix based on clustering algorithm's a results for k
14:     **end for**
15:     using connectivity matrices build a consensus matrix M_s^k for k
16: **end for**
17: **return** M_s^k

High computational complexity of clustering algorithms and iterational character of consensus methods exhibit coarse-grained parallelism and therefore are easy to parallelize. Our implementation aims at speeding up consensus methods by parallel implementation that uses widely available multi-core processors.

We present a multi-core *consensus consensus* algorithm (MCCC) that is a parallel version of the method proposed in [17]. The procedure of MCCC algorithm is described by the pseudo-code Algorithm 2.

Multicore Consensus Clustering was implemented using R language and was based on a serial implementation proposed in [22]. R packages `foreach` and `doMC` that enable parallel loop iterations using child processes were used. Note that the outermost loop in Consensus Clustering is a very good candidate for parallelization. This loop involves many reapeated runs of clustering algorithm, as well as creation of consensus matrices which is computationally intensive. Those tasks are easy to parallelize because they do not need to communicate and are indepentent. During a start of the loop a number of child processes is createad. Each process is assigned with a number of iterations and then parallel processing can take place, because processes are divided among multiple cores by an operating system's scheduler (in our case Linux). All of those processes can share memory addresses that contain a dataset, therfore copying of large memory regions is not needed [23]. When all child processes finish their iterations, the results are collected and sent back to the parent.

The parallelization is more effective when difference between k_{min} and k_{max} is large, because each process is assigned with more work. When each process has more work to do, the time needed to spawn processes and send back results is becoming smaller as a part of a whole runtime. It is also true when number of subsampling and algorithm runs (H) is large, as each iteration takes more time to finish. Inner clustering algorithm runtime and dataset dimensions are also important because of the same reason.

3   Results and Discussion

To illustrate the utility of our MCCC algorithm we performed simulations on microarray data. All simulations were performed on two processors: Intel Xeon X5650 2.67 GHz with 6 cores and 24 GB RAM. In our simulations, we have chosen K-means clustering algorithm, which is one of the most popular of partitional cluster algorithms [16]. The details of these algorithm are not reported here. We have performed experiments with $k_{min} = 2$, $k_{max} = 30$, $H = 250$, $P = 0.8$, and number of cores $c = 1, 2, 4, 8, 12$. The choice of the values of P and H was justified by the results reported in [9].

We used 5 published datasets of different sizes, each noted as Leukemia, Lymphoma, NCI60, Novartis, and St. Judge. It is worthy of mention that these datasets has become a benchmark standard in the microarray classification community [9]. Each column of a dataset corresponds to a gene, and each row to an element to be clustered. Details of the datasets are listed in Table 1. Note that Lymphoma and NCI60 datasets were preprocessed as proposed in [5].

Results of the runtime experiments over 5 datasets are given in Fig. 1. Here, each point is the arithmetic mean (log scale) of the timing results of the 10 consecutive runs. The speedup of the multi-core algorithm over single one is given in Table 2. Our multi-core CC algorithm performs up to ca. 9 times (using 12 cores) faster than the one-core CC algorithm. Note that the best results are gained

Table 1. Key features of the datasets used in the experiments.

Dataset	Experiments	Genes	Classes	Reference
Leukemia	38	100	3, acute leukemia	[11]
Lymphoma	80	100	3, lymphoma tumor	[1]
NCI60	57	200	8, cancer	[18]
Novartis	103	1000	13, tissue	[20]
St. Jude	248	985	6, acute leukemia	[25]

Table 2. Speedup of the multi-core consensus clustering over the one-core consensus clustering. Datasets are ordered by increasing size.

Dataset	Size	1 core	2 cores	4 cores	8 cores	12 cores
Leukemia	38×100	1.00	1.89	3.45	6.12	7.94
Lymphoma	80×100	1.00	2.13	3.89	6.89	8.98
NCI60	57×200	1.00	2.11	3.86	6.91	8.97
Novartis	103×1000	1.00	2.03	3.76	6.68	8.81
St. Jude	248×985	1.00	1.99	3.69	6.53	8.49

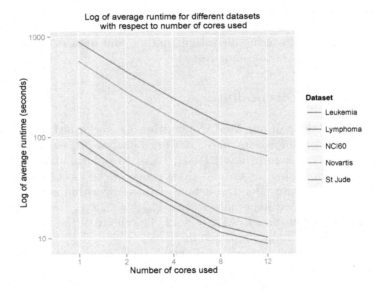

Fig. 1. Runtime performance of multi-core consensus clustering with k-means algorithm on the microarray datasets. Figure shows the dependency of the runtime (log scale) on the number of cores used. Each point averages the results from 10 repeated clusterings.

for medium-size datasets, i.e. Lymphoma and NCI60, 2.13x, 3.89x, 6.89x, 8.98x speedup, and 2.11x, 3.86x, 6.91x, 8.97x speedup, respectively. The acceleration of big data (St. Jude 248×985) is faster than for small data (Leukemia 38×100) - 1.99x, 3.69x, 6.53x, and 8.49x speedup for St. Jude, and 1.89x, 3.45x, 6.12x, 7.94x speedup for Leukemia (although not statistically significant, Wilcoxon signed rank, $p = 0.6857$).

4   Conclusion

We presented here stability-based clustering software optimized for multi-core processors. We showed that it is possible to obtain scalable performance of the compute-intensive algorithm for high-dimensional data such as gene expression microarrays.

Note that the Table 2 shows that the acceleration of computation is not directly proportional to the number of cores. More cores means less speed up. This is in accordance with the well known Amdahl's law which says that the speedup of a multi-core algorithm is limited by the time needed for the sequential fraction of it. Each time you increase the number of processors the speedup ratio will diminish.

According to [9], the modified, fast version (FC) of consensus clustering guarantees a speed-up of at least one order of magnitude with respect to the standard algorithm. It would be of interest to compare multi-core FC with single one and with multi-core CC. No less interesting would be to parallelize both fast and standard consensus algorithms using GPUs. Some work has already been done in this direction [24].

Acknowledgement and Author's Contributions

Calculations have been carried out using resources provided by Wroclaw Centre for Networking and Supercomputing (http://wcss.pl).

OU and TT designed the study and wrote the manuscript. TT implemented the algorithm and performed the experiments. All authors read and approved the final manuscript.

Availability and Requirements

Project name: mc-consensus, Project home page: https://github.com/vogatt/mc-consensus.

Operating system: Linux, Programming language: R.

License: GNU GPL, any restrictions to use by non-academics: none.

References

1. Alizadeh, A., et al.: Distinct types of diffuse large B-cell lymphoma identified by gene expression profiling. Nature **403**, 503–511 (2000)
2. Allison, D.B., et al.: Microarray data analysis: from disarray to consolidation and consensus. Nat. Rev. Genet. **7**(1), 55–65 (2006)
3. Ben-Hur, A., Elisseeff, A., Guyon, I.: A stability based method for discovering structure in clustered data. In: Pacific Symposium on Biocomputing, vol. 7 (2001)

4. Bertrand, P., Bel Mufti, G.: Loevinger's measures of rule quality for assessing cluster stability. Comput. Stat. Data Anal. **50**(4), 992–1015 (2006)

5. Dudoit, S., Fridlyand, J.: A prediction-based resampling method for estimating the number of clusters in a dataset. Genome Biol. **3**(7), research0036 (2002)

6. Garge, N., et al.: Reproducible clusters from microarray research: whither? BMC Bioinform. **6**(Suppl 2), S10 (2005)

7. Giancarlo, R., Utro, F.: Algorithmic paradigms for stability-based cluster validity and model selection statistical methods, with applications to microarray data analysis. Theoret. Comput. Sci. **428**, 58–79 (2012)

8. Giancarlo, R., Scaturro, D., Utro, F.: Computational cluster validation for microarray data analysis: experimental assessment of clest, consensus clustering, figure of merit, gap statistics and model explorer. BMC Bioinform. **9**(1), 462 (2008)

9. Giancarlo, R., Utro, F.: Speeding up the Consensus Clustering methodology for microarray data analysis. Algorithms Mol. Biol. **6**(1), 1–13 (2011)

10. Giurcaneanu, C.D., Tabus, I.: Cluster structure inference based on clustering stability with applications to microarray data analysis. EURASIP J. Appl. Sig. Process. **2004**, 64–80 (2004)

11. Handl, J., Knowles, J., Kell, D.B.: Computational cluster validation in post-genomic data analysis. Bioinformatics **21**(15), 3201–3212 (2005)

12. Kustra, R., Zagdanski, A.: Data-fusion in clustering microarray data: balancing discovery and interpretability. IEEE/ACM Trans. Comput. Biol. Bioinf. **7**(1), 50–63 (2010)

13. Lange, T., et al.: Stability-based validation of clustering solutions. Neural Comput. **16**(6), 1299–1323 (2004)

14. Levine, E., Domany, E.: Resampling method for unsupervised estimation of cluster validity. Neural Comput. **13**(11), 2573–2593 (2001)

15. Liu, Y., et al.: Understanding of internal clustering validation measures. In: 2010 IEEE 10th International Conference on Data Mining (ICDM). IEEE (2010)

16. MacQueen, J.: Some methods for classification and analysis of multivariate observations. In: Proceedings of the Fifth Berkeley Symposium on Mathematical Statistics and Probability, vol. 1, pp. 281–297 (1967)

17. Monti, S., et al.: Consensus clustering: a resampling-based method for class discovery and visualization of gene expression microarray data. Mach. Learn. **52**(1–2), 91–118 (2003)

18. NCI 60 Cancer Microarray Project. http://genome-www.stanford.edu/NCI60

19. Pirim, H., et al.: Clustering of high throughput gene expression data. Comput. Oper. Res. **39**(12), 3046–3061 (2012)

20. Ramaswamy, S., et al.: Multiclass cancer diagnosis using tumor gene expression signatures. Proc. Natl. Acad. Sci. USA **98**, 15149–15154 (2001)

21. RDevelopment Core Team: R: A language and environment for statistical computing, pp. 1–1731. R Foundation for Statistical Computing, Vienna, Austria (2008)

22. Simpson, T., et al.: Merged consensus clustering to assess and improve class discovery with microarray data. BMC Bioinform. **11**(1), 590 (2010)

23. Stevans, W.R.: Advanced Programming in the UNIX Environment. Pearson Education, India (2011)

24. Unold, O., Tagowski, T.: A GPU-based consensus clustering. Glob. J. Comput. Sci. **4**(2), 65–69 (2014)

25. Yeoh, E.J., et al.: Classification, subtype discovery, and prediction of outcome in pediatric acute lymphoblastic leukemia by gene expression profiling. Cancer Cell **1**, 133–143 (2002)

Bandits and Recommender Systems

Jérémie Mary, Romaric Gaudel, and Philippe Preux[✉]

CRIStAL (UMR CNRS), Université de Lille, Villeneuve d'Ascq, France
{jeremie.mary,romaric.gaudel,philippe.preux}@univ-lille3.fr

Abstract. This paper addresses the on-line recommendation problem facing new users and new items; we assume that no information is available neither about users, nor about the items. The only source of information is a set of ratings given by users to some items. By on-line, we mean that the set of users, and the set of items, and the set of ratings is evolving along time and that at any moment, the recommendation system has to select items to recommend based on the currently available information, that is basically the sequence of past events. We also mean that each user comes with her preferences which may evolve along short and longer scales of time; so we have to continuously update their preferences. When the set of ratings is the only available source of information, the traditional approach is matrix factorization. In a decision making under uncertainty setting, actions should be selected to balance exploration with exploitation; this is best modeled as a bandit problem. Matrix factors provide a latent representation of users and items. These representations may then be used as contextual information by the bandit algorithm to select items. This last point is exactly the originality of this paper: the combination of matrix factorization and bandit algorithms to solve the on-line recommendation problem. Our work is driven by considering the recommendation problem as a feedback controlled loop. This leads to interactions between the representation learning, and the recommendation policy.

1 Introduction

We consider the online version of the problem of the recommendation of items to users as faced by websites. Items may be ads, news, music, videos, movies, books, diapers,... Being live, these systems have to cope with users about whom we have no information, and new items introduced in the catalog which attractiveness is unknown. Appetence of new users towards available items, and appeal of new items towards existing users have to be estimated as fast as possible. Currently, this situation is handled thanks to side information available on the users, and on the items (see [2,21]). In this paper, we consider this problem from a different perspective. Though perfectly aware of the potential utility of side information, we consider the problem without any side information, only focussing on estimating the appetences of new users and the appeal of new items as fast as possible; the use of side information can be mixed with the ideas presented in this paper. Side information being unavailable, we learn a latent representation of

© Springer International Publishing Switzerland 2015
P. Pardalos et al. (Eds.): MOD 2015, LNCS 9432, pp. 325–336, 2015.
DOI: 10.1007/978-3-319-27926-8_29

each user and each item using the currently available ratings. As already argued by others (*e.g.* [16]), this problem fits perfectly into the sequential decision making framework, and more specifically, the bandit setting [9,10,20]. A sequential decision making problem under uncertainty faces an exploration vs. exploitation dilemma: the exploration is meant to acquire information in order to perform better subsequently by exploiting it; collecting the information has a cost that can not be merely zeroed, or simply left as an unimportant matter. However, in rather sharp contrast with the traditional bandit setting, here the set of bandits is constantly being renewed; the number of bandits is not small, though not being huge (from a few dozens to hundreds arms in general, up to dozens of millions in some applications): this makes the problem very different from the 2-armed bandit problem; we look for efficient and effective ways to address this task, since we want the proposed solution to be able to cope with real applications on the web. For obvious practical and economical reasons, the strategy can not merely consist in repeatedly presenting all available items to users until their appetences seem accurately estimated. We have to consider the problem as an exploration vs. exploitation problem in which exploration is a necessary evil to acquire information and eventually improve the performance of the recommendation system (RS for short). To summarize, we learn a latent representation of each user and each item, from which a recommendation policy is deduced, based on the available ratings. This learning process is continuous: the representation and the recommendation policy are updated regularly, as new ratings are observed, new items are introduced into the set of items, new users flow-in, and the preferences of already observed users change.

This being said, comes the problem of the objective function to optimize. Since the Netflix challenge, at least in the machine learning community, the recommendation problem is often reduced to a matrix factorization problem, performed in batch, learning on a training set, and minimizing the root mean squared error (RMSE) on a testing set. However, the RMSE comes with heavy flaws. Other objective functions have been considered to handle certain of these flaws [7,19].

Based on these ideas, our contribution in this paper is the following:

We propose an original way to handle new users and new items in recommendation systems: we cast this problem as a sequential decision making problem to be played online that selects items to recommend in order to optimize the exploration/exploitation balance; our solution is then to perform the rating matrix factorization driven by the policy of this sequential decision problem in order to focus on the most useful terms of the factorization. This is the core idea of the contributed algorithm we name BeWARE.

The reader familiar with the bandit framework can think of this work as a contextual bandit learning side information for each user and each item from the observed ratings, assuming the existence of a latent space of dimension k for both users and items. We stress the fact that learning and updating the representation of users and items at the same time recommendations are made is something very different from the traditional batch matrix factorization approach, or the traditional bandit setting.

We also introduce a methodology to use a classical partially filled rating matrices to assess the online performance of a bandit-based recommendation algorithm.

After introducing our notations in the next section, Sect. 3 briefly presents the matrix factorization approach. Sect. 4 introduces the necessary background in bandit theory. In Sects. 5 and 6, we present BeWARE considering in the case of new users and new items. Sect. 7 provides an experimental study on artificial data, and on real data. Finally, we conclude and draw some future lines of work in Sect. 8.

2   Notations and Vocabulary

$\mathbf{U}^T$ is the transpose of matrix $\mathbf{U}$, and $\mathbf{U}_i$ denotes its ith row. For a vector $\mathbf{u}$ and a set of integers $\mathcal{S}$, $\mathbf{u}_{\mathcal{S}}$ is the sub-vector of $\mathbf{u}$ composed of the elements of $\mathbf{u}$ which indices belong to $\mathcal{S}$. Accordingly, $\mathbf{U}$ being a matrix, $\mathbf{U}_{\mathcal{S}}$ is the sub-matrix made of the rows of $\mathbf{U}$ which indices belong to $\mathcal{S}$. $\#\mathbf{u}$ is the number of components (dimension) of $\mathbf{u}$, and $\#\mathcal{S}$ is the number of elements of $\mathcal{S}$.

Now, we introduce a set of notations dedicated to the RS problem. As we consider a time-evolving number of users and items, we will note n the current number of users, and m the current number of items. These should be indexed by a t to denote time, though often in this paper, t is dropped to simplify the notation. Without loss of generality, we assume $n < N$ and $m < M$, that is N and M are the maximal numbers of ever seen users and items (those figures may as large as necessary). $\mathbf{R}^*$ represents the ground truth, that is the matrix of ratings. $r_{i,j}^*$ is the rating given by user i to item j. We suppose that there exists an integer k and two matrices $\mathbf{U}$ of size $N \times k$ and $\mathbf{V}$ of size $M \times k$ such that $\mathbf{R}^* = \mathbf{U}\mathbf{V}^T$. We denote $\mathcal{S}$ the set of elements that have been observed, and $\mathbf{R}$ denote the matrix s.t. $r_{i,j} = r_{i,j}^* + \eta_{i,j}$ if $(i, j) \in \mathcal{S}$, where $\eta_{i,j}$ is a noise with zero mean and finite variance. The $\eta_{i,j}$ are i.i.d. In this paper, we assume that $\mathbf{R}^*$ is fixed during all the time; at a given moment, only a submatrix made of n rows and m columns is actually useful. This part of $\mathbf{R}^*$ that is observed is increasing along time. That is, the set $\mathcal{S}$ is growing along time. $\mathcal{J}(i)$ (resp. $\mathcal{I}(j)$) denotes the set of items rated by user i (resp. the set of users who rated item j). $\hat{\mathbf{U}}$ and $\hat{\mathbf{V}}$ denote estimates (with the statistical meaning) of the matrices $\mathbf{U}$ and $\mathbf{V}$ respectively. $\hat{\mathbf{U}}\hat{\mathbf{V}}^T$ is denoted by $\hat{\mathbf{R}}$. We use the term "observation" to mean a triplet $(i, j, r_{i,j})$. The RS receives a stream of observations. We use the term "rating" to mean the value associated by a user to an item. It can be a rating as in the Netflix challenge, or an information meaning click or not, sale or not, ... For the sake of legibility, in the online setting we omit the t subscript for time dependency. $\mathcal{S}$, $\hat{\mathbf{U}}$, $\hat{\mathbf{V}}$, n, m should be subscripted with t.

3   Matrix Factorization

Since the Netflix challenge [4], many works in RS have been using matrix factorization: the matrix of observed ratings is assumed to be the product of two matrices of low rank k: $\hat{\mathbf{R}} = \hat{\mathbf{U}}\hat{\mathbf{V}}^T$ [11]. $\hat{\mathbf{U}}$ is a latent representation of users, while $\hat{\mathbf{V}}$ is a latent representation of items. As most of the values of the rating matrix are unknown, the decomposition can only be done using the set of observations. The classical approach is to solve the regularized minimization problem $(\hat{\mathbf{U}}, \hat{\mathbf{V}}) \stackrel{def}{=} \operatorname{argmin}_{\mathbf{U},\mathbf{V}} \zeta(\mathbf{U}, \mathbf{V})$, where $\zeta(\mathbf{U}, \mathbf{V}) \stackrel{def}{=} \sum_{\forall(i,j)\in\mathcal{S}} \left(r_{i,j} - \mathbf{U}_i \cdot \mathbf{V}_j^T\right)^2 + \lambda \cdot \Omega(\mathbf{U}, \mathbf{V})$, in which $\lambda \in \mathbb{R}^+$ and is a regularization term. ζ is not convex. The minimization is usually performed either by stochastic gradient descent (SGD), or by alternate least squares (ALS). Solving for $\hat{\mathbf{U}}$ and $\hat{\mathbf{V}}$ at once being non convex, ALS iterates and at iteration, ALS alternates an optimization of $\hat{\mathbf{U}}$ keeping $\hat{\mathbf{V}}$ fixed, and an optimization of $\hat{\mathbf{V}}$ keeping $\hat{\mathbf{U}}$ fixed.

In this paper we consider ALS-WR [22] whose regularization term
$$\Omega(\mathbf{U}, \mathbf{V}) \stackrel{def}{=} \sum_i \#\mathcal{J}(i)\|\mathbf{U}_i\|^2 + \sum_j \#\mathcal{I}(j)\|\mathbf{V}_j\|^2$$ depends on users and items respective importance in the matrix of ratings.

This regularization is known to have a good empirical behavior — that is limited overfitting, easy tuning of λ and k, low RMSE.

4   Bandits

Let us consider a bandit machine with m independent arms. When pulling arm j, the player receives a reward drawn from $[0, 1]$ which follows a probability distribution ν_j. Let μ_j denote the mean of ν_j, $j^* \stackrel{def}{=} \operatorname{argmax}_j \mu_j$ be the best arm and $\mu^* \stackrel{def}{=} \max_j \mu_j = \mu_{j^*}$ be the best expected reward (we assume there is only one best arm). $\{\nu_j\}$, $\{\mu_j\}$, j^* and μ^* are unknown.

A player aims at maximizing the sum of rewards collected along T consecutive pulls. More specifically, by denoting j_t the arm pulled at time t and r_t the reward obtained at time t, the player wants to maximize the cumulative reward $\text{CumRew}_T = \sum_{t=1}^{T} r_t$. At each time-step but the last one, the player faces the dilemma:

- either *exploit* by pulling the arm which seems the best according to the estimated values of the parameters;
- or *explore* to improve the estimation of the parameters of the probability distribution of an arm by pulling it.

Li *et al.* [13] extend the bandit setting to contextual arms. They assume that a vector of real features $\mathbf{v} \in \mathbb{R}^k$ is associated to each arm and that the expectation of the reward associated to an arm is $\mathbf{u}^* \cdot \mathbf{v}$, where $\mathbf{u}^*$ is an unknown vector. The algorithm handling this setting is known as LinUCB. LinUCB consists in playing the arm with the largest upper confidence bound on the expected reward:

$$j_t = \operatorname*{argmax}_{j} \hat{\mathbf{u}}.\mathbf{v}_j^T + \alpha\sqrt{\mathbf{v}_j \mathbf{A}^{-1}\mathbf{v}_j^T},$$

where $\hat{\mathbf{u}}$ is an estimate of $\mathbf{u}^*$, α is a parameter, and $\mathbf{A} = \sum_{t'=1}^{t-1} \mathbf{v}_{j_{t'}}.\mathbf{v}_{j_{t'}}^T + \mathbf{Id}$, where $\mathbf{Id}$ is the identity matrix. Note that $\hat{\mathbf{u}}.\mathbf{v}_j^T$ corresponds to an estimate of the expected reward, while $\sqrt{\mathbf{v}_j \mathbf{A}^{-1} \mathbf{v}_j^T}$ is an optimistic correction of that estimate.

While the objective of LinUCB is to maximize the cumulative reward, theoretical results [1,13] are expressed in term of *cumulative regret* (or regret for short) $\text{Regret}_T \overset{def}{=} \sum_{t=1}^T (r_t^* - r_t)$, where $r_t^* = \max_j \mathbf{u}^*.\mathbf{v}_{j_t}^T$ stands for the best expected reward at time t. Hence, the regret measures how much the player loses (in expectation), in comparison to playing the optimal strategy. Standard results prove regrets of order $\tilde{O}(\sqrt{T})$ or $O(\ln T)$, depending on the assumptions on the distributions and depending on the precise analysis[1].

Of course LinUCB and other contextual bandit algorithms require the context (values of features) to be provided. In real applications this is done using side information about the items and the users [17] –*i.e.* expert knowledge, categorization of items, Facebook profiles of users, implicit feedback ... The core idea of this paper is to use matrix factorization techniques to build a context online using the known ratings. To this end, one assumes that the items and the arms can be represented in the same space of dimension k and assuming that the rating of user u for item v is the scalar product of u and v.

We study the introduction of new items and/or new users into the RS. This is done without using any side information on users or items.

5   BeWARE of a New User

Let us consider a particular recommendation scenario. At each time-step t,

1. a user i_t requests a recommendation to the RS,
2. the RS selects an item j_t among the set of items that have never been recommended to user i_t beforehand,
3. user i_t returns a rating $r_t = r_{i_t,j_t}$ for item j_t.

Obviously, the objective of the RS is to maximize the cumulative reward $\text{CumRew}_T = \sum_{t=1}^T r_t$. In the context of such a scenario, the usual matrix factorization approach of RS recommends item j_t which has the best predicted rating for user i_t. This corresponds to a pure exploitation, or greedy, strategy which is well-known to be suboptimal to optimize CumRew_T: to be optimal, the RS has to balance the exploitation and exploration.

Let us now describe the recommendation algorithm we propose at timestep t. We aim at recommending to user i_t an item j_t which leads to the best trade-off between exploration and exploitation in order to maximize CumRew_∞. We assume that the matrix $\mathbf{R}$ is factored into $\hat{\mathbf{U}}\hat{\mathbf{V}}^T$ by ALS-WR which terminated by optimizing $\hat{\mathbf{U}}$ holding $\hat{\mathbf{V}}$ fixed. In such a context, the UCB approach is based on a confidence interval on the estimated ratings $\hat{r}_{i_t,j} = \hat{\mathbf{U}}_{i_t} \cdot \hat{\mathbf{V}}_j^T$ for any allowed item j.

---

[1] $\tilde{O}$ means O up to a logarithmic term on T.

We assume that we already observed a sufficient number of ratings for each item, but only a few ratings (possibly none) from user i_t. As a consequence the uncertainty on $\hat{\mathbf{U}}_{i_t}$ is much more important than on any $\hat{\mathbf{V}}_j$. In other words, the uncertainty on $\hat{r}_{i_t,j}$ mostly comes from the uncertainty on $\hat{\mathbf{U}}_{i_t}$. Let us express this uncertainty.

Let $\mathbf{u}^*$ denote the (unknown) true value of $\mathbf{U}_{i_t}$ and let us introduce the $k \times k$ matrix:

$$\mathbf{A} \overset{def}{=} (\hat{\mathbf{V}}_{\mathcal{J}(i_t)})^T \cdot \hat{\mathbf{V}}_{\mathcal{J}(i_t)} + \lambda \cdot \#\mathcal{J}(i_t) \cdot \mathbf{Id}.$$

As $\hat{\mathbf{U}}$ and $\hat{\mathbf{V}}$ comes from ALS-WR (which last iteration optimized $\hat{\mathbf{U}}$),

$$\hat{\mathbf{U}}_{j_t} = \mathbf{A}^{-1}\hat{\mathbf{V}}_{\mathcal{J}(i_t)}^T \mathbf{R}_{i_t,\mathcal{J}(i_t)}^T.$$

Using Azuma's inequality over the weighted sum of random variables (as introduced by [18] for linear systems), it follows that there exists a value $C \in \mathbb{R}$ such as, with probability $1 - \delta$:

$$(\hat{\mathbf{U}}_{i_t} - \mathbf{u}^*)\mathbf{A}^{-1}(\hat{\mathbf{U}}_{i_t} - \mathbf{u}^*)^T \leq C\frac{\log(1/\delta)}{t}$$

This inequality defines the confidence bound around the estimate $\hat{\mathbf{U}}_{i_t}$ of $\mathbf{u}^*$. Therefore, a UCB strategy selects item j_t:

$$j_t \overset{def}{=} \underset{1 \leq j \leq m, j \notin \mathcal{J}(i_t)}{\operatorname{argmax}} \hat{\mathbf{U}}_{i_t} \cdot \hat{\mathbf{V}}_j^T + \alpha\sqrt{\hat{\mathbf{V}}_j\mathbf{A}^{-1}\hat{\mathbf{V}}_j^T},$$

where $\alpha \in \mathbb{R}$ is an exploration parameter to be tuned. Figure 1(a) provides a graphical illustration of the link between the bound, and this choice of item j_t.

Our algorithm, named BeWARE.User (BeWARE which stands for "Bandit WARms-up REcommenders") is described in Algorithm 1. The presentation is optimized for clarity rather than for computational efficiency. Of course, if the exploration parameter α is set to 0 BeWARE.User makes a greedy selection for the item to recommend. The estimation of the center of the ellipsoid and its size can be influenced by the use of an other regularization term. BeWARE.User uses a regularization based on ALS-WR. It is possible to replace all $\#\mathcal{J}(.)$ by 1. This amounts to the standard regularization: we call this slightly different algorithm BeWARE.ALS.User. In fact one can use any regularization as long as $\hat{\mathbf{U}}_{i_t}$ is a linear combination of observed rewards.

6   BeWARE of New Items

In general, a set of new items is introduced at once, not a single item. In this case, the uncertainty is more important on items. We compute a confidence bound around the items instead of the users, assuming ALS terminates with optimizing

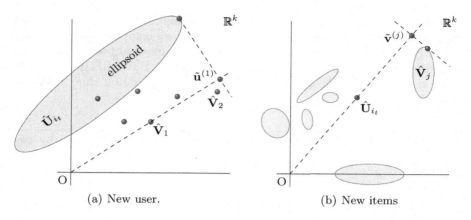

(a) New user.   (b) New items

Fig. 1. (a) The leftmost part of this figure illustrates the use of the upper confidence ellipsoid for item selection for the new user i_t who enters the game at time t. Items and users are vectors in $\mathbb{R}^k$. (One may suppose that $k = 2$ in this figure to make it in the plane.) Red dots represent items. The blue ellipse represents the confidence ellipsoid of the vector associated to the new user. The optimistic rating of the user for an item j is the maximum dot product between $\hat{\mathbf{V}}_j$ and any point in this ellipsoid. By a simple geometrical argument based on iso-contours of the dot product, this maximum value is equal to the dot product between $\hat{\mathbf{V}}_j$ and $\tilde{\mathbf{u}}_{i_t}^{(j)}$. Optimism leads to recommend the item maximizing the dot product $\langle \tilde{\mathbf{u}}_{i_t}^{(j)}, \hat{\mathbf{V}}_j \rangle$. (b) This figure illustrates the use of the upper confidence ellipsoid for item selection in the context of a set of new items. The setting is similar to the case of a new user except that the vector associated to the user is known (represented by a blue dot) while each item now has its confidence ellipsoids. The optimistic RS recommends the item maximizing the scalar product $\langle \hat{\mathbf{U}}_{i_t}, \tilde{\mathbf{v}}^{(j)} \rangle$.

Algorithm 1. BeWARE. User: for a user i_t, recommends an item to this user.

    Input: i_t, λ, α
    Input/Output: R, $\mathcal{S}$
1: $(\hat{\mathbf{U}}, \hat{\mathbf{V}}) \leftarrow \text{MatrixFactorization}(\mathbf{R})$
2: $\mathbf{A} \leftarrow (\hat{\mathbf{V}}_{\mathcal{J}(i_t)})^T \cdot \hat{\mathbf{V}}_{\mathcal{J}(i_t)} + \lambda \cdot \#\mathcal{J}(i_t) \cdot \mathbf{Id}.$
3: $j_t \leftarrow \underset{j \notin \mathcal{J}(i_t)}{\arg\max} \, \hat{\mathbf{U}}_{i_t} \cdot \hat{\mathbf{V}}_j^T + \alpha \sqrt{\hat{\mathbf{V}}_j \mathbf{A}^{-1} \hat{\mathbf{V}}_j^T}$
4: Recommend item j_t and receive rating $r_t = r_{i_t, j_t}$
5: Update **R,** $\mathcal{S}$

$\hat{\mathbf{V}}$ keeping $\hat{\mathbf{U}}$ fixed. With the same criterion and regularization on $\hat{\mathbf{V}}$ as above, at timestep t:

$$\hat{\mathbf{V}}_j = \mathbf{B}(j)^{-1}(\hat{\mathbf{U}}_{\mathcal{I}(j)})^T \mathbf{R}_{\mathcal{I}(j), j},$$

$$\text{with } \mathbf{B}(j) \overset{def}{=} (\hat{\mathbf{U}}_{\mathcal{I}(j)})^T \hat{\mathbf{U}}_{\mathcal{I}(j)} + \lambda \cdot \#\mathcal{I}(j) \cdot \mathbf{Id}.$$

So the upper confidence bound of the rating for user i on item j is:

$$\hat{\mathbf{U}}_i \cdot \hat{\mathbf{V}}_j^T + \alpha \sqrt{\hat{\mathbf{U}}_j \mathbf{B}(j)^{-1} \hat{\mathbf{U}}_j^T}.$$

This leads to the algorithm BeWARE.Items presented in Algorithm 2. Again, the presentation is optimized for clarity rather than for computational efficiency. BeWARE.Items can be parallelized and has the complexity of one step of ALS. Figure 1(b) gives the geometrical intuition leading to BeWARE.Items. Again, setting $\alpha = 0$ leads to a greedy selection. The regularization (line 4) can be modified.

Algorithm 2. BeWARE.Items: for a user i_t, recommends an item to this user in the case where a set of new items is made available.

    Input: i_t, λ, α
    Input/Output: R, $\mathcal{S}$
1: $(\hat{\mathbf{U}}, \hat{\mathbf{V}}) \leftarrow$ MatrixFactorization(**R**)
2: $\forall j \notin \mathcal{J}(i_t),\ \mathbf{B}(j) \leftarrow (\hat{\mathbf{U}}_{\mathcal{I}(j)})^T \hat{\mathbf{U}}_{\mathcal{I}(j)} + \lambda \cdot \#\mathcal{I}(j) \cdot \mathbf{Id}$
3: $j_t \leftarrow \underset{j \notin \mathcal{J}(i_t)}{\operatorname{argmax}} \hat{\mathbf{U}}_{i_t} . \hat{\mathbf{V}}_j^T + \alpha \sqrt{\hat{\mathbf{U}}_{i_t} \mathbf{B}(j)^{-1} \hat{\mathbf{U}}_{i_t}^T}$
4: Recommend item j_t and receive rating $r_t = r_{i_t, j_t}$
5: Update **R**, and $\mathcal{S}$

---

7 Experimental Investigation

In this section we evaluate empirically BeWARE on artificial data, and on real datasets. The BeWARE algorithms are compared to:

- greedy approaches (denoted Greedy.ALS and Greedy.ALS-WR) that always choose the item with the largest current estimated value (respectively given a decomposition obtained by ALS, or by ALS-WR),
- the UCB1 approach [3] (denoted UCB.on.all.users) that considers each reward r_{i_t, j_t} as an independent realization of a distribution ν_{j_t}. In other words, UCB.on.all.users recommends an item without taking into account the information on the user requesting the recommendation.

The comparison to greedy selection highlights the needs of exploration to have an optimal algorithm in the online context. The comparison to UCB.on.all.users assesses the benefit of personalizing recommendations.

7.1 Experimental Setting

For each dataset, each algorithm starts with an empty **R** matrix of 100 items and 200 users. Then, the evaluation goes like this:

1. select a user uniformly at random among those who have not yet rated all the items,
2. request his favorite item among those he has not yet rated,

3. compute the immediate regret (the difference of rating between the best not yet selected item and the one selected by the algorithm),
4. iterate until all users have rated all items.

The difficulty with real datasets is that the ground truth is unknown, and actually, only a very small fraction of ratings is known. This makes the evaluation of algorithms uneasy. To overcome these difficulties, we also provide a comparison of the algorithms considering an artificial problem based on a ground truth matrix $\mathbf{R}^*$ considering m users and n items. This matrix is generated as in [6]. Each item belongs to either one of k genres, and each user belongs to either one of l types. For each item j of genre a and each user i of type b, $r_{i,j}^* = p_{a,b}$ is the ground truth rating of item j by user i, where $p_{a,b}$ is drawn uniformly at random in the set $\{1, 2, 3, 4, 5\}$. The observed rating $r_{i,j}$ is a noisy value of $r_{i,j}^*$: $r_{i,j} = r_{i,j}^* + \mathcal{N}(0, 0.5)$.

We also consider real datasets, the NetFlix dataset [4] and the Yahoo!Music dataset [8]. Of course, the major issue with real data is that there is no dataset with a complete matrix, which means we do no longer have access to the ground truth $\mathbf{R}^*$, which makes the evaluation of algorithms more complex. This issue is usually solved in the bandit literature by using a method based on reject sampling [14]. For a well constructed dataset, this kind of estimators has no bias and a known bound on the decrease of the error rate [12]. For all the algorithms, we restrict the possible choices for a user at time-step t to the items with a known rating in the dataset. However, a minimum amount of ratings per user is needed to be able to have a meaningful comparison of the algorithms (otherwise, a random strategy is the only reasonable one). As a consequence, with both datasets, we focus on the 5000 heaviest users for the top ~250 movies/songs. This leads to a matrix $\widetilde{\mathbf{R}}^*$ with only 10 % to 20 % of missing ratings. We insist on the fact that this is necessary for performance evaluation of the algorithms; obviously, this is not required to use the algorithms on a live RS.

We would like to advertize that this experimental methodology has a unique feature: this methodology allows us to turn any matrix of ratings into an online problem which can be used to test bandit recommendation algorithms. We think that this methodology is an other contribution of this paper.

7.2 Experimental Results

Figure 2(a) and (b) show that given a fixed factorization method, BeWARE strategies outperform greedy item selection. Looking more closely at the results, BeWARE.items performs better than BeWARE.user, and BeWARE.user is the only BeWARE strategy beaten by its greedy counterpart (Greedy.ALS-WR) on the Netflix dataset. These results demonstrate that an online strategy has to care about exploration to tend towards optimality.

While UCB.on.all.users is almost the worst approach on artificial data (Fig. 2(a)), it surprisingly performs better than all other approaches on the Netflix dataset. We feel that this difference is strongly related to the preprocessing of the Netflix dataset we have done to be able to follow the experimental protocol

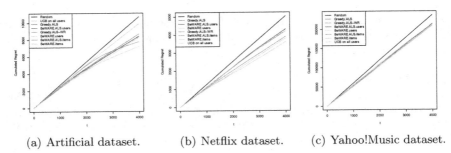

(a) Artificial dataset.   (b) Netflix dataset.   (c) Yahoo!Music dataset.

Fig. 2. Cumulated regret (the lower, the better) for a set of 100 new items and 200 users with no prior information. Figures are averaged over 20 runs (for Netflix and artificial data, $k = 5$, $\lambda = 0.05$, $\alpha = 0.12$ whereas for Yahoo!Music, $k = 8$, $\lambda = 0.2$, $\alpha = 0.05$). On the artificial dataset (a), BeWARE.items is better than the other strategies in terms of regret. On the Netflix dataset (b), **UCB on all users** is the best approach and BeWARE.items is the second best. On the Yahoo!Music dataset (c), BeWARE.items, Greedy.ALS-WR and UCB all 3 lead to similar performances.

(and have an evaluation at all). By focusing on the top ~250 movies, we only keep blockbusters that everyone enjoys. With that particular subset of movies, there is no need to adapt the recommendation user per user. As a consequence, UCB.on.all.users suffers a smaller regret than other strategies, as it considers users as n independent realizations of the same distribution. It is worth noting that the regret of UCB.on.all.users would increase with the number of items while the regret of BeWARE scales with the dimensionality of the factorization, which makes BeWARE a better candidates for real applications with much more items to deal with.

Last, on the Yahoo! Music datatset (Fig. 2(c)), all algorithms suffer the same regret.

7.3   Discussion

In a real setting, BeWARE.items has a desirable property: it tends to favor new items with regards to older ones because they simply have less ratings than the others, hence larger confidence bounds. So the algorithm gives them a boost which is exactly what a webstore is willing. Moreover, the RS then uses at its best the novelty effect associated to new items. This natural attraction of users for new items can be very strong as it has been shown during the Exploration & Exploitation challenge at ICML'2012 which was won by a context free algorithm [15].

The computational cost of BeWARE is the same as doing an additional step of alternate least squares; moreover some intermediate calculations of the QR factorization can be re-used to speed up the computation. So the total cost of BeWARE.Items is almost the same as ALS-WR. Even better, while the online setting requires to recompute the factorization at each time-step, this factorization changes only slightly from one iteration to the other. As a consequence, only a few ALS-WR iterations are needed to update the factorization. Overall the computational cost remains reasonable even in a real application.

8   Conclusion and Future Work

In this paper, we have bridged matrix factorization with bandits to address in a principled way the balance between exploration and exploitation faced by online recommendations systems when considering new users or new items. We think that this contribution is conceptually rich, and opens ways to many different studies. We showed on large, publicly available datasets that this approach is also effective, leading to efficient algorithms able to work online, under the expected computational constraints of such systems. Furthermore, the algorithms are quite easy to implement.

Many extensions are currently under study. First, we work on extending these algorithms to use contextual information about users, and items. This will require combining the similarity measure with confidence bounds; this might be translated into a Bayesian prior. We also want to analyze regret bound for large enough number of items and users. This part can be tricky as LinUCB still does not have a full formal analysis, though some insights are available in [1].

An other important point is to work on the recommendation of several items at once and get feedback only for the one. There has been some work in the non contextual bandits on this point [5].

Finally, we plan to combine confidence ellipsoid about both users and items. We feel that such a combination has low odds of providing better results for real applications, but it is interesting from a theoretical perspective, and should lead to even better results on artificial problems.

Acknowledgements. Authors acknowledge the support of INRIA, and the stimulating environment of the research group SequeL.

References

1. Abbasi-yadkori, Y., Pal, D., Szepesvari, C.: Improved algorithms for linear stochastic bandits. In: Proceedings of NIPS, pp. 2312–2320 (2011)
2. Agarwal, D., Chen, B.-C., Elango, P., Motgi, N., Park, S.-T., Ramakrishnan, R., Roy, S., Zachariah, J.: Online models for content optimization. In: Proceedings of NIPS, pp. 17–24 (2008)
3. Auer, P., Cesa-Bianchi, N., Fischer, P.: Finite-time analysis of the multiarmed bandit problem. Mach. Learn. **47**, 235–256 (2002)
4. Bennett, J., Lanning, S., Netflix, N.: The Netflix prize. In: KDD Cup and Workshop (2007)
5. Cesa-Bianchi, N., Lugosi, G.: Combinatorial bandits. J. Comput. Syst. Sci. **78**(5), 1404–1422 (2012)
6. Chatterjee, S.: Matrix estimation by universal singular value thresholding. preprint (2012). http://arxiv.org/abs/1212.1247

7. Dhanjal, C., Gaudel, R., Clémençon, S.: Collaborative filtering with localised ranking. In: Proceedings of AAAI (2015)
8. Dror, G., Koenigstein, N., Koren, Y., Weimer, M.: The Yahoo! music dataset and kdd-cup 2011. In: Proceedings of KDD Cup (2011)
9. Feldman, S.: Personalization with contextual bandits. http://engineering.richrelevance.com/author/sergey-feldman/
10. Kohli, P., Salek, M., Stoddard, G.: A fast bandit algorithm for recommendations to users with heterogeneous tastes. In: Proceedings of AAAI, pp. 1135–1141 (2013)
11. Koren, Y., Bell, R., Volinsky, C.: Matrix factorization techniques for recommender systems. Computer **42**(8), 30–37 (2009)
12. Langford, J., Strehl, A., Wortman, J.: Exploration scavenging. In: Proceedings of ICML, pp. 528–535. Omnipress (2008)
13. Li, L., Chu, W., Langford, J., Schapire, R.E.: A contextual-bandit approach to personalized news article recommendation. In: Proceedings of WWW, pp. 661–670. ACM, New York (2010)
14. Li, L., Chu, W., Langford, J., Wang, X.: Unbiased offline evaluation of contextual-bandit-based news article recommendation algorithms. In: Proceedings of WSDM, pp. 297–306. ACM (2011)
15. Mary, J., Garivier, A., Li, L., Munos, R., Nicol, O., Ortner, R., Preux, P.: ICML exploration and exploitation 3 - new challenges (2012)
16. Shani, G., Heckerman, D., Brafman, R.I.: An MDP-based recommender system. J. Mach. Learn. Res. **6**, 1265–1295 (2005)
17. Shivaswamy, P.K., Joachims, T.: Online learning with preference feedback. In: NIPS Workshop on Choice Models and Preference Learning (2011)
18. Walsh, T.J., Szita, I., Diuk, C., Littman, M.L.: Exploring compact reinforcement-learning representations with linear regression (2012). CoRR abs/1205.2606
19. Weston, J., Yee, H., Weiss, R.J.: Learning to rank recommendations with the k-order statistic loss. In: Proceedings of RecSys, pp. 245–248. ACM (2013)
20. White, J.M.: Bandit Algorithms for Website Optimization. O'Reilly, USA (2012)
21. Yue, Y., Hong, S.A., Guestrin, C.: Hierarchical exploration for accelerating contextual bandits. In: Proceedings of ICML, pp. 1895–1902 (2012)
22. Zhou, Y., Wilkinson, D., Schreiber, R., Pan, R.: Large-scale parallel collaborative filtering for the netflix prize. In: Fleischer, R., Xu, J. (eds.) AAIM 2008. LNCS, vol. 5034, pp. 337–348. Springer, Heidelberg (2008)

Semi-Naive Mixture Model for Consensus Clustering

Marco Moltisanti[✉], Giovanni Maria Farinella, and Sebastiano Battiato

Image Processing Laboratory – Dipartimento di Matematica e Informatica,
Università degli Studi di Catania, Catania, Italy
{moltisanti,gfarinella,battiato}@dmi.unict.it

Abstract. Consensus clustering is a powerful method to combine multiple partitions obtained through different runs of clustering algorithms. The goal is to achieve a robust and stable partition of the space through a consensus procedure which exploits the diversity of multiple clusterings outputs. Several methods have been proposed to tackle the consensus clustering problem. Among them, the algorithm which models the problem as a mixture of multivariate multinomial distributions in the space of cluster labels gained high attention in the literature. However, to make the problem tractable, the theoretical formulation takes into account a Naive Bayesian conditional independence assumption over the components of the vector space in which the consensus function acts (i.e., the conditional probability of a $d-$dimensional vector space is represented as the product of conditional probability in an one dimensional feature space). In this paper we propose to relax the aforementioned assumption, heading to a Semi-Naive approach to model some of the dependencies among the components of the vector space for the generation of the final consensus partition. The Semi-Naive approach consists in grouping in a random way the components of the labels space and modeling the conditional density term in the maximum-likelihood estimation formulation as the product of the conditional densities of the finite set of groups composed by elements of the labels space. Experiments are performed to point out the results of the proposed approach.

1 Introduction

The definition of clustering encloses a wide range of different techniques, all of them aiming to group similar objects according to a similarity or distance function. The factors in this definition, together with the choice of the cluster model (e.g. connectivity model, centroid model, distribution model, etc.) lead to the high variability in the clustering algorithms family [4]. Among the different employments of clustering algorithms, the Bag-of-Words model is one of the most popular, especially in Computer Vision community. In that field, the feature vectors, which may be extracted using different techniques, are used as the inputs for clustering. Then, the normalized histograms of the labels distribution over each image are computed and used as a representation of the image itself. This representation is powerful in terms of compactness, because it needs less space

© Springer International Publishing Switzerland 2015
P. Pardalos et al. (Eds.): MOD 2015, LNCS 9432, pp. 337–346, 2015.
DOI: 10.1007/978-3-319-27926-8_30

than the original image and the representation, and in terms of the semantic meaning of the representation. The collection of all the clusters is also called a vocabulary, and it can be used to represent other images. This representation can be used in different ways. For example, in [1,5] it used to build textons in order to focus on the textures of the considered images. In [2], the clustered space is used to learn a set of linear discriminant classifiers to perform red-eyes removal on face images. In [3], two vocabularies built on different feature spaces are aligned in order to achieve a compact representation which takes into account different aspects of the image (i.e. gradients and textures).

In [13], Kleinberg defines some desirable properties, proving that there is no clustering function able to satisfy them all together:

Scale-Invariance: insensitivity to changes in the units of distance measurements;

Richness: every partition of the data space S should be a possible output of the algorithm;

Consistency: changing the distance function to reduce intra-cluster distances and augment inter-cluster distances, the output partition should be the same.

Finding a consensus partition, though, poses new problems, according to Topchy *et al.* [19]:

1. Find a "good" consensus function, able to solve the label correspondence problem and to deal with all the component partitions;
2. Ensure the diversity of input clustering;
3. Estimate the how "good/bad" the input clusterings can be in order to obtain a successful combination.

Although these questions have been addressed in supervised classification researches, it is not possible to apply those solutions in a straightforward manner in an unsupervised context, basically because of the absence of labeled data.

The choice of the combination technique is critical in order to produce a clustering ensemble. A wide review of different approaches is given in [10], especially focusing on different consensus functions. Among others, it is noteworthy to mention the methods based on categorical clustering including the co-association-based hierarchical methods [7–9,19], hypergraph algorithms [11, 12,18] and boosting framework [17].

In this paper we extend the method proposed in [19] using a Semi-naive Bayesian approach instead of a pure Naive Bayesian in the derivation of the consensus function. The Semi-naive formulation for classification problems has been well investigated in the machine learning field [14,20,21]. An interesting application of this approach can be found in [15], where the Semi-naive classifier is employed for keypoint recognition purposes.

The paper is structured as follows: in Sect. 2 we recall the Consensus Clustering method proposed in [19]. In Sect. 3 the proposed semi-naive bayesian approach is explained. Finally, in Sect. 5 we draw the conclusions and give hints for some future works.

2   Consensus Clustering via Expectation-Maximization

Topchy *et al.* [19] modeled the problem using a Gaussian Mixture Model (GMM) in order to find the consensus partition by solving a Maximum Likelihood optimization. Given N data points, $\mathbf{X} = \{\mathbf{x}_1, \mathbf{x}_2, \ldots, \mathbf{x}_N\}$, they consider the outcomes of H different clustering algorithms, each of which establish a partition in the feature space. They refer to the partitions as $\mathbf{H} = \{\pi_1, \pi_2, \ldots, \pi_H\}$. It is straightforward that every clustering algorithm assigns each data point $\mathbf{x}_i$ to a partition:

$$\mathbf{x}_i \rightarrow \{\pi_1(\mathbf{x}_i), \pi_2(\mathbf{x}_i), \ldots, \pi_H(\mathbf{x}_i)\}, \qquad i = 1, \ldots, N$$

Therefore, each data point $\mathbf{x}_i$ has two representation: the first is a $d-$dimensional vector that lies in original the feature space, while the second is a vector with H elements that belongs to the labels space (Table 1). The vector composed by the labels for the $i-$th data point will be named $\mathbf{y}_i$. The whole labels set will be denoted as $\mathbf{Y} = \{\mathbf{y}_1, \ldots, \mathbf{y}_N\}$. The rationale behind this approach is that the labels can be modeled as random variables, drawn from a GMM. Hence, the probability for each label $\mathbf{y}_i$ can be expressed as in Eq. 1, where α_m, with $m = 1, \ldots, M$, are the mixture coefficients and θ_m are the parameters of each component of the mixture.

$$P(\mathbf{y}_i|\Theta) = \sum_{m=1}^{M} \alpha_m P_m(\mathbf{y}_i|\theta_m) \tag{1}$$

Using this model under the assumption that the data points are independent and identically distributed, the consensus partition can be found optimizing as the partition which maximize the probability, for each $\mathbf{y}_i$, of having been drawn from the $m-$th mixture. Hence, the problem can be formulated as finding the GMM's parameters that maximize the label-to-mixture assignment probability.

$$\Theta^* = \arg\max_{\Theta} \log L(\Theta|\mathbf{Y}_i). \tag{2}$$

where L is a likelihood function, as defined in Eq. 3

$$\log L(\Theta|\mathbf{Y}) = \log \prod_{m=1}^{M} P(\mathbf{y}_i|\theta_m) = \sum_{i=1}^{N} \log \sum_{m=1}^{M} \alpha_m P_m(\mathbf{y}_i|\theta_m) \tag{3}$$

Table 1. Data representation.

				π_1	$\cdots$	π_H
$\mathbf{x}_1$	x_{11}	$\cdots$	x_{1d}	$\pi_1(\mathbf{x}_1)$	$\cdots$	$\pi_H(\mathbf{x}_1)$
$\mathbf{x}_2$	x_{21}	$\cdots$	x_{2d}	$\pi_1(\mathbf{x}_2)$	$\cdots$	$\pi_H(\mathbf{x}_2)$
$\vdots$						
$\mathbf{x}_N$	x_{N1}	$\cdots$	x_{Nd}	$\pi_1(\mathbf{x}_N)$	$\cdots$	$\pi_H(\mathbf{x}_N)$
Original features				Labels		

To complete the definition of the model, it is needed to specify the conditional probabilities for the labels vector $\mathbf{y}_i$ (see Eq. 4) and the probability density for each component (see Eq. 5). In [19], the authors assume that the components of $\mathbf{y}_i$ are conditionally independent.

$$P_m\left(\mathbf{y}_i|\theta_m\right) = \prod_{j=1}^{H} P_m^{(j)}\left(y_{ij}|\theta_m^{(j)}\right) \tag{4}$$

$$P_m^{(j)}\left(y_{ij}|\theta_m^{(j)}\right) = \prod_{k=1}^{K(j)} \vartheta_{jm}(k)^{\delta(y_{ij},k)} \tag{5}$$

Note that the probabilities $\vartheta_{jm}(k)$ sum up to 1. In Eq. 5, the function δ is a classic Kronecker delta function and the index $k = 1, \ldots, K(j)$ is used to enumerate the labels in the j-th input mixture.

The solution to the consensus partition problem can be found optimizing Eq. 1, hypothesizing the existence of a set of hidden variables $\mathbf{Z}$ and estimating the values of each $\mathbf{z}_i$ using the Expectation-Maximization algorithm. For completeness sake, in Eqs. 6, 7, 8 we report the formulas to compute the parameters of the mixture with the EM algorithm.

$$E\left[z_{im}\right] = \frac{\alpha'_m \prod\limits_{j=1}^{H} \prod\limits_{k=1}^{K(j)} \left(\vartheta'_{jm}(k)\right)^{\delta(y_{ij},k)}}{\sum\limits_{n=1}^{M} \alpha'_n \prod\limits_{j=1}^{H} \prod\limits_{k=1}^{K(j)} \left(\vartheta'_{jn}(k)\right)^{\delta(y_{ij},k)}} \tag{6}$$

$$\alpha_m = \frac{\sum\limits_{i=1}^{N} E\left[z_{im}\right]}{\sum\limits_{i=1}^{N} \sum\limits_{m=1}^{M} E\left[z_{im}\right]} \tag{7}$$

$$\vartheta_{jm}(k) = \frac{\sum\limits_{i=1}^{N} \delta\left(y_{ij},k\right) E\left[z_{im}\right]}{\sum\limits_{i=1}^{N} \sum\limits_{k=1}^{K(j)} \delta\left(y_{ij},k\right) E\left[z_{im}\right]}. \tag{8}$$

3   Semi-Naive Bayesian Consensus Clustering

In order to model the problem in a Semi-Naive way, we relax the Bayesian Naive assumption [15,16], by grouping the labels and imposing that the labels belonging to the same group are drawn from a probability distribution, while the groups are conditionally independent. In [19], it is assumed that the labels $\mathbf{y}_i$ are conditionally independent, as modeled in Eq. 4, in order to make the problem tractable. Nevertheless, some relationship among the elements of the vector $\mathbf{y}_i$ may exist, because of the intrinsic nature of the data; in facts, $y_{i1}, y_{i2}, \ldots, y_{iH}$

are the outcomes of the H clustering algorithms run on the $i-$th data point, and it is reasonable to suppose that the labels are somehow related one to each other. Özuysal *et al.* proposed in [15] a Semi-Naive Bayesian approach to classify image patches. The key idea is to group the variables in small subsets, assuming every group to be conditionally independent from each other, and considering the elements inside the group to not be conditionally independent. We build on this idea to reformulate the consensus clustering proposed in [19]. Thus, given the H labels in $\mathbf{y}_i$, we create S partitions of size $D = \frac{H}{S}$ mutually conditionally independent. Thus, the probability becomes:

$$P_m \left(mathbf{y}_i | \ mathbf{f}\theta_m\right) = \prod_{s=1}^{S} P_m^{(i)} \left(F_{is}|\theta_m^{(i)}\right). \tag{9}$$

In Eq. 9, $F_{is} = \{y_{i\sigma(s,1)}, y_{i\sigma(s,2)}, \ldots, y_{i\sigma(s,D)}\}$ are the labels belonging to the $s-$th group, while $\sigma(s,j)$, $j = 1, \ldots, D$ is a random permutation function within the range $1, \ldots, H$. The labels F_{is} are dependent, thus the probability $P_m^{(i)} \left(F_{is}|\theta_m^{(i)}\right), s = 1, \ldots, D$ has to be expressed as a joint probability over the elements of $\mathbf{y}_i$ (see Eq. 10).

$$P_m^{(i)} \left(F_{is}|\theta_m^{(i)}\right) = P_m^{(i)} \left(y_{i\sigma(s,1)}, y_{i\sigma(s,2)}, \ldots, y_{i\sigma(s,D)}|\theta_m^{(i)}\right) \tag{10}$$

We define now an enumeration function T to assign a unique numerical label to each of the elements in F_{is}, $i = 1, \ldots, N$, $s = 1, \ldots, S$. The values of T lie in the range $\{1, \ldots, K(1) \times K(2) \times K(S)\}$. As shown in Sect. 2, $k = 1, \ldots, K(j)$ is an index referring to the labels in the $j-$th clustering.

$$T(F_{is}) : \{1, \ldots, K(1)\} \times \{1, \ldots, K(2)\} \times \ldots \{1, \ldots, K(D)\} \longrightarrow \mathcal{N} \tag{11}$$

We can now formulate the probability density (see Eq. 12) for each group F_{is} in the form of a multinomial trial, as in [19].

$$P_m^{(s)} \left(F_{is}|\theta_m^{(s)}\right) = \prod_{k=1}^{K(1) \times K(2) \times K(S)} \vartheta_{sm}(k)^{\delta(T(F_{is})),k)} \tag{12}$$

The consensus partition can still be found using the EM algorithm using the new equations formulated above. Thus, the expected values for each component of the hidden variables vectors $\mathbf{Z} = \{\mathbf{z}_1, \ldots, \mathbf{z}_N\}$ can be computed from Eq. 13 using Eq. 12 as the component probability, together with the mixture weights α (Eq. 14) and the mixture parameters ϑ (Eq. 15).

$$E\left[z_{im}\right] = \frac{\alpha'_m \prod_{s=1}^{S} \prod_{k=1}^{K(1) \times \ldots \times K(S)} (\vartheta_{sm}(k))^{\delta(T(F_{is}),k)}}{\sum_{n=1}^{M} \alpha'_n \prod_{s=1}^{S} \prod_{k=1}^{K(1) \times \ldots \times K(S)} (\vartheta_{sn}(k))^{\delta(T(F_{is}),k)}} \tag{13}$$

$$\alpha_m = \frac{\sum\limits_{i=1}^{N} E\left[z_{im}\right]}{\sum\limits_{i=1}^{N}\sum\limits_{m=1}^{M} E\left[z_{im}\right]} \tag{14}$$

$$\vartheta_{sm}(k) = \frac{\sum\limits_{i=1}^{N} \delta\left(T_{is}, k\right) E\left[z_{im}\right]}{\sum\limits_{i=1}^{N}\sum\limits_{k=1}^{K(1)\times\ldots\times K(S)} \delta\left(T_{is}, k\right) E\left[z_{im}\right]}. \tag{15}$$

4   Experimental Results

To test our approach, we used the well-known Two Spirals dataset. This dataset has been proposed by Alexis Wieland[1]. The key feature of this dataset is that the points form two spirals as shown in Fig. 1. For our experiments, we chose to use 1000 data points.

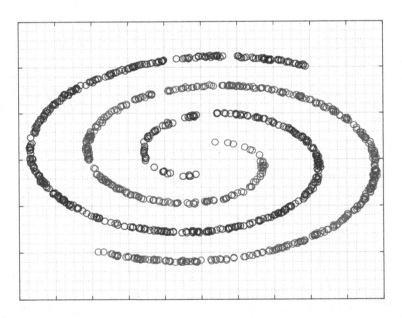

Fig. 1. Plot of the Two Spirals dataset with 1000 data points.

The experiments have been performed varying the parameters of both the original Naive [19] and the proposed Semi-Naive algorithms. In the first case, the parameters are the number of input clusterings H and the number of clusters

---

[1] http://www.cs.cmu.edu/Groups/AI/areas/neural/bench/cmu/.

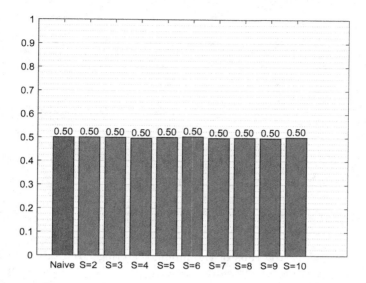

Fig. 2. Mean accuracies over 10 different runs, averaging over the parameters K and H. The first bar on the left represents the accuracy value obtained with the original Naive method [19], the next bars represent the accuracies obtained using the proposing method varying the number of groups S.

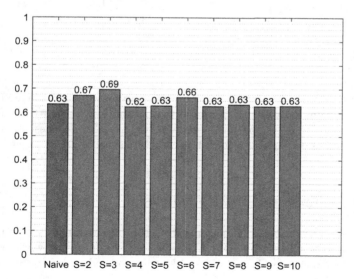

Fig. 3. Max accuracies over 10 different runs, averaging over the parameters K and H. The first bar on the left represents the accuracy value obtained with the original Naive method [19], the next bars represent the accuracies obtained using the proposing method varying the number of groups S.

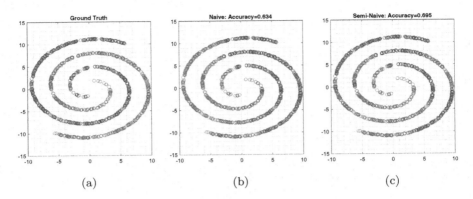

Fig. 4. Visual comparison of the results.

K to be generated by the runs of the input clusterings. H takes values in the range $\{5, \ldots, 50\}$, while K varies in the range $\{2, \ldots, 20\}$. In addition to these parameters, the number of groups S has been taken into account, considering the range $\{2, \ldots, 10\}$.

The results, obtained over 10 different runs of the experiments, are presented in Figs. 2 and 3. We computed the accuracy as the ratio between the number of elements correctly classified over the total number of elements to be classified. As shown in Fig. 2, the mean values are not very significant, both for the Naive and Semi-Naive approaches. This is because the algorithms need a fine parameters tuning step, in order to find the combination that best fits the problem. Hence, we considered the best results in terms of accuracy over all the runs and over all the parameters, as shown in Fig. 3. The best accuracy obtained for the Naive Bayesian method is 0.634, while for the Semi-Naive the best result is 0.695.

It is interesting to visualize how the two methods partition the plane. The Naive consensus (Fig. 4b) splits the plane in two, as a linear classifier would do, while the labeling produced by the Semi-Naive consensus (Fig. 4c) has a different behavior.

5   Conclusions and Future Works

In this paper, we propose a Semi-Naive Bayesian algorithm to tackle the problem of Consensus Clustering. Our approach derives from the work of Topchy et al. [19], in which the Consensus problem is modeled using a Gaussian Mixture Model. We extend this method relaxing the assumption on the conditional independence of the labels, and proposing a formulations where the labels are organized in groups, and inside each group a correlation among the labels is imposed.

Future works could involve the application of the proposed method to build Consensus Vocabularies to better represent images for the food classification task, hence extending our recent work [6] based on Naive Bayesian Consensus. Moreover, new experiments could be run on different datasets, with higher dimensionality to better understand the behavior of the proposed approach.

References

1. Battiato, S., Farinella, G.M., Gallo, G., Ravì, D.: Exploiting textons distributions on spatial hierarchy for scene classification. J. Image Video Process. **2010**(7), 1–13 (2010)
2. Battiato, S., Farinella, G.M., Guarnera, M., Messina, G., Ravì, D.: Red-eyes removal through cluster based linear discriminant analysis. In: 2010 17th IEEE International Conference on Image Processing (ICIP), pp. 2185–2188. IEEE (2010)
3. Battiato, S., Farinella, G.M., Puglisi, G., Ravì, D.: Aligning codebooks for near duplicate image detection. Multimedia Tools Appl. **72**(2), 1483–1506 (2014)
4. Estivill-Castro, V.: Why so many clustering algorithms: a position paper. ACM SIGKDD Explor. Newsl. **4**(1), 65–75 (2002)
5. Farinella, G.M., Moltisanti, M., Battiato, S.: Classifying food images represented as bag of textons. In: 2014 IEEE International Conference on Image Processing (ICIP), pp. 5212–5216 (2014)
6. Farinella, G.M., Moltisanti, M., Battiato, S.: Food recognition using consensus vocabularies. In: Murino, V., Puppo, E., Sona, D., Cristani, M., Sansone, C. (eds.) ICIAP 2015 Workshops. LNCS, vol. 9281, pp. 384–392. Springer, Heidelberg (2015)
7. Fred, A., Jain, A.K.: Robust data clustering. In: IEEE Conference on Computer Vision and Pattern Recognition, vol. 2, pp. 2–128. IEEE (2003)
8. Fred, A., Jain, A.K.: Data clustering using evidence accumulation. In: International Conference on Pattern Recognition, vol. 4, pp. 276–280. IEEE (2002)
9. Fred, A., Jain, A.K.: Evidence accumulation clustering based on the K-means algorithm. In: Caelli, T.M., Amin, A., Duin, R.P.W., Kamel, M.S., de Ridder, D. (eds.) SPR 2002 and SSPR 2002. LNCS, vol. 2396, pp. 442–451. Springer, Heidelberg (2002)
10. Ghaemi, R., Sulaiman, N., Ibrahim, H., Mustapha, N.: A survey: clustering ensembles techniques. Eng. Technol. **38**(February), 636–645 (2009)
11. Karypis, G., Aggarwal, R., Kumar, V., Shekhar, S.: Multilevel hypergraph partitioning: applications in VLSI domain. IEEE Trans. Very Large Scale Integr. VLSI Syst. **7**(1), 69–79 (1999)
12. Karypis, G., Kumar, V.: A fast and high quality multilevel scheme for partitioning irregular graphs. SIAM J. Sci. Comput. **20**(1), 359–392 (1998)
13. Kleinberg, J.: An impossibility theorem for clustering. In: Advances in Neural Information Processing Systems, pp. 446–453 (2002)
14. Kononenko, I.: Semi-naive bayesian classifier. In: Kodratoff, Y. (ed.) EWSL 1991. LNCS, vol. 482. Springer, Heidelberg (1991)
15. Özuysal, M., Calonder, M., Lepetit, V., Fua, P.: Fast keypoint recognition using random ferns. IEEE Trans. Pattern Anal. Mach. Intell. **32**(3), 448–461 (2010)
16. Pazzani, M.J.: Constructive induction of cartesian product attributes. In: Feature Extraction, Construction and Selection, pp. 341–354. Springer (1998)
17. Saffari, A., Bischof., H.: Clustering in a boosting framework. In: Proceedings of Computer Vision Winter Workshop (CVWW), St. Lambrecht, Austria, pp. 75–82 (2007)

18. Strehl, A., Ghosh, J.: Cluster ensembles–a knowledge reuse framework for combining multiple partitions. J. Mach. Learn. Res. **3**, 583–617 (2003)
19. Topchy, A., Jain, A.K., Punch, W.: Clustering ensembles: models of consensus and weak partitions. IEEE Trans. Pattern Anal. Mach. Intell. **27**(12), 1866–1881 (2005)
20. Zheng, F., Webb, G.: A comparative study of semi-naive bayes methods in classification learning. In: Proceedings of the 4th Australasian Data Mining Conference (AusDM 2005), pp. 141–156 (2005)
21. Zheng, Z., Webb, G.I., Ting, K.M.: Lazy bayesian rules: a lazy semi-naive bayesian learning technique competitive to boosting decision trees. In: Proceedings of the 16th International Conference on Machine Learning (1999)

Consensus Decision Making in Random Forests

Raja Khurram Shahzad[1]([✉]), Mehwish Fatima[2], Niklas Lavesson[1],
and Martin Boldt[1]

[1] Blekinge Institute of Technology, 371 79 Karlskrona, Sweden
{rks,nla,mbo}@bth.se
[2] COMSATS Institute of Information Technology, Lahore, Pakistan
mehwishfatima.raja@gmail.com

Abstract. The applications of Random Forests, an ensemble learner, are investigated in different domains including malware classification. Random Forests uses the majority rule for the outcome, however, a decision from the majority rule faces different challenges such as the decision may not be representative or supported by all trees in Random Forests. To address such problems and increase accuracy in decisions, a consensus decision making (CDM) is suggested. The decision mechanism of Random Forests is replaced with the CDM. The updated Random Forests algorithm is evaluated mainly on malware data sets, and results are compared with unmodified Random Forests. The empirical results suggest that the proposed Random Forests, i.e., with CDM performs better than the original Random Forests.

1 Introduction

One of the main challenges for anti-malware vendors is to detect or classify an unknown malware. The unknown malware are also referred to as zero day malware. The existing detection techniques, i.e., signature based (pattern matching) and rule based are incapable of detecting a zero day malware. To address this problem, researchers have borrowed different approaches from different domains including supervised learning and investigated their applicability for the malware detection. In Supervised learning, a model is generated from the labeled data set for the malware classification. The generated model is commonly referred to as classifier and is further used to classify malware and benign files. Experimental results have indicated that a combination of multiple classifiers (ensemble) such as Random Forests (RF) may perform better in comparison to single classifier. Random Forests[1], is created by generating the desired number of decision tree classifiers (also known as base learners) [1]. For the classification, an instance is given to each tree in RF, which then returns its prediction about the given instance. The decision of each tree is considered as a vote for obtaining the final decision. The final decision of RF is based on the majority rule, i.e., the class obtaining the majority of votes is the output. As an ensemble, RF is expected to perform better in terms of prediction accuracy than single base learners [2].

---

[1] http://www.stat.berkeley.edu/~breiman/RandomForests/cc_home.htm.

© Springer International Publishing Switzerland 2015
P. Pardalos et al. (Eds.): MOD 2015, LNCS 9432, pp. 347–358, 2015.
DOI: 10.1007/978-3-319-27926-8_31

Typically, the predictive performance of a classifier is evaluated by estimating its error rate, i.e., the proportion of misclassified instances. In case of RF, the error rate may be affected by the presence of noisy features in the data set and majority of votes to a wrong class [3,4]. The final decision of the RF algorithm is a multi-classifier decision-making process and is generally referred to as the group decision-making in the decision theory [5]. The final decision of the group may vary from the decision of an individual participant in the group. Thus, the group decision may not be supported by the whole group, which is a drawback of majority rule in context of unanimous agreement within the group. A unanimous decision is critical for problems such as malware classification, where the misclassification cost is very high in terms of losses to the user.

To address the problems of majority rule, a consensus decision-making (CDM) method is suggested [5]. For the CDM method, all group members strive to reach an optimal outcome while catering the concerns of each member as much as possible. We hypothesize that the prediction accuracy of the RF algorithm can be improved by incorporating CDM. For integrating CDM in RF, the majority decision of Random Forests is replaced by CDM. Later, modified RF algorithm is compared to the baseline, i.e., traditional Random Forests implementation in WEKA [6] on a number of data sets using different evaluation measures.

The remainder of this paper is organized as follows: Sect. 2 provides a background of Random Forests and decision-making theory. Section 2.1 discusses the related work. Section 3 discusses theoretical foundations regarding CDM. Section 4 presents the experimental setup, while Sect. 5 discusses the results from the experiment and Sect. 6 concludes the paper.

2   Background

Random Forests is an ensemble of decision trees. For creating a RF, a specific number of trees are generated through bootstrap sampling. Due to the random selection of nodes during each tree generation, each tree in RF varies in the classification accuracy [2,7]. Each generated tree in RF is tested with the out of bag data, i.e., the data, which is not used for the training. The average misclassification of Random Forests is known as the out of bag error estimate. For the outcome RF uses the (un-weighted) decisions from each tree and provides a decision based on the majority rule. It is indicated that group decision-making, where a problem is decomposed into smaller sub-problems, performs better in multiple problem domains such as decision theory, artificial intelligence, fuzzy sets theory and expert systems [8].

The group decision-making includes either the majority rule, autocracy (veto), and consensus vote. Contrary to the majority rule, in the veto, a designated member of the group or group of specific members may decide the outcome of the group. Both methods, i.e., majority rule and veto have their benefits and drawbacks. However, in both methods, the decision from a subgroup of members is ignored and outcome of the group cannot be referred as a decision that is supported by each member of the group. To address this problem, consensus voting is suggested [5]. In general, the word consensus refers to an agreement[2]. However, in case of the group decision-making, the word consensus is distinct from the common meaning and refers to a process in which all members of the set C collaborate to reach a solution that is supported by all the members of the group regardless of their individual assessment [5].

2.1   Related Work

Random Forests: The ideas of random decision forests and Bagging are presented in 1995 and 1996 respectively [9,10]. These two concepts served as the base for the development of RF in 1999. In 2001, it is presented that RF does not over-fit because of *Law of large numbers* [1]. In 2008, the basic theorem of RF is further enhanced by a series of theorems that established the universal consistency of averaging rules [2]. Since the idea of RF is presented, it has been used in different domains such as medical science, biology, bio-informatics, computer security, image processing, malware classification [11], and many others [7]. Different variations of Random Forests are also investigated by researchers to improve the prediction accuracy [12]. Some researchers have calibrated RF [13], while some have used Random Forests for the selection of important variables [14]. RF has also been improved for obtaining predictions from imbalance data sets [15].

Decision Making: A group of individuals, for solving a given task, may select a suitable option from the set of alternatives using different methods such as the majority rule [16], multiple winner, proxy voting, and veto [17]. These concepts are further extended by the social choice theory, which is a theoretical framework to attain a group decision from the participants while considering the individual preferences [18]. Different theories such as social decision scheme [19], quantitative decisions [20] and consensus decision-making are investigated. The idea of consensus decision-making is presented for the selection of a suitable candidate among multiple candidates using both individual judgment and group judgment [5].

Malware Classification: The task of malware classification is generally considered as a binary classification problem. RF algorithm is used for detecting the malware on computer systems, mobile phones and network data streams. RF has outperformed other algorithms such as Bagging, boosting, and decision trees for the detection of unknown malware [21,22].

3   Consensus Decision-Making in Random Forests Algorithm

This section explains the consensus decision-making algorithm. The consensus decision-making process can be divided into two stages, i.e., consensus stage and

---

[2] http://www.merriam-webster.com/dictionary/consensus.

selection stage. The consensus stage consists of several rounds where the preferences of each expert for the alternatives are evaluated to reach the solution. The iterative nature of the process helps the experts to reduce the differences between their opinions before concluding an outcome. The selection stage provides the subset of the most suitable alternative or a solution set. Different strategies may be further applied, (if required), to obtain the solution set.

3.1 Consensus Stage

In the consensus stage, decisions from the individual classifiers are collected and each decision is given a weight, which is further used to calculate the weighted group decision. The obtained weighted decision is re-evaluated iteratively until the convergence is achieved. The consensus stage is described as follows:

1. *Vector of Classifiers*: In Random Forests, $k > 1$ tree classifiers are generated from Bootstrapping and a vector of generated classifiers is obtained.
2. *Initial decisions (Predictions)*: Each classifier classifies the given instance and provides a vector of decisions about the n alternative classes. A decision matrix of $k \times n$, which gives the decisions from all classifiers about all alternative classes is generated.
3. *Criterion Weights = Criteria × Predictions*: The prediction of each tree classifier is multiplied with the selected criterion to obtain its weighted decision. For the experimental purpose, the out of bag error (OOB) [1] is selected as the criterion to evaluate decisions of generated tree classifiers. If a classifier is able to correctly predict the classes and OOB for that particular classifier is zero, the decision of the classifier is multiplied by 1. In all other cases, the decision of the classifier is multiplied by $1 - OOB$. This procedure reflects the confidence level of the classifiers for each classification.
4. *Aggregation*: The first aggregation step combines the values for each alternative class. This generates score vectors, one for each classifier and for each class after aggregation. These score vectors are used to generate the score matrix (S).
5. *Recursive Aggregation over Classifiers*: The OOB of each classifier is used to indicate the confidence level of the classifier for predictions. Thus, each classifier defines a vector of confidence for alternative classes. These vectors are used to construct a matrix R. The diagonals of matrix R are the degree of confidence that each classifier has in the correctness of its prediction. The matrix R differs at each step. Consequently, for each step the weighted mean aggregation is applied over the result of the previous step:

$$T = R \times S$$

6. *Next Iteration*: For the next aggregation step, following assignment is performed: $S = T$. The process is repeated for each class until the convergence is achieved. Suppose the number of aggregation steps are p, then after p aggregation steps:

$$S_p = R_p^T \times \cdots \times R_1^T \times C^T = (C \times R_1 \times \cdots \times R_p)^T$$

7. *Iteration Termination*: After the individual judgment, multiple iterations are performed, which combines the multi-classifier scores per class to obtain the overall score for each class, which leads to final ranking of all the classes. However, it is necessary to determine, how the iterations will stop. For this particular study, if the difference between the sums of two iterations is less than $1 \times e^{-}5$, the iterations are stopped and convergence is achieved.

3.2   Selection Stage

The selection stage provides the outcome of the RF. The selection stage receives the weighted means in the form of decisions from the consensus stage and the class with the highest weight is considered as the outcome.

3.3   Example and Explanation of Algorithm

Assume, a RF of 10 trees is generated using WEKA from a malware data set, which contains both malware files and benign files. An instance of malware file is given to this Random Forests. The task is to perform a binary classification, in which '1' represents the presence of a malware in the file (or a malware file), and '0' represents a benign file. Each generated tree contains (assumed value) OOB and has predicted the class of the given instance (see Table 1). For simplicity, assume that the decision vector of each tree (classifier) contains only outcome. Table 1 also presents the other required information such as the weight given by the tree to its decision (W_1), i.e., $1 - OOB$, and weight given to rest of trees

Table 1. Initial state

Trees	P*	OOB**	W_1^a	W_2^b
T1	0	0.25	0.75	0.027777778
T2	0	0.20	0.80	0.022222222
T3	0	0.15	0.85	0.016666667
T4	0	0.50	0.50	0.055555556
T5	1	0.30	0.70	0.033333333
T6	1	0.65	0.35	0.072222222
T7	1	0.30	0.70	0.033333333
T8	0	0.80	0.20	0.088888889
T9	1	0.25	0.75	0.027777778
T10	1	0.30	0.70	0.033333333

*Initial Predictions,
** Mean Absolute Error
a Self Weight, i.e., $1 - OOB$
b Weight given to each classifier in RF ($OOB_n/9$)

individually (W_2), i.e., $OOB/9$. These values are further used for calculating the weighted aggregated mean and remain constant throughout the process.

To obtain the weighted decision, the prediction of each tree classifier is multiplied with its W_1. It is worth noting that if the OOB of a particular tree is zero, the decision of the tree will be multiplied by '1'. To calculate the score matrix for each tree; sum of the prediction P_n from each tree is multiplied by W_1, and sum of decisions from other trees is multiplied with the OOB of current tree. The obtained score is divided by 10 for calculating the aggregated weighted mean. The score matrix of selected iterations, i.e., initial iteration, ith iteration and final iteration is shown in Table 2.

Table 2. Score matrix

Trees	Initial scores	Intermediate scores	Final scores	Predictions
T1	0.125	0.0560	0.000450078	1
T2	0.100	0.0458	0.000371326	0
T3	0.075	0.0351	0.000287487	0
T4	0.250	0.0995	0.000781605	1
T5	0.190	0.0673	0.000524192	1
T6	0.295	0.1205	0.000941675	1
T7	0.190	0.0673	0.000524192	1
T8	0.400	0.1352	0.001079901	1
T9	0.175	0.0585	0.000450079	1
T10	0.190	0.0673	0.000524192	1

* If Score is $< 1 \times e^-5$, prediction is class '0' otherwise prediction is class '1'.

The iterations are stopped, if the difference between the sum of ith iteration and $i+1$ iteration is $< 1 \times e^-5$. Moreover, the mean of last iteration is taken and the score below the mean is considered as the prediction for the class '0' and score $>$ mean is considered as the prediction for the class '1'. In this example initially, five trees have predicted the class as malware and five trees have predicted the class as benign. In such cases, majority rule cannot determine an outcome. When the majority rule is replaced with CDM, majority of trees have indicated the presence of a malware, which helps in determining the outcome.

4   Experiment

The aim of the experiment is two folds. First, to evaluate the impact of CDM in the Random Forests algorithm in comparison to the original RF algorithm for the task of malware classification. Secondly, to validate the generalizability of modified algorithm. The proposed changes may be used for the multi-class classification problems, however, the experiments are performed only for the binary classification. Hereafter, the modified Random Forests with the CDM will be referred to as Consensus Random Forests (CRF). Two types of experimental data sets are used, i.e., a generated data sets for the malware classification and two data sets taken from a machine learning repository [23]. These data sets may also be categorized according to their size, i.e., number of instances or features. All data sets are in the Attribute-Relation File Format (ARFF)[3], which is a structured ASCII text file that includes a set of data instances along with a set of features for each instance [24]. ARFF files are used as an input to models generated by CRF and RF. The experiments are performed with Random Forests of different number of trees.

4.1 Data Sets

The data sets from UCI repository are Forest Covertype data set[4] and Blogger data set[5]. The Forest Covertype data is generally considered as one of the largest data sets available for machine learning experiments [25]. This data set contains 581012 instances with 54 features. This data set is preprocessed to transform from multi-classification to binary classification problem[6]. While Blogger Data Set is relatively small and contains only 100 instances with six features [26]. The data set is used to classify users' trends in cyberspace into two distinct groups, i.e., professional bloggers (regular bloggers) and seasonal bloggers (irregular bloggers).

Malware Data Set is generated for malware classification. The malware data set contains 800 instances of both malware programs and benign programs for Windows operating system. Malware programs are gathered from Lavasoft[7] repository and benign programs are gathered from two different sources i.e., an online software repository CNET Download.com[8] and from a clean installation of Windows OS. The collected benign files are checked with commercial anti-virus products to eliminate the probability of false negatives. Out of 800 examples, the malware class contains 400 instances, and the benign class contains 400 instances. The generated data sets is disassembled using nsdisasm[9] utility of Ubuntu[10] to extract different pieces of information such as byte code, OpCode (operation code is the part of an assembly instruction that specifies the operation to be performed), text strings, and other information. The extracted information is further used to represent the malware and benign examples for the classification task [27]. However, OpCode representation as n-gram has produced better results than other representations. Some researchers showed that *4*-gram, i.e.,

---

[3] http://www.cs.waikato.ac.nz/ml/weka/arff.html.

[4] http://archive.ics.uci.edu/ml/datasets/Covertype.

[5] http://archive.ics.uci.edu/ml/datasets/BLOGGER.

[6] http://www.csie.ntu.edu.tw/~cjlin/libsvmtools/datasets/binary.html.

[7] http://www.lavasoft.com.

[8] http://download.cnet.com/windows.

[9] http://manpages.ubuntu.com/manpages/gutsy/man1/ndisasm.1.html.

[10] http://www.ubuntu.com.

$n = 4$ produces optimal results. Thus, the size of n-gram in the experimental data set is four, i.e., 4-gram [4].

From the disassembled output only OpCodes are extracted by using a parser and other information is discarded. Disassembly and parsing have generated a large number of OpCode sequences, i.e., n-grams. Many of these sequences may not have any useful contribution in the classification task. Thus, it is crucial to select the most contributing sequences without affecting the classifier accuracy. In the malware detection domain, each generated sequence is analogous to a term in a text document. Thus, to find the most valuable sequences, Term frequency-Inverse document frequency *Tf-Idf* from the text categorization field is used [28]. Top 1000 sequences of benign and malware are selected by using the *Tf-Idf*. These sequences are further used as features to represent a malware or a benign instance and generate ARFF files.

Table 3. Classification results with 10 trees in random forests

	TP rate	FP rate	Precision	Recall	F-Measure	Accuracy	AUC
UCI data sets							
Forest covertype data set							
RF[a]	0.953	0.048	0.953	0.953	0.953	0.952	0.989
CRF[b]	0.953	0.048	0.953	0.953	0.953	0.953	0.989
Blogger data set							
RF	0.790	0.330	0.783	0.790	0.782	0.790	0.848
CRF	0.830	0.279	0.827	0.830	0.824	0.830	0.852
Malware data sets							
4-gram data set							
RF	0.904	0.096	0.906	0.904	0.904	0.903	0.967
CRF	0.916	0.084	0.918	0.916	0.916	0.916	0.974

[a] Random Forests with majority rule.
[b] Consensus Random Forests.

4.2   Evaluation Measures

The performance is evaluated using 10-fold cross-validation. Confusion matrices are generated by using the response of both classifiers. The following four measures define the elements of a confusion matrix from algorithms used in experiment: True Positive (TP), False Positive (FP), True Negative (TN), and False Negative (FN). These elements are used to determine the True Positive Rate ($TPR = \frac{TP}{TP+FN}$), False Positive Rate ($FPR = \frac{FP}{TN+FP}$), True Negative Rate, ($TNR = \frac{TN}{TN+FP}$), False Negative Rate ($FNR = \frac{FN}{TP+FN}$), Recall, and Precision, which are further used to calculate the composite measures, i.e., Accuracy ($ACC = \frac{TP+TN}{TP+TN+FP+FN}$), Area Under ROC (AUC), and F-Measure

Table 4. Classification results with 100 trees in random forests

	TP rate	FP rate	Precision	Recall	F-Measure	Accuracy	AUC
UCI data sets							
Forest covertype data set							
RF[a]	0.953	0.048	0.953	0.953	0.953	0.963	0.989
CRF[b]	0.963	0.036	0.963	0.963	0.963	0.963	0.995
Blogger data set							
RF	0.850	0.219	0.848	0.85	0.848	0.85	0.839
CRF	0.850	0.219	0.848	0.85	0.848	0.85	0.849
Malware data sets							
4-gram data set							
RF	0.940	0.060	0.940	0.940	0.940	0.940	0.987
CRF	0.943	0.058	0.943	0.943	0.942	0.942	0.988

[a] Random Forests with majority rule.
[b] Consensus Random Forests.

$(F1 = 2 \cdot \frac{Precision \cdot Recall}{Precision + Recall})$. ACC is the percentage of correctly identified classes. For some data sets, ACC can be a reasonable estimator of performance (the performance on the novel data). However, if data sets are imbalanced, the ACC metric may be used as a complementary metric with area under ROC. ROC is plotted as a result of TPR on the x-axis in the function of FPR on the y-axis at different points. AUC is commonly used when the performance of a classifier needs to be evaluated for the selection of a high proportion of positive instances in the data set [24]. However, AUC has the benefits of being independent of class distribution and cost [29]. F-Measure is the harmonic mean of precision and recall. These evaluation parameters are used to compare the individual performance of RF and CRF.

5   Results and Analysis

The experimental results are presented in Tables 3 and 4. It is worth noting that presented results are the average result of both classes. Table 3 presents the results of RF and CRF with 10 trees. Table 4 presents the results of RF and CRF with 100 trees. Both tables present the results of TP rate, FP rate, Precision, Recall, ACC, AUC and F-Measure.

The result's analysis can be broadly divided into two parts, i.e., overall discussion and interpretation of results on all data sets and data set specific discussion and interpretation. It is worth noting that there is no difference between RF and CRF in terms of generated number of trees and obtaining the classification. For both experiments, CRF performs better than RF by increasing the TP and TN and decreasing the FP and FN. Table 3 suggests the improvement in results for all data sets except the Forest cover type data set. The Forest cover type data set is a large data set with 500,000+ instances. Thus, hundreds of instances classified correctly or incorrectly may not affect the results of the composite measures if average results are presented. However, in case of middle size data sets and small size data sets such as malware data set and Blogger data set, the difference in the number of instances in the elements of a confusion matrix produces the significant difference in composite measures. When comparing the results of Tables 3 and 4, it is clearly indicated that the increase in number of trees, improves the classification results for larger data sets. For the smaller data set, the difference in results is ignorable. Another factor, which is not presented in both tables is running time of experiments. Both experiments have consumed the similar amount of time for the selection of features and generating trees. However, when the decision part of the CRF is executed, the execution time of algorithm is significantly affected with the number trees. In the CRF algorithm, the score matrix for each tree is calculated and this process is performed iteratively until the convergence is achieved. Among all the data sets, the longest time to obtain predictions is for the CRF on the Forest cover type data set as for every instance, iterations are performed. However, for the other data sets, if the resources consumed are compared with the improvement in results, the CRF with 100 trees may be recommended.

It is worth noting that in experiments, the convergence is achieved between 15 to 20 iterations. To verify this, the numbers of iterations are manually increased from the 20 iterations to 40 iterations; however, no difference in results is found. The performance of the RF and CRF depends upon the number of selected features and quality of selected features for the generation of trees. However, to keep the selection procedures similar for both algorithm, no further pre-processing was performed. For these experiments the number of selected features is small. For the Forest Cover type data set, six features out of 54 are selected for the classification. For the malware data set, 11 features are selected out of 1000. Another contributing factor towards the performance of CRF is OOB of generated trees, which is used for calculating the score matrix. If the generated set of trees in RF is having a zero OOB, then there may not be a difference in the performance of RF and CRF. However, if the data is noisy, and generates trees that contain high OOB, the CRF is more useful as it uses OOB value for the prediction. If OOB of a tree is high, generally the good prediction results may not be obtained using RF. However, CRF uses the OOB to change the decision of trees. When the predicted outcome of a tree is multiplied with its OOB, the distance between actual class and predicted class increases or decreases. This process continues, until the prediction of that particular tree falls clearly in one class. This characteristic of CRF moves the borderline cases to a distinct class case and improves the classification results.

6   Conclusion

Random Forests has attracted researchers due to its randomness during tree generation and improved classification results compared to single classifiers. However, for obtaining the final decision, RF uses majority rule, which is not an optimum option for all situations especially for the malware classification task. Thus, to improve the decision mechanism, this paper introduces the consensus decision making in RF. To empirically evaluate the effect of changes, two different experiments are performed. Each experiment contains a large, medium and small data set. Two different number of trees, i.e., 10 and 1000 are used for experiments. The experiment results suggest that the modified algorithm improves the classification accuracy. The results also suggest that the modified algorithm with increased number of trees may be used for larger data sets. While, the modified algorithm with 10 trees may be used for medium and small data sets. For the future work, we plan to extend our experiments for the multi-class malware classification with more parameterization.

References

1. Breiman, L.: Random forests. Mach. Learn. **45**(1), 5–32 (2001)
2. Biau, G., Devroye, L., Lugosi, G.: Consistency of random forests and other averaging classifiers. J. Mach. Learn. Res. **9**, 2015–2033 (2008)
3. Li, H.-B., Wang, W., Ding, H.-W., Dong, J.: Trees weighting random forest method for classifying high-dimensional noisy data. In: IEEE 7th International Conference on e-Business Engineering (ICEBE), pp. 160–163 (2010)
4. Shahzad, R.K., Lavesson, N.: Comparative analysis of voting schemes for ensemble-based malware detection. J. Wirel. Mob. Netw. Ubiquitous Comput. Dependable Appl. (JoWUA) **4**(1), 98–117 (2013)
5. Tsiporkova, E., Boeva, V.: Multi-step ranking of alternatives in a multi-criteria and multi-expert decision making environment. Inf. Sci. **176**(18), 2673–2697 (2006)
6. Hall, M., Frank, E., Holmes, G., Pfahringer, B., Reutemann, P., Witten, I.H.: The WEKA data mining software: an update. ACM Spec. Interest Group Knowl. Discov. Data Min. (SIGKDD) Explor. Newslett. **11**, 10–18 (2009)
7. Verikas, A., Gelzinis, A., Bacauskiene, M.: Mining data with random forests: a survey and results of new tests. Pattern Recogn. **44**(2), 330–349 (2011)
8. Vanicek, J., Vrana, I., Aly, S.: Fuzzy aggregation and averaging for group decision making: a generalization and survey. Knowl.-Based Syst. **22**(1), 79–84 (2009)
9. Ho, T.K.: Random decision forests. In: Proceedings of the 3rd International Conference on Document Analysis and Recognition, vol. 1, pp. 278–282. IEEE (1995)
10. Breiman, L.: Bagging predictors. Mach. Learn. **24**(2), 123–140 (1996)
11. Shahzad, R.K., Lavesson, N.: Detecting scareware by mining variable length instruction sequences. In: 10th International Information Security South Africa Conference, pp. 1–8 (2011)
12. Robnik-Šikonja, M.: Improving random forests. In: Boulicaut, J.-F., Esposito, F., Giannotti, F., Pedreschi, D. (eds.) ECML 2004. LNCS (LNAI), vol. 3201, pp. 359–370. Springer, Heidelberg (2004)
13. Boström, H.: Calibrating random forests. In: Seventh International Conference on Machine Learning and Applications, pp. 121–126 (2008)
14. Genuer, R., Poggi, J.-M., Tuleau-Malot, C.: Variable selection using random forests. Pattern Recogn. Lett. **31**(14), 2225–2236 (2010)
15. Khoshgoftaar, T.M., Golawala, M., Van Hulse, J.: An empirical study of learning from imbalanced data using random forest. In: 19th IEEE International Conference on Tools with Artificial Intelligence, vol. 2, pp. 310–317 (2007)

16. Risse, M.: Arguing for majority rule. J. Polit. Philos. **12**(1), 41–64 (2004)
17. Farrell, D.M.: Electoral Systems: A Comparative Introduction. Palgrave Macmillan, Basingstoke (2001)
18. Elster, J., Hylland, A.: Foundations of Social Choice Theory. Cambridge University Press, Cambridge (1989)
19. Davis, J.H.: Group decision and social interaction: a theory of social decision schemes. Psychol. Rev. **80**(2), 97–125 (1973)
20. Davis, J.H., Stasson, M.F., Parks, C.D., Hulbert, L., Kameda, T., Zimmerman, S.K., Ono, K.: Quantitative decisions by groups and individuals: voting procedures and monetary awards by mock civil juries. J. Exp. Soc. Psychol. **29**(4), 326–346 (1993)
21. Shabtai, A., Moskovitch, R., Feher, C., Dolev, S., Elovici, Y.: Detecting unknown malicious code by applying classification techniques on opcode patterns. Secur. Inf. **1**(1), 1–22 (2012)
22. Shahzad, R.K., Haider, S.I., Lavesson, N.: Detection of spyware by mining executable files. In: International Conference on Availability, Reliability, and Security, pp. 295–302 (2010)
23. Bache, K., Lichman, M.: UCI machine learning repository (2013)
24. Witten, I.H., Frank, E., Hall, M.A.: Data Mining: Practical Machine Learning Tools and Techniques: Practical Machine Learning Tools and Techniques. The Morgan Kaufmann Series in Data Management Systems. Elsevier Science, USA (2011)
25. Lazarevic, A., Obradovic, Z.: Data reduction using multiple models integration. In: Siebes, A., De Raedt, L. (eds.) PKDD 2001. LNCS (LNAI), vol. 2168, pp. 301–313. Springer, Heidelberg (2001)
26. Gharehchopogh, F.S., Khaze, S.R.: Data mining application for cyber space users tendency inblog writing: a case study. Int. J. Comput. Appl. **47**(18), 40–46 (2012)
27. Shabtai, A., Moskovitch, R., Elovici, Y., Glezer, C.: Detection of malicious code by applying machine learning classifiers on static features: a state-of-the-art survey. Inf. Secur. Tech. Rep. **14**(1), 16–29 (2009)
28. Salton, G., Wong, A., Yang, C.S.: A vector space model for automatic indexing. Commun. ACM **18**, 613–620 (1975)
29. Provost, F.J., Fawcett, T., Kohavi, R.: The case against accuracy estimation for comparing induction algorithms. In: Proceedings of the Fifteenth International Conference on Machine Learning. pp. 445–453. Morgan Kaufmann Publishers Inc. (1998)

Multi-objective Modeling of Ground Deformation and Gravity Changes of Volcanic Eruptions

Piero Conca[1]([✉]), Gilda Currenti[2], Giovanni Carapezza[1], Ciro del Negro[2], Jole Costanza[3], and Giuseppe Nicosia[1]

[1] Department of Computer Science, University of Catania, Catania, Italy
pieroconca@gmail.com
[2] Istituto Nazionale di Geofisica e Vulcanologia (INGV), Catania, Italy
gilda.currenti@ingv.it
[3] Istituto Italiano di Tecnologia (IIT), Milan, Italy

Abstract. Inverse modeling of geophysical observations is becoming an important topic in volcanology. The advantage of exploiting innovative inverse methods in volcanology is twofold by providing: a robust tool for the interpretation of the observations and a quantitative model-based assessment of volcanic hazard. This paper re-interprets the data collected during the 1981 eruption of Mt Etna, which offers a good case study to explore and validate new inversion algorithms. Single-objective optimization and multi-objective optimization are here applied in order to improve the fitting of the geophysical observations and better constrain the model parameters. We explore the genetic algorithm NSGA2 and the differential evolution (DE) method. The inverse results provide a better fitting of the model to the geophysical observations with respect to previously published results. In particular, NSGA2 shows low fitting error in electro-optical distance measurements (EDM), leveling and micro-gravity measurements; while the DE algorithm provides a set of solutions that combine low leveling error with low EDM error but that are characterized by a poor capability of minimizing all measures at the same time. The sensitivity of the model to variations of its parameters are investigated by means of the Morris technique and the Sobol' indices with the aim of identifying the parameters that have higher impact on the model. In particular, the model parameters, which define the sources position, their dip and the porosity of the infiltration zones, are found to be the more sensitive. In addition, being the robustness a good indicator of the quality of a solution, a subset of solutions with good characteristics is selected and their robustness is evaluated in order to identify the more suitable model.

1 Introduction

Mt Etna is one of the best monitored and most studied active volcanoes worldwide. Since the Eighties a large number of multiparametric geophysical surveys

© Springer International Publishing Switzerland 2015
P. Pardalos et al. (Eds.): MOD 2015, LNCS 9432, pp. 359–370, 2015.
DOI: 10.1007/978-3-319-27926-8_32

have been carried out on the ground surface to gain insights into the activity of the volcano. One of the first historical dataset dates back to the 1981 eruption, which is remembered because of its intensity in terms of effusive rate and amount of lava emitted, despite the relatively short time duration of the eruptive activity. Attempts had been made to separately model the recorded dataset [2, 3, 15]. Among the different hypotheses formulated, Bonaccorso [2] interpreted the geodetic observations (leveling and EDM) by suggesting the activation of two magmatic intrusions oriented northward: the initial deeper one starting from the summit craters and the shallower one feeding the final effusive fractures. This hypothesis was considered later on to implement a computational model of the 1981 eruption [3], with the purpose of getting a more comprehensive picture of the intrusive mechanism related to the 1981 flank eruption of Mt Etna through a joint inversion of all the available dataset (microgravity, leveling and EDM). A multi-objective optimization was performed to search the space of the model parameters and find a solution that closely fits the geophysical measurements [6, 13, 18]. In order to explain the discrepancy between the intrusive volumes estimated by geodetic and gravity data, the model was modified to account for the porosity of the host rock. That model was optimised by means of the evolutionary multi-objective optimization algorithm NSGA2 [8]. This paper provides insight into the optimization of the computational model proposed in [3]. In particular, it presents further investigation of the optimization capabilities of NSGA2 and, in addition, it also applies the single-objective DE algorithm to evaluate its performance with respect to the NSGA2. The paper also presents the results of a sensitivity analysis of the model in order to identify the parameters that have higher influence on its performance. Finally, an analysis of the robustness of a set of solutions is presented.

2 Single-Objective and Multi-objective Optimization

Geophysical inversion in volcanic areas focuses on exploiting data from different monitoring techniques (geodesy, gravimetry, magnetism), physical models and numerical approaches in order to identify likely magmatic sources and gain insights about the state of the volcano. Indeed, the geophysical observations collected on a volcano are the surface expressions of processes that occur deeply within the volcanic edifice. Magma migration and accumulation generate a wide variety of geophysical signals, which can be observed before and during eruptive processes. Magma ascent to the Earth's surface forces crustal rocks apart engendering stress and displacement fields and producing variations in the gravity field due to modifications in the subsurface density distribution. Ground deformation and gravity changes are generally recognized as reliable indicators of unrest, resulting from the uprising of fresh magma toward the surface. Measurements of these geophysical signals are useful for imaging the spatio-temporal evolution of magma propagation and for providing a quantitative estimate about the magma volume rising from depth. Deformation and gravity changes are generally interpreted separately from each other using physics-based models, which provide an estimate of the expected geophysical observation produced by volcanic sources. The consistency of interpretations from different observations is qualitatively checked only a posteriori. An integrated geophysical inversion based on both data set should prove a more efficient and accurate procedure for inferring magmatic sources and minimizing interpretation ambiguities. The geophysical inversion is formulated as an optimization problem, which searches the magma source parameters (location, geometry, volume, mass, etc.) $\mathbf{m} = \{m_1, \ldots, m_p\} \in M$ in order to minimize the misfit between the values of geophysical observations and their respective values estimated by the physics-based forward model. The joint inversion of different geophysical observables implies that the misfits for each i-th dataset are simultaneously minimized:

$$f_i(\mathbf{m}) = \|g_i(\mathbf{m}) - d_i^{obs}\| \quad \text{for} \quad i = 1, \ldots, k. \tag{1}$$

where f_i is an objective function and denotes the difference between the value calculated through $g_i(\mathbf{m})$ (forward model) and the observed value d_i^{obs} for each i-th geophysical observable. Therefore, the joint inversion of a multiparametric geophysical dataset can be regarded as a multiobjective optimization problem (MOP). Solving this problem means to find the set of model parameters $\mathbf{m}^*$ that satisfies a set of constraints and optimizes the objective function vector, whose elements are the objective functions:

$$\mathbf{m}^* = \min_{\mathbf{m} \in M} F(\mathbf{m}) \quad \text{with} \quad m_j^{min} \leq m_j \leq m_j^{max} \text{ and } j = 1, \ldots, p, \tag{2}$$

$$\text{where } F(\mathbf{m}) = [f_1(m), f_2(m), \ldots, f_k(m)].$$

Here, we set up a MOP to infer the models space parameters $\mathbf{m}$ of the magmatic sources by jointly inverting the microgravity, leveling and EDM (Electroptical Distance Measurements) data gathered spanning the 1981 Etna eruption. Gravity measurements were performed using spring-based relative gravimeters along a profile circumventing the Etna edifice. Gravity changes were computed by differencing the measurements carried out from two surveys in August/September 1980 and July/August 1981, before and after the eruption. Concurrently, levelling surveys were also performed to measure elevation changes of the ground surfaces. Moreover, discrete horizontal deformation were also measured in September 1980 and May 1982 and in October 1979 and June 1981, using the EDM networks in the SW and NE area, respectively. The pattern of these geophysical dataset support the volcanological evidence that the 1981 Etna eruption was characterized by magma intrusions through fractures into the rocks. This geophysical process is simulated mathematically using solutions devised in [11,12] by solving analytically the elasto-static and gravity equations for modeling displacement and gravity changes induced by rectangular fluid-driven fractures. Two intrusive sources and two associated surrounding zones of pre-existing microfractures, which were filled with new magma are considered following the results reported in Carbone et al. [5]. Since the forward models are nonlinear operators, it calls for using robust nonlinear inversion methods. In the frame of multi-objective optimization techniques, we investigate the NSGA2 algorithm.

In order to improve the search for solutions, the population of solutions and the number of generations are increased with respect to the experiments reported in [3]. In particular, the size of the population has been increased from 500 to 1,000 individuals, while the number of generations has been increased up to 10,000 from the value of 800. In addition, the single-objective optimization technique of Differential Evolution (DE) has also been used to optimize the parameters of the model. This technique evolves a population of solutions without calculating the derivatives of the objective function. The parameters that control the DE algorithm are the *scale* and the *crossover probability* that in our case have, respectively, the values 0.8 and 0.7. The population contains 1,000 individuals and is optimized for 10,000 generations, in order to perform the same number of objective function evaluations as NSGA2 and therefore provide a fair comparison. In this context the three misfits used for the multi-objective optimization (leveling, EDM and gravity) are combined into a single-objective function which is expressed by the following formula:

$$\phi(x_i) = \sqrt{\left(\frac{err_{\text{leveling}}(x_i)}{\sigma_{\text{leveling}}}\right)^2 + \left(\frac{err_{\text{EDM}}(x_i)}{\sigma_{\text{EDM}}}\right)^2 + \left(\frac{err_{\text{gravity}}(x_i)}{\sigma_{\text{gravity}}}\right)^2} ; \quad (3)$$

where x_i is the ith individual and σ_h are the data uncertainties. An estimate of the data uncertainty is obtained by the standard deviation of each measurements dataset, which is of 0.05 m for the leveling, 0.12 m for the EDM, and 35 μGal for the gravity data. The best solutions generated by the optimization techniques NSGA2 and DE are plotted in Figs. 1 and 2. The figures show that the NSGA2 with a population of 1,000 individuals and 10,000 generations produces better results with respect to the same algorithm using a population of size 500 and 800 generations. By contrast, the solutions generated by the DE algorithm combine lower EDM and leveling errors than NSGA2, but are not able to minimize all measures at the same time, as shown in Fig. 2. The similarity of the output

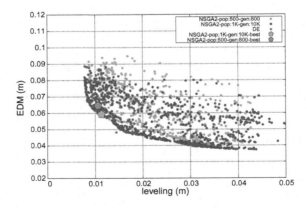

Fig. 1. Leveling error and EDM error of the solutions generated by the optimization techniques NSGA2 with two different parametric configurations and DE.

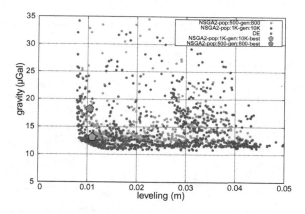

Fig. 2. Leveling error and gravity error of the solutions obtained.

values, which are concentrated in a very small region of the space of values, indicates that these solutions present little differences. This result contrasts with the large diversity of the solutions provided by NSGA2. Moreover, the values of several parameters coincide with the bounds of their respective intervals, this seems to indicate that DE is not able to search the space of parameters effectively. This could be related to the fact that this technique was natively developed for unconstrained optimization, and therefore could be more suitable to that problem rather than constrained optimization. A manual selection, performed by an expert, of the solutions found is displayed in Table 1. Moreover, a map of the Etna and the values generated by the these solutions (found by NSGA2 with a population of 1,000 individuals and 10,000 generations and with a population of 800 individuals and 500 generations) is displayed in Fig. 3.

3   Sensitivity Analysis

Sensitivity analysis (SA) is an important tool for the study of a model [14]. In fact, SA can help understand the behaviour of a model by evaluating the impact of its input parameters on the output. This information could be used, for example, to focus on a subset of parameters when optimization is performed. Moreover, SA allows to the unveil the relations between different parameters.

Concerning the model of the 1981 eruption of Mt Etna, SA is used to identify the characteristics of the magmatic intrusions whose variations affect significantly the output of the model and those which affect it marginally and are, therefore, less relevant. There are several techniques for SA, in our context the technique by Morris and the Sobol' indices were used evaluate the sensitivity of the model.

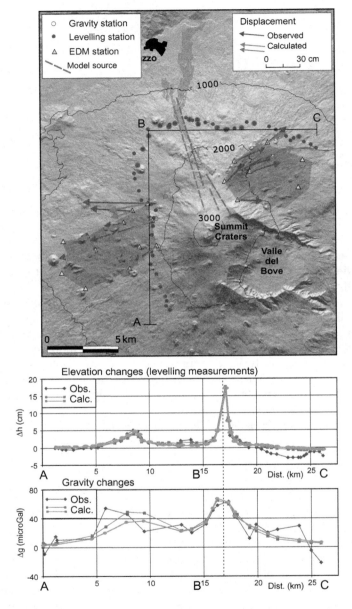

Fig. 3. Map of the Etna showing the locations of the measurement stations and the deformations measured by the EDM sensors and those calculated by the model. The plots at the bottom show the measured values (blue line) and the calculated values of, respectively, elevation and gravity changes for the NSGA2-500-800 (red line) and NSGA-1K-10K (green line) models. The details of the model parameters are reported in Table 1 (Color figure online).

Table 1. Ranges of the values of the parameters and optimal solutions selected by an expert.

Series Parameter	Min.	Max.	NSGA2	DE	NSGA2 [3]
North source					
Z_1^N, depth of the top, m b.s.l	20	20	20	20	20
L^N, length, m	4,000	8,000	6,251	6,184.2	6,703
H^N, height, m	200	500	209.42	200	231.7
W^N, tensile opening, m	0.5	2	1.54	2	0.93
ϕ^N, azimuth (from the north)	−35	−15	−15.69	−31.18	−16
X^N, northing of top center, m	4,181,250	4,186,250	4,185,594	4,184,628	4,184,924
Y^N, easting of top center, m	496,750	499,250	497,887	498,736	497,970
δ^N, dip (from the east)	45	145	111.67	113.02	88.1
$\Delta\rho^N$, density contrast, Kg/m^3	100	500	114.8	100	116.8
North infiltration zone					
D^N, depth, m	500	2,000	1,430.76	829.43	1,325
H_I^N, height, m	100	2,000	335.68	1,999	576.5
$U{\cdot}\rho^N$, thickness·density Kg/m^2	0	50,000	18,943.01	4,118.51	13,146.76
South source					
Z_1^S, depth of the top, m b.s.l	100	1,000	505.07	841	404
L^S, length, m	1,000	5,000	2,446.51	3,024.73	3,589
H^S, height, m	500	2000	1,028.12	883.3	1,140
W^S, tensile opening, m	2	6	5.43	5.99	5.2
ϕ^S, azimuth (from the north)	−30	10	−29.05	−16	−30
X^S, northing of top center, m	4,180,000	4,181,277	4,181,277	4,180,741.2	4,181,004
Y^S, easting of top center, m	496,500	501,000	499,533.6	499,844.31	499,998.3
δ^S, dip (from the east)	45	145	118.4	111.08	131.1
$\Delta\rho^S$, density contrast, Kg/m^3	100	500	114.82	100	116.8
South infiltration zone					
D^S, depth, m	500	2,000	1934.93.79	2,000	1,589
H_I^S, height, m	100	2,000	976.65	2,000	1,409
$U{\cdot}\rho^S$, Kg/m^2	0	50,000	47,904.93	19,135.64	34,485.43
Objective function and robustness					
$err_{leveling}$			0.0112	0.0144	0.0106
err_{EDM}			0.0595	0.0482	0.0646
$err_{gravity}$			13.06	13.79	18.15
Global robustness			0.2646	0.2591	0.2618

3.1 Morris Technique

The method by Morris is one of the techniques used to analyse the sensitivity of the model to variations of its parameters [10]. This global optimization technique follows a path through the input space by modifying the value of one parameter at a time and measures the response of the model. In particular, in order to

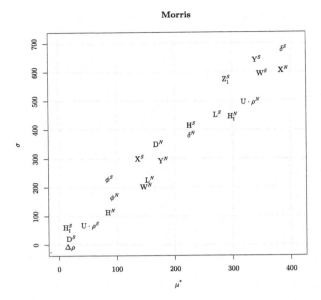

Fig. 4. Sensitivity analysis by means of the Morris method. The parameters on the upper right corner affect more largely the behaviour of the model.

quantify such response, the mean and the standard deviation of the changes to the model output are calculated for each variable. Since the mean can assume negative values, a normalization is performed. The results are shown in Fig. 4. The points of the plot near the origin of the axes have small values of mean and standard deviation and are, therefore, associated with parameters whose variations cause negligible effects to the output of the model. The other points, especially those in the top right corner, indicate large variations of the mean and are associated with parameters that strongly affect the model output when they are varied. The plot also reveals that the relationship between inputs and outputs are nonlinear since the magnitude of the effect of the variation of a parameter is related to the values of other parameters. This is suggested by the fact that large values of standard deviation are observed. In particular, these parameters control the characteristics of the deeper magmatic intrusion are its dip (δ^S), easting position (Y^S), opening (W^S), length (L^S) and depth (Z_1^S), as well as northing position (X^N), height (H_N) and thickness·, density and dip δ^N of the model of the shallower magmatic intrusion. These results are in agreement with those obtained on volcanomagnetic models performed on similar source geometries [5].

3.2 Sobol' Indices

Sobol' indices represent an effective method for estimating the sensitivity of a nonlinear model [9]. This technique, assuming that the inputs are independent, performs a decomposition of the output variance of the model in order to generate a set of indices. The higher the value of an index, the more important the effect of the parameter associated with that index in determining the output of the model [14,16]. The results, shown in Fig. 5, display the estimated value of each index along with its maximum and minimum values. They are in accordance with those obtained by the Morris technique, with the exception of the parameter δ^S, which in this case is not considered to affect the output.

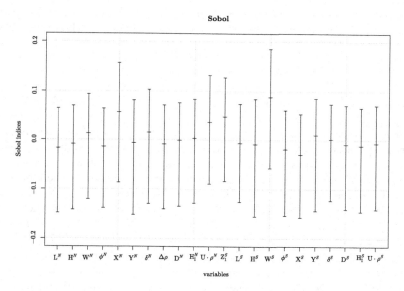

Fig. 5. Sensitivity analysis by means of the Sobol' indices.

4   Robustness Analysis

The minimization of the objective function is of primary importance for the selection of a model. However, it is not the only measure of its quality and a robustness analysis can help choose among a selection of optimal or sub-optimal solutions [1]. As a matter of fact, in many applications, if two solutions have the same objective function value, the solution which undergoes smaller variations of its objective function value when its parameters are perturbed should be preferred. For example, in the optimization of a biological model, robust solutions are preferrable as they mimic the ability of organisms to operate under different stress conditions [4,17]. In order to measure the robustness of a model, here we use the method proposed in [17]. Given a solution Ψ, a perturbation is defined as $\tau = \gamma(\Psi, \sigma_r)$, where the function γ having the form of a stochastic noise with normal distribution and standard deviation σ_r is applied to the solution Ψ. A set T consisting of several perturbations τ of Ψ is generated. A sample τ is robust to the perturbation of magnitude dictated by σ_r if the difference between the value of the objective function ϕ in correspondence of τ and the value in correspondence of the reference solution Ψ is smaller than ϵ, as expressed by the following equation:

$$\rho(\Psi, \tau, \phi, \epsilon) = \begin{cases} 1, & \text{if } |\phi(\Psi) - \phi(\tau)| \leq \epsilon. \\ 0, & \text{otherwise.} \end{cases} \tag{4}$$

An estimate of the robustness of a system Ψ is obtained by performing a set T of trials and then calculating the rate of successful trials, which is given by:

$$\Gamma(\Psi, T, \phi, \epsilon) = \frac{\sum\limits_{\tau \in T} \rho(\Psi, \tau, \phi, \epsilon)}{|T|}. \tag{5}$$

Robustness analysis is global when all the parameters are varied at the same time, while it is local if a parameter at a time is considered. Although local robustness allows to evaluate how a solution "reacts" to perturbations of specific input parameters, we believe that performing a global robustness analysis in this context is more meaningful, as it allows to observe the result of the joint perturbation of the parameters of the model (which determine the characteristics of the sources and the infiltration zones). In particular, we calculated the robustness of the solutions that we found and the robustness of the solution reported in [3], whose parameters are displayed in Table 1. The parameters of the robustness analysis have the values: $\sigma_r = 0.01$ and $\epsilon = 0.0071$, where the value of ϵ corresponds to one tenth of the minimum objective function value of NSGA2 according to the single-objective function (1), while the number of trials $|T| = 10,000$. The NSGA2 instance with a large population size and number of iterations has the highest robustness, with a value of 0.2646, while the solution reported in [3] has a slightly smaller robustness with a value of 0.2618 and the solution obtained by DE has a value of 0.2591, the lowest of the three techniques.

5   Conclusions

This paper has presented the results of the optimization of the conceptual model of the 1981 eruption at Etna volcano proposed in [3]. This model hypothesizes that the eruption was generated by two magmatic intrusions that developed in the northern flank of mount Etna. Two techniques have been used to perform the optimization of the model: the single-objective Differential Evolution technique and the multi-objective NSGA2 technique with increased population size and number of generations with respect to the original paper. The optimization performed using NSGA2 provides improved solutions with respect to those presented in [3], while DE was not able to provide good combinations of all output measures. Moreover, the solutions obtained by DE have very similar characteristics, while those found using NSGA2 feature a high diversity, this provides more meaningful information regarding the characteristics of a model. An analysis of the robustness of a selection of optimal solutions obtained was performed in order to evaluate if they were able to provide a stable output when their parameters were perturbed. Such analysis revealed that the new solution obtained by NSGA2 shows slightly higher robustness with respect to the solution previously obtained, this entails that such solutions are less susceptible to variations of their values. An analysis of the sensitivity of the model was also performed in order to identify the parameters that more significantly affect the output of the model and those which cause little effect on it. Two different methods were used: the Morris technique and the Sobol' indices. They revealed that the parameters of the model that control the characteristics of the deeper magmatic intrusion are its easting position, opening, length and depth, and the parameters that control the shallower magmatic intrusion are its position, height and thickness, density and dip. Moreover, the Morris technique highlighted that the relations between the input parameters are nonlinear.

The new optimal solution found by NSGA2 (Fig. 3, Table 1), although similar to the solution reported in [3], shows some differences. Particularly, the northern shallow source has a deeper infiltration zone and the southern source is both shorter and deeper. Since the sensitivity analysis showed that these parameters are those that may significantly affect the model outputs, the new optimal solution is preferable to the previous one. Moreover, the Morris and Sobol analyses show that the optimization problem is more sensitive to those parameters, which directly reflect their influence on the ground surface by controlling the wavelength and the extent of the geophysical variations. As expected, the sensitivity of the optimization model is also dependent on the network configurations of the measurement points. Particularly, in the 1981 Etna eruption case study no measurements were available in the more affected summit area that could have been helped in better constraining the extension of the source, especially the length and the position of the shallower intrusion.

A set of directions for the future developments of this study have been outlined. The search for solutions could be extended by the use of further optimization techniques, such as the immune-inspired algorithm opt-IA [7]. This would help shed light on the characteristics of the techniques that are effective at dealing with this optimization problem. Moreover, the information provided by the sensitivity analysis could be used to improve the optimization. For instance, the search for solutions could focus on the parameters that more largely affect the output of the model and neglect those which produce little or no variations. In addition, the information about the robustness could be used to select a set of solutions among the optimal ones found or to guide the optimization process.

References

1. Bertsimas, D., Brown, D.B., Caramanis, C.: Theory and applications of robust optimization. SIAM Rev. **53**(3), 464–501 (2011)
2. Bonaccorso, A.: The March 1981 mt. etna eruption inferred through ground deformation modeling. Phys. Earth Planet. Inter. **112**, 125–136 (1999)

3. Carbone, D., Currenti, G., Del Negro, C.: Multiobjective genetic algorithm inversion of ground deformation and gravity changes spanning the 1981 eruption of etna volcano. J. Geophys. Res. Solid Earth **113**(B7) (2008)
4. Costanza, J., Carapezza, G., Angione, C., Lió, P., Nicosia, G.: Robust design of microbial strains. Bioinformatics **28**(23), 3097–3104 (2012)
5. Currenti, G., Del Negro, C., Nunnari, G.: Inverse modelling of volcanomagnetic fields using a genetic algorithm technique. Geophys. J. Int. **163**, 403–418 (2005)
6. Cutello, V., Lee, D., Nicosia, G., Pavone, M., Prizzi, I.: Aligning multiple protein sequences by hybrid clonal selection algorithm with insert-remove-gaps and block-shuffling operators. In: Bersini, H., Carneiro, J. (eds.) ICARIS 2006. LNCS, vol. 4163, pp. 321–334. Springer, Heidelberg (2006)
7. Cutello, V., Nicosia, G., Pavone, M.: Exploring the capability of immune algorithms: a characterization of hypermutation operators. In: Nicosia, G., Cutello, V., Bentley, P.J., Timmis, J. (eds.) ICARIS 2004. LNCS, vol. 3239, pp. 263–276. Springer, Heidelberg (2004)
8. Deb, K., Pratap, A., Agarwal, S., Meyarivan, T.: A fast and elitist multiobjective genetic algorithm: Nsga-ii. IEEE Trans. Evol. Comput. **6**, 182–197 (2002)
9. Iooss, B., Lemaître, P.: A review on global sensitivity analysis methods. ArXiv e-prints, April 2014
10. Morris, M.D.: Factorial sampling plans for preliminary computational experiments. Technometrics **33**(2), 161–174 (1991)
11. Okada, Y.: Internal deformation due to shear and tensile faults in a half-space. Bull. Seismol. Soc. Am. **82**(2), 1018–1040 (1992)
12. Okubo, S.: Gravity and potential changes due to shear and tensile faults in a half-space. J. Geophys. Res. Solid Earth **97**(B5), 7137–7144 (1992)
13. Pardalos, P.M., Resende, M.G.: Handbook of Applied Optimization. Oxford University Press, Oxford (2001)
14. Saltelli, A.: Sensitivity analysis for importance assessment. Risk Anal. **22**(3), 579–590 (2002)
15. Sanderson, T., Berrino, G., Corrado, G., Grimaldi, M.: Ground deformation and gravity changes accompanying the March 1981 eruption of mount etna. J. Volcanol. Geoth. Res. **16**, 299–315 (1983)
16. Sobol, I.: Global sensitivity indices for nonlinear mathematical models and their monte carlo estimates. Math. Comput. Simul. **55**(3), 271–280 (2001). The Second IMACS Seminar on Monte Carlo Methods
17. Stracquadanio, G., Nicosia, G.: Computational energy-based redesign of robust proteins. Comput. Chem. Eng. **35**(3), 464–473 (2011)
18. Xanthopoulos, P., Pardalos, P., Trafalis, T.B.: Robust Data Mining. Springer Science & Business Media, New York (2012)

Author Index

Printed in the United States
By Bookmasters